PLEASE SEND TO:

FRANCES F. L. BEATTY
AND
WILLIAM S. WILSON

KEEPERS OF THE TREASURE

A BOOK ABOUT RAY

ELLEN LEVY

THE MIT PRESS

CAMBRIDGE, MASSACHUSETTS LONDON, ENGLAND

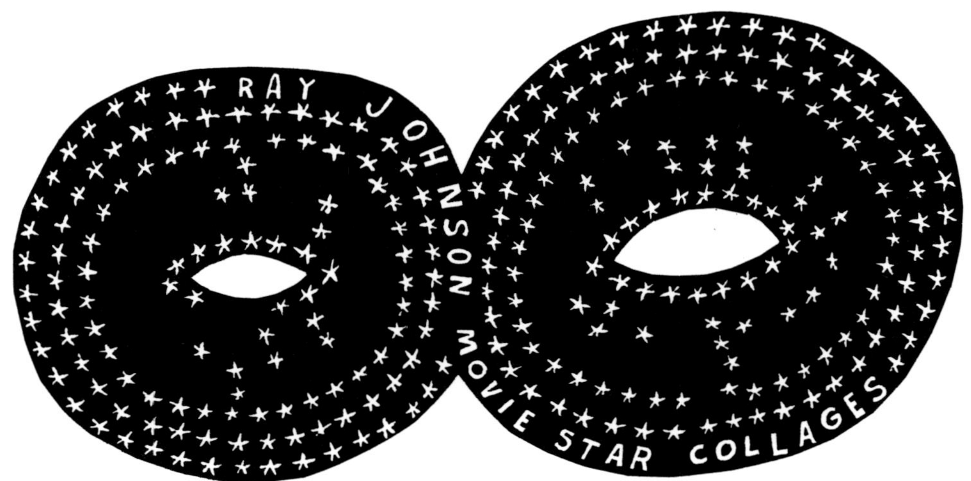

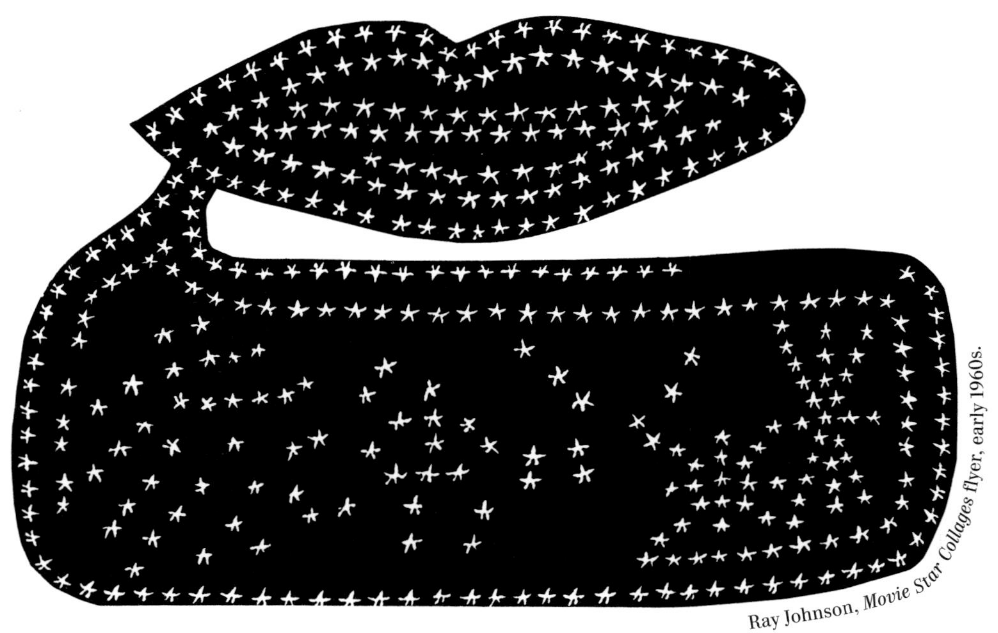

Ray Johnson, *Movie Star Collages* flyer, early 1960s.

CONTENTS

PRELUDE

This book tracks the development of Ray Johnson's art and artistic career from his arrival at Black Mountain College in 1945 until his death in 1995. As will become evident from the first page onward, however, both the art and the career present unusual challenges to their would-be chronicler. Johnson's professional progress was marred by gaps and reversals, his practice was split among several incommensurate genres, and his artwork is often ephemeral or inaccessible, and in some cases both. "I'm difficult, impossible," Johnson warned the curator of his final museum show, referring to his by then notorious impulse to flout art-world norms. This impulse became the bane of curators, dealers, critics, and collectors, but also gave his work the aliveness, riskiness, and wit that drew them to the art in the first place.

The volatile virtues of Johnson's art came as a revelation to me on first encounter, at a show of his collages in the early 2000s. Ultimately, it was exactly the difficulty of capturing those qualities, of keeping up with Johnson as he proceeds along his twisty, chasm-ridden way, that drew me into writing about him. The sheer strangeness of the path that Johnson forged through the world of art, meanwhile, seemed to call for a corresponding strangeness in the writing that would involve the reader, too, in Johnson's difficulties. Yet although Johnson's art may be difficult of access in certain respects—hard to get a grasp on, even hard to get the chance to see—in others, it is eminently accessible. Johnson's work is highly complex and formidably intelligent, and I have tried to do full justice to those qualities. But the work is also fleet-footed and very, very funny, and I wanted to do justice to those qualities as well.

The book's structure is therefore designed to evoke the character of the art, in all its complexity and volatility and humor and lightness of being. Johnson had an inborn penchant for making rapid-fire connections among often wildly disparate persons, things, and events, a crucial faculty for the collagist and creator of social networks that he became. The story this book tells likewise proceeds by association. Each chapter is divided into sections that function as variations on a given theme, sometimes building on the theme sequentially, sometimes moving out from it and circling back. The themes themselves are taken directly from Johnson's art and writings, and each embodies an aesthetic question that drove the artist's work forward.

In the first, introductory, chapter, the basic facts of Johnson's biography and the essential elements of his art practice are seen through the prism of his fascination with proper names, which function in his work both as aesthetic building blocks and signs of the ambivalent attitude toward public recognition that garnered him the title, "New York's most famous unknown artist." Chapter 2 covers a period of artistic self-discovery in which Johnson takes lessons learned and connections made at Black Mountain College and transforms them into the idiosyncratic mix of collage, performance, and correspondence he comes to call "moticos." Chapters 3 and 4, "ICE" and "Fan Club," offer views of roughly the same span of years in the mid-nineteen-sixties from different perspectives, narrating, first, the crystallization of the formal principles that will guide Johnson's art-making and then, the coming into focus of the ethical stakes of his practice, which are rooted in a critique of the culture of fame. This critique flowers in the art of the early nineteen-seventies discussed in chapter 5, work in which Johnson appoints himself the historian of the New York art world as that world itself becomes historical. The artist's inventive but also self-undermining struggle to evade the institutionalization of his work within an increasingly institutionalized art world propels the story in chapter 6, "Silhouette University." That story ends in 1980, with Johnson's exit from the commercial gallery system. The fifteen years that follow, the subject of the final chapter, find the artist in a retrospective mood, restaging old episodes and images through the dream motif of a little theater, and reworking collages with a new fluency that also bears the stamp of valediction. A brief coda deals with Johnson's suicide and the meanings projected onto that act by the artist himself and his survivors.

The summary above would suggest that the book's story of artistic development unfolds in chronological order. And it does, but not faithfully so, sometimes more and sometimes less, a strategy aligned with one of the driving questions for Johnson, the question of how to represent time in art. In the first chapter, I cite Johnson's own objections to the conventions of biography, including the rule that one should start with the subject's birth and move forward from there, step by methodical step. For Johnson, the fiction of history as an unbroken, forward-directed continuum was of a piece with the fiction of the unitary self, to which I would add, in the special case of the artist's biography, the fiction of the cohesive oeuvre. Time, the self, the artist's practice, were for this artist always already bent, split, various. In terms of structure, then, this is a collagist's story, a collection of fragments recomposed into a palpably discontinuous whole.

In terms of focus, the book tells what I will call an "art story," as opposed to a life story. "If it's not in the art, it's not in the book," was the self-imposed rule that guided my decisions throughout. It is a rule made easier to follow by the fact that the countless mailings that Johnson sent to hundreds of correspondents over the course of his life fall—or rather, were placed by the artist—under the rubric of "correspondence art," and so form part of his official oeuvre. "Official," though, may be too absolute a word to use in connection with this artist. It would be truer to say that Johnson's mail occupies an ambiguous space between the background to which most artists' correspondence is consigned, and the foreground reserved for what would usually be considered the artwork proper. Johnson had a disquieting talent for complicating distinctions.

Above all, Johnson made it hard to distinguish his life from his art. ("If it's not in the art" works as a rule only so long as one can say what is and isn't considered part of the art.) It is not just that he seems never to have taken a day off from making art, but that, when not in the studio, he seemed always to be performing as "Ray Johnson," court jester of the New York art scene. Yet however theatrical his behavior, Johnson was not, in the usual sense, putting on a show. The face that he showed to the world was at once his true face and a mask—the true face of the person who inspired a deep attachment in his friends (throughout his life, Johnson attracted an extraordinary number and variety of friends) and the mask of the persona that kept those friends, as they all said, from ever really knowing him. I do not pretend to know him better than they did. My chief aim here is to tease out some threads in Johnson's art and his thinking about it as they changed over time, so that future viewers might feel better oriented in the dynamic, ambiguous space in which the art unfolds.

No artist can be well understood without a supply of orienting histories. This is a first attempt to sketch the full arc of Ray Johnson's career: *a* book about Ray, certainly not *the* book. The visible gaps in my account thus also serve as a somewhat theatrical means of conveying the anxious sense that the task I had taken on would have to remain unfinished. There is so much more to say about Johnson's rich and expansive body of work, so much more to say about his work's consequential relation to the art of his day and ours; so many more art stories to tell, alongside stories of the life yet to be told. (Then there are all those interesting friends, each worth a book of their own ...)

Then again, that is the good news, if not for the writer whose book is done, then for all those who someday find themselves unable to resist the difficulty that is Ray.

GIAMBATTISTA BODONI (1740-1813)
SON OF A PRINTER OF PIEDMONT.
AFTER GAINING EXPERIENCE AND FAME AS SUPERINTENDENT OF THE PRESS
OF THE PROPOGANDA IN ROME
BODONI BECAME IN 1766 THE HEAD OF THE DUCAL PRINTING HOUSE AT PARMA,
WHICH HE SOON MADE THE FOREMOST OF ITS KIND IN EUROPE.
HIS "MANUALE TIPOGRAFICO", COMPLETED BY HIS WIDOW IN 1818,
CONTAINS 279 PAGES OF SPECIMENS OF TYPES,
INCLUDING ALPHABETS OF ABOUT THIRTY FOREIGN LANGUAGES.
HIS EDITIONS OF GREEK, LATIN, AND ITALIAN, AND FRENCH CLASSICS,
ESPECIALLY HIS HOMER,
ARE CELEBRATED FOR THEIR TYPOGRAPHY.
IN TYPE-DESIGNING HE WAS AN INNOVATOR,
MAKING HIS NEW FACES ROUNDER, WIDER, AND LIGHTER,
WITH GREATER OPENNESS AND DE'LICACY.
HIS TYPES WERE RATHER TOO RIGIDLY PERFECT IN DETAIL
THE THICK LINES CONTRASTING SHARPLY WITH THE THIN, WIRY LINES.
IT WAS THIS FEATURE, DOUBTLESS, THAT CAUSED WILLIAM MORRIS'S CONDEMNATION
OF THE BODONI TYPES AS "SWELTERINGLY HIDEOUS."

DEAR JOHN
HOW ARE YOU AND ELAINE AND YOUR WORK?
WHAT DO YOU DO AT AYER?
ASAWA IS A BIT DISAPPOINTED IN HER WORK IN MEXICO.
SHE PONDERS OVER CO-OPERATION AND INDIVIDUALISM.
RUDOFSKYS ARE VISITING HERE
AND DRIERS RETURN SOMETIME TODAY.
I WONDER HOW YOU TWO ARE AND WHAT YOU ARE DOING.

Ray Johnson to John Urbain, ca. 1947–1948, letter written on class notes with Bodoni "R."

A NOTE ON THE TYPE

> Josef Albers brought a font of Bodoni, his personal favorite, with him from Bauhaus on his way to Black Mountain College, where he would, among other responsibilities, begin supervising the college's printing program.—Philip Blocklyn, "'It's Right the Way It Is': Printing at Black Mountain College," *Journal of Black Mountain College Studies* 12

From Parma to Black Mountain via Dessau, the trail leading from Giambattista Bodoni to Ray Johnson is a long one. In Bodoni's era individual characters (punches) were meticulously carved by hand, a technique inevitably leading to the introduction of quirks and idiosyncrasies magnified by the scale of the punch and skill of its cutter. The choice of which original cuts to reference is a quandary that has occupied numerous typographers in the centuries since, as they sought to create typefaces of uniform coherence, capturing the essence of Bodoni's distinctive style.

As the pages of this book attest, uniform coherence was rarely if ever an ambition of Ray's when it came to type. His hand-drawn letters are a clear departure from the mechanised geometry championed by László Moholy-Nagy at the Bauhaus and carried to Black Mountain by Josef Albers. Ray's Bodoni is typically anomalous and could not be accused of being "too rigidly perfect," an accusation Ray levels at Bodoni in his accompanying biography.

The text that follows is set in Bodoni Parmigiano, designed by Riccardo Olocco and Jonathan Pierini. Direct quotations from Ray Johnson are set in **bold**. Chapter dividers and the book's cover incorporate an extended interpretation of Ray's Bodoni by Rosa Nussbaum.—RN

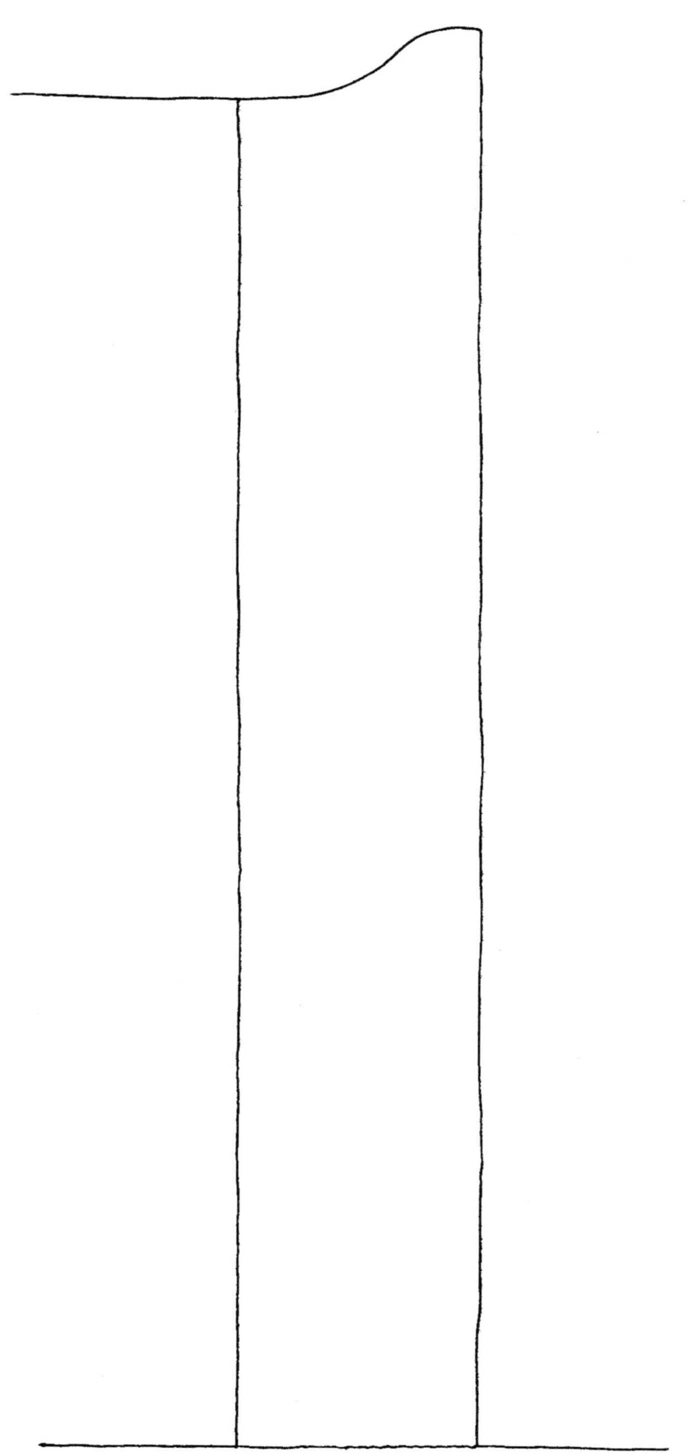

THE OTHER RAY JOHNSON

PRESENTING RAY JOHNSON.
WHAT'S IN A NAME?

I

It begins with a birth, the birth of an epithet. On April 11, 1965, Grace Glueck, who covered the art world for the *New York Times*, reported that

> The Willard Gallery on East 72nd Street is having a retrospective (OK—call it an introspective) of works by Ray Johnson, who may well be New York's most famous unknown artist. Though Johnson's collages have for years been creeping into first-rate collections, he's never before had a gallery show.
>
> "**I've never believed in the gallery thing**," said Johnson, a baby-bald young man in a leather motorcycle jacket. "**But at the same time I've been dying for a show. Ambivalence, you see. I visit collectors with a box of collages wrapped in newspaper under my arm, like a Fuller Brush Man. That pleases me. I've shown them on Mies Van Der Rohe tables all over town.**"

"New York's most famous unknown artist." This phrase has trailed Ray Johnson since the day the *Times* critic coined it, a Homeric tag that indicates his uncanny knack for almost seizing his claim to fame, only to sink again into the realm of the unknown. All artistic reputations have their vagaries, but the perpetual flickering of this artist's fame seems less accidental than willed. **Ambivalence, you see**, is our hero's mythic attribute. Ray Johnson wanted to be famous, and he wanted to remain unknown, and he clung to the belief, whose absurdity he relished, that it was possible to be both at once.

It ends with a death. On January 13, 1995, two teenagers walking past a bridge in Sag Harbor, Long Island heard a splash and turned to see a man swimming seaward through the freezing water. The next day, Ray Johnson's body was found floating near the shore. The news could not help but come as a shock, but as the artist's friends began to reflect on this act, they came to see it as, if not inevitable, then curiously consistent with the Ray they knew.

Johnson once confided to a friend—he was joking and also not joking—that **the biggest problem is my ghost, which some day when it is all over with and I am also a ghost you will perhaps know about**. He was thirty when he typed these words, young to be thinking about his ghost, or ghosts. But there was already something wraithlike about Johnson, with his high, light, toneless voice, his perpetual Buster Keaton deadpan, and his tendency, much remarked on by his friends, to vanish midstream. "One of Ray's art forms was the disappearance," said his friend, the critic and translator Henry Martin. "You'd be walking down the street with Ray, and he moved, he moved on the basis of images. He would see an image, which would remind him of somewhere else. And he would just abandon you and then go off to somewhere else."

Still, this is not a ghost story. Ray Johnson was elusive to an extreme, but his self-creation also involved the making of tangible objects in the hundreds and thousands, most of them either complex, meticulously crafted bas-relief collages intended for display in public and private collections, or pieces of "correspondence art," complex, deliberately rough-edged assemblages of ephemera, distributed by the artist, via the post or by hand, to an ever-expanding network of correspondents day after day, year after year, until the day it was all over with. For whose eyes these latter works were intended, apart from those of their original recipients, it is difficult to say. Nor is it easy to say how the correspondence pieces relate to the collages, works that Ray Johnson made for exhibition but then did everything he could to keep out of the public eye. One must also gauge the relation of the collages and the correspondence to the artist's performances in theaters, galleries, and college auditoriums. These appearances, which Johnson sometimes referred to as "Nothings," are not to be confused with his disappearances, which can also be seen as performances.

Or not. When Ray's friend Billy Name compared him to their mutual friend Andy Warhol, who hid behind the elaborate persona he had invented for himself, Billy claimed that nonetheless, "Andy was still like a person," whereas "Ray wasn't a person. He was a collage or a sculpture. A living sculpture, you know. He was Ray Johnson's creation." Ray Johnson made it difficult to tell his life and art apart. Difficult, but not impossible. This is not, or not exactly, a life story. This is an art story.

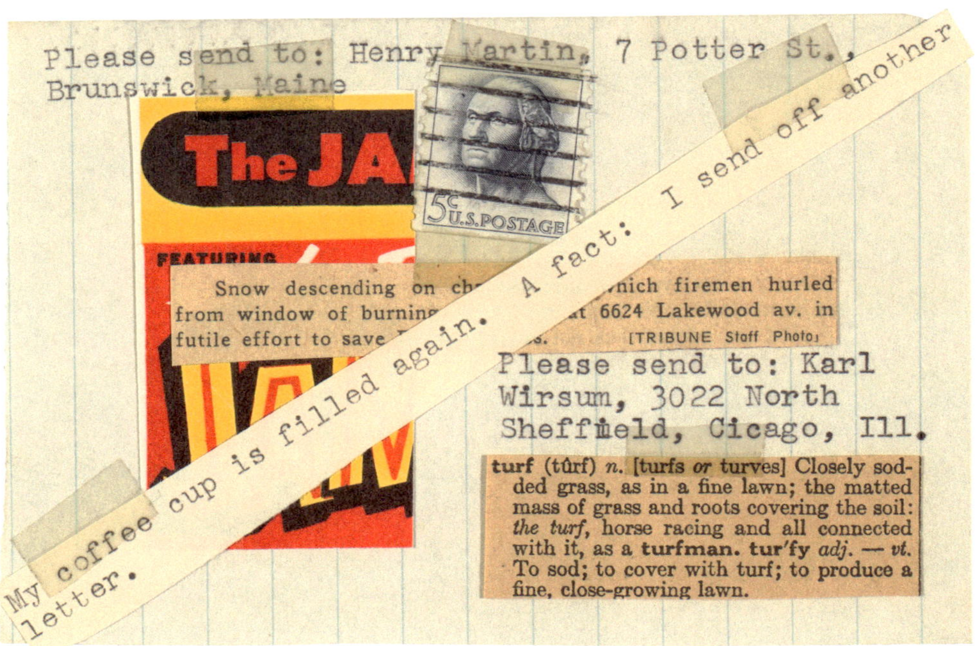

Ray Johnson, please-send-to for Henry Martin and Karl Wirsum, March 6, 1963.

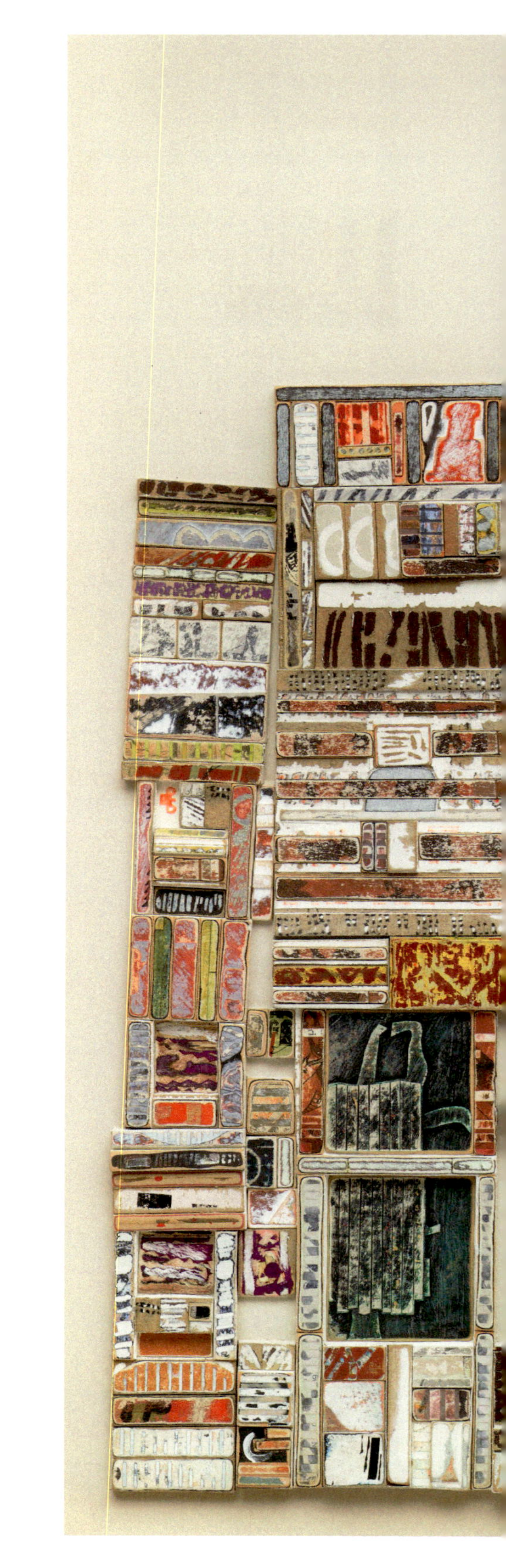

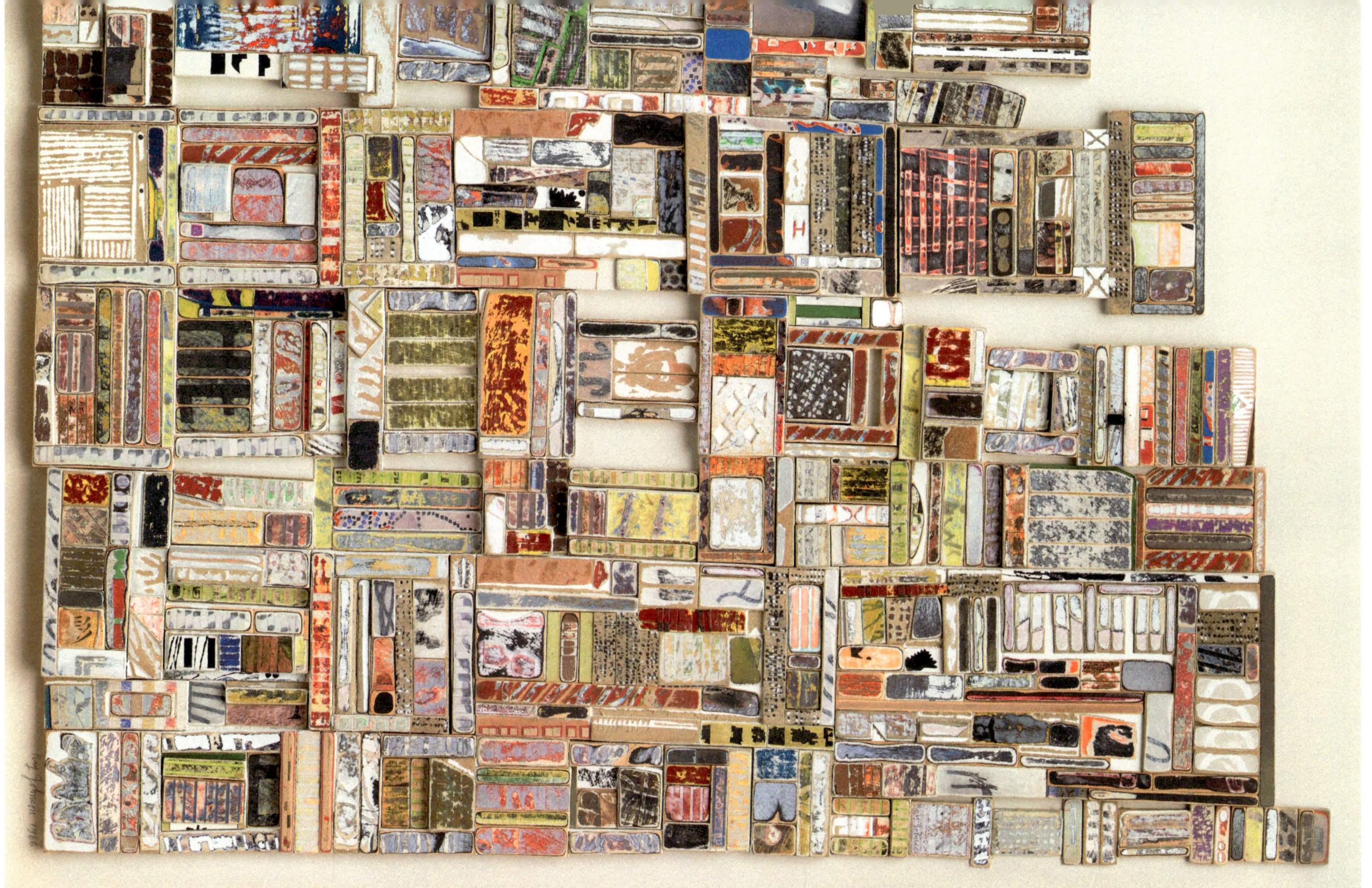

Ray Johnson, *January/February* (1966).

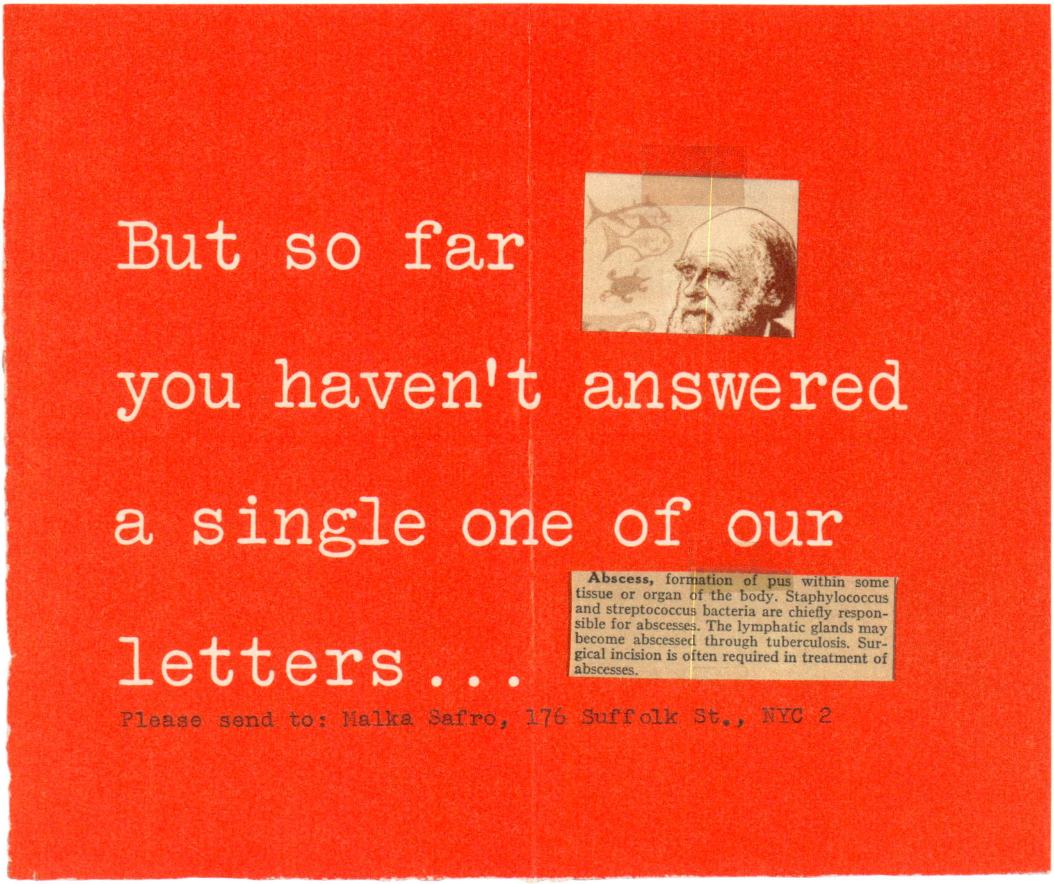

But so far

you haven't answered

a single one of our

letters...

Abscess, formation of pus within some tissue or organ of the body. Staphylococcus and streptococcus bacteria are chiefly responsible for abscesses. The lymphatic glands may become abscessed through tuberculosis. Surgical incision is often required in treatment of abscesses.

Please send to: Malka Safro, 176 Suffolk St., NYC 2

Ray Johnson, please-send-to for Malka Safro, 1963.

II

In autumn 1962, William S. (Bill) Wilson came into possession of a page torn from a book with the promising heading, **THE RAY JOHNSON STORY**, and a text that begins, “I was born in 1914 in a solid, three-story brick house in a large Midwest city.” Bill Wilson had begun keeping a file on Ray Johnson shortly after the two met, in 1956, when Wilson was starting a dissertation on Chaucer at Yale and Johnson was already a cult figure on the scene in New York. The file would grow into an immense archive of materials by, for, and about Ray Johnson, which, after Wilson died in 2016, would enter the collection of the Ryerson & Burnham Art and Architecture Archives at the Art Institute of Chicago. While he lived, Wilson tended to his growing cache day after day, year after year, as he taught, raised a family, and published fiction and criticism and here and there a piece of the never-to-be-completed book about Ray that he intended as his magnum opus. But Wilson’s archive itself is a book about Ray, the book without which no others might have been written. For as he arranged and rearranged the scraps in the plastic sleeves of the binders loaded onto the shelves that lined the parlor of his crumbling Manhattan townhouse, the archivist was reconstructing the connections among a dizzyingly complex set of events and players, a drama that was dissolving into the ether as he worked. It was a pursuit at least as quixotic as the study of medieval literature. Ray, meanwhile, encouraged and abetted his friend Bill’s monumental and monumentalizing efforts on his behalf even as, in his ambivalence, he mocked and undermined every effort, including Bill’s, to narrate The Ray Johnson Story. The page mentioned above, for instance, contains the opening of William Burroughs’s *Junky*, with addition by Ray Johnson.

When approached by critics and scholars in search of verifiable facts about his life and work, Ray Johnson exhibited a theatrical disrespect for the conventions of their craft. Take the hapless interviewer assigned in 1968 to record Johnson for the Archives of American Art at the Smithsonian Museum in Washington, DC. She begins, as is customary, at the beginning. “Where were you born—I mean by that your birthplace, your family and religious background, and were your parents artists themselves?”

Your beginning questions prompt a certain silence, he replies, with characteristic unhelpfulness. **Thinking of one’s childhood as a tape, if one is born and begins to live the way this tape begins, things go very slowly.** By “this tape,” Johnson means the magnetic audiotape unspooling in the interviewer’s recorder, unwieldy then and useless now. Then again,

Ray Johnson seems to view all media as at once eternally viable and always already obsolete. **I saw a marvelous movie last night that cost five cents,** he continues, **You put a nickel into it. It's an old nickelodeon. And you're able to control the speed. It can go very slowly or very fast. You can make it stop and you can sort of go at it at your own rate of interest. So that, in a certain way, my childhood was like that. Many years later...** The nickelodeon is a thing of yesterday, but for Johnson that means both "just yesterday" and "many years ago."

"PONEY EXPREZZ" reads the saddlebag of the rider in an old engraving that Ray Johnson pasted into one of his high-school sketchbooks, an image of a comically outmoded past that contains the seeds of the artist's future status as "the father," or "grandfather," or "even the 'sugar dada,'" of the aesthetic practice known as correspondence art or mail art. This is one claim to fame that Johnson has retained, in certain circles, through all of his reputational vicissitudes. He was by no means the first artist to play with postal materials, but he was, it is said, the first to treat the postal system itself as an artistic medium. Just as some painters make one see paint as paint, and not merely a means to a descriptive end, the movements of Johnson's missives through the post traced luminous paths like contrast dye, making his correspondents conscious of the system as a system, as a branching, buzzing network, and not just as a means of getting one's letters from here to there. "Ray Johnson plays the U.S. mails like a harp," wrote Bill Wilson, recipient of some of the artist's greatest chamber pieces.

One day in 1958, Ray handed Bill a card marked, **Please send to—/ Remy Charlip**, a friend who was a member of Merce Cunningham's dance troupe and a children's book illustrator. The card bears an image of a hand, palm out, offering the viewer a selection of strange squiggly things that on closer inspection turn out to be fishing lures. It soon became apparent that the card itself was a lure, the first step in a complex dance whose moves were at once errant and carefully choreographed by Ray, who kept luring in more friends, and soon, people who were not Ray's friends, at least not in the traditional sense, also joined the dance. One of these pen pals, artist Ed Plunkett, described how the please-send-to thing worked in a 1977 memoir.

> I was soon sending things to Ray and then began to receive mailings from him. The envelopes contained tidbits of disorganized collage scraps or proto-pop elements such as labels and pictorial material from the comic strips or newspaper pix, often transformed with drawings. Usually there were instructions to mail certain things to other people. Thus my mailing list expanded. Further, when I sent

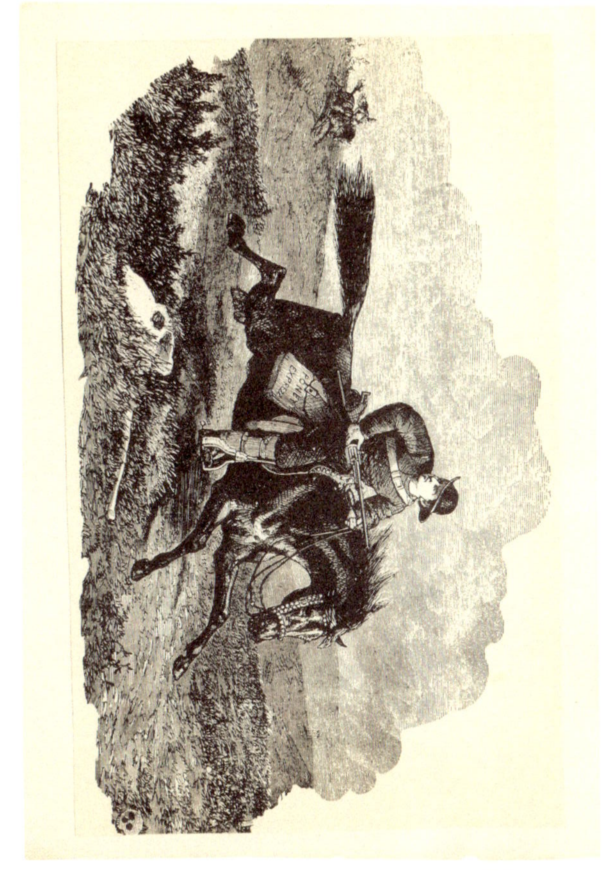

Ray Johnson, high school scrapbook, ca. 1944.

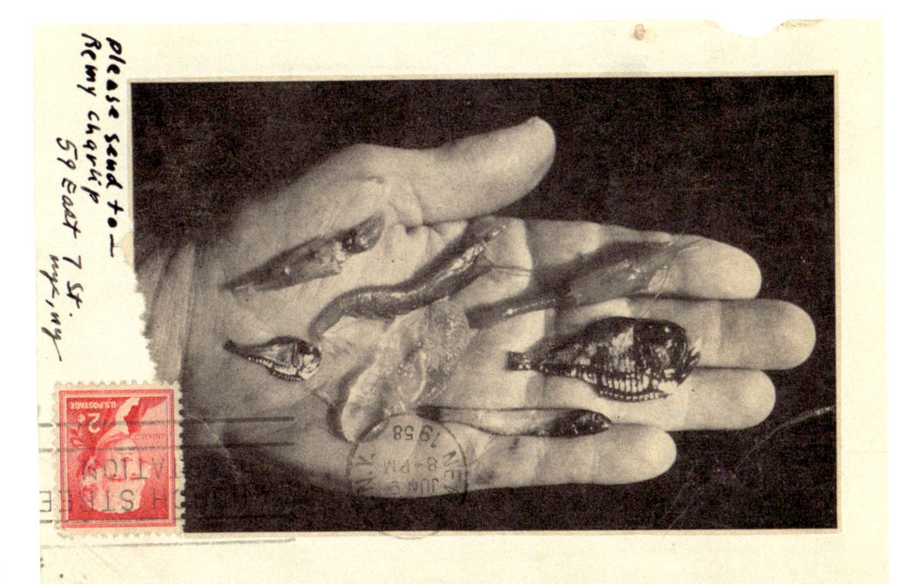

Ray Johnson, first please-send-to for Remy Charlip, September 6, 1958.

things to unknowns, they responded with mailings to Ray, or to other unknowns. Now I was corresponding with people I did not know and possibly was never to meet. It was possible to communicate with someone on one level without knowing them on any other, and this added to the mystery of it all.

It all seems rather less mysterious now, of course. In the hindsight of the present-minded, Johnson has acquired a reputation as an avatar of things to come, "The Zen Master of the Social Network." In 1962, Ed Plunkett half-jokingly suggested that Ray call his then nameless gang of mailers The New York Correspondence School, a reference to the so-called Painters of the New York School, whose expressionist style still held considerable sway. Johnson took the suggestion, although he sometimes spelled it "correspon*dance*." The participants in the Correspondance School became friends without ceasing to be strangers, bound one to the other through a radiating web of chain-letters in a new form of community. Ray Johnson's end coincided with the end of the letter as an expressive form and the beginning of the end of the post as a communication system. Prescience is an artistic power.

III

Ray Johnson, a prophet of the social network in its now familiar, dematerialized, virally spreading form? Could be. Although this could also be the kind of historical just-so story that drove Johnson himself to insist that **Mail art has no history, only a present**. Which is not to say that the artist had no interest in history, but that he had no use for history of a certain sort. That is why he objects to the interviewer's where-were-you-born question, as to her slowly unspooling tape. Both stand, at the moment of their exchange, for what the essayist Walter Benjamin, another born objector, referred to as "historicism." Historicists, said Benjamin, assume that our stories unspool in "homogenous, empty time." "They believe," added Benjamin's friend Siegfried Kracauer, "that they can grasp historical reality by reconstructing the course of events in their temporal succession without any gaps."

Mail art has no history, only a present. What past it has "can be seized," as Benjamin put it, "only as an image which flashes up at the instant when it can be recognized and is never seen again." The anti-historicist sees a present shot through with gleams of the past, like shards of mirror strewn on the street. For such a one, history takes the form of an assemblage of meaningful fragments, rescued, if just barely, from the meaningless flux of time. In a word: collage.

Over a snapshot of himself as a toddler, Ray Johnson has printed the one-word manifesto,

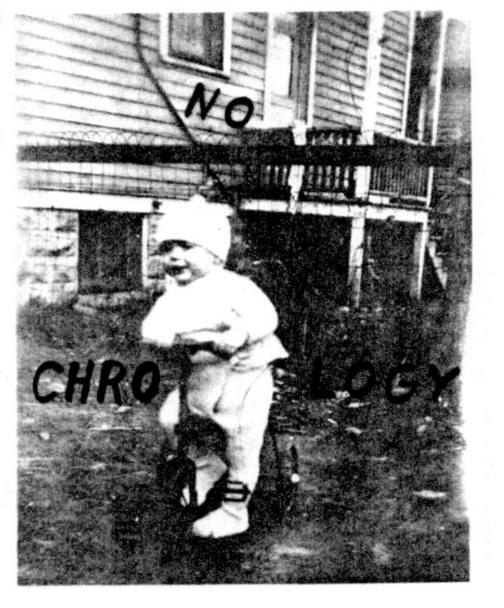

Ray Johnson, *CHRO NO LOGY* mailer, ca. 1983.

by which he means not *no* sense of temporal order, but a discontinuous one, punctuated by gaps and abrupt juxtapositions. This was Ray Johnson's way of telling stories, the collagist's way—although one's way of telling stories is as much a matter of character as it is an aesthetic choice. Seen in broad outline, as a type, Johnson shared a character—cool, ironic, enigmatic—with other artists of his generation, like Andy Warhol and Jasper Johns. Or like the poet John Ashbery, who said once, under questioning, that "My own autobiography has never interested me very much. Whenever I try to think about it, I seem to draw a complete blank. There is the title of a Japanese film by Ozu, 'I was born, but…' That's how I feel about it."

"Ray Johnson likes to tell interviewers that he was born in Idaho, Potato or, alternatively, Birthmark, North Dakota," critic Rosalind Constable noted in a 1970 profile. Johnson had been running this line since at least 1963, when "An Interview with nosnhoJ yaR," a collaboration between the artist and his art critic friend David Bourdon, appeared in *Artforum*. There, Bourdon poses a series of more or less serious questions on artistic matters to Johnson, only to receive predictably impossible answers—"What future do you see in collage?" **I hear my refrigerator humming and my kitchen sink drip**—waiting until the last moment to raise the you-were-born issue.

> Q: You are remarkably reticent about giving out biographical information. Born in 'Idaho, Potato,' etc. Wouldn't people be more thrilled and chilled to learn that you were really born in Detroit?
> Johnson: **I liked Giuletta** [*sic*] **Masina in Cabiria. She does interesting work and I do not have the slightest interest in where she was born or when.**

One can find cut-out images of Giulietta Masina, the wife of the director Federico Fellini and star of some of his greatest early films, including *Nights of Cabiria* (1957), in Johnson's communications from the mid-to-late 1950s.

i like STARS, reads the caption beside a fragment of Masina's face in a collage-book the artist made for Remy Charlip, although Masina was also a kind of anti-star, known for playing mousy nobodies who long in vain for love and glamour. Ray Johnson had a taste for fame, but he was still more interested in the dialectical relation between the known and the unknown, stars and nobodies. **So when you ask me about my being born,** Johnson explains, trying to clarify the issue for the interviewer from the Smithsonian, **to receive in the mail the other day a listing of twenty-five people named Ray Johnson in Minneapolis, each of them having been born at a different time and each one having a different childhood, I'm not really that important. All twenty-five Ray Johnsons should perhaps speak at the same time. I mean, my ideas turn this way. I think we're inclined to think of things as too important. There's so much unimportance among people.**

IV

Ray Johnson was born on October 16, 1927, in Detroit, Michigan, the only child of Eino Johnson, a factory worker at Ford Motors, and Lorraine Polkki Johnson, a housewife. The elder Johnsons belonged to a community of Finns whose forbears emigrated to Michigan's Upper Peninsula to work in the copper mines. Ray, who showed a talent for drawing from an early age, refined his skills at Detroit's Cass Technical High School, a selective public preparatory school with a strong arts program, from which he graduated in 1945. In the fall of 1945, he entered Black Mountain College in North Carolina, the famous experimental school for the arts, where he studied with Josef Albers, a lasting influence on Johnson's artistic thinking and methods. Through Black Mountain, Johnson made other influential connections with peers like Hazel Larsen Archer, Ruth Asawa, Robert Rauschenberg, Norman Solomon, and Stan VanDerBeek, and teachers John Cage, Merce Cunningham, and Willem and Elaine de Kooning. Johnson fell in love with another teacher, sculptor Richard Lippold, and moved with him to New York City in 1950; their romantic attachment lasted for a quarter-century, throughout which Lippold remained married to his wife, Louise.

In 1968, Johnson's friend Andy Warhol was shot by Valerie Solanas and Johnson himself was mugged at knifepoint when he went out to get the papers reporting the shooting. Shortly after these incidents, Johnson moved to the north shore of Long Island, where he lived until his death in 1995. During his lifetime, Johnson traveled outside the United States only twice, briefly, both times to Canada.

When Johnson left Black Mountain in 1948, he was a painter of geometric abstractions in the Albersian style; by the mid-1950s, he was producing both paintings and collages, as well as experimenting with the kinds of mailings he would soon codify as "correspondence art." In 1958, he destroyed most of his paintings and thereafter worked in three main artistic modes, all governed by collage principles: exhibition collage, correspondence art, and performance. That same year, Johnson sent his first known *please-send-to* mailing; in 1961, he staged the first of the performances he called *Nothings*; and in 1968, he held the first in a series of performance-style *Meetings* for members of his mail-art network, known as the *New York Correspondance School.* The artist's first one-person exhibition at a major commercial gallery was held in 1965 and the last, just thirteen years later, in 1978. Johnson officially announced his exit from the gallery world in 1980-and would show only in non-profit venues for the remainder of his life. In the ensuing years, Johnson increasingly avoided the public eye, while maintaining a daily practice of making art in all his characteristic modes to the end.

None of these facts is interesting unless one is interested in Ray Johnson. To be interested in him, however, one must first know something about him, and this artist's way of disappearing has made him hard to know. Hence the number of people who think of Johnson as what we call *a name* in the world of art has remained small relative to those whose eyes light up at the mention of the names of friends of Ray like John Cage, Christo and Jean-Claude, Chuck Close, Bruce Conner, Joseph Cornell, the de Koonings, Jasper Johns, Louise Nevelson, Yoko Ono, Nam June Paik, Robert Rauschenberg, Ad Reinhardt, James Rosenquist, Andy Warhol—Ray knew everyone, it seems, and everyone knew Ray.

That's just gossip, some might say. But gossip, for Ray Johnson, was never just gossip; it was also one of his art forms, as essential to his way of thinking as his "disappearances." One critic describes a Meeting of Johnson's New York Correspondance School as "a New York opening without a show, that is, a place for gossip, which is, after all, Johnson's medium." Which is true, although it might be truer to say that Johnson's medium is names, big names, medium-sized names, or no-names, accreting to no apparent end. And yet Johnson did have his ends in view. Like a gossip columnist, he may have elided the narrative that connects the names, but he trusts you—assuming you are the kind of reader who likes such lists—to fill in the gaps for yourself. One difference between Ray Johnson and a gossip columnist: If you think you are *not* the kind of reader who likes to pore over lists of names, trying to work out the connections between them, Johnson would persuade you otherwise.

Every name in *Robert Rauschenberg*, in order of appearance: **Larry Rivers, Ludwig Bemelmans, Andy Warhol, Oyvind Fahlstrom, Her Royal Highness Queen Christina of Sweden, Mrs. Armand G. Erpf, Moki Cherry, Mrs. Jacob W. Javits, David Budd, August Heckscher, Keven McCarthy, Mark Rothko, Billy Kluver, Robert Rauschenberg, Jeffrey Postter, Anne Ryan, Ellen Johnson, James Rosenquist, Jeanne Miles, Penelope, Barnett Newman, Chryssa, Robert Scull, Jack Youngerman, Marquis Bernard-Alexis Poisson, Ad Reinhardt, E. Box, Hummingbird, Lyman Kipp, Roy Lichtenstein, Alex Hay, Jill Johnston, Alexander Liberman, RAY JOHNS Betsy Ross ON**

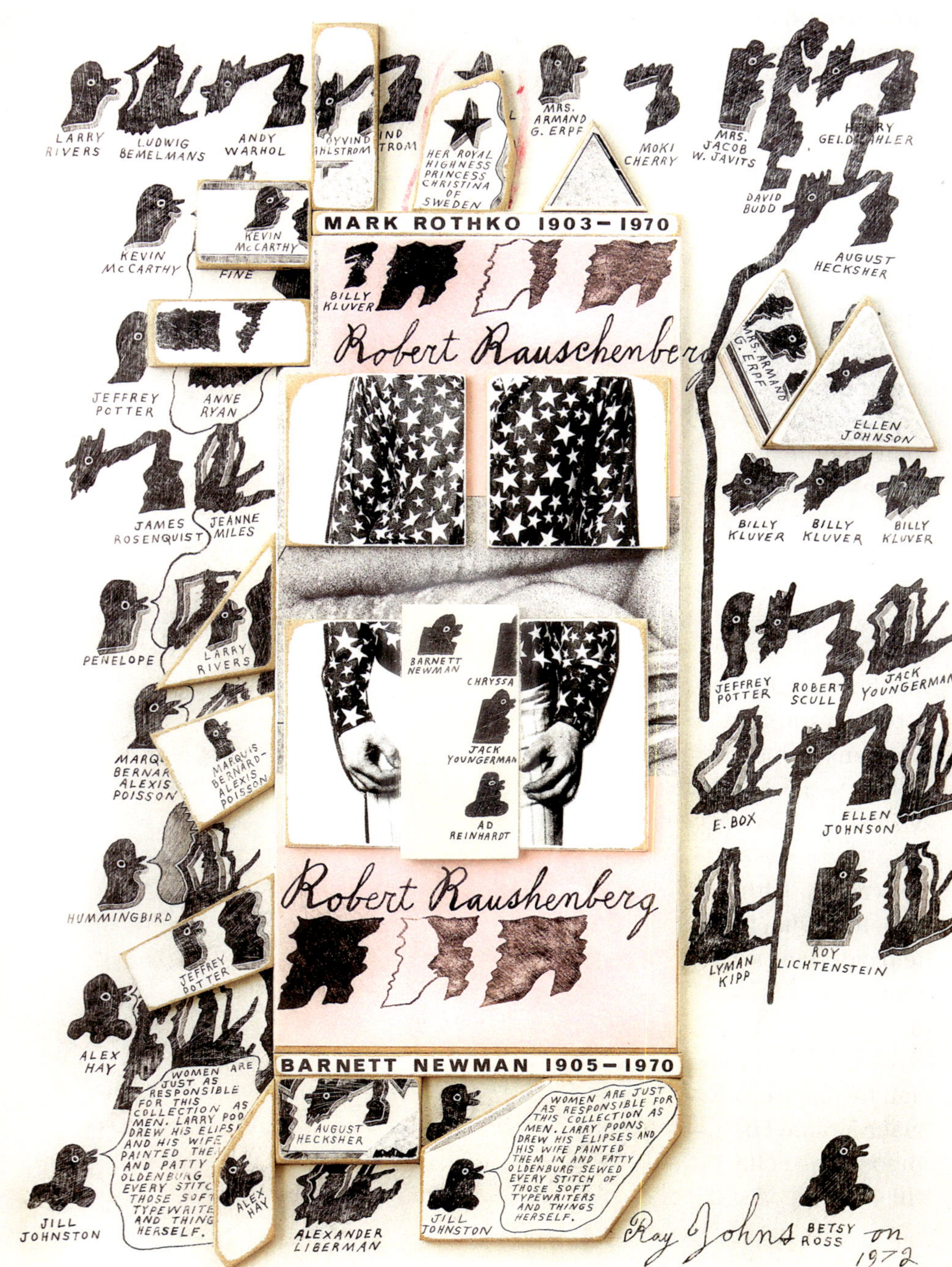

Ray Johnson, *Robert Rauschenberg* (1972).

V

What is the first question you ask a stranger? Not, where were you born, but: What's your name?

Johnson's exhibition collages of the early- to mid-1970s are often structured around loosely gridded charts of proper names, prompting critic Lawrence Alloway to observe at the time that "In Ray Johnson's collages words and images are inextricable; the denotation of proper names and the chains of visual associations tangle and unravel." In the 1972 collage *Robert Rauschenberg*, for instance, the name of flag-maker Betsy Ross interrupts the artist's stylized signature at lower right, sending our gaze up toward the star-spangled shirt of the central figure, labeled as art-star Rauschenberg, whose ex-partner, as we may recall, if we are up on our art-world gossip, was flag-painter Jasper Johns. Many of Johnson's name-filled collages are based on the "seating chart" flyers on which he listed invitees to the Meetings of his New York Correspondance School and other performance events. For the names in this piece, however, the artist drew on an actual gossip column, an account by *New York Times* reporter Charlotte Curtis of a dinner hosted by Rauschenberg for Queen Christina of Sweden in October 1972, whose guest list Curtis describes as a daring mix of "Mr. Rauschenberg's SoHo friends and a sprinkling of refugees from the tipper [*sic*] East Side."

From the downtown side of the roster, way down at the bottom of the picture, Jill Johnston, "the selfstyled 'lesbian nationalist' who rarely goes anywhere these days without a purple and white 'Dyke' button pinned to her United States Marine Corps jacket," delivers a diatribe about the wives of the art stars, whose craftwork gets scanted in the official accounts. "Women are just as responsible for this collection as men. Larry Poons drew his ellipses and his wife painted them in and Patty Oldenburg sewed every stitch of those soft typewriters and things herself." According to Curtis, Johnston's words were "rewarded with applause, mostly from the women," although the *Times* columnist, already incredulous to find herself at what "was perhaps the most unusual interpretation of a black-tie party since somebody dressed a monkey in a dinner jacket and seated it next the hostess," likely did not join in the applause. But Ray Johnson finds himself siding with the women.

Johnson sides with the women in part because he knows that as a gay man he may be viewed as feminine and so discounted. A photographic image, framed between the upper and lower portions of "Rauschenberg"'s torso in the collage features Johnson's lips, oddly vaginal in this context, while a cardboard tile effaces the torso's crotch. (Using the coded language of the day, Curtis snidely refers to Rauschenberg's girlish way of "settling his wavy shoulder-length coiffure with a bobby pin over each ear.") Still, it is not the politics of sex and gender per se that concern Johnson here so much as it is the politics of the art world. He identifies with Patty Oldenburg and Thalia Poons because he fears that, like them, he will be forgotten despite the essential role he played in the history of art.

For the contributions of the artist's wives have been scanted not only because they are women, but also because of the nature of the artistic labor they perform. Thalia Poons fills in the dots and Patty Oldenburg, like Betsy Ross, sits and sews: their work is accretive, rather than inventive. Ray Johnson knows that collage is generally held in lower esteem than painting or sculpture because it, too, may be seen as less than inventive, as a mere matter of gathering the scraps and stitching them together. To this mongrel mix, he adds a layer of gossip, that quintessentially feminine activity, a move, one would think, that could only further damage his chances in the art world. Then again, the tension between the material and social aspects of the image, a tension keyed up by the artist's anxiety over the professional rejection that he at once dreaded and invited, produced a kind of collage that no one had ever seen before. "Johnson merely explained the work," Lawrence Alloway recalls, "by saying he was name-dropping."

VI

The irony that a name-dropper like Ray Johnson should have such an utterly common name never escaped him for long. Writing to a new correspondent in 1968, Johnson offered the following in place of a self-description:

> **There is a Ray Johnson negro dancer. There is a Ray Johnson sculptor who studied with de Creeft, whose wall telephone was the best sculpture. There was a Ray Johnson who sold hardware on Madison Avenue. There's a Rayfield Johnson in the book. One year I sent them all Xmas cards. I want to get them all 14 of them to a N.Y.C.S. Meeting.**

There's a Rayfield Johnson in the book, i.e. the telephone book, the exact opposite of the name-dropper's list. In **the book**, everyone gets a listing and the names scroll by in a meaningless blur: **so much unimportance among people**, although, for the right reader in the right mood, the phone book's virtual forest of name-columns may induce a sense of the numerical sublime. In the gossip column, a precious handful of names, nothing in themselves, shine bright with the reflected light of our envy. Johnson loved both kinds of list; even more, he loved the friction you can produce by rubbing one kind against the other.

Johnson Furniture Co.
Rev. G. Adolphus Johnson
Johnson Garage, Inc.
Garfield Johnson
Gaylord Johnson
Gaylord Johnson
Mrs. Gearline Johnson
MRS. Genevieve Johnson
Mrs. Genevieve M. Johnson
George Johnson
George Johnson
George Johnson
George Johnson
George Johnson
George Johnson
George Johnson
George Johnson
George Johnson, JR.
George B. Johnson
George B. Johnson

1955

To
Mr. Alfred Barr, Jr.
Modern Museum
11 West 53 St.
nyc, ny

Ray Johnson to Alfred Barr, Jr., 1955.

It is 1955, says the postmark on the envelope, and Ray Johnson is nobody, or nobody much, certainly not yet enough of a name in the art world to ring a bell with the addressee, Alfred Barr, founding director of the Museum of Modern Art. The artist suggests as much when he stacks up a list of Johnsons taken straight from the phone book in the place where his return address should be. And yet, just as a cat may look at a king, any Johnson who wants to can mail something to Barr, or to Dorothy Miller, then MoMA's head curator, who that year also received one of Johnson's envelopes with a phonebook-listing on the left. You could say that writing to Barr and Miller was a careerist move, an impatient up-and-comer's bid for attention from the powers-that-be. And it was, except that, even back then, sending a letter was not an approved means of building your art career. Moreover, when Miller opened her envelope, she found a collaged image at the top of which Johnson had scrawled **To stay out is the problem**, a strange message for a twenty-something unknown artist to send to a prominent cultural gatekeeper, not to mention something of a performative contradiction, since he had just slipped this letter under her door, so to speak. For the rest of his life, the artist would lead museum officials, gallerists, collectors, and critics in this same baffling dance, one step forward and two steps back.

VII

Ray Johnson's ***A BOOK ABOUT DEATH*** is one of his strangest and most enigmatic projects. The "book," never constituted as such, consists of thirteen unbound prints designed one by one between 1963 and 1965, each mailed

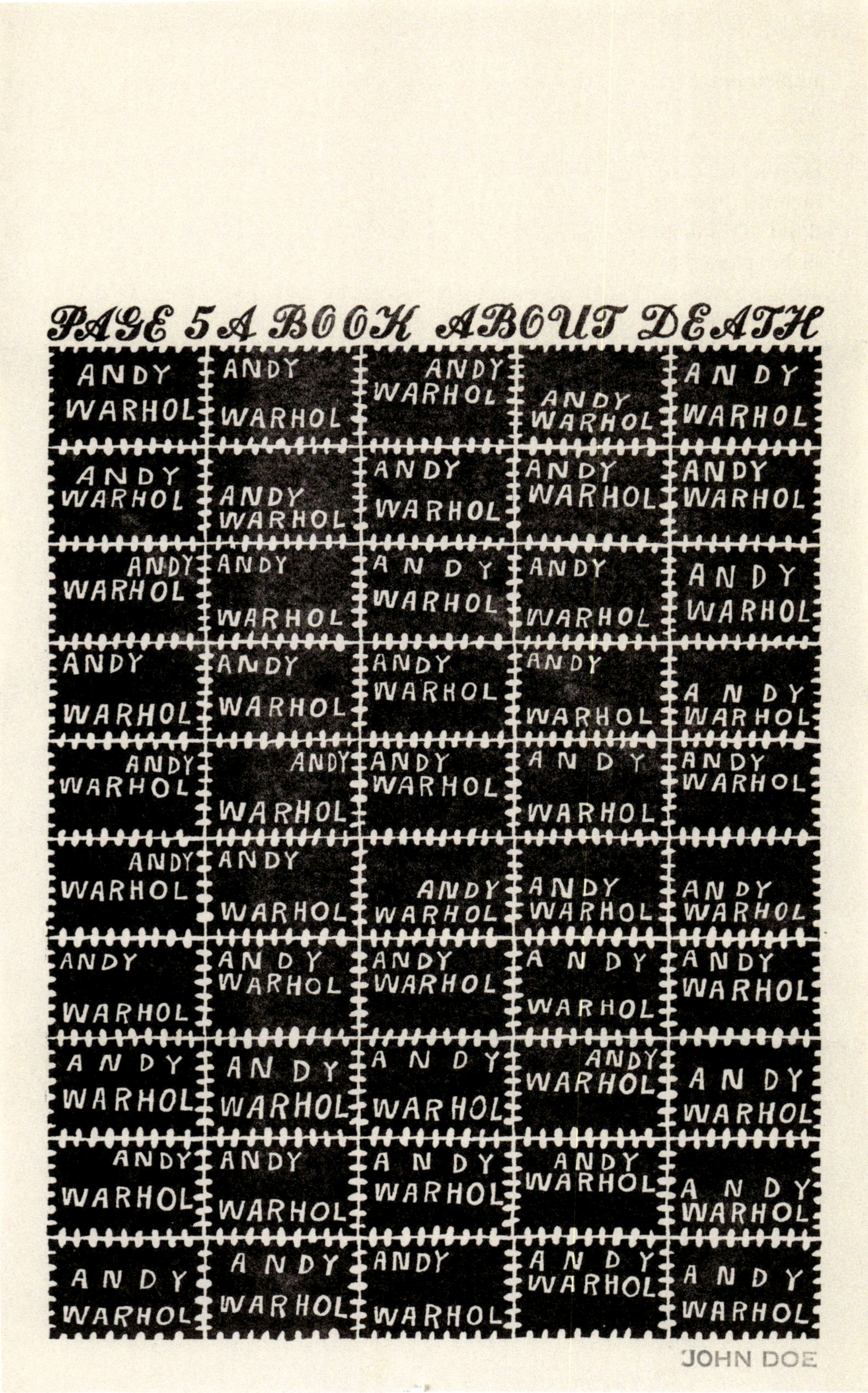

PAGE 5 A BOOK ABOUT DEATH

ANDY WARHOL	ANDY WARHOL	ANDY WARHOL	ANDY WARHOL	ANDY WARHOL
ANDY WARHOL	ANDY WARHOL	ANDY WARHOL	ANDY WARHOL	ANDY WARHOL
ANDY WARHOL	ANDY WARHOL	ANDY WARHOL	ANDY WARHOL	ANDY WARHOL
ANDY WARHOL	ANDY WARHOL	ANDY WARHOL	ANDY WARHOL	ANDY WARHOL
ANDY WARHOL	ANDY WARHOL	ANDY WARHOL	ANDY WARHOL	ANDY WARHOL
ANDY WARHOL	ANDY WARHOL	ANDY WARHOL	ANDY WARHOL	ANDY WARHOL
ANDY WARHOL	ANDY WARHOL	ANDY WARHOL	ANDY WARHOL	ANDY WARHOL
ANDY WARHOL	ANDY WARHOL	ANDY WARHOL	ANDY WARHOL	ANDY WARHOL
ANDY WARHOL	ANDY WARHOL	ANDY WARHOL	ANDY WARHOL	ANDY WARHOL
ANDY WARHOL	ANDY WARHOL	ANDY WARHOL	ANDY WARHOL	ANDY WARHOL

JOHN DOE

Ray Johnson, *A BOOK ABOUT DEATH*, page 5.

out as it emerged to various correspondents. Some pages came with a request for funds to produce the next in the series. In 1963, Andy Warhol offered to cover the printer's costs for page 5 and in response received a sepulchral take on his own *S&A H Green Stamps*, painted the year before. Warhol's green stamps are a kind of money; Johnson's Warhol stamp is a kind of tombstone, "Andy Warhol" on a slab, ad infinitum. (A copy of the Warhol page that Johnson sent to David Bourdon, a close confidant of both Ray's and Andy's, is marked with an additional ink stamp: **JOHN DOE**, the name on the toe-tags of the morgue's unknowns.) Warhol, just then riding his first wave of success, had become a name.

"I know you are but what am I?" one can imagine Johnson and Warhol wondering when they first met, sometime between 1955 and 1956, probably through their work in graphic design, a practice for which each revealed a talent while in art school. Both men pursued jobs in commercial illustration while they geared up for careers in the fine arts, although Warhol's immense success in that line would dwarf Johnson's sporadic efforts. Both were born to working-class immigrant families in middle-American industrial towns and, once they got to New York, both cultivated the mien of the cooler-than-thou cosmopolitan to the point of seeming affectless, a mask designed both to conceal and to reveal their shyness, gayness, and emotional oddity. Each became the wallflower center of an extrovert coterie. Both were refined draftsmen who first made their names as artists with pictures based on crudely altered found imagery.

Johnson took the first step in that direction with *Elvis #1 (Oedipus)* (ca. 1956–58), one of a set of star-photo collages that curator Henry Geldzahler would dub "the Plymouth Rock of the Pop Art movement." Back then, Warhol was still staking his hopes of art-world success on delicate homoerotic drawings that gallerists hesitated to show. It wasn't until 1962 that he began making paintings from star-photos, having hit, the previous year, on the pop style that would bring him fame. In the meantime, however, Johnson had abandoned his proto-pop experiments. No one would confuse his work with Warhol's going forward. Still, the uncanny resemblance between the two artists' earliest star-pictures is more than skin-deep. The ripping sound as they first tore materials from fan magazines to make art signaled the start of a lifelong preoccupation for both artists with the utopian-dystopian implications of a society built on the promise and threat that in the future, everyone will be famous for fifteen minutes.

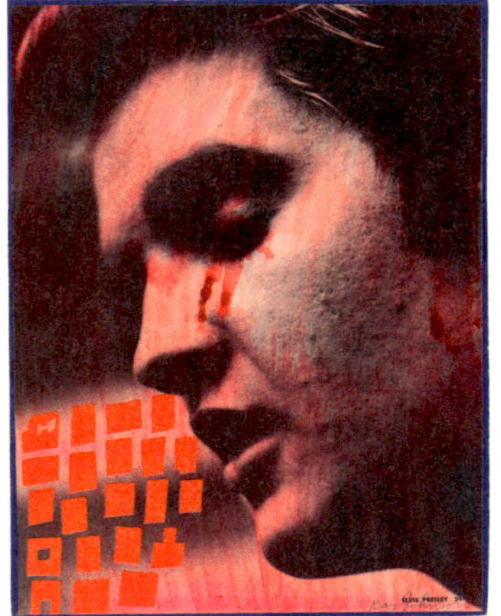

Ray Johnson, *Elvis Presley #1 (Oedipus)* (1956–58).

VIII

Johnson inscribed Warhol's name into the ***BOOK ABOUT DEATH*** in 1963, a big year, Ray knew, for Andy, the year of the blockbuster show of *Elvises* at Ferus Gallery, the first serial *Disasters*, the *Race Riots*, and the *Silver Lizzes*. It was also the year that Ray Johnson made a name for himself among Warholites by connecting up his increasingly famous friend Andy with his never-to-be-famous, though always somewhat notorious, friend Billy Linich, who in 1964 would move into the Factory, silver its walls, serve as its house photographer, and acquire the suitably Superstar-ish appellation Billy Name. In 1963, however, Ray was still reporting back to Billy from Andy's pre-Factory studio space.

Dear Billy Linich, I though you'd be interested to know that Larry & Thalia Poons and I visited Andy Warhol where we saw his recent paintings of Liz Taylor as we heard "That Little Town Flirt" and saw his recent paintings of Liz Taylor as we heard "That Little Town Flirt" and saw his recent paintings of Liz Taylor as we heard "That Little Town Flirt" and saw his recent paintings of Liz Taylor as we heard "That Little Town Flirt" and saw his recent paintings of Liz Taylor as we heard "That Little Town Flirt" and saw his recent paintings of Liz Taylor as we heard "That Little Town Flirt" and saw his recent paintings of Liz Taylor as we heard "That Little Town Flirt" and saw his recent paintings of Liz Taylor as we heard "That Little Town Flirt" and saw his recent paintings of Liz

Are Johnson's iterations of his brush with Warhol's iterations of his "Little Town Flirt" homage or satire? As is often the case with this artist, it is hard to tell the difference. Meanwhile, the differences between Warhol's paintings and Johnson's mailing in terms of scale (wall-sized/palm-sized), medium (stable/fragile), and intended audience (wide/intimate) are all too obvious. These are the differences that would determine the ever more widely divergent trajectories of their respective careers in the years to come. At the same time, Johnson's little text piece stresses some under-the-skin affinities. Warhol's silkscreen is a crude means of achieving the desired blurring effect; the carbon paper Johnson uses to reprint his text is even cruder. This crudeness seems a calculated denial of the fact that the culture was in the advanced stages of what Walter Benjamin dubbed the age of the work of art's technical reproducibility. Is a little blur in the redoubled registration all it takes to get the aura back?

The same and yet not The same and yet not The same and yet not The same

Dear Billy Linich, I thought you'd be interested
to know that Larry & Thalia Poons and I visited
Andy Warhol where we saw his recent paintings of
Liz Taylor as we heard "That Little Town Flirt"
and saw his recent paintings of Liz Taylor as we
heard "That Little Town Flirt" and saw his recent
paintings of Liz Taylor as we heard "That Little
Town Flirt" and saw his recent paintings of Liz
Taylor as we heard "That Little Town Flirt" and
saw his recent paintings of Liz Taylor as we heard
"That Little Town Flirt" and saw his recent paintings
of Liz Taylor as we heard "That Little Town Flirt"
and saw his recent paintings of Liz Taylor as we
heard "That Little Town Flirt" and saw his recent
paintings of Liz Taylor as we heard "That Little
Town Flirt" and saw his recent paintings of Liz

Dear Billy Linich, I thought you'd be interested
to know that Larry & Thalia Poons and I visited
Andy Warhol where we saw his recent paintings of
Liz Taylor as we heard "That Little Town Flirt"
and saw his recent paintings of Liz Taylor as we
heard "That Little Town Flirt" and saw his recent
paintings of Liz Taylor as we heard "That Little
Town Flirt" and saw his recent paintings of Liz
Taylor as we heard "That Little Town Flirt" and
saw his recent paintings of Liz Taylor as we heard
"That Little Town Flirt" and saw his recent paintir
of Liz Taylor as we heard "That Little Town Flirt"
and saw his recent paintings of Liz Taylor as we
heard "That Little Town Flirt" and saw his recent
paintings of Liz Taylor as we heard "That Little
Town Flirt" and saw his recent paintings of Liz

DEPOSITORS CONTRACT

The above rules, regulations, conditions, limitations, and the rights and remedies herein provided are cumulative, and not exclusive of any rules, regulations, conditions, limitations, rights and remedies, provided by any other agreement between the depositor and this Company, or by law.

Ray Johnson to Billy Linich, ca. 1963.

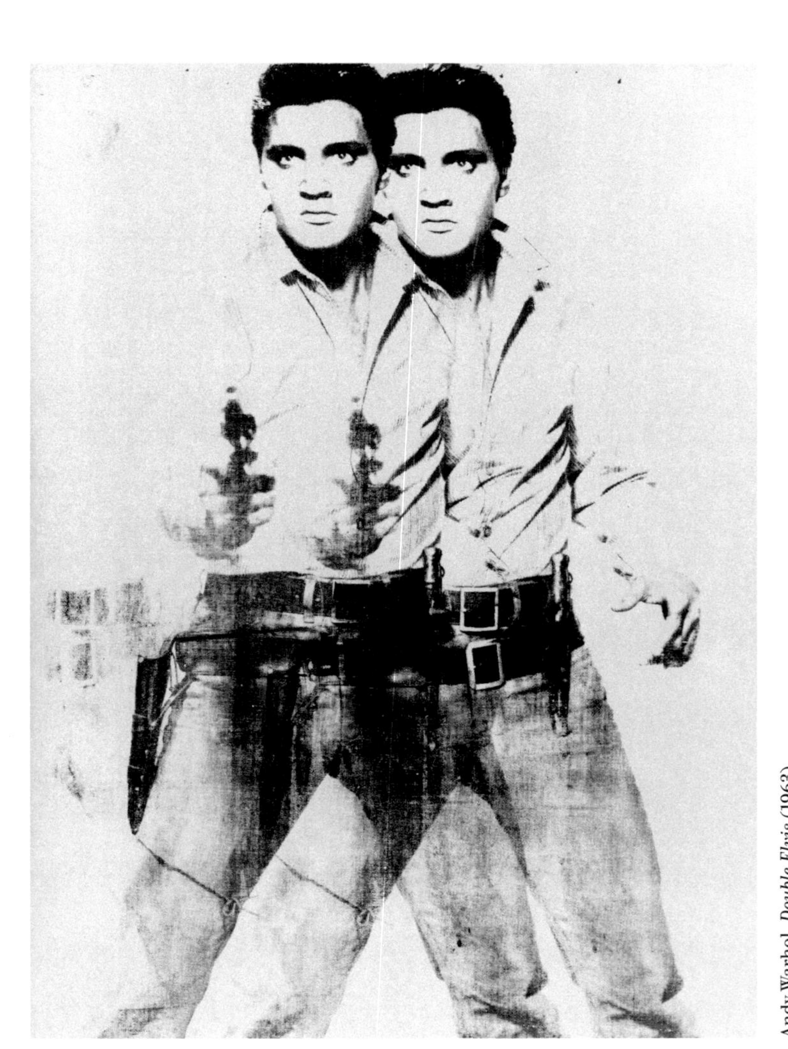
Andy Warhol, *Double Elvis* (1963).

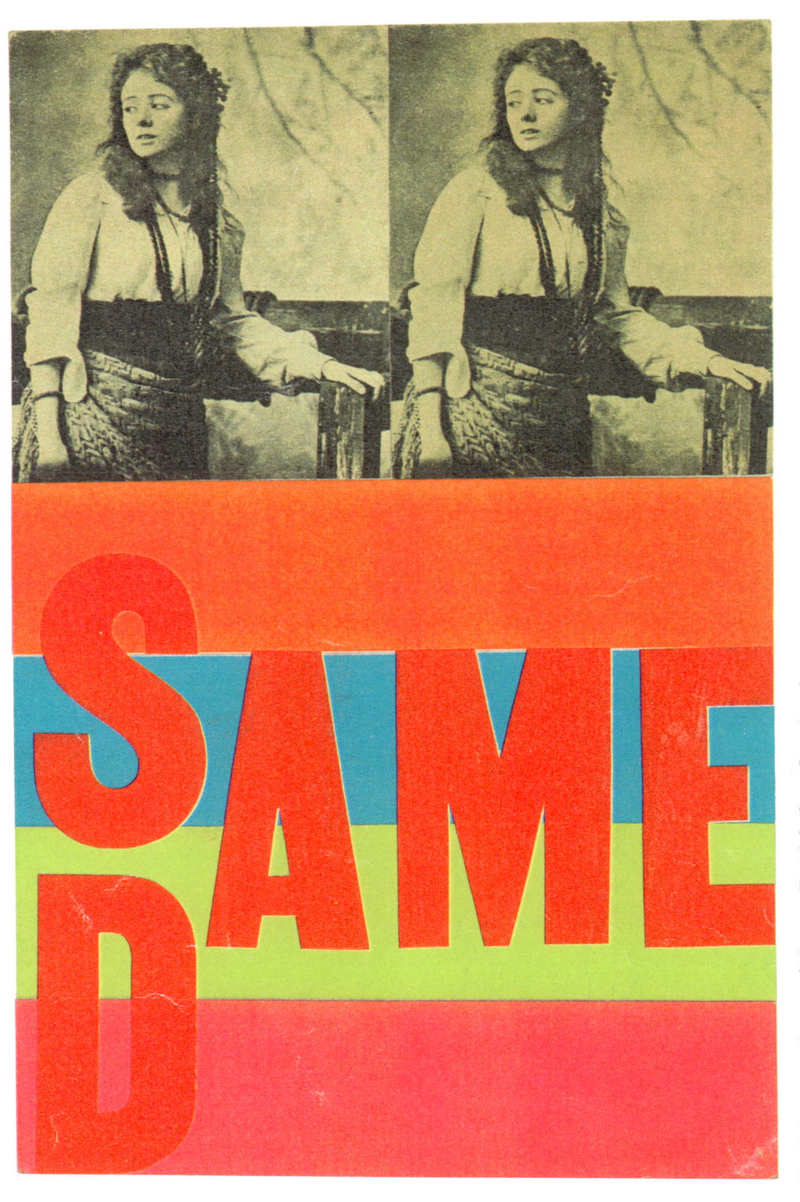

Ray Johnson to Norman Solomon, *Untitled (Same Dame)*, n.d.

IX

In the mid-1950s, Johnson mailed a collage featuring two identical photos of a turn-of-the-century beauty and the letters **S/D/AME** to Norman Solomon, a friend from Black Mountain who was a painter, a photographer, and a world-class wiseacre in the mold of William Demarest, the actor to whom director Preston Sturges gives the final word in his 1941 comedy of mistaken identity, "The Lady Eve." "Positively the same dame," Demarest groans, shaking his head, as he shuts the door on Barbara Stanwyck and Henry Fonda, who can't seem to take in the fact that the Stanwyck he has in his arms is the same dame as the Stanwyck he married. (Long story.) Of course, being an actor, Stanwyck always goes by a different name in her movies—in the case of "The Lady Eve," where she plays a con woman playing an aristocrat, two different names—although, being a star, she is nonetheless always "Barbara Stanwyck" as well as the character she plays. (Like many stars, Barbara Stanwyck also had a "real" name: Ruby Catherine Stevens.)

Ray Johnson was interested in stardom as, among other things, a special case of a universal phenomenon. Each of us has a name and a set of photographic images by which others may identify us, personal markers that nonetheless can and will float free of our persons and circulate in our absence. We all, that is, have our ghosts.

"THE [*sic*] KNOW WHAT'S IN A NAME—Linda Lee, left, of Chinatown, and Linda Lee, of Old Tappan, N.J., see the sights along Mott St., New York City," reads the caption under the photo accompanying a news item that Johnson clipped and sent to Bill Wilson in 1963. "LINDA LEE, MEET LINDA LEE. When Linda Lee, 11, picked up the New York Herald Tribune last February in Old Tappan, N.J., and saw a picture of Linda Lee, 11, along with a story about the Chinese New Year, she wrote Linda Lee a letter suggesting a pen pal relationship."

Underneath the headline Johnson has typed **Linda Lee 111, metts** [*sic*] **Linda Lee, 111 and Linda Lee, 111 (in 1963).** This intervention is typical Ray weirdness, which is to say, weirdness with a point. Read the story's lede again. "When Linda Lee, 11, picked up the New York Herald Tribune last February in Old Tappan, N.J., and saw a picture of Linda Lee, 11, along with a story about the Chinese New Year, she wrote Linda Lee a letter suggesting a pen pal relationship." By the time one gets to that third "Linda Lee," the name starts to float free of its referent. Encountering one's double at once reinforces one's sense of identity—she is like me—and renders it uncanny—but what does it mean, to be "like me"?

ONE TWO THREE HERE COMES LINDA LEE THREE FOUR FIVE LOOK AT HER JIVE, Johnson has penned on a scrap of paper sent together with the *New York Herald Tribune* clipping (cf. "Mr. Lee" by the Bobbettes, 1957). The notion of a third, ghostly "Linda Lee, 11" makes the graphic artist in him see the Arabic 11 as a Roman double-I. Linda Lee I, Linda Lee II, Linda Lee III. As the I's multiply, identity jives and jumps. Ray Johnson loved the graphic quality of the English pronomial "I," whether formed like a pillar or a simple line. For him, it was the symbol of a sensation, the sensation of a subject always in the process of shedding its subjectivity, of becoming something else. A postcard Johnson sent to Norman Solomon in 1958 reads, in its entirety,

Even now, as
I write I

The next year, Norman received a card from Ray across which he had scrawled:

I AM NORMAN SOLOMON

X

When Jasper Johns had his first solo show at Leo Castelli's gallery in 1958, *Art News* noted that the auspicious debut "place[d] him with such better-known colleagues as Rauschenberg, Twombly, Kaprow and Ray Johnson." Unlike Robert Rauschenberg, Cy Twombly, and Allan Kaprow, Ray Johnson had an overly common last name, so the *Art News* writer included his first name as well. More significantly, unlike these peers, Johnson had not yet had a solo show with a major gallery, making it something of a mystery how the writer came to rank him with the others in the first place. Three years after the MoMA curators received their puzzling mailings from a phonebook's-worth of Johnsons, "Ray Johnson" had already become a name—of sorts.

Shortly after the *Art News* piece on Johns's debut came out (it made the cover), Johnson made ambivalent mention of it in a letter to a newish but already dear confidant, May Wilson, Bill's mother. Still at that time a housewife and Sunday painter living in suburban Maryland—she was perhaps the only member of Johnson's Correspondance School to have signed up for an actual correspondence-school art course—May would move to Manhattan eight years later, at the age of sixty-one, to pursue a career as a maker of unsettlingly grotty junk assemblages and sexually subversive collages. Bill, who had mixed feelings about having his mother on the scene, nonetheless wrote a laudatory article in which he coined the nickname by which May would become known, "The Grandma Moses of the Underground." Ray was drawn to May Wilson's as yet somewhat suppressed wild side from his first visits home with Bill. He encouraged her ambitions, offering generous critiques of the artwork she sent him and letters full of inside dope and inside jokes about the art world.

I have not seen Arts in which I am highly sculptural, reported Ray to May in January 1958. **Probably refers to the Zabriskie collage show,** "Collage in America," a wide-ranging group exhibition at Zabriskie Gallery which included Johns, Kaprow, and Rauschenberg along with Johnson. **Although it may refer to the other Ray Johnson. There are five of us in the Manhattan phone book. I am number five on the Dada Hit Parade, according to January Art News. Others being Raushenberg, Johns, Twombley, Kaprow and myself. That's probably me they are referring to although it may be one of the other Ray Johnsons.**

Johnson sometimes spells Twombly's name right in his missives to others, but Rauschenberg's never, an error that seems to have been motivated by a mix of animus and rivalry. While the animus may or may not have had its justifications—**Bob Raushenberg told me once that he was my friend. I replied: No, we're not. Friends are friendly,** a moody Ray complained to Bill, also in 1958—the sense of rivalry was well-nigh unavoidable. The shadows cast by those other, unimportant Ray Johnsons may veil but cannot fully conceal the Ray who would finally, in 1965, admit to Grace Glueck that, all that time, he had **been dying for a show**. The boys in the Dada Hit Parade (yes, boys only; Jill Johnston's tirade certainly had its justifications) were just this or that side of thirty in 1958 and starting to hit their stride. For them, the race to make a name for oneself, a name that moves to the top of the list and stays there, was on.

XI

The title of *Man O'War*, a collage composed in Johnson's early-1970s style, refers to the famous racing thoroughbred, and the collage itself is centered on a horse's star-coated silhouette. Under the horse's hooves is a memorial plaque, a common feature of the abstracted celebrity portraits that Johnson turned out by the dozens in the 1970s. Two such plaques bracket the truncated central figure in *Robert Rauschenberg*, commemorating the recently departed **MARK ROTHKO 1903–1970** and **BARNETT NEWMAN 1905–1970**, big-name art-world ghosts. At first glance, the stallion in *Man O'War* might seem to be running in a different race, until you notice how what looks like a typesetter's error bends his name and dates back in the direction of the art world. The horse's cenotaph, "Man O'War, 1917–1947," thus becomes **MAN O'WARH9L7–1947**, the mangled but still recognizable signature of Ray's old friend, by that time the undisputed front-runner of their generation, at least in terms of sheer fame.

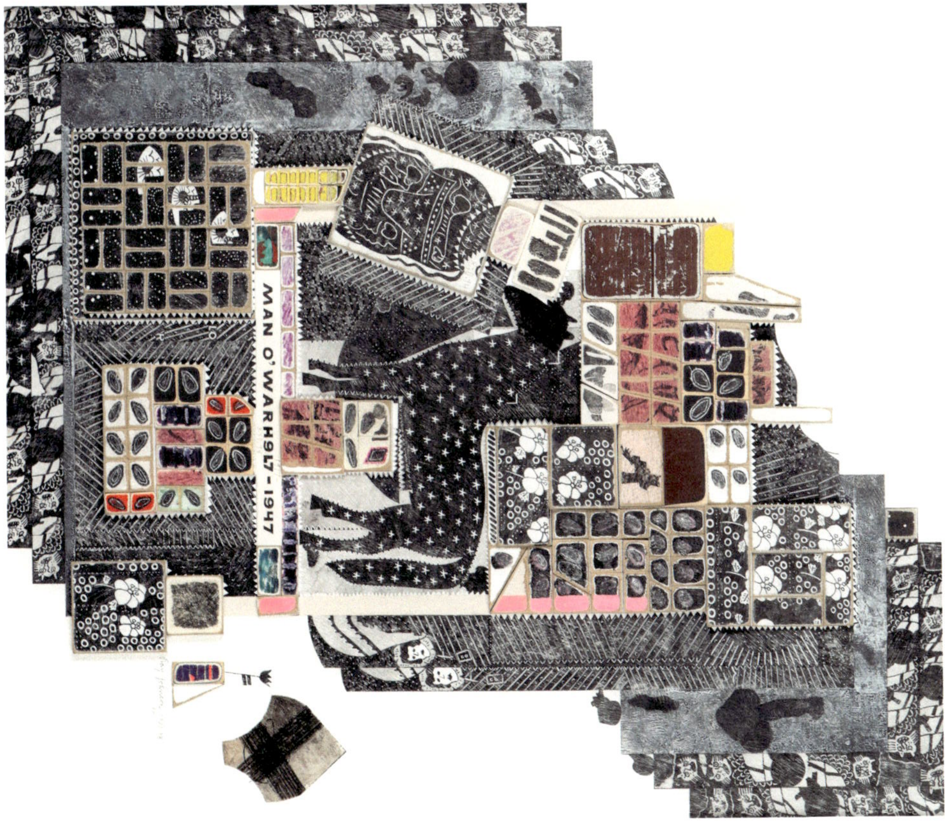

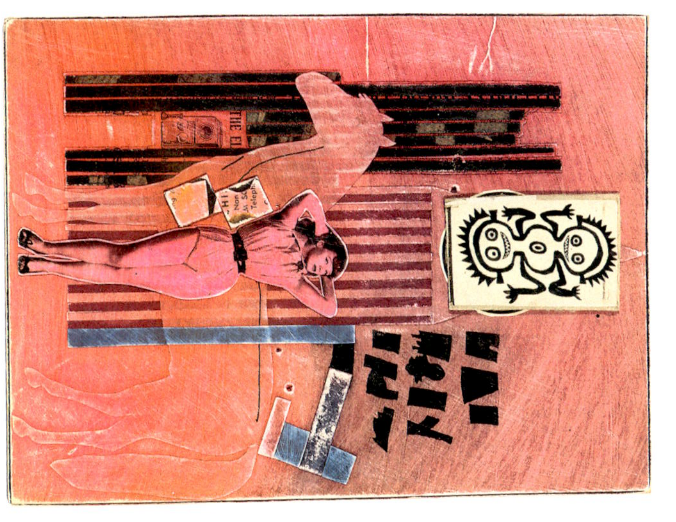

Ray Johnson, *Movie Star with Horse* (1958).

Ray Johnson, *Man O'War* (1971–88–94).

The artist's attitude toward his subject also bends and twists. This portrait of the artist as a trophy winner could certainly be taken as a jab at Warhol. Notice, on that score, how the horse-man's signature ends with "L7," 1950s slang for a total square—for example, an artist whose pursuit of uptown success cost him coolness points with his downtown friends. Then again, the more than usually strict grid that Johnson imposed on this unabashedly pretty composition, with its bursts of stars and flowers, could be read as a *celebration* of the square. The horse, meanwhile, is also a figure of identification for Johnson, always associated with his ambivalent attraction to fame. The equine silhouette in *Man O'War* has a pedigree in the artist's work that can be traced back at least as far as *Movie Star with Horse*—from 1958, that is, the year that Ray Johnson was running neck and neck with Rauschenberg, Johns, and co., **according to January Art News.**

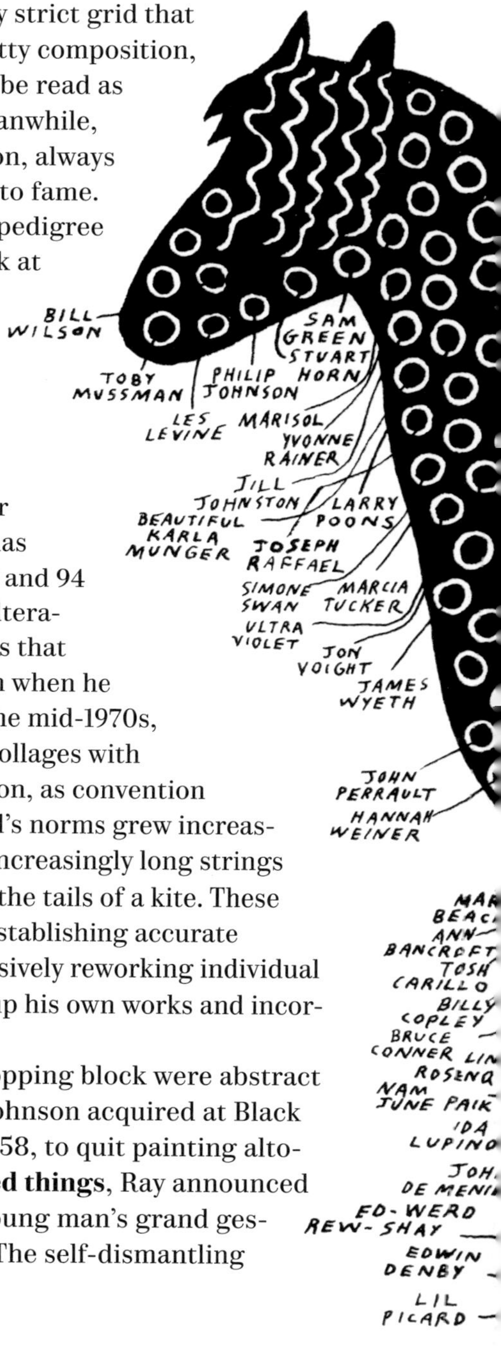

Although *Man O'War* bears the stylistic hallmarks that place it with Johnson's other "portrait" works from the early-1970s, he has given it a serial date, "1971–88–94." The 88 and 94 in this case likely refer to very minor late alterations made to the image; the 94 also tells us that this piece was still in the artist's possession when he died, at the turn of that year. Up through the mid-1970s, Johnson tended to inscribe his exhibition collages with a single date marking the time of completion, as convention dictates. But as his relation to the art world's norms grew increasingly vexed, the collages began to feature increasingly long strings of dates trailing the artist's signature, like the tails of a kite. These multiple dates index, without necessarily establishing accurate chronologies for, the artist's habit of obsessively reworking individual pictures, as well as his practice of cutting up his own works and incorporating the fragments into new pieces.

Among the works consigned to the chopping block were abstract paintings done in the Albersian manner Johnson acquired at Black Mountain, the artist having decided, in 1958, to quit painting altogether. **I went to Cy Twombly's and burned things**, Ray announced to Bill Wilson, in October of that year, a young man's grand gesture of renunciation and self-recreation. The self-dismantling impulse embodied in that gesture, however, would not only persist but would become ever more integral to Johnson's artistic process. Collage is the art of reassembling the fragments of a broken world without pretending they can ever be joined again into a whole. Ray Johnson practiced collage in this sense, but still more, his was an art of auto-collage. The half-assembled puzzle of his oeuvre shows a portrait of the artist as Frankenstein's monster, each painful seam exposed.

XII

Ray Johnson, auto-collagist, was as thrifty with motifs as he was with materials. The horse makes another appearance in a photocopied mailing, undated but likely created soon after November 5, 1969, when Johnson encountered Rosalind Constable, who was thinking of writing an article about him, at his New York Correspondance School's **When It Rains It Pours** meeting at the School of Visual Arts. Tethered to the animal's outline by dozens of little lines, are names drawn from Johnson's

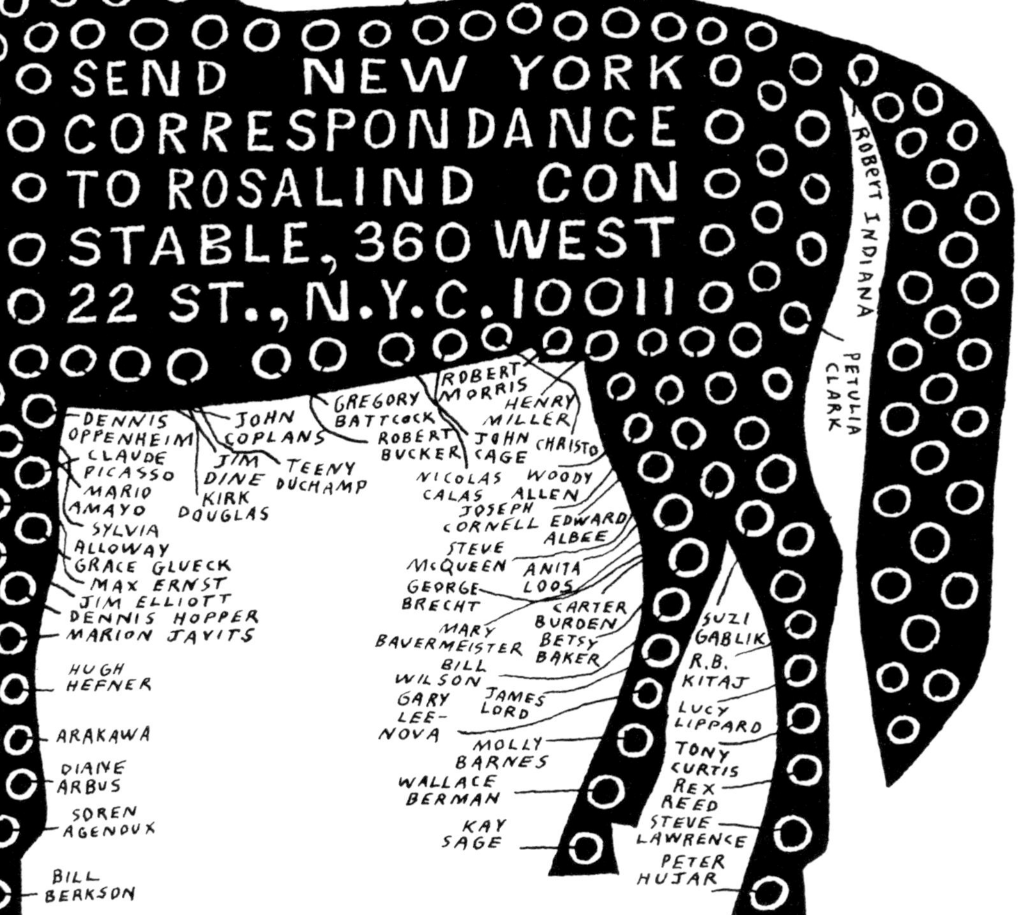

Ray Johnson, NYCS mailer with Rosalind Constable horse, ca. 1969.

then-current concentric circles of intimates, art-world allies, and celebrity fascinations. The horse itself is covered with circles, rather than the stars that bedeck the artist's Man O'War: the one is designed to range around the social network, the other to hang on a wall, above and apart.

Constable's own name, inscribed on the horse's flank, has been broken in two so as to make a pun on "Stable," a home for a horse, of course, but also a term for a gallery's roster of artists and the name of a Manhattan gallery that hosted shows of very early works by Rauschenberg, Twombly, and Warhol. Following the journalist's name is her home address. After Constable told Johnson that she wanted to write an article about him and his work, he issued the please-send-to order and she was barraged by mailings from the members of the NYCS, including "A letter from Ray Johnson saying: **Andy Warhol said he wanted to be quoted as saying 'Ray Johnson's letters are entertaining.'**" All this left her more amused than surprised, since "this was not the first time I had been on Johnson's mailing list, for back in the fifties I had interviewed him in his stark white studio on slummy Suffolk Street on the Lower East Side. A day or two later I received from Johnson a small envelope containing a small quantity of dust."

XIII

From 1937 to 1967, Rosalind Constable held the best job one never knew existed, as "Time-Life's avant-garde specialist," writing a newsletter on the latest in cutting-edge culture that circulated only among certain editors at the Luce Corporation, the publisher of virtually every magazine you might expect to find on a mid-century coffee table. In 1962, Ray's friend John Wilcock profiled Constable for the *Village Voice,* a scruffy newsprint weekly that was the very antitype of a Luce glossy. "Rosie Constable saves Henry Luce a great deal of money in getting an education for himself," a colleague quipped to the reporter. Wilcock nonetheless judged it "a pity" that Constable's newsletter was strictly an in-house affair, since "The Constable Report, always interesting, is often brilliant in its blending of disparate facts into a comprehensive entity."

That description could apply just as well to the work of Ray Johnson, another tracker of who's who in the avant-garde and drawer of previously unsuspected connections, whose charts and lists of names were mailed around to a select group, interoffice memos of a kind. That Johnson himself saw an overlap between his purview and Constable's is implied in an offhand comment he made in a letter-to-the-editor that was published in the *Village Voice* in 1964: **Those Jasper Johns alphabetized paintings might just as well have been a listing of Rosalind Constable trend-setters or taste-makers.**

It is not easy to reconstruct the context of this remark, which appears mid-way through the letter to the *Voice*. In the first place, Johnson is referring, of course, to Jasper Johns's great series of pictures featuring the letters of the alphabet, stenciled and arranged in order in a grid, works that, much like Johns's series of numbers, and somewhat like his flags, targets, and maps, play on Dadaist notions of foundness, on the one hand, and modernist notions of painterly flatness, on the other. Johnson conveys his grasp of the dynamic at work in these pictures with his usual economy in a 1965 mailing to Wilson, where he has taken a magazine page featuring an image of a Johns numbers painting and cut a hole through the photo's caption so as to emphasize the words "FLAT IMAGES," then taped a cut-out from another Johns image half-way over the hole. (Thin as the mass-produced-magazine page may be, it is not *utterly* flat.) "DYE," reads the cut-out, a reminder that while Johns rendered some of his letter and number charts in bright primary colors, others in the series are restricted to a palette of dull lead-grays, and a suggestion that Johns's compulsion to repeat these rigid litanies of letters and numbers has a tinge of the death-drive.

The nominal occasion for Johnson's letter was an advertisement that had recently run in the *Voice* for *Home Movies*, a musical one-act by the painter and professional wrestler Rosalyn Drexler and the playwright and preacher Al Carmines. The ad took the form of a letter offering a defense of Drexler and Carmines' production, which had been deemed

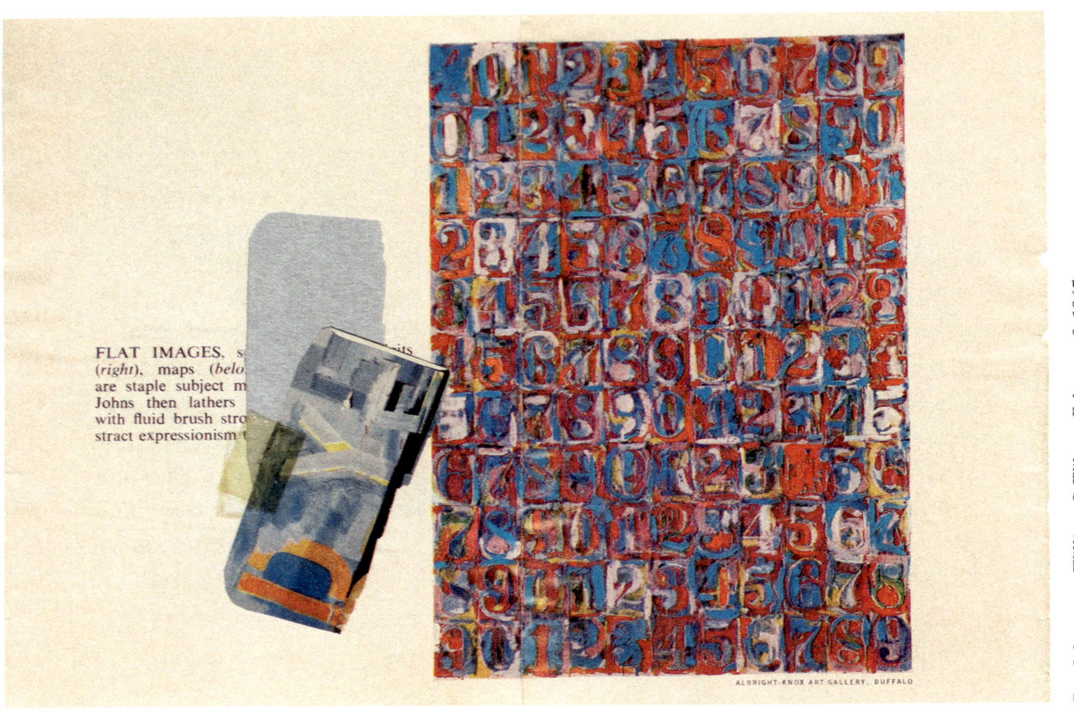

Ray Johnson to William S. Wilson, February 2, 1965.

"of questionable worth and taste" by the *New York Times*; signatories to the letter included several of Johnson's friends in the art and theater worlds, among them Jasper Johns and the founders of the Living Theater, Julian Beck and Judith Malina. Malina and Beck themselves were no strangers to controversy, as Johnson reminds us in a barbed reference to Malina's brief imprisonment after having turned the Living Theater's 1963 trial for tax evasion into a riotous performance piece. **I remember when Julian Beck and Judith Jailbird were forever listing their sponsors down the left side of their stationery**. Bill Wilson preserved a Living Theater program from that period in his archive, and it is quite a list—

Lionel Abel
Horace Armistead
John Cage
Joseph Campbell
Dollie Pierre Chareau
Merce Cunningham
Jean Cocteau
Elaine de Kooning
Willem de Kooning
Jean Erdman
Wallace Fowlie
Paul Goodman
Lou Harrison
Erick Hawkins
Frederick Kiesler
Willard Maas
James Merrill
Betty Parsons
Tibor de Nagy Gallery
Parker Tyler
Amos Vogel
Oscar Williams
Tennessee Williams

—a list Johnson himself could scarcely improve on, with its mix of names well-known and cult, downtown and uptown, crossing fields, classes, and generations, shot through with a hot-pink thread of those-who-know queerness.

The sentence in the letter about Beck and Malina is immediately followed by the reference to Johns and Constable, a seemingly free association motivated by a peculiar sort of envy. Johnson envied the social connections that Beck and Malina leveraged for their sponsorship, just as he envied those that Drexler and Carmines leveraged in their defense, connections that anyone might envy as a sign of social power, but that only Johnson would covet because they enabled the making of great lists. Rosalind Constable appears here as another enviable list-maker.

But Jasper Johns was not that kind of list-maker, nor was the reclusive artist known for his social reach. He was enviable, however, in other ways. In 1958, writing to Bill Wilson about Johns's debut at Castelli, Ray's satirical edge was blunted by self-pity. **Jasper Johns has a sell-out of his show. Modern Museum bought four. Alfred Barr bought one for his wife. Those American flags. Targets, etc. [...] How is May. How is you. I am sick, sick, sick. But on to the art world I go. To that uptown opening. Boo hoo.**
It could be the out-paced racehorse in Johnson boo-hooing again when he implies that, like Constable's insider reports, Johns's austere alphabets

are just gossip in high-toned drag. Still, it is such a strange thought, counterintuitive, to say the least. Turn the thought on its head, though, and you get the curiously plausible suggestion that Johnson's manifestly gossipy interest in names is, at its root, just as impersonal and as reliant on given-not-made structures as Johns's compulsive repetitions of letters and numbers. Johnson understood that compulsion from the inside. He had his own thing for letters and numbers, which derived in part from a Johns-like need to speak without speaking, to render the elements of expression inexpressive, thing-like.

One consequence of this need to render the personal impersonal, for Johnson as for Johns, is that letters often become interchangeable with numbers. In June of 1963, a few months after Bill received Ray's mailing regarding Linda Lees I, II, and (possibly) III, Ray sent Bill a mini-collage with a clipped-out etymological history of the letter J, which, according to the clipping, is a "modified form of I," to which "a curve was added ... to distinguish it when it stood as an initial." That scrap has been taped to a page on which Ray has re-typed an editor's note from New Directions' 1957 edition of Arthur Rimbaud's volume of prose poems, *Illuminations*. The note explains how a poem originally titled "H" came to be mistakenly retitled "Antique II" by an earlier editor. A printer's error turned the letter into a number.

Page 123. H. Formerly this poem was incorrectly entitled "Antique II." De Lacoste offers the following explanation of how the title "H" disappeared: After several printings the letter "H" became so worn that it lost its crossbar and became the Roman numeral II. Someone then decided that it must be the sequel to the preceding poem which, in Berrichon's order, was Antique, hence "Antique II."

J, 10th letter of Eng. alphabet, modified form of I; was the last letter to be added to the alphabet. In Lat. *I* had the consonant sound of *Y*, as well as being a vowel. In the 14th cent. a curve was added to *I*, to distinguish it when it stood as an initial; thus the present form of *J*.

Ray Johnson to William S. Wilson, 1963.

Someone once asked me if I was an S. or an M.
I replied "I was J."

Johnson explained, in a November 1968 letter to his friend the artist Nam June Paik, firmly deflecting what seems to have been a personal question in the direction of the impersonal.

Johnson's personal-impersonal love for lettering is partly a matter of need. But it is also a matter of craft, derived from the rigorous training in the elements of design that he received, first in high school, and then, crucially, from two of his favorite teachers at Black Mountain, painter Josef Albers and graphic designer Alvin Lustig. From Albers, known for his endless series of images of squares on squares on squares, Johnson also took the grid-as-given. The structuring grid remains clearly visible under even the busiest of his compositions and always governs his lists of names. This structure, too, is held in place by the counterforces of psychic need and aesthetic commitment.

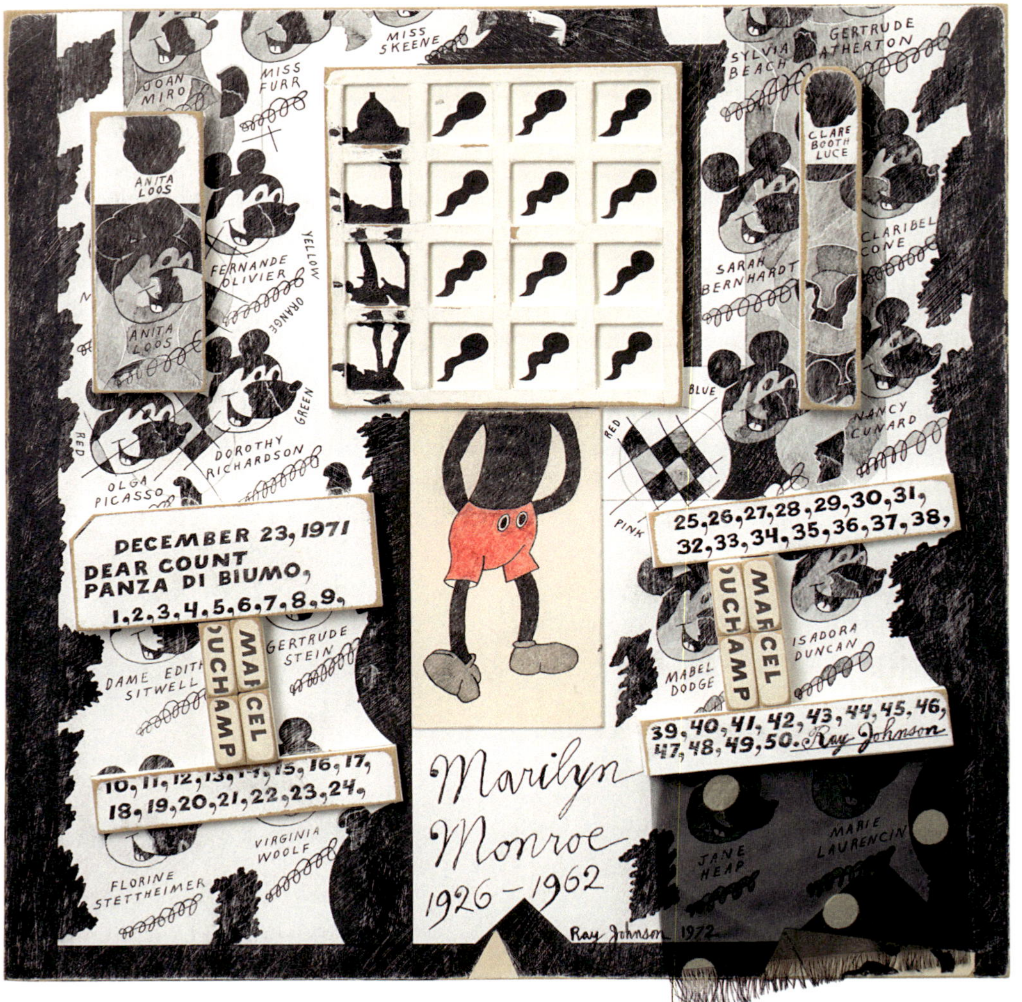

Ray Johnson, *Marilyn Monroe, 1926–1962* (1972).

XIV

As Andy Warhol assumed his longed-for place in the floodlit world of famous faces, Ray Johnson went the other way, retreating, like Jasper Johns, into a private world governed by puzzling symbols and coded words. Still, like Warhol (and quite unlike Johns), Johnson kept an eye trained on the fame-world. He just viewed it from a very different angle.

In Johnson's celebrity portraits, fame's power inheres not in the magnetic star-image but, more tenuously, in the abstracted star-name. All that remains of the putative subject of his 1972 collage, *Marilyn Monroe 1926–1962*, is the star's named-and-numbered cenotaph. A recognizable star-body does occupy the picture's center, but it belongs to Mickey Mouse, whose head, cut off from its trunk, multiplies to fill the compositional grid. Each repetition of the mouse-head is attached to a different name, all belonging to real or fictional women associated with the early twentieth-century avant-gardes, with two exceptions: painter Joan Miro, whose name an English speaker might mistake for a woman's, and Clare Boothe Luce, wife of Time-Life publisher Henry Luce and a popular playwright who had a big hit with *The Women*. As in *Robert Rauschenberg*, made the same year, Johnson identifies here with women whose names he fears may be lost to history.

The name "Mickey Mouse," meanwhile, is nowhere to be found among the heads, but those in the habit of tracking Johnson's line of thought will arrive at the mouse's name by association, through Monroe's, with which it shares its initials, *MM*. When read from Johnson's oblique angle, the star-name—the last vestige of fame—devolves into mere letters. Then there is the letter—as in postal message—that the artist has cut up and refit into the grid of the Monroe portrait, whose words have devolved into a series of numbers. What might it have said? Addressed to the collector Count Giuseppe Panza di Biumo (a count for a Count) and signed by Johnson, one imagines it was yet another bid for recognition on the artist's part.

XV

One could make the case that the names in Johnson's art are impersonal insofar as they are (doubly, punningly) disembodied, signifiers cut adrift from their signifieds, then conscripted to march in rows under identical cartoon heads. One could even argue that for Johnson, writing is just another form of drawing, so that, in a name-chart piece like *Robert Rauschenberg*, the names are no more or less significant than the morphing, glyph-like shapes he pairs with them to mark the squares of the inevitable grid. In the end, though, unlike Jasper Johns' gridded alphabets, which only look like gossip columns to Ray's X-Ray eyes, Johnson's name-charts are as much sociological as they are formal. Those names do conjure a world, "forming a neat political cut through the artist-critic-dealer-collector Big Apple," as Mary Josephson put it in her 1973 review of Johnson's **History of the Betty Parsons Gallery**, "at, of course, Betty Parsons."

It took some nerve in 1973 for a critic to suggest, as Josephson does in her review's first sentence, that "Formalism's art-from-art DNA linkages are still, despite bandwagon antiformalists, a beautiful historical model." The overwhelming sensuousness of mid-century abstraction had nurtured a breed of critics who trained viewers to keep their eyes on the canvas. But as Allan Kaprow observed in his prophetic essay "The Legacy of Jackson Pollock," there was a tendency in Pollock's work, unnoted by his critical contemporaries, that would inexorably steer his truest heirs away from pure painting. Their art, the art of Johnson's generation, would call for new modes of historical and philosophical explanation. Josephson herself admits that formalismà la Clement Greenberg had become a bit of a closed circuit, a kind of addiction, a way for "history [to] get a high from its own processes." "One way out"—Johnson's way out, according to Josephson—"is to piggyback not on art history but the *art scene*—its rumors, gossip, oral traditions." The art scene is flimsy and trashy, as historical sources go; still, "maybe Johnson's Kleenex version of history is trying to tell us something we don't want to hear."

The piece is brilliant edge to edge. After he read it, Johnson promptly organized a Meeting for Josephson at the Paula Cooper Gallery. Did he or did he not know at the time that "Mary Josephson" was one of the pseudonyms of Brian O'Doherty, critic and artist, and himself one of the great limners of the contours of the art scene? O'Doherty later claimed that Johnson did not know, that Johnson tried to get in touch with Josephson through him, O'Doherty, in his role as editor of *Art in America*, the place where the review appeared. "Mary Josephson, one of my alter egos, wrote about him sympathetically. He wanted to meet her. So ... I had to hide Mary." Every name on a Ray Johnson list is a rabbit hole.

In the late-1960s, after he had his first major gallery shows, and as he began to formalize the activities of the New York Correspondance School, Ray Johnson adopted as his signature icon a crudely drawn rabbit-head. The correspondence-school simplicity of its rendering suggests that the icon is rooted in the Duchampian ethic that held that everyone and anyone could be, in fact already is, an artist. Rows of identical rabbit-heads spread across the name-charts, each accompanied by its singular name, at once the sign and the negation of personal identity. The rabbit-head inspired the apt title of *How to Draw a Bunny*, a 2002 Ray Johnson documentary by John Walter and Andrew Moore that for the first time spread Johnson's reputation beyond the tight circles of cult followers and aficionados of the "artist's artist" who had until then kept his name alive.

The rabbit is also a trickster figure—Br'er Rabbit, Bugs Bunny, the creature who lures Alice down the fateful hole.

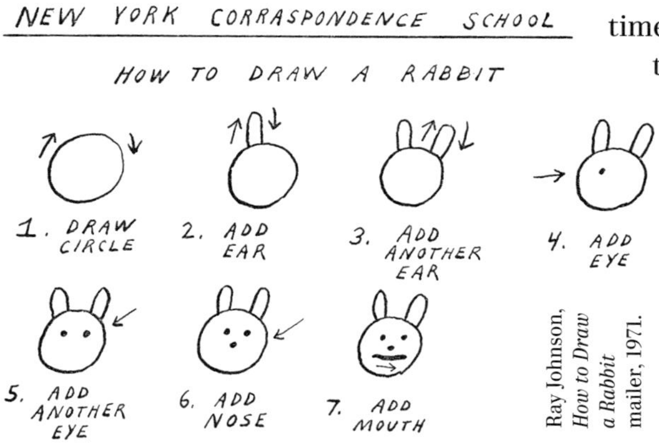

Ray Johnson, *How to Draw a Rabbit* mailer, 1971.

“The Key Was on the Table,” reads the newpaper caption under a still from the 1933 film version of *Alice in Wonderland* that Ray clipped and sent to Bill in 1964. Just before this scene, the book tells us, Alice had been chasing the White Rabbit only to find herself suddenly alone in a hall lined with locked doors. Seeing the key, her “first idea was that it might belong to one of the doors of the hall, but alas! either the locks were too large, or the key was too small, but at any rate it would not open any of them.” One knows how she felt.

XVI

“Maybe Johnson’s Kleenex version of history is trying to tell us something we don’t want to hear.” What that might be, Josephson/O’Doherty doesn’t say, although she/he does call Johnson one of “our best critics”; in other words, his art may be “at best minor, but his subject may not be. It’s a bit like a still-life painter who manages to tell us more about history than a big history painter.” What a beautifully, perfectly equivocal assessment—major critic, minor artist, major subject, minor genre.

“A chronicler who recites events without distinguishing between major and minor ones acts in accordance with the following truth: nothing that has ever happened should be regarded as lost for history”—words to live by from Walter Benjamin, the original Kleenex historian. Yet even those who espouse Benjamin’s credo may find it hard at times to resist playing the ranking game. “In a more pedagogic mood I rendered account of the comparative ranks of the great figures who emerged from the *déconfiture* of Pop sensibility, noting in terse phrases the positionings of Lichtenstein, Warhol, Rosenquist, Oldenburg, and Jim Dine. Offhandedly, I dispatched Wesselman, Indiana, Marisol, and Johnson to the status of evaporations,” the critic Robert Pincus-Witten recalled, with some chagrin, in 1977. “That assessment appeared in May 1970 and by the very end of the month, Johnson had already had a rubber stamp made up which read ‘EVAPORATIONS BY RAY JOHNSON’”.

The evaporations stamp can be seen at the bottom of a NYCS please-add-to-and-send mailing, along with a drawing of a snowball and the words, As soon as it melts.... No one will even remember it! This caption expresses both Ray Johnson’s deepest fear and his deepest wish—that the disappearance might be not merely one art form among others in his repertoire, but his true métier. The name that embodies this talent for evanescence, the name Johnson ultimately attached to his aesthetic as a whole, is **Nothing**.

Ray Johnson, NYCS mailer, March 15, 1972 (please-add-to with Snowball).

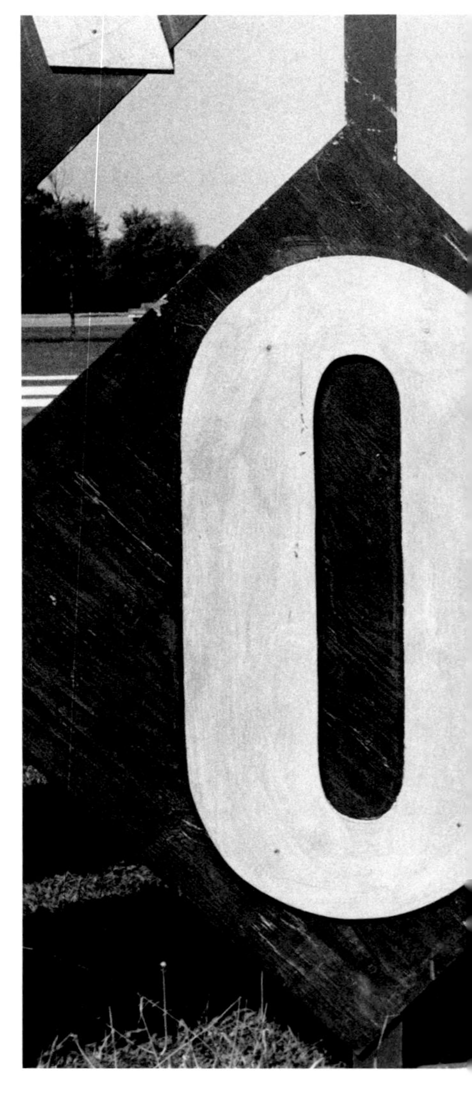

RAY JOHNSON

HAND-LETTERED ~~PAINTED~~

NOTHING

Ray Johnson, mailer, ca. 1994.

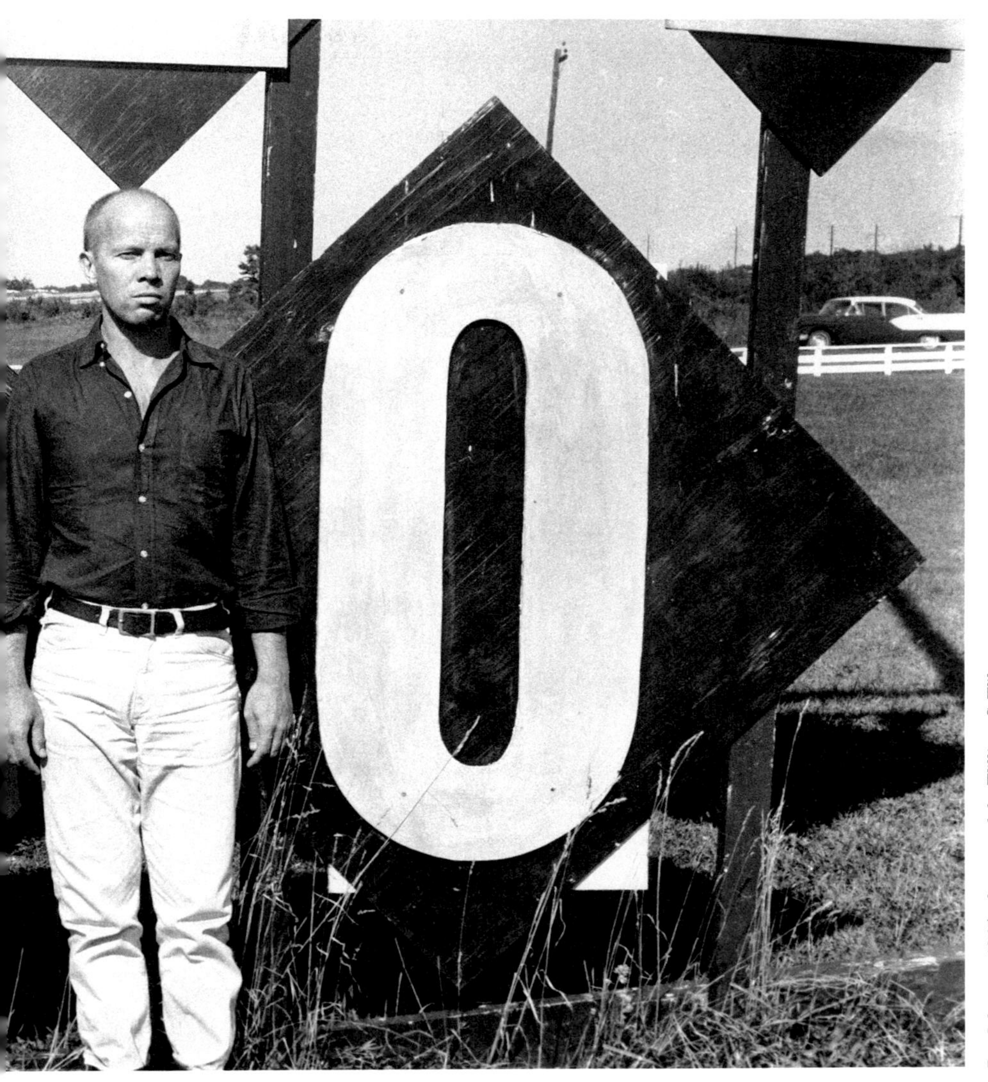

Ray Johnson, 1965, photograph by William S. Wilson.

Officially introduced by the artist as an improvised mockery of Allan Kaprow's Happenings, inflected by its appearances in the work of his friend John Cage, "Nothing" gave a name to something that seems always to have been present in Ray. **Remember what Asawa said in class one night**, he wrote to a Black Mountain classmate in 1947, **the Taoism philosophy of nothing ness being everything-ness. I feel that way.** But while Johnson's **Nothing** may have been founded in the kind of Zen openness practiced by Cage, it soon acquired a sharper edge. There is a negativity that clears a space, a negativity that propels the dialectic on its twisting-turning way, and a negativity that *wounds*. Ray Johnson's genius for the negative was a double-edged gift.

In the months before it was all over with, Johnson sent messages and made calls that might have rung alarm bells for their recipients had they come from anyone else but Ray. One such recipient was Frances Beatty, formerly vice president, then president, of Richard Feigen & Co., the gallery with which Johnson was most closely associated during his period of showing in galleries. After the artist's death, Beatty became the director of the Ray Johnson Estate.

> Richard and I tried for 17 years to do a Ray Johnson show. Ray was totally ambivalent. In the mid-1980s he said **I've got it, Frances, we'll have**, pause, **Nothing in the show**. He wanted to be famous, but he realized if he ever was famous, it would be the end of his activity as an artist.
>
> He called me about five days before he died and he said: **Frances, I think I'm finished doing this Nothing I'm involved in. I'm going to do Something, and you're going to be able to do the show.** And he laughed his sweet Ray laugh, and then he jumped off the bridge. It was a complete performance.

"Nothing that has ever happened should be regarded as lost for history," says Walter Benjamin. Then again, he also says, "The past can be seized only as an image which flashes up at the instant when it can be recognized and is never seen again." Ray Johnson gets this dilemma; he can bear, if only just, the Benjaminian thought that if you wish to seize hold of a memory as it flashes up at a moment of danger, you must be prepared, in the next instant, to release your grasp. That memory, that image, that thing we most don't want to and need to hear must be lost and found and lost and found and lost and found again. If "Johnson's Kleenex version of history is trying to tell us something we don't want to hear," it may be Nothing, whatever Johnson means by that. The "void," perhaps—to quote Benjamin one last time—into which "every image of the past that is not recognized by the present as one of its own threatens to disappear irretrievably."

“He moved on the basis of images.” An image flashes up, then the next, and the next. Ray Johnson lived a spider’s life, day in, day out, spinning his intricate, fragile, dangerous metonymic webs. Just ask Bill Wilson:

> He was so intent on constructing fields of relations that anything that entered his life must yield interrelations, or else not exist for him. Yet for Ray, interrelations were evanescent, always about to evaporate like dew. His relations with other artists existed only in his consciousness of them, a consciousness he had long planned to end by drowning. So, even in astonishingly full moments of immediacy and indeterminacy, he sensed that relations were ultimately nothing.

XVII

> **Bill, // A response immediately. Sort of a “don’t jhmp”. That’s jump. What with all the stories I’ve had of “suicidal Bill Wilson”. Today letters from all my new friends. Yours the most answerworthy because the most “hit”. May telling of her trip to the hospital still in the future. A babbling thing from Anne about how it is black after fire.**

At this time, Bill Wilson was still in grad school at Yale, and it was driving him crazy. “Anne” is Ann Ubinger—another name persistently misspelled by Ray—Bill’s artist wife-to-be. **That’s jump**. Ray Johnson loved typos, for their contingency and materiality. This one led to the association, **A ghost immediately. Sort of a “ghost jump”. That’s ghost. What with all the stories you might have heard about “Ray Johnson’s ghost”. No letter today from my ghost.**

Bill had invited Ray to New Haven, but **I don’t think I can come down the dates you mention. Although the man called today to say the projected advertising thing I was involved with fell through and I will not make those thousands of daollars** [*sic*]. **So I have no money unless the New York Times sends some. But the biggest problem is my ghost, which some day when it is all over with and I am also a ghost you will perhaps know about.**

Regarding **the projected advertising thing** and **the *New York Times***: Johnson had been trying to make a living doing graphic design, without much success, although the work he did do was beautiful. His most successful, and, as it has turned out, most enduring, piece of graphic work is his cover for New Directions’ 1957 edition of Arthur Rimbaud’s *Illuminations*, with its pre-Roy-Lichtenstein ghost-in-the-machine Ben-Day dots. This image of the artist as a rude young man became a signature motif for thrifty Ray from then on.

“Je est un autre,” Rimbaud announced in a letter, a grammatically impossible phrase, translated in the New Directions *Illuminations* as “I is some one else,” although a frequently cited alternative is the more literal, “I is an other.”

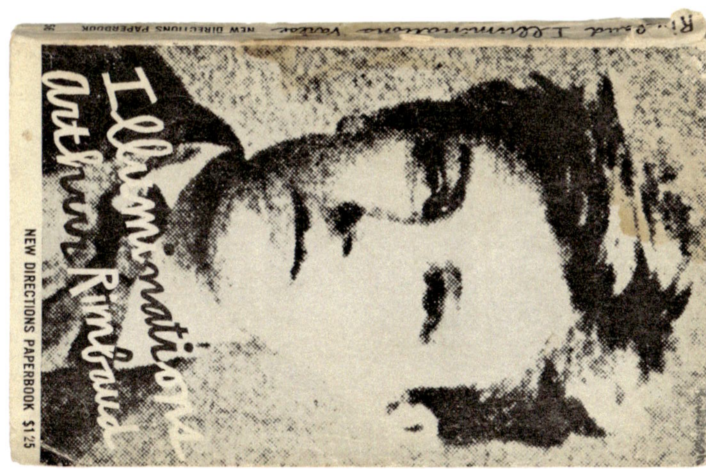

Ray Johnson, cover design for Arthur Rimbaud's *Illuminations*, 1957 ed.

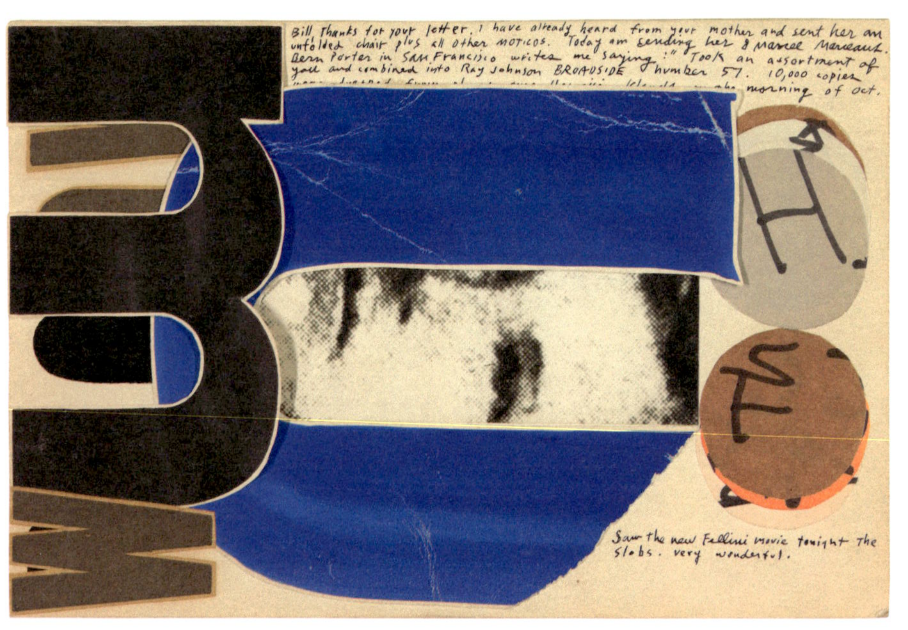

Ray Johnson, *Untitled (Rimbaud)* (1956).

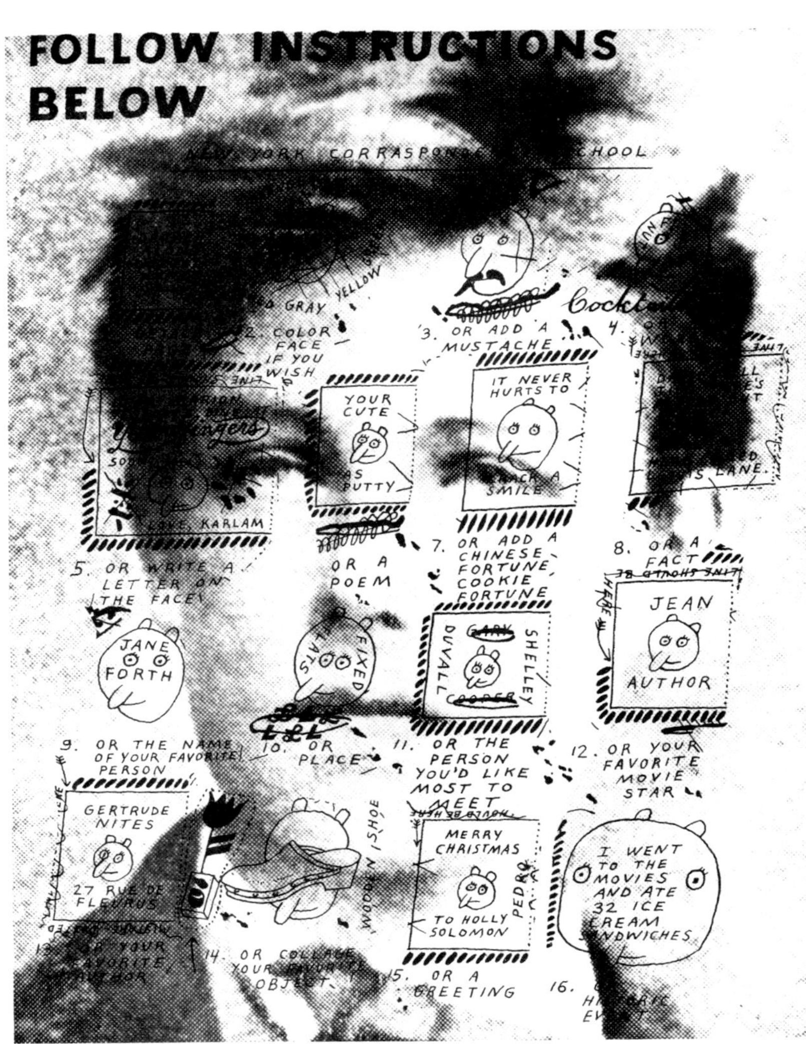

Ray Johnson, *Rimbaud Face Mailing*, 1971.

December 30, 1966

Dear Bill Wilson,

I returned home—after being in the Village—by subway and thought and thought and had an idea that a Ray Johnson died and another Ray Johnson is about to begin and he shall have a new name and I shall have to be Ray Johnson but I am this other person.

BOMBAY

RAY
born Dec. 30, 1966

[at the bottom of this note are three ink-stamps, printed sideways:]

JOHN DOE
JOHN DOE
JOHN DOE

There is the Ray Johnson who bridled when asked where he was born, and then there is this other Ray, so eager to let Bill know he had just been born somewhere between the Village and lower Manhattan at the end of 1966. Why 1966? It was the year that Ray Johnson found himself as an artist. But that's not the important thing here. The important thing here is the relation between Ray Johnson and **this other person**—who is Ray Johnson, who died and now lives under another, yet same, name. The important thing is the name, each one shining with its own peculiar, distant light out of an ever-shifting constellation of names. **I'm intrigued and interested in an incredible galaxy of people,** said Johnson in speaking of his portraits, although, he added, with characteristic sangfroid, **Since I cut everything up, they're all people in a kaleidoscope.** Each twist of the lens brings some names to the fore, as others spin out of sight. But just because we can't see them doesn't mean they are not still there. **There's so much unimportance among people.** And, at the same time, all the importance in the world.

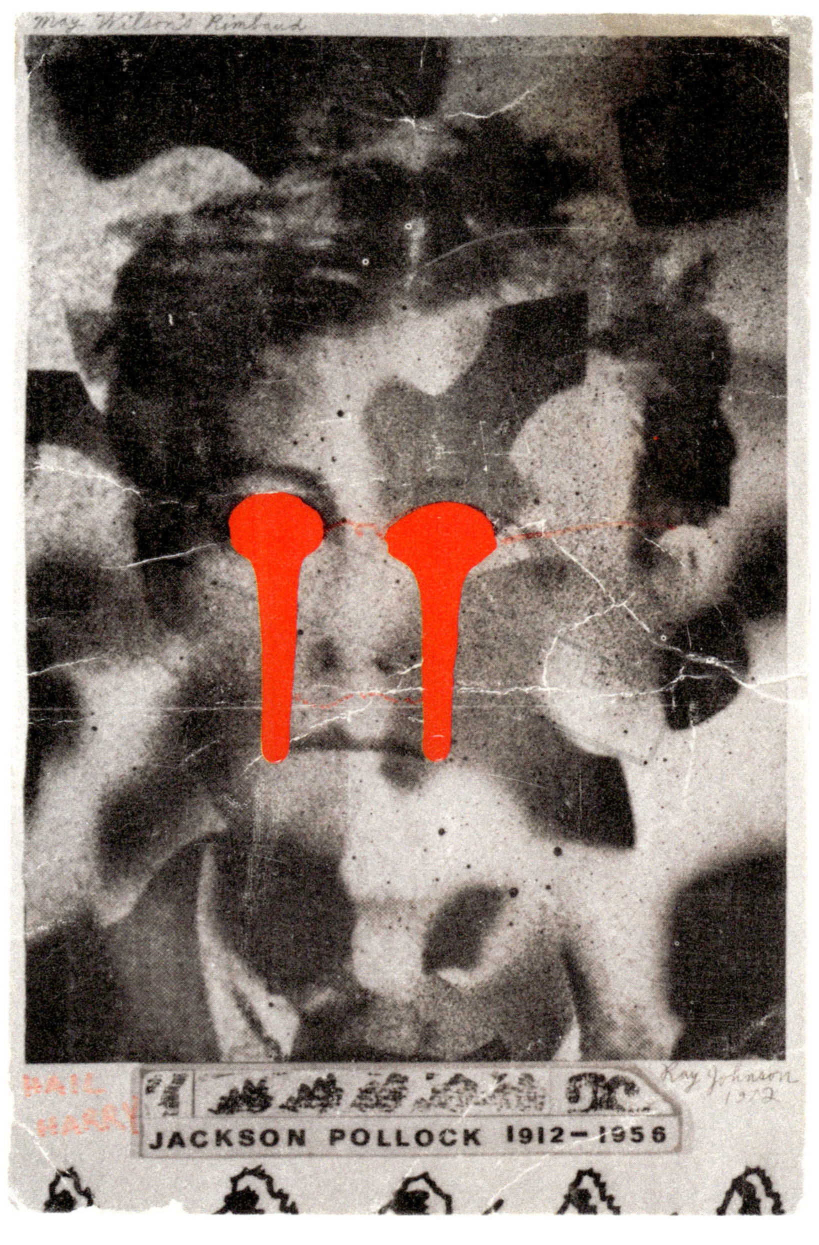

Ray Johnson, altered invitation card for "Ray Johnson's History of the Betty Parsons Gallery," 1973.

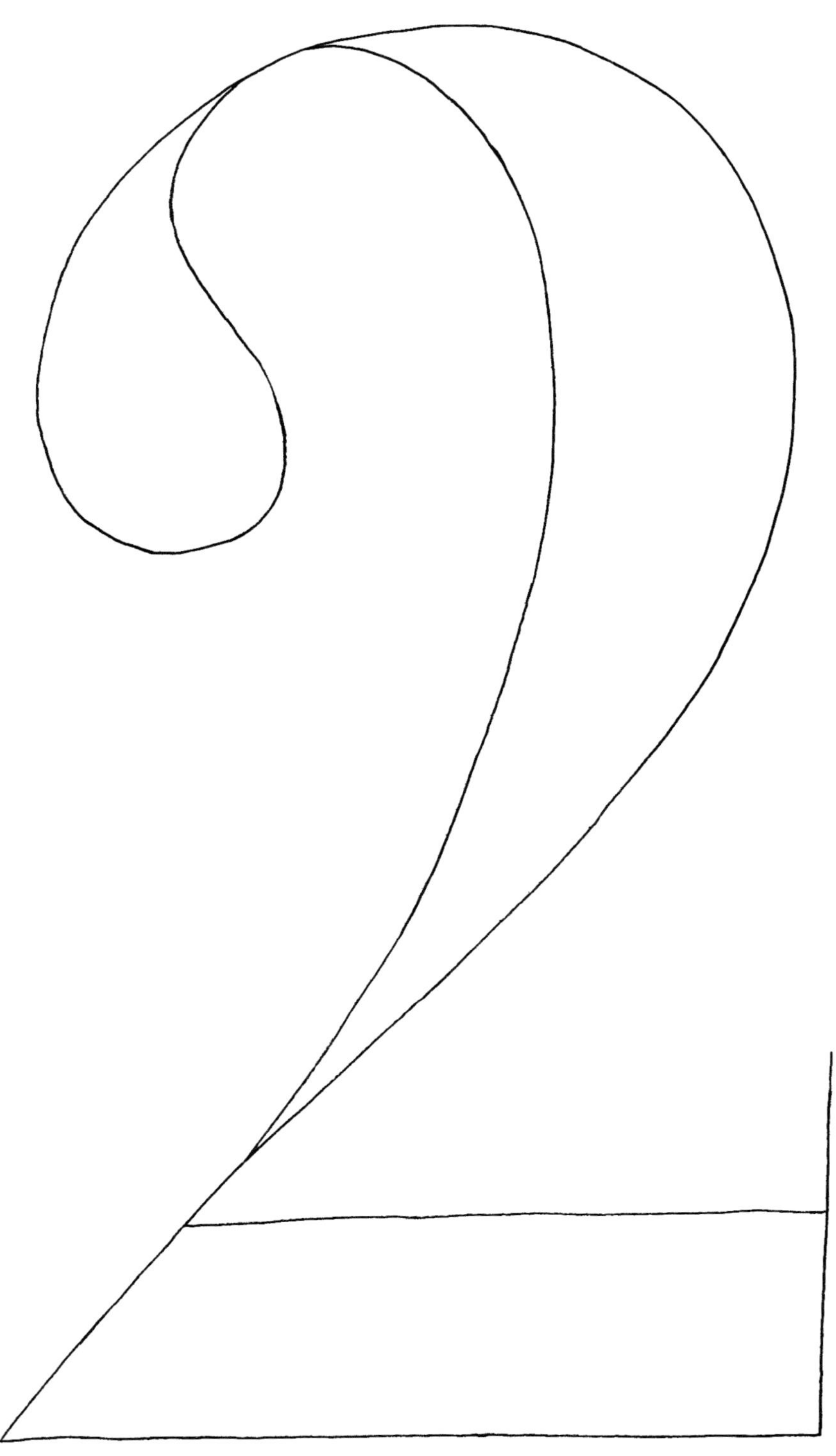

1945–1965

HOMELESS FORMS:
FROM BLACK MOUNTAIN TO *A BOOK ABOUT DEATH*

I

connoisseur of chaos

I

A. A violent order is disorder; and
B. A great disorder is an order. These
Two things are one. (Pages of illustrations.)

Detail from Ray Johnson to Frances X. Profumo, February 13, 1953.

A. A violent order is disorder; and
B. A great disorder is an order. These
Two things are one. (Pages of illustrations.)
—Wallace Stevens, "Connoisseur of Chaos"

II

A picture of the artist and art critic Suzi Gablik, taken in the fall of 1955 at Gablik's behest by her friend, the photographer Elisabeth Novick (a favorite in later years at *Vogue* and *Harper's Bazaar*), might be more accurately described as a picture of a woman rendered unidentifiable by an avalanche of paper scraps, descended from who knows where. The scraps, moreover, are not just any scraps, but made things, artworks of a kind that Ray Johnson had recently decided to call "moticos." What is a moticos? Around the time the picture of Gablik was taken, Johnson himself posed this question on a flyer sent out to multiple correspondents.

On at least one occasion, Johnson also buttonholed passersby on the street and asked them to respond to a series of questions on the topic, for instance:

Did you ever read moticos or do you know the story of moticos?
If you knew nothing about a moticos except its title is "MO" would you want to see it or not?
How often do you go to the moticos?
Do you understand moticos?

The answers he received tended to be understandably nonplussed.

A shipping clerk: *I haven't the slightest idea.*
A laundry helper: *I don't know.*
A salesman: *I don't know what the hell it means.*
A store manager. *I don't know.*
A nun: *Is it a motto or something?*

I intended to ask a hundred people but after the first sixteen I got kinda discouraged, the artist confessed to John Wilcock of the *Village Voice*, whose piece on Ray Johnson ran in the paper's very first issue, in October 1955. Ray had just turned twenty-eight. "i read some of your moticos. the others i didn't dig. but i like the whole idea," Wilcock had written to Johnson that August, "and a story about you would fit beautifully." Fit beautifully, that is, with Wilcock's notion of the kind of downtown character that he would feature for the next ten years in his column, *The Village Square*. Wilcock ends that first column with the following excerpts from Johnson's manifesto, or poem, or motto, or something:

> **The next time a railroad train is going its way along the track, look quickly at the sides of the box cars because a moticos may be there. Whether the train is standing still or speeding past you, a moticos Don't try to catch up with it. It wants to go its way. But have your camera ready to snap its picture. It likes those moments of being inside the box ...**
>
> **The best way is to go about your business not thinking about the silly moticos ... so go your way and go to sleep when you will. The moticos does that too and does not worry about you. Perhaps you are the moticos. Destroy this. Paste the ashes on the side of your automobile and if anyone asks you why you have ashes pasted on the side of your car, tell them.**

Does that answer your questions? **There will be no questions, hence no need for answers**, Johnson insists, toward the end of the piece. Yet the moticos question, which had been forming in the artist's mind for some time, had become by then *the* question for him, one that could not and would not be dismissed for a decade to come.

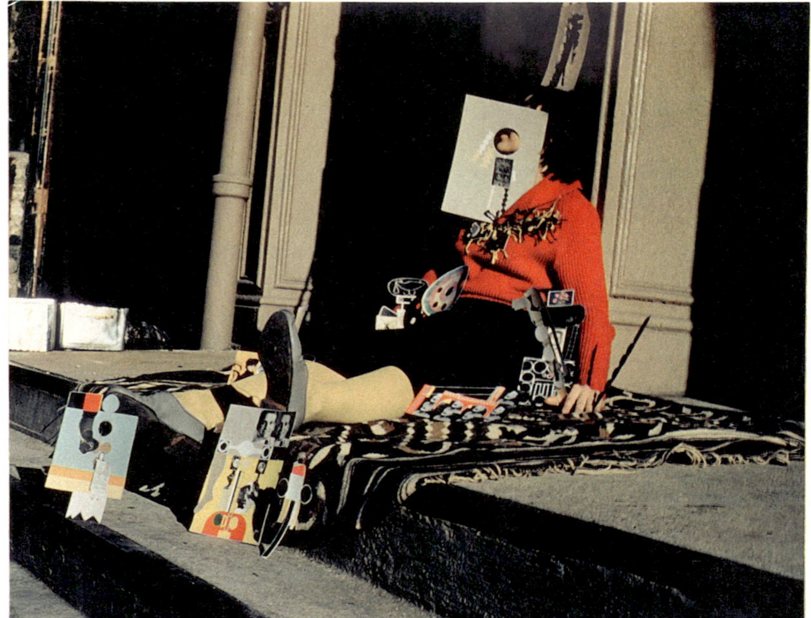

Suzi Gablik with Ray Johnson moticos, photograph by Elisabeth Novick.

WHAT IS A MOTICOS ?

The next time a railroad train is seen going its way along the track, look quickly at the sides of the box cars because a moticos may be there. Whether the train is standing still or speeding past you, a moticos   Don't try to catch up with it. It wants to go its way. But have your camera ready to snap its picture. It likes those moments of being inside the box. When your film is printed and the moticos is finally seen, it will not be seen, unless you paste the photograph of the moticos on the side of a box car so someone can see the moticos or take its picture. It may appear in your daily newspaper. Someone may put it there. Cut it out. Save it. Treasure it. Make sure it is in a box or between the pages of a book for your grandchildren to find and enjoy.

The moticos is not only seen on railroad trains, but on   It really isn't necessary to see the moticos or know where it is because   I have seen them. Perhaps I might point them out to you. The best way is to go about your business not thinking about silly moticos because when you begin seeing them, describing what they are or where they are going is   So just make sure you wake up from sleeping and go your way and go to sleep when you will. The moticos does that too and does not worry about you. Perhaps you are the moticos. Destroy this. Paste the ashes on the side of your automobile and if anyone asks you why you have ashes pasted on the side of your car, tell them.

Or write the word moticos on the top of your automobile. It loves moving and rain water. Not so many people will wonder what it means. There will be no questions, hence no need for answers. And if you have an automobile, drive to pleasant places because   Have you seen a moticos lately? Perhaps you have. They are everywhere. As I write this I wish someone were here to point one out to me because I know they exist.

Ray Johnson, *WHAT IS A MOTICOS?* (short version), 1955.

What is a moticos? Wilcock asked. **They're really collages—paste-ups of pictures and pieces of paper and so on—but that sounds too much like what they are, so I call them moticos**, Johnson explained. **It's a good word because it's both singular and plural and you can pronounce it how you want.** Johnson's casual tone here belies the feverish energy with which he had been pursuing his collage work over the past year or so, an activity that threatened to displace the painting that up until then had been the focus of his ambition. The artist had amassed hundreds of small-scale paste-ups—their size was limited by that of his preferred support, the cardboard rectangles laundries use for folding men's shirts—and wasn't quite sure what to do with them. First, he tried to sell them to people on the street, then, when that didn't work, thought of selling them through the mail. To that end, according to Norman Solomon, Johnson

> made a mailing list of some fifty or so names of collectors, some of them quite well-to-do. The next step was to make an announcement and some sort of description list of the collages, perhaps by titling them individually.
>
> Which he did. But he wanted a name for the group.
>
> Ray asked me, "**What do you think I should call them?**" My most recent anthropological readings had been about Eskimos. I said, "How about calling them Eskimos?" Ray, seeing that I was reading the dictionary, asked what word I was studying just then. I said, "Osmotic."

The letters rotated in air, shifted, stopped: **MOTICOS**. It would be a kind of brand-name, like Schwitters' *Merz*.

III

Ever see any KURT SCHWITTERS paintings or constructions? Johnson asked a friend from Black Mountain College in 1947. **He was a post-war German DADA artist who raided the junk heaps and put together wonderful texture things and created from all the mess that was postwar Germany.**

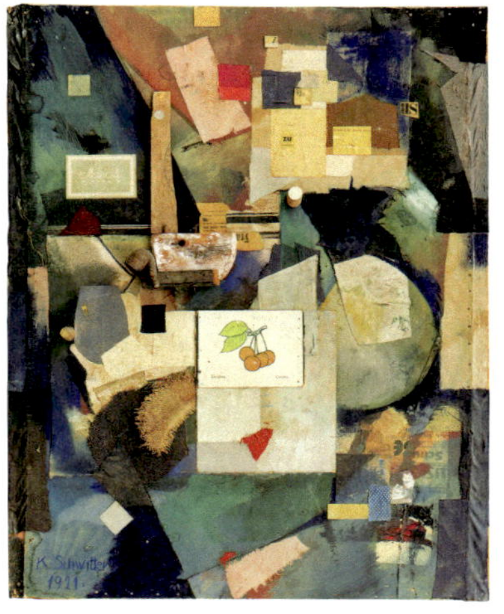

Kurt Schwitters, *Merzbild 32A: The Cherry Picture* (1921).

What, Schwitters asked himself, should I call these **wonderful texture things?** Spawned from a trashed ad for the *Kommerzbank* that the artist recycled into an early collage, the Merz label eventually attached itself to Schwitters's work in multiple media: there would be Merz pictures, Merz poems, Merz performances, Merz graphics, Merz installations. "My aim is the total Merz art work, which combines all genres into an artistic unity," Schwitters declared; an aim never to be achieved, however, for "Create it ourselves we cannot, because we too would only be parts of it, mere material." For Ray Johnson, it was a failure to aspire to.

The word *Merz* has overtones of shit (*merde*) and money (*kommerz*), money as shit, the waste thrown off by capital in the first world war and its aftermath. Schwitters and his Dada friends mined **the mess that was postwar Germany** for art that turned trash, not into treasure, but into more expressive trash. In the midst of a boom following on a second world war, after a visit to his friend Suzi's new apartment, Ray blissfully contemplated the mess that was mid-century New York: **everyone is moving, everything is being torn down—every city block is debris for neo-dada artists to piece back together.**

To piece back together—and do what with? You can try to sell your little Schwitters-esque constructions on the street, or you can market them to collectors via a primitive form of direct mail advertising, or you can mail them as gifts to friends, or you can mail them to friends to try to sell to *their* friends. In 1956, a hopeful Ray mailed off a large packet of moticos to his close friend from Black Mountain, sculptor Ruth Asawa, who by that time had happily settled in California. Her children, she said, loved the gifts he sent, but his art met with a strangely mixed response.

> Do you want me to send back the moticos. The reactions are all different. Some completely indifferent, some fascinated. All of them more interested in your thoughts than the moticos, your motivation to do them.

People don't want to buy them, because they're paper etc. and they curl up. Are they missing something?

In the event, she kept them. Half a century later, with their mother ailing, Asawa's children sent some moticos off to auction.

Don't try to catch up with it. It wants to go its way. But which way is its way?

IV

At the time of the moticos photo shoot with Gablik and Novick, Johnson was living at 2 Dover Street, in the shadow of the Brooklyn Bridge. It was the second of the artist's three downtown Manhattan apartment-studios, all of them located on the rough edge of the Lower East Side, all of them small, cheap, and monastically spare—spare except on the rare occasions when works came out of the closet to be arrayed for a showing.

Such studio showings, for collectors or fellow artists, while often theatrical in the Ray manner, were still recognizable as a certain kind of art-world ritual. The moticos showings, staged outside the studio, were harder to categorize or even describe; hence Suzi's desire to have one, at least, captured on film. "That day," wrote Bill Wilson, "Ray carried boxes of moticos down seven flights to be photographed in sunlight." Down, out, back to the street, back to the mess that makes one ask, what happened here?

In 1953, on the cusp of the moticos years, Ray mailed a friend a copy he had made of a poem by Wallace Stevens, "Connoisseur of Chaos," which begins with the propositions, "A. A violent order is disorder; and/ B. A great disorder is an order." Like any properly dialectical set, these two thoughts prove hard to hold together in one's mind. Ray Johnson reveled in the chaos wreaked by market forces—**everyone is moving, everything is being torn down**, everywhere heaps of debris for the taking. At the same time, he knew enough to fear the predatory order behind the rich disorder. And so, while one Ray Johnson was mailing out moticos flyers to the collectors on his list, the other Ray Johnson was already plotting ways to keep his art beyond the market's grasp. **Destroy this. Paste the ashes on the side of your automobile and if anyone asks you why you have ashes pasted on the side of your car, tell them.**

According to Bill Wilson, after the Dover Street photo shoot, Ray in fact "took the moticos around the corner into the alley, where he burned them to ashes." Wilson connects this act with Johnson's systematic destruction just a few years later of every painting he had ever made, barring those held back by friends who listened not to the voice commanding, **Destroy this**, but to the one whispering, **Cut it out. Save it. Treasure it. Make sure it is in a box or between the pages of a book for your grandchildren to find and enjoy.**

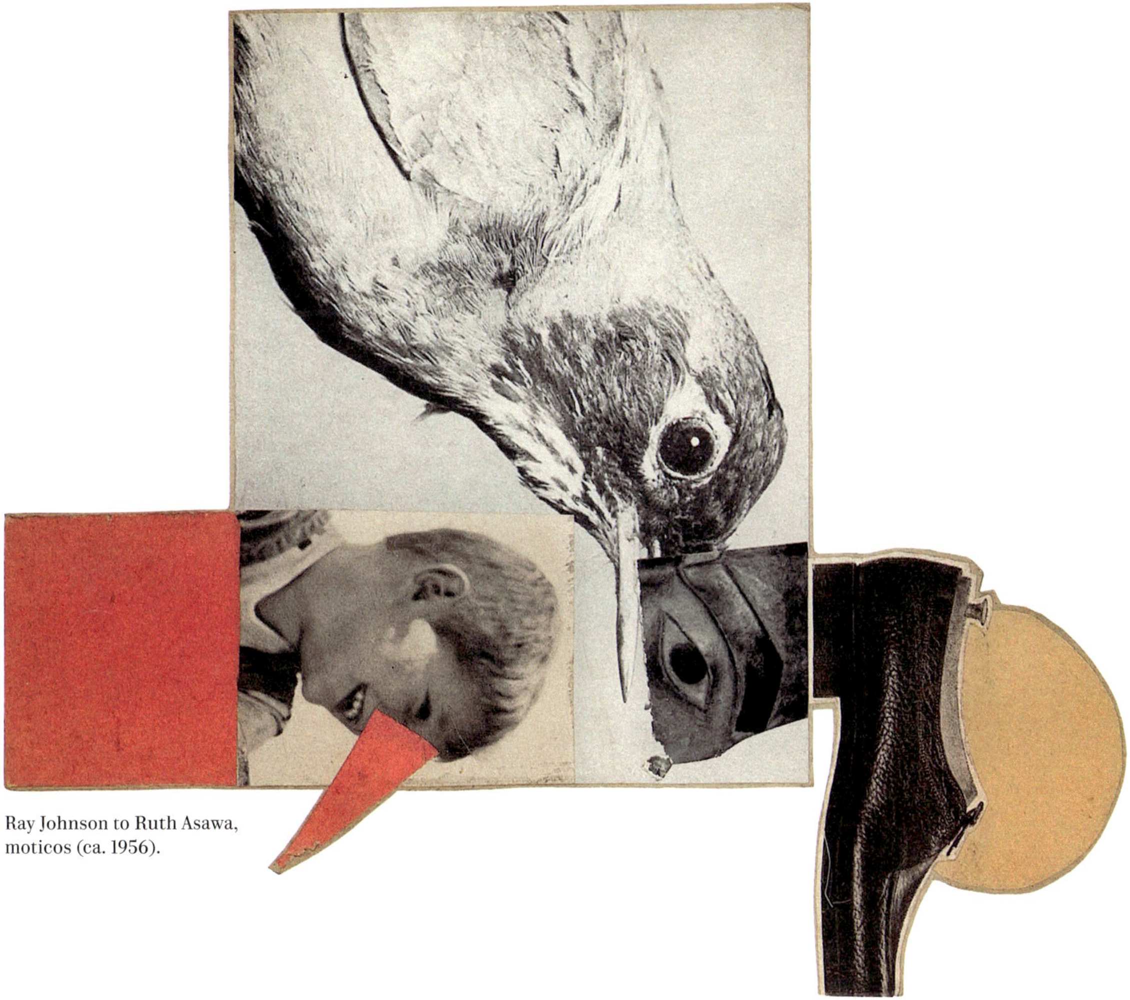

Ray Johnson to Ruth Asawa, moticos (ca. 1956).

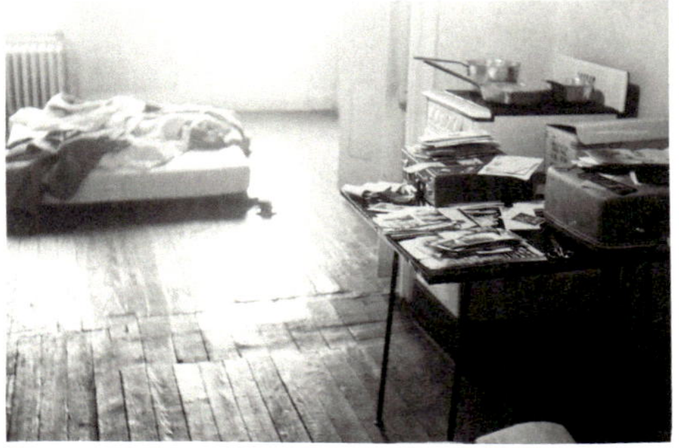

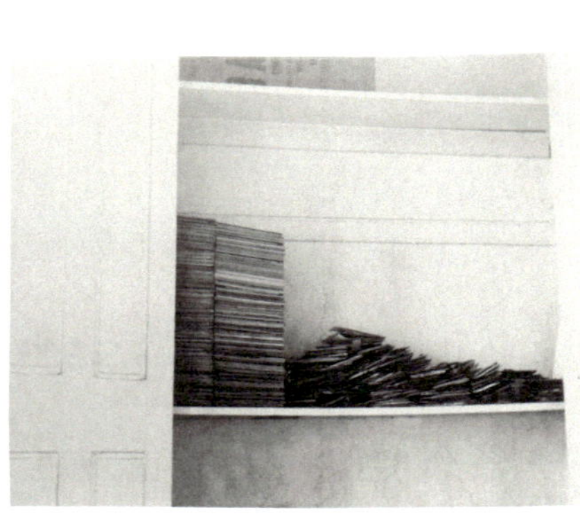

Ray Johnson's apartment at 176 Suffolk Street, 1963, photographs by William S. Wilson.

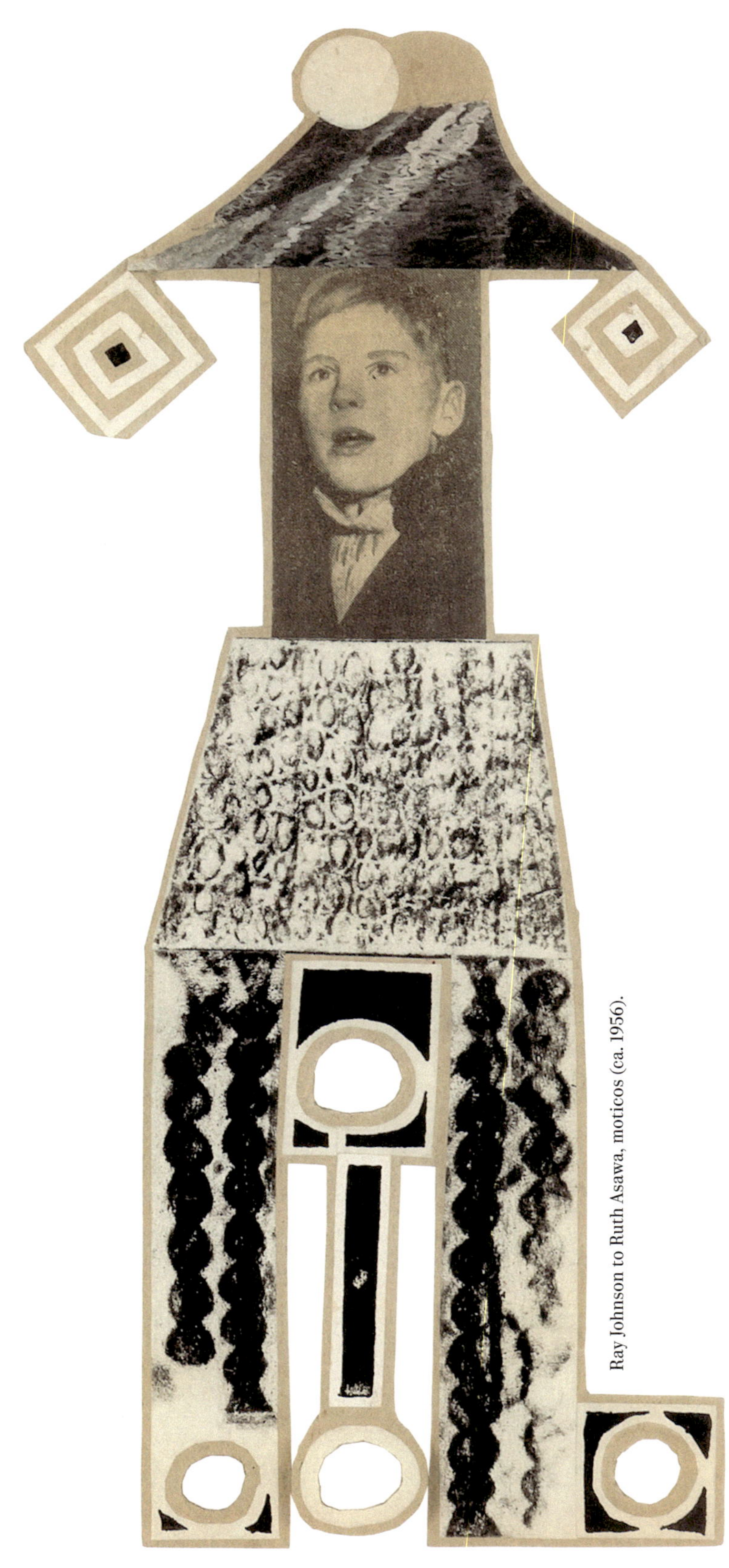

Ray Johnson to Ruth Asawa, moticos (ca. 1956).

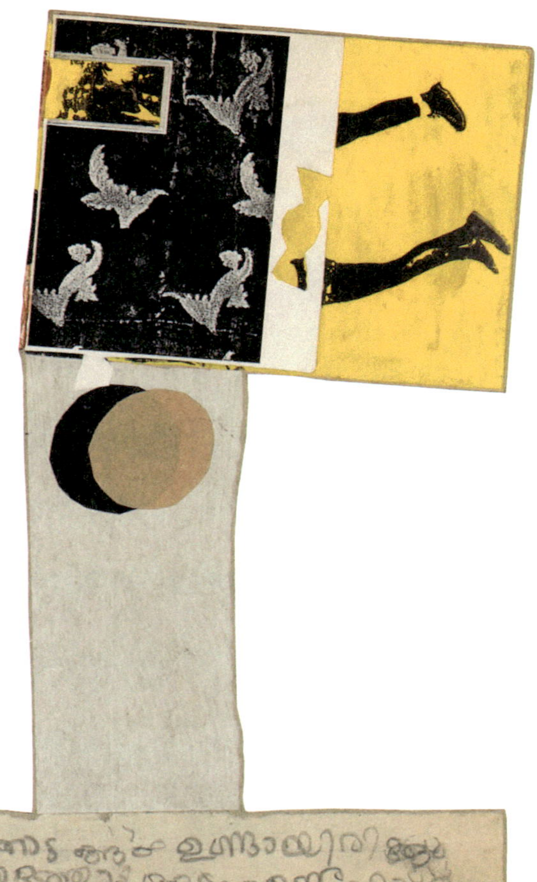

Ray Johnson to Ruth Asawa, moticos (ca. 1956).

The moticos wants the impossible, then; it wants to be destroyed *and* to be preserved. Granted, to be found at some future time, by chance, **in a box or between the pages of a book**, a mystery for the grandchildren of yesterday's **neo-dada artists to piece back together** for themselves, is a tenuous enough form of preservation. What if the box molders in the attic, the book gathers dust on the shelf, the children stay down in the street playing their neo-neo-neo-dada games?

"B. A great disorder is an order." Which is to say, leave everything to chance? No. The Stevensian connoisseur of chaos must confect a new order out of disorder while managing somehow not to reproduce the violence inherent in the originary order. On Dover Street, the neo-dada artist patiently inserts the moticos between the slats of a derelict shipping pallet one after another until the slats are full.

Have your camera ready to snap its picture. It likes those moments of being inside the box. But the moments before and after? Novick's exposures can memorialize but can't capture the life the moticos takes on in Ray's hand as it arcs between the jumble in the storage box and the assemblage that never quite jells into what most of us would call an order. Still, the moticos pictures, especially those with Johnson in them, have their own fascination. Connoisseurs of characters like John Wilcock would always be drawn more to that Ray Johnson, the enigmatic presence on the scene. The artist was—and it is clear he knew he was—a great photographic subject. Then again, Asawa's friends, who hadn't seen the photos, told her they were "more interested in your thoughts than the moticos, your motivation to do them." It was the artist's motivation, the animating thoughts behind the art, that drew them.

Motive: from the Latin *movere*, to move. **It loves moving and rain water**. Johnson could sense, with the others, that something was moving about him, something that was not exactly him, an "it" that had its own motivations. **It wants, It likes, It loves,** he wrote of the moticos. Even Ray was not sure yet, I think, just what **It** was. But at least it had a name.

V

In February 1956, Jiro Yoshihara, a Japanese businessman-turned-painter, and his confederate, the artist Shozo Shimamoto, together sent Jackson Pollock copies of a journal that Yoshihara had recently founded in connection with an artists' collective he had also founded. Both the group and the magazine were called *Gutai*, a term compounded from the words for "instrument" and "body." Initially inspired by the kind of materialized gesture represented in Pollock's drip paintings, the Gutai aesthetic soon

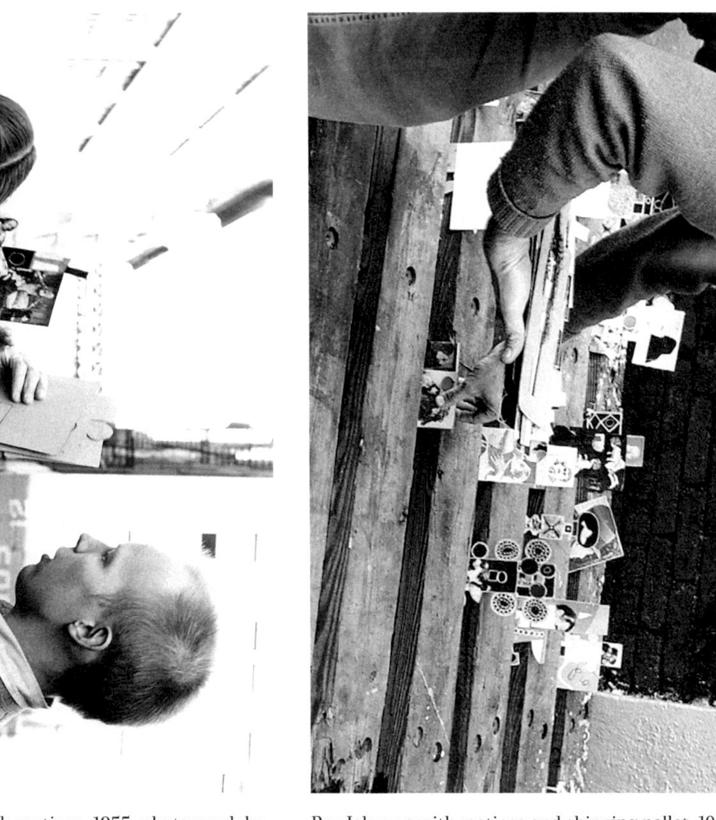

Ray Johnson and Suzi Gablik with moticos, 1955, photograph by Elisabeth Novick.

Ray Johnson with moticos and shipping pallet, 1955, photograph by Elisabeth Novick.

expanded to include the more explicitly body-centered work of certain artists who followed in Pollock's wake. (Allen Kaprow, inventor of the Happening, was another early recipient of issues of *Gutai.*)

After Pollock died, in August 1956, a friend of his, the collector and critic B. H. Friedman, found the *Gutai* issues among the painter's effects and soon after wrote to Yoshihara to express his interest in the group. Not long after that, Yoshihara received a letter that began, **Bob Friedman showed me your very interesting magazines recently and suggested I send you something of my work since you expressed interest in what younger artists are doing.** The letter's writer proceeds to offer an account of his artwork that highlights its dynamic quality.

Most of my work is collage which I call MOTICOS. I send out a monthly newsletter about the work I am doing which takes the place of a formal exhibition. The works cannot be exhibited in the usual way because they constantly change, like the news in the papers or the images on a movie screen ... Some of those MOTICOS are tied with string to a panel; some of them are used as one group. Those MOTICOS are moved by the wind or the weather; just like dead leaves, the heat preserves them.

The works ... constantly change. And yet, in Johnson's telling, the forces that drive the change seem to emanate from somewhere outside the artist himself. The moticos are used, moved, preserved—but by what or by whom? Johnson's moticos are inert in themselves, **just like dead leaves**, like the leaves in Shelley's poem about the West Wind, "from whose unseen presence the leaves dead/ Are driven, like ghosts from an enchanter fleeing." This unseen force is at once, adds the poet, "Destroyer and preserver."

The Romantic in need of motivation seeks the supernatural in nature. The neo-Dada, sifting through the urban debris, seeks lost connections among persons. (Cached in each commodity, says Marx, is an estranged social relation. Trash it, and you release the ghost.) Johnson's moticos is a connector, half thing and half thought, inherently inert yet charged, at times, with an uncanny supra-personal energy. His accomplice, Gablik, thus finds herself moved, as **by the wind or the weather**, to preserve Johnson's art from the daemon who would send it all up in flames if he could. **When your film is printed and the moticos is finally seen, it will not be seen.** It may nonetheless leave traces of its unseen presence in certain gestures and words, a few of which Gablik would retrace in 1964 in a brief essay, accompanied by some of the Novick photos, published in *Location*, a short-lived but starry journal edited by critics Thomas Hess and Harold Rosenberg and the future novelist Donald Barthelme.

> Like information in a newspaper, the images on a movie screen, the collages of Ray Johnson are constantly changing and new ones come

> to take their place. Ultimately, they take the form of mailings, surprises, presents, which he distributes complexly according to the rules of a private game. It is a question of waiting, not for time to finish the work, but for time to indicate something one would not have expected to occur.

What is a moticos? A thing that gives way to an indication, a gesture toward "something one would not have expected to occur." Gablik lifted the first and last sentences in the passage above from Johnson's writings; he and she were close conspirators back then. "In the end," as Gablik saw it in 1964, gesturing toward their friendship, "the moticos are more involved with intimacy than with any public occasion." On Dover Street, the photographer clicks away, and yet—or so the story goes—what happens in the box, stays in the box: just two friends at play.

VI

Then again, we are talking about the art world, an always unstable mix of public sphere and private enterprise, where even the most intimate of spaces may serve as the stage for exhibitions and competitions. In 1958, the year that *ArtNews* introduced Jasper Johns as "the newest member of a movement among young American artists to turn to a sort of neo-Dada," a movement that includes "such better-known colleagues as Rauschenberg, Twombly, Kaprow and Ray Johnson," Ray Johnson tells May Wilson, **I loaned my dear friend Suzi a painting called Trampoline which has four pink plastic fish hanging on it**, then feels compelled to add, **At Suzi's, she has a Bob Raushenberg** [*sic*] **across from my painting. His has a parachute attached.**

One collage **has four pink plastic fish hanging from it**, the other **has a parachute attached.** Both pieces, in other words, include elements capable of being **moved by the wind or the weather.** To the casual observer, they are just bits of string; to the future conservator, a perpetual headache. To Johnson and Rauschenberg, though, they are indications, pointers in the direction of a quixotic dream, a dream they share, of a fundamentally mobile art.

In 1955, the year of the parachute piece, the year of the moticos installations, Rauschenberg signaled his sense of affinity with Johnson by inviting him to collaborate on a new work, a mixed-genre construction of the type that Rauschenberg would come to call a "combine." Like the moticos, Rauschenberg's combines were collages of a sort, the sort that gestured at the Dada notion of a total artwork that might, as Schwitters proposed, not only "combine all genres into an artistic unity," but also incorporate the creator and his collaborators, as if they too were "only parts of it, mere material."

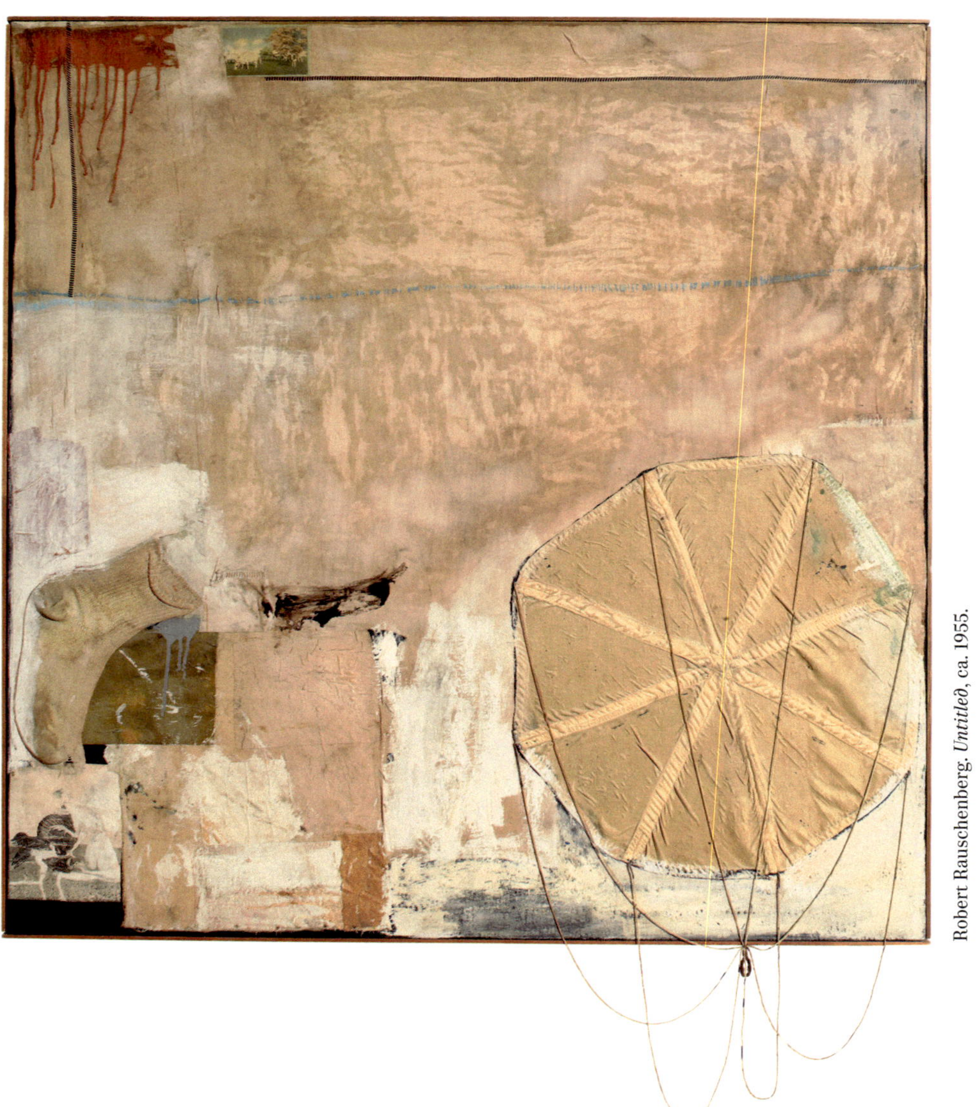

Robert Rauschenberg. *Untitled*, ca. 1955.

The combine, like the moticos, like the *Merzbild*, was not so much a thing in itself as it was trace evidence of the artist's actions and relations.

The actions and relations embodied in the combine that Rauschenberg had mentioned to Johnson are exceptionally well-documented. The artist conceived the piece, he said, as a "protest" aimed at the selection committee for a high-profile annual group exhibition hosted by the Stable Gallery, in which he had previously shown work. Although Rauschenberg himself had again been asked to contribute to that year's Annual, he was peeved that, despite his recommendations to the committee, "there had not been any new artists invited to exhibit," and so, as he tells it, "I invited four artists: Jasper Johns, Stan Vanderbeek, Sue Weil and Ray Johnson, to give me works to be built into my collage." The artist's selection was freighted with personal significance. Johnson and VanDerBeek were connections from Black Mountain College, where Rauschenberg and Weil, then married to one another, had spent a brief but crucial period together; Weil was now the artist's ex-wife, and Johns his current romantic partner. As the deadline for the Stable show approached, however—again, as Rauschenberg tells it—"only two paintings," by Johns and Weil, "were ready in time to be installed into the major piece." The contributions by these two intimates were embedded in little boxes with doors that can be opened and shut, while a program for a concert featuring John Cage, Rauschenberg's mentor at Black Mountain, was affixed to the surface of the collage.

Twelve years after its debut, Rauschenberg's collage, newly titled *Short Circuit* in memory of the workaround that went into its making, served as the centerpiece of *Art in Process: The Visual Development of a Collage*, a show at the Finch College Museum of Art in Manhattan. Before the show opened, Elayne Varian, the museum's director, wrote to Johnson, whose work would also hang in the show, to ask if he could send her "a short note regarding the Rauschenberg invitation to you to participate in his collage." His reply is revealing, although perhaps not in quite the way Varian might have hoped.

I have no remembrance of being asked by Robert Raushenberg in 1955 to incorporate my work in any work of his incorporating the work of Sue Weil and Jasper Johns.

I do remember at that time a small orange tree Bob and Sue had. Also, on a small island off the coast of Connecticut, Sue's mother had a large house, I carried a book on Taoism and quoted lines to them about emptiness and nothing. Years later the house burned.

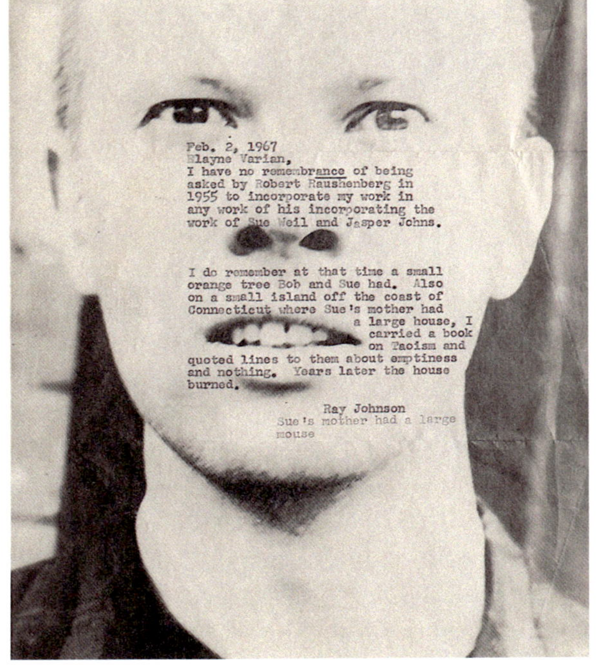
Feb. 2, 1967
Elayne Varian,
I have no remembrance of being asked by Robert Raushenberg in 1955 to incorporate my work in any work of his incorporating the work of Sue Weil and Jasper Johns.

I do remember at that time a small orange tree Bob and Sue had. Also on a small island off the coast of Connecticut where Sue's mother had a large house, I carried a book on Taoism and quoted lines to them about emptiness and nothing. Years later the house burned.

Ray Johnson
Sue's mother had a large mouse

Ray Johnson to Elayne Varian, February 2, 1967.

Also lost in that fire was a group of early Rauschenberg paintings whose relatively orderly geometries bespoke the influence of Josef Albers's teaching at Black Mountain; the artist had stored them at the Weil house after they failed to sell in his first solo show, at Betty Parsons' gallery, in the spring of 1951. By that time, Rauschenberg had begun his marriage-ending affair with painter Cy Twombly, with whom he would return to Black Mountain later that year. **I went to Cy Twombly's and burned things**, Ray Johnson would tell Bill Wilson in 1958, those things being his own early paintings, abstractions of a rigorously Albersian kind. (At Black Mountain, Johnson was an Albers acolyte, while Rauschenberg found Albers's model "beautiful" but "impossible" to follow.) Did Johnson mean for us to draw a connection between the two burnings, both of which left half-effaced but still traceable paths leading back to Albers's classroom at Black Mountain? Maybe. It was a small world, certainly.

The piece by Johnson that Gablik hung facing Rauschenberg's parachute seems not to have survived, although one can find a description of it among a list of works that the artist sent to his lawyer (and Gablik's boyfriend) Harry Torczyner in 1965: **"Four Pink Fish," oil on board with string and plastic fish attached, in wooden frame, measuring 3½ by 4 feet, painted in 1956.** Johnson's painting-with-fish, then, was scaled to rival the combine painting, at roughly five feet square, minus the strings. Rauschenberg would continue to work on a grand scale—he was always inventing new ways to command space—but Johnson would never do so again—no single work made after he **burned things** measures more than three feet square. The parachute now hangs in a museum; the other piece, who knows? Does it matter? Perhaps not, if it is true what Gablik says of Johnson's collages, that "[i]n the end they are more involved with intimacy than with any public occasion." Yet it is also true that the face-off with Bob at Suzi's, on display for all their friends to see, mattered to Ray.

VII

Robert Rauschenberg, his biographer Calvin Tomkins tells us, "met Jasper Johns one winter night in 1954 on the corner of Madison Avenue and Fifty-Seventh Street," introduced on the fly by Suzi Gablik, a friend of Rauschenberg's from Black Mountain "who happened to be one of the few people Johns knew in New York." By the following summer, the two men were ensconced in neighboring lofts on Pearl Street, near Manhattan's tip. Johnson's Dover Street apartment was just a few debris-filled blocks north; a few blocks south was Coenties Slip, described by critic Holland Cotter as "a filled-in deep-water inlet that had once been the city's main landing place for wooden ships," where, "while Abstract Expressionism was flourishing uptown, a number of younger painters and sculptors interested in a very different kind of art lived and worked in deserted sailmaking lofts." The ad-hoc Coenties colony included Robert Indiana, Ellsworth Kelly, Agnes Martin, James Rosenquist, Lenore Tawney, Bill Wilson's future wife Ann Ubinger, and Jack Youngerman, whose then wife, actress Delphine Seyrig, was a few years out from her who-is-*that* turn in *Last Year at Marienbad.*

The living spaces along this stretch were cold but quiet and graced with river-light. His gaze drifting up from his worktable, Johnson could see **Little boats—big boats continuously on the river.** Up and down the streets, artists grazed on the debris, even the very un-Dada Agnes Martin, who staked out some early grids with boat spikes and bottle caps. One could think there, clear away the inner debris. One could also, as Cotter suggests, take one's distance from the prevailing modes of gestural abstraction. An undated Ray Johnson please-send-to, addressed to **Robert Clark Indiana/ c/o Stable Gallery**, includes a postcard on which Johnson has typed a fragmentary phrase—"the abandoned piers 5, 6, 7 and 8, the sycamores (as Hoosier as a tree can be) ..."—pulled from "Coenties Slip," a memoir by Indiana published in the catalogue for a 1963 show of his own work. Also folded into the envelope is a collaged-on page from a 1964 article by critic and curator Sam Wagstaff titled "Paintings to Think About," which begins, "For a number of contemporary American artists, whose works tend away from Expressionism in a more austere direction, the composer John Cage has been an intellectual guide."

The photos accompanying Wagstaff's article show art meant to exemplify the style that was coming to be known as minimalist: boxy sculptures by Tony Smith and Robert Morris, Jasper Johns' empty frame in gray-on-gray, and an unusually severe piece by Indiana—the black-and-white *DIE*—which Johnson has mischievously sweetened into **[HONEY] PIE**. Wagstaff's initial reference to Cage, however, points toward another aesthetic strain, related to but separable from minimalism, which the critic identifies as "conceptual, idea art, as opposed to retinal or visceral." Wagstaff goes on to quote Cage himself on art made to appeal primarily to the eye or the gut—"There

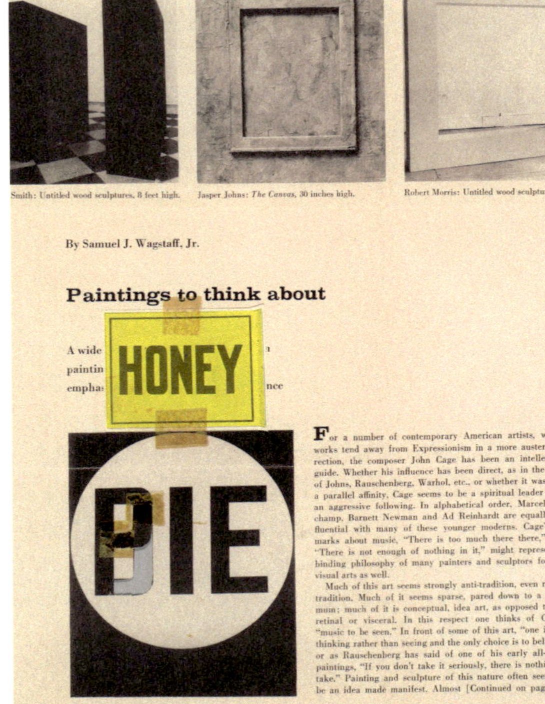

Smith: Untitled wood sculptures, 8 feet high.

Jasper Johns: *The Canvas*, 30 inches high.

Robert Morris: Untitled wood sculpture, 6 feet high

By Samuel J. Wagstaff, Jr.

Paintings to think about

A wide … n
paintin
empha… nce

For a number of contemporary American artists, whose works tend away from Expressionism in a more austere direction, the composer John Cage has been an intellectual guide. Whether his influence has been direct, as in the case of Johns, Rauschenberg, Warhol, etc., or whether it was just a parallel affinity, Cage seems to be a spiritual leader with an aggressive following. In alphabetical order, Marcel Duchamp, Barnett Newman and Ad Reinhardt are equally influential with many of these younger moderns. Cage's remarks about music, "There is too much there there," and "There is not enough of nothing in it," might represent a binding philosophy of many painters and sculptors for the visual arts as well.

Much of this art seems strongly anti-tradition, even recent tradition. Much of it seems sparse, pared down to a minimum; much of it is conceptual, idea art, as opposed to the retinal or visceral. In this respect one thinks of Cage's "music to be seen." In front of some of this art, "one is left thinking rather than seeing and the only choice is to believe," or as Rauschenberg has said of one of his early all-white paintings, "If you don't take it seriously, there is nothing to take." Painting and sculpture of this nature often seems to be an idea made manifest. Almost [Continued on page 62]

Robert Indiana: *Die*, 6 feet high.

Ray Johnson to William S. Wilson, n.d.

is not enough of nothing in it"—versus the kind of art, Cage's own kind, before which "one is left thinking rather than seeing and the only choice is to believe." The debris-loving jokester Johnson is no one's idea of a minimalist, but a conceptualist? One recalls Asawa's friends, "All of them more interested in your thoughts than the moticos." The moticos already hung half-way between thing and thought. How much nothing, Ray Johnson had begun to wonder, was enough?

"For a number of contemporary American artists, whose works tend away from Expressionism in a more austere direction, the composer John Cage has been an intellectual guide," especially to those young painters, composers, and poets who made the swerve toward "conceptual, idea art, as opposed to retinal or visceral" via the classes in experimental composition that Cage taught at the New School for Social Research from 1956 to 1961. From this cohort came friends who would play significant roles in Johnson's life, including Fluxus artists George Brecht and Dick Higgins, poet Jackson Mac Low, and expressionist painter turned maestro of Happenings Allan Kaprow. But Johnson's access to Cage, while equally direct, was of a different kind.

VIII

John Cage first came to Black Mountain College in the summer of 1948, Johnson's last semester there. Over the course of that memorable session, Cage gave twenty-five mini-concerts of the music of Erik Satie, capped by a production of a rarely performed play by Satie, *The Ruse of Medusa*, which starred painter Elaine de Kooning and architect Buckminster Fuller, with choreography by Merce Cunningham and décor by de Kooning and her husband Willem, all of them summer faculty who were new to the college. Near the bottom of the program's credit's list under "SPECIAL PROPERTIES," is a credit for "Telephone," designed by "Raymond Johnson & Forrest Wright."

At Black Mountain, Raymond Johnson was just one talented kid among many. But that summer he was suddenly swept into the grown-ups' world when sculptor Richard Lippold joined his friends Cage and Cunningham at the school, having driven from New York to North Carolina in a hearse with his dancer wife Louise and their two young daughters. The hearse would soon serve as a trysting place for Richard and baby-faced Ray, who fell deeply in love for the first and, it would seem, last time in his life. **How have I got thru life without the broken heart?** Ray marveled in 1974, when Richard at long last told him it was over, he had found somebody new. On October 12, 1994, four days before

Johnson's 67th birthday, three months and a day before his suicide, a postcard went into the mail with Lippold's address, in Ray's hand, on one side, and on the other, a pasted-on image: a photo of a baby with its heart scissored out.

In the fall of 1948, Frances X. Profumo, a poet friend of Ray's with whom Richard had also become close that summer at Black Mountain, received a letter in which Lippold confided that he, too, had fallen hard. For him, it seems, it was a first open acknowledgement, to himself as well as others, of his attraction to men, whereas "Ray can tell you that he has loved other men before me & I am not his undoing." As Richard knew, this was news to Frances, who had had her own affair with Ray. Lippold's wife Louise, meanwhile, he reports, "alternates between patience and bitterness and her well-being is my one worry." Nonetheless, "I am helpless now to do more than learn from Ray all that I need to know about myself, and have needed to know for some time." The student had become the teacher, or rather, "We have much to learn from each other. For how long I don't know, and it seems irrelevant now. We are happy in each other and this is our reality."

The plan going forward, said Richard, was for him to live with Ray "& visit my family week-ends." Their initial retreat to a house in the Pennsylvania countryside, however, left Ray missing **my friends and my mobility at school.** He was, he wrote to Frances in November, **sure of my devotion to people and the way I want to live but so unsure of other things. If you would only write me some words I would feel better.** The letter breaks off midstream and then resumes: **richard retrieved this from the stove and insists i send it to albert and ruth**, that is, Ruth Asawa and her husband-to-be, the Black Mountain–trained architect Albert Lanier. The communications among the four young friends had grown complex and fraught. **I am sure Albert condemns me and I love him very much,** Ray had fretted to Frances in a note enclosed with Richard's initial confession. And in the corner of a letter from Ray to Ruth, sent in January 1949, Ruth would pencil "Burn when read" before forwarding the page to Frances.

A few months later, Johnson came to New York, perching at first in the Lippold family's apartment (**Louise said to send her love to you**, he lets Frances know, soon after arriving) before moving to a Harlem studio, where Richard would come and go. In the summer of 1951, Richard and Ray headed downtown at the suggestion of Lippold's friend Cage, who had found a place by the East River. Composer Morton Feldman lived in the building, too. *Harper's Bazaar* found the ménage piquant enough to merit an item, published in July 1952.

Fresh, seemingly capricious winds in music, sculpture, and painting come from a ramshackle structure at 326 Monroe St. in New York, in the shadow of the Williamsburg Bridge. There, in a neighborhood of grime and garlic, four friends—experimental, even stratospheric artists—have established three uncluttered studios with a view of the East River. They call it, after their landlord, the "Boza Mansion." The four, seen above in a de luxe hearse, are Richard Lippold, owner of the somber vehicle, who uses it to cart his family and sculptures (his "Variation No. 7: Full Moon" is on view at the Museum of Modern Art); composer Morton Feldman; John Cage, the first to discover and settle in the old tenement; and Ray Johnson, painter.

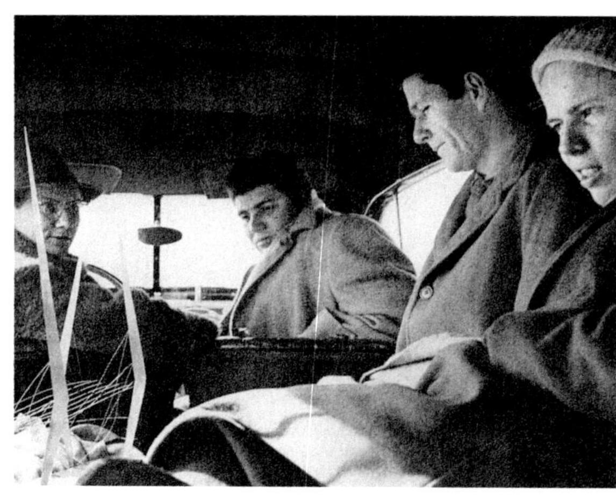

Photograph from "Four Artists in a 'Mansion,'" *Harper's Bazaar*, 1952. Left to right: Richard Lippold, Morton Feldman, John Cage, Ray Johnson.

Four artists, three studios. The *Harper's Bazaar* blurb writer delicately omits to mention that Lippold divides his time between Johnson's apartment and the Lippold family home and makes no mention at all of another notable part-time occupant, choreographer Merce Cunningham, Cage's partner in art and life. In a letter sent in the fall of 1951 to a friend still at Black Mountain, Ray affects nonchalance as he evokes the heady atmosphere at the Bozza Mansion (the garlic-averse reporter, perhaps not used to Italian spelling, also omitted the second "z"). There, his ascetic digs are brightened by

violets from Mrs. Cage [artist Xenia Cage, John's former wife]**— grass from the country and a beautiful weed, a present from John, a chrysanthemum bush. He says you can fry the leaves in batter and eat them. He took us to a new Japanese restaurant very good. The four of us had dinner here last night. I cooked Chinese pork with anise which everyone liked. Richard has a drawing of a bird that Morris Graves sent via Marion Willard who was West. He is finishing his hanging instruction today—he is polishing sheets and then must lacquer [...] Today I start a new painting. Merce back from a few weeks vacation in Rockport, looking like a blond mulatto—so tan. Little boats—big boats continuously on the river.**

IX

I have nothing to say
and I am saying it

said John Cage repeatedly, one evening in 1949. The phrase functions as a leitmotif in the composer's "Lecture on Nothing," which he was delivering for the first time to a group of New York artists, most of them associated with Abstract Expressionism, who had begun to meet regularly at a downtown space known as The Club. Cage conceived the talk at least in part as a provocation—another repeated phrase, "It is not irritating," suggests that the speaker's audience may find it so and one painter, Cage later recalled with relish, "stood up part way through, screamed, and then said, while I continued speaking, 'John, I dearly love you, but I can't bear another minute.'" He remained a valued member of the Club nonetheless. While he may have judged that "there was not enough of nothing" in his Club compatriots' paintings, Cage's talent for negation brought to their discussions something they might otherwise have lacked, a bracing sense of internal distance.

(The year before Johnson's first brush with Cage at Black Mountain, he hears his friend Asawa speak in class of **the Taoism philosophy of nothing ness being everything-ness**, and thinks, **I feel that way**. Three years after that, he moves in across the hall from John. Life is a dream.)

Life was a dream, once. In 1972, when historian Martin Duberman published *Black Mountain: An Exploration in Community*, the first full-scale study of the college, Johnson mailed out copies of a snarky burlesque of his background interview with Duberman, under the heading, **Norman Solomon's Doberman Interviews Ray Johnson**.

> **Doberman: First of all, don't be too alarmed, Mr. Johnson. I am a talking dog and I want to ask you a few questions about Black Minute College. Woof.**
> **Johnson: I have nothing to say.**

It goes downhill from there.

> **Doberman: According to our records, you were a student at Black Minute College for 3 arf years.**
> **Johnson: I was a student there for <u>3</u> arf minutes....**
> **Doberman: What did you <u>do there</u> for those 3 arf minutes?**
> **Johnson: I don't remember.**
> **Doberman: Which 3 arf minutes in <u>what arf year</u> were you there? In the Albers bow wow years? In the Olson woof years?**
> **Johnson: Arf.**

Doberman: You don't sound very "college-educated" to me. Are you sure you were at Black Minute, that experimental galaxy of talent?
Johnson: I don't think I was.
Doberman: Do you know John Cage?
Johnson: Who?

"I have nothing to say." **I have nothing to say.** Johnson's delayed echo of Cage's kōan hovers, as is his wont, between mockery and tribute. The mockery is partially aimed at Duberman of course, but it is also intertwined with the memories that flicker up in Johnson's note to Elayne Varian regarding his relationship with Rauschenberg.

Rauschenberg's perfectly empty *White Paintings*, produced at Black Mountain in 1951 under Cage's influence, were immediately seized on by Cage as exemplary artworks. The set of indistinguishable canvases covered in flat-rolled white house paint were not things to be looked at, Cage said, but occasions for looking, "airports for the lights, shadows, and particles." They were also the avowed inspiration for the composer's similarly exemplary *4'33"* (1952), whose title specifies the time in which the composition's listeners are to observe a silence. Listen again to the flat declarative sentences that Johnson offered up to Varian in lieu of a direct answer to her query. **I carried a book on Taoism and quoted lines to them about emptiness and nothing**. Ray Johnson, like Robert Rauschenberg at his most Cagean, practiced that kind of negation. **Years later the house burned.** Ray Johnson practiced that kind of negation, too.

Cage's aesthetic is often associated with the first kind of negation, the kind that opens onto silence and emptiness. But that aesthetic also has a punk-destructive side. As Johnson worked through this Cagean opposition, he began to refer to the conceptual aspect of his practice as **Nothing**, or rather, *a* **Nothing**, two negatives equaling a positive.

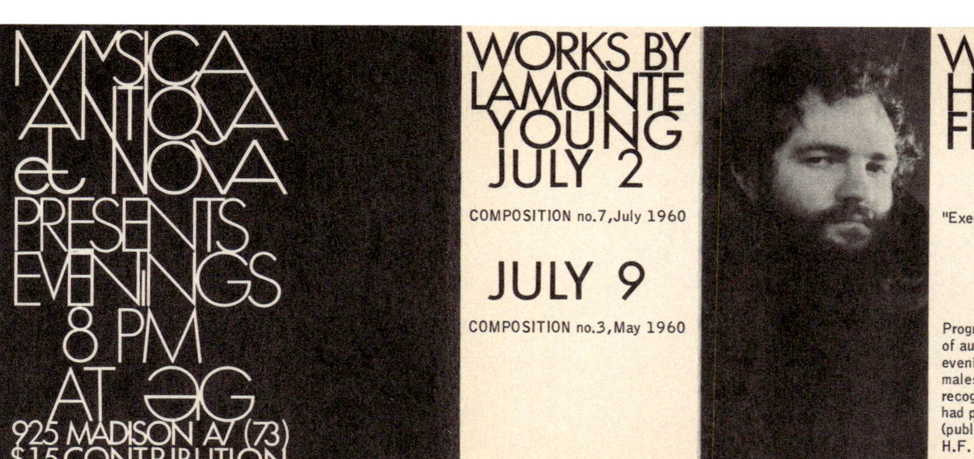

X

Nothing officially entered Johnson's lexicon in 1961, when George Maciunas, the self-appointed leader of the conceptual art group Fluxus, invited Johnson to give a performance, one of a series curated by Maciunas at the AG Gallery, an unfinished space uptown on Madison Avenue. The flyer for the series features announcements of ambitious *WORKS* and portraits of the artists as intense young men. Among them, the announcement for *NOTHING BY RAY JOHNSON* sticks out like the bandaged thumb in the accompanying photo, a portrait of the artist as a bloody pain.

Accounts of that first **Nothing** vary, but roughly and in brief: having kept his audience waiting until somewhat late in the evening, Johnson arrived carrying an armful of wooden dowels, possibly found on the street en route, and proceeded to drop them down the stairs leading to the gallery's upper floor, making a clatter that startled gallery-goers and a mess that endangered their upward progress. That was it. Years later, Johnson spoke of having been **influenced** in this action by John Cage, **who was a friend of mine.**

That evening, though, it was the Happenings of Allan Kaprow, another Cage acolyte on the ascent, that were foremost in Johnson's mind. The Happenings were relatively elaborate events, involving constructed environments, props, and scripted instructions for both performers and audience, while still leaving ample room for unscripted actions and reactions and thereby satisfying the Cagean call for "enough nothing" in art. These events had a punk-destructive aspect (the audience for one Kaprow event was first imprisoned in a box, then attacked by a man with a power mower), along with a touch of Romantic afflatus. "Happenings are not just another style," Kaprow declared in 1961, but "a moral act, a human stand of great urgency, whose professional status as art is less a criterion than their certainty as an ultimate existential commitment." Johnson's response

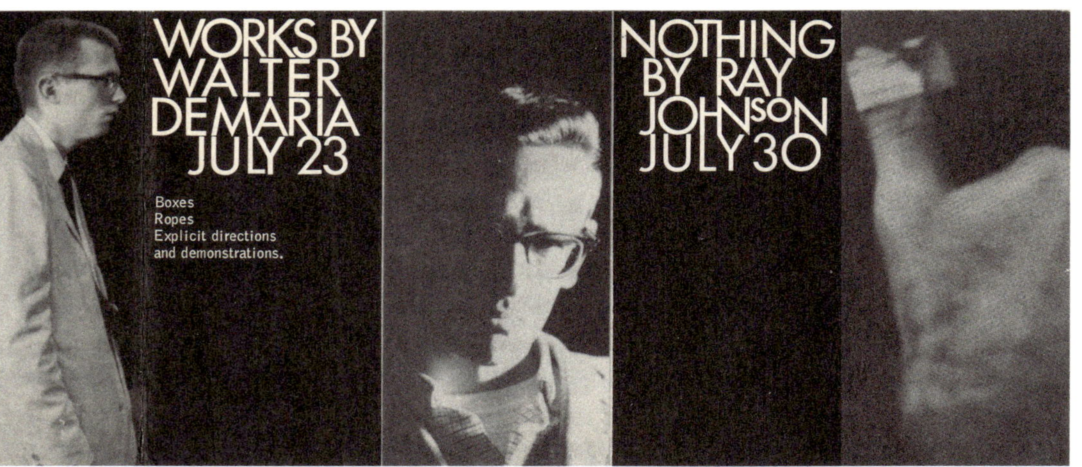

Flyer for performance series at AG Gallery, 1961.

to these performances and their accompanying rhetoric was to compress and deflate. The corner-of-the-eye, what-was-*that*? Nothing is the Happening's afterimage, its negative. Or maybe just another mocking echo.

Doberman: Why did you go to Black Minute?

Johnson: I don't remember.

Doberman: Do you have any quickie sex stories about the life there?

Johnson: No, I don't.

Doberman: Did they teach you to be so negative?

Johnson: Yes.

Doberman: Now we're getting somewhere! Did they conduct classes on "How to Print Negatives?"

Johnson: You fucking dumb dog!

Did they teach you to be so negative? Ray Johnson's perversity, his inability to let self-seriousness go by unmocked, was all his own. But by the time he left Black Mountain, he had acquired the beginnings of a sense of how he might put his native negativity to, yes, serious artistic use. **Did they conduct classes on "How to Print Negatives?"** During his time at the college, Johnson also became highly skilled at graphic design, a practice that he would try, and fail, to use to make a living while he struggled, in his first years out of school, to establish himself as a painter. But those same skills would prove central to Johnson's correspondence art, which mixed hand-made elements with printed circulars, visually arresting advertisements for nothing.

In 1987, Allan Kaprow put together *A Tribute to John Cage: Prepareð Box for John Cage*, a limited edition of works by various hands. Ray Johnson's contribution, a mailer from 1983 titled **An Interview**, consists of a four-part diagram with the explanatory preface, **When I lived across the hall from John Cage on Monroe Street (1950s)/ I made & gave to him:**

The gift for Cage was a wooden box, **painted flat black** inside and out on four sides and sealed on one end

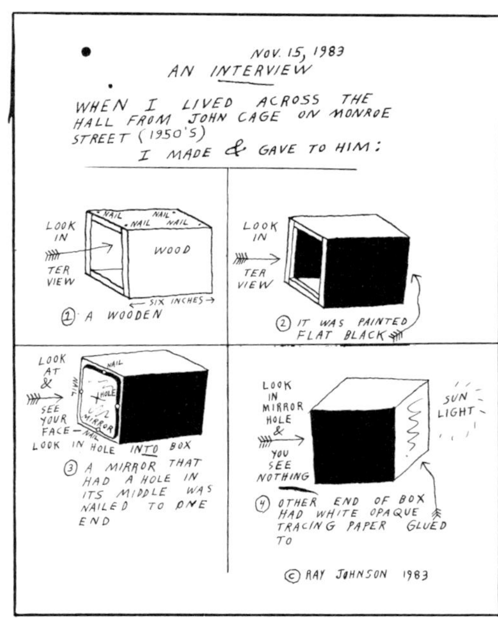

Ray Johnson, *An Interview* flyer, November 15, 1983.

with a mirror pierced with a peephole and **white opaque tracing paper** on the other. **Look/ in/ ter/ view**, Johnson instructs the viewer. Unable to resist a peephole, you move toward it. You see your face in the mirror. Closer. One eye focused on the tracing paper at the box's other end, **you see nothing**. With **sun light** behind it, framed by **flat black**, the paper's translucency renders its whiteness dimensionless. In a sidebar to a study of Kaprow and the Happenings, art historian Judith Rodenbeck describes Johnson's box as an "anti-Brunelleschian construction" designed to frustrate every expectation that we bring to works of art: it offers "no internal view, no inter-subjective dialog, no *costruzione legittima*," the trick of perspective that translates art's space into ours. The *White Paintings*, also produced under Cage's spell, likewise aim to block our efforts to see art as a mirror or window, inducing the kind of blindness that leads, it is to be hoped, to insight. Again, set beside Rauschenberg's full-length-mirror-sized panels, which now hang in various configurations in various museums, Johnson's little box might not look like much, but, again, who knows, since it either no longer exists or never did exist except in the artist's imagination.

What can one say in **An Interview**'s favor? It is "more involved with intimacy than with any public occasion," although whether that is a virtue remains to be seen. It provokes frustration to the point of complete exasperation. You see yourself and then you don't, and then you bump your nose on the mirror and then you see nothing, really nothing. Whereas Rauschenberg's panels, so frustrating to critics at the time, turn out to be—or rather, always already were, as Cage recognized instantly—screens for projection, "airports for the lights, shadows and particles."

No one could beat Ray Johnson at the game of frustration. Ask any interviewer. Woof.

XI

> Germans to Teach Art Near Here [photo]; Professor Josef and Frau Albers, above, of Dessau, Germany, where they taught art in the famous Bauhaus school there until Hitler's policies caused it to close recently, this week joined the faculty of Black Mountain College at Blue Ridge to conduct an art department in the college.
>
> —*Asheville Citizen*, December 5, 1933

John Cage sometimes taught in a formal capacity, but his lessons were also transmitted to a whole generation of artists by informal and even invisible means, like mushroom spores. Whereas Josef Albers's practice, in the studio and at the writing desk as well as in the classroom, was pedagogical through and through. Between 1922 and 1958, he played crucial roles in the development of three historically significant art programs, first at the Bauhaus, then at Black Mountain, and finally, at Yale University. As a teacher, Albers emphasized systematic training in the basics of visual form, such as line, shape, and especially color. As an artist, he is best known for the extensive series of systematic studies in juxtaposed color that unscrolled decade after decade under the rubric *Homage to the Square*.

When Sam Wagstaff spoke of "retinal" art in "Paintings to think about," Josef Albers was precisely the kind of artist he had in mind. A book about Albers's teaching takes its title from the phrase in which the painter summed up his highest goal as educator: "to open eyes." One can hardly imagine an aesthetic more diametrically opposed than his to an art that has as its goal that, as Cage put it, "one is left thinking rather than seeing." But if one takes a step back and sees Albers's art in the context of his work as a teacher and institution-builder, he can begin to look more like a conceptual artist. There is an Albers whose true medium is not paint but school.

To put this in more balanced terms, while Albers was indeed a formalist at heart, his approach to form was at once aesthetic and social. In a book on the teaching of Albers, Cage, and Buckminster Fuller at Black Mountain, Eva Diaz spells out this dialectic: "Attentiveness to details of form meant, to Albers, an alertness to the ways in which an individual was sited in the larger field of social relations." Having shaped and been shaped by the communal ethos of the Bauhaus and Black Mountain, Albers came to believe, Diaz writes, citing the artist, that "art was intelligible only within a community of understanding—'recognizing oneself and developing oneself in relationship to others.'" Like his student Ray Johnson, Josef Albers may be viewed as a creature and creator of networks.

Which is not to say that Albers would recognize himself in this description, nor, for that matter, would the Ray Johnson who was Albers's devoted student for three years at Black Mountain. **In Design there are many people who flock to hear the clear, wise, and constructive ideas of Albers,** Ray reported to his parents early in his apprenticeship, and apparently the ideas were taking. **I am starting to do some new paintings in oil on very brightly colored backgrounds showing squares or circles of color overlapping to produce a mixture of two colors.**

This Ray Johnson was then and would remain the kind of formalist who needed the communicative resources afforded to him only in the making and viewing of visual art. He thought and felt through color, through graphic punch, through composition that brought order to his world without betraying its inherent disorder. Like his teacher Josef Albers, that is, Ray Johnson was, in both a simple sense and a more complex one, an art-school artist. But Albers never aimed to make the social aspect of his work apparent in his art, whereas, from the moment he began to wonder what a moticos was until the day he died, Johnson would struggle to make art that fused the social and the sensuous without scanting either aspect. It would prove to be, as Kurt Schwitters could have told him, a heartbreaking project. Still, quixotic as Johnson's project may have been, it was also a logical outgrowth of his education.

XII

When the Archives of American Art at the Smithsonian Institution sent someone to speak with Johnson in 1968 for their collection of interviews with significant figures in the American art world, the interviewer, Sevim Fesci, began with a question that implied that the artist's vocation might be traced back to his beginnings: "Where were you born, I mean by that your birthplace, your family and religious background, and were your parents artists themselves?" Johnson waved her off, in part because he objected to such questions on principle. But he also knew that Fesci was pointing in the wrong direction. The answer to the question of how he became the artist he was, an artist for whom the social fabric was as malleable a medium as paint, had less to do with family than with institutions. Black Mountain College is part of that answer. This leaves the question of how a midwestern factory worker's son got to Black Mountain.

A classroom photograph of Josef Albers shows him crouched over a piece of paper on which he is demonstrating something to an attentive student, Hazel Frieda Larsen (Archer), whose photographs would provide a matchless chronicle of life at Black Mountain. To Hazel's left is her friend Ray, seen wearing the letter sweater of his alma mater, Cass Technical High School, which back then was the only selective public high school in Detroit. Founded with the needs of the city's bourgeoning car industry in mind, Cass Tech offered pre-professional programs, including one in commercial art and

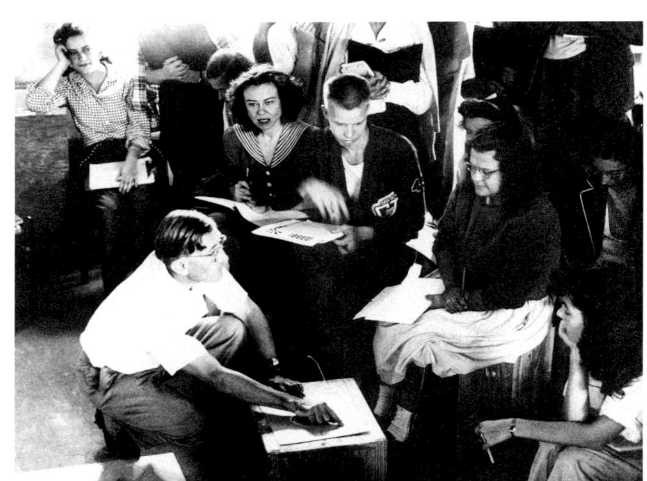

Josef Albers teaching at Black Mountain College, ca. 1945–48. Seated, center: Ray Johnson, Hazel Larsen (Archer).

design. A middle school art teacher took note of Ray's talent and urged him to apply.

When Ray had reached his senior year, a piece in the student newspaper portrayed him as one of the school's success stories, while giving a glimpse of the Ray who was already ambivalent about success as it is usually portrayed.

> Outstanding in the Art Department is Ray "Baldy" Johnson. Those who know him say he illustrates the horrible example of the brush cut. [photo] Ray is president of the Advertising Art Club, and has recently won a scholarship to the Art Students' League in New York.
>
> His hobbies are fishing, painting, Gene Tierney, and June Allyson.
>
> **My greatest ambition**, offered Ray wistfully, **is to buy a farm, live on it, and paint for the rest of my life.**

A quarter-century would then pass before wistful Ray would buy the Manhattanite's equivalent of a farm, a house in suburban Long Island, where he could take his distance from the art world. But while he was in high school, the outlines of the other Ray, the one who would cut an indelible figure on the New York scene in the 1950s and '60s, had also begun to emerge.

There are lectures on Monday night, movies on Tuesday, art class on Friday, art class on Saturday, lecture on Sunday. I lead a very busy life, this Ray reports to Arthur Secunda, a friend from Cass Tech whose family had moved away to New York. After some of Johnson's letters to Secunda appeared in *Corresponðence: An Exhibition of the Letters of Ray Johnson*, a 1976 show at the North Carolina Museum of Art, the artist began to refer to these early mailings when asked about the origins of his New York Correspondance School. As Johnson himself remarks in one interview, the Secunda letters are full of the usual high school stuff, **what dance I was going to, and what cheerleaders I was running around with, all of that embarrassing drivel**. But they also exhibit, on page after page, **things that I'm still doing today**, the fluid, antic mix of word and image that makes a Johnson mailer recognizable at a glance.

The letters also reveal a Ray who, for all his comic deflections, is growing more serious about art. Scribbling off to the side one **Friday morning in Art Comp. Class**, Ray gives "Art" a detailed account of the Friday night **figure class** he has been attending at **the Institute** with another Cass Tech student, Pete DiCresce, then pleads with his correspondent to **send me something you did in your life class. Please send a drawing, not a cartoon. Your cartoons are swell, but you also can draw. Please follow my advice, son**. The too-perfectly named Art is for Ray a new kind of friend, a fellow artist, like Pete, or like the "George T" Ray mentions in his next paragraph.

There is a Michigan Artist Show in the gallerys [*sic*] of the Institute now. I plan on seeing it tonight. On opening night, there were high class gents and dames in evening dress and George T. says that it was a classy affair.

Ray's new friends share with him not only a vocation, but a world. Art doesn't need to be told that that **the Institute** is the Detroit Institute of Arts, where he, like Ray, attended classes and lectures to supplement his studies at Cass Tech. In 1927, Johnson's birth year, the DIA opened the doors of its new, ambitious Deco-classical building and began to realize the vision of its director, William (Wilhelm) Valentiner, a German-trained art historian who would oversee the provincial institution's transformation into one of the

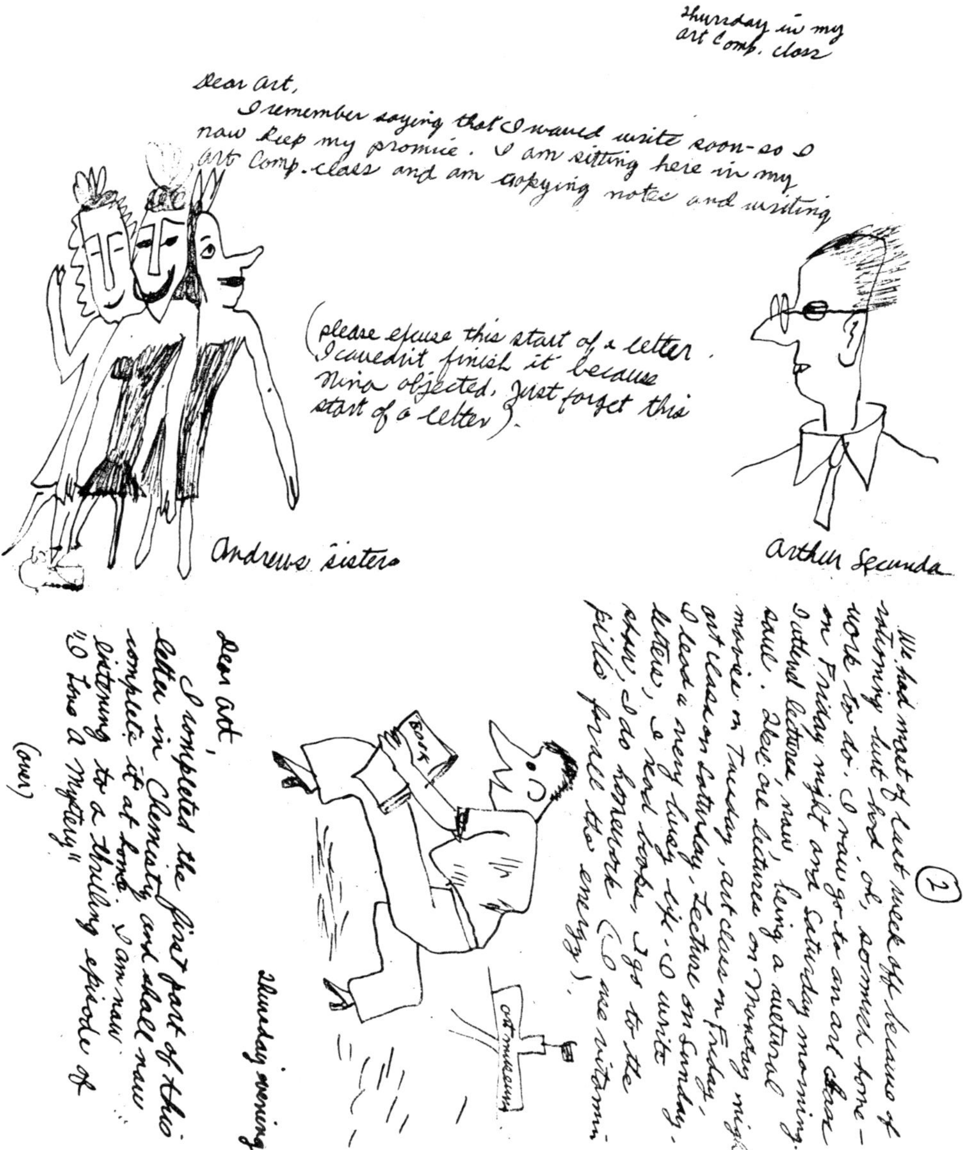

Thursday in my art Comp. class

Dear Art,
I remember saying that I would write soon-so I now keep my promise. I am sitting here in my art Comp. class and am copying notes and writing

(please excuse this start of a letter. I couldn't finish it because Nina objected. Just forget this start of a letter).

Andrews sisters

Arthur Secunda

(2)

We had most of last week off because of returning but boy, oh, so much home-work to do. I now go to an art class on Friday night and Saturday morning. I attend lectures, now, being a cultural soul. There are lectures on Monday night, movies on Tuesday, art class on Friday, art class on Saturday, Lecture on Sunday. I lead a very busy life. I write letters, I read books, I go to the show, I do homework (I use vitamin pills for all the energy).

Thursday evening.

Dear Art,
I completed the first part of this letter in Chemistry and shall now complete it at home. I am now listening to a thrilling episode of "I Love a Mystery"

(over)

Ray Johnson, letter to Arthur Secunda, ca. 1943.

country's great universal museums. In 1945, the year that Ray headed off to Black Mountain, Valentiner stepped down from his position, although he would linger on to curate one last show, the show that Johnson describes in a query included in a packet sent to Bill Wilson 1965.

Dear Sirs, // In 1945–46 you had a sculpture exhibit at your museum with Lachaise's portrait of John Marin, his floating woman, a prehistoric goddess of fertility and perhaps R. Lippold's Hills are not Empty. Is it possible to obtain a catalogue of this exhibit organized by Dr. Valentiner?

Valentiner was a specialist in Netherlandish painting, but the director's tastes and principles also committed him to connecting the institution to its time and place. He commissioned Diego Rivera to wrap the museum's central court in murals, curated shows of cutting-edge contemporary art ("confusing and controversial," per one review that Ray pasted in his high school scrapbook), and co-sponsored the Annual Exhibition for Michigan Artists with the Detroit Artists Market, a co-op gallery where a teenage Ray sometimes put his drawings up for sale. As Ray writes to Art about this **Michigan Art Show**, one can see him beginning to grasp the way school connects to the museum which connects to the gallery which connects, somehow, to the sphere of **high class gents and dames in evening dress**: all the ingredients one needs to make an art world.

XIII

According to Bill Wilson, Pete Di Cresce, fellow artist, was the first true love of Ray Johnson's life. They had just one sexual encounter, initiated by Ray, followed by a rebuff from Pete. Ray then slipped Pete a smoldering self-portrait, captioned, **What's say let's be buddies?** Afterward, Ray and Pete remained friends-in-art. Sometime during their senior year, Ray left him this note.

Pete—next Sat. nite, I get out of work at 6—I have to eat my supper downtown—why don't we both go to the Russian Bear and have a good time and then go from there. Why don't you bring something for Stan and Zubel to criticize. It'll be a good criticism.

It'll be a good criticism. If you are serious about your work, as Ray reminded Art,

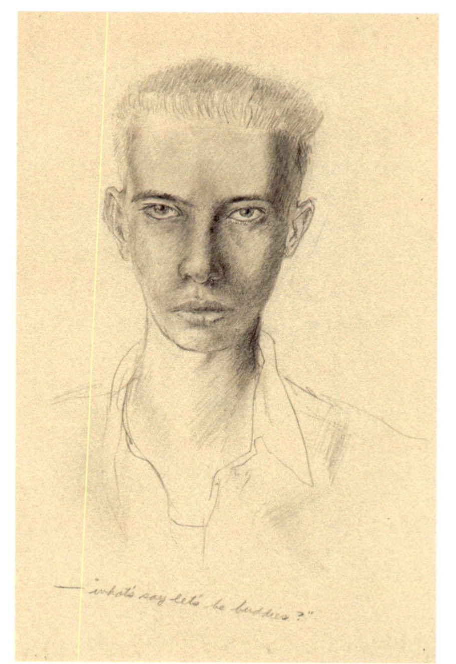

Ray Johnson to Pete Di Cresce, ("What's say let's be buddies"), n.d.

you must share it with other artists, and this, as he reminds Pete here, entails engaging in the art-world ritual of the critique. But first, supper at the Russian Bear in downtown Detroit, an unofficial clubhouse for local artists, among them the up-and-coming painters Stanley Twardowicz and Zubel Kachadoorian, both of whom had taught at the Ox-Bow School of Art in Saugatuck, Michigan the previous summer, when Ray attended along with other students from Cass Tech. Twardowicz would later try his luck in New York, with some success, a development Johnson flags in a 1964 mailing to Bill Wilson, which includes a cut-out image of a painting captioned, "Twardowicz, Number 11, 1955. Purchase." It had been bought straight from the studio by the Museum of Modern Art.

Ray Johnson projects his art worlds onto a moebius strip. **R. Lippold's Hills are not Empty** arrives in Detroit (**perhaps**) at the behest of **Dr. Valentiner** just after Ray has left for Black Mountain and three years before R. Lippold makes Ray's dream of true love with a fellow artist a reality. Stan Twardowicz would go on to have the career as a painter that Johnson veered away from a decade after their paths had crossed at the Ox-Bow School. That summer of 1944 in Saugatuck, Ray would make a new close friend, an artist named Elaine Schmitt, whose dancer sister, Betty, would convince Elaine, Ray, and Elaine's friend from a teacher's college back home in Wisconsin, Ruth Asawa, to apply to this amazing school where Betty had already begun her studies, this place called Black Mountain.

XIV

The art world was a small world for Ray Johnson in his first years in New York, a world largely bounded by his art-school circle. He was living with his teachers on Monroe Street. He was working at the Orientalia Bookstore, managed by another Black Mountain College alumnus, lighting designer Nick Cernovich, likely the place where Ray picked up the **book on Taoism** from which he read to Bob Rauschenberg and Sue Weil about **emptiness and nothing**. The circle widened as waves of students Ray had missed at the college arrived in New York from North Carolina. "I met Ray in December 1950," Norman Solomon recalled, "at the Woolworth's in New York City at 39th Street and Fifth Avenue," where Johnson had come with Hazel Larsen and Solomon with painter Dorothea Rockburne. **I sent this on a postcard to Dorothea**, Johnson would type on a card sent to Bill Wilson circa 1970, "this" being Henry James's great statement on "relations": "Really, universally, relations stop nowhere, and the exquisite problem of the artist is but to draw, by a geometry of his own, the circle within which they shall happily appear to do so." Through his art,

Ray Johnson sought to give aesthetic shape to social networks while at the same time evoking their boundlessness. In that art, he would keep circling back to these Black Mountain years.

During those years, however, Ray Johnson was still trying to work out a geometry of his own by faithfully following **the clear, wise, and constructive ideas of Albers**. All through the spring and summer of 1951, he labored over what he described to Frances Profumo, partway through the work, as **the most complex painting I have ever attempted**. That painting, *Calm Center*, is one of the few to survive Johnson's efforts to burn and chop away this chapter in his history.

Albers's ideas centered on the relational nature of color, the way no color is perceived in isolation, but, rather, in dynamic interaction with the colors that surround it. In the *Homage* series, Albers confined his

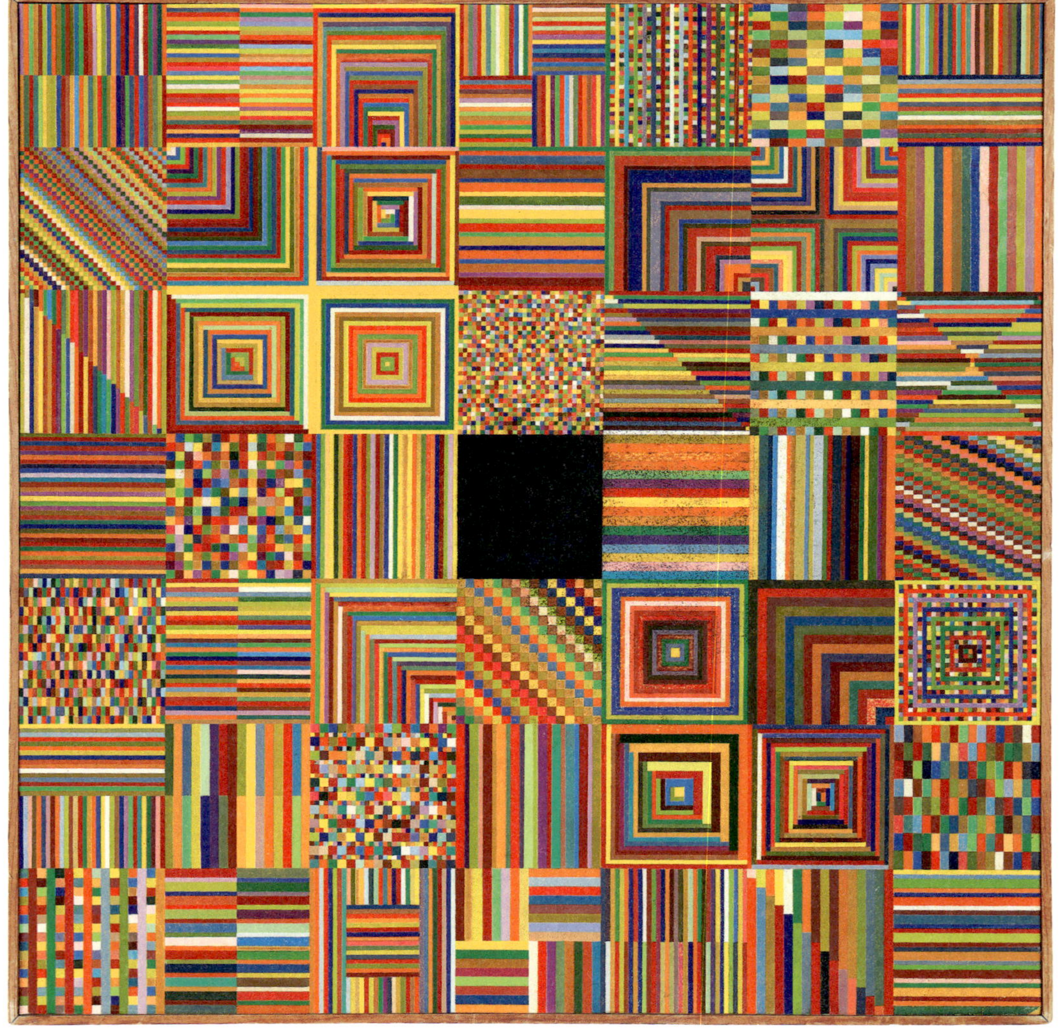

Ray Johnson, *Calm Center* (1951).

experiments in the retinal effects produced by the juxtaposition of colors to the space he referred to as the "prison" of the square. An artist can find freedom in constraint. In each *Homage* image, the given pattern of three or four layered squares lets the artist know just where to stop, while Albers's conception of the project as a potentially endless series tells us that really, universally, relations stop nowhere.

Is Johnson's *Calm Center* a unique work or a series? The artist composed the painting square by square, reporting to Frances in June that **Twenty seven squares are finished**, out of **49 in all.** The range of colors in the painting is wide and the relations among them complex; the forms are limited to variations on the square (square, rectangle, or rectilinear bar), obsessively arranged and rearranged, square by individual square. The tension between restricted form and expansive palette holds the whole composition tight, and yet the impression *is* of a series, or maybe an exhaustive catalogue. The sensory effect is not merely retinal, but eye-popping—"like looking at the underside of a starfish and seeing the thousands of moving feet," said one critic who saw the painting the year after it was made, hanging in a show sponsored by the American Abstract Artists Group. In a letter sent to Frances in October, Ray describes the sensation he was after as a **riot of violent color surrounding the calm black.** The syncopated colors do violence to the eye because they will not let it rest. They represent a version of relations that stop nowhere, as against the good infinity of **emptiness and nothing** embodied in the central square.

The October letter registers Ray's reaction to Frances's response to a photograph of *Calm Center* he had sent her. **When you say my painting is "mosaically beautiful" it distresses me because though it reminds one of weaving, mosaics or embroidery it still remains a painting**, it begins. **It reminds one of weaving,** and if one has just come from Black Mountain, it reminds one, more specifically, of the weavings of Anni Albers, who consciously exploited the elements of syncopation and infinitude already built into the patterns that a loom produces. In 1947, eagerly anticipating the Albers' return to school from a sabbatical in Mexico, Ray writes to his parents that he **is painting an old salad bowl the outside enamel black shiny and the inside texalite white dull** to put potato chips in at the welcome home party he will throw for the couple and that he has **painted Anni's bedroom all white because it is her favourite color**. When an artist paints a bowl, or a room, does it still remain a painting? In 1965, Johnson will begin to make mosaics out of little cardboard tiles, a crucial turn in the development of the signature style he will refer to as "collage-painting." But in 1951, he must resist the implications of his friend's astute critique because he still remains a painter in the strictest sense. What else could he be?

When painter Allan Kaprow found himself confronting the same question in the mid-1950s, he turned, as Johnson did, to collage, a practice that soon led him, like Johnson, to take his art out of the studio and set it in motion. In 1958, the year that Johnson **went to Cy Twombly's and burned things**, Kaprow published an essay, "The Legacy of Jackson Pollock," in which he claimed that Pollock (Pollock the fictive hero of painting, Pollock the historical marker), having taken painting to what seemed its utmost verge, "left us at the point where we must become preoccupied and even dazzled by the space and objects of our everyday life." Now, suddenly, "Objects of every sort are materials for the new art: paint, chairs, food, electric and neon lights, smoke, water, old socks, a dog, movies, a thousand other things." One could say that in this list paint is presented as just another thing among things, no longer a special thing apart. Then again, since Kaprow places it first on the list, one might wonder if paint retains for him a vestige, at least, of its former preeminence.

Ray begins his October letter to Frances by querulously objecting to her calling his painting "mosaically beautiful," **because though it reminds one of weaving, mosaics or embroidery it still remains a painting**. He then informs her, in a seeming non-sequitur, that **Sometimes at sunset the river is the same tone as the sky and the buildings in Brooklyn seem to float in the air.** In fact, he is still talking about painting. Ray is telling Frances that paint is *not* like light or air or water, not just another thing among things—even if, when his gaze drifts up from his worktable, he sees things moving and changing outside the studio and thinks, if only I could do *that*. But paint has its own life, a life apart, laid down stroke by unchangeable stroke. Lest his friend miss the point, the artist leaves off the usual concluding **Ray** and ends the letter with three brushy daubs, two in pure primaries, one in calm black.

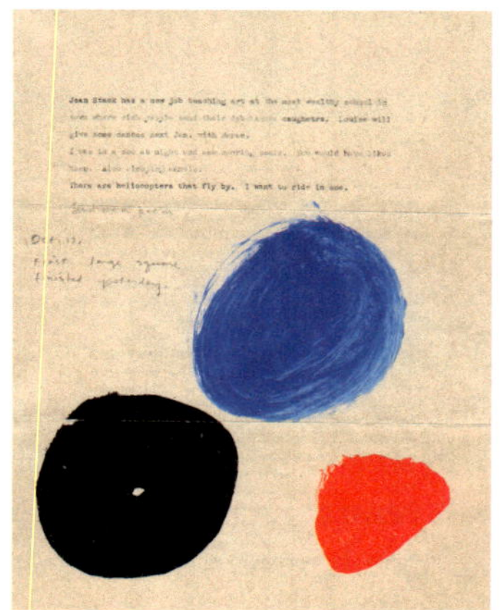
There are helicopters that fly by. I want to ride in one.

Ray Johnson letter to Frances X. Profumo, October 17, 1951.

XV

Of the dozens of envelopes that Frances received from Ray in the first few years after he left Black Mountain, the majority enclose letters just like anyone else's—words jotted on blank sheets, meant to convey information, thoughts, and feelings as they pass through the writer's mind. Some enclosures, though, do include the kind of striking visual elements Johnson's correspondents would come to expect in their Ray-mail—drawings, stylized lettering, the occasional bits of collage, and, in that one October letter, paint. Among the most striking is a 1949 mailing consisting of twenty-one square cardboard tiles, which could be seen in hindsight—which is always false to experience—as prophetic of Johnson's mid-1960s shift to a mosaic method of construction.

these are fragments of my painting daedalus, Ray explains on one of the tiles. On another, he relays some Black Mountain gossip: **i saw anni at the mondrian show** (*Piet Mondrian: Paintings 1910 through 1944*, at the Sidney Janis Gallery, where the Dutch painter's *Victory Boogie-Woogie*, with its eye-popping syncopated squares, was on view); **i go tomorrow to see hazel's photos at modern museum.** The remaining puzzle-pieces are abstracts in orange and black, to be assembled at the receiver's whim.

Like any artist's letters, Ray's record excitement at breakthroughs and frustration with blocks. One **depressing** rainy day in March 1953, Ray complains that **I am painting, painting, painting, but it is paining**, a setback he implicitly contrasts to his friends' advances.

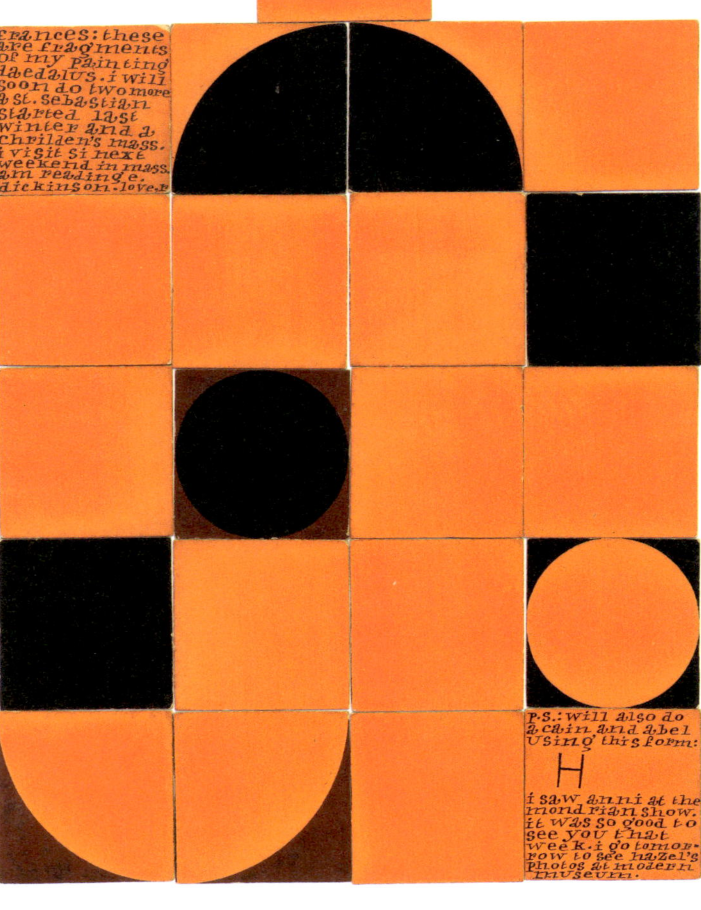
frances: these are fragments of my painting daedalus. i will soon do two more a st. sebastian started last winter and a chrilden's mass. i visit si next weekend in mass. am reading e. dickinson. love, r

p.s.: will also do a cain and abel using this form:
H
i saw anni at the mondrian show. it was so good to see you that week. i go tomorrow to see hazel's photos at modern museum.

Ray Johnson puzzle-letter to Frances X. Profumo, autumn 1949.

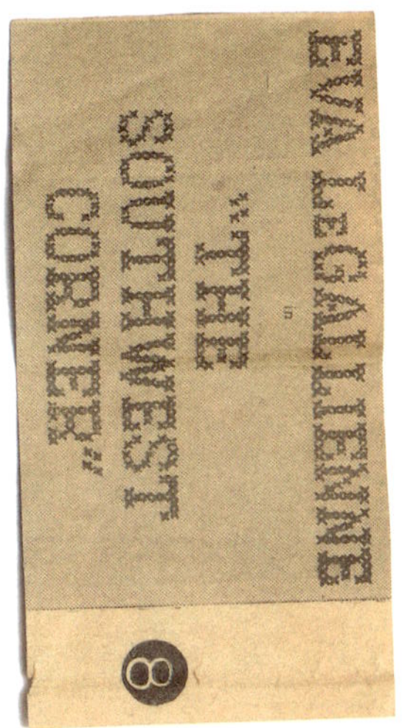

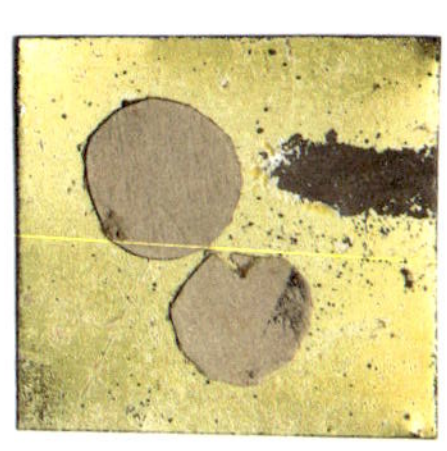

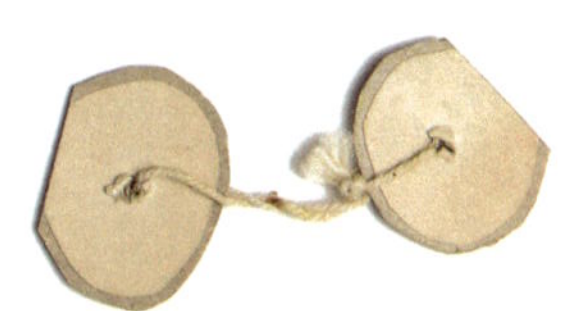

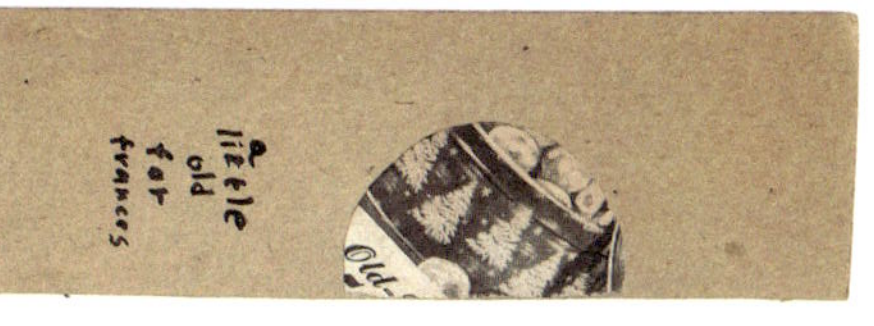

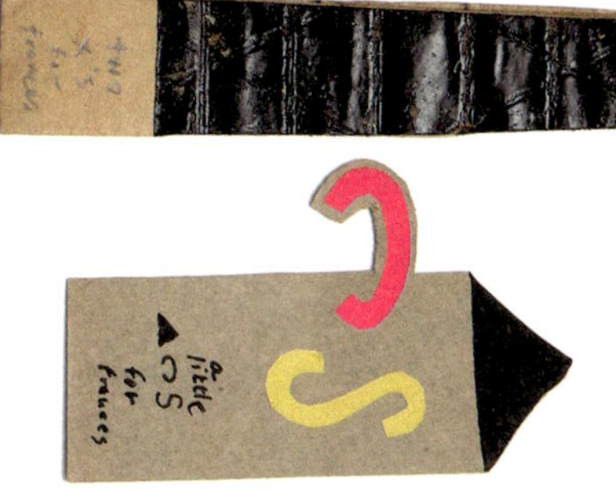

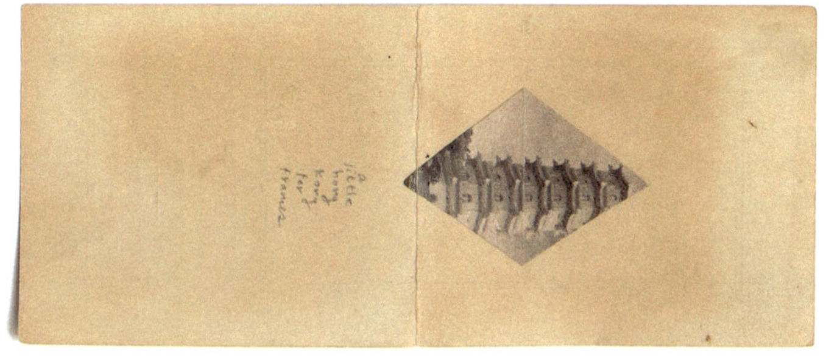

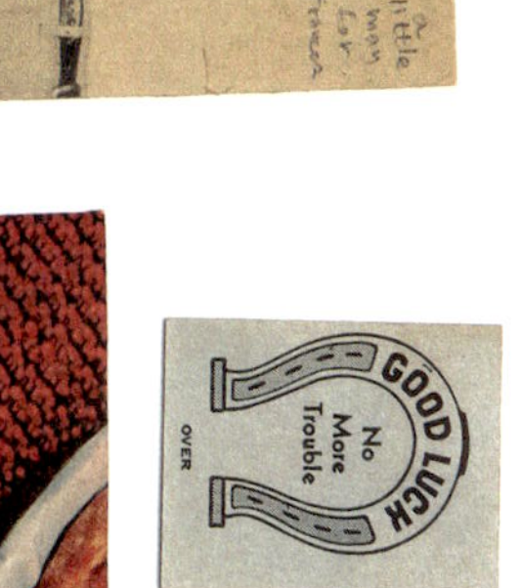

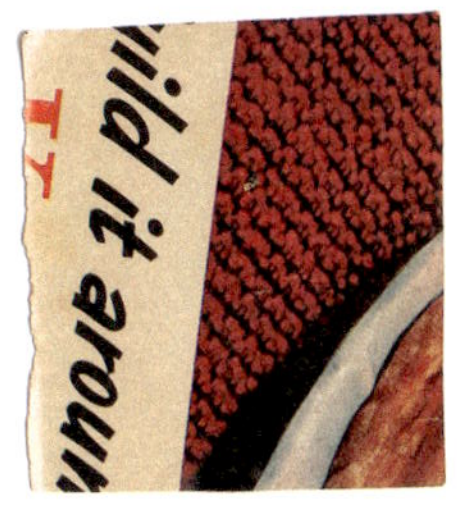

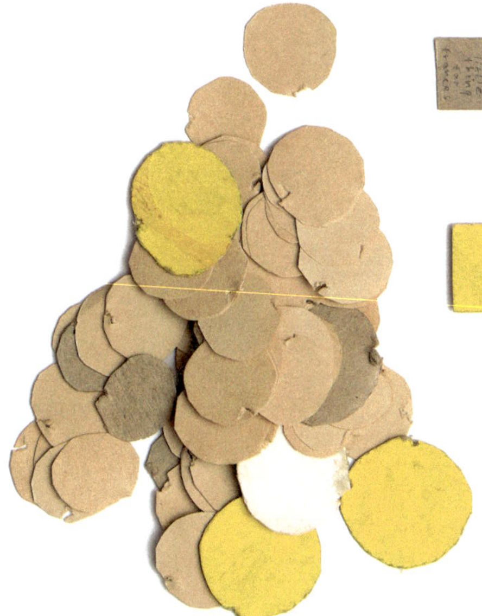

Ray Johnson moticos packet for Frances X. Profumo, ca. 1955.

Merce called me last night. He was back from Urbana where he gave a dance concert that was well received and John's music concert for magnetic tape was a shocker. One might see the moment captured in this letter as just another low point on the graph of inevitable ups and downs, or one might see it as a turning point. For, as it happens, from this moment on, Ray's mailings to Frances will contain fewer and fewer words and more and more images: mostly funny clippings, at first, and then, beginning in 1955, also packets of small, charming, highly personalized collages.

In October of 1955, Frances will receive the first in a series of clues as to the name Ray has just given to the little things he has been sending. Others on Johnson's mailing list, both intimates and strangers, would receive similar envelopes around this time, each return-addressed with a stack of actual phonebook business listings balanced atop the fictive "Mo Tea Co.," located at 2 Dover Street, where Johnson had moved in 1953 after the Bozza Mansion was torn down. **If you knew nothing about a moticos except its title is "MO" would you want to see it or not?** Ray Johnson asked strangers on the street one day in 1955. Beats me, they said. What is a moticos? The answer, it turns out, is twofold. A moticos is:

(a) a thing, unique, that falls from the envelope, still aglow with its junk-heap aura, into a unique recipient's palm;

(b) an idea, and thus, in theory, infinitely reproducible, with as many potential recipients as there are addresses.

Like the rest of today's—or rather, yesterday's—mail, a moticos may be as particular as a letter or as generic as an advertisement. Open the envelope and see what's inside.

Ray Johnson, envelope mailed to Frances X. Profumo, October 25, 1955, detail.

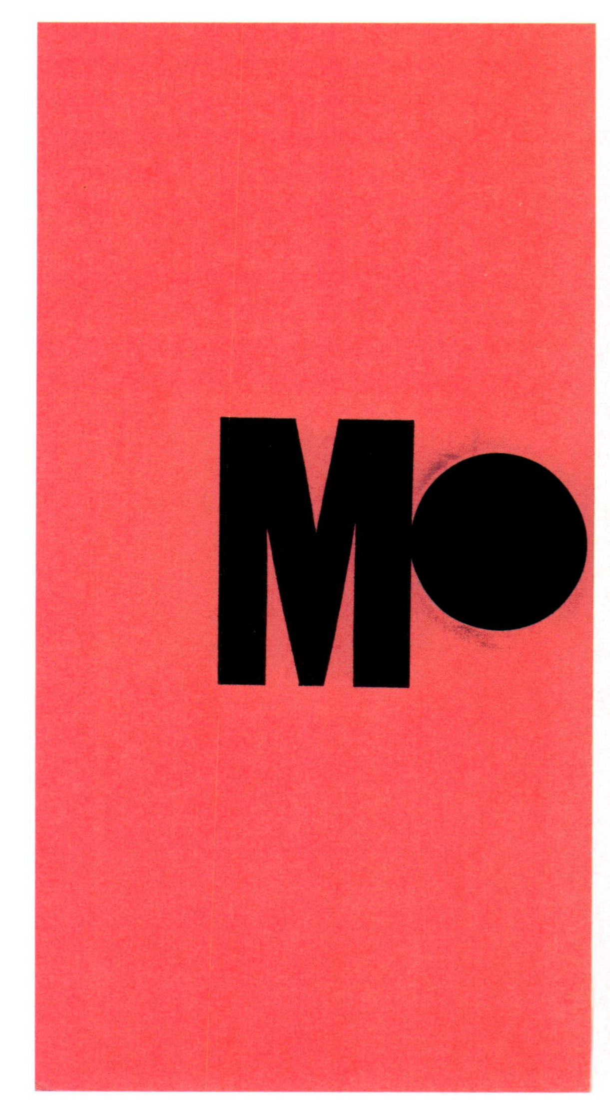
M

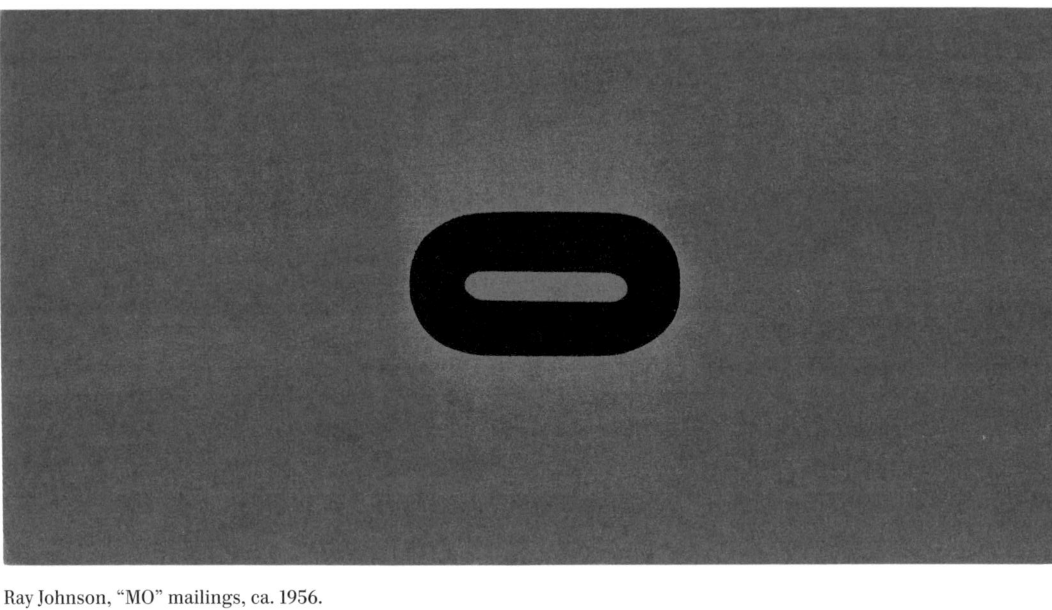

Ray Johnson, “MO” mailings, ca. 1956.

XVI

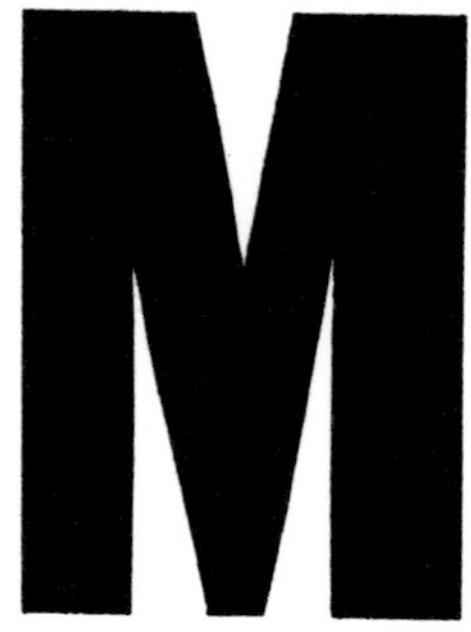

is for *matière*.

In hindsight (tricky hindsight), the advent of the moticos appears to herald the formation of Ray Johnson's Correspondance School, a project that will place him in a line of idea-artists descended from Marcel Duchamp via John Cage. The moticos moment also marks the beginning of the end of Johnson's efforts to fashion himself a painter in the style of Josef Albers. And yet, in its way, the moticos is as indebted as Johnson's paintings were to Albers's teachings.

In the letter home that records Johnson's earliest efforts to put Albers's precepts to work in paint, **showing squares or circles of color overlapping to produce a mixture of two colors,** art student Ray also speaks of a signature Albers exercise known as the *matière* study. *Matière*, he explains to his parents—he wants them to understand, this is important to him—**is a French word, meaning matter in English. Matiere** [*sic*] **has to do with the surface qualities of materials. He**, Albers, **showed us examples from magazines of photographs and advertising drawings that were done by artists who were conscious of the feel of things. It is much more exciting to have a pleasant touch sensation from objects than none at all.**

Albers's studies in the interaction of color appeal mainly to the eye. But the *matière* work links sight to touch, the moment of contact between hand and world. Hence, Albers instructed, "the use of tools is initially limited" in such work, the better to "achieve intimate contact with the material through one's own fingertips." The essay in which he offers this and other guidelines for the promulgation of the *matière* technique, "Teaching Form Through Practice," was published in a 1928 issue of the journal of the Bauhaus, where Albers first developed the *matière*. Albers also lays emphasis here on the economy of form that stems from what he calls "the activation of negativa (of remainders, intermediate, and negative values)." Such "negative values" are for Albers both aesthetic—"heightened interest, stronger effect, and greater unity are generated," he says, when an artist exploits negative space to make maximal use of minimal means—and a matter of economy in the practical sense. Artist Fritz Horstmann wryly observes that as a "school with very little funding in the depths of the Great Depression," Black Mountain "was a perfect place to further develop the *matière*—an exercise that is best done with found materials and scraps from the waste bin."

albers garden has good soil, begins a little ode to Albers's *via negativa* that Ray wrote in 1947 and sent to a Black Mountain friend who had left for New York,

soil made out of trash + garbage-
growth, creation, construction, invention
out of everything—every quality,
every feeling, every material, every
person. everything has some
use—can be turned into
something wonderful-
good soil out of garbage-
matieres out of the dump-

A list that Albers made in 1928 of possible materials for the *matière*—"corrugated cardboard, wire mesh, cellophane, transparent plastic, labels, newspapers, wallpaper, straw, gum, matchboxes, confetti and paper streamers, gramophone needles, and razor blades"—is as catholic in its way as the list that Cage's student Allan Kaprow would compose thirty years later, finding himself "preoccupied and even dazzled," as Albers hoped his students would be, "by the space and objects of our everyday life." The *matière* studies were arrangements of just such objects, disposed to heighten contrasts of texture and shape, and to produce a sense of surprise, as once familiar things, now repurposed, turn strange to the eye. When asked about the *matière* effect in a late-life interview, Ruth Asawa described one her friend Ray Johnson made—"nobody could see what it really was"—which, on closer inspection, turned out to be gauzy tent caterpillar nests laid on rough-textured metallic sheets. Like most other such pieces, it has long since disappeared. "Longevity was not a priority," explains critic Michael Beggs, since "these were temporal, didactic creations made for a moment of apprehension or disbelief in the classroom." Albers meant for the *matière* to have a mayfly life. And yet, at the same time, he also meant for it to have an afterlife. And so, Beggs writes, "Instead of keeping favorite *matières*, as he did with work in other media, Albers used photography to document them."

In 1956, Ray Johnson received a commission, the first of several, to design a book cover for James Laughlin's New Directions press. It was a plum assignment, William Carlos Williams's *In the American Grain.* The artist brought along photographer John D. Schiff to Williams's place in New Jersey and came back with a roll of shots of the poet's hand, palm out, back pressed into masses of foliage. The hand functions in these photos both as a wonderful texture thing in itself and as the sign of the "haptic," a term often used in connection with Albers's *matière* studies.

Ray Johnson, cover design for William Carlos Williams's *In the American Grain*, 1956 ed.

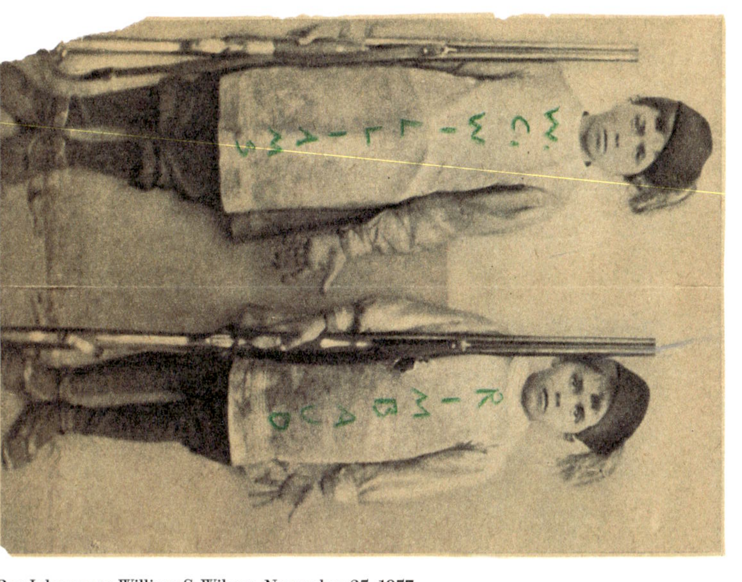

Ray Johnson to William S. Wilson, November 25, 1957.

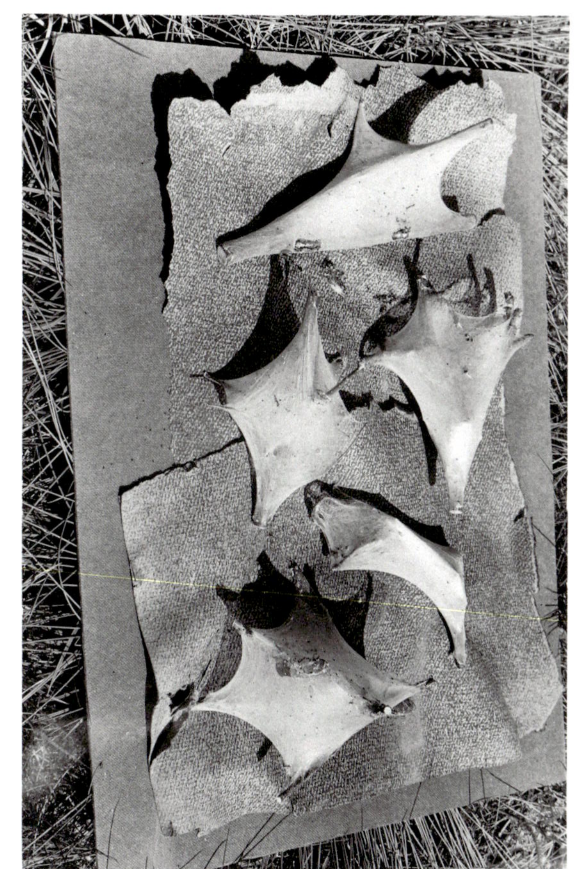

Ray Johnson, *Matiére* study, Black Mountain College, ca. 1947–49, photograph by Ted Dreier.

The Oxford English Dictionary defines *haptic* as "relating to the sense of touch, in particular relating to the perception and manipulation of objects using the senses of touch and proprioception," *proprioception* being, it says, "the perception of the position and movements of the body." Proprioception is a sixth sense which would prove crucial to certain kinds of post-painterly art practice. The mythic Jackson Pollock invoked by artists like Kaprow and the members of the Gutai group is the Pollock one finds in the films and photographs by Hans Namuth, which depict the painter as a kind of dancer, his consciousness wholly given over to the movements of his body in relation to the space and objects of his art. Ray Johnson's ineluctable grace while placing moticos on a pallet or dropping dowels down the stairs stemmed from this same kind of concentrated self-inhabitation, the expansion of the sense of touch into a sense of the body's being in the world.

The intent body in motion; the impermanent arrangement of objects; the archival capture, in images and/or words, of the encounter between person and thing: this volatile triangle composed Ray Johnson's *beau idéal*, imprinted early and returned to over and over, from this angle and that.

XVII

A vintage photo-postcard shows two solemn child-soldiers, the taller of whom is identified, in Johnson's hand, as "W. C. Williams," and the smaller as "Rimbaud." Bill Wilson, the card's recipient, knew that Ray had just completed his second cover for New Directions, the one for Arthur Rimbaud's *Illuminations* with the grainy Ben-Day dot rendering of the poet's face. And Ray knew that Bill had had a friendly exchange with Williams (also "Bill" to his friends) the previous year regarding the poet's epic-in-progress, *Paterson.* (Williams's reply to Wilson's query—"you have been extremely alert," the poet assured the professor—is preserved in Bill Wilson's Ray Johnson archive). Bill and Art, Bill and Ray, comrades in arms. Their drill apparently requires the postcard's poet-soldiers to rotate their arms outward to display their open palms, the same direction, more or less, that Johnson must have given Williams when he met him at his home just outside Paterson, New Jersey.

On a subsequent card, a giant and his little friend reprise the act with uplifted arms for the same audience of one. This second show of hands is postmarked November 12, 1958. A few days later, Bill would write to another friend to ask that she return the paintings Ray had given her to be submitted to "the burning." "Ray Johnson has not been wrong yet," the ever-loyal Bill averred, "& I trust him to make out of the ashes, what we had never seen before & would not otherwise see." Four months after Bill issued his impassioned plea, Ray sent his friend Dorothy Podber, then co-director of the Nonagon Gallery, a card onto which he had pasted an ad for "THE BURNING MAN by Stephen Longstreet A rich, vibrant novel of the life and loves of a painter who becomes a giant in the world of modern art."

Ray Johnson had caught a glimpse, in the mailings and the moticos, of something he had never seen before, something the paintings had lacked, that was uniquely his. And this something had begun to make a name for him, of sorts, in a world of art that now extended beyond his Black Mountain circle. "Let me tell you that Judith and I find that a moticos in the morning mail is worth a cup of coffee every morning for month. Were they to stop there would be a vacuum in my life," Julian Beck, cofounder of the Living Theater, avowed in 1955. Johnson had begun to attract a new kind of friend, the kind who was also a devoted fan.

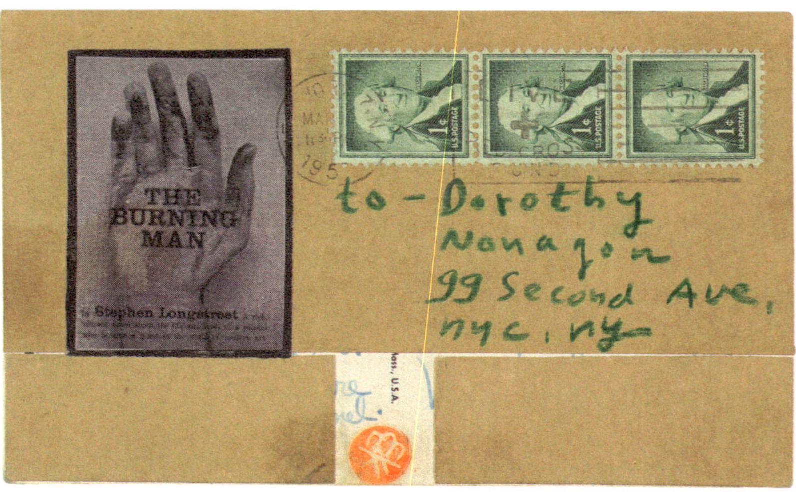

Ray Johnson to "Dorothy Nonagon" (Podber), March 1959.

Ray Johnson, postcard to Bill Wilson, November 12, 1958, verso.

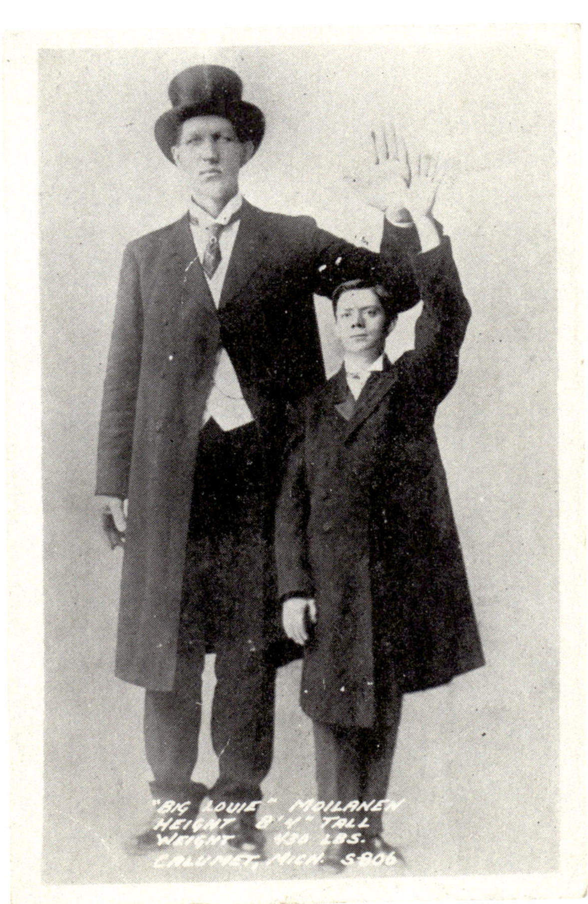

Ray Johnson to William S. Wilson, November 12, 1958, recto.

By the time he named the moticos, Johnson had had two solo exhibitions of his art, one in a New York bookstore and the other in a Boston print shop run by a Black Mountain friend. It wasn't yet much of a career, judged by the usual art world metrics, or by comparison with the progress of peers like Johns, Kaprow, or Rauschenberg. But by 1955, Johnson did have the beginnings of what would grow, over time, into a considerable cult following. And he saw from the start that this—his status as a cult figure, his friend-fans, the whole star/fan complex—like **every quality, every feeling, every material, every person**, could be repurposed as the stuff of art.

In 1955, Elvis Presley was still a hillbilly singer with a cultish reputation. Then, all at once, on the heels of the release, in early 1956, of "Heartbreak Hotel," his first single to become a million-seller, came the hit album, the notorious TV appearances, and the first star turn in a movie. By year's end, Elvis had undeniably become a name. Sometime in the two years after the star began his precipitous ascent, Ray Johnson took a copy of a publicity still of Presley looking like something a Greek might have sculpted, washed it with red paint, tattooed it with mysterious shapes, and called the finished product *Oedipus*.

Henry Geldzahler's description of this image as "the Plymouth rock of the Pop Art movement" has proven almost as enduring as the "most famous unknown artist" label. One often finds Geldzahler's phrase in art-historical accounts of Andy Warhol's star-portraits, to which Johnson's work stands, the critics say, as a half-forgotten precursor. The Warhol connection in turn—in a fine ironic twist—lent cachet to *Oedipus*, which would become the most widely reproduced and exhibited of Johnson's works. Stardom is a universal currency.

Stardom is a universal currency that each artist cashes out in his own way. Warhol limned his stars in elegantly spectral veils of color on screen-sized canvases. They are made for the eye, like Albers's squares, unfolding, like the squares, in a potentially endless series. The scant handful of proto-pop portraits that Johnson produced in the 1950s started with the same kind of glamor shots that Warhol worked from (Ray and Andy were known to shop together sometimes for movie stills and magazines), then got progressively grungier with the application of washes and streaks and thick squares of paint, junky paste-ups, and salvaged shirtboard backings.

Johnson's stars speak volubly of the artist's hand, an effect that the artist underscores in his second Elvis portrait, made from a photo in which the singer uses his fingers to palpate his own face. The proto-pop portraits are also—this is an effect no reproduction can convey—lightweight and small-scale, made to be held in hand by their recipients, to whom they were invariably given, not sold. Stardom is a universal currency that may also, or so Johnson and his friends seemed to believe, circulate within the confines of a gift economy. Within the circle that the artist draws, by a geometry of his own, the intensified recognition that we call fame may be transferred among friends who are one another's fans, although it is a special kind of fame, contained, concealed from outsiders.

The moticos, said Ray's friend Suzi, "are more involved with intimacy than with any public occasion." Can this be said of Johnson's proto-pop images? The fame these images have attained relative to the rest of Johnson's oeuvre derives from the glamorous photos that undergird them, which retain their frank appeal to the fan who maintains faith in the star's supernatural power. Glamour is like lightning; one can't hold it in one's hand. What is a moticos? Not this, exactly, Ray Johnson realized, as he turned back from Plymouth rock.

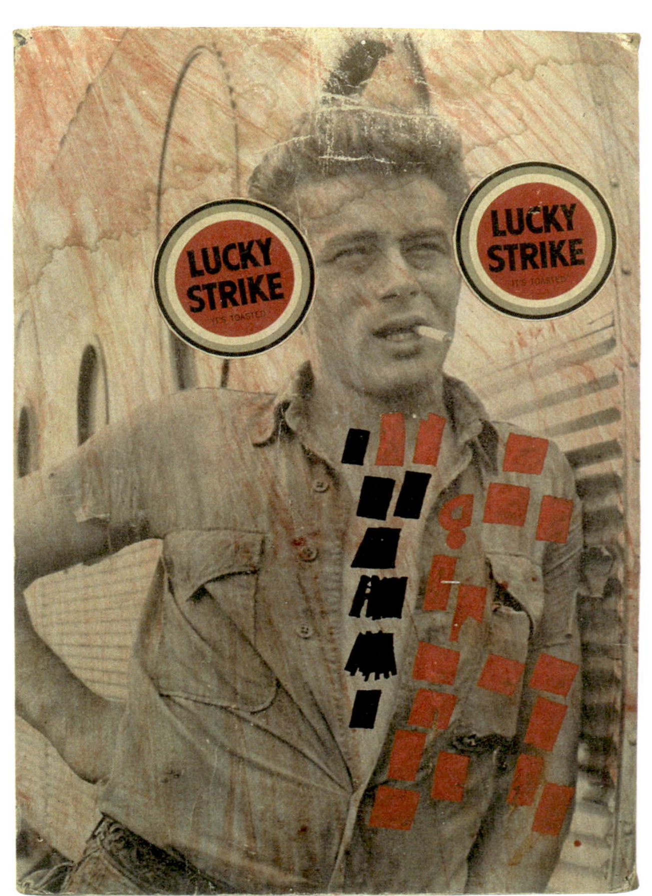

Ray Johnson, *James Dean (Lucky Strike)* (1957).

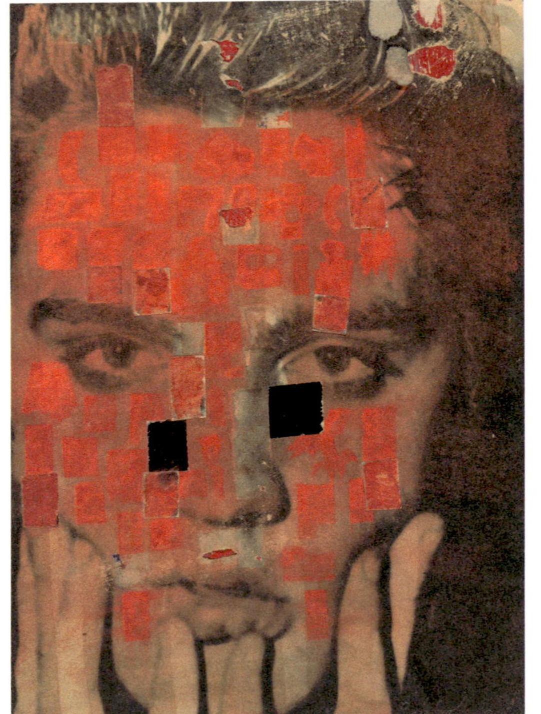

Ray Johnson, *Elvis Presley #2* (1956–58).

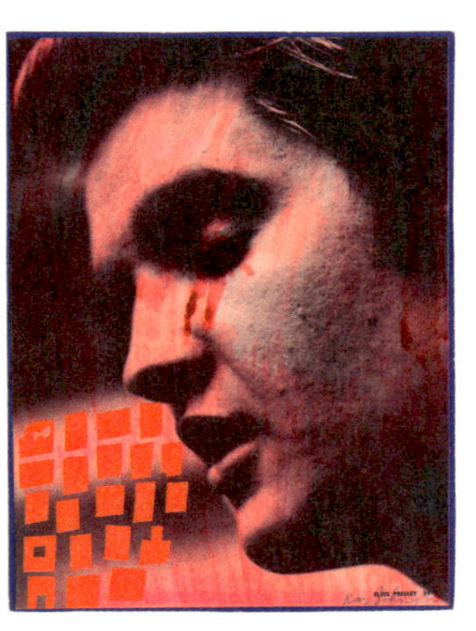

Ray Johnson, *Elvis Presley #1 (Oedipus)* (1956–58).

XIX

I'm the only painter in New York whose drips mean anything, Johnson joked about the watery red streaks descending from the shadowed socket of his Elvis Oedipus—a joke that, as usual, he also means us to take seriously. His drips speak of the old myth of Oedipus, who "was left thinking rather than seeing" after his awful stumble into self-knowledge; of the newly minted myth of Elvis, who sang in a wine-dark groan of a hotel with "room/ For broken-hearted lovers/ To cry there in the gloom"; of the fast-receding myth of Pollock, whose drips were portrayed by some as the purest instance of pure painting and by others as cris de coeur. The drips speak, too, in an undertone, of the painter's masochistic taste for blood and tears, a taste his broken-hearted Elvis might be thought to share.

Johnson would give that thought another turn in a sequence of James Dean portraits that followed in the train of *Oedipus*. Rumors circulating within the gay underground had it that Dean himself was a masochist, with a fetish for being burnt with cigarettes (in one proto-pop piece, Dean's face is flanked by labels cut from packs of Lucky Strikes), but even for those not in the know, the actor's image would be forever shadowed by the car crash that ended his short life in 1955. Frank O'Hara wrote an elegy for Dean soon after that, in which the poet fused his private sense of Dean's sexuality with public knowledge about his death, depicting the star as "a spirit eager for the punishment/ which is your only recognition."

When O'Hara's poem appeared in *Poetry* in 1956, the magazine received a letter of complaint. "The James Dean necrophilia has penetrated even to the upper regions of our culture," its writer grumbled, adding, with that "penetrated," a touch of homosexual panic to his policing of the boundary between high and low. O'Hara's dear friend Bunny Lang had warned him that the Dean poem was "too out" and told him "you'll be sorry" to have published it. He wasn't, but the self-abasing note O'Hara strikes at certain moments in the poem—"I speak as one whose filth/ is like his own," he says of Dean—suggests how much its conception cost this naturally buoyant writer. O'Hara was not given to making public statements. His poems, like Johnson's moticos, are typically intimate in tenor and were often circulated via ingeniously restricted routes; he chose to publish a remarkably small portion of the many hundreds he wrote before his own too-early death in 1966. As the first editor to collect O'Hara's work, Donald Allen, would discover, the only extant copies of many of the poems were to be found in old mail that the poet's correspondents thankfully had saved.

XX

I'm the only painter in New York whose drips mean anything is, among other things, a joke addressed to the kind of viewer who insists that the expressionist's drips are nothing but pure paint. Then again, this viewer might retort, one can mean too much. One can be the kind of painter whose work is too explicit, too chatty, even, the kind of painter that the lovers of pure paint call "literary." When, as would often happen in the years to come, someone said Ray Johnson was "a poet," the artist sometimes bristled with annoyance and sometimes blushed with pleasure, and sometimes did a bit of both at once.

Ray Johnson was a poet who wrote in no known language. What is a moticos? An image, a thing, an idea, a transitory link between persons, a neologism and an idiolect.

That first Elvis speaks in drips, but also in another painted language that issues from the mouth as a cloud of squarish shapes, miniature abstractions cut loose from their Albersian moorings. In his letter to Jiro Yoshihara at *Gutai*, Johnson explains the derivation of these shapes, which appear in greater variety on a printed flyer he sent along with the letter. **The enclosed page shows small black patterns reduced in size, silhouettes of the MOTICOS**. The page was one in a series of mailers that Johnson produced from the mid-1950s to the early 1960s as a means of promoting his graphic design business. One understands from Johnson's explanation to Yoshihara that the shapes on the flyer are purely contingent, the accidental residue of an image-making process. Still, it is hard to shake the sense that they also constitute a kind of alphabet or sign-language. This sense grows stronger when one views the moticos-silhouette flyer side-by-side with others in the series, like the one on which silhouetted figures spell out "Ray Johnson Drawings" in semaphore, or one that tells funny little children's-book-style animal stories as it runs through the alphabet: **rattlerattlerattlerattlerattle/ snakessnakessnakessnakes/ twisttwisttwisttwisttwist/ upupupupupupupupupup/ veryveryveryveryveryvery/ wellwellwellwellwellwell**

The graphic designer works in a space where word and image meet and merge. Ray Johnson felt at home there from the outset.

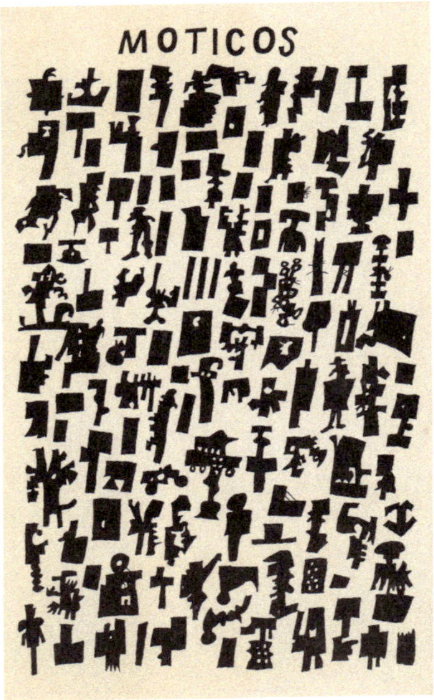

Ray Johnson, *Ray Johnson Design* flyer (*Moticos*), 1956.

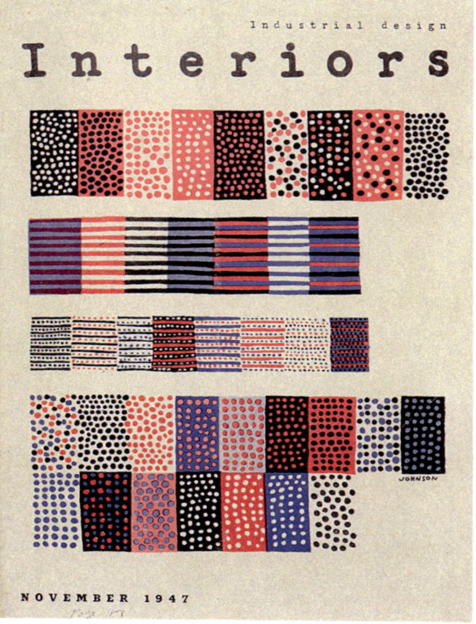

Ray Johnson, cover design for *Interiors* magazine, November 1947.

aaaaaaaaaaaaaaaaaaaaaa
birdbirdbirdbirdbird
cancancancancancancancan
dododododododododododo
easyeasyeasyeasyeasyeasy
flyingflyingflyingflying
gamesgamesgamesgames
highhighhighhighhighhigh
inininininininininininin
jjjjjjjjjjjjjjjjjjjjjjjjjjj
skyskyskyskyskyskyskysky
littlelittlelittlelittlelittle
monkeysmonkeysmonkeys
nevernevernevernevernever
openopenopenopenopenopen
peanutspeanutspeanutspeanuts
quicklyquicklyquicklyquickly
rattlerattlerattlerattlerattle
snakessnakessnakessnakes
twisttwisttwisttwisttwist
upupupupupupupupupupup
veryveryveryveryveryvery
wellwellwellwellwellwell
sixsixsixsixsixsixsixsixsixsix
youngyoungyoungyoungyoung
zebraszebraszebraszebraszebras
rayrayrayrayrayrayrayray
johnsonjohnsonjohnsonjohnson
2dover2dover2dover2dover2dover
streetstreetstreetstreetstreetstreet
newyork38newyork38newyork38
re.2-0375re.2-0375re.2-0375re.2-0375

Ray Johnson, *Ray Johnson Design* flyer (*A Bird Can Do Easy Flying...*), ca. 1955–56.

RE.2-0375

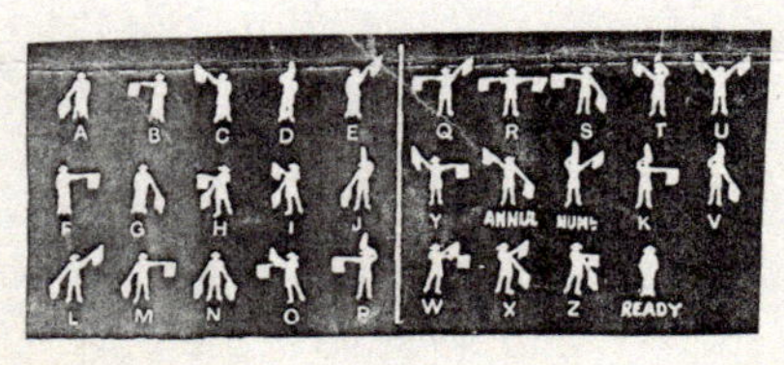

Ray Johnson, *Ray Johnson Design* flyer (*Semaphore*), 1956.

IF TEARS

ARE DROPPED
ON A DRY PIECE
OF PAPER, STAINED
WITH THE
JUICE OF THE PETALS
OF MALLOWS
OR VIOLETS,

THEY WILL CHANGE
THE PAPER TO A
PERMANENTLY
GREEN COLOUR.

Ray Johnson design
176 Suffolk St. NYC.
Canal 82271

Ray Johnson, *Ray Johnson Design* flyer, (*If Tears Are Dropped*), ca. 1961.

In high school, he was president of the Advertising Art Club. While he was still in college, Josef Albers got him a commission to design the cover of *Interiors* magazine, with results that did the teacher proud. Johnson would go on to create distinctive designs for book covers, record album covers, magazine layouts, window displays, advertising posters, even scarves. But he never quite made a commercial go of his design work. He wasn't much of a businessman, you could say, or you could say he was an instinctive subverter of commercial systems, and you would be right, either way.

You can see this in the designs themselves. A successful graphic must be all message, and all image, all at once, and the intended message must be crystal clear to its intended audience. Johnson gets the formula backward, somehow. The image-words on the flyers he used to market his skills are charged with ambiguity, like a poem, or a spell. They fascinate, when what they should do is communicate.

I'm the only painter in New York whose drips mean anything, Ray Johnson said. Funny. Funny because meaning is a funny thing. Whether one's meanings mean anything depends so much on where and to whom one chooses to convey those meanings.

XXI

When *Gutai* published a two-page spread on Johnson's work in 1957, the editors used as illustrations three of the design flyers along with the first page of Johnson's letter describing the moticos. They seem to have viewed the flyers not as commercial promotions but as some sort of fine art—Yoshihara refers to the moticos page as "that fancy form you sent us" in his letter informing Johnson that they wanted to do a piece on him. "You are so new and original. We were all surprised and interested in it very much." The fascinating ambiguity of the designs made sense to them in the context of the story Johnson told about his moticos, a story that fit with the Gutai artists' own commitment to an art that was fundamentally mobile. **I send out a monthly newsletter about the work I am doing which takes the place of a formal exhibition. The works cannot be exhibited in the usual way because they constantly change, like the news in the papers or the images on a movie screen.** The flyers, like newsletters, bear evidence of events now past, always slipping from the interested reader's grasp. **The New York Correspondence School has no history—only a present**, Ray Johnson would claim, later in his history, when it had become clear that what he meant by "a present" was both the ever-fleeting moment and a gift.

In 1955, Ray Johnson figured that one thing he could do with the still-nameless collage-objects he had been making was to market them by mail. "The next step," as Norman Solomon tells it, "was to make an announcement and some sort of description list of the collages, perhaps by titling them individually. Which he did." Unfortunately, or fortunately, depending on which side of the art/commerce divide you stand, Ray Johnson's idea of a description list was even more hopelessly poetic than his ideas for the design flyers he had begun to make at the same moment.

A list from 1955 bears the title, **NEW MOTICOS**, followed by these numbered items.

1. **God is a penny bank**
2. **for ylla**
3. **ka**
   f
   ka
   ylla
4. **a dollar bill with Kafka over it (are those children holding hands or passing money?) (collection Black Mtn. College)**
5. **—Feder thinks the word "toupee" arouses too many ludicrous or unpleasant thoughts in prospective purchasers. He thinks the word "Tashay," which he invented, sounds pleasant and French.)**
6. **BIGGEST LAUGHING SCREAM OF THE YEAR**

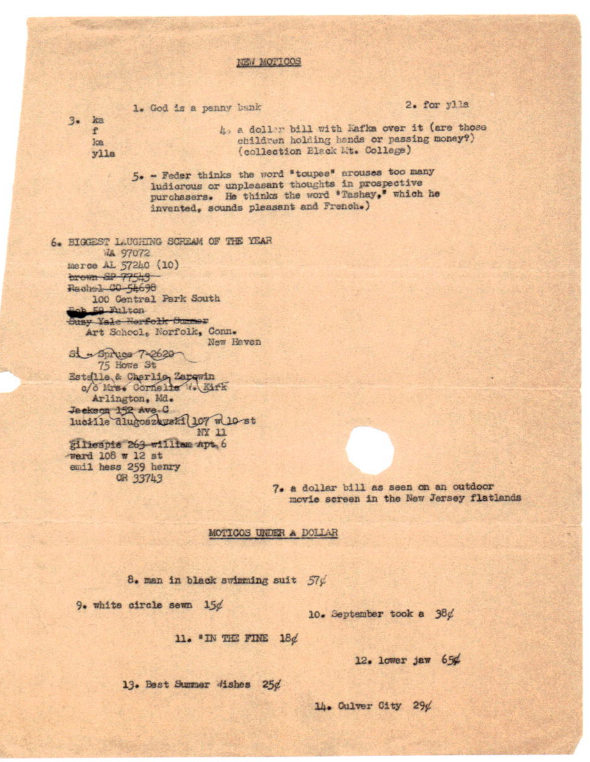

NEW MOTICOS

1. God is a penny bank

2. for ylla

3. ka
f
ka
ylla

4. a dollar bill with Kafka over it (are those children holding hands or passing money?) (collection Black Mt. College)

5. - Feder thinks the word "toupee" arouses too many ludicrous or unpleasant thoughts in prospective purchasers. He thinks the word "Tashay," which he invented, sounds pleasant and French.)

6. BIGGEST LAUGHING SCREAM OF THE YEAR
WA 97072
merce AL 57240 (10)
~~brown SP 77549~~
~~Rachel CO 54698~~
100 Central Park South
~~Bob 59 Fulton~~
~~Susy Yale Norfolk Summer~~
Art School, Norfolk, Conn.
New Haven
~~SL - Spruce 7-2620~~
75 Howe St
Estelle & Charlie Zarewin
c/o Mrs. Cornelia W. Kirk
Arlington, Md.
~~Jackson 152 Ave C~~
lucille dlugoszewski 107 w 10 st
NY 11
~~gillespie 263 william Apt 6~~
ward 108 w 12 st
emil hess 259 henry
OR 33743

7. a dollar bill as seen on an outdoor movie screen in the New Jersey flatlands

MOTICOS UNDER A DOLLAR

8. man in black swimming suit 57¢

9. white circle sewn 15¢

10. September took a 38¢

11. "IN THE FINE 18¢

12. lower jaw 65¢

13. Best Summer Wishes 25¢

14. Culver City 29¢

Ray Johnson, *NEW MOTICOS* mailer, 1955.

Next comes a series of listings from Johnson's own address book, partially crossed out. (Ray Johnson's address books deserve a book of their own.) Finally, scattered randomly across the bottom third of the page are **MOTICOS UNDER A DOLLAR: man in black swimming suit 57¢; white circle sewn 15¢; September took a 98¢; "IN THE FINE 18¢; lower jaw 65¢; Best Summer Wishes 25¢; Culver City 29¢.** There seem to be no records of what any of the "fifty or so…collectors, some of them quite well-to-do" whom Solomon said Johnson initially had in mind as the readers of such a list thought when they received their copies.

Johnson's moticos mailers do not make the kind of sense an artist should when making a sales pitch to collectors, or to the gallerists and museum curators Johnson also put on his moticos mailing lists. Another list from 1955, **OLD MOTICOS**, forms a solid, page-filling block of print. Nowhere on the page does it say that the run-on phrases represent individual artworks, that they are for sale, or that they are by Ray Johnson. But that does not mean they do not mean anything. One can still glean clues as to the nature of the moticos if one is willing to plunge in.

> **Rear guard action by Fernando gets desired results as he gives Arlene the snapping towel treatment With every cup a juggling performance is give free A slot machine at one end; a manicure at the other Audrey Hepburn on one side; Mickey Mouse on the other Moons, Gertrude Stein 1. you 2. you 3. you Let's call a spade a sp Holding a golf ball and a check Johnson's back plaster music Crescent moon over the Port of New York Authority w-pan, as it were a Sty a witness with a c Robert Trachtenberg A ring on the little finger of the left hand of a painist** [*sic*] **Yellow crescent; yellow fan; yellow coat Right arm; the boots are too large for the feet 26 are magenta; 59 are yellow; 57 are white, and a blue wing Ten are green A poem for Jasper Elephant**

One finds signs in this passage of Johnson's Albersian interest in pure color and shape—**Yellow crescent; yellow fan; yellow coat**—as well as evidence of his taste for transgressive and theatrical gestures—**Rear guard action by Fernando gets desired results as he gives Arlene the snapping towel treatment With every cup a juggling performance is given free**—and for the specifics of proprioceptive experience—**the boots ... too large for the feet**, the **ring on the little finger of the left hand of a painist** [*sic*]. One sees that Johnson sees in the typewriter's keyboard not only a means of making meanings but also a set of alphabetical and numerical designs that have their own independent aesthetic value. **Let's call a spade a sp**; **a witness with a c**. He is sensitive to the different perceptual impacts of **57** and **Ten**.

Correspondents of Johnson's who had actually seen the moticos would have known that they are often double-sided (**Audrey Hepburn on one side; Mickey Mouse on the other**), meant to be turned over in the hand. They would know, too, that the moticos traffic in faces, as the

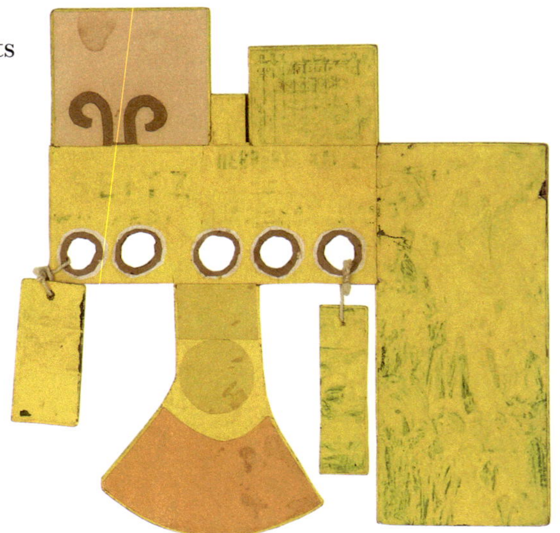

Ray Johnson, *Untitled (Yellow Moticos)* (1953).

list-poems traffic in names, names famous, semi-famous, and unfamous, all waiting to be recognized by **1. you 2. you 3. you**.

All the names in **OLD MOTICOS**, in order of appearance: **William Holden, Billy Graham, The Dalai Lama, Margaret Truman, The Sitwells, Fernando, Arlene, Audrey Hepburn, Mickey Mouse, Gertrude Stein, Johnson's, Robert Trachtenberg, Jasper, Three Marlon Brandos, Alan Hovhanness, Virginia Woolf, Ethel, Mr. Ferrer, Genet, Lincoln, Remy's, Kline, Stella, Dear Ray Johnson, Cordially, Sam Kramer, World famous dancers La Guta and Leslie, Colette, Eudora Welty, Suzi, Martha Graham, Jack, Jack, Empson, Pound, Rexroth.**

But is a moticos list really meant to be parsed like a poem, broken down into its component ideas? The New Critic William Empson, whose name appears in the penultimate line of **OLD MOTICOS**, writes of poetic ambiguity in general that "In a sense it cannot be explained in language, because to a person who does not understand it any statement of it is as difficult as the original one, while to a person who does understand it a statement of it has no meaning because no purpose." Empson also warns that to understand a poem, you:

(a) must have assimilated a fair amount of information regarding the poem's content and context;

(b) must be "experienced in the apprehension of verbal subtleties or of the poet's social tone";

(c) must "become the sort of person that can feel at home in, or imagine, or extract experience from, what is described by the poetry";

(d) must, of course, "have included it among the things you are prepared to apprehend."

It is a lot to ask of a reader. When Ray Johnson's most indefatigable interpreter, Bill Wilson, got his PhD in English, the New Criticism was at the height of its reign. Wilson knew what it meant and had what it took to become an expert close reader of Johnson's densely coded verbo-visual argot and to teach others what he learned. (Where poetic ambiguity is concerned, Empson advises, "the educator [that mysterious figure]" will be more "helpful" than "the analyst," that pinner and killer of meanings.) To read a poem, you must want to learn a new language, one that is native only to that poem's writer.

The relationship between poet and reader is a form of intimacy: the thing between the two of us, the thing only we understand, the thing that turns to ashes in the glare of any public occasion. The relationships that Johnson cultivated with his friend-fans during the moticos years served as a blueprint for the kinds of intimacy he would always aim to generate through his art. But in those years, Johnson was also coming to realize that to transform intimacy into art, the intimist must find a way to imply, in the art, that the space of intimacy is open to all comers (since really, universally, relations stop nowhere). His art must be as specific as a letter and as generic as an advertisement.

Ray Johnson was just beginning to grasp the key to his synthesis of the particular and the abstract, the personal and the social, the tacit and the explicit. It was a solution that had always been close at hand; maybe that is what made it hard to see at first. When, in 1984, an interviewer asked Johnson about "the philosophy" behind his practice, with the benefit of hindsight, the artist could see it plain as day. **I mean, all of these things have a specific meaning. I see it as the task of myself as an artist to evaluate, to determine what the meanings of these things are. And they have a formal structure. But that takes place in the privacy of my studio. And in the privacy of the U.S. and international postal system.** Meaning depends on context, and the context that made Johnson's meanings mean what he meant them to mean was the mail.

XXII

The postal system is the most public of institutions. In theory, no citizen stands beyond its reach. Yet the post is also a guardian of our privacy, tasked with ensuring that the seals on all those mysterious squares and rectangles remain unbroken until they reach the hands of their intended recipients. The postal system differs, in its respect for privacy, from the communications systems that have succeeded it, systems to which Johnson's correspondence network has often been compared. Postal communication is at once absolutely public and absolutely private. In our digital communications, the public and the private interfuse in ever-new mutations.

The postal system came to offer Johnson an ingenious solution to a problem that emerged during the moticos years, the problem of how to synthesize the antithetical poles of his practice. But it could not help him when it came to solving two other major problems. One was the problem of how to make a living as an artist. The other was the problem of how to gain an audience for his art.

Ray Johnson, terrible businessman and incorrigible subverter of commercial systems that he was, stipulated that the mail that circulated through his network of correspondents must never, under any circumstances, be put up for sale. Mail art was not that kind of art: to sell it was to despoil it. To meet his worldly needs and wants (which were always modest, but still), Johnson would have to make another kind of art, art of a style distinct from that of the mail art, that could be sold. I refer to this kind of art as Johnson's "exhibition" work, since, to some extent, he conceived of it as such. Some of it would be sold, both privately and through galleries, and some of it would be shown in traditional commercial and non-commercial art venues.

Johnson's relations with the organizers of art exhibitions, however, were always fraught. This was especially true of his relationships with art dealers, but he could be difficult as well with the personnel of museums and other non-profit institutions. Sometimes the difficulties he caused were conceived, and perceived, as works of art in themselves. Still, even Johnson's greatest admirers among the art professionals came to approach him with a certain wariness. The distance Johnson maintained from the core institutions of the art world ensured that he would always have trouble gaining and keeping an audience for his art. Of course, his correspondents were a kind of audience. But an audience is in essence a public creature; the word "audience" originally denoted a hearing in the judicial sense. Ray Johnson had to have known that for his art to live beyond him, it would have to find an audience in this sense, an abstract social entity that had the power to pass judgment on the work, a process of judgment that would, moreover, take place in contexts not of the artist's choosing.

At some moments, Johnson thought of the moticos as exhibition art, a thing a collector might hang on the wall. At others, he thought of it as the central figure in a performance, an entity that loved moving and rain-water, that could evaporate or be burnt to ash once the dance was done. In the end, however, the moticos proved too ephemeral for the collectors and too material, too appealing to the eye and hand, for those who preferred Nothing in their art. What is a moticos? A homeless genre, though whether homeless by accident or by design it is hard to say. In 1959, Ray summarized his current dilemma by means of an art-historical quotation inscribed on a card he sent to his friend Diana Epstein.

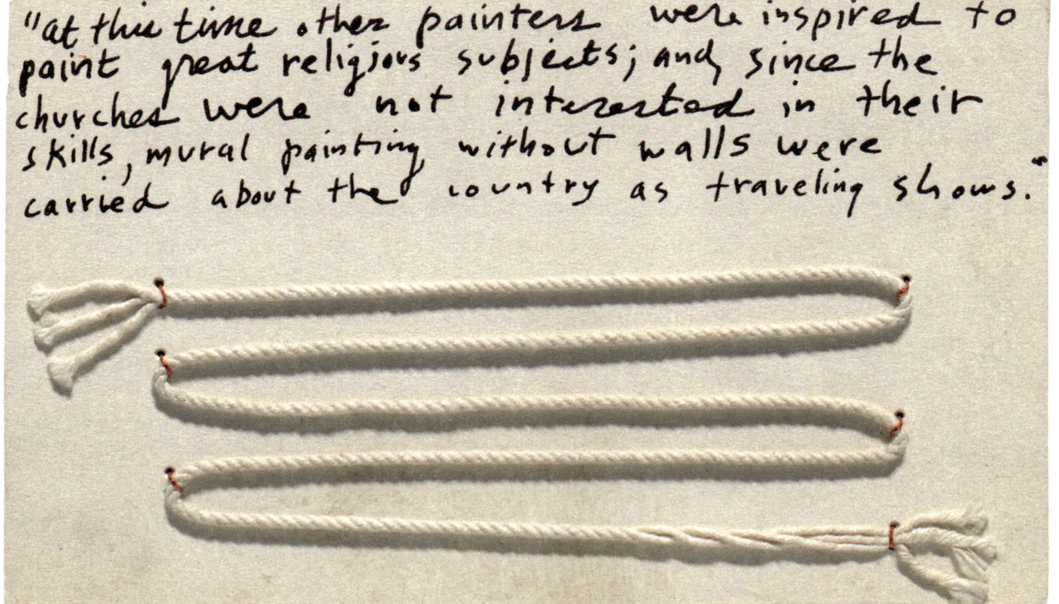

Ray Johnson to Diana Epstein, n.d.

By the end of the 1950s, Johnson had begun to feel at home in the postal system, a place where everything is always on the move, more at home, it seemed, than in the art world, which had so far shown scant interest in his skills. Was it possible, he wondered just then, that he could solve the problems he now saw staring him in the face, the problems of money and of audience, within the context of the post? The answer, in the end, was no. But some dead ends may become ends in themselves. In the early 1960s, the more worked-over, Schwitters-like moticos gradually disappeared from the mailings, doubtless to the disappointment of friends who had grown accustomed to finding **wonderful texture things** in the mail. The going of the moticos left a gap, and in that gap, Ray Johnson constructed a great Rube Goldberg machine, the kind of contraption that gets you nowhere in life and everywhere in art, and named it **A BOOK ABOUT DEATH**.

XXIII

A BOOK ABOUT DEATH (hereafter abbreviated as **ABAD**) is:

1. Not exactly a book. Starting in March 1963 and ending in February 1965, Ray Johnson created a set of thirteen images to be reproduced via photo-offset lithography at a commercial print shop, the same method of production Johnson had used for the flyers advertising his design work. Johnson never bound the pages into a book. He also orchestrated the distribution of the pages such that no single recipient would receive the full set of thirteen.
2. Not exactly thirteen pages. The last page in the series is clearly marked **PAGE 15**, and Johnson's correspondence contains sketches for and discussions of designs for additional pages.
3. Not exactly titled **A BOOK ABOUT DEATH**. On page 1, the title page, Johnson kicks up the front leg of the "K" so that "BOOK" may read as "BOOP" (his icon-language would later come to include a simplified rendering of the face of cartoon flapper Betty Boop). On the final page, the artist rechristens the work **BOOM ABOUT DEATH**.
4. Not exactly about death. Pages 1 and 6 include quotations from news items that recount the deaths of toddlers in bizarre accidents; page 12 commemorates the death by suicide of someone Johnson knew. There are no direct references to death on the remaining ten pages.

It is relatively easy to say what **ABAD** is not. It is very difficult to say what it is, or what it means. **ABAD** seems designed to petrify the would-be interpreter. Perhaps that is what makes it deathly.

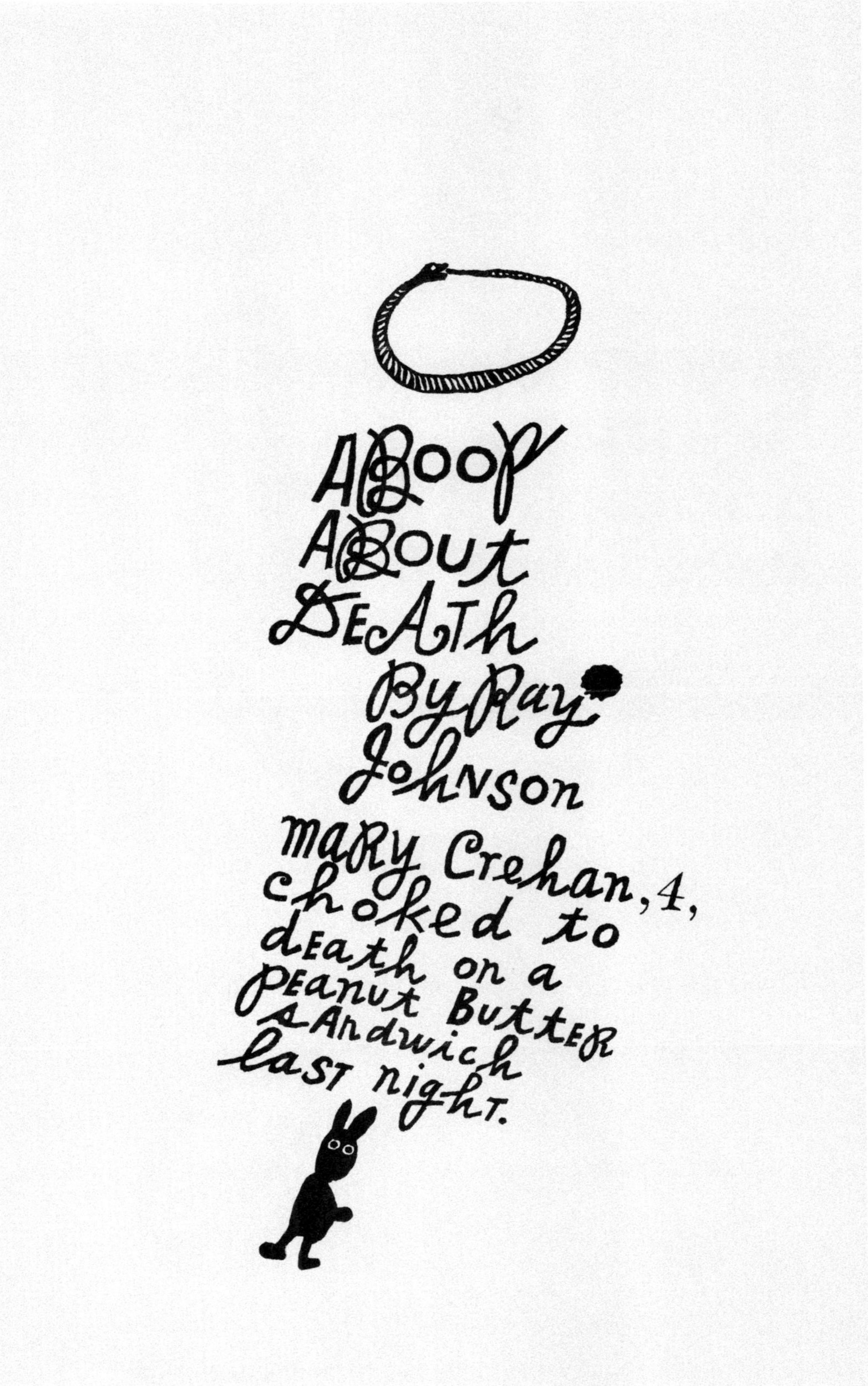

A BOOK
ABOUT
DEATH
BY RAY
JOHNSON

MARY Crehan, 4,
choked to
death on a
peanut butter
sandwich
last night.

Ray Johnson, *A Book About Death*, p. 1.

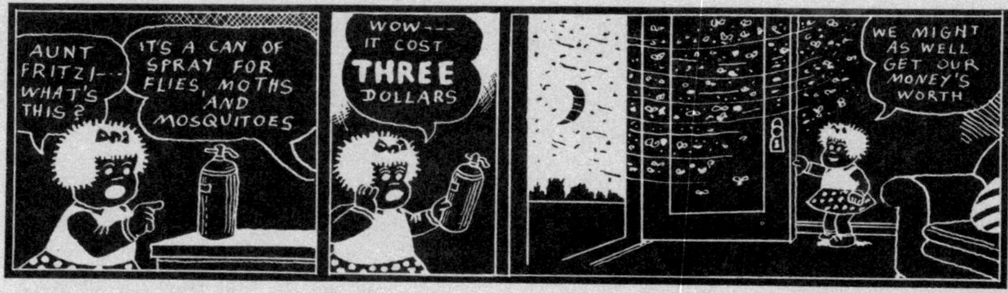

8АБАВУ

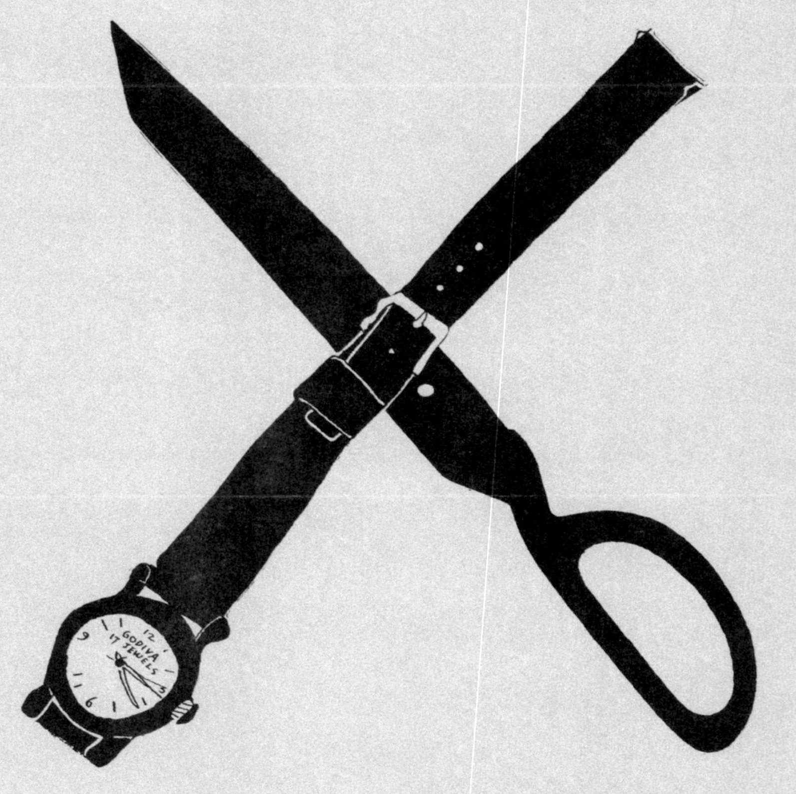

Ray Johnson, *A Book About Death*, p. 3.

XXIV

In 2009, when an art space in Amsterdam held an exhibition on **ABAD**, Bill Wilson wrote the text for an associated volume titled—naturally—*A BOOK ABOUT A BOOK ABOUT DEATH*. In it, Wilson glosses Johnson's book page by page. The glosses are full of indispensable information and insights. They are also often as esoteric as the material they purport to unpack. "Cryptography" can refer either to the act of encoding secret messages or to the act of decoding them. *ABABAD* does both at once, producing impasses that mirror the aporetic style of **ABAD**, where, as even the indefatigable Wilson must admit, "Ray, in coding with improvised rules which no one but he understands, has reached a point at which no reader can decode the code."

The page that prompts this comment is page 3, printed, as Wilson tells us, on September 10, 1963. At the top of the page is a reprint, in negative, of a comic strip from Ernie Bushmiller's long-running series *Nancy*. The sheet's bottom half is covered by a large X formed by a wrist-watch, its band cut and laid flat, crossed with one half of a pair of scissors. Wilson makes what he can of these elements. As for the string of symbols in the middle of the page, they derive, he explains, from a word that Johnson had often seen on posters advertising events in the then-thriving Ukrainian community on the Lower East Side. "Ray had been told that the word," spelled in Cyrillic, "indicated 'dance' in Ukrainian, but he read it as he wrote it in the roman alphabet, '3ABABY.'" 3ABABY had become a running joke between Bill and Ray before the inception of **ABAD**, a joke that had something to do with the twin daughters born to Bill and Ann in 1961 and something to do with the triangular relationship of Bill, Ann, and Ray.

Still, Wilson's privileged information gets him only so far. He cannot see why Johnson has turned the accustomed "3" here into an "8"—it is this move that provokes him to claim that the artist "has reached a point at which no reader can decode the code." Wilson does remark that the substituted number "is pronounced as the word 'ate,' as in 'ate-a-baby.'" But he does not connect that observation to another bit of knowledge that he discloses earlier in *ABABAD* in connection with the little girl's death mentioned on Page 1, his knowledge that "Ray was aware that Ann and Bill Wilson had had a daughter who had died shortly after her birth." Ann and Bill had three baby girls, but only two survived. This is dark. Dark like the grave. And darker than the obscurest of obscure poems. Is **ABAD** a book about the breaking of the connections through which we make meaning, in language and in life?

XXV

You could say, conversely, that it is about the making of such connections. The names of many of Johnson's closest friends appear in the pages of **ABAD**, worked into the designs in ingenious ways. On page 11, May Wilson's first name appears in a song lyric overlaid on the reprinted image of a twisted-wire café chair that features in one of Johnson's design flyers. In the legend that runs up the page's left edge, "May" gets twisted into the anagram, "Amy," in a reference to the poet Amy Lowell, then twisted once again into "Ami," which, as May's son Bill points out, is French for "friend." The friend's name here is bound to a repeated motif, the wire chair, that is in the process of becoming part of Johnson's nascent icon-language. **ABAD** is a work of cryptography.

It is also a work of iconography, a vocabulary lesson in Johnsonese. For instance:

8 MAN SHOW: An art exhibition with a rotating cast of contributors that existed only as a set of announcement cards that Johnson sent around to his correspondents during the early 1960s.

ROBIN GALLERY: Fictional art space whose name was a play on the word "robbing"—as in the hold-up pictured on page 4 of *ABAD*—which is one way to short circuit a market economy; it also alludes tothe names of two venues where Johnson's work appeared in actual group shows, New York's Reuben Gallery and Batman Gallery in San Francisco. Batman showcased West Coast grunge-collage artists like Bruce Conner and George Herms, both of whom would join the ranks of Johnson's friend-fans. On page 4, **GEORGE HERMS** is linked, via his name, with an East Coast friend of Ray's, **GEORGE BRECHT** (born George Ellis MacDiarmid), artist, composer, and founding member of Fluxus. Ray Johnson is an associative thinker. It all connects up, like the ouroboros-snake with its tail in its mouth on page 1 of **ABAD**.

GEORGE
JOHNS
MAN
RAY
HER B
RECHT
MS (Malka Safro)

Ray Johnson, detail from *A Book About Death*, p. 4.

SNAKE: Slippery skin-shedder and Ray Johnson's spirit animal. One snake appears on page 1 and another on page 15 (13). On page 10, there are four, which take the forms of a tiny caduceus, an **ADVERTISEMENT** for nothing in particular that Johnson once placed in the *Village Voice*, a **BRICK SNAKE** associated here with Ann Wilson, and a black arabesque signed "Karl Wirsum."

KARL WIRSUM: A painter who would become known, later in the 1960s, as a member of the Hairy Who, a group of Chicago artists whose comic-book-psychedelic imagery, like the work of the West Coast collagists,

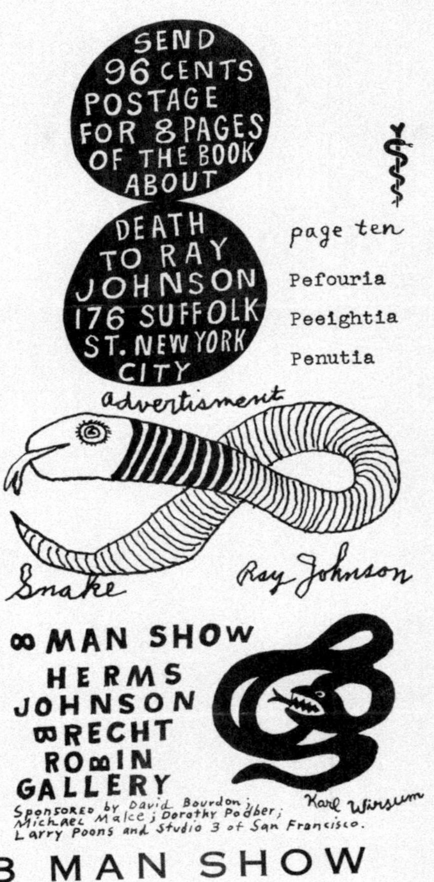

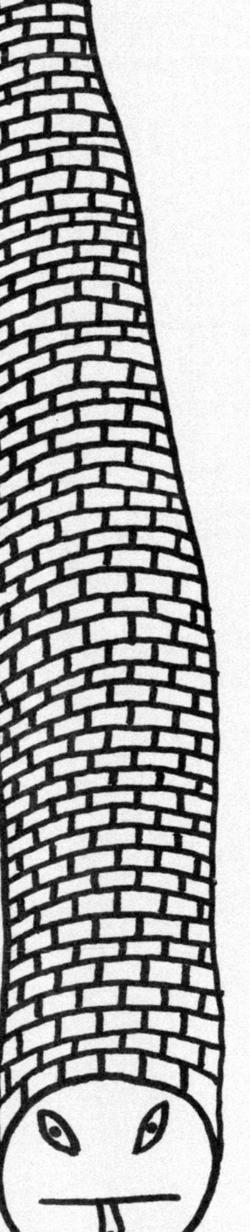

8 MAN SHOW

GEORGE BRECHT

GEORGE HERMS

RAY JOHNSTON

ROBIN GALLERY

A

BRICK SNAKE

FOR ANNE WILSON

Ray Johnson, *A Book About Death*, p. 10.

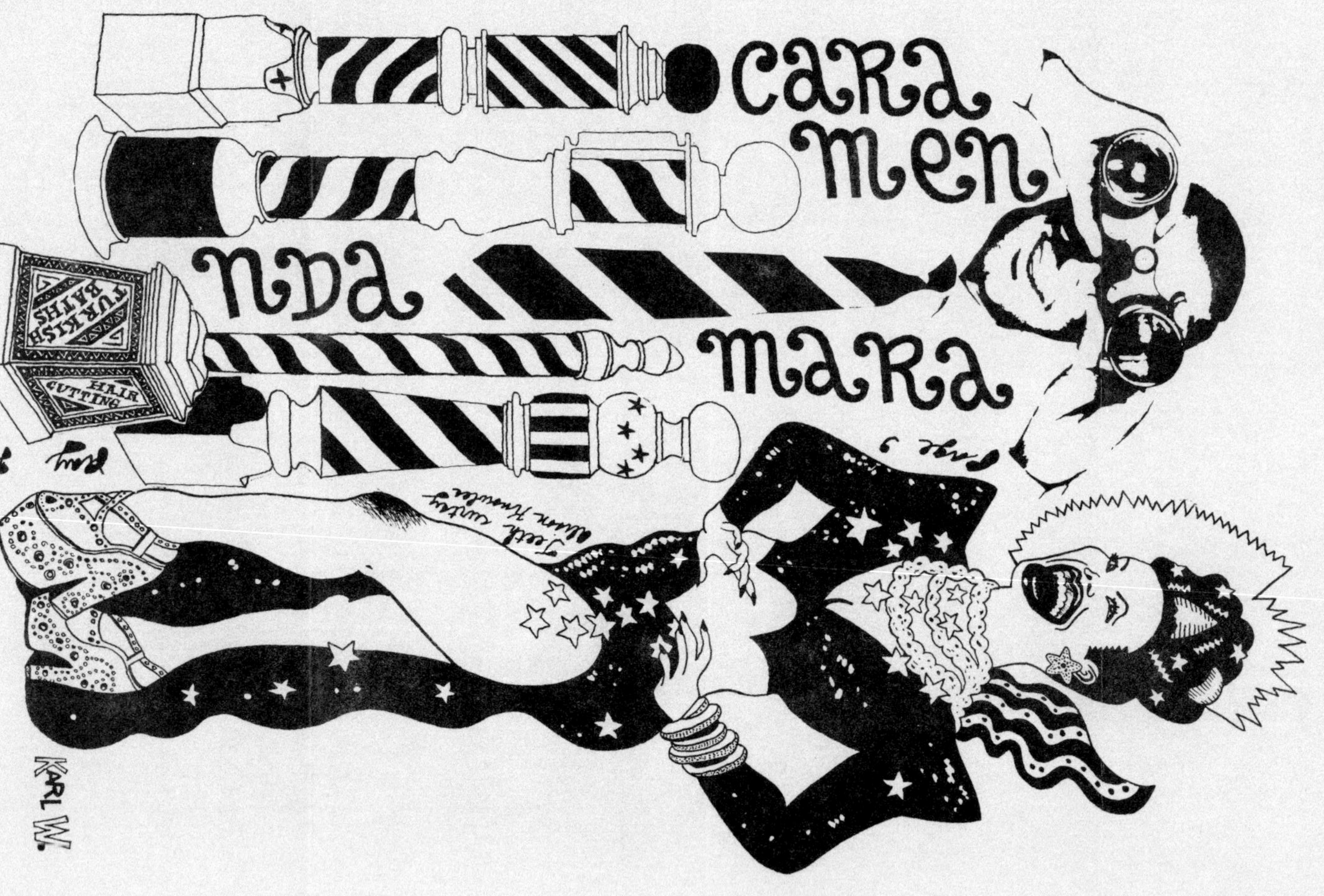

Ray Johnson, *A Book About Death*, p. 9.

offered a funky alternative to the colder, sleeker art styles of sixties New York. When Johnson began **ABAD**, Wirsum was twenty-three and just getting going after graduating from art school. Through a former teacher, he met Ed Plunkett, the Johnson correspondent who had joked that the artist should call his web of mailers the New York Correspondence School. Introduced by Ed, goofy Karl and witty Ray clicked instantly. Wirsum's name appears twice more in **ABAD**, as "Karl W.," under drawings he made following Johnson's specifications, one of the flamboyant star Carmen Miranda (a favorite of teenage Ray's) and the other of a statue of a figure identified as **Samuel S. Cox, the letter carrier's friend**.

On these two pages, Johnson has signed **Ray J.** under his half of the page in a hand resembling Wirsum's. Connection here verges on identification. Wilson observes that binoculars feature in the design of both of the Wirsum collaborations, which suggests to him that Ray "wanted to see the sight which saw the objects through the eyes of other artists." Once Johnson abandoned pure painting, collaboration became integral to his work at every level, even to work that remained confined to the privacy of the studio. Collage is always a collaboration, if only with the spirits released from the debris.

XXVI

The final page of Ray Johnson's never-to-be-closed **BOOK** went to the printer on February 19, 1965, five days after the publication of the first collection of Ray Johnson's art in book form—that is to say, in a book with a cover, binding, and publisher. That volume, *The Paper Snake*, was the brainchild of Dick Higgins, another Fluxus artist, who had founded Something Else Press in 1963, in part, he has said, in order to work with Johnson, who had been branded "an outsider" to Fluxus by the group's imperious chief, George Maciunas. Higgins calculated, however, that, if he had his own press, "I ran no risk of offending would-be Pope George if I published Ray Johnson." *The Paper Snake* was the fledgling publisher's second venture, after a volume of his own writings.

In his Ray-book, Higgins fragments Johnson's texts and images and scatters the pieces across the pages in a collage as eccentric as, but in a style quite different from, any of Johnson's own assemblages. Johnson was ambivalent about the project; control of his meanings had been wrested away. And then there was the problem of publication itself. Writing to May Wilson in November 1964, Ray moaned that **I got proofs today for the Dick Higgins book on Ray Johnson and I always find anything in public or print an embarrassment because I'm so dumb. But it's going**

through and is called Paper Snake, a title I did not ask for. I wanted it to be Papa R. Snake. According to Higgins, Johnson did give *The Paper Snake* its title.

Ray gives, and Ray takes away. The last page of **ABAD** features an image of a letter-opener labeled **NORMAN SOLOMON'S KNIFE** (Ray could be sharp, but Norman was *cutting*), with **PAPA R SNAKE** engraved on its blade. While their friendship survived this jab, Ray nonetheless managed to hit Dick where it hurt. In a moment of what some might call madness, Higgins had asked Johnson "what the book should cost; he said immediately '**$3.47**,' a thoroughly unusual price. I gagged, knowing that I was unlikely ever to recover my investment in the project at that rate, but I used that price anyway."

The thrill of dancing with Ray always had its price. Dick knew this going in, having been a friend-of-Ray in good standing since 1959. It had begun to seem like something of a scandal to him, and the other friend-fans, that Ray had not yet had a major gallery show. Whose fault was that, though? Sure, the art world did not get Johnson as it should have, but still, Higgins could not resist a gentle jab of his own, in the form of a card on which he has repeatedly retyped, "Yes, Ray, it seems that on Manhattan Island there are no art galleries." In April 1965, two months after the final page of **ABAD** went to press, Ray Johnson would have his first solo show at a major Manhattan gallery, a development by which he was unambivalently pleased for once. But he could not stay pleased for long. The commercial art world would never feel like home.

One could see **ABAD** as a last-ditch attempt by the artist to avoid taking his art public, a path that led, Johnson believed, to embarrassment, and might yet lead, he feared, to something worse than that, something one might call "death"—with the caveat that "death" is a more ambiguous word than one might have thought before reading Johnson's **BOOK**. Instead of publishing **ABAD**, then, Johnson disseminated selected pages by mail and by hand to friends and strangers on his list.

Does that make **ABAD** mail art? In some ways, yes, and in some ways, no, for two important reasons. Unlike his other printed flyers, which were one-offs, made to be fed at will or whim into the ongoing flow of correspondence, Johnson conceived the pages of **ABAD** as a unified work of fine art, a thing that had its own life apart from the normal flow of correspondence. Furthermore, unlike any of his other mailings, the pages had their price. Or rather, the pages had two prices. One, which Johnson made clear on the page in so many words, was the price recipients were expected to pay for postage. The other price was paid by individual patrons whom Johnson solicited to cover his production costs. In the days when **painters**

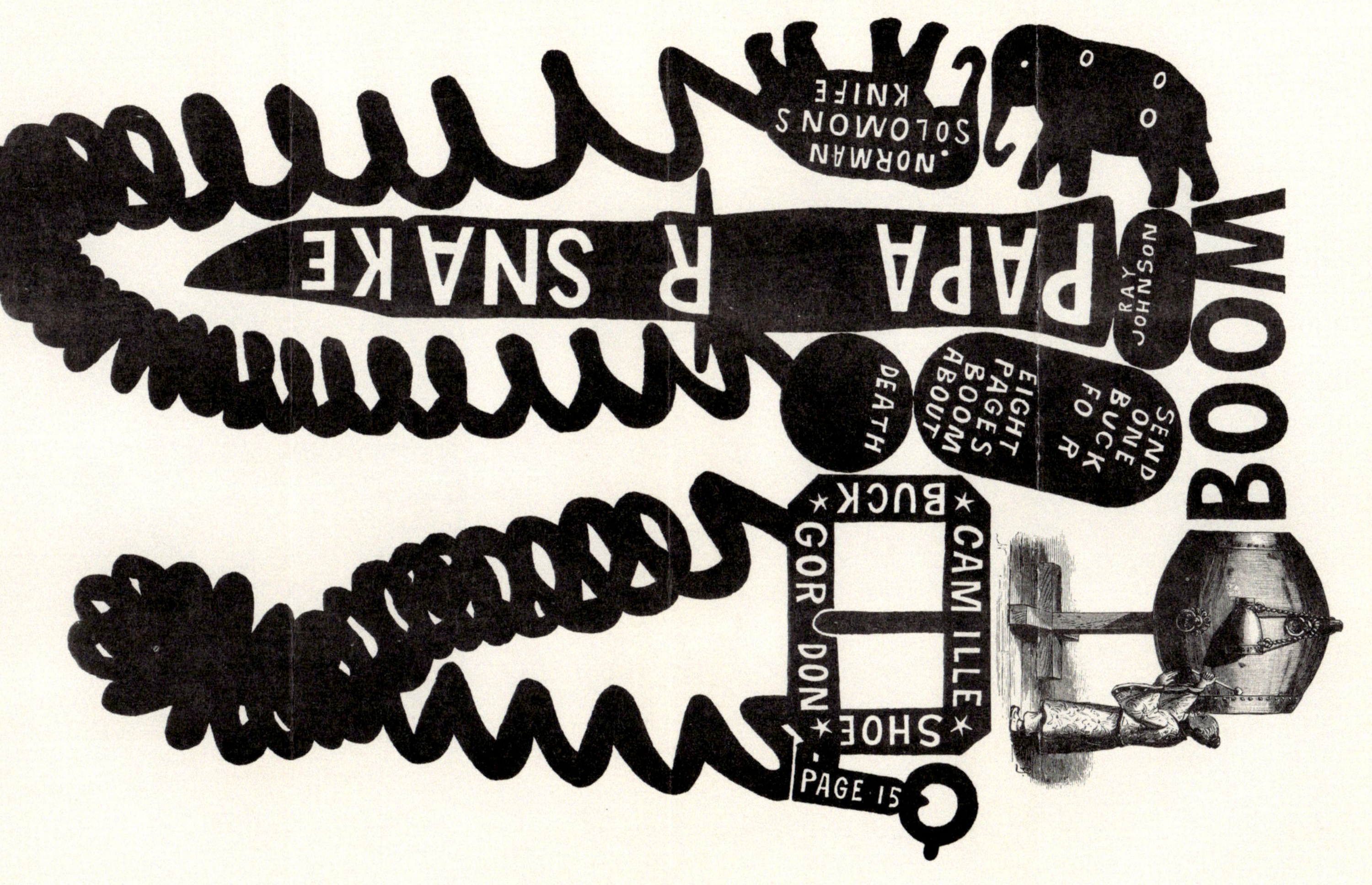

Ray Johnson, *A Book About Death*, p. 15.

Yes, Ray, it seems that on Manhattan Island there
are no art galleries. on Manhattan Island there
Yes, Ray ,it seems that on Mahnattan Island there
Yes, Ray, it seems that on Manhattan Island there
are no art galleries. on Manhattan Island there
are no art galleries. on Manhattan Island there
Yes, Ray, it seems that on Manhattan Island there
are no art galleries. on Manhattan Island there
Yes, Ray, it seems that on Manhattan Island there
Yes, Ray, it seems that on Manhattan Island there
are no art galleries. on Manhattan Island there
are no art galleries. on Manhattan Island there

SUBJECT TO FINAL REVIEW & CERTIFICATION
3RD REQUEST
M. FERREIO
CHIEF OF POL
REN SCHED.

Dick Higgins to Ray Johnson, February 26, 1965.

SEND 96 CENTS POSTAGE FOR 8 PAGES OF THE BOOK ABOUT DEATH TO RAY JOHNSON 176 SUFFOLK ST. NEW YORK CITY

Ray Johnson, detail from *A Book About Death*, p. 10.

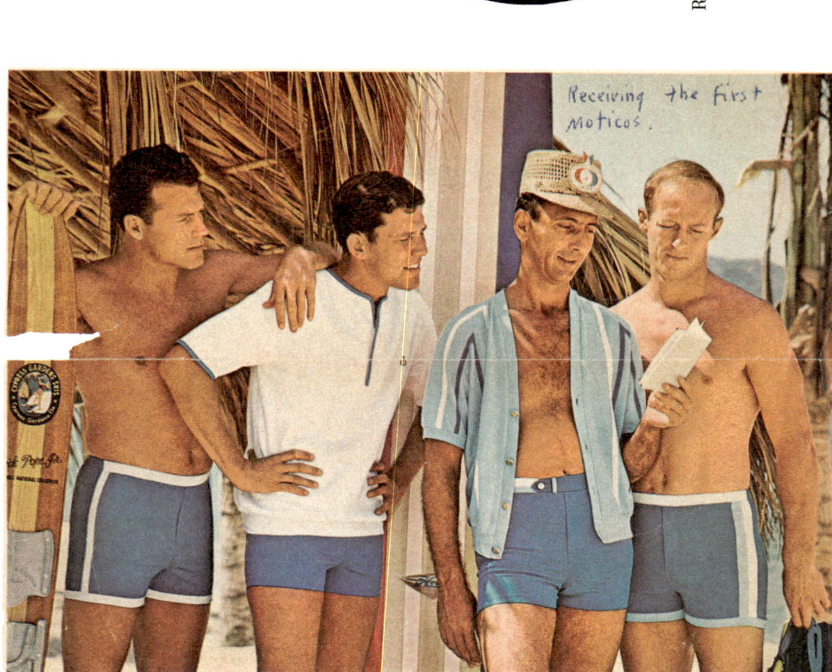

Ray Johnson to William S. Wilson, ca. May 1965.

were inspired to paint great religious subjects, a painter might insert a portrait of his patron in a corner of the picture. Johnson rendered his tribute by incorporating his sponsors' names in the page design.

As a practical alternative to the more conventional means by which artists of Ray Johnson's day made a living and gained an audience, **A BOOK ABOUT DEATH** was an unmitigated failure. The workarounds Johnson seems to have had in mind were at once outmoded—patronage, really?—and too far ahead of their time, eerily anticipating our world of advertisers for Nothing who live by clicks. As art, **ABAD** fascinates, yet obdurately refuses to invite even the most engaged of readers all the way in; it is coded without being intimate. Which is not to say it fails as art. If nothing else, it brought the moticos idea to a perfect dead end.

XXVII

In April 1965, Johnson wrote to Dorothy Miller, the MoMA curator whose attention he had been trying to attract for a decade or more, and who seemed finally to have been taking an interest in him. **Dear Dorothy Miller,/ You asked several weeks ago about moticos. I guess these pages from Book About Death could be filed under that./ With best wishes,/ Ray Johnson**. Was it already time to file away his just-completed **BOOK**? Shortly thereafter, Ray forwarded Bill his note addressed to Miller, along with a nostalgic image of three surfer dudes crowded around a fourth, who is holding what looks like a letter. Ray has added his own caption to the photo: **Reading the first moticos**.

M is for medium. By 1965, Johnson had found his, although it no longer had a name. It was too soon for "network," and too late for **moticos**. One might see the moticos years as a transitional period in the artist's evolution, the phase when **It sheds the feathers, skin, etc., before a new growth**, as Johnson wrote of the moticos in another mid-1950s mailer. **It is a very short space of time,** this first skin-shedding phase, or at least, it may seem so in retrospect. **It is for a moment; at this moment; at any moment.** Ray Johnson lived in time, like anybody else; like any other artist, he would try one thing, then another, not knowing how it would work, or how it would be received. But he also had an uncanny way of standing simultaneously inside and outside history, of being the creature both of **this moment** and of **any moment.** (It is this here-yet-there-ness that the camera loves.) Johnson wanted his to be a story without history, without chronology. Yet he also imagined an art whose whole history might unfold, fan-shaped, from a single moment. In the moticos, we can see, at moments, this artist's whole career in miniature, or rather, projected on a moebius loop.

Among the scores of old acquaintances who rushed to record their memories just after Johnson died was Hilton Kramer, once chief art critic for the *New York Times*, and later, a leading cultural conservative of the Reagan era. Kramer would write some of the meaner reviews Johnson was to receive, and Johnson would mock him mercilessly in return. And yet, in hindsight, all of that seemed to fall away. "We met at a party at a friend's house on the Upper East Side of Manhattan," Kramer recalled, "in the winter of 1952–53":

> Like Ray, most of the other guests at that party were alumni of Black Mountain College in Asheville, N.C., where they studied with Josef Albers and also came under the influence of John Cage.... It didn't take long to understand that Black Mountain had, for better or for worse, left a deep imprint on the lives of everyone who had been there. This was certainly true of Ray, whose art cannot be fully understood, I think, in isolation from the ideas of both Albers and Cage. Yet what most impressed me about Ray at the time was that despite his apparently sunny disposition and his extraordinary good looks, he already sounded like a man in mourning for his life. (He was then in his mid-20's.)

It is a person of 20 years or more having the same intelligence as a child from 8 to 12 years old.

It is sure to die sometime. (If you are interested in receiving the future Moticos announcements, please let me know or your name will be dropped from the mailing list).

It made a great impression on me at the time because just about everyone else at that party—myself included—was in a state of high excitement about the New York art scene and eager to become a part of it. Ray, on the other hand, seemed already to be preparing to drop out.

It is the hard, rainbow-colored lining of the shell of certain oysters.
It is thought or feeling that makes one act.
It is anyone who tries to deceive people by tricks, stories, and jokes.
The wind moves the leaves.

Most sincerely,
Ray Johnson

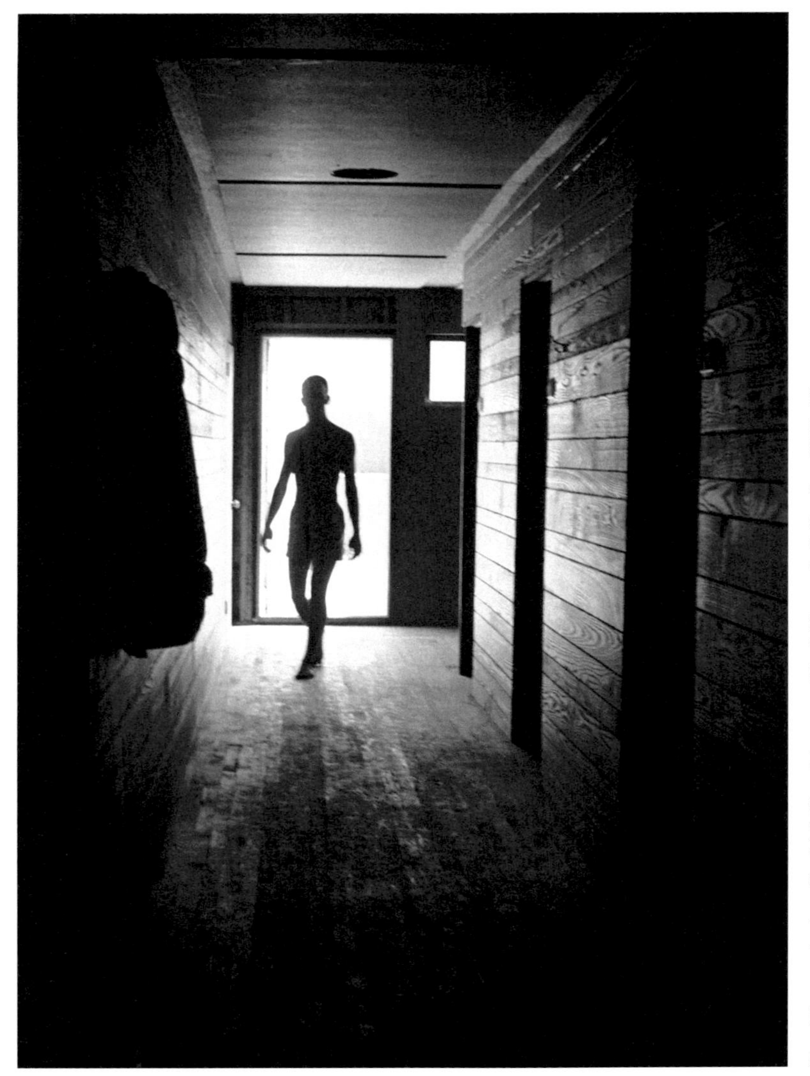

Hazel Larsen Archer, *Untitled (Ray Johnson at Black Mountain College)*, c. 1945-48.

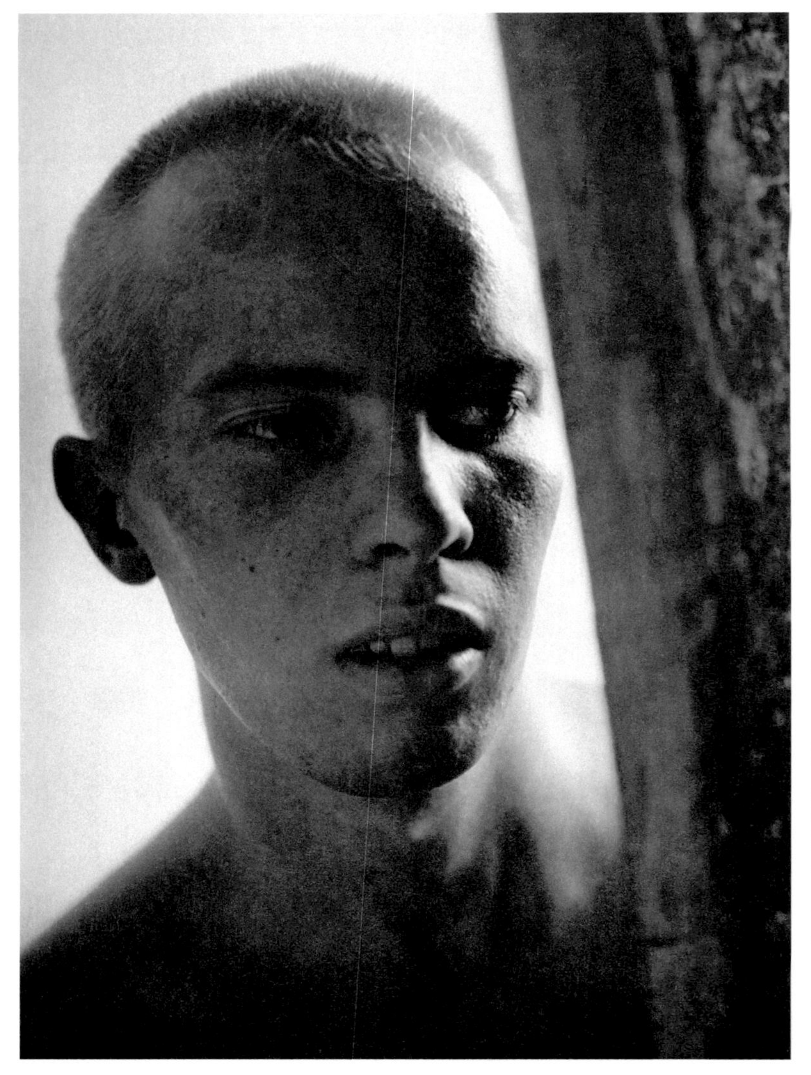

Hazel Larsen Archer, *Untitled (Ray Johnson at Black Mountain College)*, c.1945-48.

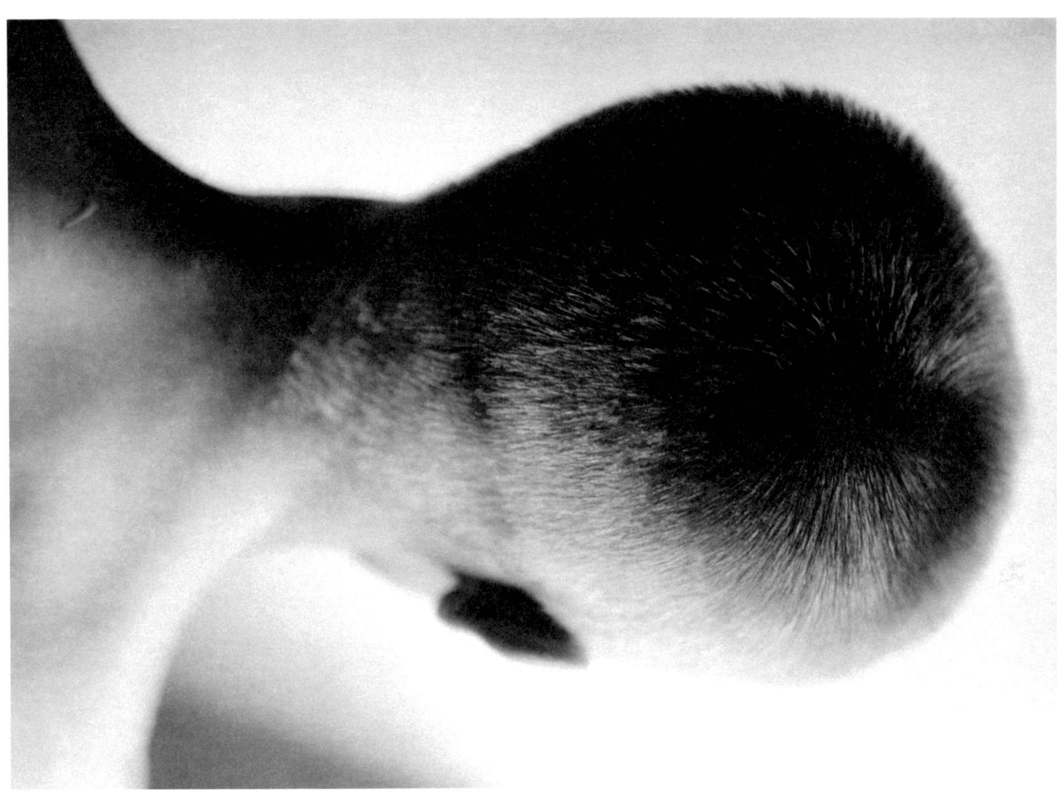

Hazel Larsen Archer, *Untitled (Back of Ray's Head)*, c.1945-48.

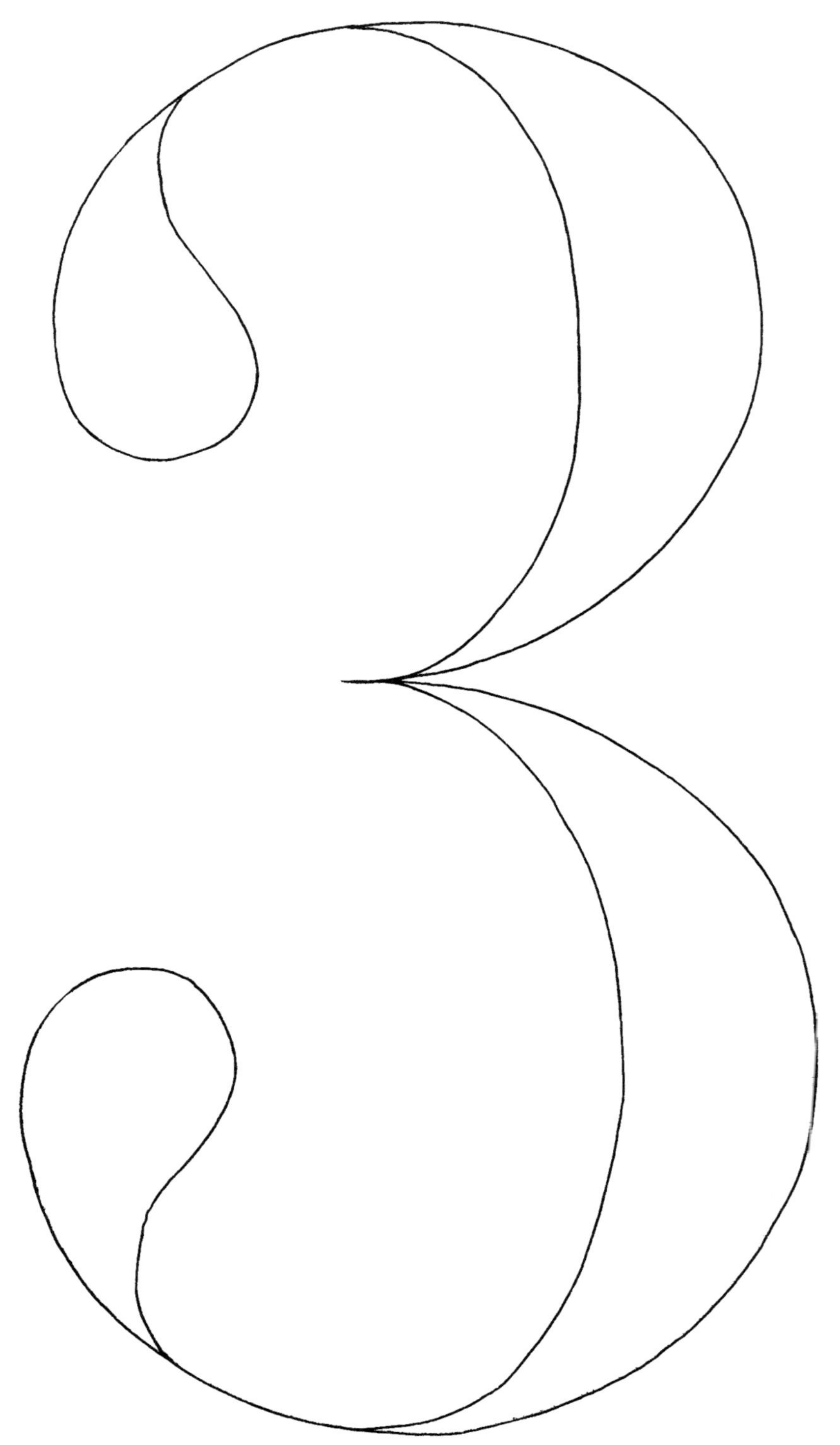

1964–1967

CRYSTALLIZATIONS: CORRESPONDENCE ART AND MOSAIC COLLAGE

I

> The different portions of this complicated structure stand, of course, in the most manifold logical relations to one another. They can represent foreground and background, digressions and illustrations, conditions, chains of evidence and counter-arguments. When the whole mass of these dream-thoughts is brought under the pressure of the dream-work, and its elements are turned about, broken into fragments and jammed together—almost like pack-ice—the question arises of what happens to the logical connections which have hitherto formed its framework.—Sigmund Freud, "Part C: The Means of Representation in Dreams," in *The Interpretation of Dreams*, vol. VI, *The Dream-Work*

> Driven by winds and ocean currents, pack ice is a mixture of ice fragments of varying size and age that are squeezed together and cover the sea surface with little or no open water.—*The American Heritage Science Dictionary* (2005)

"Now could you tell me which artists have influenced you most?" Sevim Fesci asked Ray Johnson in their 1968 interview, at which Johnson first balked (**I think I'm probably against influences**), then offered what sounded like a Zen parable, or an account of a dream. He had seen a photograph in *Time* magazine of the French novelist J. M. Leclezio captioned "Fire and Ice," which interested him **because the last three years of my work has been a long period of ice, which was suddenly close to fire and produced a flow of water. And I can see that the flow of water is very difficult to handle and channel and the ice was really very ideal because of its frozen state and it didn't take very much fire to melt and there are all these forms of water to contend with.** Fesci, baffled, quickly changed the subject.

But if one looks at the work Johnson produced in the three years prior to their conversation—not such a long period, in terms of sheer time, but packed with incident and discovery—one sees that the notion of "ice" was indeed central to that work. Something jelled for Johnson between 1965 and 1968, and then it dissolved, and the forms came in a flood. He became the artist he was meant to be and he began to drown: two versions of the same story.

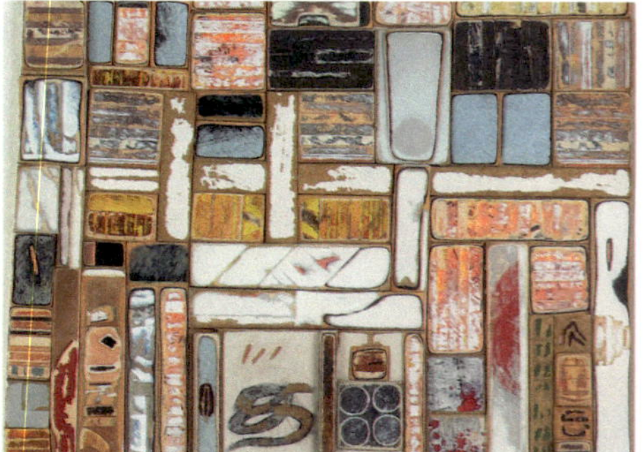

Ray Johnson, *ICE* (1966), detail.

II

> **There exists for me this lovely spring April day a problem of what to do with a Correspondance situation involving 62 composed letters addressed to people mostly who have received other such letters with similar contents. Each envelope contains eight articles consisting of worthless scraps also collages of encyclopedia fragments scotchtaped to backgrounds and parts of other letters.**

This **Correspondance situation** may have been a problem of Ray Johnson's own making but that is not to say that it was not a serious problem. **At the moment I wish to be taken quite seriously**, he avers, at the close of an essay-mailing titled **Correspondance Art**, in which he lays out the problem with unusual explicitness. It is the problem of his art's place in the world, no less. It is also a question of art-qua-art's place in his work. **There is obviously very little art work of merit in these letters and their presentation which is deliberately crude and unappealing. Any aesthetic is gushed during the tender period of letter composition.**

April Fool's Day, 1964. A recording angel hovers by our correspondent as he tenderly considers which scraps to send to whom, **carefully arranged in strict sequence of small upon larger upon larger pieces making a kind of filing system comfortable to the author.** A comfort destined to be disturbed, alas, as **The arrangement can be easily altered by a careless viewing such as occurs during the opening of a letter and contents picked at according to a momentary whim as to what one does like a child when it grabs a xmas present**. The angel of the aesthetic nervously rustles its wings as the careful arrangements get disarranged and years go by and the scotch tape dries out and the collages, already made **deliberately crude and unappealing**, fall apart in their envelopes and the envelopes themselves disappear into the backs of drawers and attics and wastebaskets. Somewhere along the way the angel, guardian of art and memory alike, takes flight, and one is left with the problem of what to do with such traces of the author's intentions as remain.

> **There are mostly no instructions as to what to do or what was the author's intent. The "author's intent," we have heard, has something to do with studies of poverty and quite primitive economics.**

So how do you propose to deal with the problem?

> **The problem will be solved by one of two answers. The bulk of the material will be dumped upon Michael Malce or Lawrence Alloway of the Guggenheim Museum. Malce has kindly taken in such bundles before addressed to him at his gift shop on Eighth Street ... He also**

kindly has purchased the postage stamps which allow the letter to reach it's [*sic*] **destination.**

Ray Johnson lived always in conditions of monk-like austerity and in his early years in New York was sometimes desperately, "ketchup-soup" (**add half hot tap water and mix**) poor. Correspondence was his one extravagance, but all that postage and photocopying would not pay for itself. Friends with access to official mailrooms and a willingness to bend the rules played essential roles in this regard: IBM, the Juilliard School, and Hertz Car Rental all became generous if unwitting benefactors of the New York Correspondance School during its first decade. Gift shop owner Michael Malcé, although a small proprietor, had likewise shown himself to be **a true friend of contemporary art** who could be counted on to mail off **yet another bundle. But**

But

the Correspondance School is not too interested at this time in a happy ending to it's [*sic*] **efforts. Such activity as junk mailing pieces necessarily go unnoticed and may be considered non-art.**

One might think, given that Johnson was devoting ever-greater portions of each day to working on mailings which, unlike the moticos that preceded them, were designed for maximal ephemerality and minimal visual appeal; given also that, unlike the moticos, which the artist did try to market, however quixotically and ineffectually, the Correspondance School mailings were distributed free of charge and came with the tacit proviso that recipients refrain from selling them or risk Johnson's wrath; one might think, I repeat, that the chance that these pieces might **be considered non-art** was one that Ray Johnson would be willing, perhaps even happy, to take. The growing collection of ink stamps that Johnson had begun to have custom-made to adorn his mailings by then included one that expressly cautioned, **THIS IS NOT A WORK OF ART**. Then again, the first stamp Johnson had made, and the one that appeared most frequently on the mailings, read **COLLAGE BY RAY JOHNSON**, a ratifier designed to distinguish the mail pieces from the exhibition collages, which Johnson always signed by hand. Both stamps appear on a 1964 mini-collage Johnson sent to artist John Willenbecher, one at the top, one at the bottom, suspending its scotch-taped scraps in the space between non-art and—something like art.

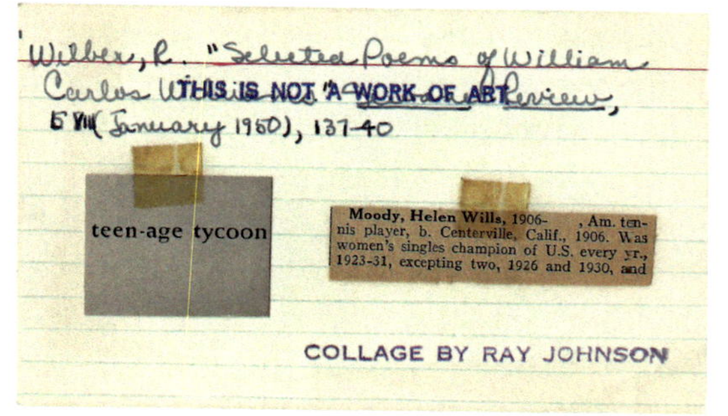

Ray Johnson to John Willenbecher, September 29, 1964.

When Johnson's first major New York solo show opened at the Willard Gallery in 1965 and Grace Glueck of the *New York Times* interviewed him for the article in which she dubbed him "New York's most famous unknown artist," Johnson had to admit that although **I've never believed in the gallery thing ... at the same time I've been dying for a show. Ambivalence, you see.** Ambivalence is a sustained suspense; the more sustained the suspense, the more we long for resolution. **Would sending the stuff to a Museum and Curator assure these little baby seeds of an Art classification?** the thirty-six-year-old famous unknown Ray Johnson found himself wondering as he contemplated his stacks of mail. Stranger things had happened in the art world in the half-century since Marcel Duchamp had managed to get his urinal-turned-*Fountain* rejected by an exhibition committee whose members had vowed to accept every artwork submitted to be shown. Art may survive, even thrive on, rejection, but it cannot bear to **go unnoticed.** So—**Should Mr. Alloway get his first package of monstrous letters? Will he consider this gift satire, art activity or nonsense?**

It is unclear whether Lawrence Alloway received the monstrous package of letters. The Guggenheim curator had, however, already expressed interest in a different package—"I want very much indeed to see your box of 100 Collage" [*sic*]—in a 1963 note responding to a mailing sent by Johnson, whom he was then "very much looking forward to meeting." Alloway, who left his post at the Guggenheim in 1966 to return to criticism, would prove one of Johnson's more sympathetic readers, granting the artist his ambivalence while honoring his intent. "Johnson said of his correspondence school that it is 'secret, private, and without any rules,' but there is a disconcerting precision to his letters," the critic observed in 1977.

Alloway may have been disconcerted in part by the precision with which Johnson's artwork tracked his own critical thinking. In his best-known essay, "Network: The Art World Described as a System," written in 1972, Alloway surveys changes in the art world that he sees as stemming from a wider cultural shift wherein "all of us are looped together in a new and unsettling connectivity." As older structures of social connection get taken up into rationalized networks, individual persons and things are increasingly reduced to nodes in the system—an "unsettling" prospect, as Alloway suggests—and the system itself becomes the primary object of critical inquiry. What Alloway terms the "output" of the art-world-as-system thus consists, he says, not of individual works of art, but of "the distribution of art, both literally and in mediated form as text and reproduction."

The act of composing and distributing my letters ... has become my entire artistic expression for the last year or so, reason enough, Johnson

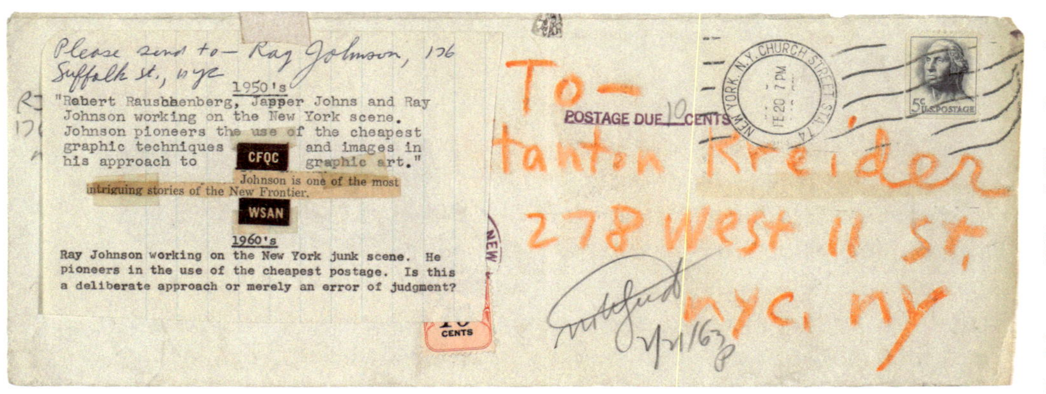

Ray Johnson to William S. Wilson, September 10, 1964.

had come to believe by that spring of 1964, for his efforts **to be taken quite seriously.** When the artist wondered if sending his mail to Alloway at the Guggenheim might garner it **an Art classification**, he had come to understand what he was up to well enough to guess that the classification would be granted, if at all, not to the letters seen as a collection of individual works, but as a sign of **art activity**, at once the output of a systematized network and a satire on such systematization. It was not so much the letters that were monstrous as the New York Correspondance School itself. The question now was whether Ray Johnson would prove to be master of his monster.

III

Michael Malcé, a Greenwich Village gift shop proprietor, hung out with the downtown theater types in Johnson's orbit, like lighting designer Johnny Dodd and dancer Fred Herko, who were both sometime actors in Warhol's movies, and choreographer David Gordon and his wife, dancer Valda Setterfield, who worked part-time in Malcé's shop before their performing careers took root. Gordon and Setterfield's path would lead them from Johnson's friend James Waring's company to Judson Dance Theater and its offshoots, and eventually, to Gordon's own company, for which Setterfield danced when she wasn't dancing with Merce Cunningham. Meanwhile, Gordon went on designing eye-catching window displays for Malcé as the shop moved further uptown and its stock shifted from gifts to funky collectibles like Mickey Mouse watches and vintage comics. Eventually, Malcé would parlay his knack for spinning junk into gold into a career as an influential dealer in Americana. "Michael, he's the pioneer of camp," testified loyal customer Andy Warhol.

1960s Ray Johnson working on the New York junk scene. He pioneers in the use of the cheapest postage. Is this a deliberate approach or merely an error of judgment? In a scrap-on-scrap collage sent to Bill Wilson in the fall of 1964, Johnson parodies his critics ("Ray Johnson, a pioneer in the use of the cheapest graphic techniques": John Coplans, *Pop Art, USA*, 1963) while returning to the thoughts about the **Correspondance situation** that had bedeviled him that spring. Although the New York junk scene had its charms—funky things, funky people—it could never offer the assurance of an Art classification that a museum might. Junk carries only the assurance of its own ephemerality. It is like dance that way.

Metaphysique d'ephemera: a term coined by Joseph Cornell to describe his own inimitable way of spinning junk into gold, rearranging finds from New York's streets and dime stores into otherworldly dioramas packed into homemade wooden boxes and sealed behind glass. Initially at least, these constructions, too, raised doubts as to whether they belonged in the museum under an Art classification or in the gift shop with the rest of the collectibles. Cornell's first solo show, in 1932, was advertised as "toys for adults" and a review of his second, in 1939, called it "a holiday toy shop of art for sophisticated enjoyment." The artist's gallerist Julien Levy set prices low and marketed the works as Christmas gifts.

"Ray Johnson is to the letter what Joseph Cornell is to the box," declared Nicolas and Elena Calas in 1971. Nicolas had once been a regular contributor to *View* magazine, mid-century Manhattan's house organ for Dada and Surrealism, whose editors were among Cornell's earliest supporters. In his 1977 piece on Johnson, Lawrence Alloway cites the Calases' remark approvingly, taking it to mean that "both artists come out of the collage tradition but both have expanded it drastically." Having made the connection, though, Alloway leaves it at that, as do the Calases, apparently taking it for granted that we will grasp the implications of their pairing of Cornell and Johnson.

IV

A fan letter from Johnson to Joseph Cornell, dated November 25, 1966, begins, as it should, with a compliment: **I saw your beautiful ICE at the Modern Museum for the first time this week**. Only, the Cornell that Johnson saw at the Museum of Modern Art, a "box of ice cubes encased in sumptious [*sic*] blue velvet," as Cornell himself described it in a 1940 letter to Charles Henri Ford, co-editor of *View*, is not called *ICE* but *Taglioni's Jewel Casket*. *ICE* is, however, the title that Johnson gave to a collage featured in his second solo show at the Willard Gallery, held in the spring of 1966. One wonders if Johnson, a longtime regular at MoMA, had really failed to notice Cornell's sumptuous showpiece before that November, or if, rather, Johnson thought it might be time at last for Cornell to notice *him*.

By the end of 1966, Johnson had reached what felt to him like a crossroads. In November, he writes to Cornell, and in December, he confides to Bill Wilson his **idea that a Ray Johnson died and another Ray Johnson is about to begin and he shall have a new name and I shall have to be Ray Johnson but I am this other person**. By the following February, it's official. "At this particular moment," artist Lil Picard seems pleased to report in *The East Village Other*, "Ray Johnson announces in a new collage, not yet shown anywhere, his death." The announcement takes the form of a tombstone that gives its maker's dates as 1927–1966, beside which are inscribed the birth and death dates of the irresistibly named Wanda Gàg, author of the bestselling children's book, *Millions of Cats*.

One obvious landmark had been passed. Richard Lippold, who had been showing at the Willard Gallery since the mid-1940s, put in a word for Ray with Marian Willard, the gallery's founder, and her husband and partner, Dan Johnson. In April 1965, at the relatively advanced age of thirty-seven, Ray Johnson finally had a solo exhibition at a major New York gallery. The artist was, you could say, more than ready for his close-up. **I have this form to fill out for Art in America**, he kvetched to May Wilson back in 1962. **I am considered New Talent ha, ha. I am Old Talent.** The 1965 Willard show featured forty-one works, including a few of the early paintings that had survived "the burning" (most of these belonged to Lippold, less scrupulous than some of Johnson's friends about his wishes and more protective of his art). A careful perusal of the gallery's sales list, though, reveals an odd fact. Thirty-eight of the pieces in the show bear dates ranging between 1951 and 1960, while only one is dated 1964, two are from 1965, and there are no works at all from 1961, 1962, or 1963. In other words, Ray Johnson's first big gallery exhibition had more the air of a retrospective than a debut.

What was Johnson doing during those missing years? He was discovering that the monstrous **Correspondance situation** could absorb as much time as he would give it. He was mailing off the pages of **A BOOK ABOUT DEATH,** among other things a thought-experiment in the creation of a space for exhibition outside the museum-gallery complex. He was performing in public, occasionally—the early 1960s were the **Nothing** years—and in private, constantly. He was participating in group exhibitions, then satirizing them in the form of announcements for fictional group exhibitions, which his friends Andy Warhol and David Bourdon themselves then satirized in the form of an advertisement they placed in the *Village Voice* in September 1964, while Johnson was in Bellevue Hospital recovering from a bout of hepatitis. (Close readers of the ad for "RAY JOHNSON & other Living Americans" might be tipped off by the show's odd hours: "7–8, Mon., Wed., Fri.; 2:30–4 Tues., Thurs., weekends & holidays.")

Bourdon and Warhol's prank drew on insider gossip about the parade of notables who turned Johnson's hospital visiting hours into an ongoing art

8 MAN SHOW 3

MRS. BRECHT

IDA FINE

KAY JOHNSON

WOODPECKER GALLERY

Ray Johnson, "phantom postcard" (Woodpecker Gallery), 1968.

8 MAN SHOW

GEORGE BRECHT

GEORGE HERMS

RAY JOHNSTON

ROBIN GALLERY

Ray Johnson, "phantom postcard" (Robin Gallery), 1968.

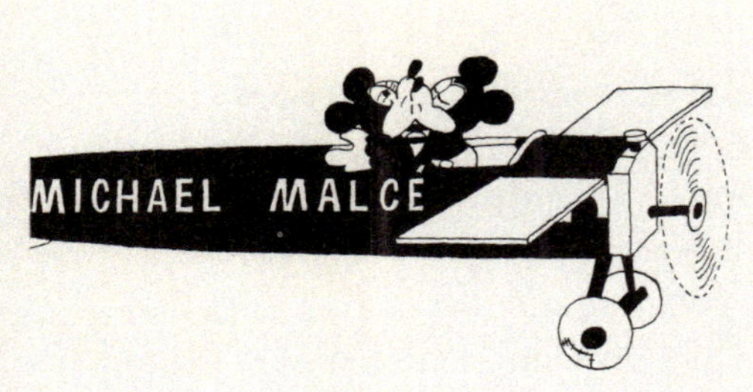

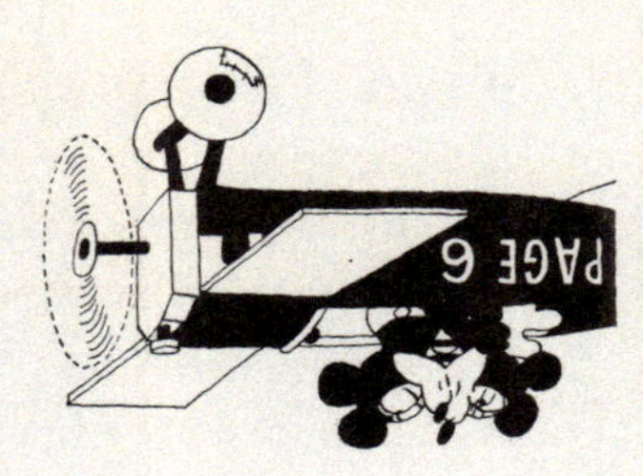

P O R T U G A L A N E S
I A P I N T O 2 Y E A R S
O L D W A S C U T E R E
C E N T L Y W H E N S H E
S T E P P E D O N A L I
V E W I R E W H I L E C R
U S H I N G G R A P E S
I N H E R B A R E F E E T

Ray Johnson, *A Book About Death*, p. 6.

world event (Warhol's assistant Mark Lancaster arrived **wearing an elegant English blue suit made by the Beattle's** [*sic*] **tailor**). It also drew on insider knowledge of Johnson's peculiar position in the art world, famous yet unknown, famous for being unknown, famous for showing his work rarely, and then seldom where you would expect it. **Is this a deliberate approach or merely an error of judgment?** An unanswerable question, which would hang over Johnson to the end of his life and beyond. Still, by 1964, he had begun at least to recalibrate his approach. Just two years earlier, he was all prickly with May about *Art in America*.

> **They want photos of six of my best recent works ha, ha. Which "Please send to's" shall I have photographed? What collections and owners of these works they want to know ha, ha. Nobody wants these "please send to's" so how do I know who owns them or where they are and who at this very moment is pasting a sequin on one of my major works? ... See you in Art in America, May, maybe I'll send a photo of something of yours. Maybe I'll send a Bruce Connah** [*sic*]**. I'm very angry about this, damn them. Why can't I be a good boy?**

Johnson was too deep in the weeds at that point to see what his mailings might have to do with the kinds of "works" that institutions and collectors would hang on their walls. His subsequent reflections in **Correspondance Art** show him beginning to get some distance, beginning to come to grips with the dialectical quality of the mailings, their suspension in a space between the junk shop and the museum. Yet even there, he frames the situation—**there exists for me ... a problem**—in oddly passive terms, as if this were not where he had expected or intended to find himself.

V

Johnson had always loved to draw—his closest cousin vividly recalls "Ray at a very tender age with pencil and paper scurrying across the floor with his scribblings." Did he love to paint? He struggled so with the medium throughout his twenties and gave it up with such vengeful satisfaction; then again, violent struggle and rejection may also be signs of love. He had, in any case, a strong appetite and sure feel for color, which Albers's tutelage stimulated and refined. His were "meaningful colors, from the most delicate closeness to the most vibrating intensity," as Lippold puts it, in a catalogue-style essay that may have been written to accompany Johnson's third Willard show, in 1967. Lippold also speaks there more generally of Johnson's devotion to what was most difficult and of his "incredible technique, not an end in itself, but a servant to the complexity of his total art." In his late-blooming mid-thirties, Ray Johnson found himself committed to correspondence art, a conceptual practice in which visual appeal, while not entirely absent, was nevertheless beside the point. But his hand and eye still ached to make other kinds of delicate discriminations, to arrive at what Wallace Stevens calls "sudden rightnesses" and to pause there, relieved.

To pause but not to stay. Johnson first tried to sell the moticos. Then the moticos told him, **It loves moving and rain water**, **It wants to go its way**, and he found ways to set and keep it in motion, even at the risk of its disappearance and dissolution. In the New York Correspondance School, he discovered a veritable perpetual motion machine, designed to maximize the operations of chance and change on whatever got fed into its gears and to minimize the significance of ownership for the receiver. **Nobody wants these "please send to's" so how do I know who owns them or where they are and who at this very moment is pasting a sequin on one of my major works?** Johnson knew, too, that such uncertainties about authorship and value would cling to the mailings even as they inevitably succumbed to inertia, coming to rest in folders and boxes, perhaps just for a time, perhaps forever.

Still, for reasons both psychological and practical, he could not dispense with the need to make works that institutions and collectors could hang on their walls. A 1963 scrap-on-scrap collage marked **Please send to George Brecht** juxtaposes two dictionary definitions: "naïve. adj. artless, ingenuous, unaffectedly simple, unsophisticated," and "exhibit. n. A display, something shown, a thing shown before a court as evidence. To show, to display; to reveal by outward sign, as to *exhibit* anger." The furious urge to exhibit was always at war in Ray with the desire to maintain a childlike artlessness.

I spoke with Diane di Prima and Bob Morris on the telephone about the problem of my "style" and whether or not I had one, and Bob Morris thought I <u>definitely</u> had one, Johnson crowed to George Brecht in January 1963. This was the year when Robert Morris—ex-painter turned performer and sculptor—can be said to have found his own style, as evidenced in his first New York solo show that fall at the Green Gallery, a turning point for the tendency not yet known as Minimalism. Although Morris's surging confidence may have been contagious in the moment, Johnson would soon return to worrying over the problem of his "**style.**" Why put the term in quotes? Perhaps because he knew that for him it was a question not so much of style per se but of how his **Correspondance situation** could or could not be related to the kinds of collages he had been making for exhibition in years past.

The collages Johnson chose to hang at Willard in 1965 did have a dominant style: gestalt compositions constructed from frame-filling abstract please send to - George Brecht, 315 woodbridge ave., Metuchen, New Jersey

naïve (nä ēv′) *adj.* Artless, ingenuous, unaffectedly simple, unsophisticated. **-′ly** *adv.* — **-′ness** *n.*

exhibit (eg zib′it) *n.* A display; something shown; a thing shown before a court as evidence. — *vt.* To show, display; to reveal by outward sign, as, to *exhibit* anger. **-′itive** *adj.* — **-′itor, -′iter** *n.* — **-′itory** *adj.*

Ray Johnson please-send-to for George Brecht, 1963.

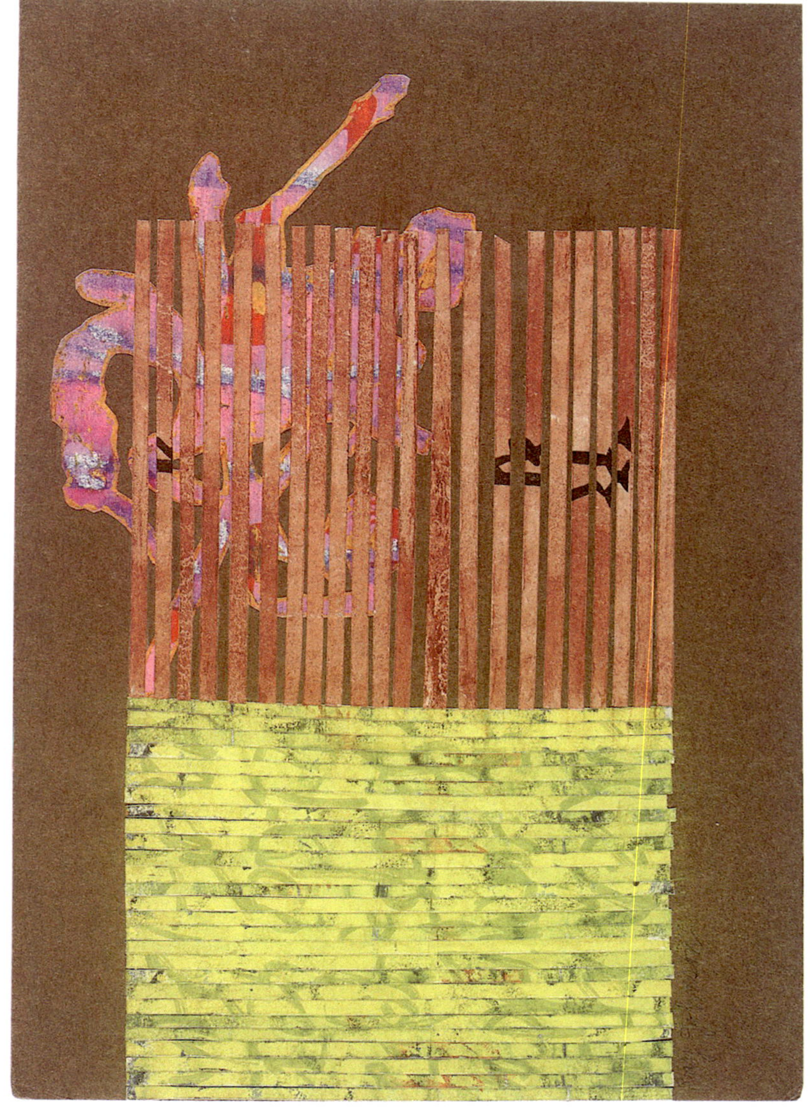

Ray Johnson, *Caged* (1959).

and semi-figurative shapes, themselves constructed from previous works that were cut into strips and fitted closely together. The strips, with their quasi-geological striations, taken together with the quality of Johnson's color, which oscillates, as Lippold says, between "delicate closeness" and "vibrating intensity," give the images energy, especially as one draws near to take in the details. Yet when one steps back again, that energy seems at war with the overall design—a conflict made literal in a collage called *Caged*, where the straight strips box in a snake-like squiggle in shocking pink. The relation between the public and the intimate, as between whole and part, handled with a juggler's lightness in the moticos and the correspondence art, turns stiff with tension here.

In April 1966, Ray's friend George Ashley, then toiling at the offices of Hertz Car Rental, afterward a performer and administrator with Robert Wilson's theater company when it was still a hippie circus, not the European opera-house darling it would become, wrote to May Wilson to give her the lowdown on the opening of Johnson's second exhibition at Willard. Having run through the list of Johnson regulars who came to show their support—Norman Solomon, James Waring, composer Albert M. Fine, "STAN VAN DER BEEK, filmmaker, who brought Ray Johnson a gift, a 3" paint brush," "the Wilsons' friend who torments TV sets" (the video artist Nam June Paik, who was at the time occupying a floor of Bill and Ann Wilson's ramshackle Chelsea townhouse), and Ray's best friend and muse, Toby Spiselman, whom Ashley escorted, bringing her "a small reddish-blue carnation" to complement her "pinky-lavenderishy costume, very pretty"—and having transmitted to May his "vision" of "RAY JOHNSON, in a wide wale corduroy jacket, turquoise in color, cut like a blazer; ivory chinos and turquoise canvas shoes," Ashley came to the meat of the matter:

> and the ART , , , well, it is very difficult to describe, but perhaps,
> well, freer than last year,
> and less dependent on a single major shape (the pagodaish that seemed to be here and there last year) and very, very clean and purposeful, and brilliantly detailed, multi-leveled, intricate in the variety of little shapes used and the variety of decoration, coloring really very fine but very hard to tell you about

George couldn't show May what he meant. Not only were photography and photographic reproduction more cumbersome affairs back then, but Johnson's post-1965 collages remain difficult to photograph and reproduce, for reasons to be discussed later. As Ashley says, they are also hard to describe, in part because they are generically indeterminate, neither collage nor painting, firmly composed yet suspended precariously between material states, like sheets of closely packed ice.

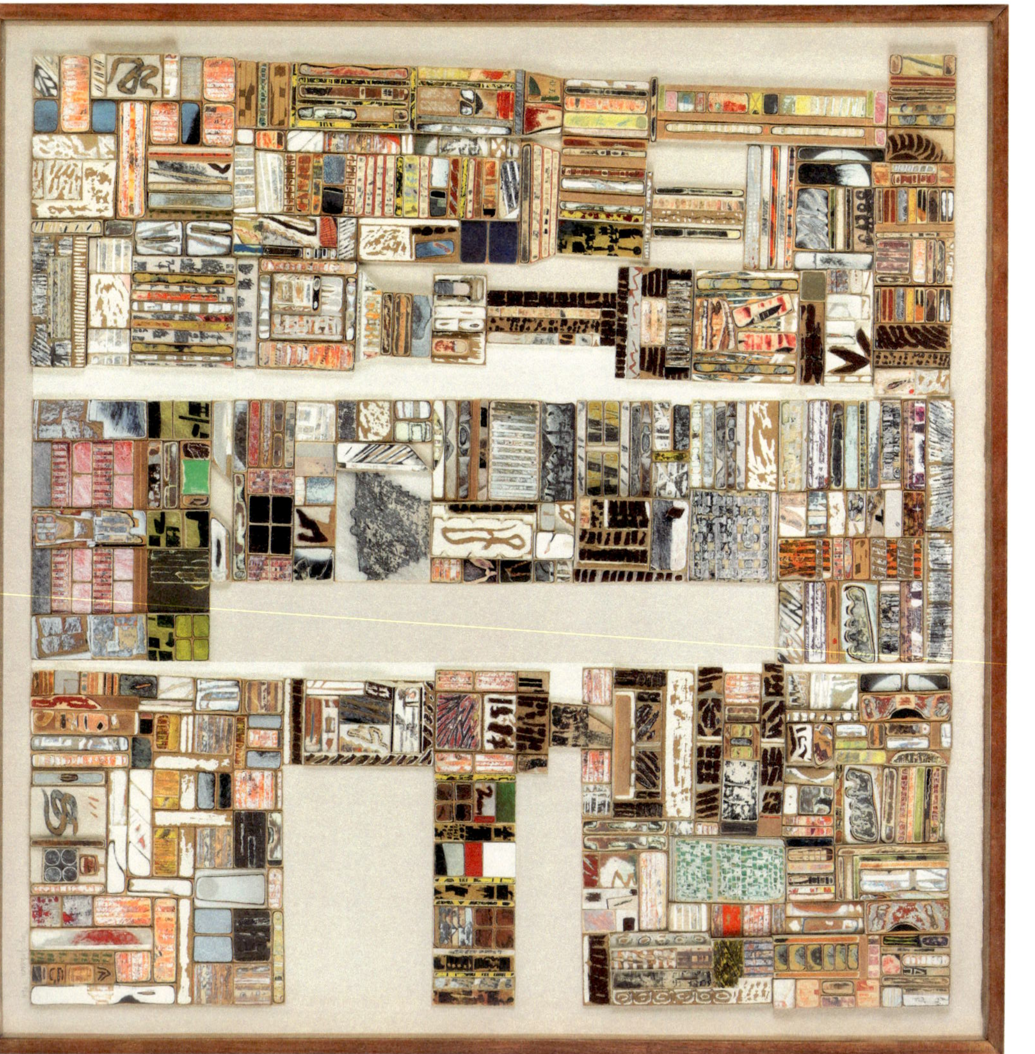

Ray Johnson, *ICE* (1966).

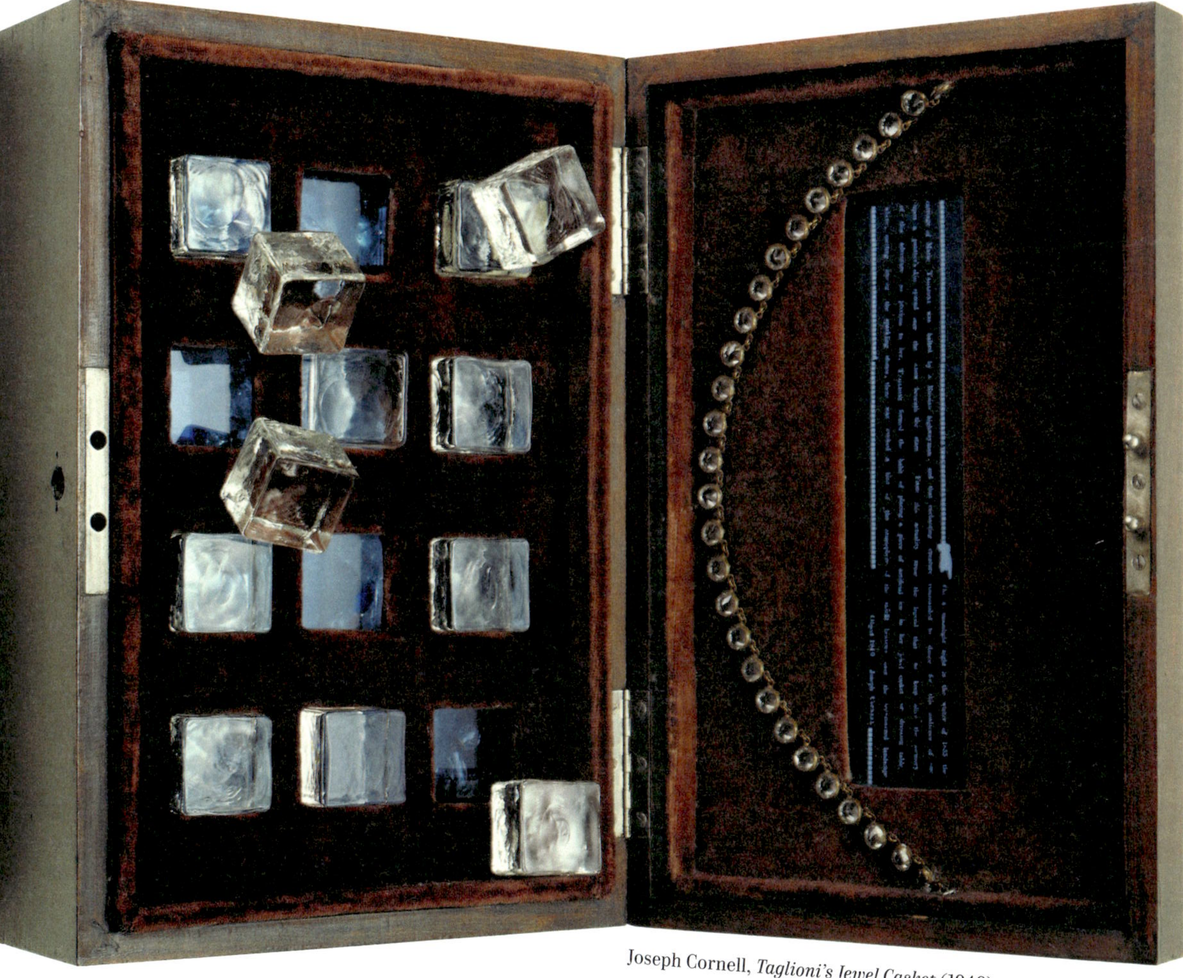

Joseph Cornell, *Taglioni's Jewel Casket* (1940).

VI

The majority of Joseph Cornell's boxes have glass fronts, like store windows, but *Taglioni's Jewel Casket*, which Ray Johnson (mis)identifies with his own *ICE*, belongs to a group of boxes that are more like salesmen's cases, with lids that shut. With the lid open, the "diamond" necklace, attached by the ends to the edges of the lid, assumes its parabolic curve. Across the distance enforced by MoMA's vitrine, you can see but not read the text framed at the center of the lid. Cornell's urge to produce unmanageable tensions in his art between the intimate and the public, forcing curators to choose between letting viewers come too close or holding them at too great a distance, was something Johnson understood all too well. **I was going to write to the Art Institute of Chicago**, he informs Cornell in his fan letter, **telling them I thought that a work of yours that they had screwed to the wall was not properly exhibited and that it should be in a glass case if it has to be seen by droves of people.**

Was it not meant to be seen by droves of people? Could it conceivably have been meant, like a letter, for an audience of one?

In the case of *Taglioni's Jewel Casket*, the curious droves who wish to read the legend on the lid must settle for Cornell's words as transcribed on the museum label (also known in the business as a "tombstone").

> On a moonlit night in the winter of 1855 the carriage of Maria Taglioni was halted by a Russian highwayman, and that ethereal creature commanded to dance for the audience of one upon a panther's skin spread over the snow beneath the stars. From this little actuality arose the legend that, to keep alive the memory of this adventure so precious to her, Taglioni formed the habit of placing a piece of ice in her jewel casket or dressing table drawer where melting among the sparkling stones, there was evoked a hint of the starlit heavens over the ice-covered landscape.

ICE and jewels, the ephemeral and the everlasting. Although a funny thing about Cornell's ice is that it is as durable as his dime-store gems; and unlike the necklace, which moves with the movement of the lid, his twelve glass cubes have fixed places within the velvet grid that rests on a sheet of blue glass, suspended an inch or so above the actual bottom of the case, where glass chips and jewelry fragments are left to shift unseen, vestiges of the kind of chance meetings and partings this work memorializes.

VII

> **I'm not a painter. I'm a collagist. I deal with things that are constantly being chopped up and shuffled and moved around. What I deal with**

> **is what you have in a kaleidoscope, when you have pieces of ground glass in a cylinder and simply give it one slight turn and you have a complete change of pattern and reflection of light and color. And it's changed the next moment by another slight switch. That's the way my imagination works. That's my working process in the studio.**
>
> —Ray Johnson, radio interview, 1984

If a collector or institution is to hang a work on the wall, the work must stop moving and changing long enough to allow itself to be hung. The work must decide, at that point, whether its need to keep moving outweighs its need to hang on a wall. The work may be ambivalent about the prospect of being seen by droves of people, but it may nonetheless hesitate to renounce the possibility that it might be—*seen*, that is—altogether. A compromise formation: the work stops moving and changing and allows itself to be hung but it finds a way, or several ways, to register its ambivalence. What happened in 1966 is that Ray Johnson finally found a compromise he could live with, a process that would produce unmoving images that conveyed the possibility that they might be **changed the next moment by another slight switch**. The key to that process was a piece of concretized ambivalence akin to Cornell's unmelting cube.

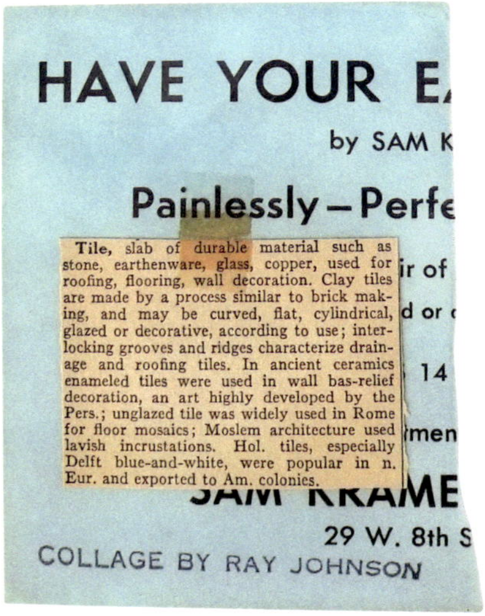

Ray Johnson to Henry Martin, June 16, 1964.

From an encyclopedia entry on "Tile" taped onto a scrap-on-scrap collage that Ray sent in 1964 to his friend Henry Martin, we learn that "In ancient ceramics enameled tiles were used in wall bas-relief decoration, an art highly developed by the Pers." The *tesserae* ("cubes" or "dice") in Roman and Byzantine mosaic-work were made of stone or glass. When the prominent critic Dore Ashton reviewed Ray Johnson's 1966 show at the Willard Gallery, she confessed that she had previously known the artist only as "a founder of a correspondence school" who had paradoxically managed "to get a reputation based on missives only the receivers knew about." Now, she seems surprised to find, "He also makes pictures. Or rather," not pictures, exactly, but "missives that are construed on a surface and exhibited on walls, communicating with anybody, not anybody special ... Many of his collages are composed of tiny plaques, put together to make shapes whose meaning escapes me. But the intimate little messages—the painted or scratched or even nearly blank tesserae—are intriguing in themselves."

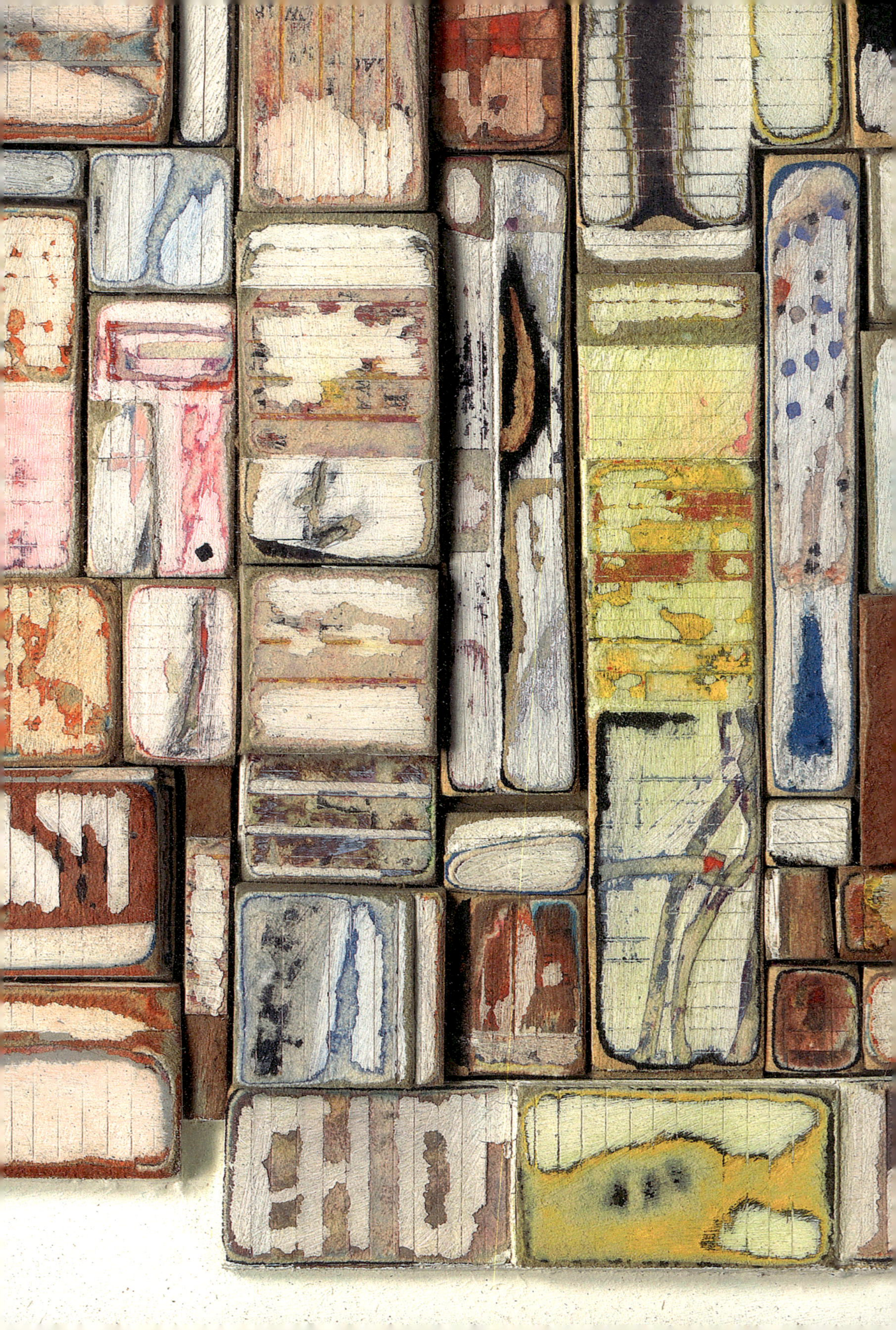

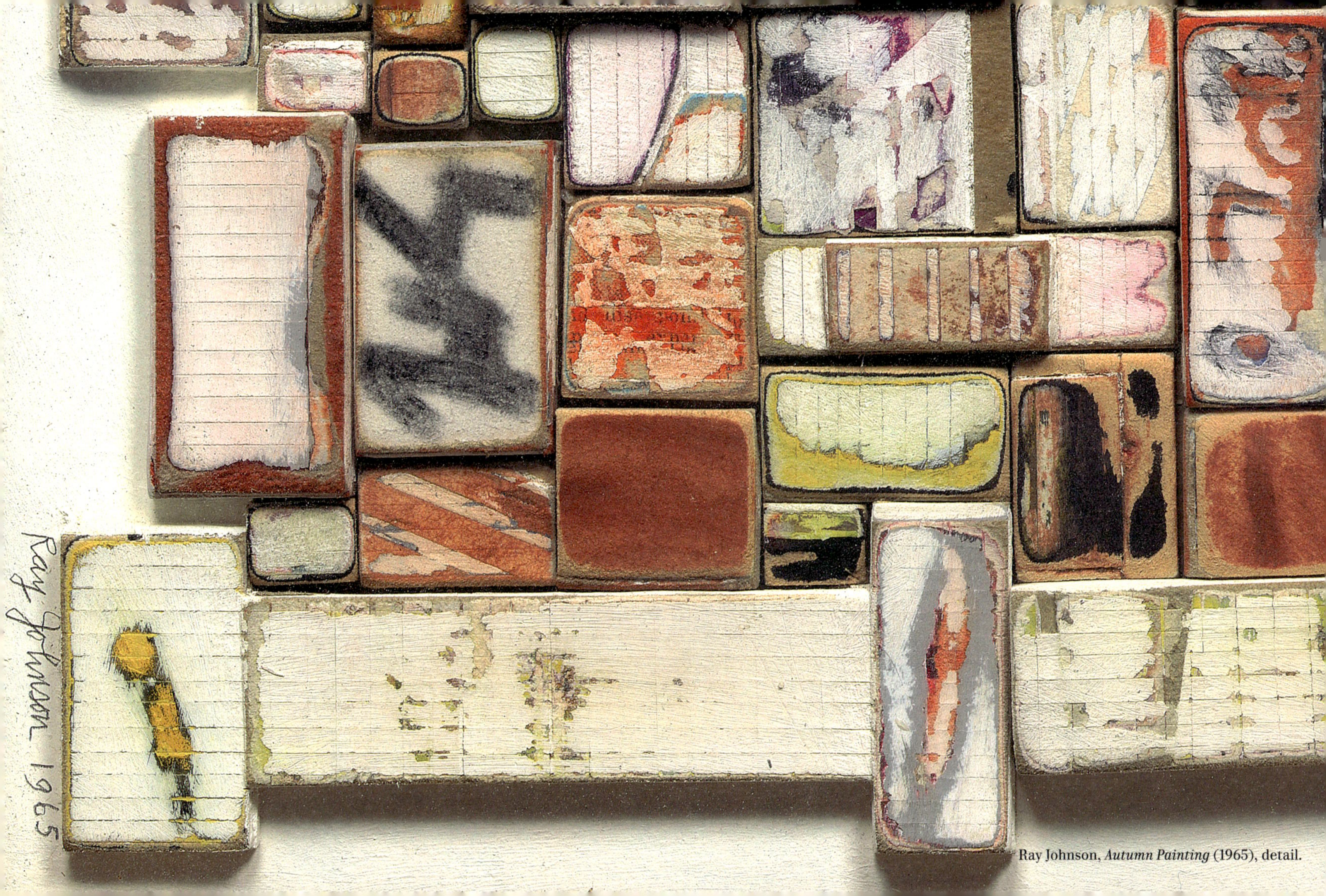

Ray Johnson, *Autumn Painting* (1965), detail.

Like the strips that preceded them, the tesserae seem to speak of past lives, of having been part of some other image-message, an impression accentuated by the sandpapering and other deliberate degradations to which Johnson energetically subjected his fragments. (A friend recalls being distracted by the sandpaper's constant "ch-ch-ch-ch-ch-ch" back of Ray's voice on the phone.) The strips, though, are always subordinate to the shapes they form, whereas each of the tiles may be imagined as independent from the others with which it has been provisionally arranged. They invite the viewer to see them, as Ashton does, as "intriguing in themselves." Each one is a tiny painting, or as Ashton would have it, message, or to be more accurate, perhaps, a small sculpture or structure, since the bits of cardboard, again unlike the strips, are built up to various levels of relief, although to see them as three-dimensional objects the viewer must come in very, very close—and it is an effect that only the very best photography can capture, and even then, it will likely get lost in reproduction—a problem surely anticipated by Johnson.

"The intimacy of approach is important to the kinds of responses he wants to elicit," Ashton warns. "Only those who care will take the trouble to examine the details and thereby enter into Johnson's mood." Remember, this is an assessment, sympathetic and sensitive but wary of special pleading, of the first set of artworks Ray Johnson had ever made not just in the hope but in the *knowledge* that they would soon be hung on a gallery wall to be seen by "anybody, not anybody special." Certain of the more elaborate arrangements of tesserae, like *ICE*, or *January/February*, which Marian Willard and Dan Johnson would keep for themselves for a decade before handing it over to a museum, were dazzlingly complex tours de force, enacted at twice or three times the scale of the shirtboard collages from the 1950s that filled the first Willard show. Yet even these showpieces were still, somehow, not quite public, not for just anybody, it turns out, "only those who care."

In October 1966, Johnson retyped the entirety of Ashton's review on stationery printed with the heading "Memo from the desk of ... GEORGE ASHLEY," appending a brief note to the recipient.

> **Bill, after you left I discovered the French word**
for umbrella is pap
parapluie
But still don't know what L'ABEILLE is.
Johnson's mood.

L'Abeille-Enseigne I is the title of a late collage by Joseph Cornell. The collage was reproduced next to Johnson's 1965 tesserae-assemblage *Pink above* at the end of Dore Ashton's column of exhibition reviews, in which a piece on Cornell's show at the Schoelkopf Gallery precedes the one on Johnson's show at Willard. Ashton remarks there on Cornell's habit of not dating his works, appropriate, she thinks, given that the aging techniques to which he submits his materials create a nostalgic sheen that situates them "outside of linear time." What Ashton calls Cornell's "blurred" temporality also derives from his practice of recycling materials from piece to piece, as in another 1966 collage featuring the "L'ABEILLE" sign, which reveals it to be the name of a nineteenth-century company that ran a "Mail Coach to Waterloo." L'ABEILLE, in other words, as I think Johnson knew, is a mailer-bee. Moody Ray, so intimate, so far away.

VIII

A "little actuality," Cornell calls the encounter of the ballerina and the bandit on the snow beneath the stars. Yet how does one verify the existence of a dance for an outlaw audience of one?

10/17/65 Dear James Waring,
Twenty copies of Pocket Theatre were left in the back of an uptown 2nd Avenue bus. So was the piece of cardboard with two staples in it.
Also two more Pocket Theatres.
At Edward Oleksak's front door were left 12 more Pocket Theatres.
Picture of Terrence [*sic*] Stamp was left in Andrew Sherwood's mail box.
Two original James Warings left in Paul Kilb's mail box at 344 Third Avenue. Also George Deem catalogue.
Five gold grapes left in mail box of Ennis Desk Co. on 3rd Avenue.
Two gold grapes thrown into a sand pile.
Figure 8 gold round beads left in middle of 3rd Avenue.
Green Gallery envelope addressed and posted to David Bourdon.
Sequin string dropped in front of a news stand.
Small piece of plastic dropped by a barber pole.
Plastic jewell [*sic*] put in a mail box.
Masayuki Nagare's statement about stones dropped in middle of 42nd Street.
Ann Arbor flyer posted to James Waring.
Artschwager catalogue addressed and mailed to Bourdon.
Dan Flavin announcement dropped near barber pole.
For therapeutic nutritional support information tossed at two pigeons.

Like Ray Johnson, James Waring is a figure as elusive as he is legendary. He wrote well and wittily, made lovely collages in a style that owed much to Johnson's moticos, but was best known as a choreographer and dance teacher, many of whose students, like Lucinda Childs, David Gordon, Deborah Hay, Fred Herko, Yvonne Rainer, and Valda Setterfield, would go on to perform at Judson Dance Theater. Johnson's name frequently appears in Waring's programs including that of *The Pocket Follies*, at the Pocket Theatre, "an entertainment by 28 poets, painters, actors, dancers, and musicians," per the *Village Voice*, June 6, 1963. "Proceeds will benefit the recently formed Foundation for Contemporary Performance Arts," initially created by John Cage, Jasper Johns, and Robert Rauschenberg to help fund performances by the Merce Cunningham Dance Company: **something**, as Ray might put it, **to do with studies in poverty and quite primitive economics.**

Athletic announcement in foreign language left in mail box of Antiques de France.
Rosenquist Green Gallery announcement to Waring posted.
8 × 10 glossy photo of "7 Faces of Dr. Lao" dropped in mail box on 57 Street.
8 × 10 glossy photo "Black Pit of Dr. M" and Yektai announcement and homework page left at Cinema I.
Contents of Akron, Ohio letter dumped in garbage can East 61 Street. Envelope saved.
Small envelope accidentally dropped at 62 Street.
Free zinnia seeds put in mail box of Act III.
Small original James Waring left in wooden milk carton in front of Horn and Hardart.
Wadsworth Atheneum dance announcement posted to Waring.
Also post card of Empire State Building.

You might classify the string of little actualities that Johnson reports on to Waring under the heading of correspondence art, even if only some items end up in mailboxes, and still fewer are sent through the post. Or, given that the artist is addressing his choreographer friend, you might think of it as a performance, albeit in the absence of an audience, at least one that conceives itself as such (surely the pigeons looked up, if only for a second). (Johnson to Lippold, December 1957: **Merce's concert last night. I was so impressed by the complete devotion to dance of himself and his dancers that it didn't really matter if there was an audience there because they were so beyond mere entertainment.**) You might even find yourself tempted to label Johnson's topographical scatter of objects a collage, although this would require you to grant "collage" a sense, and a spatial field, expanded to the breaking point.

"Both artists come out of the collage tradition but both have expanded it drastically." A funny thing, in one sense, to say about crafters of intimacies like Johnson and Cornell, so committed to working on a shrunken scale, while knowing that placing limits on the scale at which they worked virtually guaranteed their reputations would remain similarly limited. A Klee or a Morandi may astonish us every now and then, but the law of the Salon, go big or go home, seems to find new applications for every generation of visual artists.

And yet, when Ray Johnson emerged, blinking, from his rabbit hole of a **Correspondance situation** in the mid-1960s, he was indeed reborn as an expansive artist, expansive in more than one sense, although never in a sense that would fully reveal itself to the naked eye. His art expands only under analysis, like a dream, and then only if one permits oneself to enter into the dreamer's mood. His art is message, image, and performance all at once. As in a dream, the various levels of expression combine to form a single dynamic structure.

> The different portions of this complicated structure stand, of course, in the most manifold logical relations to one another. They can represent foreground and background, digressions and illustrations, conditions, chains of evidence and counter-arguments. When the whole mass of these dream-thoughts is brought under the pressure of the dream-work, and its elements are turned about, broken into fragments and jammed together—almost like pack-ice—the question arises of what happens to the logical connections which have hitherto formed its framework.

The dream, like the collage, traffics in second-hand materials that have been "broken into fragments and jammed together." The verbal and visual grammars that govern our daylight way of making sense lose their force; "the logical connections which have hitherto formed its framework"—this then that, this because that—give way to the riskier logics of juxtaposition and association. The interpreter of dreams learns to leapfrog from fragment to fragment, to follow phantom trails that spiral down into obscurity.

The dream, unlike the collage, is fluid and fleeting. Reach for it and it dissolves like ice in the grasping hand.

The dream, like dance, is fluid and fleeting. The dream is a dance for an audience of one.

IX

On April 22, 1964, Ray Johnson drafted a letter to Jill Johnston, dance critic of the *Village Voice*, of which he then made several different copies, a sign that its message was meant for more eyes than just hers. The letter centers on Johnston's own dancing.

Jill,

Your dance last night at Andy Warhol's party was one of the very best dance [*sic*] **I have ever seen. How very brilliant to incorporate the foil-covered pipe over the juke box. You must have spent your child-hood hanging on jungle jims.**

You did a very beautiful thing. I am glad you didn't fall or the pipes didn't. I'm glad you didn't fall on your head or cut yourself.

It was breathtaking [...] **Thank you, Jill, for what I thought would not allow me to sleep last night it was so frightening to see you dangle from that pipe but I did sleep and you did hang and I was impressed.**

Johnston (**my sister Jill**, Johnson called her in one mailing, in reference to their kindred surnames) was an unorthodox critic who had turned her *Voice* column into "a forum," as she said, "for covering or perpetrating all manner of outrage," although, as Johnson's letter to her suggests, her style of outrage, much like his, had a charming tinge of childlike naïveté. Johnson's fellow faux-naïf Andy Warhol, also charmed by Johnston, showcased her in two early films, *Jill and Freddy Dancing* (1963) and *Jill Johnston Dancing* (1964). In *Jill and Freddy*, made soon after Warhol acquired his first Bolex camera, Johnston and Fred Herko improvise together on a rooftop. At first, Warhol keeps them both in frame but then gets fascinated by Johnston's wild parody of the kind of balletic grace the princely Herko effortlessly embodies and leaves him behind to track her as she ping-pongs from corner to corner. By the time he made his second film with Johnston, Warhol knew to have more reels on hand. Set loose in the Factory, newly silvered edge to edge with paint and foil by Ray's old friend Billy Name, Johnston uses every object in her path—a moving-dolly, a rug, a mop and bucket, a banana, cans of paint—to bring the space to hectic life. In the film's last shot, Jill shimmies up the bathroom doorway and Billy's spotlight bouncing off the silver, silver everywhere haloes her in a blaze of glory.

We know that Johnson witnessed the filming of *Jill Johnston Dancing* because Billy Name photographed him there just then, standing by Warhol's side, sporting a (short-lived) beard. But Ray does not write to Jill about the dance preserved on film, he writes to her about a dance no one will ever see again. He writes to her about it as if she had performed it for him alone. The dance persists for him as an afterimage, a night thought teetering on an edge between the kind of dream that makes you want to go on sleeping and the kind of nightmare that jerks you awake. **You did a very beautiful thing.** But what makes it so beautiful is also what makes it so frightening, the risks she takes, the potential for disaster. **I am glad you didn't fall or the pipes**

didn't. I'm glad you didn't fall on your head or cut yourself.

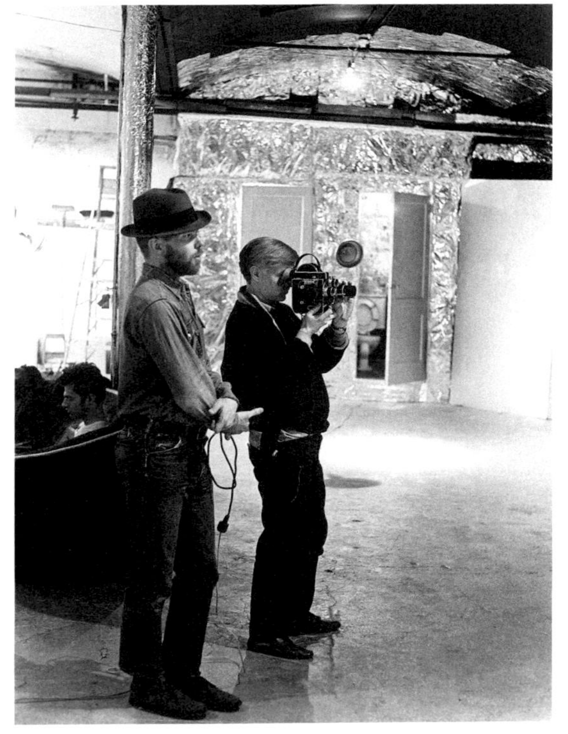

Billy Name, "Andy Warhol filming *Jill Johnston Dancing*" (1964).

Glad, or disappointed? Jill made admiring reference to Ray in her *Voice* columns, ending one eye-rolling account of an evening at the Harkness Ballet ("Wonder if there's any grafitti in the lady's room") with a vow to "submit a petition for Ray Johnson to give the world its next 'Firebird'." But when interviewed about their relationship shortly after his death, she said, "I didn't correspond with Ray because he scared me. I found him kind of intense." Johnston first met Johnson, she recalled then, at "a Fluxus-type performance" where "he was running around outside the audience with Albert Fine. Just running around and creating his own event." "A kind of ecstatic joke," the interviewer suggested. "I don't know that it was ecstatic," Johnston replied, "It was disruptive. One noticed."

By the mid-1970s, Jill Johnston had transferred her energies from art to politics and re-made her name as the author of *Lesbian Nation: The Feminist Solution*. **I am glad you didn't fall or the pipes didn't.** Eventually, though, something had to give. Johnson and Warhol were both drawn to Johnston's exuberant sexual line-crossing, the way her dancing set girlish grace against boyish daring to simultaneously celebratory and subversive effect. But neither man would follow her into the streets when the time came. Each tried to keep the wilder currents of the time contained within his own art, with mixed success.

X

"Bang!" went the little gun that Dorothy Podber pulled from her purse with a gloved hand one fall day in 1964, shortly after she had walked into the Factory, having asked first if she could shoot some pictures, by which it was thought she meant, naturally, with a camera. The bullet went into the collective foreheads of four freshly silkscreened *Marilyns* stacked neatly against the wall, to be known ever after as the *Shot Marilyns*. In 1989, the red *Shot Marilyn* set a record price at auction for Warhol's work, a record that was topped in 1998 in the sale of the orange version, which was again shattered in 2022, when *Shot Sage Blue Marilyn* went for $195 million, the highest auction price paid to date for any twentieth century artwork. A touch of violence makes the art world sit up. Warhol's immediate response to the shooting, though, was to try to repair the canvases as best he could and to ban Podber from the premises for life. "She's too scary," he said.

Podber was, others said, "a witch," "a terrorist," "a marvelous, evil woman," "the wildest, most way-out, extraordinary creature who ever walked the earth." She handed out methamphetamines to her friends like candy and ran an illegal abortion referral service as well as a business cleaning doctor's offices that doubled as a drug theft ring. Podber was kept by a banker and a corrupt politician before falling for one Lester Schwartz, a magnetic stevedore who had previously portioned his favors between Ray's friends Julian Beck and Judith Malina, the couple who ran the Living Theater. For a few years in the mid-1950s, Podber codirected the Nonagon Gallery on East 6th Street, famous for its jazz nights, on one of which Charles Mingus recorded his celebrated *Jazz Portraits: Mingus in Wonderland*. Before the *Marilyns* incident, though, Dorothy Podber was best known on the downtown scene as Ray Johnson's partner in crime.

Like the *Marilyns* incident (for which Ray either was or wasn't present, depending upon whom you ask), Podber and Johnson's joint offenses might be classed as art crimes, mere performances. Even so, they were performances calculated to make their audiences cringe, gag, startle. The two might barge into your apartment, for instance, and start playing the recordings of stutterers made by speech therapists that Johnson had found on one of his garbage-can treasure hunts. They might hand you a gift package that when opened would disclose a decomposing rat or raccoon, should you have been so unlucky as to encounter them during what they proudly referred to as their "dead animal phase." Or you might, if you were a collector, be invited to a showing of work at Johnson's studio only to find the space completely empty, and as you looked around, puzzled, suddenly see Podber burst out of a closet, laughing demonically.

Whisperings about the pair's antics made the rounds, forming part of Ray Johnson's peculiar early fame. At least some readers of the *Village Voice* thus may have been expected to get the joke when Johnson paid to place an image of a rat with his name spread across its side amid the gallery announcements in March 1966. This was Johnson's second advertisement-for-nothing; the first, published two years earlier in the same paper, featured a drawing of a snake commissioned from Karl Wirsum, an image that Ray would immediately recycle into his ongoing **BOOK ABOUT DEATH**.

In his *Voice* ads, Johnson deftly mocked the relentlessly dull visual template and mercenary grind of conventional art-world advertising while registering his continuing uneasiness with the whole gallery scene. The ads were versions of Johnson's signature dance, running around outside the audience, just running around and creating his own event. Which is not to say that Ray Johnson had his relation to his audience entirely under control.

XI

A mailing without an addressee.

> **Another dream 1.17.67**
> **The room I live in has two windows. They are frosted white. I cannot see out and no one can see in.**
> **In my dream I discover from across the way that one can see in from a distance. That surprises me very much.**
> **I wake up. The windows are opaque and I cannot see out**

XII

Suddenly, if you wanted to see a lot of Ray Johnson collages all in one place, you no longer had to be one of those clued-in collectors or curators waiting for him to show up with **a box of collages wrapped in newspaper under my arm, like a Fuller Brush man**. That kind of tightly controlled way of showing his work **pleases me**, the artist insisted to Grace Glueck in 1965. But by the end of 1966, Johnson had had his second solo exhibition at Willard in the spring and his first solo exhibition at Richard Feigen's gallery in Chicago in the fall and had works featured in two major museum shows, including one—at last—at the Museum of Modern Art in New York. And he was, despite all misgivings, pleased. **Suzi sent the Dore Ashton kind words from London and Pink Above was reproduced next to a Cornell and I am so very happy,** Ray let Richard know in October in a note that ended with a loving **Sleepy head it was nice to talk to you on the telephone last night murky moon** and a grinning snake in place of a signature.

Also in 1966, Johnson received an award for painting from the National Institute of Arts and Letters that came with a grant of $2,500, an amount equal to seven years of his rent on Suffolk Street. At the awards ceremony, Johnson took the chance to speak with an attendant member of the Institute, the great modernist Marianne Moore, whom he had been trying to draw into his circle of correspondents for over a decade. Johnson's initial interest in the poet seems to have been sparked by his Black Mountain friend Frances Profumo, a poet herself, whose family knew Moore.

galleries galleries galleri

Recent Paintings
MARCH AVERY
April 1st thru April 17th
WAVERLY GALLERY
103 WAVERLY PLACE, N.Y.C.

leonard March22-Apr. 16
baskin
drawings & sculpture
BORGENICHT 1018 madison

NELL
BLAINE
Recent
Painting
from
St. Lucia
and England
opening April 5
POINDEXTER
21 W 56

PHOTOGRAPHS
NICHOLAS DEAN
APRIL 3-29
HICKS STREET GALLERY
BROOKLYN HEIGHTS

SOCIAL PROTEST
DOOMSHOW
COLLAGE PAINTINGS
STANLEY FISHER
OPENS APRIL 1 8 PM
STRYKE GALLERY
86 E 10 ST.

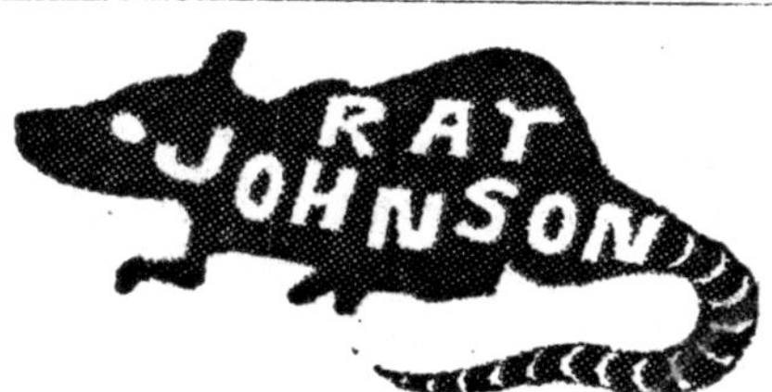

Ray Johnson, advertisement in the *Village Voice*, March 31, 1966.

PHILLIP KING
SCULPTURE
Opening Wed. 5-7 PM Apr. 6
RICHARD FEIGEN
GALLERY • 24 E. 81, N.Y.C.

John *thru April 13*
LANGFORD
PAINTINGS
De Mena Gallery
453 E. 88 (nr. York) SA 2-3527

MARZELL
APRIL 1-22
ASPECTS • 100 E. 10 ST.

Korn

ROSA

WILLIAM
McI
new p
Champ
Pou

M
PERID

ORIG
Remarkab
C
1046 Madis
COA
969 3rd Av.
Both Galle
Both Ga

HEN
me
C
Narrator
Th
B
Sa

galleries galleries galleries galleries

58e79

REXLER

AR 6 - APR 4
UGH
d scrolls
ll Gallery
ege,
N. Y.

A.
ER
dison (68)

thru Apr. 17
GRAPHS
From $15 up
ERY
.) 10 am-7pm
ALLERY
M to Midnight
on. Thru Sun.
On Sundays.

OORE:
form
IAL
Collingwood
House
St.
ights
9 PM
on

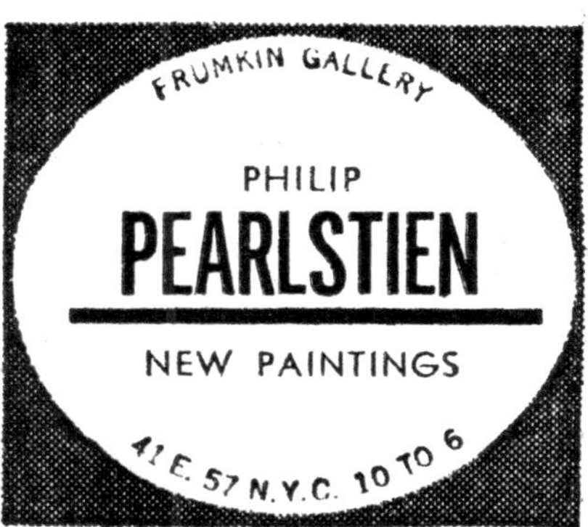

POSTMA
NICHOLS
HERDMAN

Paintings

Opening: Apr. 1 thru Apr. 17
Thurs.-Sun., 1-6:30 pm
JUDSON GALLERY 239 Thompson St.

NOW THRU APRIL 6

RED WHI-TE BLUE

BEUKENKAMP	KENDALL
DOWLING	MENEELEY
FRANKENTHALER	PRENTICE
GOODNOUGH	RIVERS
GREENSTEIN	SHAW
INDIANA	VANDERBURG

AT FREDERICK TEUSCHER 53 W 83

873 6036

MARY STEELE PAINTINGS

OPENING FRI., APR. 1, 8-10 PM
TUES.-SUN. 12-5:30 THRU APR. 21
BRATA GALLERY
56 THIRD AVENUE

GAMES WITHOUT RULES
IN COLLABORATION WITH
NICOLAS CALAS

MAR 29 — AP. 16
FISCHBACH
799 MADISON

TOM DOYLE

DWAN • 29 W 57

Ray's post-college letters to Frances are full of Mooreiana—clippings, copied-out poems, collages, a report on a reading—and in 1953, he managed, with his friend's help, to inveigle Moore into visiting his Dover Street studio. Unfortunately for Ray, the sixty-five-year-old Moore was just then at the outset of a period in which she unexpectedly found herself a sought-after public figure, having long been famous among poetry insiders but unknown elsewhere. Deluged by obligations, she had little time for new acolytes. Moore's responses to Johnson's further attempts at contact through the mail and once, at a party at their mutual friend Charles Henri Ford's, were polite but perfunctory and came to a definitive end in 1967 with a two-sentence note: "Thank you very much Mr. Johnson, but I am compressing myself rather than expanding. Don't be disappointed, I do have to be a hermit."

Ray was disappointed. But he was also more interested than ever in the vagaries of fame, and he knew that Moore's late-life fame derived not so much from her poems as from her appearances in magazines and on television and on the streets of New York in her perennial black broadcloth cape and George Washington tricorne hat, cutting a figure at once reassuringly old-fashioned and disturbingly androgynous. Like Johnson, that is, Moore became a walking advertisement for her art, although, in her case as in his, the performance also threatened to distract the audience from the art as art.

Not long after his encounter with Moore at the awards ceremony, Johnson abstracted her tricorne hat into a stylized silhouette and appropriated the image for his own use. He began a series of exhibition collages that centered on the hat icon. Four of them would hang in *Art in Process: The Visual Development of a Collage*, the 1967 show at Finch College Museum of Art whose curator, Elayne Varian, had written to ask Johnson about his involvement in the making of the show's centerpiece, Robert Rauschenberg's *Short Circuit*, and received the mystifying yet revealing reply in which he denied remembering being asked by Rauschenberg to contribute to the combine but did recall visiting Rauschenberg and his former wife Sue Weil at Weil's parents' house. **I carried a book on Taoism and quoted lines to them about emptiness and nothing. Years later the house burned.**

"Some say the world will end in fire / Some say in ice," wrote the aptly named Robert Frost.

Art in Process was the first of three significant group exhibitions to include Johnson's work in 1967, alongside another pair of solo shows at Willard and at Feigen. A letter written in February of that year to his friend Soren Agenoux begins with gloomy Ray repeating his complaint about having been labeled "New Talent" by *Art in America* back in 1962, then all at once his mood brightens and he relays the news of the upcoming shows at Willard and Finch and the Lil Picard piece featuring **My death notice a la Wanda Gag**. Johnson's pivot here from shadow to sunshine turns on a coded phrase that will recur in other mailings and images. **Soren, the Fire has melted the Ice and there is a flow of water**.

In his poem, Frost equates ice with hate and fire with desire. Johnson fuses the two urges, Freudian-style, in a spare, sharp tesserae-piece from 1966 titled *IRE*, the word inked at the center of the picture in subtly striated block letters. A blood-red crescent pendant from the "R" just barely suggests a "C" concealed beneath that, should it emerge, would turn IRE into ICE. Below the word is a pyramid of frozen flame and above it, a tile-on-tile picture-in-picture murmuring its message from the past to those who care. Come here, says the picture, I want you here. Stay away, says the word, I can't tell hate from love, **damn them. Why can't I be a good boy?**

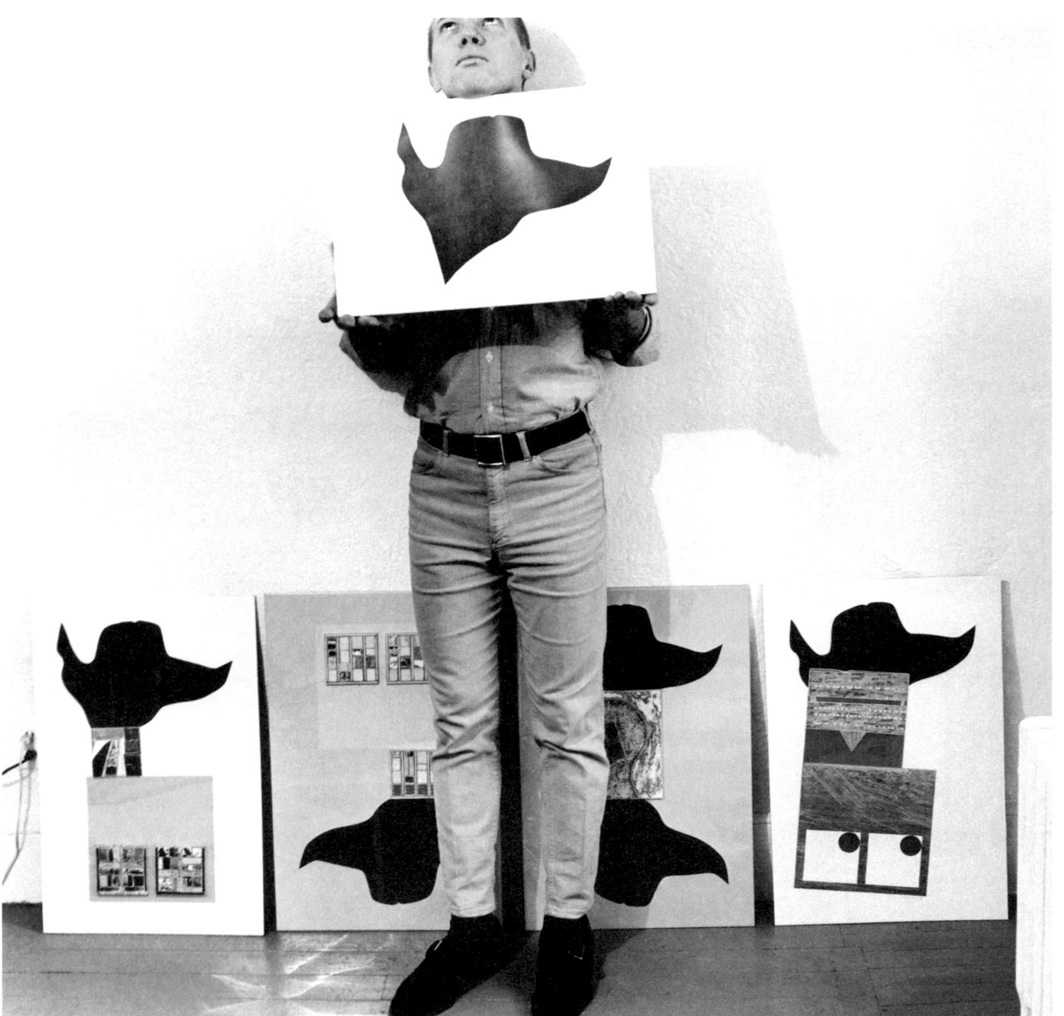

Ray Johnson with Marianne Moore hat collages, 1967, photograph by William S. Wilson.

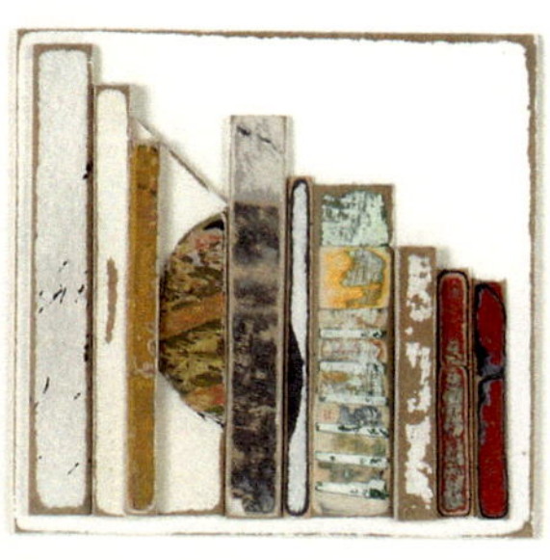

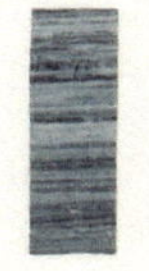

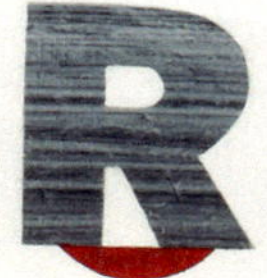

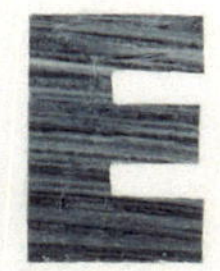

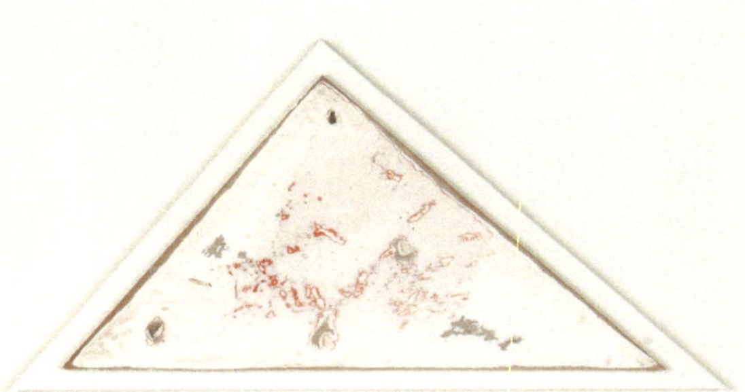

Ray Johnson, *IRE* (1966).

XIII

And the white space in which the tiles and lettering float, what does it say? So much white space, as much like a page as a canvas, yet neither page nor canvas.

Collagists, like all collectors, are prone to *horror vacui*, the dread that drives them to cram every available inch with stuff. But the sine qua non of collage is white space, not so much a medium as an element, like fire or water, the matrix where image and word meet and merge. "The book, as a total expansion of the letter, must directly take on the letter's mobility, opening a space for the invention, via correspondence, of a game, as yet unknown, which may sustain the fiction," proclaimed Stephane Mallarmé, who first made the page visible as white space through the unfolding of his lyric riddle, "Un coup de dés jamais n'abolira le hazard" (A throw of dice will never abolish chance).

By "fiction," Mallarmé means not "page-turning story in which you can lose yourself" but a piece of artifice that makes you conscious of its material existence even as it takes its distance from the rest of the material world. His pathbreaking picture-poem was not a collage but it was in the air when Braque and Picasso invented collage as a fictional form and the magpie Picasso picked up Mallarmé's visualized page and found a rhyme for it in the painterly realm. Lest we miss the connection, the painter spells it out in one collage in black and white. For "un coup de dés," he gives us the cut-up phrase "un coup de thé" ("théâtre," halved) on a newspaper scrap slotted into a penciled armature that recedes and advances as the white space that floats it solidifies and dissolves, like a sheet of ice.

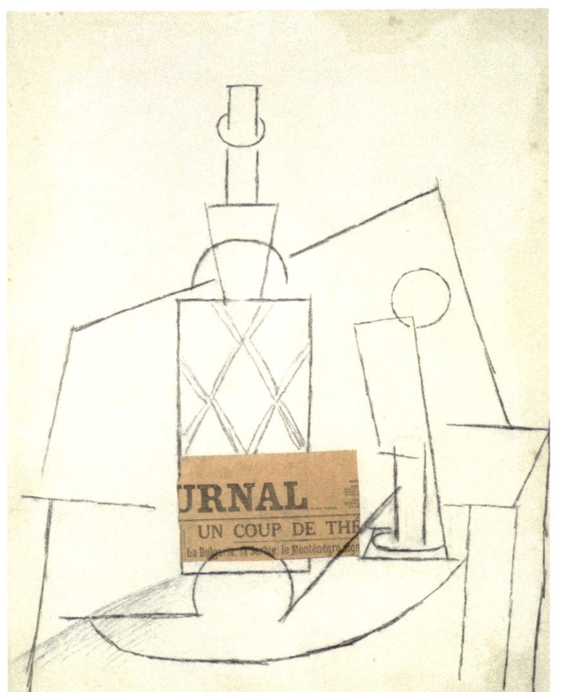

Pablo Picasso, *Bottle, Glass, & Wine Bottle on a Table* (1912).

Although Johnson had shown a facility for collage since his time at Black Mountain, he seems not to have grasped the meaning of white space, that is, the meaning it had for him, until that crucial period between 1964 and 1966. The ground in his early exhibition collages was usually washed with color and/or paved with strips; the moticos, too, were given color washes and/or filled edge to edge with image-fragments. His official compositions were still held together by painterly means. But the fragments that tumbled out of the envelopes that had begun to make their way through the correspondence network were scotchedtaped together here and there but otherwise loose, like **what you have in a kaleidoscope**. When Mallarmé spoke of "a total expansion of the letter," he was not, of course, referring to postal correspondence. Yet Johnson was like Mallarmé insofar as he conceived of the alphabetic letter as at once a transmitter and a blocker of meanings, a thought and a thing. And Johnson's **BOOK ABOUT DEATH**, that strange fusion of collage, correspondence, and graphic design, was nothing if not an effort mobilize the page, to launch it into space as the opening move in a previously unknown game.

Johnson's letters succeeded where his *BOOK* failed. As he worked through the implications of the **Correspondance situation**, he found the open space he needed on the streets punctuated by trash cans and mail boxes, on the surfaces where correspondents spread the contents of their envelopes, and finally, most precariously, on the walls where his tiles played out their chamber dramas frame by frame. *Un coup de théâtre*: "a sudden or sensational turn in a play," **simply give it one slight turn and you have a complete change of pattern and reflection of light and color. The fire has melted the ice and there is a flow of water**. A throw of dice will never abolish chance.

XIV

The sole artwork in Johnson's first show at Willard that bore a date of 1964, was a white monochrome suspended, as the works to come would be, between painting and collage. Johnson titled it *Balshazzar's Feast*, after a museum label that curator Sam Wagstaff had sent to him, having filched it from the frame that once held an oil sketch for a British academic painting from 1821, which depicted an episode from the Old Testament Book of Daniel. The sketch remains in the collection of the Wadsworth Atheneum, where Wagstaff then worked.

Johnson affixed the label to his own picture's frame as an inside joke, or rather, a joke inside a joke, addressed to an audience of one. For *Balshazzar's Feast* had originally started off as a portrait of Wagstaff that Johnson titled "Dimple," after one of the movie-star-handsome curator's striking features. In a letter to Wagstaff dated December 8, 1963, Johnson writes that he has finished the portrait, which measures six feet long by two feet wide and **is all white except for the dimple which is a black**

shape 6 ½ inches at the top area of the drawing which being inked runs down the surface to the bottom. I would like for you to see the drawing soon, he added, which Wagstaff did, only to receive another letter from his portraitist on December 28 proposing to **add a second black shape in the top area exactly like the first but of course it would create a different situation than the original situation**. A series of missives followed recording Johnson's next moves in the game: **Today I turned "Dimple" upside down**; **Today I hung "Dimple" in my john**; and finally, inevitably, **Last night I hit "Dimple" with a hammer and destroyed it.** The play of gestures that displaced the portrait can be traced nonetheless in *Balshazzar's Feast*, which is constructed entirely from pieces of "Dimple"'s frame, its mute surface punctuated only by the plaque transferred from another frame by Johnson via Wagstaff.

Is it still a portrait of the curator? It speaks of curatorial concerns: the frame, the label with its tombstone birth and death dates flanking the name of the once celebrated, now forgotten artist. Johnson refers to it as **The "Balshazzar's Feast" aspect of my portrait of you** in a letter to Wagstaff from December 1964. But the change of title registers a shift in Johnson's focus. In the story of King Belshazzar ("Balshazzar" is the label-maker's spelling), the ruler's decadent fête is interrupted by the appearance of a disembodied hand that "wrote over against the candlestick upon the plaster of the wall of the king's palace." Wise men are summoned, "but they could not read the writing, nor make known to the king the interpretation thereof," necessitating a visit from Daniel, famous for his "interpreting of dreams, and declaring of riddles, and loosing of knots." The letters, the riddler Daniel says, spell the ruler's doom. "God hath numbered thy kingdom, and brought it to an end." Hence our expression, "the writing on the wall."

The wall presents a problem to the writer of enigmatic letters. If he hangs them there for anyone to see, he risks baffling and terrifying, or worse, non-plussing, his audience. Something tells him, nonetheless, that the message must be delivered on schedule. *Balshazzar's Feast* marks the pivotal moment after which Ray Johnson would begin, for the first time, to leave visible significant swathes of the white paperboard support onto which the collage elements are affixed. He began to recognize that the support does more than support, that it is a dynamic element in itself, like the tiles, at once independent of the other elements and interactive with them, mobile in stillness. The white space signified for him a breathing space in which he need not choose, or might at least defer choosing, between competing modes of presentation: visual and verbal, vertical and horizontal, public and private. The artist has walled off the scene of discovery using the whitened slats of the frame. **The room I live in has two windows. They are frosted white. I cannot see out and no one can see in.** No one can, and yet, one can. **In my dream I discover from across the way that one can see in from a distance. That surprises me very much.** Although if, from a distance, one could see the writing on the wall, one might still have to ask the riddler Ray for his interpretation. And he might be as surprised as anyone to find himself saying, as Daniel did to Belshazzar, it is time for a new regime.

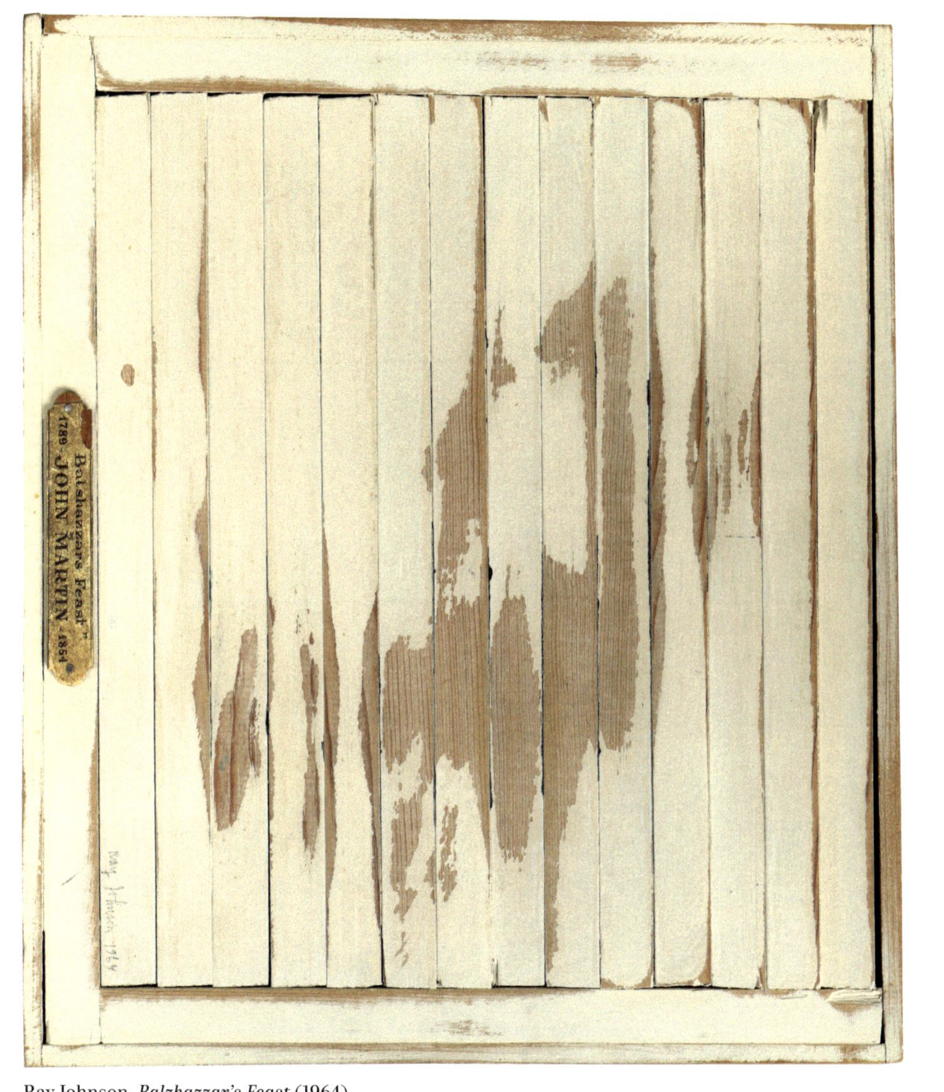

Ray Johnson, *Balzhazzar's Feast* (1964).

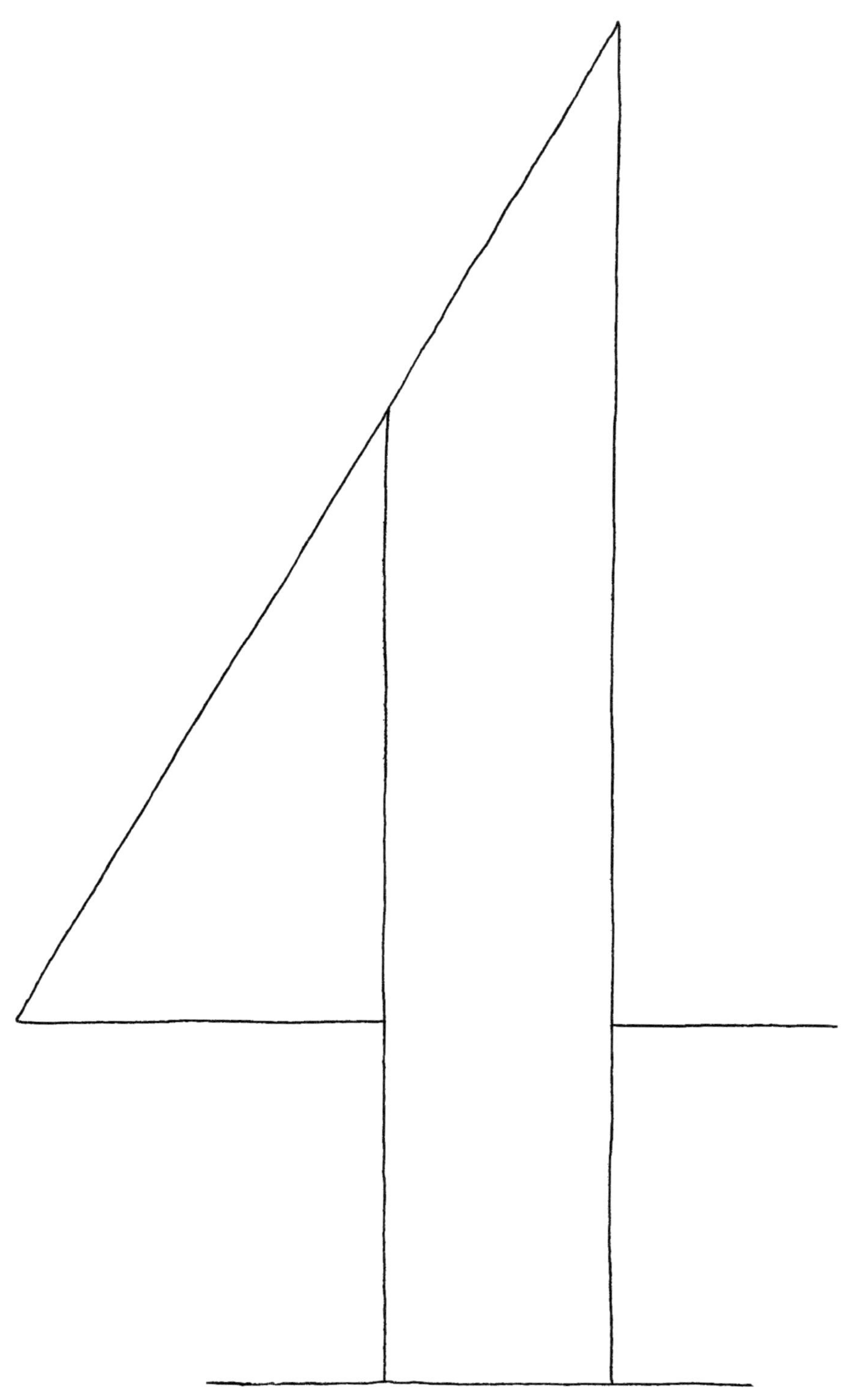

1963–1968

FAME AS A FORM OF ART, FAME AS A FORM OF DEATH

I

Philip Leider, the founding editor of *Artforum*, began corresponding with Ray Johnson in 1964 at the instigation of Johnson's critic friend, David Bourdonand in 1967 finally published their triangulated exchanges in the magazine. In one missive, Johnson takes a jab at the *New York Times*' Hilton Kramer, who had given his second show at Willard an exceptionally nasty pan. **Golly gee, I wonder if Milton Kramer is going to say something nice about me soon, gosh I just don't know what he will think (gush!) he SAID IN PRINT! that Paul Klee just wasn't one of the "greats."** As evidence, perhaps, that at least some people count *him* as **one of the "greats,"** Johnson adds a postscript alerting Leider that **I have asked Richard C of Johnson City Fan Club**—a mail artist and devoted Ray follower, who really did live in Johnson City—**to give you a blast.**

Leider knows how the game is played.

Gee, Ray, how can you think it would matter to *any* of us girls here at the Ray Johnson Fan Club of Sin City *what* Nickie Hilton thinks about a guy like you? We wouldn't care what he said, even in print, even on the whole front page of the *NEW YORK TIMES*. In our hearts you're the best!

Do you really think we here at RJFCSC can't see that all he's trying to do is make a rep for himself by putting down Cassius Klee? Why before you came along we had a great picture of a little tinker toy and swore allegiance every single morning to the CKFCSC.

Sue-Ann X

The art world is like junior high school, Leider implies, when it is not like the most brutal of boxing matches. (By the time these letters were sent, champion of the ring Cassius Clay had changed his name to Muhammad Ali and was in the news for his refusal to fight in Vietnam.) Leider's little satire also airs what was by then an open secret, that Johnson's correspondents were as much like fans as they were like friends. Johnson was a cult figure—one almost wants to say he was born that way—and the New York Correspondence School lent form and meaning to the cult. Leider indicates his interest in this meaning without venturing a guess as to its nature. But he makes clear his distaste for the who's in, who's out game of "the greats," a feeling Johnson seems to bring into focus, although the editor already had his doubts. In 1970, Leider went on a speed-fueled walkabout to the Southwestern desert with Richard Serra, memorialized the trip in a gonzo-style "goodbye essay," quit the magazine, and took his distance from the New York art world.

II

Bill Wilson took the notion of the Ray-cult as seriously as anyone could, while keeping in mind that taking Ray seriously was a risky business. In 1963, Bill christened the collection of Johnsonalia he had been amassing since he and Ray met "The Archives of the New York Correspondence School" and sent an official AOTNYCS questionnaire around the Johnson friend-fan circuit. The first part of the questionnaire contained general requests for information and materials; the second part was fill-in-the-blank. The participants seem to have enjoyed the blank-filling—a sampling of whimsical, poetic responses from Carolee Schneemann (1963 was the year of her genre-shattering *Eye Body: 36 Transformative Actions for Camera*) may be taken as representative.

I walked about the city one night with Ray Johnson and saw ________
refuse, recollection, carpets, wish bones,

and did keep walking and kneeling down,,

and left him carrying a tomatoe.

Ray Johnson mailed to me messages, images poems, terrors.

Ray Johnson left in my mailbox an oversized glove.

The most significant or insignificant mailing I ever received from

Ray Johnson was black and white.

Through Ray Johnson I met an uncertain beast.

But the questionnaire's implicit demand that respondents take the Ray-business as seriously as Bill did met with resistance, as seen in the form of the grammar-school gold star that Schneemann pasted in place of the requested "Critical exegesis of Ray Johnson's work."

The questionnaires soon fell out of circulation. The responsibility for producing the sort of critical exegesis of Ray Johnson's work that Wilson believed it deserved would fall to Wilson himself, a responsibility not to be laid down until he himself was. Bill was a born exegete, and the Book of Ray offered him the prospect of a fathomless supply of beautiful puzzles.

A pair of Johnson mailings from 1963 may be read, through the occlusions of Ray's usual ambiguity and ambivalence, as thank-you notes for Bill's activities on his behalf. The first, sent in February, contains a piece of found correspondence, a category of scrap avidly collected by Johnson for enclosure in his mail packets. The ink stamp at the top of the sheet identifies it as issuing from "The LARRY CARINGI Fan Club." It is addressed, in a round, childish hand, to Irene Selznick, the daughter of Louis B. Mayer and onetime wife of David O. Selznick, both legendary Hollywood producers, who was herself at the time of this letter's composition a recently retired producer of Broadway plays.

Dear Miss Selznick,

This is Susan May, Larry Caringi's president. I guess you have heard about Larry's great movie called The Victors. I'm hoping that you will help Larry in any way you can. I'm sure that Larry will appreciate any help you can give him. Remember we want to thank you for your help and kindness.

As always,

Pres. Susan May

Below May's signature, Ray, who never could resist a play on names, has typed instructions to **Please send to** his fan and Bill's mother, **May Wilson**. And who was Larry Caringi? Hard to say, given that he appeared in a minor role in just one film, the aforementioned *Victors*, a star-studded box office failure released in 1963. The letter, in other words, is addressed to someone adjacent to power on the behalf of someone adjacent to stardom by a fan who styles herself president of her fugitive organization. Is this the most that can be hoped for from the fledgling AOTNYCS?

The second mailing, from July, conveys a sweeter, simpler message. The envelope addressed to Ann and Bill has been sent, says the return address, by **A fan.** The assembly depicted in the enclosed photo, too, consists only of fans, a portrait of the NYCS as a mutual admiration society.

III

Bill and Ray met in 1956. That year, sociologists Donald Horton and R. Richard Wohl published a paper titled "Mass Communication and Para-Social Interaction: Observations on Intimacy at a Distance." Their argument, much-cited in the subsequent literature, centers on the advent of what they identify as a new genre in the relatively new medium of television, which they term the "personality program." We know it as the talk show and are by now familiar with its most salient feature, the "host," a performer whose direct address to the audience creates, say Horton and Wohl, an unprecedented "illusion of intimacy." By comparison with the exoticized Hollywood stars who preceded them, television's domesticated host-personae seem to betoken a closing of the distance between star and fan.

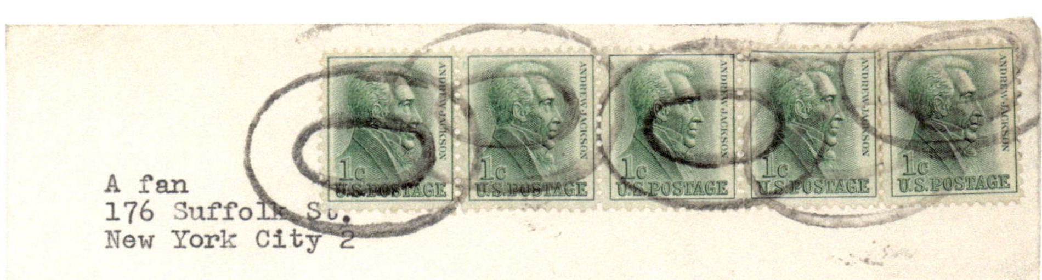

A fan
176 Suffolk St.
New York City 2

Anne & Bill Wilson
458 West 25 St.
New York City, N.Y.

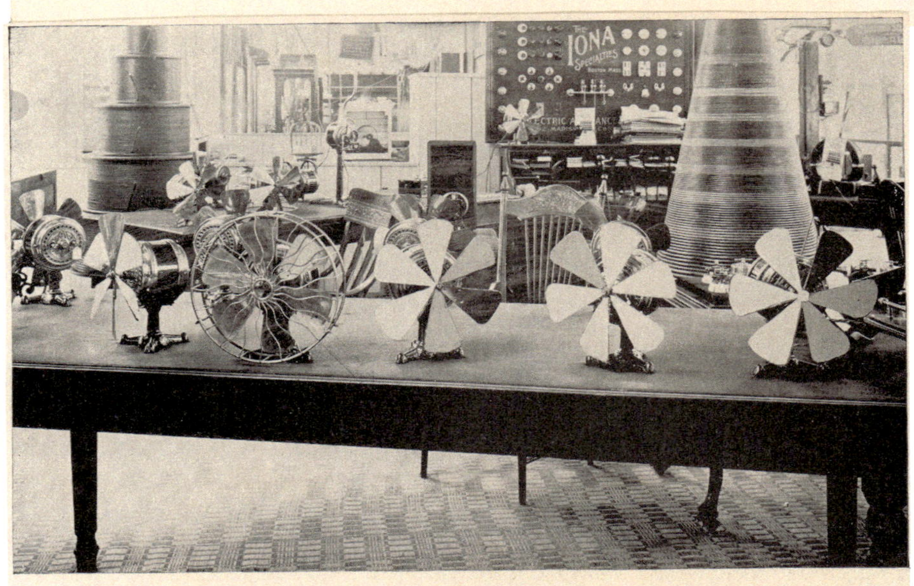

ELECTRIC FANS

Ray Johnson to Ann and Bill Wilson, July 21, 1963.

> The persona offers, above all, a continuing relationship. His appearance is a regular and dependable event, to be counted on, planned for, and integrated into the routines of daily life. His devotees "live with him." [...] Indeed, their continued association with him acquires a history, and the accumulation of shared past experiences gives additional meaning to the present performance. This bond is symbolized by allusions that lack meaning for the casual observer and appear occult to the outsider. In time, the devotee—the "fan"—comes to believe that he "knows" the persona more intimately and profoundly than others do; that he "understands" his character and appreciates his values and motives.

The more time and exegetical energy the fan devotes to his chosen figure, the more persuaded he is that the distance between them may be closed. However, since, as Horton and Wohl remind us, "the one-sided nature of the connection precludes a progressive and mutual reformulation of its values and aims," in fact the intimacy the devotee longs for must forever remain out of reach.

When the lopsided relationships of the parasocial realm fail to satisfy, what is one to do? Every now and then, driven mad by frustration, the fan may give in to the frankly antisocial urge to smash the screen, reach through and touch the star. As the movies keep reminding us, this story cannot end well. Ray Johnson became a fan of the cultish comedian Sandra Bernhard after he saw her on a talk show promoting Martin Scorsese's 1982 film *The King of Comedy*, a classic instance of the fans-gone-rogue genre, in which Bernhard plays a lost soul who helps to kidnap the talk show host with whom she is obsessed. Johnson, a man of multiple obsessions, could sympathize; he was always trying to get his idols to join his game. Some, like Joseph Cornell, might be induced to play along, but when others, like Marianne Moore, chose to keep their distance, it could take some time before Ray would accept no for an answer. He wasn't dangerous but his persistence could be unsettling.

Unsettling and unsettled, unsettling because unsettled. Johnson understood from within the fan's need for intimacy, but caught in an unceasing oscillation between the roles of cultist and cult object, he also felt the star's need for privacy. Meanwhile, the rules of celebrity culture require that the conflicting needs of star and fan alike remain unmet. Nonetheless, say Horton and Wohl, the fan may still eke out some compensation for his devotion to the media personality, to the extent that their (admittedly one-sided) relationship presents the devotee with "opportunities for the playing of roles to which the spectator has—or feels he has—a legitimate claim, but for which he finds no opportunity in his social environment."

Imagine you are a medievalist with a Yale degree who would rather die than live out your days in some peaceful college town. You meet this guy, this creature, for whom life is an unending performance yet who can play no role other than that of his authentic self. Should this personality address you, and you respond to his address, you could find yourself drawn into his otherworld, which turns out to be connected to your world by a magic portal that proves surprisingly easy to access. His appearance in your world will become a regular and dependable event, to be counted on, planned for, and integrated into the routines of daily life. And the routines of daily life will thus be transformed.

IV

"And what I assume you shall assume/ For every atom belonging to me as good belongs to you," Walt Whitman tells us, from his side of the portal. Even the least skeptical of readers has wondered at some point, Is this to be believed?

To correspond with Ray Johnson was to assume the role of artist. Through the two-way portal of the mails, one could actually make contact with the NYCS network's host, albeit at a distance, and through such touching-at-a-distance, take on some of his power—a power that was, however, exceptionally frangible. "LA STAR QUI NE SE PREND PAS POUR UNE STAR," reads an early-sixties scrap Ray sent to Bill: the star who doesn't think she is a star. One had to remember that Ray-world wasn't *the* world, that the host's radiance fades at the network's edge.

The art world isn't *the* world, either, although it sometimes acts as if it thinks it is. The serenely skeptical Marcel Duchamp devised one marvelous test after another to see just how small a gesture it might take to annex that world's power to confer the name of artist. In the process, he underscored that power's contingent quality, its way of being there and not there, like the "50 cc. of Paris air" supposedly enclosed in a druggist's glass ampoule so labeled by the artist. The ampoule's organic silhouette, a swelling volume culminating in a swan's-neck-hook and water-drip-tip, would be added by Johnson in the early 1970s to the store of malleable motifs out of which he built a private sign-language. But Johnson had had this vial and its labeler on the brain at least since 1963, when he addressed a puckish query to David Bourdon.

LA STAR
QUI NE
SE PREND PAS
POUR
UNE STAR

Ray Johnson to William S. Wilson, n.d.

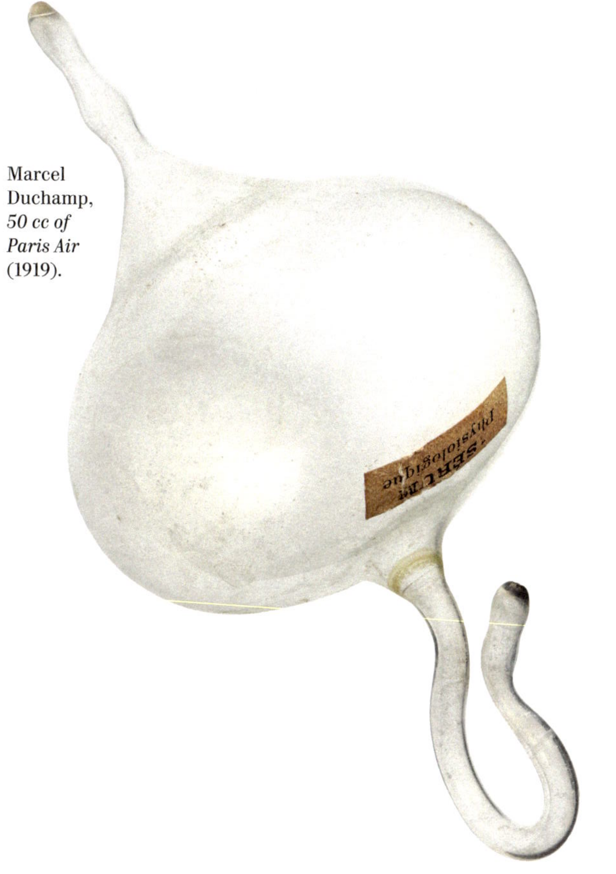

Marcel Duchamp, *50 cc of Paris Air* (1919).

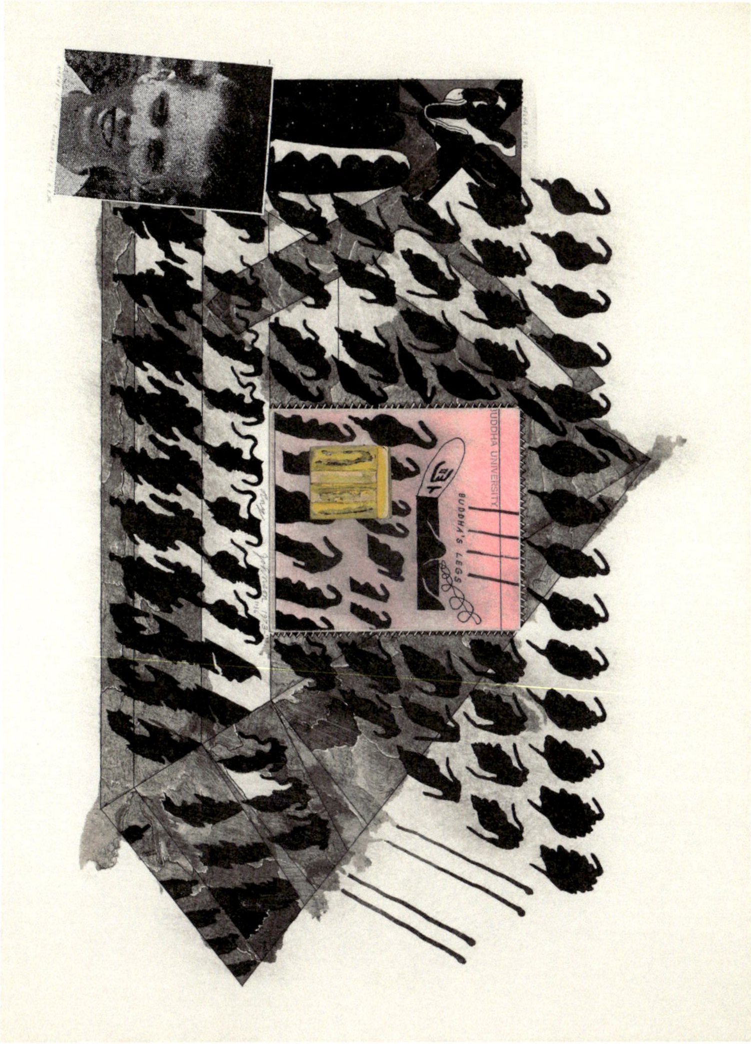

Ray Johnson, *Buddha's Legs* (1973).

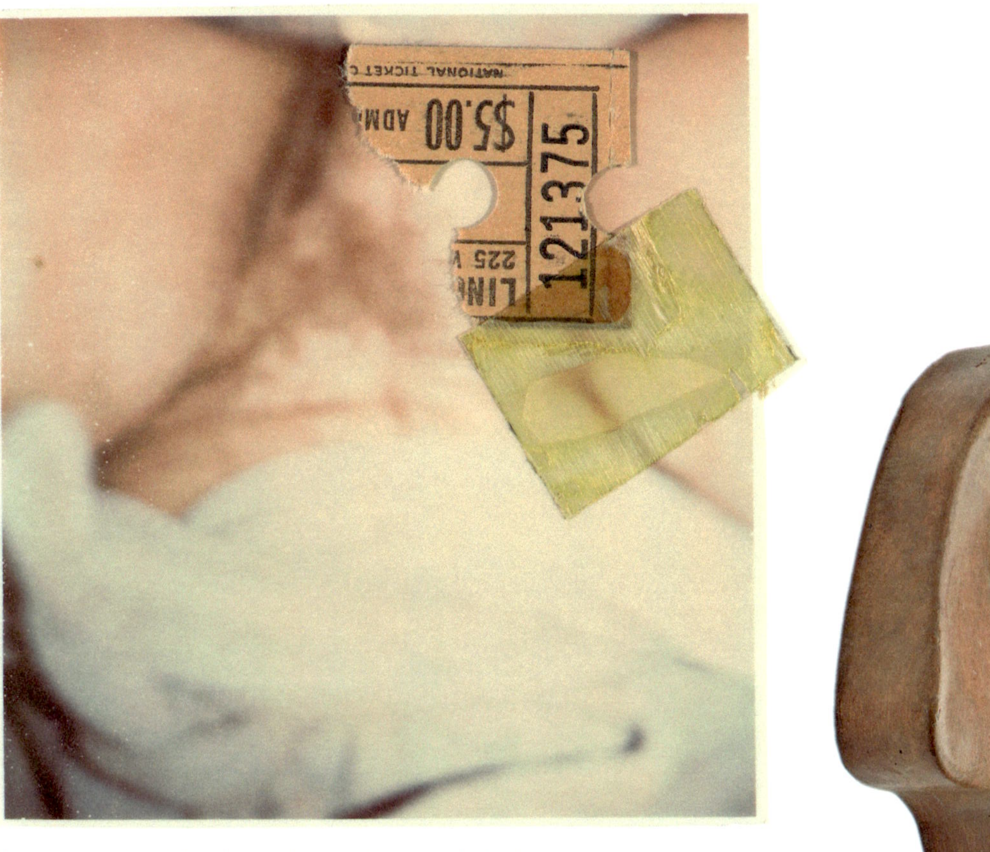

Ray Johnson to David Bourdon, mailing dated February 26, 1963.

Marcel Duchamp, *Female Fig Leaf* (1950/61).

I am trying to find information about Duchamp's object 'Hair de Paris', the flask filled with Paris hair, 1919. Is that in the Philly collection? I wonder what Duchamp meant in Show magazine when he said "Can't you just smell the stench in the hair?"

A riddle: How did hair get into Duchamp's "Air"? By way of answer, Johnson has affixed to the page a scrap-on-scrap collage that matches a punched ticket corner with a photo of a woman's crotch, two found echoes of a less ethereal Duchamp piece, *Female Fig Leaf*, a life-cast of a vulval notch. The *Fig Leaf* made its New York debut at the Rose Fried Gallery in 1953, but it would be another ten years before its next US appearance, in the epoch-making Duchamp retrospective at the Pasadena Museum of Art. This exhibition, the first full-scale survey of the artist's work by an American museum, was the most ambitious of a series of events marking the fiftieth anniversary of Duchamp's sensational entry onto the American scene via the 1913 Armory Show, where his *Nude Descending a Staircase* became that event's great *succès de scandale*. Johnson cites "Duchamp: Fifty Years Later," an interview with the artist in the February 1963 issue of *Show* magazine, in his letter to Bourdon, one of a cluster of mailings from that year that refract this Duchampian history through a Johnsonian prism.

Karl Wirsum, for instance, received a snack-cake souvenir card bearing instructions on how to perform The Great Marvelmo's "'Sinking-Rising Egg' Trick" to which Johnson taped a magazine clip describing Duchamp's *Nude Descending* as "the Helen of Troy of modern art—it launched a thousand quips and caused a furor when it won first prize, hanging upside down at the controversial Armory Show in 1913."

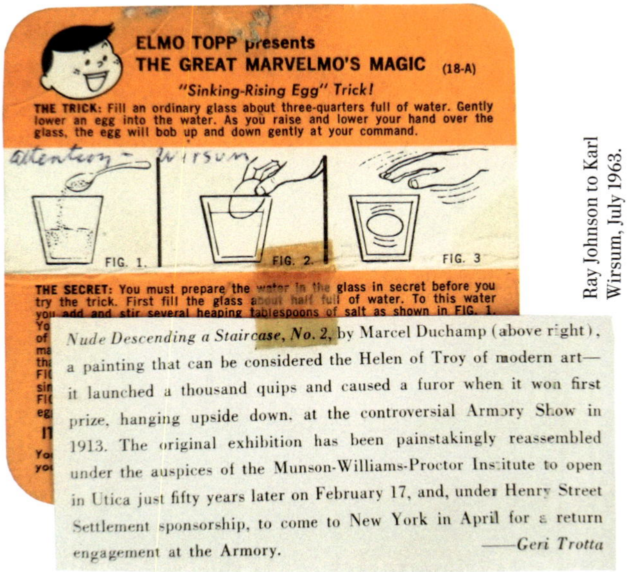

Ray Johnson to Karl Wirsum, July 1963.

"IT'S STRANGE, BUT THERE'S SOMETHING ABOUT IT THAT I LIKE—" says the viewer of "Nude Descending a Fire Escape" in another clip. Beauty is in the eye of the beholder, who is learning to like to be outraged and amused.

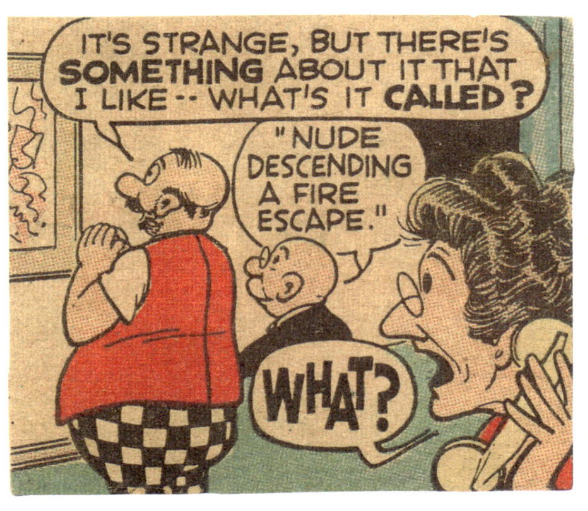

Ray Johnson to William S. Wilson, 1963.

The *Nude Descending* cartoon was part of a packet sent to Bill Wilson that also included a cut-out of a Yale lock (Bill's badge of honor, Bill's stigma) and an anagram scramble in Ray's hand, at once desultory and pointed—**TAR TEAR STAR TEA RST ART EAR**—with the pasted-on rubric, "BAD TASTE." In 1961, Marcel Duchamp, his star once again on the rise, gave a lecture at MoMA in which he explained that his choice of everyday objects for the artworks known as Readymades had been "based on a reaction of *visual* indifference with at the same time a total absence of good or bad taste ... in fact a complete anaesthesia." Was this to be believed?

V

A society column in the October 21, 1967 *Chicago Daily News* devoted to the goings-on at the opening of "Pictures to Be Read, Poetry to Be Seen," the inaugural exhibition of Chicago's Museum of Contemporary Art, was accompanied by a photo with the caption, "Mrs. Claes Oldenburg (left) in a see-through minidress and Toby Spiselman were getting as much attention as the art. Toby was wearing the art, too. Artist Ray Johnson attached a dead woodpecker to a wooden square for Toby to wear." Spiselman's demure glance deflects attention even as her dress attracts it, ever the star who doesn't think she is a star.

The MCA's founding director, Jan Van Der Marck, had chosen ten collages in Johnson's new style to hang in the show, including *ICE*, the Wanda Gag memorial, and two variations on the theme of Marcel Duchamp's "Comb," a "rectified" readymade from 1916—the rectification consisting of words neatly inscribed along the comb's edge. A letter from Van Der Marck to Johnson, sent in the run-up to the opening of *Pictures to Be Read*, indicates that Johnson had requested that the curator purchase five hundred plastic combs of a certain make, which Van Der Marck was having trouble locating, although he was willing, he said, to keep looking. The curator was all in on the Duchampian game, having staked his fledgling institution's reputation to a show that took its inspiration, as he wrote in the catalogue's introduction, from the artist's "Large Glass." Hewing close to Duchamp's rebarbative edge, Van Der Marck steered

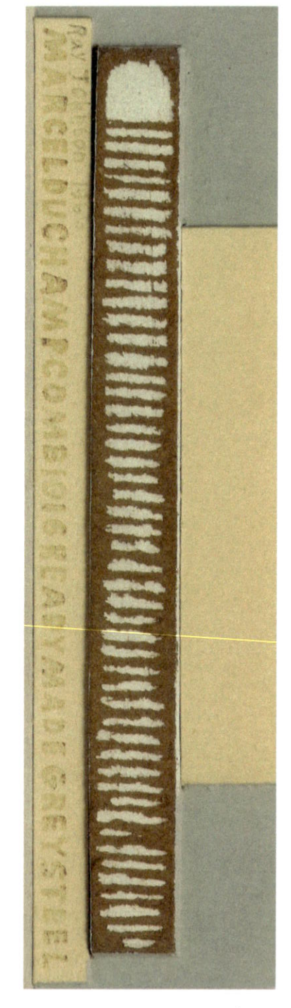

Ray Johnson, *Stele* (1966/67), detail, with lettering: “MARCELDUCHAMPCOM-B1916READYMADEGREY-STEEL.”

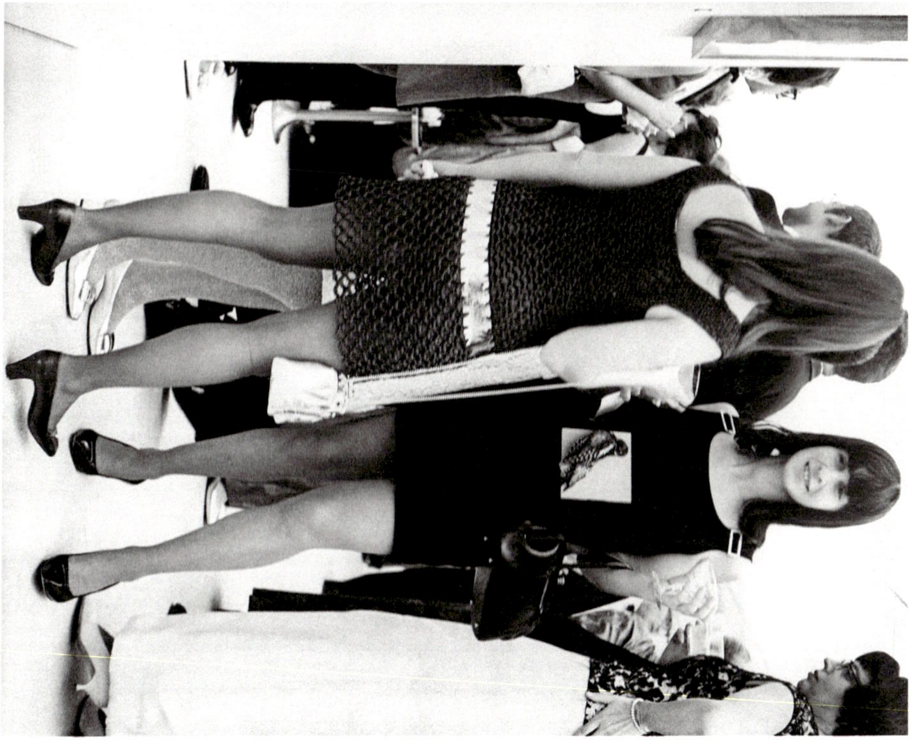

Toby Spiselman at the opening of “Pictures to Be Read, Poetry to Be Seen” with woodpecker on board by Ray Johnson, October 21, 1967.

clear of market-friendly heirs to the mantle like Johns, Rauschenberg, and Warhol, choosing instead to show a group of under-knowns: Shusaku Arakawa, Gianfranco Baruchello, Mary Bauermeister, George Brecht, Oyvind Fahlström, Johnson, Allan Kaprow, R. B. Kitaj, Alison Knowles, Jim Nutt, Gianni-Emilio Simonetti, and Wolf Vostell.

Critic Harold Rosenberg covered *Pictures to Be Read* for the *New Yorker*, where he describes it as "explicitly dedicated in the Duchamp–Cage tradition of reaching away from art towards things and symbols that happen to fall within the artist's field of vision." True enough. But Rosenberg had made his name championing the vigorous strain of abstraction he called "action painting," and he remained wary of what he saw as the come-what-may attitude shared by many of the show's artists, with their Happenings and aleatory assemblages. The critic names Johnson, "known for the charming paper cut-outs he sends through the mails," as one of several assemblagists who "give the impression of being so totally immersed in art that it doesn't matter whether they make it or find it." Rosenberg was the sort to admire, even envy, those who live "immersed in art." But he also worries that artists who equate finding with making have taken a wrong turn in pursuit of "an impossible ideal, the dream of a world in which all actions are intended to be forgotten in the moment of their fulfillment"—a world, that is, without art as this critic knows it.

Rosenberg views art that blurs the distinction between making and finding somewhat differently in "Collage: Philosophy of Put-Togethers," an essay published in 1975, eight years after the Chicago show. There, he suggests that "the mingling of object and image in collage, of given fact and conscious artifice," has an important role to play insofar as it "corresponds to the illusion-producing processes of contemporary civilization." For like collage, "twentieth century fictions"—Rosenberg's charged examples are "documents waved at hearings by Joseph McCarthy" and Stalin's appropriation of Lenin's corpse—"are rarely made up out of whole cloth, perhaps because the public has been trained to have faith in 'information.'" In its blurring of fact and fiction, collage thus bears the at once dubious and real distinction of encapsulating "the primary formula of the aesthetics of mystification of our time." Collage mimics the patchwork veil drawn over the workings of inhuman power and, in so doing, brings home to art "the absurdity of representing things and images in a universe of forces and energies."

In 1967, Rosenberg may have dismissed the artworks at the MCA as mere "projections of ideas," utterly "without scale, sensuous appeal or passion," the qualities he had learned to love in the paintings of Pollock, de Kooning, & Co. But by 1975, he seems to have come to terms, not without regret and by his own route, with the historical inevitability of the turn toward "the Duchamp-Cage tradition." As Rosenberg saw, the Duchampian turn augured, first, the ascendance of art that seeks to channel dematerialized forces and energies and, second, the concomitant pathos of art that remains stubbornly attached to things and images.

What kind of art did Ray Johnson make? The first kind; also, the second kind.

VI

Dear Harold,

Anything anyone would say I would chop up and do something else with it so if something is something else to begin with

(space)

Ray Johnson opens the second of two letters he sent to Harold Rosenberg shortly after *the New Yorker* printed the review of *Pictures to Be Read/ Poetry to Be Seen* with this pictorial-poetic distillation of the essential elements of his art: the constant chopping and recycling of materials; the commutable relation of word and image; and, last but not least, **(space)**, nothing in itself and yet the without-which-nothing catalyst of unstoppable movement and change.

The first of Johnson's two letters to Rosenberg opens with a complaint. In the review, the critic had truncated the title of one collage, *His art looks old timey eccentric and Chinese-modern to me today. William T. Wiley 1967*, which was, the artist grants, an exceptionally long title, but still, **I would be upset if my woodpecker had been called a pecker.** (Rosenberg and Johnson had crossed paths at the MCA opening, where Ray's bird, on Toby's dress, was a *succès de scandale*.) More caveats follow. The artist chastises the critic for referring to the collage as a "box," a genre Rosenberg associates in the review with Johnson's beloved Cornell. **My collage-paintings**—Johnson's preferred term for his exhibition works—are, he explains, **planned** not for the Cornellian shadowbox **but for the "frame" with the background spaces following the old and beautiful proportions. Ha ha**, Ray seems to feel compelled to add (ever the jester), only to go back to explaining, in all earnestness,

> **Yes, I am known at this time for my past mailings but never never never for my "paper cutouts". Anything I may have cut out is probably scotch-taped or glued to a background and rubber-stamped "collage by Ray Johnson", solidly affirming what it is.**

This is not quite true, as Johnson must know, and Rosenberg suggests as much in his reply. "I seemed to remember the moticos as pictures of cut-outs, or maybe I had in mind the things we reproduced in location." (Three years before, Rosenberg, then co-editor of *Location*, had published Suzi Gablik's piece on Johnson and the moticos.) "That's what you get for affecting people's imaginations—they get even by imagining things," the critic chaffs, tactfully allowing the artist an out, without quite letting him off the hook. However, Rosenberg goes on to say, taking Johnson up on the tacit invitation to engage, "I won't go along with you on the boxes. A frame is a species of box. ... If it surrounds an absolutely flat image, like a tape around a banknote, or even a border, it would be wrong to call it a box. But a house can be 'framed' between two hills or it can be boxed between two hills."

Johnson's response to Rosenberg's critique is characteristically indirect, involving a twisty story about the placement of two postage stamps **in one of those damn moticos I make**, but it ends with a sincere expression of gratitude for **your kind letter** and is signed, **Seriously**. It was a moment when the artist needed to be taken, and to take himself, seriously, to believe that the art-problems he was struggling with were serious problems; hard for anyone, but exceptionally hard for an artist like Johnson, for whom the jester's mask was not just a protective shell, but integral to the practice of his art.

VII

It was a moment. Johnson's move into gallery and museum exhibition in 1965 changed the whole equation of his art. One bit of finicky phrasing in the first letter to Rosenberg—**I am known at this time for my past mailings**—seems meant, for instance, as a nudge to the critic to shift his attention from the mail art to the exhibition work. Then there is the artist's somewhat puzzling objection to Rosenberg's reference to his "charming paper cutouts." Of course, Johnson knew that affixing cut-out materials to a surface at once does and does not transform them from something found into something made. He knew, as well as Picasso or Ernst or Schwitters, that collage thrives on the tension between the found and the made, "the mingling of object and image," "of given fact and conscious artifice." But found material does function differently in Johnson's mail art than it does in his exhibition pieces, and in the exchange with Rosenberg we catch him in the process of registering this difference.

When he first began using the **collage by Ray Johnson** stamp, in 1961, Johnson was still mailing out **those damn moticos**, frameable fusions of collage, painting, and drawing, along with loose scraps and more casual constructions. Within a few years, though, the division had widened between

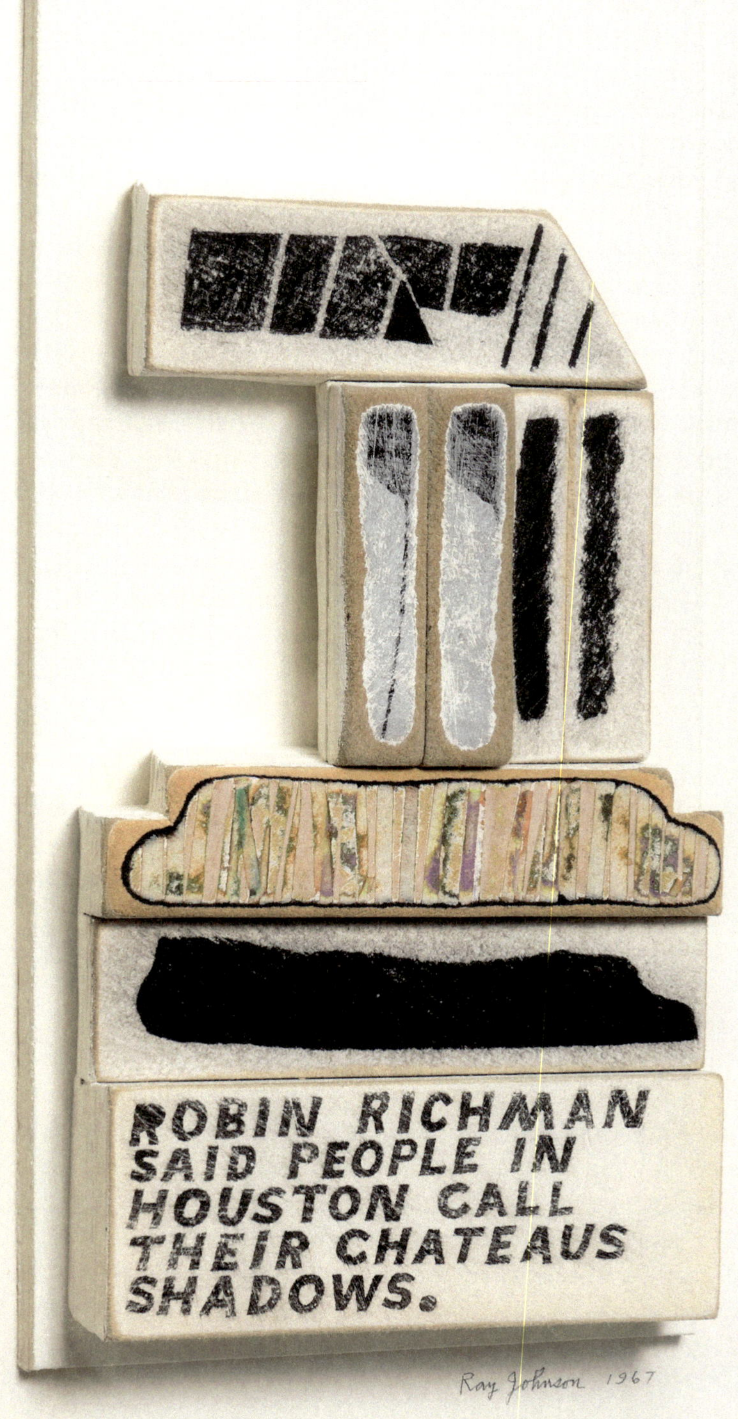

Ray Johnson, *Chateaus Shadows* (1967).

work **planned for the "frame"** and work destined for the envelope. As minimally crafted scrap-on-scrap pieces began to fill the mail packets, the **collage by Ray Johnson** imprimatur honed its message. "This is art," the stamp now said, in an unmistakably Duchampian tone, "because, and only because, I say so."

At the same time, Johnson began to build his exhibition work around the tesserae, fragments of larger works generated within the studio itself. The tesserae are in a sense found objects, and the parent blocks that they were cut from often incorporated materials found outside the studio. But the tiles always have a painterly look, the look of the studio. They *look* made, not found.

From a distance, the tesserae look like little paintings, but from up close one can see that they are three-dimensional, more like little sculptures. Or to be more precise, since their backs are flat against the support surface, the tiles are bas-relief, occupying neither the quasi-real space of sculpture nor the fully imaginary space of painting. Rosenberg associates Johnson's bas-reliefs with Cornell's shadowboxes because they both stake out a kind, if not quite the same kind, of in-between space. Johnson maps his territory in a 1967 collage in which a multicolored tile-cloud casts a (real) shadow on its own painted shadow, which hovers above a plaque that says **ROBIN RICHMAN SAID PEOPLE IN HOUSTON CALL THEIR CHATEAUS SHADOWS.**

How real is a Texan *chateau*? How unreal is a shadow that appears and disappears as the viewer moves and the light changes? What to call Ray Johnson's medium? **It is interesting,** Johnson writes in 1971 to Richard Feigen & Co.'s gallery manager Lotte Drew-Bear (yes, what a name!), regarding works from his recent show there, **that you refer to "Jacqueline Kennedy," "Sure Too," "Nina" and "Henry Fonda Foot" as "drawings" in your August 11th letter since the Feigen/Chicago identification labels on the back of the "two returned to me" (I would call them paintings although Harold Rose**

[Johnson leaves a space here]

enberg in the New Yorker called them "boxes") identify "Nina" and "Henry Fonda Foot" as "collages."

I would call them paintings, but not everyone would. Johnson knows, for instance, that if you are a museum curator and you want to get a collage from storage, you go to look for it not among the paintings or sculptures but in the Department of Drawings and Prints. For the curator, the distinction between drawing and painting is a matter of support surface, paper vs. canvas. Johnson knows, too, that the Department of Drawings and Prints is the red-headed stepchild of the institution, perpetually overshadowed by its golden sibling, Painting.

"The work strikes the eye immediately as very accomplished, finished, framed in wood and glass, no loose ends. R.J. is a poet-painter. To what extent collage is like poetry, collage gets like literature in that it must be read, scrutinized, collage is small on/with paper." So begins a review in *Arts* magazine of Johnson's solo show at Willard Gallery in 1967 that Ray's friend Toby Spiselman spotted before Ray did and sent on to him.

Johnson's reply suggests that he was a bit overwhelmed by the reviewer's praise. **Got your envelope with the review in it and am quickly trying to write down what I think and feel (like WOW).** With Toby, Ray let down the mask, knowing that she would think as he thought, feel as he felt. She would understand why it takes him half a page before he even gets to the review, why he first has to tell her that he **thought I would see Blow-Up again and duplicate the clothes the hero wears**, that he **Read about M. Moore in Times last night and wrote her a letter I will probably not mail**, and that he has **been thinking for days of taking one of your xerox and glue** [*sic*] **to thick cardboard relief and it being a Ray Johnson made of your images but my bit would be the shadows and the relief and the build-up.** The implication being that they are in this together.

It feels good to be called a poet-painter, he finally says. It feels good even if it means making the kind of art that is "small on/with paper," that is thereby also, as the reviewer says, "intimate, must be seen up close for a long time, demands attention"—neither the kind of art that evinces the "visual indifference" professed by the true-blue Duchampian nor the kind that museum curators tend to build their displays around.

But in the "small on/with paper" world he shares with Toby, Ray plays the hero, the radiant center of the story. In one letter to him, she retypes the definition "in my dictionary" of the "ray flower. Also ray floret," a "marginal" species of the flower genus aster, from the Greek for "star." "Aster" is also, she adds, a biological term for "a star-shaped figure of achromatic substance" with "radiating fibers called the aster rays."

What I assume you shall assume. If he is a star-shaped figure, so must she be.

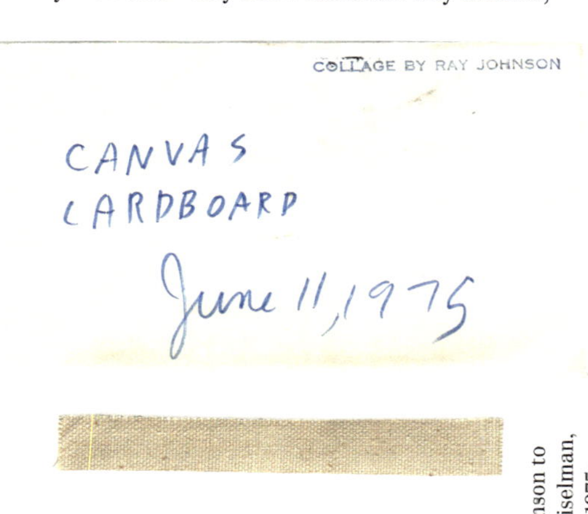

Ray Johnson to Toby Spiselman, June 11, 1975; envelope and enclosures.

IX

Two hands veil the face in Johnson's *Duchamp with Star-Haircut*, the downstage hand of the poser in a photograph affixed to a large square tile, and the offstage hand of the artist, ch-ch-ch-ing away at the tile with his sandpaper. They are meant to remind us of the two hands that frame the face of Marcel Duchamp in a portrait of the artist as his feminine alter ego, Rrose Sélavy, hands that belonged not to the artist but to a female friend. We are also meant to think of another Duchamp portrait, of the artist with his hair shaved in the shape of a shooting star, an effect Johnson reproduced by having his friend Toby Spiselman don his own watch cap, accessorized for the occasion with a toy sheriff's badge.

Duchamp's friend and frequent collaborator Man Ray took the Rrose Sélavy photo and may have taken the star-tonsure one as well. Johnson, knowing this, emphasizes the photographer's role, writing "Photo Joe Filzen" signature-style under the portrait of Toby-as-Duchamp, in letters slightly larger than—and parallel to—his own signature. Filzen was not, as it happens, one of Johnson's many friend-collaborators. But he did take a striking picture of Ray's face, partly concealed by Ray's hand, curved in and be-ringed, Sélavy-style. Filzen's photo first appeared on the poster-announcement for Johnson's 1968 solo exhibition at Richard Feigen's gallery in New York (where he had recently expanded from Chicago) and was subsequently, inevitably, taken up by Johnson to be copied, chopped, and fed into his endless flow of images.

The Feigen show opened two days before an event for which Johnson had great hopes. **The N.Y.C.S. is planning a big April 1 "Meeting" with a cast of thousands**, he informed Lotte Drew-Bear in February 1968. **It will not be a party or a happening but I hope expressive of a "new form."** In May, he sent an official report to Jan Van Der Marck.

The New York Correspondence School held its first Meeting April 1st [April Fools, a sacred day for jester Ray] **at the Religious Society of Friends Meeting House in New York City (built in 1890 same year Mark Tobey was born). I felt it was a great success bringing the public the private letter-writer world**.

By all accounts, nothing much happened at this first *Meeting* beyond some milling and peacocking around and this, it seems, was the point. A Meeting was a Nothing "with a cast of thousands," every one a star, but with just one host: "R.J. in white, white ... ringed by people, by snakes ... the master puppeteer ... no strings," according to notes taken by one participant just after the fifth Meeting, in September 1968.

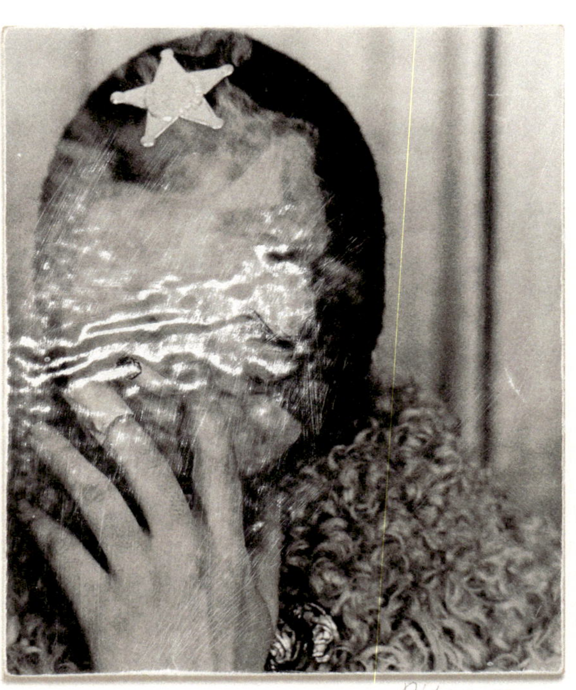

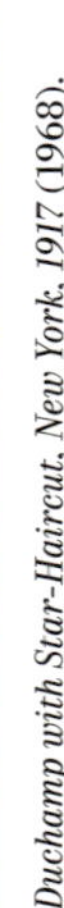
Ray Johnson, *Duchamp with Star-Haircut, New York, 1917* (1968).

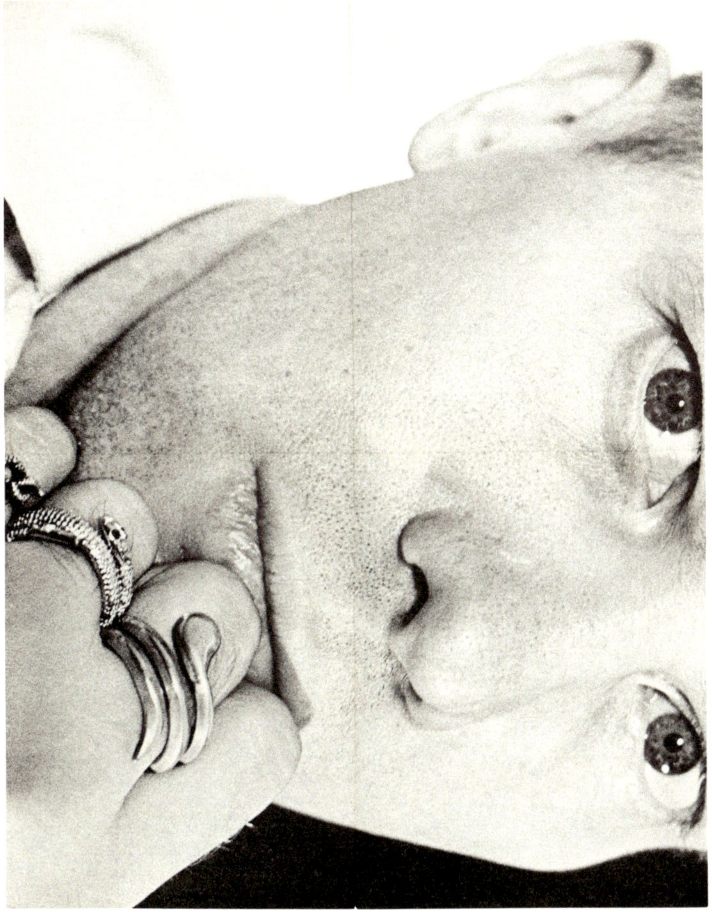

Joe Filzen, *Ray Johnson* (1968).

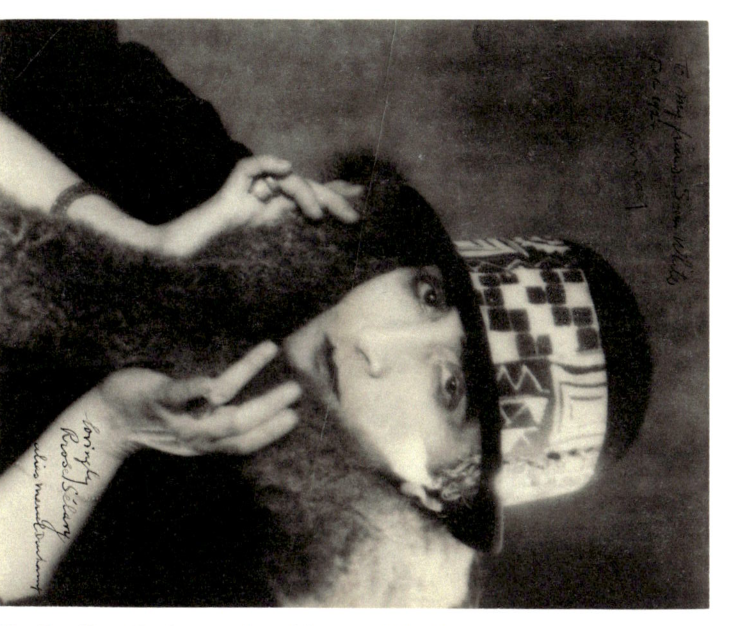

Man Ray, *Marcel Duchamp as Rrose Sélavy* (ca. 1920–21).

A Meeting was **not**, Johnson insisted again in a letter to poet Jackson Mac Low, **a party or a "happening" to meet say how do you do all other actions words ideas depends on who is or isn't there**. It was a networking event, in other words, in a peculiarly strict sense, made up of **actions words ideas depends on who is or isn't there**, assembled with perfect indifference to aesthetic form. The idea being, as Johnson explained to Van Der Marck, to turn **the private letter-writer world** inside out, to make manifest the branching forces and energies implicit in each intimate exchange between one correspondent and another.

Johnson was excited about the possibilities inherent in his "new form," too excited for once to play the jester. He gives Van Der Marck the details regarding two more Meetings scheduled in June (he would hold seven altogether that first year), then sketches the big picture.

Our secretary Toby Spiselman, an IBM mathematician, had contacted IBM about our meetings. They are interested. Tomorrow she goes to the United Nations to discuss an international Meeting. We met with Hannelore Hahn last Saturday, who works for Mr. Hoving [Thomas Hoving, director of the Metropolitan Museum of Art] **and discussed New York City Meetings so you see we are going in every direction. Our idea is to hold these meetings gratis but eventually to be sponsored by organizations to pay for postage, mailings to be designed by N.Y.C.S. members and let us use their buildings to meet and "do our thing."**

Spiselman features in this story, as the public-facing member of Johnson's corporate "we." This is the story behind *Duchamp with Star-Haircut*, a portrait of a friendship in the process of becoming an institution. It is a two-faced portrait, at once public and private, female and male, the face effaced by hands we can and cannot see.

X

Toby Spiselman was indeed a mathematical researcher at IBM who was working toward a PhD in mathematics from Yale when she met Bill Wilson who was also getting his degree and who introduced her to Ray in the summer of 1959. Toby was there at the beginning, a charter member of the innermost inner circle of friend-fans, and she would be there at the end, the only one of that original circle who would maintain real intimacy with the ever-more-elusive Ray. She was the one who would bury Ray's ashes.

In the first years of their friendship, though, Toby was just one of a set of female co-conspirators constellated around Ray. The feral, flamboyant ones, like Dorothy Podber and May Wilson, tended to eclipse the mild-mannered wits like Spiselman and Marie Tavroges (first secretary of the NYCS, so dubbed for her willingness to send out Ray-mail at the expense of her employer, the Juilliard School). But as much as Ray needed someone like Dorothy, he needed someone like Toby still more.

Ray Johnson the cult figure, the Ray of the zillion Ray-stories, was, as Billy Name once quipped, a "living sculpture, you know. He was Ray Johnson's creation." Name went so far as to say that "Ray wasn't a person," unlike Andy Warhol, who was still at least somewhat "like a person." Name had glimpsed, he thought, a private Warhol who differed from the public version, while Johnson's persona was of one impenetrable piece. Was this to be believed? The consensus among those I have spoken to about Ray Johnson is that "No one really knew him" although some have felt compelled to add, "except Bill, maybe? Or Toby. Or, I don't know, Richard Lippold." If you care about someone, it is painful to think that they may have lived without ever experiencing real intimacy. In that spirit, I would say, yes, Toby. And for a time, Richard Lippold. (Neither of whom I spoke to. And Bill said he never really knew Ray, no one did.)

Ray was a person, but a person who lived for art to a point where he convinced others, and perhaps at times even convinced himself, that any aspect of his life that could not be assimilated into his art should not be considered part of the Ray Johnson Story. One might think that such a sacrifice of life to art would hollow out the artist's privacy, leaving only the public shell. And yet Johnson's art was an art of intimacy, a kind of art that requires you to draw close, then closer still, to see what he means for you to see. A dance for an audience of one.

Toby was that one. She was, of all his cast of thousands, the one star who truly didn't think she was a star. She was the one who lived for Ray, so that he could live for art.

Oc tobe r 16,
1967

Dear Ray,
This is some of my blood for
your Birthday. It was taken
from my left arm today. It
might solve the bed bug problem.
Before you goto sleep pour
the blood on the floor. Then
when you turn on the lights
and all the little bed bugs
wake up they will dring the
blood instead of biting you.
If it works I will give you
some blood every day for the
rest of my life. Happy Birthday
I love you. *Toby*

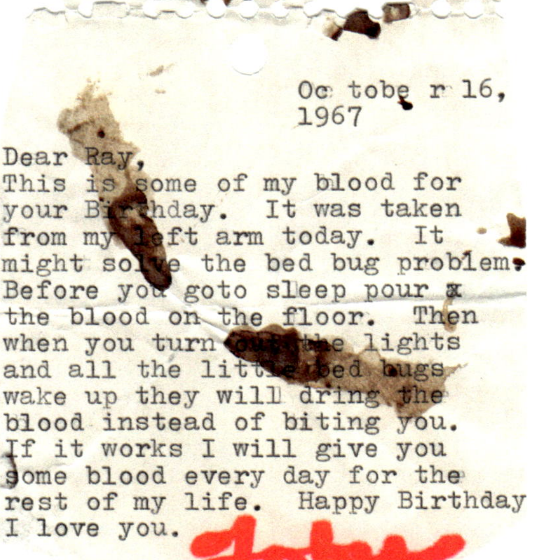

Oc tobe r 16,
1967

Dear Ray,
This is some of my blood for
your Birthday. It was taken
from my left arm today. It
might solve the bed bug problem.
Before you goto sleep pour x
the blood on the floor. Then
when you turn out the lights
and all the little bed bugs
wake up they will dring the
blood instead of biting you.
If it works I will give you
some blood every day for the
rest of my life. Happy Birthday
I love you. Toby

Toby Spiselman to Ray Johnson, October 16, 1967.

And so, when he was ready to bring to the public his private letter-writer world, Toby Spiselman became the face of Ray Johnson's strangely public privacy. The face effaced.

XI – STAR-SHAPED FIGURES 1

March 23, 1964

Pat dear, Natalie's sister Lana has left Jax and is here in New York studying stud ying acting and do you have her address? Wasn't Wood good in Love With [*sic*] **Proper Stranger those cute Macy's dresses she got to wear although Lana is much more glamorous in those pink Jax things,**

gushes Ray Johnson the cultist, the fan of fans, in a letter addressed to Patty Oldenburg, who stitched the soft sculptures and performed in the happenings of her artist husband Claes. Patty was to Claes as the flickering starlet Lana Wood was to her sister Natalie, that is, famous more by association than in her own right.

Natalie Wood was a big star in a Hollywood that was shrinking in the wake of the spread of television and the breakup of the studio system. As a child, she was indelible in the 1940s Christmas chestnut *Miracle on 34th Street* and as a teen, in the 1950s classic *Rebel Without a Cause*, but her mid-'60s vehicles, like so many American films of that period, have mostly vanished from memory. In 1963, Wood was nominated for a Best Actress Oscar for her performance in the kitchen-sink romance *Love with the Proper Stranger*, costarring Steve McQueen, who makes a glamorous entrance in Johnson's next sentence.

Had cock tails the udder day with Steve McQueen and his wife Thalia at the Plaza, Ray reports, an unlikely claim with a grain of truth. Johnson's **cock tails** probably weren't served at the Plaza and certainly were not shared with Steve McQueen, by then enthroned as the movies' "King of Cool." But "Thalia" *was* the distinctive name of the wife of the artist's artist friend Larry Poons, who, like McQueen, maintained a serious sideline in motorcycle racing, and whose own star had begun to rise two years earlier with a boost from Johnson. "What's that?" asked Ray when he spotted *Cripple Creek*, the first of Poons's "dot" paintings, on a visit to his studio, after which he sent over a friend, Metropolitan Museum curator Henry Geldzahler, who brought gallerist Dick Bellamy, who brought collector Robert Scull, and it was off to the races for Larry.

The names keep dropping, fading before they hit the ground. There's **little Sue Lion**, that is, eighteen-year-old Sue Lyon, her career already sputtering after her scandalous 1962 debut in Stanley Kubrick's film version of *Lolita*, **with that great new husband of hers Hampton Fancher the Third**, a tv cowboy of scant renown. But who cares how famous he is? **Is he cute. I have this picture of him from Photoplay on my wall of him in his underwear wow**. Which leads to thoughts of **the ever-so-great photos of Paul Kilb**, known, insofar as he is known at all, as the star of *Twice a Man*, directed by Gregory J. Markopoulos, a big name in the small world of queer avant-garde cinema.

Twice a Man came out in 1963, a breakout year for queer film, the year of Kenneth Anger's *Scorpio Rising*, Jack Smith's *Flaming Creatures*, and Andy Warhol's *Blow Job*. With Hollywood's recession, space had opened up for new kinds of films and new ways of viewing. Gay filmmakers like Anger, Markopoulos, Smith, and Warhol were cinema cultists turned cult cineastes, scavenging from the ruins of movie conventions past the fragments of a language for their own unconventional experience. In the letter to Patty Oldenburg, Johnson traces his version of this path as he shifts his identification from clause to clause—now a falling movie starlet, now a rising art-world star, now the "wrong" kind of Photoplay voyeur, the kind who looks at the boys who are meant for girls, now the rare right kind of art-house viewer, the kind whose ever-shifting perspective allows him to see cinema whole.

Ray Johnson was the kind of movie fan who went to see everything. He was also the kind of network-oriented thinker for whom all star systems interlocked. Stardom, to such a mind, is a radically relative state. Johnson had an eye for the frayed edges of fame: for the fame-adjacent, by marriage or blood, for the "period" star who wears her obsolescence like a halo, for the rarified reputations strictly confined to the art world or the art house. Which is not to say he could entirely shake off the common dream of real, true stardom. If you could be any star, who would you be?

Of course my favorite movie star of all time is Louise Nevelson when she walks down those stairs at the end of Nine and A Half wow. An instant art-house hit when it debuted in 1963—foreign films also benefited from Hollywood's decline—*8½* stars Marcello Mastroianni as the doppelganger of the film's director, Federico Fellini, who even lent the actor his signature black hat with its swooping brim. A late bloomer, sculptor Louise Nevelson first achieved fame in the 1950s, when she was in her fifties, for her monumental monochrome bas-relief wall pieces cobbled together out of found scraps of wood. With her theatrical get-ups (a penchant for major headgear earned her the nickname, "The Hat") and imperious gaze, she also proved to be a great photographic subject.

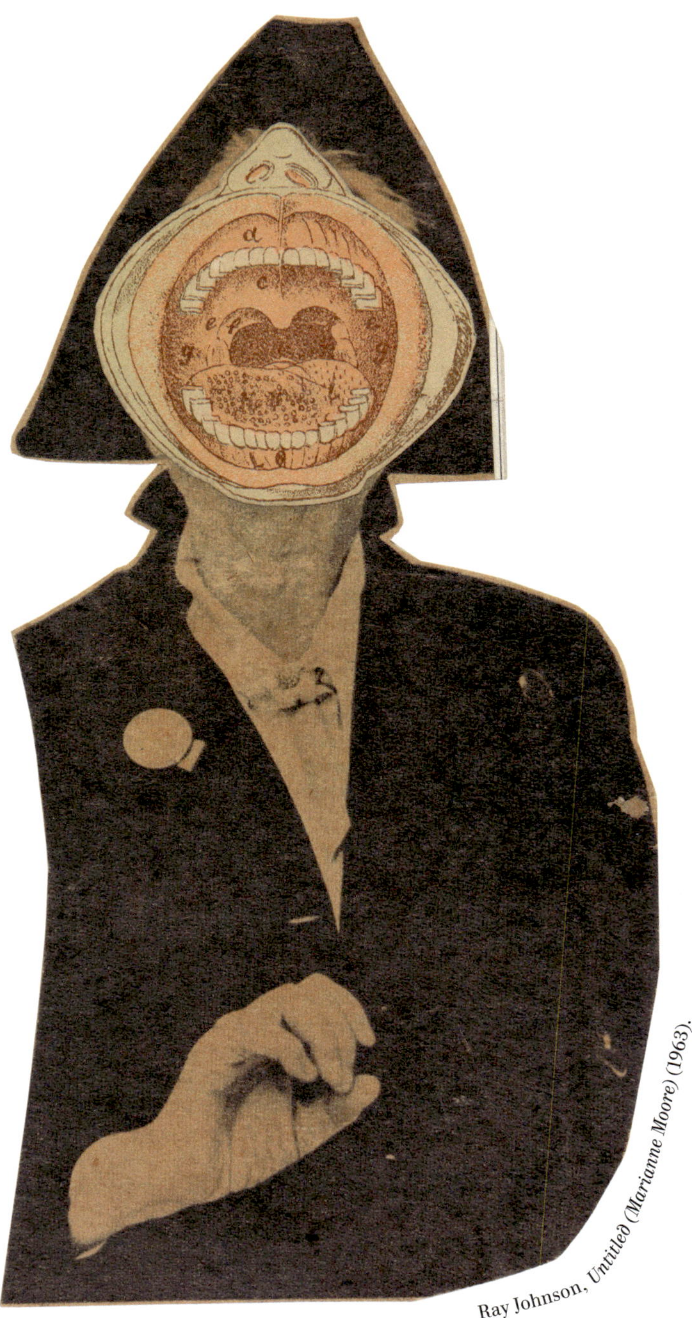

Ray Johnson, *Untitled (Marianne Moore)* (1963).

Ray Johnson with Marianne Moore hat icon, photograph by William S. Wilson.

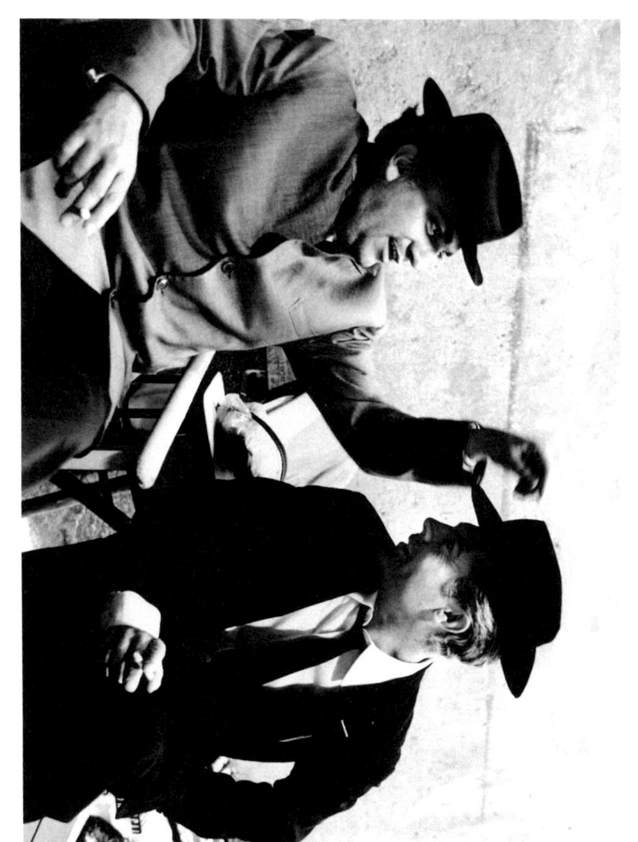

Tazio Secchiaroli, *Federico Fellini and Marcello Mastroianni, 8 1/2 backstage, Rome 1962.*

Nevelson was that discomfiting thing, an artist of the second sex and the first water. Her performance for the camera, like Mastroianni's as Fellini, served at once to advertise and to distract from her creative power. She staged her art in the unmapped space between the second and third dimensions. Such ambiguities can inspire a certain ambivalence. Is Ray Johnson's **favorite movie star of all time** a star, really? Let us say, a star-shaped figure.

XII – STAR-SHAPED FIGURES 2

IS MARIANNE MOORE MARIANNE MOORE? is the title of a text of indeterminate genre written by Ray Johnson in 1966 in response to an essay that Bill Wilson was writing, which itself was a response to Johnson's series of collage-paintings featuring the artist's iconic rendering of Marianne Moore's signature black tricorne hat. "Ray so disapproved of my academic writing," Wilson would later write, "that he wrote an essay about Marianne Moore's hat to show how it should be done." Johnson leaps from association to association in the text with his usual quicksilver speed while deploying his typewriter, as Wilson notes, to give "an expressive significance to the marks of ink on paper, and to the spaces around the marks." **It feels good to be called a poet-painter.**

Moore, Ray Johnson's favorite poet of all time, was, like him, an associative thinker of great speed and agility. Another Moore fan, John Ashbery, once wrote that reading her is "like a ride on a roller coaster." However confident one feels upon boarding, "in no time at all, one is clutching the bar with both hands, excited and dismayed at the prospect of 'ending up in the décor,' as the French say of a car that drives off the road." Bill Wilson, ever undismayed by Ray's swerves, reads **IS MARIANNE MOORE MARIANNE MOORE?** as a variation on the Johnsonian theme of "twoness," of Johnson's "sense of himself as two," as "himself and his twin, ghost or other double," a sense of split-ness that the artist then projects onto the world at large. Is Marianne Moore Marianne Moore? Yes and no. For as the coaster starts to pick up speed, Johnson's redoubled subject encounters an unlikely twin.

> **I clipped a page from Life magazine showing Marilyn Monroe's tomb stone which read Em Em 1926–1962. I was impressed by her dates. Like Joe. (Joe D.). Joe De Em. Joe Death. A playing card figure this way also that way.**

The chasm that divides Marianne Moore from Marilyn Monroe is bridged for Johnson by the redoubled double-arch of their initials, **Em Em.** Wilson (first name, William) also notices—of course, he would—that "looking at the letter *M* as a visual design, it is seen to be usually identical to its upside down reversal, the letter *W*." **A playing card figure this way also that way.** Bill and Ray, Ray and Bill. **As William Wilson signing off on the telephone said Tah Tah I did not get it and he said it was hat hat backwards.**

But what if one does not think this way also that way? Are there still connections to be made between Marilyn and Marianne? In a postwar society bent on putting women back in their places, the two MMs were taken up as the embodiments of sexual extremes—the spinster and the sexpot—and fed into the maw of an increasingly voracious culture industry. Both were photographed by Richard Avedon and Cecil Beaton, both were featured in *Life* magazine. Still, as even Johnson must admit, **Marianne Moore certainly is not Marilyn Monroe.** One was a real, true star, if there ever was one. While the other, as Moore's biographer Linda Leavell points out, "was not famous enough to be identified by name in the *Life* headline"—"Life Goes on a Zoo Tour with a Famous Poet"—just "famous enough to be called 'famous.'"

Ray Johnson would have savored the pathos of this distinction. (Marianne Moore, New York's most famous unknown poet.) He also shows signs here of savoring Monroe's brand of pathos, the doomed quality that, at least in retrospect, could be seen to suffuse her every gesture as she hastened to her terrible tabloid death. **(Joe D.). Joe De Em. Joe Death.** After the breakup of the star's ten-month marriage to Joe DiMaggio, the baseball great remained his ex's biggest fan to the end. Or rather, to the end and beyond. DiMaggio would be the one to make Monroe's funeral arrangements and send weekly roses to her grave, the very roses one would see, no doubt, if one turned to the **page from Life magazine showing Marilyn Monroe's tomb stone which read Em Em 1926–1962.**

XIII

Is Ray Johnson Andy Warhol? Only if one could imagine a Warhol famous enough to be called "famous" but not quite famous enough to be identified by name. Or a Warhol who would render the star-image barely recognizable, as Johnson does in his first-ever Monroe portrait, from 1958, a strip-collage in shades of fuchsia. One would also have to account for the very un-Warholian hand that curves toward Marilyn's sliced-up, color-soaked silhouette, as if it were about to cup the pin-up and carry her away. A shape is just a shape, it says. Anyone with a scissors can cut

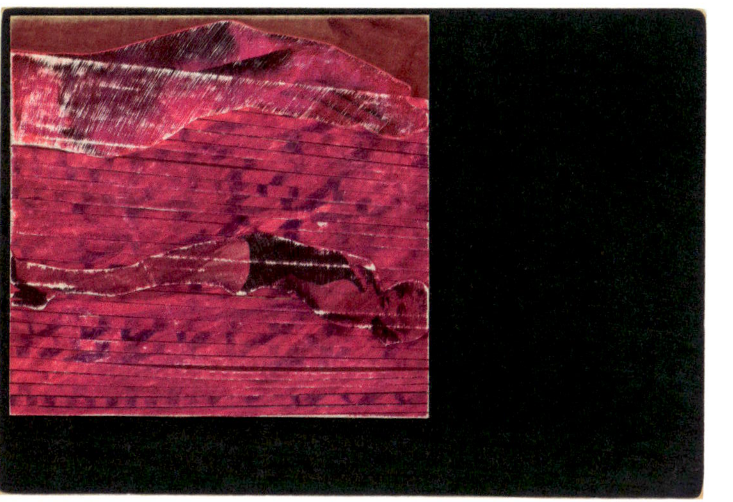

Ray Johnson, *Hand Marilyn Monroe* (1958).

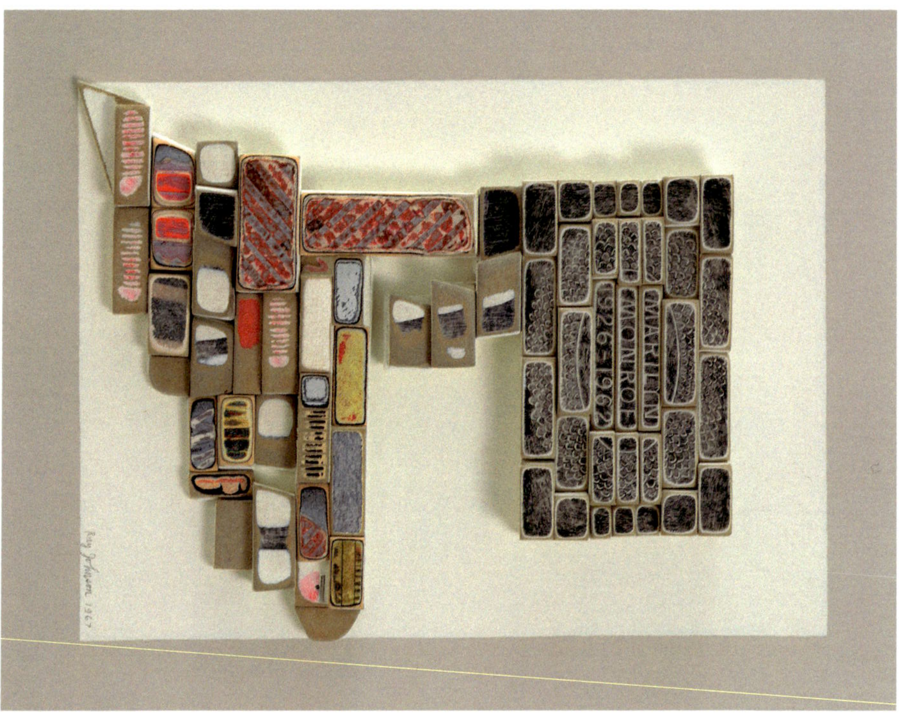

Ray Johnson, *2nd Marilyn Monroe* (1967), with “tombstone” and “roses” tesserae.

a star down to size. Palm-size, in this case. The whole image is no bigger than a page.

The actual Warhol's first Monroe painting, the *Marilyn Diptych*, from 1962, is larger than life, over six feet high and almost ten feet long. Its obsessive focus, a focus that it shares with every subsequent Warhol *Marilyn*, is the face that made the star a star, a face that was in "real" life at once masklike and perpetually, uncannily mobile. The twenty-five repetitions of the face on the diptych's left side are hyper-legible, slathered with garish warpaint; the black-on-silver repetitions on the left shimmer and fade. Monroe had been dead only a few weeks when the artist first put squeegee to canvas.

The word "icon" may denote either a diagrammatic sign or an image of a sacred being. Warhol's Marilyn is both, although with an accent on the sacred. She is his secret sharer, the closest he will ever come to real, true stardom.

Johnson's Marilyn is a shape, just recognizable, a set of letters and numbers etched into paper or stone. A sign among other signs, whose meaning shifts with the syntax.

Marianne Moore certainly is not Marilyn Monroe. In collage, Marilyn's head could be put on Marianne's body. One can pretend to be someone one is not. Children's play. I'll be you and you be me. Be my valentine. Ray Johnson wearing Marianne Moore's hat.

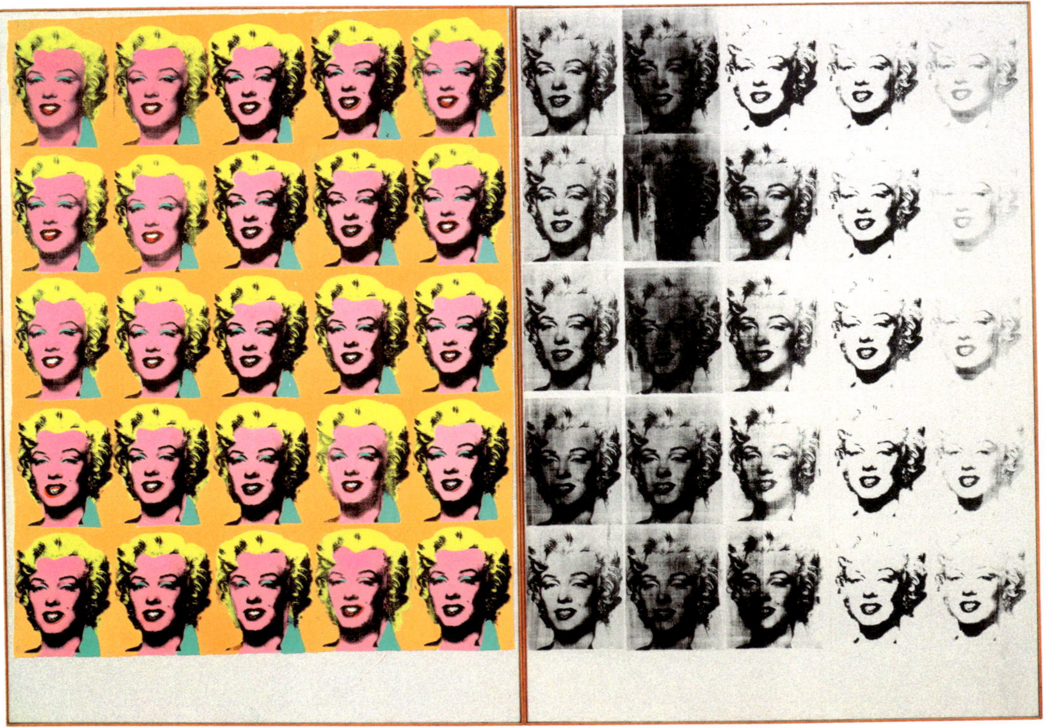

Andy Warhol, *Marilyn Diptych* (1962).

XIV

Some guys have it. Some guys never will.

On September 30, 1965 Ray Johnson sent Bill Wilson a copy of a 1932 photograph from the files of the LAPD depicting the scene of the alleged suicide of Paul Bern, the husband of movie star Jean Harlow, just four months into their marriage. The photo has been neatly sliced in two and is accompanied by a piece of paper bearing the typed motto, **Some guys have it. Some guys never will.** A mailing sent a few days later discloses the source of the motto: an ad for a line of men's grooming products featuring a photograph of a pair of shapely masculine buttocks sheathed in gleaming leather, onto which Ray has pasted a photograph of himself, sheathed in his favorite studded jacket, looking flirtatiously over his shoulder at the photo-booth camera.

"Some guys have it." Ray Johnson had it. The camera loved him. The other guys in the cruising grounds he frequented both before and after his break-up with Richard Lippold went for his butch-martian look. Bill Wilson, who was deep in the closet back then, admired Ray's relative openness about sexual matters as well as his sexual confidence.

"Some guys never will." Ray Johnson never would have it, that thing that makes a star a star. Was it a matter of character? Yes. Of luck? Yes. Of choice? Yes, absolutely. "His favorite word was 'failure,'" Henry Martin would say after Ray was gone. **A playing card figure this way also that way.** This way, eternal glamour, that way, a death's head. Andy Warhol was drawn to fame's dark reverse as much as Johnson was. Warhol's art is full of death. But failure is also a kind of death, a death-in-life, a social death, and that Warhol could not face.

Take, for instance, Warhol's response to Fred Herko, a crush who shows up in several of the artist's early films, including *Jill and Freddy Dancing*, and an extraordinary *Screen Test*, in which the dancer first tries to ward off the camera with a demonic glare, and then, defeated, disappears behind eyes turned suddenly, eerily empty. Herko "was brilliant but not disciplined—the exact type of person I would become involved with over and over and over again in the sixties," Warhol ruefully recalled in his 1980 memoir, *POPism: The Warhol Sixties*. The problem with Herko and others of his type, he saw in retrospect, was that they were "too gifted to lead 'regular lives,'" yet "too unsure of themselves to become real professionals."

But Herko's restiveness under Warhol's kino-eye speaks of resistance, not insecurity. Not everyone dreams, as Warhol did, of donning the armor of the "real professional" and battling one's way to the peak of success.

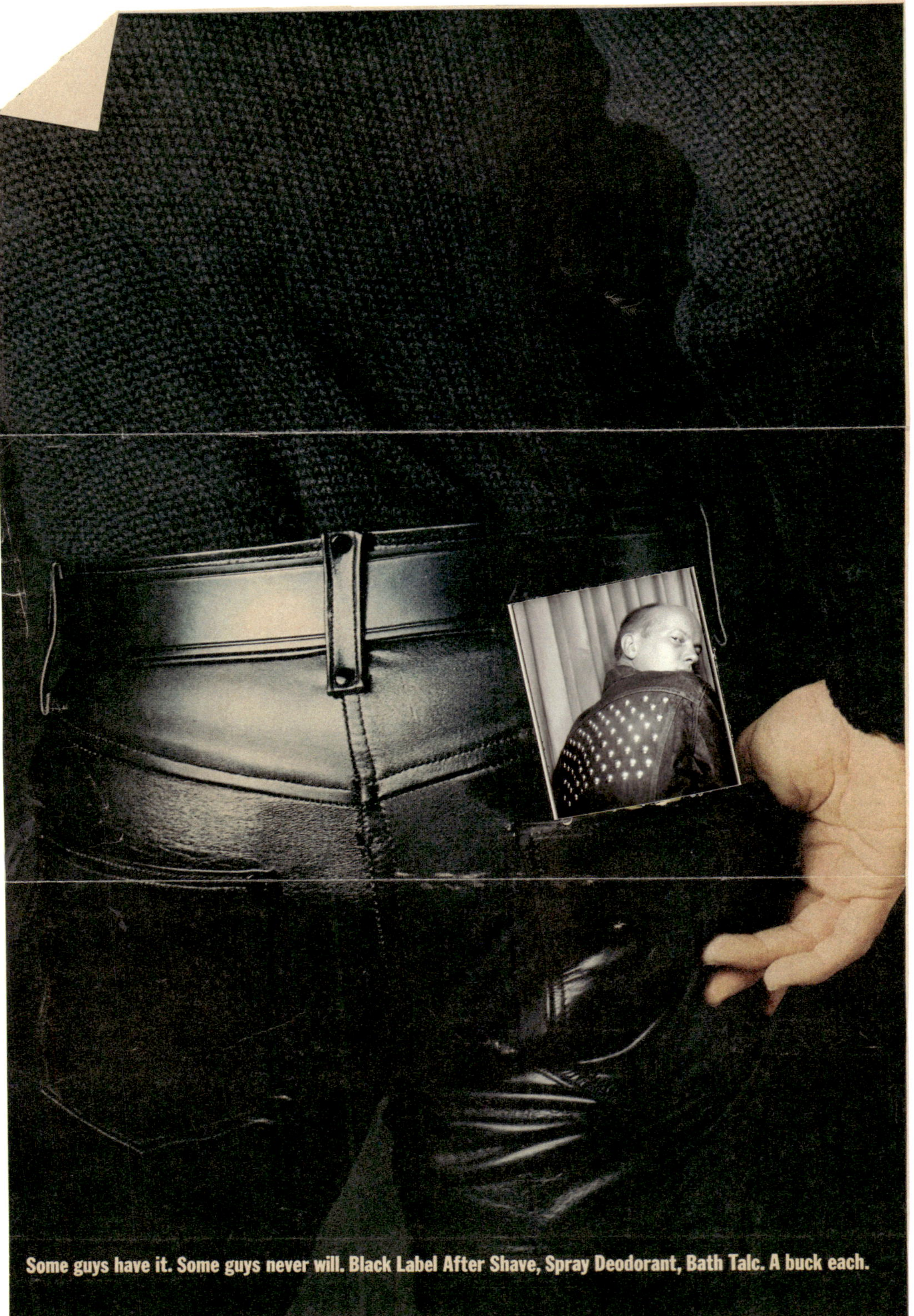

Ray Johnson to William S. Wilson, May 10, 1965.

Ray Johnson, *A Book About Death*, p. 12.

Looking down from that height, the artist might well breathe a sigh of relief at having outdistanced the crowd of untamable freaks on whose backs he made his name. Yet, as critic Paisid Aramphongphan shrewdly remarks, the fragmentary portrait of Herko that emerges in *POPism* suggests that the dancer nevertheless lingered in the art-star's mind as the image of "everything Warhol was not, the idea of not getting it together hovering in the background: a projection, perhaps a fantasy, even a repressed desire."

Fred Herko certainly is not Andy Warhol. Yet one may see the dancer as the artist's dark reverse. Ray Johnson did, in 1964, after Herko danced out their mutual friend Johnny Dodd's fifth-floor window to the sound of Mozart's Coronation Mass and died in the street below. Herko was high on speed, as usual, but still, said Dodd, his only audience, the dancer appeared to have calculated the effect of his performance: "the time and the place were right, the decor was right, the music was right." The memorial page for Herko that Ray appended then to his **Book About Death** was modeled on the one he had made for Warhol just the year before.

In fact, Bill Wilson tells us, Johnson simply reused the original mechanical depicting a sheet of stamps bearing Warhol's name. To this, he super-added a row of stamps with Herko's name and, above them, two circles containing the words, **SEND 96 CENTS POSTAGE FOR 8 PAGES OF THE BOOK ABOUT/ DEATH BY RAY JOHNSON 176 SUFFOLK ST. NEW YORK CITY**. The artist then blacked out all but three letters in the first three words of the second circle, leaving only D, R, and Y, and then proceeded to do the same to Warhol's name in the stamps below, with the result, Wilson observes, that "the DY of Andy suggests the DY of Fred's other nickname, Freddy, while the R of Warhol matches the R in Herko." One name is pursued by the other's ghost, in a dance performed under the sign of Death by RaY.

XV

You would never know, from reading Ray Johnson's mail, that the United States in the 1960s was regularly rocked by explosions of public violence and waves of revolutionary fervor. Like others of his ilk, Bill Wilson marched for social justice and against the war. When he made the mistake of suggesting Ray might join him, the artist responded by mailing off a pair of please-send-to's via David Bourdon that link Bill to Jean-Paul Marat, the Jacobin purist best known to an art purist like Johnson from Jacques-Louis David's painting depicting the revolutionary lying dead in his bath, victim of an assassin's knife. In David's painting, we receive the shock of history through a scene of intimate violence. This, Ray Johnson understood.

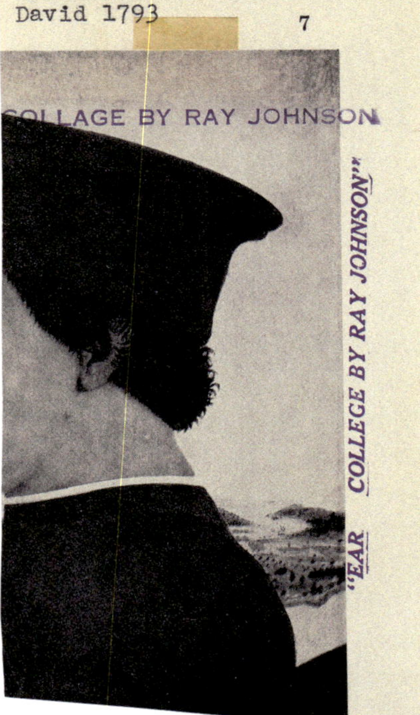

Send to Wilson Archives

The French revolutionist Jean Marat was slain by an assassin who sneaked up with a knife while he was relaxing in his bath with a book.

COLLAGE BY RAY JOHNSON

Ray Johnson, please-send-to's for "Wilson Archives," May 31, 1966.

> A May story, as told by Bill Wilson.
>
> My mother, May Wilson, lived in a one-room studio apartment at 208 West 23rd Street, next to the Chelsea Hotel. She became friends with Valerie Solanas, so I became acquainted with Valerie, chatting with her or Jackie Curtis in the blocks they animated on 23rd Street near 7th Avenue. In 1968, Valerie asked Wilson, who was sixty-three years old, for permission to keep her laundry under her sofa-bed. To amuse guests, Wilson would pull Valerie's laundry-bag from under her bed, fold the cloth to show the outline of a gun, and explain with a wink that the stiff object was Valerie's laundry.

Actor and playwright Jackie Curtis, who plays no further role in this story, belonged to the set of personalities in orbit around Andy Warhol who came to be known as Warhol Superstars. The Superstars sometimes acted in Warhol's films, but their status derived less from these appearances than from their sheer proximity to Andy, combined with a knack for entertaining a kind of knowing delusion about the nature of their fame. The Superstars gave the impression that they believed that the small world presided over by Warhol, the one in which they were famous, was the only one that mattered, even as they intimated that "real" stardom is also a delusion, more widely shared than theirs, perhaps, but still poignantly limited in space and time.

Valerie Solanas, the star of this story, was a stray dog of a writer whose best-known work is the hilarious, scabrous *SCUM Manifesto*, the founding document of her one-woman feminist movement, The Society for Cutting Up Men. In 1965, Solanas moved into the Chelsea Hotel and began trying—and trying and trying—to get Andy Warhol to produce a play of hers with the evocative title *Up Your Ass*. The artist wanted none of it, but to get her off his back, he gave Solanas a small part in his 1967 film *I, a Man*, where she does a quite funny turn as a version of herself, a butch hustler given to arguing with her johns. But Valerie was no Superstar. Her delusions pressed too close.

> So for months Valerie kept her pistol under my mother's bed, in an apartment where my three children sometimes played, obviously with none of us grasping that if a gun goes under my mother's bed in the first act, it must be fired in the last act.

The last act unfolded on June 3, 1968, when Valerie Solanas pulled her gun out from under May Wilson's bed and took it to the Factory and shot Andy Warhol in the chest. Although the artist survived, he would never entirely recover from the assault in either body or mind.

That night, Ray Johnson went out **to buy the papers to read about Andy and on Suffolk St.** found himself pursued by a group of toughs one of whom **I could not help but notice holding a switchblade with a rather long blade so then I began to walk faster I began to run and was chased** but managed to outrun his pursuers and flag down a police car, then thought better of it and walked away and **got the papers and taxied up to Toby's where I asked for a stiff drink.**

I ran like a bunny. I escaped. But history was catching up with Ray. The letter I quote above is signed **SCARED BUNNY**. At the bottom of another letter from that summer, dated at the top June 3, Johnson has scrawled **5:10 pm/Andy/Warhol/shot/June 5/Kennedy shot**. That would be presidential candidate Robert F. Kennedy, who like his brother, President John F. Kennedy, before him, now lay dead of an assassin's bullet.

On July 18, 1968, Johnson took a page from the *Village Voice* and inked on it a gun-like shape encircling the words, "some friends/ temporarily. His lockers/ be emptied by the end of/ month, so he needs a truck/ some muscle and a safe place/ He would like to/ old public." By that time, Ray had already moved with his few sticks of furniture and many boxes of art to the north shore of Long Island, where he would live and work for the rest of his days. An item toward the bottom of the *Voice* page mentions Johnson in connection with a new underground newspaper and at the very bottom the artist has pasted a news-clip headlined "Youth Dies of Wounds." **Warhol shot. Kennedy shot**. It was an explanation of sorts, the only one Ray Johnson would ever offer, for why he left the city then and never looked back.

scenes

Continued from preceding page

the dancers drifted off with the drummer, bespeckled but unbowed, but clothed.

ON JUNE 1 Christine Domaniecki gave Andrew Demetrius a birthday present. It was a shirt made in France. The motif was the American flag—a few stripes, a field of blue with an assortment of stars on it in front, and the same in back.

Christine, Andrew, and five of their friends from a blues group called the Free went to Dutchess County [illegible] urth of July [illegible] a ren[illegible] rig[illegible] ca[illegible]

[illegible] othe-que[illegible] spend Fri[illegible] ntima-tions[illegible] ndered with[illegible] some of th[illegible] e clear that [illegible] Befo[illegible] ma[illegible] qu[illegible] And j[illegible] o so, [illegible] side [illegible] own [illegible] ar- [illegible] il [illegible] y fo[illegible] ch[illegible] and [illegible] and [illegible] e next m[illegible] as thrown in[illegible] out on bail and [illegible] trial.

The story of Andrew's shirt is it's not what you wear, it's who you are and where you wear it. Andrew had worn it all through June in and around New York City and nothing happened. Also American flag shirts have lately become a very chic item among the rich Southampton summer people and the current issue of Seventeen magazine has two girls wearing flag outfits on the cover. But apparently flag clothes just don't make it in Dtuchess County.

STASHED RAT PACK-STYLE in basements, closets, and subway lockers around the city is a collection of rare magazines, art books, old prints and offbeat memorabilia [illegible] in with all kinds of ordin[illegible] ratpack junk. The stash belongs to Maurice, the famous white - maned, bearded magazine - seller who is a familiar walking landmark in Greenwich Village coffee shops and bars where he has peddled his papers for a very long time. A recent fire destroyed some of Maurice's collection and put him in St. Vincent's Hospital where he was treated for burns and had a hernia operation that he'd been putting off for years. He is out now: sick, broke, and more desperate than ever. If you want to [illegible] he can be contacted at [illegible] the home of some friend[illegible] ying temporarily. His lockers [illegible] to be emptied by the end o[illegible] month, so he needs a truck [illegible] some muscle and a safe plac[illegible] [illegible] all. He would like to [illegible] old public[illegible] ns and donate [illegible] use-ums and librar[illegible]

IT IS A LITTLE difficult for me to write up the new bi-monthly newspaper that just came out with its first issue because it has no name. Not having a name makes perfectly good sense because the basic idea of its publisher, 22 - year - old artist Steve Lawrence, was to put out a "non-verbal communication."

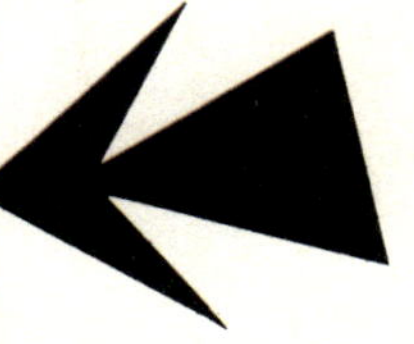

At a quick glance it looks like yet another underground newspaper until you notice its almost total lack of words.

As big as the New York Times, its 16 raunchy pages of drawings, photos, montages, and special effects were done by Paul Fisher, Peter Hujar, Ray Johnson, Billy Name, Joseph ~~Raphael~~ Raffael, Elizabeth Staal, and Stanley Stellar.

Different artists, photographers, and collagists will contribute to each succeeding issue with absolutely no censorship of what they want printed. Because of this freedom no attempt will be made to sell on the newstands. Subscriptions for the first five issues are $5 sent to Steve Lawrence, 188 Second Avenue, New York City. In Manhattan they will be hand delivered and elsewhere mailed first class.

—Howard Smith

Youth Dies of Wounds

TRACY, Calif., Dec. 6 (UPI) — Dr. Richard Fine, in charge of a first aid station at the concert, said an unidentified young man had died of stab wounds.

Ray Johnson to unknown recipient, July 18, 1968.

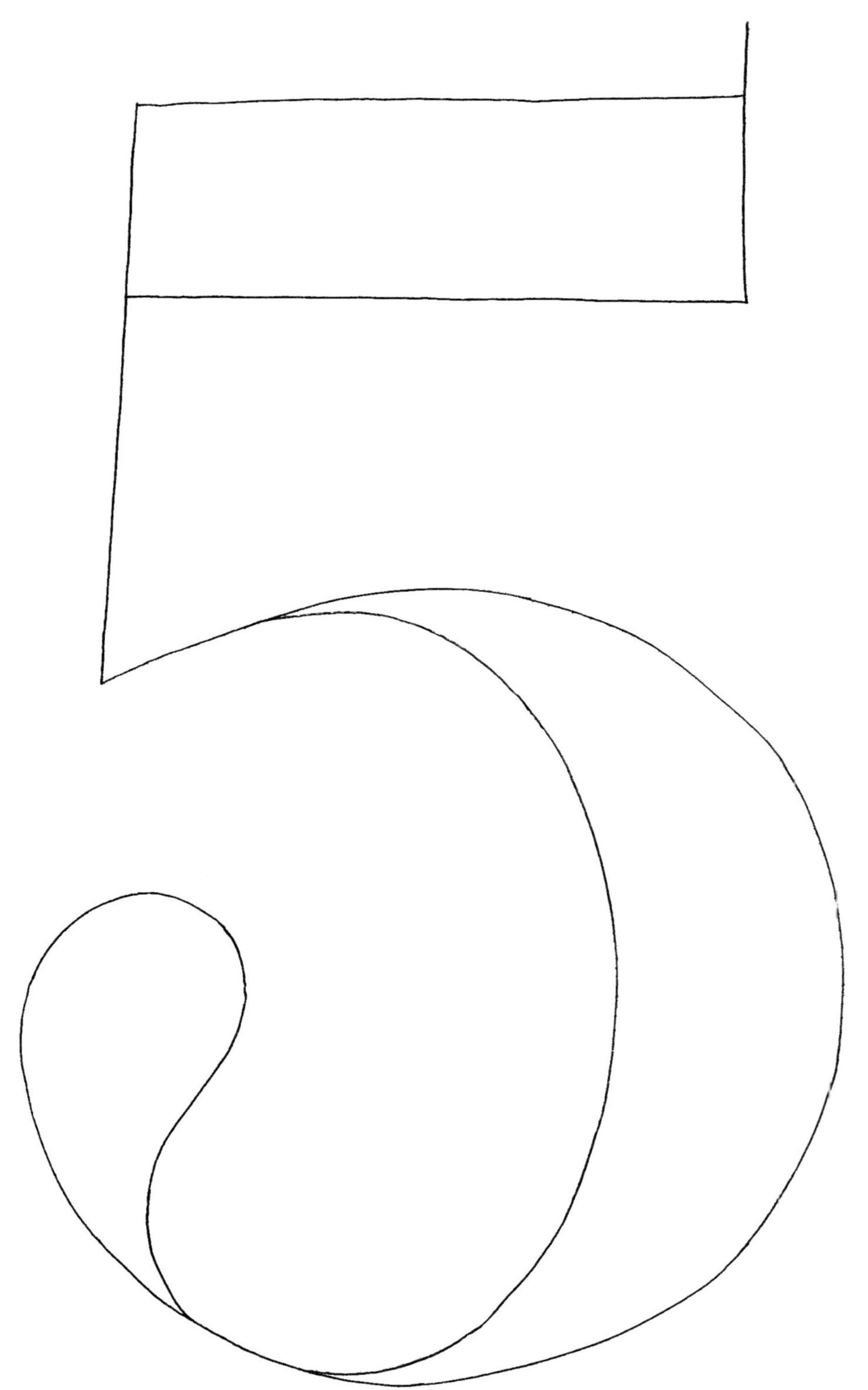

RAY JOHNSON'S HISTORY OF

1969–1973

THE ART WORLD VIEWED
FROM OUTER SPACE

I am into some new way of thinking which has to do with the present and the future and the past and the future being presented in the past.
—Ray Johnson to Suzi Gablik, April 28, 1973

I

At the turn of the 1970s, Ray Johnson had History on the brain, which is not to say that he had a concept, more like a tickle that provoked him to free-associate his way toward **some new way of thinking** in letters to understanding friends and acquaintances. The critic John Gruen, who had **been so kind to me and the New York Corraspondence** [*sic*] **School in the past** was asked in the summer of 1971 for his reaction to Ray's **thoughts of proposing to the Museum of the City of New York a show of my memorial works dedicated to the historic greats of New York Past**, a project that would have the bonus of enabling the artist **to get my hands on old letters, files of photos, etc.** of the kind one imagined beautifully moldering in the archives of that under-visited institution, just waiting for a present-future-past-minded thinker like Johnson to slip them into his time loop-de-loop.

Anticipating that the critic might nonetheless judge this dusty repository of New York Past an unsuitable venue for a show of new art, Johnson explains that **The art gallery situation being what it is in a shaky manner, I turn to the shaky Museum**. A very Johnsonesque solution, responding to one seismic disturbance in his professional life by moving his operations to even shakier ground. Meanwhile, the artist would seem to have contradicted the claim about the art gallery situation earlier in the letter, when he boasts to Gruen that, of the set of memorials to various historic greats on view **at my last Dollar Bill Show at Feigen**, he **was delighted that the Whitney Museum purchased Anna May Wong, that Carmen Miranda and Marilyn Monroe were also purchased, and that Mishima & four others will go to Larry Aldrich Museum for a show this summer**.

Was he on the edge of success? Or the edge of failure? All one can ever say for sure is that Ray Johnson lived on the edge. The years from 1969 to 1973 would nonetheless mark a peak for Johnson, measured in terms of public visibility and of frenetic activity. These were the years when he would come as close as he ever could to wanting and having what most people would call a career. Even so, viewing the present, as was his wont, from the perspective of the future, he saw himself already as a thing of the past.

II

John Gruen's most recent gesture in support of Johnson and his School was a capsule review in the form of a missive.

> Ray Johnson: New York Correspondence School (Whitney Museum, 945 Madison Ave.): Dear Ray Johnson, I think your show (the letters, the postcards, the envelopes, the scraps of paper, the messages, the pictures and drawings, and, above all, the cryptic enclosures) are startling, informative, dazzling, telling, hilarious, daring, delicate, involving, endearing, fresh, stimulating, imaginative, delicious, diverting, delightful, mysterious, ambiguous, dizzying, alive, transitory, ephemeral, effervescent, playful, spontaneous, airy, joyful, crazy. (*New York Magazine*, October 5, 1970)

"Ray Johnson: New York Correspondence School," on view at the Whitney from September 2 to October 6, 1970, would have been the artist's first solo show in a museum had it not been a group show. Johnson had written in November 1969 to curator Marcia Tucker proposing **an exhibition <u>The New York Correspondance School</u> to be shown in the first floor back gallery**, the smallest and least prestigious of the museum's exhibition spaces, although also its most public one, just off the lobby to the left of Marcel Breuer's marvelously overscale elevators. The shaky status of the show's proposed contents would match that of the proposed venue. **The art works exhibited would be the letters, postcards, drawings and objects contributed at my request from the several hundred New York Correspondance School international artist and writer "members."**

If there were any museum curator in town at that moment who might be expected to respond to such a proposal with anything more than a laugh and a shake of the head, it would be Tucker, then in her first year at the Whitney. Her programmatic ambitions can be gleaned from her description of the works in her debut exhibition there, *Anti-Illusion: Procedures/Materials*, as evidence of "an art that presents itself as disordered, chaotic, or anarchic," that "deprives us of the fulfillment of our aesthetic expectations and offers, instead, an experience which cannot be anticipated nor immediately understood." She wrote this knowing, of course, that one person's provocative anarchy may be another person's inexcusable mess. "Anti-Illusion" was predictably condemned in the *New York Times* by Johnson's old nemesis Hilton Kramer for "giv[ing] one much to think about but very little to see."

Kramer was still more dismissive when the Correspondance School show opened, sniffing that "What you or I might deem fit for the wastebasket, the Whitney Museum of American Art judges worthy of its exhibition space." Having received his share of Ray-sendings in the past, the critic conceded that, "As something to receive in the mail, a Ray Johnson work is often a delight—a very, very brief delight. But," he concludes, with a not-too-regretful sigh, "the current show at the Whitney doesn't persuade me that the ultimate home for this work is a museum." The *Times* had a kind of negative genius in those days for promoting critics who would make even the least venturesome cultural historian of the future feel superior.

For all his fogyism, though, Kramer did have a point. Once the contributions to the show began to pour in, Johnson found himself worrying, as he put it in a letter to Tucker, about how to set off the **gems** from **what Bill Wilson would call 'slush'**. His first idea was that they show **the "bulk" things lumped into a kind of shrine-altar** and otherwise make the room **look as empty as possible and a severe selection of the "better items" show what is possible to receive through the N.Y.C.S.** "Better items" versus "bulk": the quotation marks around these terms suggest that Johnson felt some embarrassment about submitting this work to conventional aesthetic judgment, for wanting to give the museumgoers not just something to think about, but something to see.

Then again, the artist himself may not have been fully persuaded that the mailings belonged in the gallery—**in fact I liked very much the way they were stored in the storage room neatly tucked away**, he muses, just after offering his recommendations for the installation. After all, **I myself in my studio have to keep all the mailings I receive every day in the mail in cardboard boxes piled on top of each other.**

It likes those moments of being inside the box, Ray wrote of the moticos. As long as it remains in the box, it has a future. In the future, it may escape and make an ambiguous, dizzying, alive, transitory, ephemeral appearance. It may give delight—a very, very brief delight. Painful to say, but isn't delight brief by nature? "He who binds himself to a joy/ Does the winged life destroy," cautioned the joyful William Blake. "But he who kisses the joy as it flies—"

III

—risks being thought insufficiently serious. In the November 1970 issue of *Artforum*, critic Kasha Linville faintly praises the results of Johnson's efforts at the Whitney as "an image-word ragout that's best enjoyed and not analyzed." For, although "the NYCS involves issues of time, chance, and dissemination of information," Johnson's way of treating these issues is not the "sober way" of "current conceptual art efforts." Linville can't quite see him, then, "as a conceptual artist. Instead, he is more a solicitous host" of an amusing, if anarchic, "diversion." As for his "meticulous, nostalgic collages[that] have been seen in galleries since the mid '60s," they are, simply, "minor." "Since the mid '60s"—it is only 1970, yet it sounds so long ago.

IV

The art gallery situation being what it is in a shaky manner, I turn to the shaky Museum. Richard Feigen believed in Ray Johnson's gallery work and had been happy to show as much of it as he could as often as he could since the mid-sixties, despite disappointing sales. However, the week after Johnson suggested to John Gruen that his meticulous, nostalgic collages might be fit for the museum of New York Past, the artist wrote to Feigen's Chicago gallery manager, Lotte Drew-Bear, to let her know that **I have discussed with Richard & Michael** [Findlay, Feigen's New York associate] **leaving the Feigen Gallery**. Even then, ambivalent as always, he wondered, **Would it be foolish** for Feigen **to have another Ray Johnson show? I have no idea what gallery affiliation I will stumble into in the near future. The horizon looks bleak horizon.**

The art gallery situation seemed unsettled, if not entirely bleak, to others besides Ray at that moment. In October 1968, Paula Cooper, most recently the director of the Park Place Gallery, an artists' co-operative, opened her own space in the gritty industrial district just south of Greenwich Village. Cooper specialized in the kind of sober-minded minimal and conceptual art that Marcia Tucker would showcase at the Whitney the following year, uningratiating work that seemed curiously at home on the unwelcoming streets of the neighborhood soon to be known as Soho. Over the next two years, Cooper would be followed by a few adventurers from uptown like Leo Castelli's former gallery director Ivan Karp and Feigen's charming young right-hand man Michael Findlay, as well as downtown artists' collectives like the group at 112 Greene Street, two members of which, Tina Girouard and Gordon Matta-Clark, were also founders of the area's first proper eatery (and artists' co-op and ongoing happening), Food.

They were just a handful of shops in a nowhere location, but they shook that sensitive creature, the art market, or rather, they were a sure sign that the market had already begun to tremble. One night in September 1971, three years after Cooper staked her claim in no-man's-land, Leo Castelli, the New York art world's grand duke, and its duchess-in-exile, Castelli's Paris-based ex-wife Ileana Sonnabend, along with the established gallerists John Weber and André Emmerich, hosted the simultaneous openings of their new Soho galleries, each occupying a full spacious floor of a building in which Castelli and Emmerich owned shares. This was a dealers', rather than an artists', co-op.

The *succès de scandale* of that evening was provided by British performance artists Gilbert & George, up on a table, in businessman tweeds, their faces and hands bronzed, singing a music-hall ditty over and over in the manner of music-box automata, an incongruous manifestation of the things of the past in the space of the future. When Ray Johnson stopped by Sonnabend in October, as he reported to his old friend Diana Epstein, the pair **were still singing "Underneath the Arches" and a crowd of people sat on the floor watching them so I walked over and smacked a Tender Buttons sticker (not very good glue, my dear) on the lower right corner of their table**. Tender Buttons was the Gertrude Stein–inspired name of the jewel-box button shop run by Epstein and her partner in life and business, Malka Safro. Johnson had designed his friends' store's logo, featured on the inadequately sticky sticker.

The logo, a four-holed black button, appears twice on a sales-slip mailing to John Willenbecher, also from October 1971. The first button is printed on the slip; the second is drawn on a scrap and marked **PLEASE SEND TO GEORGE AND GILBERT**. The words and image on the scrap are both x-ed out in memory of the response to Johnson's intervention, which made **the gallery Director...very very very angry wants to know what I think I'm doing we converse I explain it's all Art and George comes down from table to fix tape machine I dare to speak to him says "Hi, George I've always wanted to meet you I'M Ray Johnson"-the gallery Director gets VERY VERY angry and says they're "LIVING SCULPTURES" and "don't TALK" and I say why don't you put up a sign so I guess I've been 86'd out of**

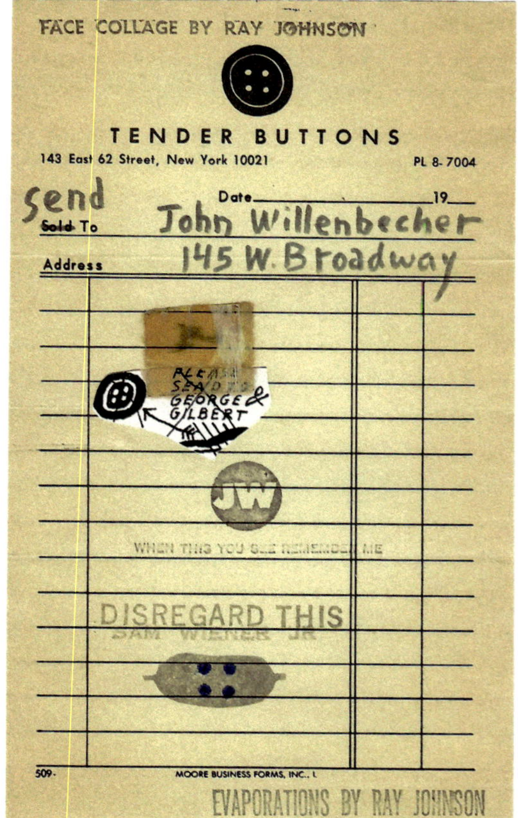
FACE COLLAGE BY RAY JOHNSON
TENDER BUTTONS
143 East 62 Street, New York 10021 PL 8-7004
send
Date 19
Sold To John Willenbecher
Address 145 W. Broadway
PLEASE SEND TO GEORGE & GILBERT
JW
WHEN THIS YOU SEE REMEMBER ME
DISREGARD THIS
SAM WIENER JR
509-
MOORE BUSINESS FORMS, INC.
EVAPORATIONS BY RAY JOHNSON

Ray Johnson to John Willenbecher, October 1971.

Sonnabend gallery after that. Also we smacked a Tender Button (not very good glue my dear) right in middle of lovely pine board entrance on stairs to Castelli gallery.

Ray Johnson would never have a show at a Soho gallery. Richard Feigen, feeling at odds with the times, closed his downtown space in 1971 and stopped showing new art shortly thereafter, refashioning himself as a secondary market dealer with a flair for mixing moderns with old masters.

V

Ray Johnson would never live, as many artists on the scene then did, in a Soho loft, having fled the scene the summer before Paula Cooper made her move downtown for the North Shore of Long Island, where he would first rent a modest house **with a Joseph Cornell attic** and then, in 1969, buy another modest house, known as the Pink House for its original color although he painted it gray. There he would receive mail for the rest of his life.

At first, the isolation took adjusting to: **its like being in jail out here with sunshine**, Ray confided to May Wilson in July 1968. **A body was found floating in the bay one morning. My cold water doesn't work. I do not have a refrigerator. Miss you too.**

A body was found floating in the bay one morning. Not the first floater to be noted in passing in Ray Johnson's mail, nor the last. Now, though, he had moved closer to the sea. Like Joseph Cornell before him, he found the beaches of Long Island to be as rich in usable debris as any city street. In 1969, the French artist Ben Vautier asked Johnson to contribute an "action, gesture, or idea" to Vautier's *FESTIVAL OF NON-ART*, conceived as a set of events that would take place simultaneously all around the world. Johnson sent a letter that begins, **Last night I delivered a letter in a court and I went into a gas station to find out where the court was** and segues from the real gas station to a fantasized scene of Vautier **selling anti art gasoline** and **fixing flat anti art tires** to a **French dinner** cooked by museum curator Jean-Patrice Marandel to a meal of **anti art strawberries at a new place out here called International Pancakes**. And then a pause; and then one last change of scene. **I walked along the beach today and I found a fragrant Russian Leather cologne bottle and I saw an elegant yacht basin and wonderful trees.** It is an art scene, but one for which court rulings on what is and isn't art seem to have receded into some dim, distant past.

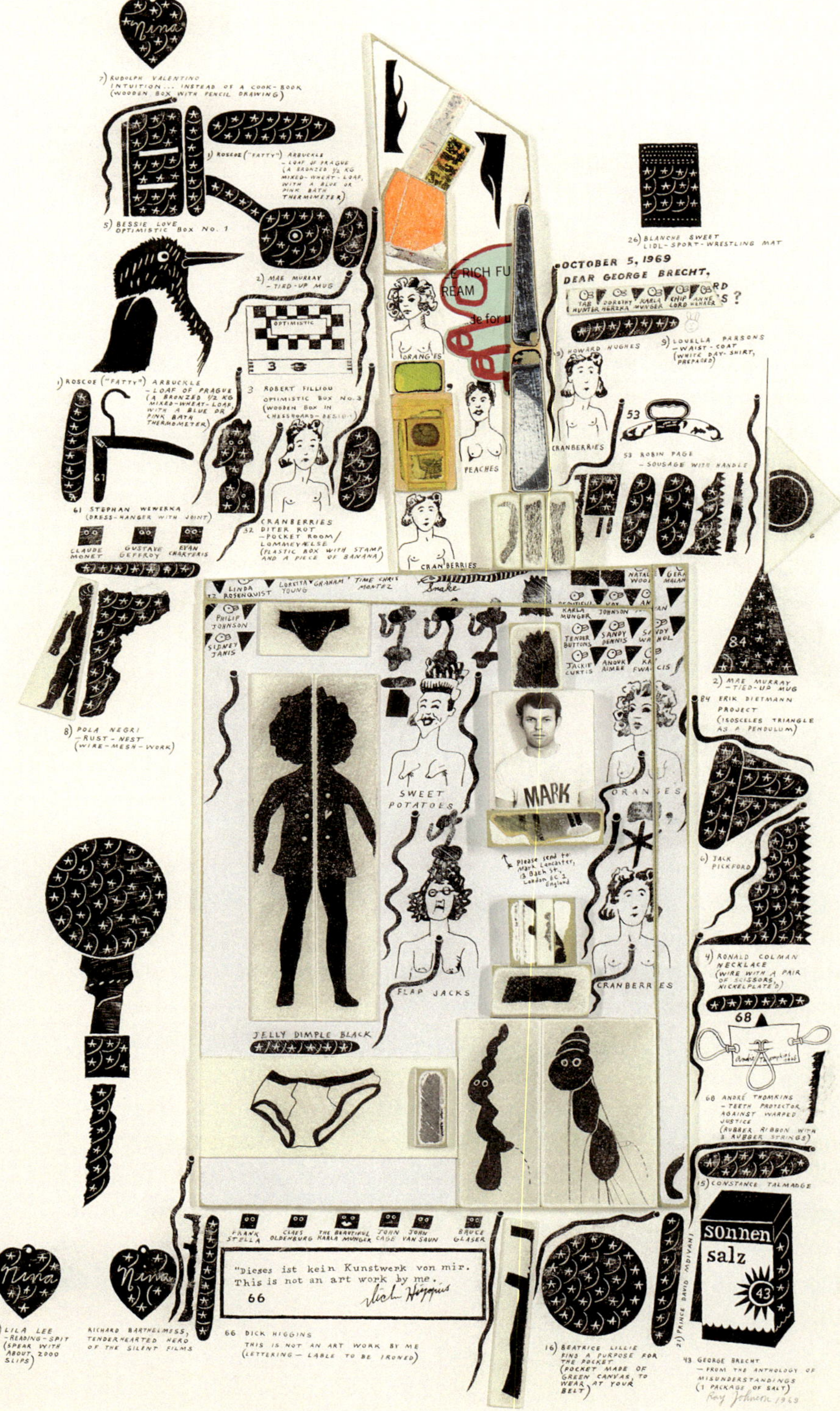

Ray Johnson, *Mark* (1969).

In 1964, British painter Mark Lancaster suddenly found himself at the center of the New York art scene after he took up his art-school teacher Richard Hamilton's suggestion to give Andy Warhol a call when he got to the States. Like other prepossessing young people who had wandered into the Factory before him, Lancaster was recruited to stretch canvases and silkscreen and make the occasional film appearance. When Ray Johnson was in Bellevue recovering from hepatitis in the fall of '64, Warhol also deputized Lancaster to go to Johnson's bedside "as a 'get-well present,'" after which, naturally, "Ray started mailing me things." Early in their correspondence, Lancaster sent Johnson a photograph of himself in a T-shirt that read "MARK," which Richard Hamilton's wife Terry had commissioned another art student she knew, David Hockney, to make as a gift for Lancaster. In 1969, Ray jotted Mark's then-current address below the picture he had received some years before, which now holds the center of a complex collage.

Which is not to say that the photograph occupies the actual center of the collage. Rather, it has been placed one square to the right of and half a square below the axis of the grid that underpins the visual field. Mark's nicely symmetrical facial features and dead-frontal gaze tug against his asymmetrical placement; his head has also been apposed to the head of a silhouette of Shirley Temple, which has been sliced straight down the center to emphasize its near-symmetrical shape. The original of this Shirley can be found in a 1958 strip collage that Johnson describes in a 1966 letter to his young friend Henry Martin as **rather Dubuffet or Klee-like sandpapered up brown with a flirt skirt rather like a cookie. Slight heart.** Martin was in the process of purchasing the piece as a replacement for another early Ray collage lost in a robbery (heartbreak). Henry, always one of Ray's greatest admirers, was also in the opening stage of a years-long campaign to convince the collector, gallerist, and Duchamp scholar Arturo Schwarz to take an interest in Ray's art. Schwarz had recently enlisted Martin to assist him with a monumental undertaking, the first catalogue raisonné of Duchamp's work.

Ray Johnson, *Shirley Temple* (1958).

Mark Lancaster had his own Duchamp connection, as Johnson lets Jan Van der Marck know in a brief note, undated but likely from 1967, since Johnson mentions that **Richard Hamilton is in town for his show at Iolas**, which took place that year. **Richard Hamilton is in town for his show at Iolas and part 2 of the JA N painting will be included in it a small photo of Mark Lancaster an English painter who photographed Richard Hamilton constructing his Duchamp glass**—a sentence, like so many by this writer, that begs for an extended gloss.

VII

> **Richard Hamilton is in town for his show at Iolas and part 2 of the JA N painting will be included in it a small photo of Mark Lancaster an English painter who photographed Richard Hamilton constructing his Duchamp glass, which I undretsand** [*sic*] **is in the Colpey** [*sic*] **collection.**

Duchamp Glass: Hamilton's 1965–66 reconstruction of Marcel Duchamp's *Large Glass*. The project was financed by artist William Copley, a friend of Ray's and a close associate of Duchamp (who made Copley the steward of his final work, *Étants Donnés*); hence, **the Colpey** [*sic*] **collection.**

Richard Hamilton: protean artist who is best known for two works, the Duchamp project and *Just what is it that makes today's homes so different, so appealing?*, a 1956 collage that, like Ray Johnson's mid-1950s Elvis images, is often cited as a harbinger of Pop art.

the JA N painting: a collage tribute to Jan Van der Marck that Johnson created in the run-up to the curator's 1967 debut exhibition at the Museum of Contemporary Art Chicago, *Pictures to Be Read, Poetry to Be Seen*, which would also include other works by Johnson. In assembling the show, Van der Marck had taken the *Large Glass* as his conceptual lodestar.

part 2 [of the JA N painting]: The reference is unclear, and Johnson's slippery syntax does not help. Was the artist already at work on the version of *Mark* he would complete in 1969? Or did he scrap a 1967 version and start again later? Did he mean to imply that a piece including the photo of Lancaster would hang in Hamilton's show at the Iolas Gallery? (In 1978, Iolas would host Ray Johnson's last-ever show in a commercial gallery.)

VIII

Once Ray Johnson and his boxes had moved away—though not that far away—from the center of the New York art world, the art world moved to the center of his art, or to be more precise, to the center of the art he made for the art market. The art market is not identical to the art world, but it exerts a powerful centripetal force on that world's components. *Mark* marks the moment when Johnson began to map the interrelations among those components in collage terms. The kaleidoscopic shifting of his tesserae on the melting icesheet of white space would acquire—or reveal itself already to have had—a social dimension. And the anarchic dance of the mailings would submit—for the moment, for the sake of argument—to the constraints of the framed field.

The photograph of Mark in *Mark* projects out from a bas-relief picture within the picture, sliced along the top and right edges to create the suggestion of a frame. The flats on which the relief-elements float are scattered with ink drawings, many of which come with numbered captions. Each number is followed by a proper name, and most of the names are followed by the titles and descriptions of somewhat hard-to-picture objects: "*Loaf of Prague* (a bronzed ½ kg mixed-wheat-loaf with a blue or pink bath thermometer)," "*Find a Purpose for the Pocket* (pocket made of green canvas, to wear at your belt)," "*Reading-Spit* (spear with about 2000 slips)," and so on. Johnson has made helpfully realistic drawings of some of these objects. Others are represented by decorative black shapes studded with irregular white stars whose origin the avid Ray-watcher may trace to an early-1960s flyer advertising his **MOVIE STAR COLLAGES**.

The names under the star-shapes belong to personalities of the silent-film era, some still familiar (Rudolph Valentino, Fatty Arbuckle), some long-faded (Lila Lee? Bessie Love?). Those under the illustrations belong to contemporary artists and designers, including Johnson's friends Dick Higgins and George Brecht. Brecht is also hailed directly in the picture's upper right quadrant, as if at the beginning of a missive, **Oct 5, 1969, Dear George Brecht**, although the message drawn below the greeting has been tiled over. One can just make out a few letters, a question mark, and a bunny head sign-off, half-erased.

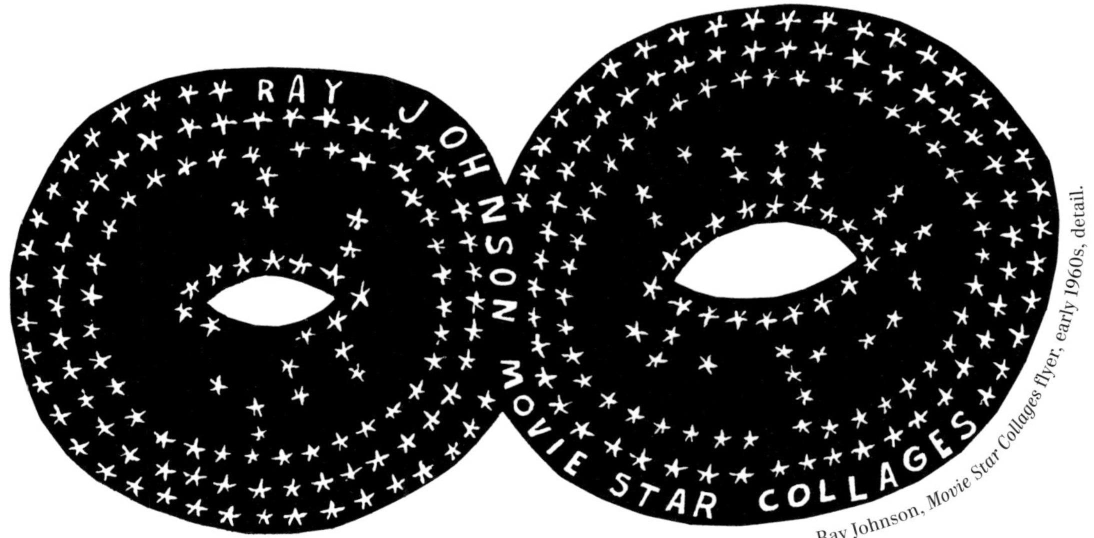

Ray Johnson, *Movie Star Collages* flyer, early 1960s, detail.

The tombstones in Johnson's previous memorial works had tested the viewer's knowledge of a name or two, but here there are so many names to take account of: names from the speechless past, names vividly present to our correspondent, and at the picture's off-center center, a name embedded in a snapshot from an era barely finished yet cut off from the now by a set of seismic shifts in the world from which it emerged. Ray's way with constellated names was no secret to **the several hundred New York Correspondance School international artist and writer "members"** then on his mailing list (both *Mark* and his proposal for the Whitney Correspondance Show date from the fall of 1969), but now, it seems, he wants to make it a matter of public record.

After holding the first Meeting of the New York Correspondance School in 1968, Johnson wrote of his **success in bringing the public the private letter-writing world**. He would not always succeed; the problems that arose in the mounting of the Whitney show would soon make clear to him just how delicate a business it was, this transfer between worlds. But it was also becoming clearer to him that the intimate experience of opening an envelope and the intimate experience of peering at the tesserae were two sides of one fact, **like a playing card this way also that way**. If he were to go on making pictures intended to hang on the walls of galleries and museums, he would have to find a way to make this fact, the fact that his art was message, image, and performance all at once, palpable to the viewing public.

IX

What are those strange objects whose word-and-image renderings fill *Mark*'s borders, forming a second frame-within-a-frame? Brecht and Higgins, as well as some of the other artists named here, like Robert Filliou and Diter Rot, had Fluxus connections, and the descriptions make the pieces sound like the kinds of market-resistant artworks—Rot's *Pocket-Room/Lommevaelse* is a "plastic box with stamp and a piece of banana"—one associates with Fluxus. Has Johnson taken these pieces from the catalogue of a Fluxus show?

The artist would have had Fluxus on his mind just then, since October 5, the date of the pictured note to Brecht, was the day after the close of the New York Avant Garde Festival. The festival, a staple of the art-world calendar, was the brainchild of frequent Fluxus collaborator Charlotte Moorman, dubbed "The Topless Cellist" after her memorable performance in Nam June Paik's *Opera Sextronique*. Johnson had participated in the event before, but this time he had pulled off a *succès de scandale*, no small feat, given that Moorman and her friends were such seasoned shockers of the bourgeoisie. On September 30, Johnson dashed off a brief report to Lotte Drew-Bear. **Last Sunday**, September 28, the first day of the festival, **I flew in a helicopter the Feigen Gallery kindly paid $100 an hour for from out here on Long Island to Ward's Island in Manhattan where for the 7th Avant Garde Festival organized by Charlotte Moorman I dropped 60 foot-long hot dogs through a round hole in the plastic bubble of the helicopter.**

It was exciting to do.

As it turns out, though, the numbered objects in *Mark* were not made for exhibition, nor were they props for a performance (although one, Robin Page's *Sausage with Handle*, is funnily reminiscent of Johnson's recent triumph). Johnson has lifted the images and descriptions from the latest copy of the catalogue of VICE-Versand, a quixotic business founded in 1966 by German collector Wolfgang Feelisch. Feelisch's idea was to produce artworks in unlimited editions to be sold via mail order (one meaning of "versand" is "mail order") at an affordable price—in 1969, each item cost eight Deutschmarks, the equivalent then of slightly less than two dollars. VICE-Versand's products are things and missives, things as missives, each a tiny act of resistance to the way things are done in the art market. A kind of performance after all.

X

... marks the spot.

"Mark" is a proper name, but also a noun and a verb, a labile word of the sort that poets love. **It feels good to be called a poet-painter**, Ray Johnson sometimes thought. Then he would remember that the heroes of the art world were strong, silent types, whether of the pure-painter or the elegant-conceptualist variety. In 1969, Johnson was embarking on the talking-pictures phase of his career. From now on, viewers of his gallery work would have to be prepared to read the fine print: so many names, so many words. So many associations to trace out, and out.

Yet, if you had asked, Ray Johnson would surely tell you that he was a visual artist first and last. Poetic he may have been, but not, heaven forbid, *literary*, a word that in the art world is always wielded as an insult. A visual artist is first and last a mark-maker, a conjurer of form out of formlessness. And, as art historian Rosalind Krauss argued in 1979, for the modern visual artist, the grid is the form of forms. The grid "is what art looks like when it turns its back on nature," Krauss wrote in "Grids" (a minimalist title suited to its moment). "It is a mapping of the space inside the frame onto itself," "a mode of repetition, the content of which is the conventional nature of art itself." Frames within frames within frames. The grid, to the critic's eye, is a visualized concept that "states the autonomy of the realm of art." It sounds like a trap, the lid of a box snapping shut.

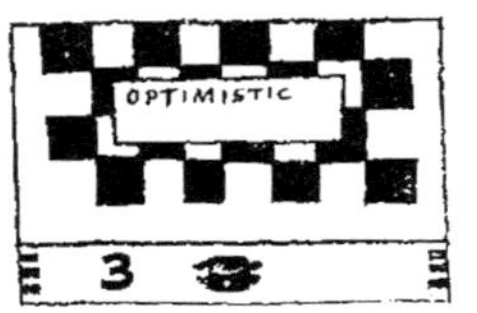

3 ROBERT FILLIOU OPTIMISTIC BOX NO. 3 (WOODEN BOX IN CHESSBOARD-DESIGN)

In his drawing of an item from the VICE-Versand catalogue, Robert Filliou's *Optimistic Box No. 3*, Johnson has left out a crucial detail. On the box's lid, below its title, Filliou has written, "so much the better if you can't play chess." If one opens the chessboard-box, one finds, pasted inside the lid, the phrase that completes the thought: "you won't imitate Marcel Duchamp." For the late twentieth-century conceptualist, this counts as optimism.

Unlike Duchamp, Ray Johnson never gave up painting, even after he gave up painting. The marks he situates at the actual center of *Mark* are just marks, evidence of the inimitable touch of the artist's hand, not manifestly meaningful, even if one suspects they may have morphed out of extant bits of Johnson's icon-language. The center of this grid is not the black square of *Calm Center*, but it is empty in its way.

The forms at the center of the grid repeat like the squares of a grid, but not exactly, since they are drawn freehand; they are irrational—blobby, curvy, asymmetrical—relative to the grid's compulsive rationality. In an interview with Henry Martin from 1984, Johnson responds to a question about his opinions on the artists of the day in his typical sideways fashion, sliding away from the present toward the past, to **a tiny and strikingly eloquent Giacometti** that he had to squat down to see and **a Francis Bacon sphinx** that reminded him of **a photograph of the sphinx seen in profile**, which struck him as **very deformed, and people always photograph the sphinx as they look at it frontally because one tries to see form rather than unform—like a portraiture concept of the nineteenth century, of Grecian wholeness, which is one viewpoint—but the unform is there as well.**

In the mid-1990s, Rosalind Krauss seemed to turn against the kind of late-modernist rationality that is represented by the grid in her writings on the *informe*, a concept, or as she says, "anticoncept," borrowed from novelist, philosopher, and prophet of body horror Georges Bataille. But the grid and the *informe* are two sides of one fact, a playing card this way also that way. *Mark* is about Johnson's need to manage the tension between form and unform as much as it is about his need to bring the public his private letter-writer world and to mark his spot on the terrain of the as-yet barely mapped realm that everyone had just begun to call "the art world."

XI

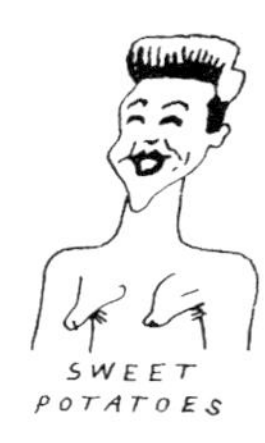

Once he was taken up by galleries, Johnson began to work to shows, spurred by deadlines to produce flights of collages, often linked by a motif or theme. In 1967, he showed his "Duchamp Combs," in 1968, "A Lot of Shirley Temple Post Cards," and in February 1970, the show for which *Mark* was made opened at Feigen's New York uptown space under the title "I Shot an Arrow into the Air It Fell to Earth in the Ear of an Artist Living in Flushing, New York Tit Show."

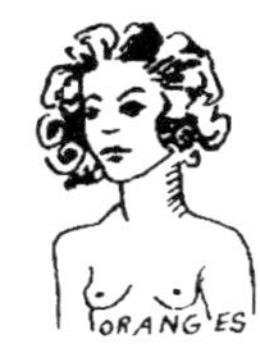

What Johnson called his "tit collages" all feature a motif **based**, as he explained to Suzi Gablik, **on a 1930s tit chart, done in comic-strip style by an anonymous artist. It's the sort of thing that schoolboys pass around.** Viz., the four nymphs that attend Mark in *Mark*, with their morphological captions: *Sweet Potatoes*, *Oranges*, *Flap Jacks*, *Cranberries*. The tit charts are embarrassing, the sort of thing that schoolboys pass around, the sort of thing that one might have wanted to look away from even in 1969. Johnson anticipated this response, which means he knew these images would generate blind spots in the viewer's field of vision wherever they appear.

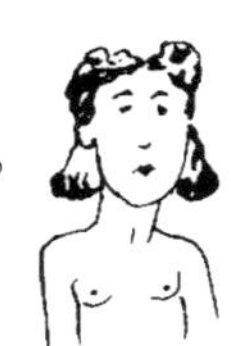

See the black square on the tile that forms the base of the notional plinth that supports the portrait-bust of Mark, with its Grecian symmetry? The tit charts are like that. And not. They are low, crude, a juvenile expression of body horror—*informe*. They are also composed of abstracted shapes broken down into categories and fitted into grids—what art looks like when it turns its back on nature.

Ray Johnson, *Mark* (1969), details.

XII

I see the tit-charts as the sort of thing that schoolboys pass around, and I see them as a blind spot akin to the black square. But "'Seeing as …' is not part of perception. And for that reason it is like seeing and again not like." Ludwig Wittgenstein makes this claim just after he has shown the reader of his *Philosophical Investigations* how the drawing of a "duck-rabbit" may induce the uncanny feeling of suddenly catching a perception in the process of becoming thought. One can see the drawing as a duck or one can see it as a rabbit but one cannot see it as both at once because one cannot *think* "duck" and "rabbit" simultaneously. And yet, as one remembers the "oh!" moment of the shift from one aspect of the image to the other, one grasps the essence of "seeing as," of how, as Wittgenstein says, "the flashing of an aspect on us seems half visual experience, half thought." Wittgenstein illustrates his argument with his own schematic rendering of this "picture-puzzle," derived from a cartoon by an anonymous artist that had been making the rounds since its debut in a German humor magazine in 1892.

Ray Johnson began using a schematic rendering of a rabbit head to sign the occasional letter in the early '60s, but it was only in 1968, with the advent of the Correspondance School Meetings, that the rabbit became his trademark icon. It was a portrait of the artist as an incorrigible trickster, and it was also, at the same time, the portrait of everyone as an artist. For, as Johnson insisted to Richard Feigen in March 1970, after they had had what seems to have been a contentious discussion of the upcoming Whitney Correspondance Show, **Everybody is a member of the NYCS. Everybody**. Everybody and anybody might find their names beneath the bunny heads on the seating-chart flyers that Johnson began to send around soon after he began holding Meetings. The printed grid into which these mini-portraits are fitted

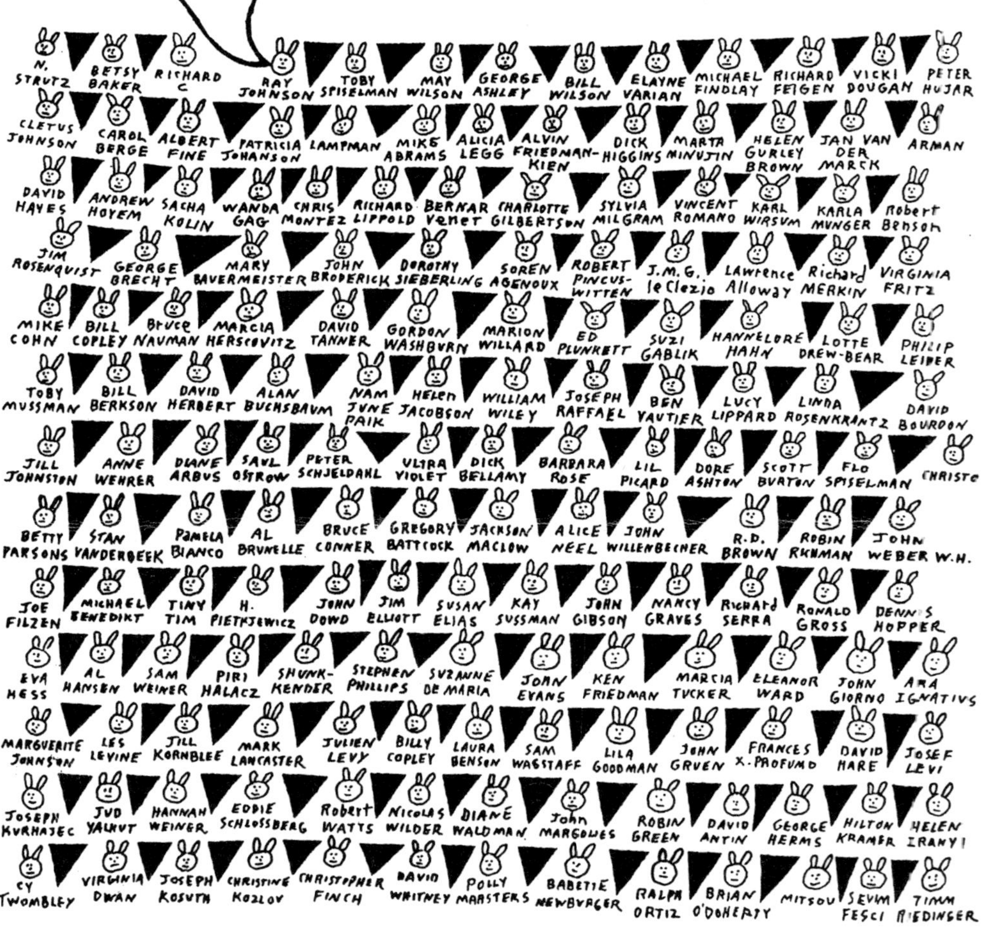

Ray Johnson, flyer for *A Mysterious New York Correspondance School Meeting*, 1968.

is bounded by the edges of the paper sheet—in practice, that is. In theory, though, as Krauss reminds us, "the grid extends, in all directions, to infinity," and viewed from that aspect, "the given work of art is presented as a mere fragment, a tiny piece arbitrarily cropped from an infinitely larger fabric."

Once they migrated from Johnson's signoffs to his seating-charts, you could see the bunny heads this way also that way, as individual portraits or as nodes in an infinitely expanding network. But could you grasp the moment of the shift from one aspect to another, a feat that was always a kind of magic trick? In late March of 1969, Johnson flew to Sacramento, where he had been invited to stage a Meeting-style event in connection with a group exhibition at California State University called *The Last Correspondence Show*. Johnson's event was titled "A Duck Named Andy" and featured a raffle—or raffael, as Ray insisted on calling it, in honor of his painter friend Joseph Raffael—for which the prize was **a duck that turned out to be a rabbit**. Having pulled off the trick, the artist added the duck-rabbit to his ever-expanding lexicon.

Pieces of a seating-chart featuring a grid of Johnson duck-rabbits have been worked into the design of *Mark*. In the block of names that rises from Mark's head like a cartoon thought-bubble, actress Sandy Dennis, the archetypal urban neurotic of '60s cinema, is seated alongside "Sandy Warhol," and Kay "Fwancis" (Francis), a 1930s Hollywood glamor girl with a slight speech impediment, is catty-corner from her art-world counterpart, "Kay Johnson." A duck named Andy and a rabbit named Ray are caught in a web of identification and desire at whose center lies a portrait named MARK, an image that can't help but remind Andy-Sandy-Kay-Ray of the good old days, before things got so terribly, tewwibly complicated.

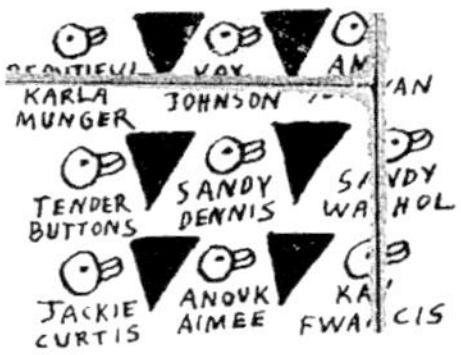

Ray Johnson, *Mark* (1969), detail.

XIII

In the spring of 1964, the philosopher Arthur Danto walked into the Stable Gallery and saw Andy Warhol's *Brillo Boxes* and walked out both vexed and thrilled. Warhol's boxes were indistinguishable, at first glance, from commercial packaging, yet Danto saw that he saw them as art. The thrill came in seeing himself "seeing as," but there remained the need to unwind the means by which the trick had been effected. That December, Danto gave a talk titled "The Artworld," in which he arrived at an insight that would fuel a lifetime of speculation. He saw, in a flash, that "To see something as art," and more particularly, to see something as art that looks, at first glance, like non-art, "requires something the eye cannot decry [*sic*]—an atmosphere of artistic theory, a knowledge of the history of art: an artworld." The philosopher produces the term "artworld" with a flourish here, as if he were pulling a rabbit out of a hat.

If you had never heard this term elsewhere, in fact, you might guess, from reading "The Artworld," that Danto had invented it. For while he does briefly acknowledge that "we cannot readily separate the Brillo cartons from the gallery they are in," and also mentions that "the history of recent New York painting" forms part of the "atmosphere of artistic theory" that one must have absorbed in order to see the cartons as art, nowhere does Danto connect his loftily theoretical "artworld" to its vernacular counterpart, the loose configuration of people and places and things and forces and ideas that his fellow gallery-goers would have offhandedly referred to as "the art world." He omits this connection in part because he is elucidating a philosophical concept for a philosophical audience, to whom the history of recent New York painting is an irrelevance. But the omission is also performative, a way of showing how the "artworld" concept works to divide those who breathe its atmosphere of theory from the rest of us. If you are the kind of person who can make the "artworld"–"art world" connection, you are also the kind of person who can see the *Brillo Boxe*s as art, and if you are not (and Danto must have suspected that some of his philosophical listeners fell into the "not" category), not.

Another thing that Danto does not say, in this case because it is something I think he did not see, is that the same conditions that made it suddenly possible to see Warhol's *Brillo Boxes* as art also made it possible, just as suddenly, to see "the art world" as a historical phenomenon. The history of recent New York painting, its sunset efflorescence of painterly abstraction, had posed an obstacle to Andy Warhol's entrée into the art world, and when he could feel it becoming a thing of the past, he made the Brillo Boxes as a fitting send-off. A few years after this, after a shooting, and a move, Ray Johnson saw in the becoming-historical of the art world another kind of opportunity. He would become its historian.

XIV

The Museum of the City of New York would never host a show of Johnson's **memorial works dedicated to the historic greats of New York Past**. But the idea that the artist had floated in his letter to John Gruen lingered. A few months after sending that letter, he typed up and copied and distributed a two-part **Plan** to assorted correspondents.

Part one consists of a list of seventeen proposed memorial works, stacked in a column in alphabetical order (**Diane Arbus 1923–1971/Paul Cezanne**

1839–1906/Walt Disney 1901–1966 . . .). The second part is a solid block of type that harks back to Gruen's exuberant review of the Whitney Correspondance Show, relaying Johnson's plans **to send "startling" letters to "court jesters," to send "informative" letters to "ubiquitous spooks plodding through shadows fruitlessly," to send "dazzling" letters to the Aunt Martha Museum, to send "daring" letters to "anyone who doesn't stay in one place anymore,"** and so on for another twenty-three headlong lines—nostalgists may pause to note the plan **to send "imaginative" letters to Jasper Johns, who was once handcuffed to Merce Cunningham during a Frank O'Hara poetry reading**—that end with the artist's pledge **to send "forget-me-not" letters to Gordon Matta's Restaurant**, Food, which had just opened in Soho the previous fall.

The contrast between the slow-scrolling death-dates of the memorials list and the letters that rush in a stream toward the very latest thing might seem to reinforce the separation between Johnson's exhibition work and his mail art and to cast the collages, once again, as things of the past and the mailings as things ever on their way to giving delight in the present moment sometime in the future. Still, these two practices do occupy the same pictorial-poetic space in Johnson's **Plan**. He is finding ways to give form to the thought that they are ineluctably connected.

Plan may also be read as a public, or at least, semi-public, statement of the artist's intent to take control of his career. Starting in the mid-1960s, impeded though he may have been by skeptical critics and by his own unremitting ambivalence, Ray Johnson had been trying every way he could to bring both his exhibition collages and his mail activities into public view. When the ground started to shift under the art world toward the end of the decade, he struggled to retain his footing in the galleries. At that same moment, though, his efforts to publicize the mail art were given an unexpected boost by the emergence of a set of correspondence networks explicitly inspired by, but independent of, the NYCS. By 1969, Phil Weidman, the curator who invited Johnson to Sacramento, could call his exhibition "The Last Correspondence Show" and expect everyone to get the joke. Mail art, too, was becoming historical.

From Sacramento, Johnson had gone on to Vancouver, to participate in *Concrete Poetry*, an exhibition at the University of British Columbia. The visit turned out to be something of a fiasco—having hung the nineteen collages he had selected for the show, Johnson then took them all down, cut his finger in the process, smeared his blood on the wall and titled the result *Blood of Concrete Poet*. Why? It is not clear. It could have to do with Ray's strong, never-to-be-explained aversion to leaving the confines of the United States; this was the first of only two such trips he would ever make. Or perhaps he thought the collages looked out of place in the exhibition, which otherwise consisted of word-and-image art in a conceptual vein. Should he have contributed some kind of mail activity instead? (After Johnson's departure, Richard Feigen would call from New York to insist that the collages be rehung. This gallerist deserves credit for his loyalty, which was always to the artist rather than the man.)

Once home, Johnson wrote to Alvin Balkind, the curator in Vancouver. Under the emphatic heading, **REQUEST**, the artist asked Balkind if, after the show closed, he would please **cut out the Ray Johnson blood March 28, 1969 to envelope size and mail it to Eleanor Antin wife of critic David Antin**. David Antin was also an experimental poet, while Eleanor was an artist who, Johnson explains, **has a collection of glass slides of all of the poets**, each slide smeared with a different poet's blood and fitted into one of the gridded slots in her *Blood of Poet Box* (1965–1968). When Antin exhibited this work, **somewhere in Queens**, Johnson tells Balkind, **They made her take it down.**

The idea to include Johnson in *Concrete Poetry* had come from a young Canadian artist, Michael Morris, to whom Johnson first wrote in 1968 after reading about a painting by Morris with the, for Ray, irresistible title, *The Problem of Nothing*. In the months following Johnson's visit, Morris, unphased by the blood on the wall, made plans with his partner Vincent Trasov and their friend Gary-Lee Nova to form a mail art collective they would call Image Bank. The name, with its corporate overtones, was meant both as a joke and as a sign of conviction, a sign that there was something fundamentally anti-personal about the artists' enterprise. The name marked a difference between Image Bank's activities and those of the NYCS. Ray Johnson's mailings had begun as an exchange of intimacies and would continue to be shaped by the dialectic between one-to-one intimacy and the kind of systematized network whose constituents are "looped together," as Lawrence Alloway would put it in 1972, "in a new and unsettling connectivity." The mail artists who emerged in Johnson's wake, however, took the networked character of their enterprise as a given. For them, correspondence as an expression of one-to-one intimacy was a thing of the past.

Just as Warhol made his way into the art world through the culture of commodities, summoning the ghostly distinction between art market and supermarket, so Johnson's epigones hoped to find their way in through the "information economy," a phrase just then coming into use. For if it were true, as Alloway thought, that individual works of art had become less significant in themselves, that art's meaning was now generated through "the distribution of works of art, both literally and in mediated form as text and reproduction," then mail art might conceivably be the art of the future. And if mail art was the future of art, it did not matter if you lived far from the geographic centers of the art world—if you lived in, say, Western Canada—because the art world was destined to become radically de-centered, dispersed across a network that was everywhere and nowhere.

If, if, if. It was a time for utopian thinking. Bands of mischievous hippies, naked as often as not, gambol across the pages of the early issues of *FILE* magazine, founded in 1972 by General Idea, a mail art collective in Toronto whose members went by the art-names AA Bronson, Felix Partz, and Jorge Zontal. Morris and Trasov followed suit, calling themselves Marcel Dot and Mr. Peanut, respectively (a photo of Trasov in full Planter's-mascot drag would grace the cover of *FILE*'s debut issue), along with their fellow Canadians Dr. and Lady Brute, Anna Banana, and the explicitly Johnsonian Corres Sponge School of Vancouver, all mail artists, all Ray-fans.

Ray is everywhere in those first numbers of *FILE*, in the mock gossip column, in the mock "best-dressed" feature, at the very top of the part mocking, part serious Top Ten List of 1972 (in the topsy-turvy world of the correspondence crowd, Warhol comes in at number 5 and Duchamp, at 11, doesn't quite make the top-top). Ray is their Marilyn.

XV

Stardom is a form of death. **Dear Deaths**, begins a letter by Ray Johnson to the obituary department of *The New York Times,* dated April 5, 1973, **The New York Corraspondence** [*sic*—when Johnson got tired of admonishing people to spell it correspon*∂ance*, he moved the "a"] **School, described by critic Thomas Albright in "Rolling Stone" as the "oldest and most influential" died this afternoon before sunset on a beach where a large Canadian goose had settled down on it's** [*sic*] **Happy Hunting Ground, was there obviously very tired and ill and I said to it "Oh, you poor thing."**

Thomas Albright's article, "New Art School: Correspondence," a celebration of the "far-reaching, far-out, potentially revolutionary" mail art movement, was published in *Rolling Stone* magazine in April 1972, the same month that *FILE* made its debut. The response that Johnson sent when Albright first wrote to him, requesting information for his article, begins graciously enough: **I would be delighted to send you material about the New York Corraspondence School and whatever visual material seems appropriate**. Then he begins to squirm.

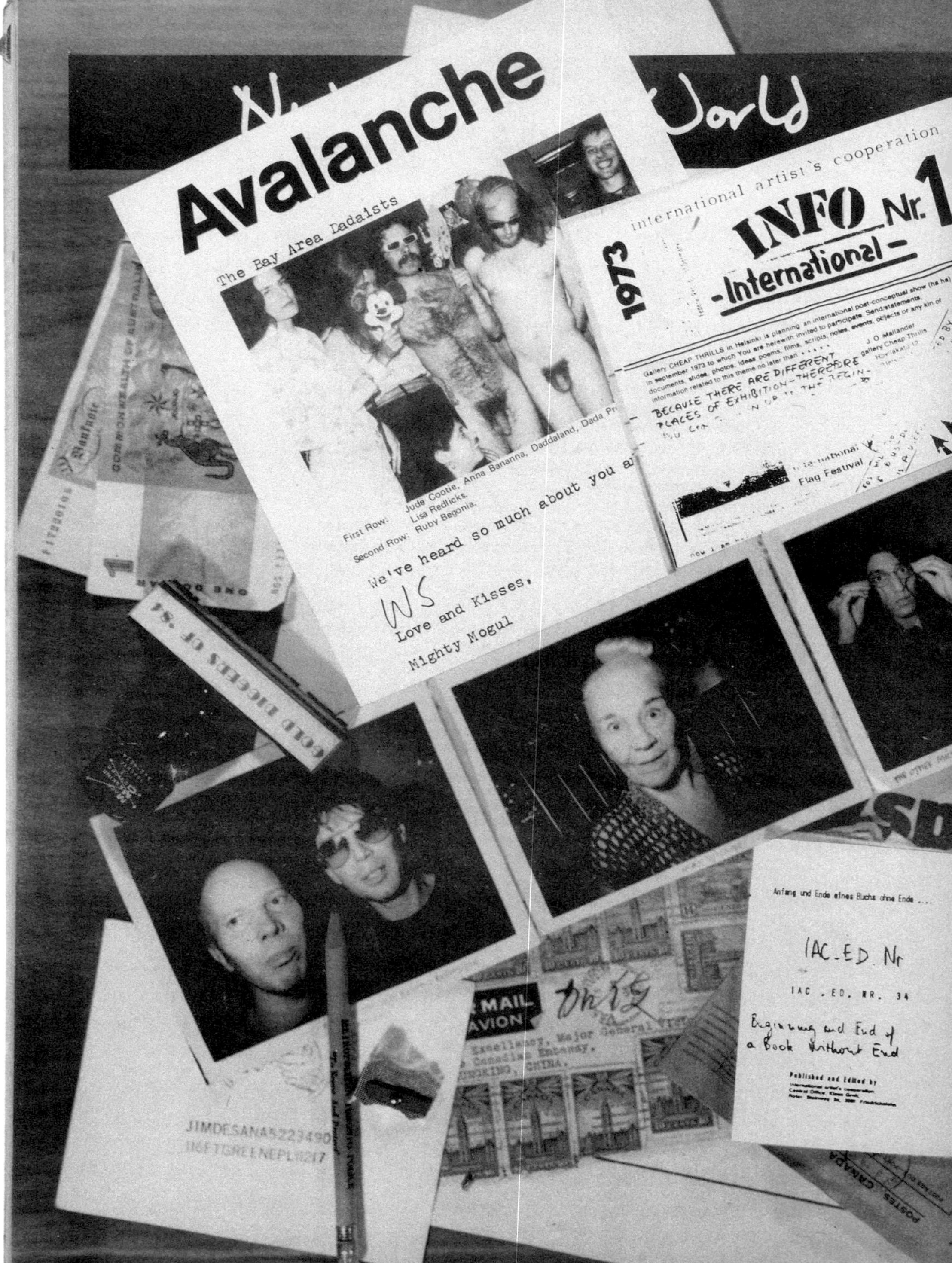
Avalanche
The Bay Area Dadaists
First Row: Jude Cootie, Anna Banana, Daddaland,
Lisa Redlicks.
Second Row: Ruby Begonia.
We've heard so much about you
WS
Love and Kisses,
Mighty Mogul
international artist`s cooperation
1973
INFO Nr. 1
-International-
BECAUSE THERE ARE DIFFERENT
PLACES OF EXHIBITION
Flag Festival
ONE DOLLAR
Anfang und Ende eines Buchs ohne Ende ....
IAC_ED Nr
IAC . ED. NR. 34
Beginning and End of a Book Without End
Published and Edited by
MAIL
AVION
JIMDESANA5223490

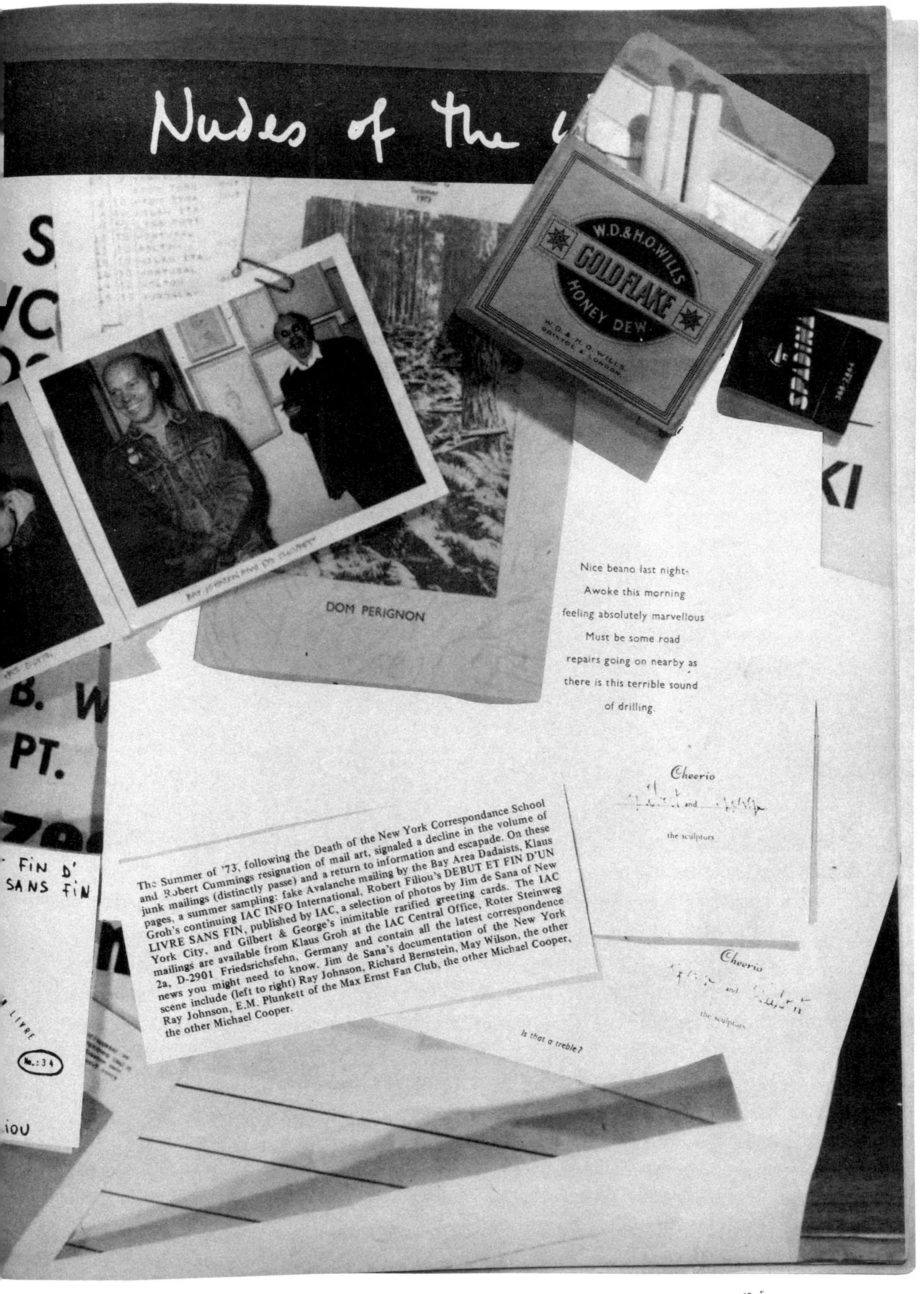

FILE, December 1973, "Nudes of the World" spread: Ray Johnson in snapshots, far right and far left; May Wilson, second from left.

I am so very tired of mailing letters and mailing material and mailing things. I have spent my whole life doing this. I am 44 years old. It aches to feel oneself becoming a thing of the past.

Then again, Johnson was nothing if not a connoisseur of the various forms that death can take. **"How beautiful!"** he remembers thinking, as he writes to *Deaths* of the way his exhausted Canadian counterpart **mustered up whatever strength it had and waddled away from me. "How like a bird—about to die yet having some courage to try to go on." And then—** and then—**it lifted it's legs and wings and shit out some black shit it was such a large heavy bird**. Ray Johnson had cultivated whatever you might call the opposite of the Midas touch, a knack for turning acceptance into rejection, gold into shit. It was a defense mechanism that would enable him to survive one form of death after another, until—it depends on how you look at it—he either lost his nerve or found the form that suited him.

Ground control to Major Tom. The end of the *Deaths* letter finds its writer far from shore. **Time to leave the Capsule. I'm stepping through the door. Tell my wife I love her <u>very much</u>**—lines Johnson has taken from the latest, latest thing, David Bowie's *Space Oddity*, a song that climbed to number 15 on the US singles chart in 1973. The name beside the bunny head sign-off is new as well: **Buddha University**. Samsara: one dies and is reborn in a new form.

XVI

The First Buddha University Meeting, dedicated to critic Mary Josephson, took place on June 9, 1973, at the Paula Cooper Gallery in Soho. Johnson wrote to Josephson to apprise her of this upcoming event in May, the month that Josephson's savvy review of Johnson's latest exhibition, "Ray Johnson's History of the Betty Parsons Gallery," was published in *Art in America*. The artist sent the letter to the reviewer care of the magazine after his efforts to elicit her contact information met with resistance from the magazine's editor, Brian O'Doherty. Johnson comments obliquely on Josephson's elusiveness at the letter's end, when he informs her that **After reading the New York Times yesterday, there now also exists <u>Emily Dickinson University</u>.**

Dickinson died uncelebrated in May of 1886. On May 22, 1973, the *Times* judged it "fitting," at long last, "that the omission be redressed with the publication of an 'obituary' of the shy and elusive person whom Mark Van Doren called the greatest woman poet"—an accolade as double-edged, in its way, as "New York's most famous unknown artist." Johnson had been a fan of Dickinson's for some time, but something in this article seems to have sealed his identification with "Amherst's inscrutable poet." "In fame, as in obscurity, Emily remains an enigma, and perhaps she would not object to that," the *Times* writer suggests. Well, yes, one thinks Ray must have thought, although one wonders if he winced at the overfamiliar "Emily," the kind of liberty we tend to take with those whose fame comes with a qualifier: famous, but a woman, famous yet unknown or, even once known, unknowable.

Then there was the article's title, "A Delayed 'Obituary.'" Johnson had an eye for awkward phrasing. And it is such a Johnsonian idea, the idea of an obituary in quotation marks, not so much the confirmation of a death as the recognition of a fame deserved but delayed; a fame that, once conferred, feels like a kind of death. Better to delay, then—but how?

"I died for Beauty," someone lets us know from the other side of the grave in Dickinson's poem #448. Emily Dickinson was always imagining a life beyond life that is not life eternal but a held pause. The one who died for Beauty, "scarce/ Adjusted in the Tomb," falls into conversation with one who died for Truth, also freshly situated "In an adjoining Room," and their talk goes on, against all odds, "Until the Moss had reached our lips— / And covered up—Our names—" This respite lasts "a Night," by the poet's measure, although the mourners—and the tombstone-carver—may hope that the names on the memorials will still be legible in time to come. Better not to say how long a time—or who, after a time, may recognize the names.

XVII

Brian O'Doherty has said that Ray Johnson did not know, when the artist asked for the editor's help in getting in touch with his reviewer, that O'Doherty had started writing reviews as "Mary Josephson" once he joined the masthead at *Art in America*. Shortly after that first Buddha University Meeting, though, Johnson was on "Mary"'s trail, joking to O'Doherty that he had begun **to suspect that everybody at Art in America doesn't exist, since Mary Josephson won't even tell me where to get a copy of "Degrees Below Zero,"** a telling reference to the fictional volume of poems that O'Doherty had attributed to his creation in her credit line. Ray knew a fellow skin-shedder when he saw one.

"Mary Josephson" was not the first, nor the last, pseudonymous alter ego Brian O'Doherty would assume—eventually, the number would come to four—but she was his only female persona. She gave him, he later said, a "long-desired" chance "to free myself from limiting malehood, to substitute another voice for that inner voice that never stops speaking." Josephson's writing career nonetheless ended when O'Doherty left the magazine.

For Johnson, by contrast, "limiting malehood" had ceased to function as a psychic baseline. Instead, he lived with a sense of gender as porous or multiple, a sensation that was always generative, but also always hedged with threats. A headline on a newspaper clipping that Ray sent to Bill in 1962 to forward to May reads "43 Seized at Artists' Ball Cleared of Masquerading." The forty-three were men, "masquerading to conceal their identity," which is to say they dressed in drag, at that time a practice punishable by law, the paper's reporter notes, as "a form of disorderly conduct." Bill and May were each fascinated, for their own reasons, by instances of unfixed identity. May pressed Ray to send her his copies of "physeek magazines"—gay erotica thinly disguised as bodybuilding guides—for use in her collages, where she would sometimes add her own head to a hunky torso and sometimes cut the musclemen into delicate snowflakes. One also finds many physique pics as well as more frankly pornographic images in Ray's mailings to Bill, who struggled to acknowledge his desire for men even after his wife Ann left him for critic Gene Swenson, who also preferred men, in 1966.

Ray understood May's need to slip the trap of gender as he understood Bill's balked urge to come out. He was born in the state of Neither/Nor. If only one could be famous and unknown, alive and dead, two and three dimensional, both and neither, in endless suspense.

If, if, if.

XVIII

A packet sent by Ray to Bill in November 1963 includes clips of three cute guys—two physique models and Hollywood star Guy Madison—and a mailing label torn from a magazine cover, which may at first glance seem unrelated to the clippings. The label is addressed to the attention of Dr. John Money, once a respected psychologist specializing in the developmental implications of the condition that was then called hermaphroditism, whose research led him to take part, beginning in 1965, in the Johns Hopkins Hospital's pioneering program in what were then called sex-change operations. Money is now notorious for his nightmarish mistreatment of a child patient who was ultimately driven to suicide by the doctor's depredations and his research has largely been discredited. In 1963, though, Money had as yet only published a few papers in obscure medical journals. How Johnson could have known about him back then—and how he got that mailing label—remain mysteries.

It is easy to see, however, how the doctor's name might have attracted the artist's attention. In the spring of 1970, Johnson wrote to Lotte Drew-Bear with the good news that he was **working on the last batch of paintings for the Dollar Bill Show**, due to open at Feigen Chicago that September, and that he **got a terrific reply from Dr. John Money at Johns Hopkins Hospital who does sex changes and he sent a great family tree type paragraph which is just what I want for the catalogue.** Money takes up Johnson's query in good spirit—"Sometimes when I am in unfamiliar places I look up Money in the phone book but I've never looked up Dollar or Bill"—and ends his letter, written, in proper NYCS style, on the inside of a flattened box of exotic tea, with a warm, "I'm so glad you wrote to me."

The Dollar Bill collage-paintings all incorporate, as the rubric implies, an actual one-dollar bill, and like most of Johnson's post-1969 exhibition works, they prominently feature proper names, some centered on a single name in the manner of the memorials, some dotted with name-clusters cut from seating charts. It is easy to draw the line that connects name to fame, and fame to money. Some of the named subjects of the "portraits" in this series were famous-famous (Marilyn Monroe, Jacqueline Kennedy Onassis, Joan Crawford), while others commanded a degree of art-world recognition (museum director René d'Harnoncourt, painter Ed Ruscha, collector Gertrude Stein). Such collisions between fame-worlds were also a staple of Johnson's post-1969 art.

Then there is the *Joe Buck Dollar Bill.* Like John Money, Joe Buck had a name ideally suited to Johnson's present needs (only more so, since "buck" means "dollar bill"). And he was famous, like the other portrait subjects—although unlike them, he was fictional, the titular character in *Midnight Cowboy*, the unlikely winner of the Academy Award for Best Picture in 1970. The win was unexpected in part because the film was rated "X"—the only film so rated ever to receive an Oscar—for scenes in which Buck, played by Jon Voight, then at the height of his epicene beauty, has sex for money with men and women. Or to be more accurate: Joe Buck, a Texan hayseed adrift in Manhattan, tries to have sex for money but keeps failing to get paid, by a schoolboy in a porn theater, by a mad preacher in the seediest of hotel rooms, and, most humiliatingly, by a true professional (Sylvia Miles) who manages to wrangle Buck's last dollar away from him at the end of their encounter.

Castello vecch
i di Stato già
occupato dal
'incendi. Qui,
ominasse seve
parete, che
pi vescovi di
fra i nobili c
scovi; nei p
rire i meda
ttestare la ri
a zecca e ab
o, che ci tran
ue si scorgono ancora negli sbiaditi affreschi del Castello e si ha notizia di
i. Di una verità spietata è quello fiammingo della Galleria Nazionale di Roma,

TALLERO D'ARGENTO DI BERNARDO CLESIO (1531).

EX-SAILOR GUY MADISON HAS ZOOMED, TO FORE FOR STAR-MAKER D. SELZNICK

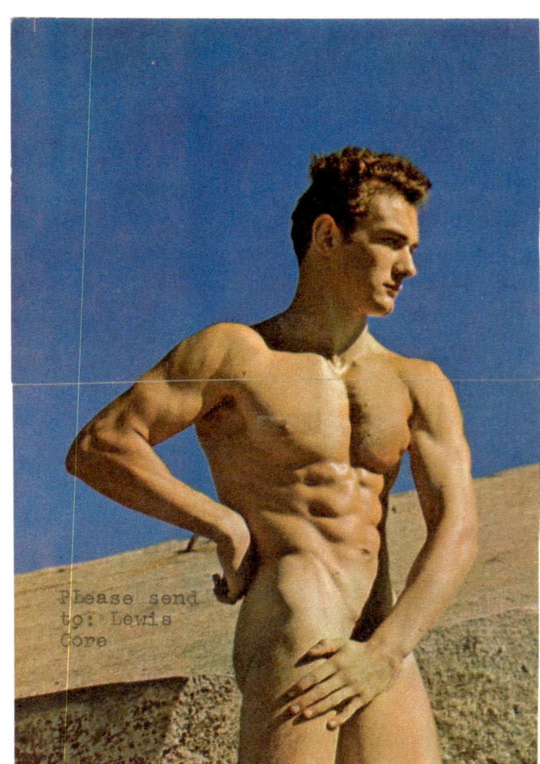

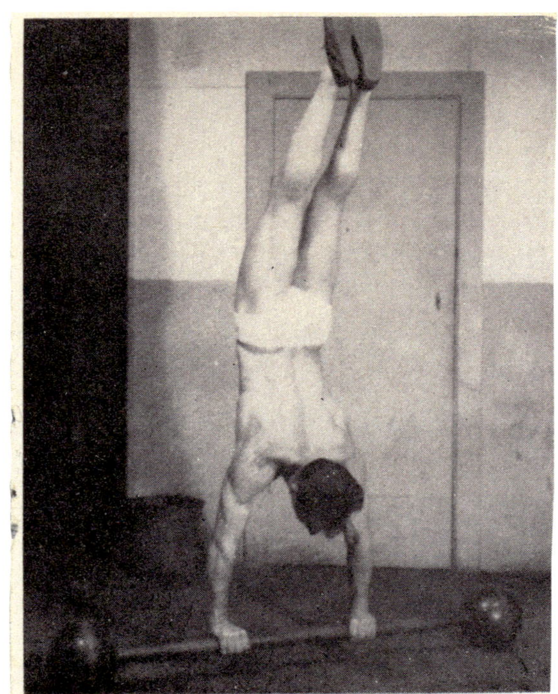

Please send to: May Wilson, 3
Dance Mill Road, Phoenix,
Maryland

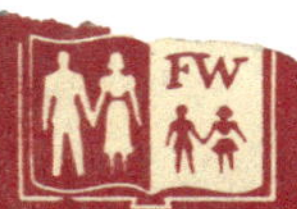

EXINGTON AVENUE, NEW K 22,

POSTMASTER:

This parcel may be opened for postal inspection

RETURN POSTAGE GUARANTEED

To:

The Johns Hopkins Hospital
Receiving Dept.
Wolfe Street Storage Bldg.
Baltimore 5, Md.

JOHN DOE

Attn: Dr. John Money
400 Phipps Clinic

Ray Johnson to William S. Wilson, November 6, 1963.

Toward the end of the film, Buck is invited to a wild party staged as a simulacrum of the scene at Andy Warhol's Factory. The filmmakers even went to the length of hiring Paul Morrissey, who directed all the movies released under the Warhol brand after Warhol lost interest in filmmaking, to orchestrate the event. They also tried to hire Warhol to play a version of himself, an underground movie director prowling around the crowd with a camera, but he demurred, and the role went to Viva, one of several Warhol Superstars featured in the sequence. When the production sent her to have her hair done at a fancy uptown salon, Viva telephoned Andy to share the thrill, but soon after she began talking, she heard shots. It was June 3, 1968, the day Valerie Solanas took her gun out from under May Wilson's bed.

At the party, Buck finally picks up a woman (Brenda Vaccaro) who seems willing and able to pay for his services, but when they get to bed, he can't perform. To spare them both embarrassment, she suggests that they play scribbage, a game in which one spells out words with lettered dice. On his first turn, Joe misspells "MONY" and his companion starts to tease him, listing other words that end in "y"—"pay, lay, fey, gay"—"Is that your problem, baby?" she asks, narrowing her eyes. No, says the movie. (The central relationship in the film is the not-not-not-gay intimacy between Joe Buck and his would-be pimp, Ratso Rizzo, played to the acting-class hilt by Dustin Hoffman.) And then again, yes. *Midnight Cowboy* wants it both ways, seeming gay while playing straight, pretending not to know how to spell MONY while cashing in. It marks a turning point in American movies: the studio system breathes its last, last gasp and rises from the ashes of the underground.

XIX

The androgynous beauty whose photograph anchors *Joe Buck Dollar Bill* is not Jon Voight but Josephine Baker, who left the U.S. for France in the 1920s to scale heights of stardom no one with her skin could hope to reach back home. Joe B. and Josephine B. It is a connection only letter-obsessed Ray could have made. But once made, one can see how that connection would then lead him to associate a famous image of Baker *en travesti* with Buck in his cowboy drag ("that cowboy crap ... that's faggot stuff, that's strictly for fags," Ratso taunts an indignant Joe). Of course, Baker is the exact reverse of Buck in key respects: female to his male, black to his white, and the kind of rags-to-riches star beside whose spectacular success the failed fantasies of characters like Joe look all the more pathetic. Still, in Johnson's eyes, the link between them is direct and strong. Lest the viewer miss it, the artist has run a strip of tesserae

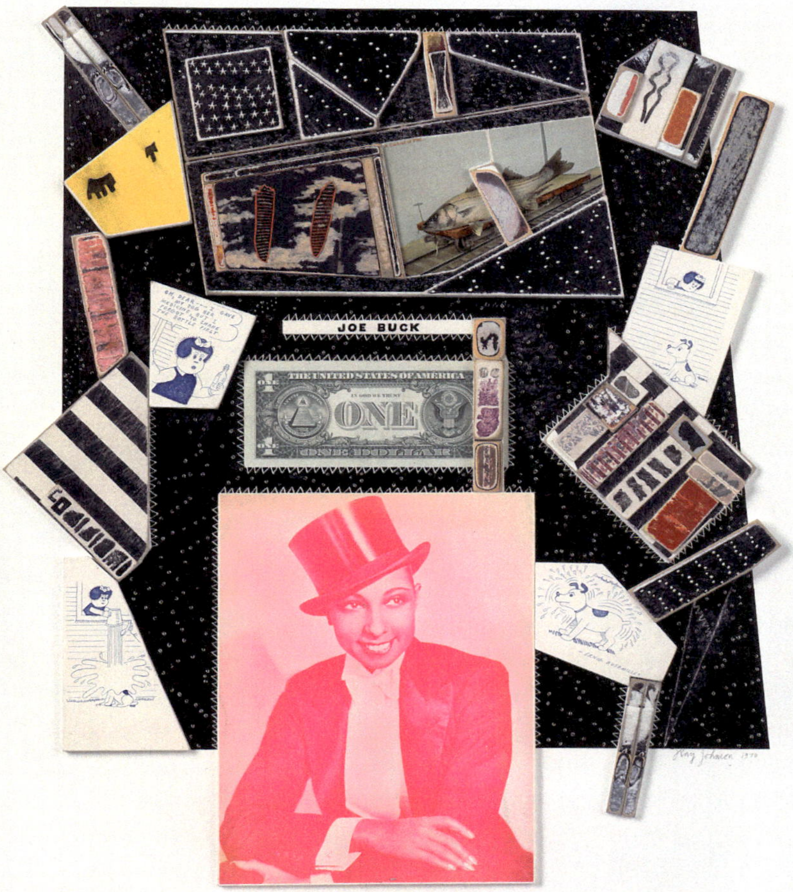

Ray Johnson, *Joe Buck Dollar Bill* (1970).

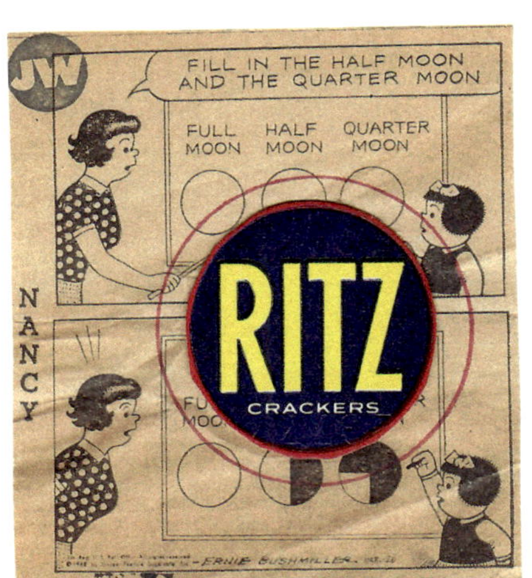

Ray Johnson to John Willenbecher, March 1969.

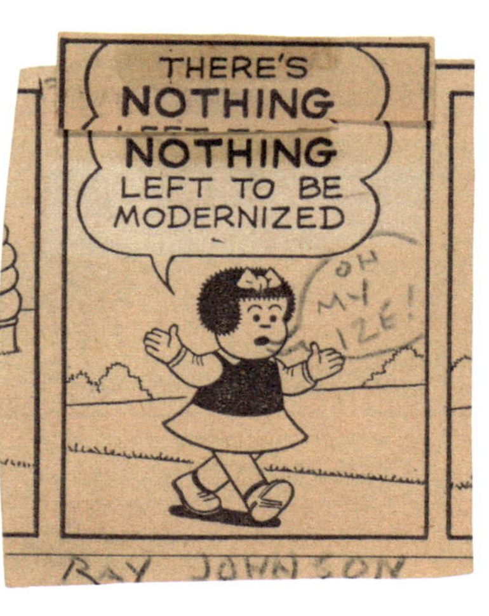

Ray Johnson to William S. Wilson, February 15, 1965.

from the right edge of the "Joe Buck" nameplate through the right edge of the dollar bill to the top right edge of the Baker photograph.

The three elements connected by the strip are centered relative to one another and to the sides of the picture frame; they are also the only pieces in the collage that are both squared-off and set square within the frame. All the other tiles are atilt on the large rhomboid shape whose edges constitute a second frame, a frame whose bounds the unrulier tiles keep breaking through. Some of the tiles are sandpapered abstracts, one bears an image from a joke postcard that depicts a fish out of water, and four others contain panels copied from Johnson's favorite comic strip, *Nancy*, by Ernie Bushmiller. At the lower right corner of the framing shape, Johnson has angled Bushmiller's signature, inscribed on the final panel, so that it points down toward his own. "Oh dear," says Nancy in the panel, "I gave my dog her medicine, but I forgot to shake the bottle first." Her characteristically backwards solution is to dump a pail of water on the unwitting pet, who must then shake madly to shed the drops.

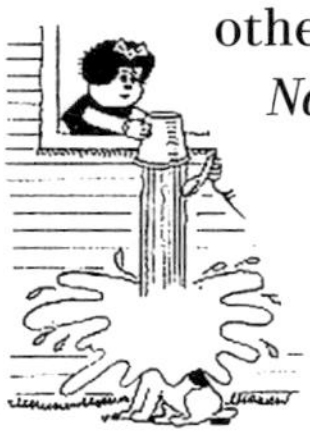

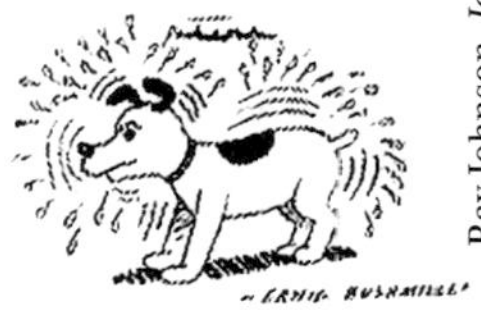

Ray Johnson, *Joe Buck Dollar Bill* (1970), details.

Nancy was a favorite as well of other artists Johnson knew, like Warhol, and Frank O'Hara's protégé Joe Brainard. They were attracted by Bushmiller's drawing style, which was so simplified as to be almost abstract, by his humor, which was so dumb as to be almost unfunny, and perhaps most of all, by his tomboyish heroine, whose name doubles as a pejorative epithet for "gay man." To these impure formalists, *Nancy* was found modernism, of a slightly bent variety.

One could view *Joe Buck* as a portrait of the artist, the joker in the pack of *Dollar Bills*. But it is more like a void where a portrait should be. The name above the dollar signifies all that Ray is not: not a true professional, like Warhol, the kind of artist who can forge a brand, and stick with it; neither the geometric purist he started out as, nor the crude cartoonist he might sometimes seem to be. Nothing in itself, this not-not-not-Ray functions as a black hole into which our categories keep collapsing. The grid that underpins *Joe Buck* is built around simple equations—buck=dollar bill, J.B=J.B—only to be riven by criss-crossing identifications. Success≠failure, boy≠girl, fact≠fiction? It would be sweet to think so, says the picture. What if, like Nancy, you are prone to getting things backward? What if, like Joe Buck, you are selling but no one is buying? In Ray Johnson's art world, the center that is money cannot hold. It cannot compete for our attention with the girl dressed like a boy, who had to leave her country to succeed, though you would never know, from her cheshire-cat smile, all she had to go through to get here.

XX

“Dear Ray,” begins a letter headed “Chelsea Hotel/Nov. 8, 1970,” and signed “Joe Buck.” “I’m dictating this to Jamie Herlihy, he’s my secretary because I don’t write all that good.” James Leo Herlihy, the author of *Midnight Cowboy* (1965), the novel on which the film is based, was born, like Ray, in 1927 in Detroit, and studied at Black Mountain, though not when Ray was there. Herlihy’s work, like that of many gay artists in that pivotal moment, was shaped by a wrenching conflict between the need to reveal and the need to conceal his sexuality. Jamie Herlihy died a year before Ray Johnson did, having long suffered from writing too little and drinking too much, but in 1970, buoyed by the film’s success, he was riding as high as he ever would. The letter from “Joe” to “Ray” ends with a postscript: “You must be some dude in person. Me, too.” Joe Buck knew a fellow fiction when he saw one.

XXI

“I like my Dollar Bill that’s in the catalog,” Joe lets Ray know, “Only I want to see the one that isn’t, too.” Herlihy is referring to *Midnight Cowboy Dollar Bill*, the second of three *Cowboy*-themed collages Johnson had planned to make (though no trace of a third one has survived). *Midnight Cowboy* shares a template with several of the other Dollar Bills, a shape that Johnson borrowed from Karl Wirsum. Before the Dollar Bill show opened in Chicago, Karl’s hometown, Ray sent him a note with a heads-up—**Karl August,/ I hope you don’t mind I’ve done four portraits of your BACK for my BUCK $$ show Feigen Sept**., with a tracing-paper cutout of a Wirsum muscleman taped over the message.

The muscleman first appeared as one of two dozen or so tattoos that spread across another bodybuilder’s back, a form that functions as a frame within the frame of a poster made to advertise the inaugural exhibition of the Hairy Who, a group of young Chicago painters who all worked in a trippy pop-cartoonish style. Wirsum outlined the torso, with its shaggy armpits exuding giant gleaming sweatdrops, but the tattoos were a collective project, and the signatures of all the members of the group can be found scattered across the figure’s back. It is a portrait of the artist as a social network, the network in which everyone is an artist.

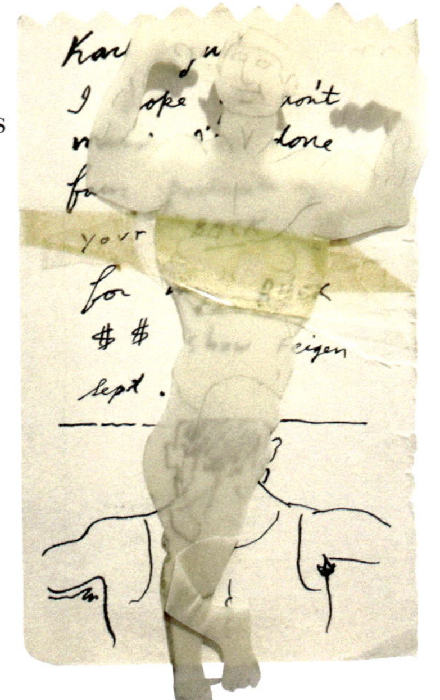

Ray Johnson to Karl Wirsum, 1970.

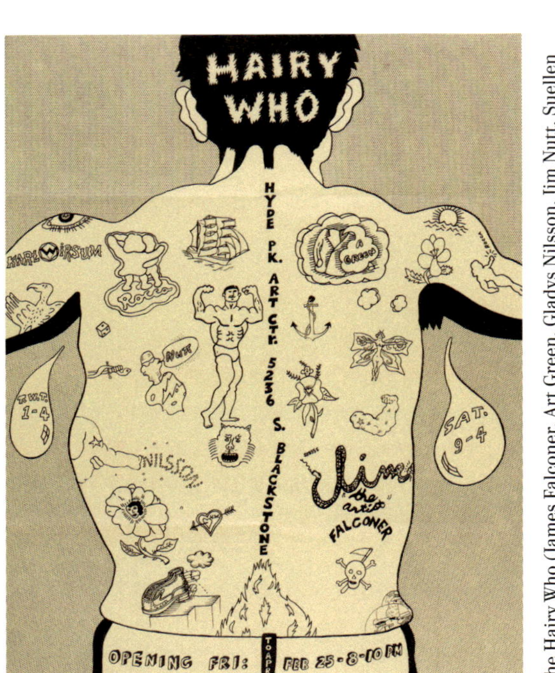

The Hairy Who (James Falconer, Art Green, Gladys Nilsson, Jim Nutt, Suellen Rocca, and Karl Wirsum), poster for the first Hairy Who group exhibition at the Hyde Park Art Center, Chicago, February 25–April 9, 1966.

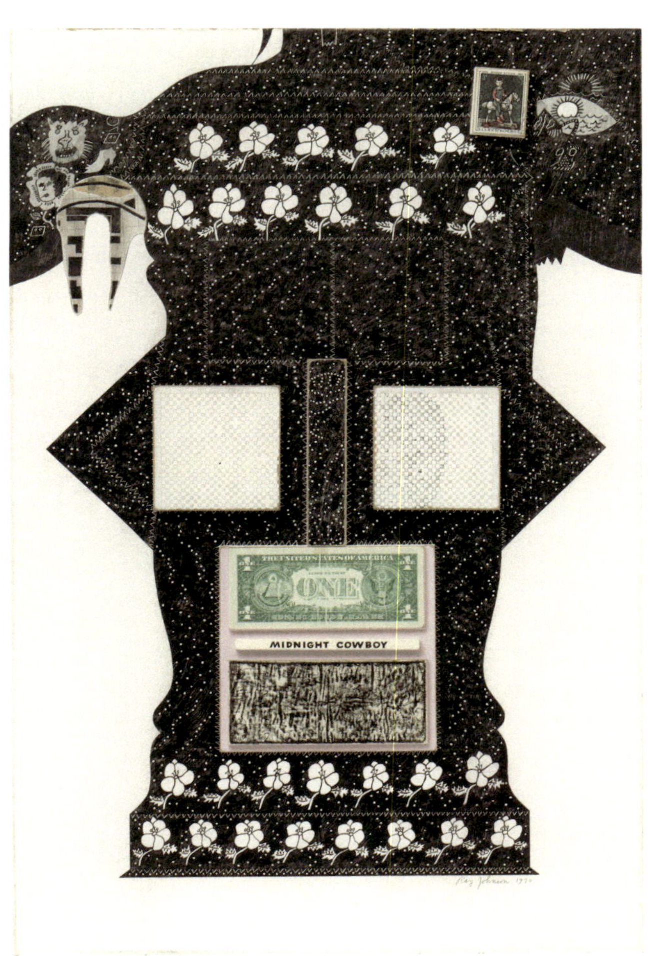

Ray Johnson, *Midnight Cowboy Dollar Bill* (1970).

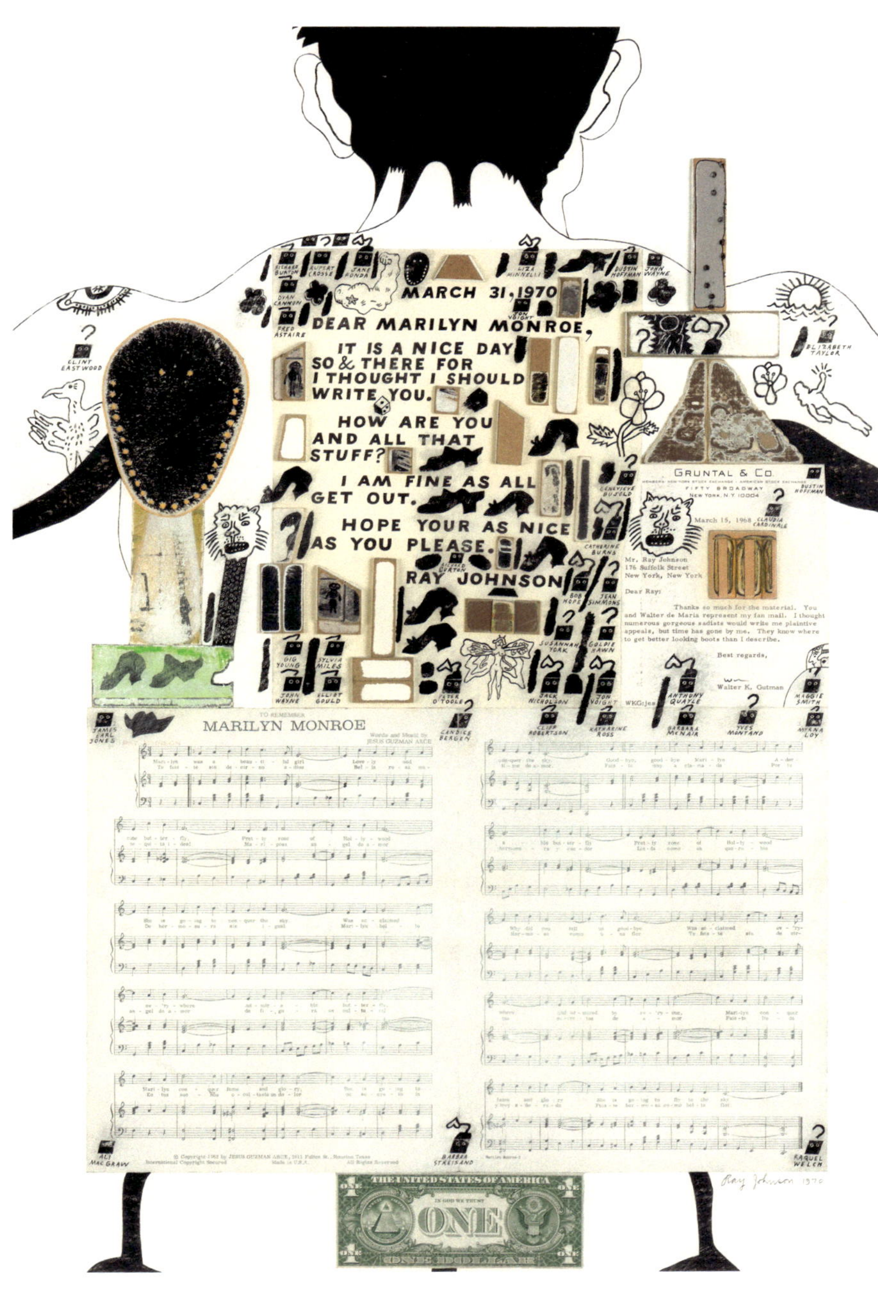

Ray Johnson, *Marilyn Monroe Dollar Bill* (1970).

Everybody is a member of the NYCS. Everybody, Ray Johnson told his dealer, who did not want to hear it. Richard Feigen's instinct told him that Johnson was a great artist, the kind of artist who might make a dealer's reputation while at the same time making him some money. The great-artist idea drives the art market and paves the path of least resistance for museum curators, art critics, and historians. Artists who embrace the opposing idea that "everyone is an artist," make things difficult for themselves and others. In the early 1970s, the everyone-an-artist concept became closely linked to Fluxus associate Josef Beuys, whose *Intuition ... Instead of a Cookbook [wooden box with pencil drawing]*—a bestseller for VICE-Versand—appears in *Mark*, where Johnson attributes it to screen heartthrob Rudolf Valentino.

If, as the logic went in those days, you could buy a Beuys through the mail for two dollars, or better yet, engage in the free exchange of mail as art, and if, moreover, you were not all that worried about sorting out the "better items" from the "bulk" things, then dealers, curators, and critics might have nothing more to do. Ray Johnson's collage-paintings were becoming ever richer and more resonant as he found new ways of integrating them into his total practice. But they were still hard to sell, in part because it was hard to untangle them from the troublesome thought that, as Ray himself would later quip, **I am an individual who is a group**.

In *Midnight Cowboy Dollar Bill*, the bill is pasted face-side down, to show the ONE on the dollar's back. ONE is a set of letters and a number and a gender-neutral pronoun and on a bill, a denomination that points to an absent source of value. ONE is an individual in the abstract, as opposed to the hairy, sweaty particular. The Wirsum torso appears as an abstracted shape in *Midnight Cowboy*. If the dollar-bill-shaped tile placed below the actual dollar bill once bore an image, it has since been rubbed out. Two eye-catchers, a curved tessera and a postage stamp with a painting of a boy riding a toy horse (a mini cowboy), have been pushed out toward the edges of the field, lest they detract from its spare elegance.

The dollar is also face-side down in *Marilyn Monroe Dollar Bill*, another Wirsum-torso image. While the torso here, unlike the one in *Midnight Cowboy*, is still visibly a body, its already inked-up flesh has been overwritten edge to edge in Johnsonese. There are tesserae, and name-chart fragments, and moticos-style silhouettes of shoes, and two oval face-like shapes—no, those are heel-prints. Ow. Among these bits of code wind the words of a faux-naif message to Marilyn that Ray might have copied from one of his found postcards, and, to the right of this imaginary missive, the artist has pasted an actual letter, typed on the stationery of the Wall Street brokerage Gruntal & Co. and dated March 15, 1968.

Dear Ray,

Thanks so much for the material. You and Walter de Maria represent my fan mail. I thought numerous gorgeous sadists would write me plaintive appeals, but time has gone by me. They know where to get better boots than I describe.

Best regards,

Walter K. Gutman

Walter K. Gutman was a rabbit-hole character par excellence. He made a fortune as a stock analyst and a name for himself sharing his wisdom on the subject in a market newsletter distinguished by an irreverent wit that garnered him the title, "a Proust in Wall Street." But he had started out as an art critic and never quite left the scene. By the time Gutman wrote to Johnson, he had, among other things, done a book with Dick Higgins, collaborated on films with the underground-director's-underground-director George Kuchar, and studied art with Jack Tworkov, painting fetishistic pictures of musclebound females that got him featured in "The Dominant Woman," a show curated by Ray's old acquaintance Elayne Varian at Finch College.

The Walter K. Gutman dollar bill: on its face, a market letter; on its reverse, a boot-heel pressed into flesh. Ambivalence, you see. As Ray Johnson was learning, ambivalence tends to undermine the value of one's currency. Why cultivate it, then? Ambivalence is worth the pain, if and only if what one wants most is a perpetual out from the existing alternatives.

XXII

Out of the art world, into the dream world.

oct 11, 1972
toby a most extraordinary dream
artists studio discovered small tree
bark pieces with words small handlettered
poems i had written on trees in an orchard
years ago with norman in conn. or mass. years
later found by these people who didn't know who
they were by. I claimed authorship.

Funny that Ray eschews capitals here until he gets to that final "I." **I claimed authorship.** But only after he has disclaimed it, leaving his works behind far from home, scattering them in the company of a friend, retrieving them through the mediation of strangers. Ray dreams of a world of happy accidents, of authority lost and found. A comic world, like the wood to which the members of the court escape in Shakespeare's *As You Like It*, where

> this our life, exempt from public haunt,
> Finds tongues in trees, books in the running brooks,
> Sermons in stones, and good in everything.
> I would not change it.

Or so the exiled Duke would have us believe. Because he believes it, while he dreams.

XXIII

Betty Parsons began making art while she was in her teens and began dealing it in the mid-1930s, when she was in her mid-thirties. A decade later she would open her own gallery and represent, among other starry mid-century names, the painters she called her "four horsemen of the apocalypse," Barnett Newman, Jackson Pollock, Mark Rothko, and Clyfford Still. Parsons was a New York art world insider if there ever was one, and yet, while she was undoubtedly in that world, she was also in some sense not of it. "She is not, for me, primarily, a dealer," wrote the critic Clement Greenberg, by which he meant that, just as "a painter is referred to as a painter's painter or a poet as a poet's poet, Mrs. Parsons' is an artist's—and critic's—gallery: a place where art goes on and is not just shown and sold." One of Parsons's artists, Saul Steinberg, put it more fancifully, describing her as "a fiction," who

> exists in the way that Raskolnikov exists, or Julien Sorel. The profession of art dealer is very difficult, very delicate. A dealer is the intermediary between two of the most important things in life—money and fame—and the fact that Betty is a fictional character makes it easier to deal with her, although it also makes things less precise.... It is good for a dealer to have a fictional side. The best dealers are like Nibelungs, keepers of the treasure. They are remote. Betty is like that.

"It also makes things less precise": this was Steinberg's tactful way of gesturing toward the inconvenient fact that Parsons's focus on making her gallery a place where art goes on came somewhat at the expense of her attention to those two most important things in life, money and fame. Artists had a way of leaving her once they had had a taste of both and wanted more. Over the years, Parsons' clout diminished, although her legend remained undimmed.

Johnson refers to the legend in a 1972 letter addressed to Parsons and her associate, Jock Truman, proposing **the idea of exhibiting works I want to create which will be Memorials to Pollock, Ad Reinhardt, Sonia**

Sekula, Barney Newman, a show that would summon up **those Tiger's Eye years remembering those first Raushenberg shows and so forth.** *The Tiger's Eye* was a little magazine that burned bright for a moment in the mid-1940s, the moment of Parsons's ascendance to art-world prominence. Edited by Ruth and John Stephan, the magazine featured the émigré Surrealists as well as many of the artists Parsons showed in those years, including Reinhardt and Newman and Sonia Sekula, a Swiss painter who had been Johnson's downstairs neighbor on Monroe Street in the early 1950s and remained a friend until she died, by her own hand, in 1963. We share a world, Johnson is saying, in his coded way, to Parsons, whom he did not actually know well (his letters to her are alternately addressed to "Betty" and "Mrs. Parsons"), although he was friendly with Truman.

Still, even if they once shared a world, Johnson's life of late had been unfolding at the outer edges of Parsons' sphere. Nervously aware of this, it takes the artist several paragraphs to get to his exhibition proposal, after some court-jester-antic attempts to bring the dealer up to date. **Since I am presently without a New York gallery,** he confesses, **I am showing this month with Arturo Schwarz in Milan where last December did** [*sic*] **a whole new show of Famous People's Mother's Potato Mashers—naturally Andy Warhol, Michael York, Jackie Kennedy Onassis and Batman**—not, Ray must have known, names to conjure with for Mrs. Parsons. Nor were the star-names he drops in connection with his latest **New York Corraspondence School Meeting for Anna May Wong to be presented June 3 at the New York Cultural Center auditorium,** where **the role of Anna May Wong will be played by Naomi Sims, famous Vogue model.** (The glamorous Sims, then at the height of her fashion-world fame, was also, as it happened, the wife of Johnson's art-dealer friend Michael Findlay.)

One could see Johnson's jester-dance here as defensive, a way of masking his fear that Parsons might reject him, or—and—one could see it as productive, part of the process of working out **some new way of thinking which has to do with the present and the future and the past and the future being presented in the past.** For Ray Johnson was, unlike Betty Parsons and the kinds of artists she championed, a lover of the ephemeral, of the foam at the tip of the cresting wave of the present; and at the same time he was, like Parsons and her kind, deeply invested in a certain moment of New York Past, a moment when all the tendencies of the previous avant-gardes, of Dada and Surrealism and painterly abstraction, seemed held in solution, and Ray and his friends had just left Black Mountain and come to the city and everything seemed possible. **Those Tiger's Eye years remembering those first Raushenberg shows**—in 1951,

Parsons gave Rauschenberg, who was in between stints at Black Mountain, his first solo exhibition—**and so forth**.

After leaving Feigen, Johnson would sell work from the back rooms of a number of firms, including Parsons's, but while he lived, he would never again have official gallery representation. In 1972, whether he knew it or not, he was on his way out of the gallery system. This was the moment that the idea that had been forming in the artist's mind crystallized around the fictional aspect of Betty Parsons, the legend of the dealer who was somehow not primarily a dealer but a keeper of the treasure—although kept for what purpose, for what moment in the future? A fictional character has no future and so could not say, but maybe a certain kind of historian could.

XXIV

"The art world," people say, as if it really were a planet unto itself. People do not speak of the other elite art-spheres this way and that is because the world of the visual arts floats, above and apart, on a sea of money and that is because works of visual art can be turned into fungible vehicles of investment as works of literature and theater and dance and classical music cannot. The story of how the art world became a world apart has yet to be written, or, at least, has yet to be written in the form of a book called something like *The History of the Art World*. But it is clear by now to most of its constituents that the art world, as they know it, is an artifact of the peculiar relationship, at once parasitic and parodic, that developed between a globalizing art market and a globalizing financial market in the decades following World War II. One sees in a flash the difference between the post- and pre-war avant-gardes in the difference between Warhol's boxes and Duchamp's Readymades. For while both the *Brillo Boxes* and the Readymades require "an atmosphere of theory" to be seen as art, unlike Duchamp's scrupulously unassuming found objects, Warhol's packages proclaim their salability with all the graphic power they can muster.

And yet the art world is not identical to the art market. It remains a "world" rather than an industry because it is not, or not yet, vertically integrated but is comprised of a kit of parts—galleries and schools and magazines and museums and fairs and auction houses—that seems, still, to have been assembled by a loony bricoleur. It can still harbor spaces, pockets of internal distance, where art goes on and is not just shown and sold. Duchamp spoke of the "infrathin," a quality the perception of which allows one to distinguish between seeming indiscernibles—this bottle-rack in the gallery and that one in the café. The distinction between the art world and the art market is like that. Or it is like the sliver of space between the support and the raised surface of a tile in a Ray Johnson collage—a space that the camera mercilessly flattens out, and that even a real-live viewer must come in very close to discern.

XXV

The endless allusiveness of Ray Johnson's collage-paintings may seem daunting to the casual viewer, but really, "All you have to know," as one reviewer of Johnson's Parsons show assured his readers, "is that Art is people together, names in proximity. Ray's Pollock is a crowd." To say that Ray's Pollock is a crowd is not quite the same as to say that everyone is an artist, nor is it exactly to say that the individual has become a mere node in a network. It is to say, rather, that Jackson Pollock, the Marilyn Monroe of Betty Parsons' art world, is a sum of energies, the collective energy generated by the inhabitants of Planet Art. In *Ray Johnson's History of the Betty Parsons Gallery*, the centripetal force around which these energies whirl is not the dollar but desire, a desire that is at once eros unbound and aesthetic sublimation.

An installation shot from the Parsons exhibition shows that the pictures were hung with their lower edges aligned and just a sliver of space left between them, a space like the gutter between the pages in an open book.

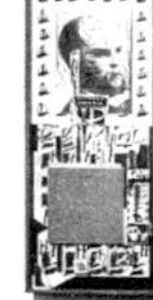
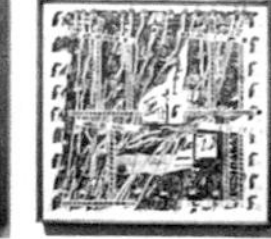
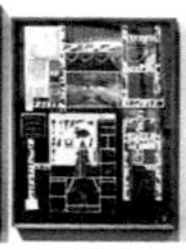
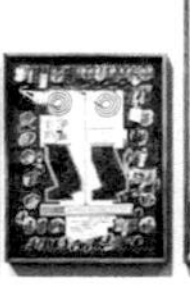
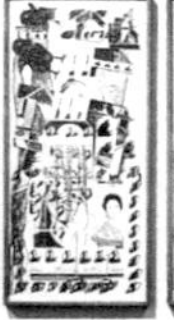
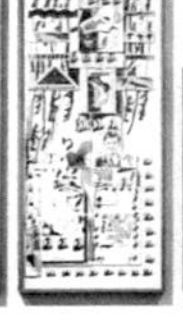
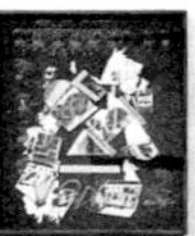
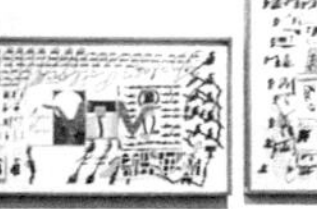
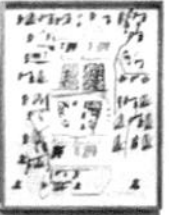
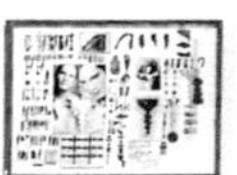

Installation photograph of "Ray Johnson's History of the Betty Parsons Gallery," 1973.

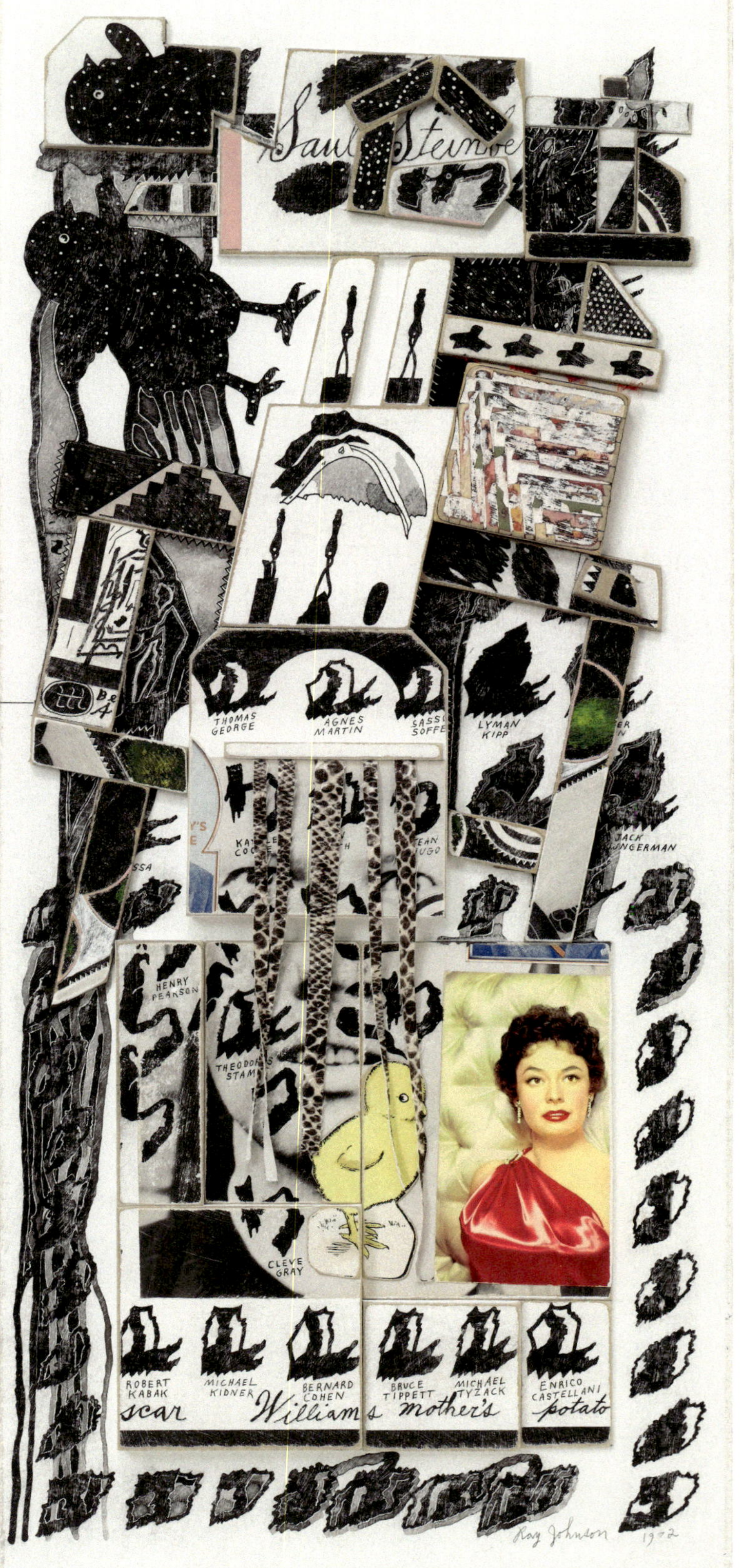

Ray Johnson, *Saul Steinberg* (1972).

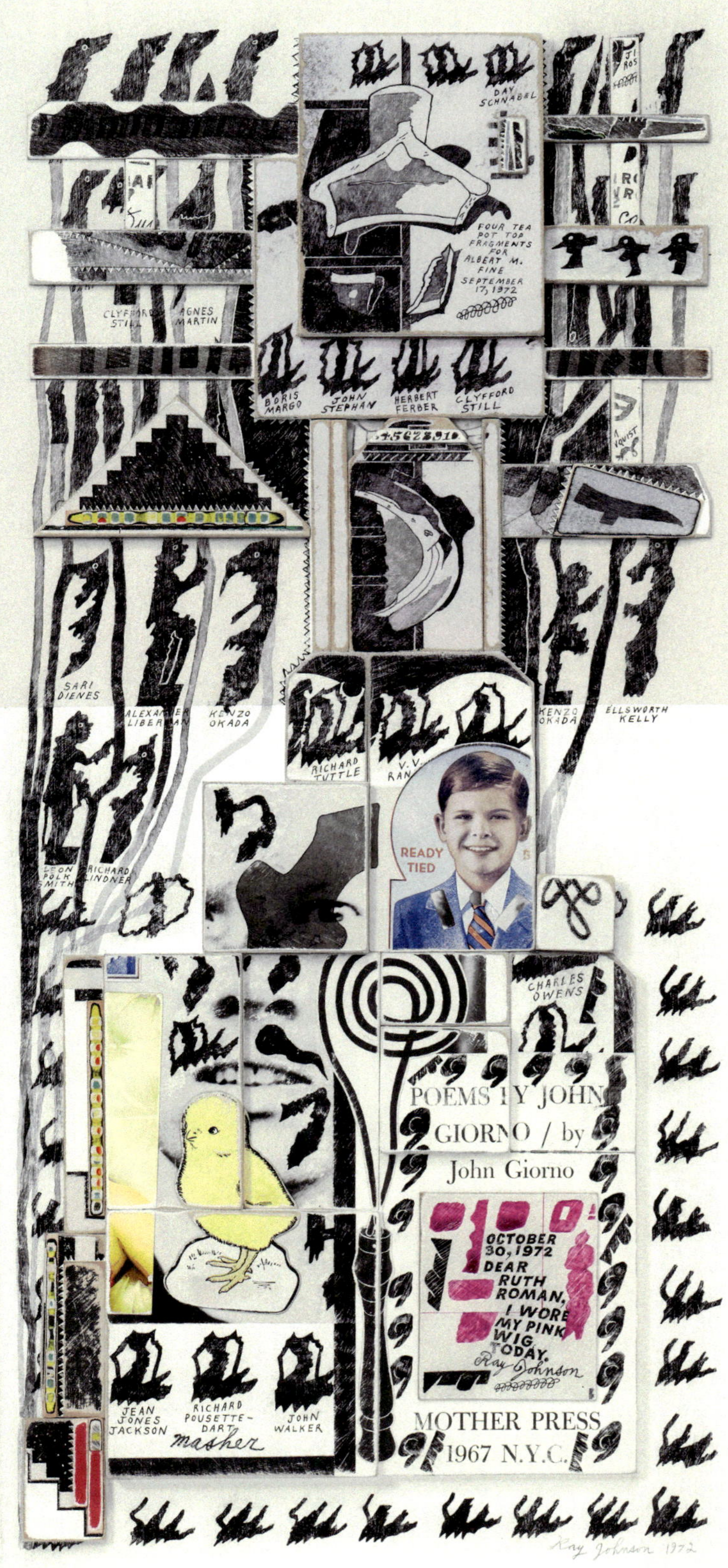

Ray Johnson, *Richard Pousette-Dart Masher* (1972).

Since Johnson always closely supervised the hanging of his work when possible, one can assume this arrangement was his idea. The pictures' alignment and proximity encourage the viewer to scan them one after another, like the pages of a book, rather than to contemplate each separately, stepping back to take in the gestalt before attending to the details, as one usually does in galleries.

At the center of the wall in the photograph, a pair of tall, narrow painting-collages anchors the ensemble. *Saul Steinberg* and *Richard Pousette-Dart Masher* are both named after artists who began showing with Parsons early on and did *not* leave her for greener pastures—Steinberg because he was a quirky comedian with an oblique relation to the art world who saw in the "remote" Parsons a kindred spirit (and who also arranged, for practical reasons, to split his representation between Parsons and her more commercially minded colleague and rival Sidney Janis); and Pousette-Dart because, although his sense of scale and touch initially led critics to place him with the best of his expressionist peers, a move out of the city in 1951 and an ineradicable mystical streak caused his work to fall out of fashion soon thereafter. But Parsons always had a place for painters' painters of his type.

The Steinberg and Pousette-Dart pictures, with their closely matched compositional programs, form a diptych, and within each picture is a smaller diptych, likewise composed of matched portraits of artists. The artist at left in both cases is Johnson himself, seen in a photograph taken by his friend Ara Ignatius, peering out at us through a blizzard of glyphs and glued-on fragments. The artists at right remain hidden, although their identities may be inferred from traces of desires past, burnt-out fires "whose embers," in the impression of one of the show's reviewers, nonetheless "still glow, ready to be fanned into flame at the breath of the visitor poring over the works."

These traces take the form of found scraps: in *Saul Steinberg*, a glamor shot of actress Ruth Roman, a star from the 1950s whose reputation did not survive the period, sheathed in flame-red satin; and in *Pousette-Dart Masher*, the title page from a book of poems by John Giorno, a ubiquitous figure on Johnson's New York scene. Johnson has superimposed his own note to Roman on the Giorno page, a note that also appears, in slightly different form, in the collage that hung to the left of the diptych on Parsons' wall, a memorial to Jackson Pollock titled *Dear Ruth Szowie*. To clinch the link between the two pictures within the pictures, the artist has placed a cutout from a vintage advertisement for a clip-on necktie, labeled "Ready Tied," above the Giorno page, and placed the cutout's sliced-off left edge by his own eye in the Steinberg collage. This dense tangle of references is knotted together by rhymes, as in a poem, and by displacements, as in a dream, and, as in a dream, the referential relay is spurred on by an insatiable wish.

The elusive objects of desire here are a matched set of luscious brunettes, Ruth Kligman and John Giorno, both artists themselves but famed for their magnetic effect on other artists. To historians of the mid-century art world, Kligman, who really did resemble Ruth Roman in her youth, will forever be the "death-car girl," in Frank O'Hara's cruel but indelible phrase, who survived the crash that killed her lover Jackson Pollock in 1956. Giorno also sidestepped into immortality early in life, when he became the subject of Andy Warhol's *Sleep* (1964), five hours and twenty minutes of film culled from a night-long session in which Andy ran his camera while John dreamed. A year after leaving Warhol, Giorno took up with Robert Rauschenberg, who designed the cover, a collage of voluptuous bodies in shades of flame-orange, for the book of poems whose title page Johnson features in his *Pousette-Dart Masher*. Devastated as Kligman was by Pollock's death, within a year, she, too, had moved on, to Pollock's eternal rival for painterly preeminence, Willem de Kooning. In Bill's studio one day, Ruth saw an abstraction with swathes of cerulean blue and cadmium yellow pinned together by V-shaped slashes of black and green and let out an exclamation, "zowie," so that was what the painter called it, *Ruth's Zowie*—a title which, like de Kooning's paintings even at their most abstract, also has something of the voluptuous body about it.

Each diptych within the diptych is two-faced, like a dollar bill. On one side, a portrait of the artist, on the other, a hidden history of the art world. You could call that history gossip, or "Kleenex history," in Brian O'Doherty's nice phrase; "gossip," this critic judged, in his review of the Parsons show, was "after all, Johnson's medium." Yet as Ray Johnson retails it, gossip gets inextricably tangled with the drives that drive the making of art, the drives to emulate and to compete, the manifest urge to look and the latent urge to touch, and back of it all, the never-to-be-explained-away desire to communicate by indirection, by rhymes and displacements, in fragments of cardboard and slashes of paint.

The artist's desire to communicate often feels, in the moment of making, like a strictly personal desire, contained within this body, this mind, and this studio, though aimed at absent others who might offer up their zowies in response. It is a rarer sort of artist who holds to the sense that art is people together, that the drives that drive the making of art are fueled by the collective energies of everyone concerned with art. Ray Johnson was that sort of artist and, at the same time, he was also an artist of the studio. When he put this contradiction to work, to make art just was to experience the sensation of being pierced through by interpersonal energies. It was a sensation akin both to the pleasures of sexual masochism—see the knot on the tile beside the beaming boy model for Ready Tied—and to the pleasures of critical analysis. Johnson's names in proximity may look like gossip at first glance, but as one turns the pages of his book, gossip thickens into social history, the kind that seeks the future in the past.

The objects of desire in the Parsons diptych are embedded in a grid of names, each belonging to an artist who showed, at one time or another, at the Betty Parsons Gallery. But with a handful of exceptions, these are not names of the sort that command wide recognition in the art world, not now, and not even then, when Johnson wrote them out under his gridded glyphs. (John Stephan, the editor of *Tiger's Eye*, is there, for instance, flanked by Boris Margo and Herbert Ferber.) They are all names of artists whom Parsons, with her discerning taste and her determination to maintain a space where art goes on, thought worth her time and ours. In commemorating them, Johnson affirms the dealer's judgment, while at the same time trying to maintain the kind of scrupulous indifference Duchamp aimed at in his choice of objects. There is pathos, certainly, in the thought of all that longing and labor, all that intelligent, interesting, beautiful work lying untouched in the vaults of museums, passed over in auctions, packed in storage units rented by guilt-racked survivors. But in Johnson's history paintings, the art world is seen from an aerial perspective, a mapmaker's perspective, from which individual dramas shrink to pinpoints.

Or maybe it is the perspective of the astronaut, uncertain of return. **Time to leave the Capsule. I'm stepping through the door.** Something like this thought, fanciful as it is, seems to have occurred at least to one other person, the critic Lawrence Campbell, who, as he scanned the image-pages on Parsons's wall, began to see in them something "more than a series of glass windows into the past—it is as if a thousand dark emeralds had been thrown from a space capsule." This simile casts Johnson's work as history as science fiction, **the future being presented in the past**. It is a story with a cast of thousands, each actor a "dark emerald," at once invaluable and obscure. It is a historical puzzle whose pieces have been scattered across space, like Johnson's dream-poems, with the hope, if not the assurance, that they may one day be recovered and reconfigured in an order that might enable us to grasp what they once meant, in themselves, and to one another.

XXVI

Johnson begins the first sentence of his proposal-letter to Parsons and Truman by mentioning that he had **a telephone conversation with Jock today about an Albert M. Fine work**, presumably a business conversation, although Fine was not represented by the Parsons Gallery. Fine's name also comes up in *Richard Poussette-Dart Masher*, making him an exception to the picture's rule that all artists named there must have shown with Betty Parsons. Johnson accents Fine's exceptional status by making him the dedicatee of a collage within the collage, *Four Tea Pot Top Fragments for Albert M. Fine,* with its own completion date, September 17, 1972. Albert M. Fine occupies his own space and time.

Albert Fine had been part of Ray Johnson's inner circle since the '50s, when Fine was enrolled at the Juilliard School of Music, where he had a reputation as a wunderkind—"simply the most highly developed musician I met at Juilliard," in the estimation of a younger classmate, composer Philip Glass, who arranged to take private lessons with Fine while he was there. But Fine wandered from what would have seemed to have been his path. "I began playing the clarinet when I was six, the piano when I was eight, composing when I was twelve, conducting when I was sixteen," he told Glass. "Then I gave up conducting, then composing, then piano and finally clarinet." His retreat from the classical music world included a stint in the ranks of Fluxus, during which Fine composed a short, complex piece for piano and voice, "Fear No Forks," with lyrics written, and read in performance, by Ray Johnson, memorializing a moment at Black Mountain when Johnson "watched Elaine de Kooning eat a hamburger with a pair of pliers." Fine's relationship to Fluxus, while not as tenuous as Johnson's, still tended toward the peripheral. Jill Johnston pairs him with Johnson in her signal memory of a "Fluxus-type performance" where Ray was "running around outside of the audience with Albert Fine. Just running around and creating his own event."

Fine had a second life as a visual artist—a favorite material was wet tea bags—and mail artist, although he showed infrequently, mostly at marginal venues. His activities were interrupted by breakdowns and institutionalizations and would be abruptly cut off by AIDS, from the effects of which Fine died in 1987 at the age of fifty-five.

(When asked, not long after Fine's death, for an epitaph, another of his friend-admirers, Richard Tuttle, offered up a beautifully twisted bit of wire he had just found on the street, which for him "symbolized that Albert has found everything he has been looking for." Back in 1972, Tuttle was a rising star in Betty Parsons's stable. His name, which appears in *Richard*

Pousette-Dart Masher, has lasted, although the reputation hit a bump in 1975, when a Whitney Museum show of Tuttle's fragile, poetic constructions curated by Marcia Tucker was judged "egregiously subordinate to the most minor of minor art" by the incorrigible Hilton Kramer and the board of the museum, fed up with Tucker's edgy choices, fired her.)

Johnson represents this life in pieces as the top of a broken tea pot, delicately rendered in ink. Fine does not belong in this history and then again, he does. To map the art world with real accuracy, Johnson knew, he had to draw its ragged edges, where the known fades into the shadowy depths of the unknown.

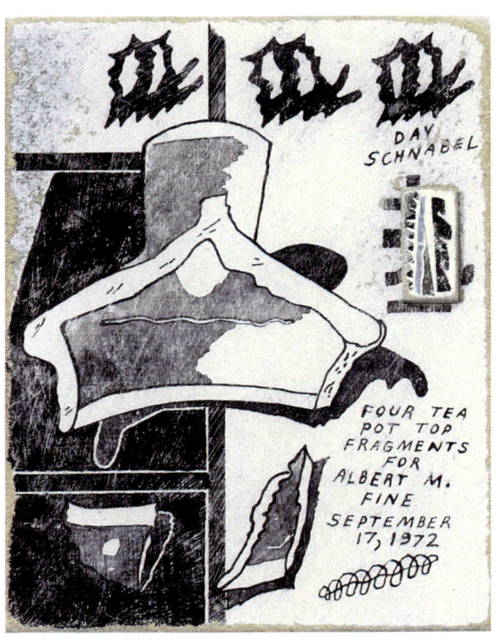

Ray Johnson, Richard Pousette-Dart Masher (1972), detail.

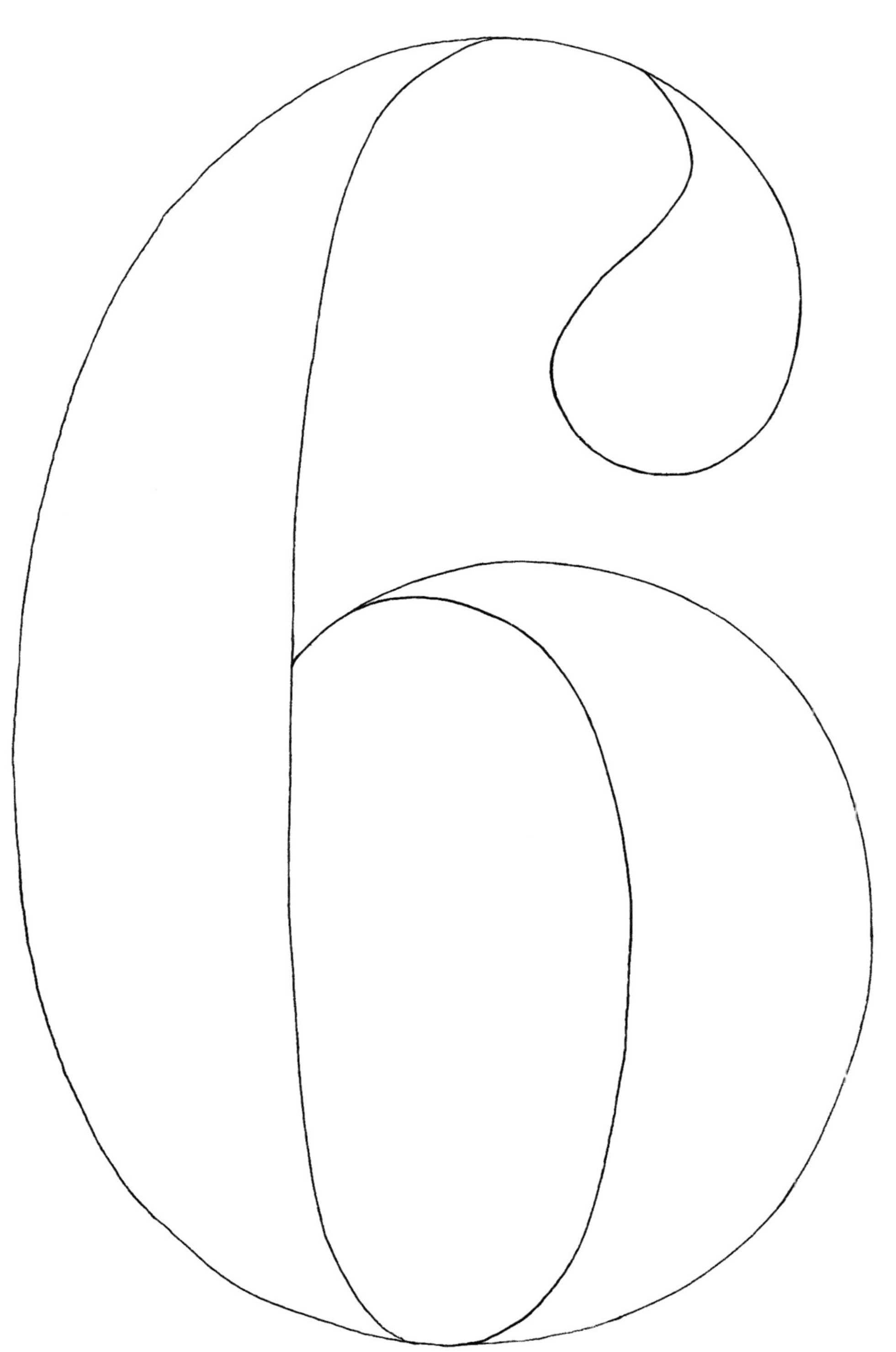

SILHOUETTE UNIVERSITY

1973–1980

SHADOW INSTITUTIONS AND THROWAWAY GESTURES

I

"How many years has it been that I've been writing about Ray Johnson?" Henry Martin wondered to Ray Johnson in a letter sent from Rome, where he had just moved from Milan, where he taught at a university until that job got lost in the wake of the student uprisings of 1968, after which he began to scrape out a living as an art critic. Martin had wandered from what would have seemed to have been the path marked out for him in his sophomore year at Bowdoin College, when he had "the enormous good fortune to study Chaucer with Bill Wilson." Bill would decamp from Maine to Manhattan when the semester was over but the two reunited when Henry came to the city in 1963 to go to graduate school in hopes of becoming an English professor like Bill, only to decamp himself for Milan on a whim two years later. Bill was a reluctant academic of the kind who make for the most charismatic teachers and Henry was the first and perhaps the purest of his many disciples.

"Milan abandoned to its fortunes after nearly six years—Henry abandoned to his after nearly thirty," Henry mock-lamented; the student by then was deeply enmeshed, like his teacher before him, in writing about Ray Johnson, writing "interminably, without haste, without interruption, without readers, without even paper." Henry first met Ray in 1962 while he was still an undergraduate down from Bowdoin on a visit with Bill and soon began receiving mail from interested parties.

After college Henry moved to the Lower East Side not far from Ray and they became friends for real, for life. "Ray was very, very open, and he was very, very kind. And I don't know, there was something about me that he liked. I was very open in my way, I think," Henry told me, much later in life. "Ray liked me because I had a particular kind of innocence." "That you maintained?" I asked, although anyone could see he had. "Well, I hope so. And one of the things about Ray was that he helped me maintain it."

II

"I showed your pictures to Schwarz," Henry reported, back in 1966, referring to photographs Ray had sent of some of the first tesserae collages, "and he said, 'How funny, I never had imagined that Ray Johnson was an Abstract Expressionist.'" Ray Johnson, painter of the New York School? An undaunted Martin would keep trying, this way and that, to convince Arturo Schwarz that Johnson was a school-master of another kind. But it was not until 1972, after Mary Bauermeister (like Ray, a well-connected yet underappreciated collagist-cum-poet) smuggled a suitcase full of Johnson's works into Italy to put before Schwarz, that the Galleria Schwarz in Milan

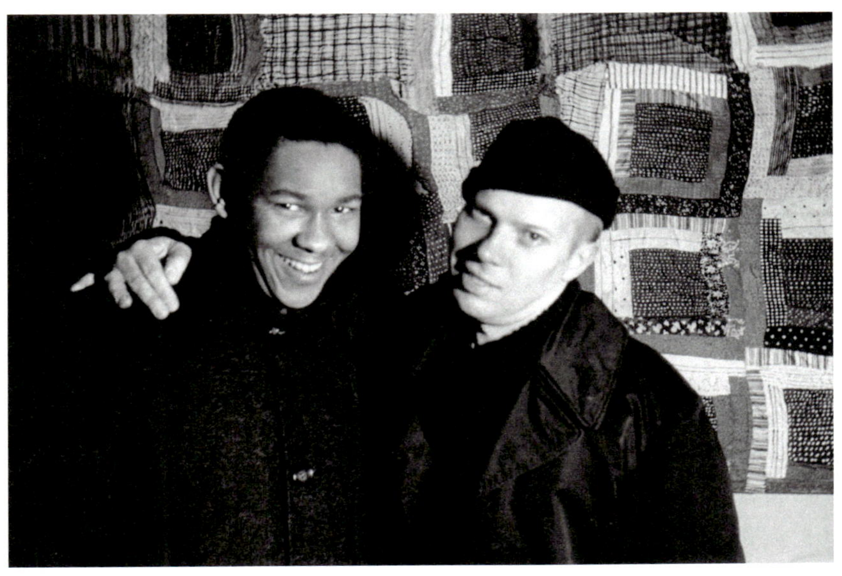

Ray Johnson and Henry Martin, 1964, photograph by William S. Wilson.

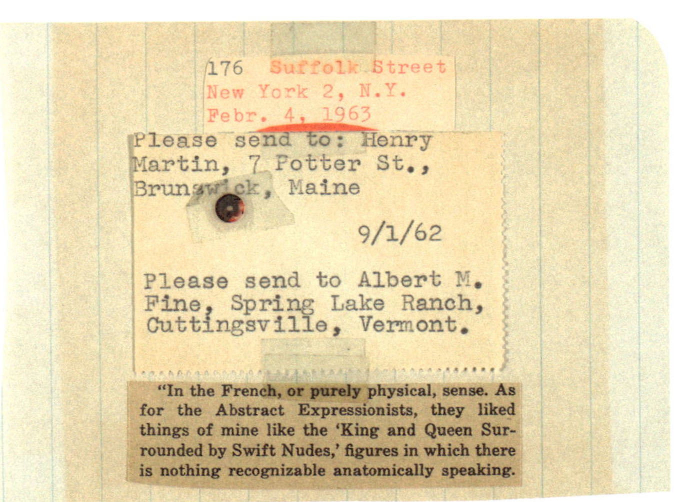

Ray Johnson, please-send-to for Henry Martin and Albert Fine, 1963.

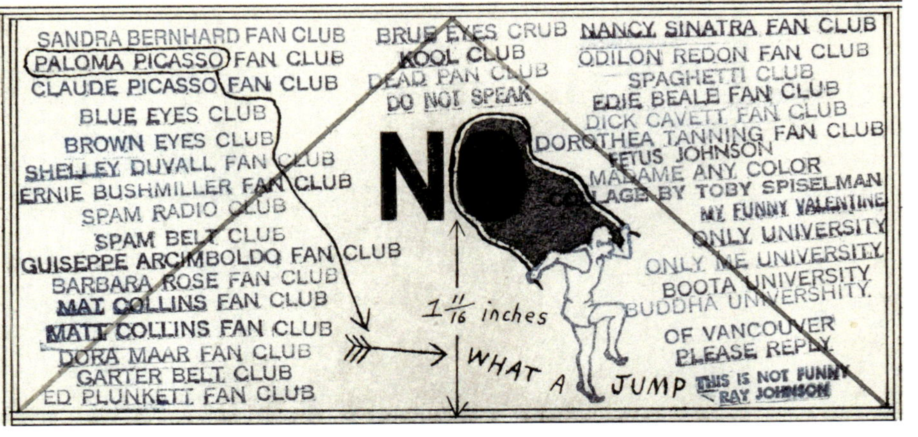

Ray Johnson, *Untitled (NO CHRO[NO]LOGY)* (1984), detail.

would host its first Ray Johnson show, with a catalogue essay contributed by Henry Martin. Johnson was thrilled to be working with Schwarz whose name had become indissolubly linked with Duchamp's through the limited-edition replicas of the artist's Readymades that the gallerist had begun issuing in 1964 and the catalogue raisonné of Duchamp's work that he published in 1969. It was a source of regret for Ray that unlike Schwarz, or John Cage, or Jasper Johns, or William Copley, or any number of others on his mailing list, he could claim no significant link to Duchamp. Finally, in 1971, he took it upon himself to establish one by calling a Meeting of the Marcel Duchamp Club.

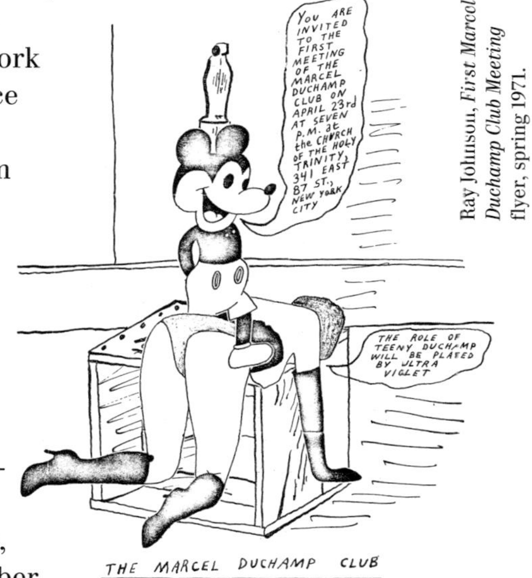

Ray Johnson, *First Marcel Duchamp Club Meeting* flyer, spring 1971.

"Who's the leader of the club that's made for you and me?" trilled the cherubic members of *The Mickey Mouse Club* at the outset of their televised meetings, the first of which was broadcast in October 1955, the month the moticos got their name. The New York Correspondance School was meant to be that kind of club, open to any bright-eyed, black-eared fan who wanted to tune in. But the enterprise had lost its youthful glow. **I am so very tired of mailing letters and mailing materials and mailing things,** Johnson would confide in the fall of 1971 to Thomas Albright of *Rolling Stone*. The internal contradictions that had driven the activity from the start were still operative; the NYCS was, as Albright wrote, at once "a continuous happening by mail" and "a sophisticated communications feedback-system," an "admixture of fantasy and logic." Yet if only by virtue of its unchallenged status as the "Oldest and most influential of the correspondence networks"—a phrase from Albright's piece that Johnson would pick up and recycle—the NYCS had become an institution, forcing its creator to confront the question, Am I an institution man?

To which the inevitably bifurcated answer was a horrified "No" followed by a rueful "Yes." Johnson's School died an ignominious death in 1973 and out of its ashes rose that highest form of institutional life, a University. Ray Johnson was still an art-school artist, but the art school model had changed. One had begun to need an MFA—as much for the connections one might make in a program as for the training one might receive—to launch one's career. Johnson's University, meanwhile, was founded in the shadow of its disreputable twin, the Fan Club, an underside of Ray's art-thought that now also acquired an official stamp. Or rather, stamps. Ray Johnson's institutions had a way of generating shadow institutions, the better for their founder to slip away into the crowd.

III

A note on Betty Parsons Gallery stationery dated February 17, 1973, in which Jock Truman lets David Bourdon know that "the Ray Johnson Joseph Cornell Valentine is available if you are interested in owning it," made its way back to Ray, who pulled it out in 1980 and overlaid it with a new motif: a tracing of a hand emanating wavy lines suggesting motion, with **the throwaway gesture** inscribed beneath.

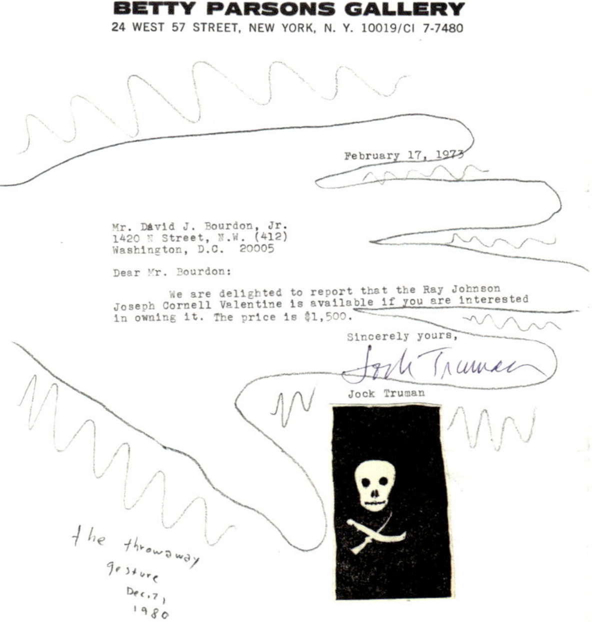

BETTY PARSONS GALLERY
24 WEST 57 STREET, NEW YORK, N. Y. 10019/CI 7-7480

February 17, 1973

Mr. David J. Bourdon, Jr.
1420 N Street, N.W. (412)
Washington, D.C. 20005

Dear Mr. Bourdon:

We are delighted to report that the Ray Johnson Joseph Cornell Valentine is available if you are interested in owning it. The price is $1,500.

Sincerely yours,

Jock Truman

Jock Truman

the throwaway gesture
Dec. 7, 1980

Jock Truman to David Bourdon, February 17, 1974, with additions by Ray Johnson, 1980.

One hesitates to say that this or that was the point where Ray Johnson strayed from his path, given that, from the start, his path seemed to consist of nothing but deviations. But looking back from 1980, one can survey, with Ray, a period when he stepped off a kind of cliff, the kind that hapless cartoon animals step off and then hang, magically, in air so long as they have not registered that there is nothing more to run on. Then again, Johnson could always do a lot with nothing. Once he realized where he stood, he would point to the air beneath with all the insouciance of a born master of the throwaway gesture.

Or, as the artist would spell it on the flyers he made for an event held at the Detroit Institute of Arts in October 1978, **The Thoreau Away Gesture**. According to one review, Johnson's DIA performance began with:

> a ream of paper (his announcements), heaved upward in a single block to flutter slowly down, beautifully illuminated by the diffuse light.

> They settled to the marble floor to form an expressionist design which was walked on during the remainder of the performance. A little later, as a deliberate prelude to the much less deliberate body of his performance, he shredded his script, threw that, and by contrast its dispersal was laconic and miniature.

Evocative as these actions were, the authors of the piece, William Graham and Tom Bloomer, nonetheless suspected that they "only served to disguise the real gesture—a magical and baffling trick." Having asked an audience member to do a headstand, "the artist knelt intently about twenty paces away." Then, "Slowly and silently extending his right arm, Ray Johnson suddenly snapped his fingers and a rain of small change fell from the man's pockets, glittering and clanging loudly on the marble floor"—the opposite of the magician's usual "play with levitation." It was a joke, the writers suggested, "about the gravity of the art world." Ray Johnson lets things—no, *makes* things—fall, leaving the art and the money on the ground. But who is the joke on, really?

IV

By the time he got to Detroit, the artist had had ample chance to practice his tricks. Between 1974 and 1980, he received more invitations to perform for an audience than in all the previous and subsequent years combined. This was not a Ray-thing; he was a boat on a rising tide. These were the years when an antitheatrical strain of performance that had developed within movements of the everyone-an-artist tendency, from the Happenings to Fluxus to the Judson Church group, came to be codified as "performance art," an individualized specialty on which one could base a career. They were also years that witnessed both a multinational economic recession that depressed the art market and a momentous increase in public arts funding in the United States. (Funding for the National Endowment for the Arts rose from about $9 million in 1970 to $150 million by the end of the decade.) Some of Johnson's performances took place at the kinds of non-profit art spaces that were springing up all over the country as the grants rained down. But the majority of his invitations came from colleges and universities, which had begun to host rounds of visiting artists who could serve as living clues as to how one might find one's way into that mysterious redoubt that everyone now called the art world.

The visiting artist was supposed to show the kids how the professionals did it. Writing in 1974 to an administrator at the New York Institute of Technology to propose a visit, Johnson dutifully listed recent accomplishments including performances at Columbia University, Oberlin College, and his stint as **an artist-in-residence last February in Illinois under a State Council for the Arts grant. For the five days I was there, we had a Correspondence Exhibition. I lectured and did performances in three Illinois towns and I also made a special show of work that was displayed. I also juried a print show. So they got their money's worth of my time and interest.** All very professional, except perhaps for the note of weariness that creeps into that final sentence.

For so long, Ray Johnson had gone without so many luxuries, including the luxury of the sustained attention of the art world, to reserve for himself the ultimate luxury of performing only unalienated labor. To have this near-impossibility as one's aim requires what Henry Martin called "a particular kind of innocence." One could even say that what non-profit institutions were paying Ray Johnson for was the promulgation of his brand of innocence, manifested in performance as a lack of calculation. An observer of Johnson's Oberlin presentation noted its "impromptu" quality and the artist's use of casual finds, as when "he did 'A Sound' which consisted of inflating and popping a sanitary glass paper bag from the Oberlin Inn." **I spin bottles. I begin with no plan. I face the void**, the artist said of his antimethodical procedures. He warned the arts administrator at NYIT that **Since my ideas about what I do concern spontanaety and consulting** [in the moment, as he typed, performatively] **Webster's Third for the correct spelling of spontaneity and custom made program for each situation of what I am presenting**, the faculty and students would just have to stay open to what came.

When the conditions were right, such openness could lead to revelations. "Dear Ray, it was so beautiful," attested Ellen Johnson (no relation, although Ray made hay with the coincidence), the art historian who had invited him to Oberlin. "I simply cannot thank you enough for what you gave to us. For many of those students, you opened doors to perceptions they didn't know they had." To more jaded viewers, Ray's sweet nothings might seem merely "an aggressively silly use of time," as critic Peter Frank described the proceedings in Detroit. Yet Frank also seemed to admire Johnson's silliness insofar as it could be "read as a kind of send-up of 'serious' performance and video artists' often self-important, self-indulgent, smugly diffident formalism." (Was Ray, like Echo, fated to survive only as a faintly mocking Sound?) Then there were those occasions when the conditions were all wrong, somehow, by Johnson's at once capricious and principled standards.

V

The negotiations by mail had gone swimmingly between Johnson and Daniel Wells, the playful young arts administrator at Western Illinois University. In a letter dated October 17, 1973, addressed to **Daniel Wwoops Wells**, Ray proposed creating **a special group of collages to be mounted in your gallery to accompany the correspondence**, rather than sending a hodgepodge of older works. **Please say yes that this is what I should do say yes.** For Ray Johnson, there was no time like the present. Wells had already gotten a sense of this in-the-moment quality from his first glimpse of the artist, in 1972, at the Wabash Transit Gallery, a student-run space at the School of the Art Institute of Chicago, where Johnson had been invited to orchestrate a correspondence exhibition and a second meeting of the Marcel Duchamp Club. Although the latter was advertised as a performance by Ray Johnson, "it was kind of funny," Wells recalled, "because he was sitting at a table and people were not really engaging with him. He was doing some work with scissors. And people kind of left him alone and I thought, that's proper; when somebody's working you hate to interrupt them." Is there anything more beautiful than somebody's absorption in work they love?

After detailing his plans for the collage exhibit, Johnson let Wells know that **Yesterday was my birthday and late at night on color television Harpo Marx suddenly played Happy Birthday on the harp and managed to hold up his hand which had five lit candles on the ends of his fingers.** Which might seem like a non sequitur but was actually a gage for actions yet to be performed. **I liked it very much and thought that was the way things should work out. I hope the February thing is as nice.** Which it mostly was: when February came around and Johnson arrived at WIU, the exhibitions of his **special group of collages** and of mail art sent in for the occasion by NYCS members and his judging of a show of student work and two of his three performances went off as well as he might have hoped.

The third performance took place at a private club, at the behest of George Irwin, a local collector, patron of the arts, and founder of the Illinois Arts Council, which sponsored Johnson's visit. The event was billed as a dinner followed by a talk by Johnson. "But," said Wells, still sounding somewhat chagrined decades later, "it turned out not to be a talk at all. He ordered somebody to get a record player and he wanted a copy of David Bowie's *Space Oddity.*" And once these were obtained, "he didn't say a word. He got up in front of these people and he played the David Bowie song so loudly that it was just ear shaving; he turned it up as high as it could go. And he was very deadpan about it." If the artist had stopped there, one might just say, that's Ray the silent comedian. There always was a tinge of hostility in Harpo's act, however cherubic his expression remained. But when the music ended, Johnson launched into a diatribe against his audience, saying they "didn't know what was going on with anything. He was almost angry; it was very strange." Or not so strange. **They got their money's worth**, which is to say, they got a glimpse, as in a funhouse mirror, of how money looks to someone who could never quite credit its worth.

VI

Although he never said so outright, Ray Johnson made it clear, by various signs, that he did not like to travel. After a 1979 visit to the Rhode Island School of Design to do "Another Throwaway Gesture," he would never again perform outside New York State. The artist first ventured outside the U.S. in 1969 to participate in the *Concrete Poetry* show in Vancouver, only to flee abruptly after leaving a smear of blood on the wall. On his second and, as it turned out, final trip abroad in 1973, which also took him to Canada, having been invited to dinner at the rambling Toronto loft inhabited by the members of the art collective General Idea and friends—by AA Bronson's rough count, the household consisted of "three women and three or four men, and Pascal who was somewhere in between"—Johnson arrived **with adhesive tape over my mouth** and proceeded to **do a Harpo Marx bit**. As Bronson remembers it, there was nothing hostile about Ray's silent-comedian act. "He just sat there and glittered, just happy as a clam," and "everybody shined for him, he was the perfect audience. He didn't interrupt." Although one could also say, he was so quiet, it was as if he wasn't there.

"it would be really beautiful if you could ever have reason to come and visit. or if you were anywhere in europe at all i'd come and visit you," Henry longingly wrote to Ray on April 10, 1973, the very day a show of collages by Ray Johnson opened at the Angela Flowers Gallery in London, which you might think was a reason to cross the pond. But no. **I think they're pissed off I didn't fly there for the opening**, an unrepentant Johnson reported on April 12 to Colin Naylor, editor of the English journal *Art & Artists*, from whom he was **Happy to get all the Angela Geraniums information. I never hear anything from her—I wrote her saying like when is my show**. Flowers had been the first European gallerist to host a Ray Johnson exhibition, in 1971; he didn't attend that opening, either. Nor did he bestir himself to get on a plane when solo shows of his work were held in Milan in 1972, 1975, and 1976, and in Naples in 1977.

In the artist's absence, his art developed a tendency to wander from its appointed path. Visitors to the Ray Johnson exhibition at the Massimo Valsecchi Gallery in 1975 may or may not have noticed a curious little note stuck on the inside of the gallery door that read, "We feel it necessary to inform the public that this show has been organized neither with the collaboration of the Schwarz Gallery nor indeed with Ray Johnson." The note was brought to Johnson's attention by Henry Martin, who had not only been to see the show ("very very beautiful") but had previously witnessed Arturo Schwarz's response to it. As Henry told Ray, "Arturo," to whom Johnson had granted the exclusive right to sell his work in Italy, "upon hearing of the show at Valsecchi, shrieked around the city like a stuck banshee or a witch in heat, called his lawyers, threatened to sue for damages, and in brief nearly gave a heart attack to everyone he could." (Hence the note.) Valsecchi, also according to the well-informed Henry, had acquired "nearly all of the potato mashers that were in your Angela Flowers show in London," where he "also picked up some things at a Sotheby's auction." The show featured "two pieces that he bought from collectors who bought them from Arturo" as well. None of Valsecchi's proceeds seem to have made their way back to Johnson, who at that moment was still struggling to wring monies owed to him out of Angela Flowers.

Ray depended much on Henry during this period to mediate for him with Schwarz and other figures on the Italian art scene and to help him track his collages' divagations. When Martin mentioned in a letter to Johnson that plans were afoot for a show of his work at a gallery called Framart, the artist replied in a panic that he had **telephoned** gallerist **Marian Goodman and Jaap Reitman**, proprietor of Soho's leading art-book emporium, and **Nobody has heard of Framart. This is confusing. Arturo has not said anything to me about Framart. What oh what is it? Is it in Naples? If that's a clue? Framart must be in Naples?** Yes, Henry reassured Ray in his next letter, the gallery was in Naples and was run by a Mr. Framart who, "rumor has it," had "been buying up all the Ray Johnsons that Arturo has to sell," Schwarz having largely bought out his own shows of Johnson's art. All these pieces had left Ray's hands years before and few would ever be seen by him again. Maintaining one's innocence has its costs.

VII

The collages that Johnson made for the shows at Galleria Schwarz in 1972 and at Angela Flowers in 1973 were entries in a series called **Famous People's Mother's Potato Mashers**, each featuring one or more stylized

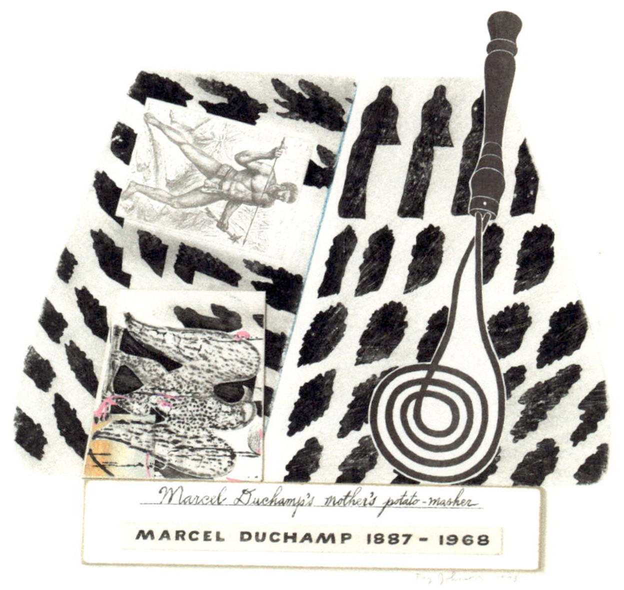

Ray Johnson, *Marcel Duchamp's Mother's Potato Masher* (1973).

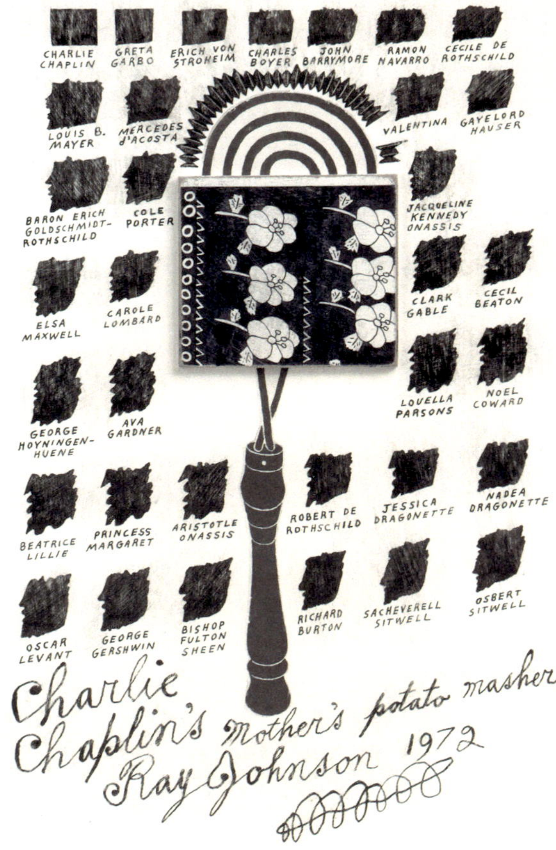

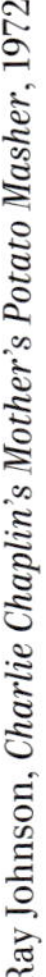
Ray Johnson, *Charlie Chaplin's Mother's Potato Masher*, 1972.

renderings of that humble kitchen tool. The model for Ray's masher had belonged to May Wilson, the mother of his friend Bill, who was famous in Ray-world if nowhere else.

Why a potato masher? Unlike, say, the dollar bill or the tit chart, the masher motif would seem to have been chosen according to the standard of "*visual* indifference, along with a complete absence of good or bad taste" that Duchamp said guided his selection of the Readymades. And yet, as with Duchamp's urinal or bottlerack or snow shovel, the longer one looks at the masher, the more formal presence it accrues since (as Duchamp surely knew) the aesthetically-inclined gazer will project charm onto the most charmless of objects. Johnson suggests that we might even see the masher as a kind of star, the kind whose very inexpressiveness breeds obsession.

This thought comes to the fore in a collage titled *Charlie Chaplin's Mother's Potato Masher*, whose ostensible star is the silent comedian, represented as a small black square. The associations that crisscross the picture's grid of names, though, trace back repeatedly to the black square next to Chaplin's, identified as Greta Garbo, a frequent presence in Johnson's assemblies. The gossip is too intricate and infra to unfurl here, but if you type the names of Cecile de Rothschild, Louis B. Mayer, Mercedes D'Acosta, Valentina, Gayelord Hauser, Baron Erich Goldschmidt-Rothschild, and Cecil Beaton into a search box, you may lose yourself—if you are so inclined—in the swirl of frustrated desires and sliding sexual identities that Garbo's obdurate blankness perpetually mobilized. Chaplin was merely speechless. Garbo radiated an indifference that, as in the case of the Readymades, was as or more charming than any intent to charm could have been.

The pictures give us the masher-as-form, a piece of vernacular abstraction enlivened by accidental tensions, the anthropomorphic curves of the handle vs. the business end's symbolic spiral. But the function of the masher is to mash, to turn form into unform, plunge after vigorous plunge. In the spring of 1965, Bill Wilson created and circulated a document titled "Invoice #4," in which Ray Johnson and May Wilson recount a series of events from the early days of their friendship. In each episode, Ray mails a work of art to May: a **collection of collage fragments by myself which had been strung on a piece of string**; **a Ruth Asawa wire sculpture I had exchanged with Ruth for a painting**; an early Larry Poons abstraction **I had around my studio for quite a while**. These artworks had not wandered from their way, they had been sent to their doom.

Upon receipt of each object, May thought, "no loss if it is lost in my work," and commenced to mash. Some of Ray's moticos she dipped in glue and stuffed into a cigar box which she painted black; “the rest of the strung cardboard became twisted into a figure eight, and is now painted red.” Having dismissed Asawa’s spider-web-delicate spheres-within-spheres as “bulky,” and having on hand “a triangular 2 × 4' wood shape, open in the center,” she “sat on the wire thing to flatten it, nailed it to the triangle, and painted it black.” The aesthetically inclined may say “ow ow ow” but May’s partner in crime **was amused by this and thought it witty to associate Asawa with the act of sitting.** After she took the Poons canvas and “stapled it in sharp creased folds to a wooden panel, painted red,” though, Ray **never had the courage to tell Larry about what had happened and said it was on tour when he asked where the painting was**.

May’s were throwaway gestures of another kind. She had the innocence of a two-year-old who doesn’t know the difference between yours and mine. She wanted to make art less, perhaps, because she was aesthetically-inclined than because she wanted to take things and make them her own. When she wasn’t mashing other people’s art, she liked especially to take tools designed to form, or deform, female bodies and minds—dolls, kitchen equipment, high-heeled shoes—and to subject them to her habitual process of gluing things together in deliberately creepy concatenations and covering the whole in a thick coat of monochromatic paint. For Ray, she was a miraculous found object, a sort of anti-star, a dispeller of charm and creator of mess. She sometimes signed her letters “Greta Garbage.”

VIII – ABANDONED CHICKENS 1

Just before Brian O’Doherty stepped down from his editorship at *Art in America* in 1974, he okayed an idea that Ray Johnson had for a piece on “Artists’ Childhood Toys.” It would eventually appear in the magazine under the title, “Abandoned Chickens,” a phrase that emerged out of a dialogue between Johnson and Morris Graves, an artist whose Zen outlook and exquisite hand Ray had long admired. Unlike other artists interviewed for the piece, Graves was not a close friend—his tetchy response to a second **attempt to obtain his baby photo** prompted Ray to **write him a post card saying “Forgive my zeal**”—but he was friends with John Cage back in the day and had, like Richard Lippold, been associated with the Willard Gallery since the 1940s. Graves was silent for so long after Johnson asked him about his favorite childhood toys, **I began to think that the long silence was the answer to my question**. Further down the page, Johnson memorializes the moment in a Cagean collage, where a bird identified as “The American Songster” repeatedly tweets out **SILENCE**.

Graves's eventual response, "abandoned chickens," was confounding in its own way, and after a bit more talk, Johnson got up the nerve to ask for an explanation. **"Oh no," he said. "A bantam chicken." "Oh, a bantam chicken," I exclaimed. Gee, I thought, I better run out to the Locust Valley library to see what a bantam chicken looks like**. This exchange, along with similar encounters that unfold across the next five pages with Ray-friends like Lynda Benglis, Christo and Jeanne-Claude, Les Levine, Marisol, Joseph Raffael, James Rosenquist, and Andy Warhol, doesn't quite count as art criticism, art history, or even art gossip. "This article is a Ray Johnson," O'Doherty alerts the reader who might startle at the syncopated mix of word and image, the found and the made, dense juxtaposition and swathes of airy white space characteristic of a Johnson page. Just what kind of Ray Johnson is it, though? Johnson had designed "please add to and send" mail-art tear-out pages for publication in magazines before, but this was not that. Nor was the piece connected to any of the artist's recent series of collages.

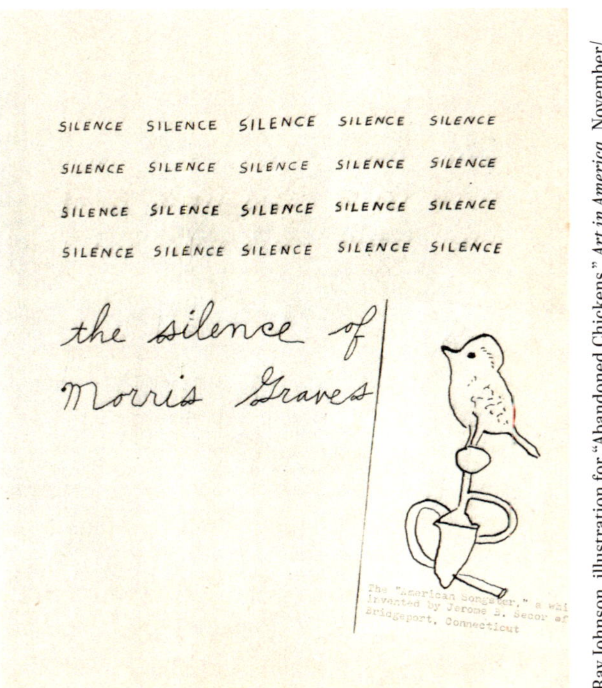

Ray Johnson, illustration for "Abandoned Chickens," *Art in America*, November/December 1974.

The article's theme bespeaks a desire to return to a time when the impulse to make art was purer and the circuit that connects mind to hand more direct. Graves's connections to Cage and Lippold take Ray back not to childhood, though, but to those dreamy days on Monroe Street when he would touch a brush to the palette, then turn to see the boats on the river. And the thought of approaching Willem de Kooning for an interview sends him into a reverie on that long-ago summer at Black Mountain when **John Cage presented his Erik Satie festival and Elaine de Kooning played the lead in The Ruse of Medusa** and **I walked with Bill and Elaine one sad evening up "the Road" when they had just heard about Gorky's death**. Ray can't get Bill on the phone, so he tracks the painter down at his home in East Hampton and is offered a painterly dinner, **a Dutch still-life of brown sausage and shad roe and pumpernickel bread with yellow butter on a white plate. We discussed Martin**

Duberman's recently published Accurate History of Black Mountain College. When I got around to a.c.t. (Artists' Childhood Toys), Bill's answer was one of the most beautiful poems I ever heard:

a

cart

and he made the drawing in two minutes with his eyes closed.

De Kooning spent every waking hour of his life that he could spare working his way back to the point where he could draw like a child. Johnson knew this, and when he asked his friend that evening **how it felt to be America's and the World's Greatest Painter**, he wasn't kidding, for once.

A hard-won innocence may be the subject of "Abandoned Chickens." But the question of its form remains. Some months after the article was published, Johnson approached Barbara Burn, an editor at Viking Press, to ask if she might be interested in his idea for developing the piece into a book. She responded affirmatively and proposed that they might meet. In May 1976, Johnson informed Burn that he now had a literary agent, Phyllis Seidel (then enjoying success with a recent discovery, Anne Rice, whose *Interview with the Vampire* was published that month). But since their last conversation, Johnson's book-concept had changed somewhat: **I have started a silhouette portrait project and have drawn Andy Warhol and William Burrough's** [*sic*] **silhouettes and hope to do Peter Beard, Mary Hemingway, Louise Nevelson and many others with a book idea in mind**, a book that would **include with the silhouettes, photos and writings scrap book style like my <u>Childhood Toys</u> article**. Oh, and—**It is starting off like the Snaking of Americans since the silhouette head-faces have my snake drawings of the last year on them. Oh, yes Dali should be included ... If only I could get Cher to sit for me.**

Are you still interested in my book ideas? She was, "in principle," said Burn, although it would be hard to tell until Johnson could present the material "in some organized fashion." Which, one suspects, the editor already suspected he could not. Nonetheless, she wanted him to know, "I'm glad that you are still doing what you do," which somehow included the making of books, just not the kind that Viking could publish. It had been a decade since Ray had sent out the last pages of **A Book About Death**, an experiment in circumventing the established institutions of publication and exhibition. Was it time to resume the study?

☐ yes
☐ no
☐ a bantam chicken

It is starting off like the Snaking of Americans since the silhouette head-faces have my snake drawings of the last year on them. Barbara Burn may well have been puzzled by this reference, but Ray had given more expansive accounts of his Snaking in other letters to friends and potential supporters. To Anne Trueblood Brodzky, editor of the magazine *artscanada*, the artist described it as **a Major Work: a collage snake of many cardboard disks 12 ½ inches in diameter which extends to fifty or a hundred feet**, bearing **specific "portraits" of art personalities such as Lynda Benglis, Joseph Cornell, Allan Kaprow, Suzi Gablik, naturally Andy and also people like Halston, Virginia Woof and James Dean. It is as though the snake ate my previous "bunny list" works**. The snake project also represented a return to Johnson's pre-1965 practice of carrying his collages around in a cardboard box and displaying them by appointment for an audience of one, only this time, as he explained to Aladar Marberger of the Fischbach Gallery, **after showing to an audience of one person, that singular person is requested by mail (since I am the New York Correspondence School) to suggest a next person to connect with the viewings**. No two showings would be the same, as the snake **gets shuffled like playing cards. The accumulated persons having seen it or on waiting lists to see it is part of the event.** The snake idea, as Ray confessed to Henry, was born out of the need for **The reality of money to survive**. And yet it quickly grew in Johnson's mind into a synthesis of everything he had done so far, **an early Motico concept** turned **Monumental Event work to document**.

The project was abandoned within a year. Johnson left behind some examples of what seem to be the original disks, often transformed by later additions. No records of the actual snake-in-process exist. But the snake-as-monument, its bold contours set off by inky shadow on one side and a shaggy mane of price tags on the other, survives, in the form of a drawing mailed to Arturo Schwarz.

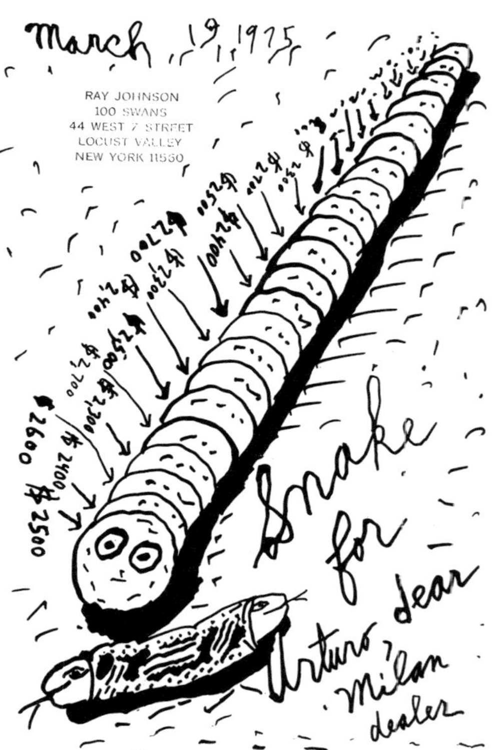

Ray Johnson to Arturo Schwarz, March 19, 1975.

X

A very gloomy letter to Arturo Schwarz, dated March 28, 1975, nine days after the snake drawing, finds Johnson mired in **a daily chore which is to destroy the New York Correspondence School**. In practice, this means **going through the boxes and boxes and boxes and boxes and boxes of material and throwing out as much as I can throw out**, a cleansing process motivated by the thought that **I myself plan to die soon**. Johnson had of course announced his death more than once before, most recently in a mailer that consisted simply of the sentence **Ray Johnson died**, with the date **June 8, 1974**. This marked the culmination of a sequence of mailings that began with a sheet bearing the similarly bald declaration, **Richard Lippold died**. It was a paper memorial to a Monumental Event. Richard had told Ray that he was in love with another man, a young Italian he met on a cruise, and it was over between them.

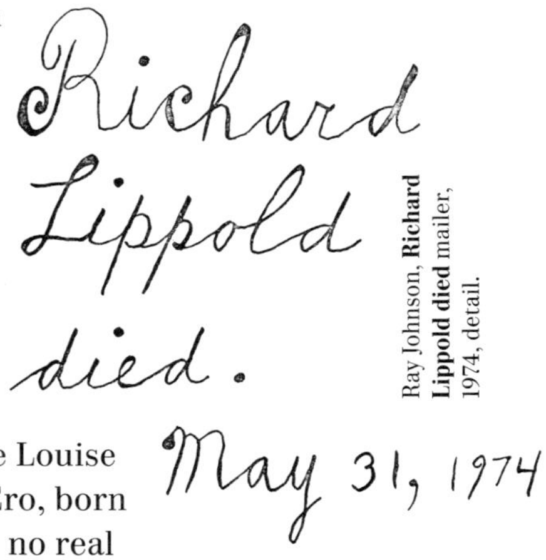

Ray Johnson, **Richard Lippold died** mailer, 1974, detail.

The intimacy the two had sustained for twenty-six years was founded in romantic passion and fed by mutual admiration, but it was also riddled with distances, both physical and emotional. Ray chose to live in Locust Valley because it was near to where the Lippolds lived, and he developed a quasi-familial closeness with Richard's wife Louise and their children, especially the youngest, Ero, born a decade after Ray and Richard met. Ray had no real place, though, in the elegant social life that Richard crafted for himself, financed by commissions for the galactic constructions in gleaming metals that at one time seemingly every ambitious modern architect had to have for his office building, theater, restaurant, or chapel. A 1966 item in the *Chicago Tribune* chronicling a party celebrating Lippold's acquisition of a custom-designed pipe organ of an opulence not seen "since the free-spending days of tycoons like the Morgans and Fricks"—"Richard always wanted two things more than anything else," one guest remarked, "a Rolls-Royce and a pipe organ"—ends on a tellingly discordant note. "Among those who attended the party were the proud builder of the organ, Schlicker, and his wife; Mrs. Anthony Bliss, wife of the president of the Metropolitan Opera" at Lincoln Center, where Lippold's golden *Orpheus and Apollo* dominated the Philharmonic hall lobby until 2014, when it was placed in storage, never to return (tastes change; names fade), "and Ray Johnson, the collagist, who had to sit very still during the recital to keep the rustling of his black leather motorcycle jacket from disturbing the performance."

Still, the relationship with Richard was formed when Ray was very, very open, and innocent in a way he never could be again, and he had remained deeply attached. Writing to George Ashley from his **summer of severe love problems**, Ray tries to make light of the situation—**Oh sob. I guess I have been lucky. Blame it on the Bossa Nova**—and lets George know he has been taking solace in a Hare Krishna (!) **with lotsa muscles and warm body and everything quite in the right place and the frontal stare and oh boy**. Then the mask falls. **One night screaming and crying in the car. This letter is not for publication**.

"This letter is not for publication": a sentence rare if not unique in Ray Johnson's oceanic volume of correspondence, and one I thought twice about quoting. The story of this break-up is not an art story. But its violence can be felt in the broken rhythms of Johnson's art-thoughts and actions of the mid-1970s; and it did leave one visible scar, at the calm center of *Calm Center*, which Richard had protected from its maker's destructive urges once, but now Ray rushed into the Lippolds' home, where the painting into which he had put so much of his youthful knowledge and talent still hung, and scratched a primitive heart into it, a negative valentine.

XI

On **February 14, 1975/Valentine's Day**, Ray recorded for Henry the words that came to him that morning as he woke up: **The New York/ Correspondence School/ has no history ... /only a present**. When, later that year, Johnson retyped **The New York Correspondence School has no history, only a present** and ratified the statement with the official stamp of **ONLY UNIVERSITY**—his latest shadow institution—and sent the page to David Bourdon, the phrase took on the appearance of an *ars poetica*. In the associative drift of the letter to Henry it also reads as a performative contradiction, since in the following sentence, Ray relays the news that **Richard C called from North Carolina wants** [*sic*] **to do a show of Ray Johnson letters**. Richard C. (for Craven) was a mail-art acolyte whose wit and style so closely matched Johnson's own that in 1968 he began to stamp his mailings **FAKE COLLAGE BY RAY JOHNSON**, with Ray's approval—the artist had so many imitators by then that it was refreshing to have the fact plainly acknowledged. Now Richard had an idea for a show, a retrospective survey of Ray's life in letters. Would the prospective subject of this history approve?

One Ray Johnson was content to live in the present, suspended in air. The other Ray Johnson was haunted by visions of **the future being presented in the past**, visions that begged to be given durable form. That Ray Johnson, the historian of the future, viewer of all things through the eyes of death, could not shake the idea that the Book was the right container for his art, for all his doubts. "'He Wrote the History Book,'" somebody insists, in the title of a poem by Marianne Moore, to which a second speaker skeptically responds, "*The* book? Titles are chaff." **The New York Correspondence School has no history**, if by "history" you mean a singularly authoritative account. *The* book? No. But—just possibly—*a* book.

Correspondence: An exhibition of the letters of Ray Johnson, curated by Richard Craven and Huston Paschal, with Ray Johnson's energetic cooperation, opened on October 31, 1976, at the North Carolina Museum of Art. The curators picked up Johnson and Toby Spiselman at the airport and when they got to the museum parking lot, Richard handed Ray the exhibition catalogue and, he said, the artist "fell to his knees, he was so pleased." In one quick, sharp glance, Johnson saw that this was the kind of book he had been dreaming of.

The catalogue was enclosed in a box-like cardboard folder **which has**, as Ray later explained to the members of his friend Marcia Resnick's Book Arts class, **my drawing on the front. The spine has instructions on how to draw a rabbit which is basically very simple. You draw a circle and add some ears.** On the back, you see **a photo of me taken by a friend named Ara Ignatius which was photographed in the New Jersey dump**, which was next to **a railroad tower and the trains go by very frequently and very fast, and he had me stand on the railroad tracks in some point of danger, which may explain the expression on my face.** Also on the back, in columns flanking a wide-eyed Ray, are the names of the hundred-plus lenders to the exhibition, correspondents from every period and byway of Johnson's art-life, from Cass Tech to Buddha University, from Arthur Secunda to Arturo Schwarz. Copies of the mailings featured in the show are fitted into the folder in two thick loose-leaf sheaves: this is not a catalogue in the usual sense, but an exhibition in book form. One could say, in fact, that the catalogue pages were not pages but prints, since, as Johnson noted to Resnick's students, the mailings were reproduced by his preferred method of offset printing, the same method he used for **A BOOK ABOUT DEATH**, pages of which he proceeded to pull out of the folder and display to the class one by one, narrating as he went: **this is a drawing of Carmen Miranda by a friend, Karl Wirsum—a friend who is a Hairy Who from Chicago who has an opening this afternoon at the Phyllis Kind Gallery whose eyelashes I once found at the bottom**

Correspondence: An exhibition of the letters of Ray Johnson (North Carolina Museum of Art, 1976), spine.

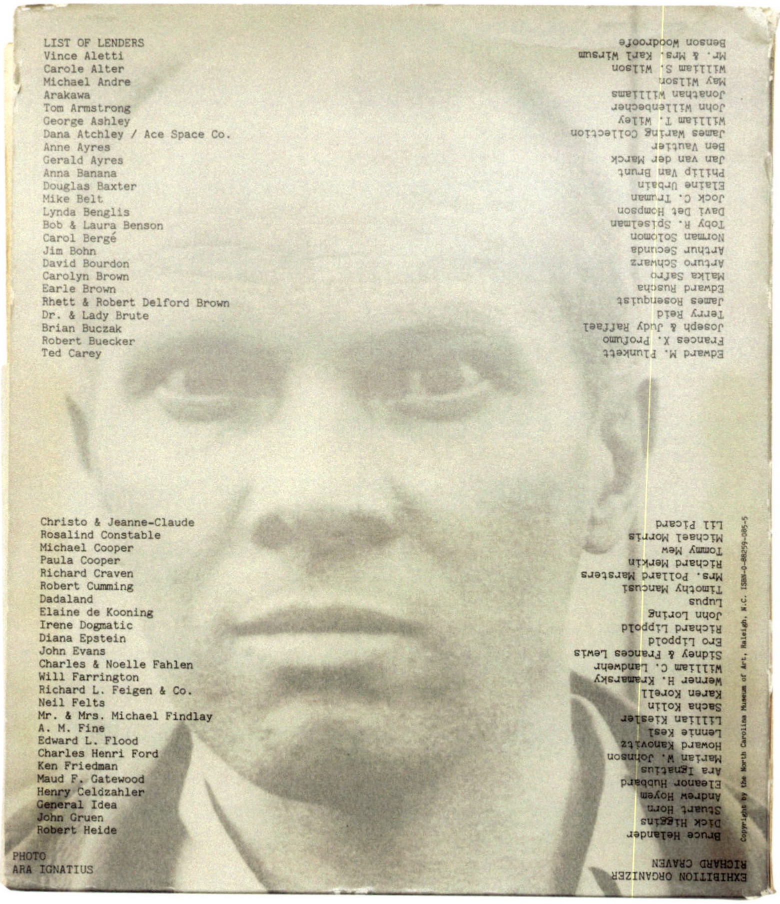

LIST OF LENDERS
Vince Aletti
Carole Alter
Michael Andre
Arakawa
Tom Armstrong
George Ashley
Dana Atchley / Ace Space Co.
Anne Ayres
Gerald Ayres
Anna Banana
Douglas Baxter
Mike Belt
Lynda Benglis
Bob & Laura Benson
Carol Bergé
Jim Bohn
David Bourdon
Carolyn Brown
Earle Brown
Rhett & Robert Delford Brown
Dr. & Lady Brute
Brian Buczak
Robert Buecker
Ted Carey
Christo & Jeanne-Claude
Rosalind Constable
Michael Cooper
Paula Cooper
Richard Craven
Robert Cumming
Dadaland
Elaine de Kooning
Irene Dogmatic
Diana Epstein
John Evans
Charles & Noelle Fahlen
Will Farrington
Richard L. Feigen & Co.
Neil Felts
Mr. & Mrs. Michael Findlay
A. M. Fine
Edward L. Flood
Charles Henri Ford
Ken Friedman
Maud F. Gatewood
Henry Geldzahler
General Idea
John Gruen
Robert Heide

PHOTO
ARA IGNATIUS

EXHIBITION ORGANIZER
RICHARD CRAVEN

Bruce Helander
Dick Higgins
Stuart Horn
Andrew Hoyem
Eleanor Hubbard
Ara Ignatius
Marian W. Johnson
Howard Kanovitz
Lennie Kesl
Lillian Kiesler
Sacha Kolin
Karen Korell
Werner H. Kramarsky
William C. Landwehr
Sidney & Frances Lewis
Ero Lippold
Richard Lippold
John Loring
Lupus
Timothy Mancusi
Mrs. Pollard Marsters
Richard Merkin
Tommy Mew
Michael Morris
Lil Picard
Edward M. Plunkett
Frances X. Profumo
Joseph & Judy Raffael
Terry Reid
James Rosenquist
Edward Ruscha
Malka Safro
Arturo Schwarz
Arthur Secunda
Norman Solomon
Toby R. Spiselman
Davi Det Hompson
Jock C. Truman
Elaine Urbain
Philip Van Brunt
Jan van der Marck
Ben Vautier
James Waring Collection
William T. Wiley
John Willenbecher
Jonathan Williams
May Wilson
William S. Wilson
Mr. & Mrs. Karl Wirsum
Benson Woodroofe

 ISBN-0-88259-085-5

Correspondence: An exhibition of the letters of Ray Johnson (North Carolina Museum of Art, 1976), back cover.

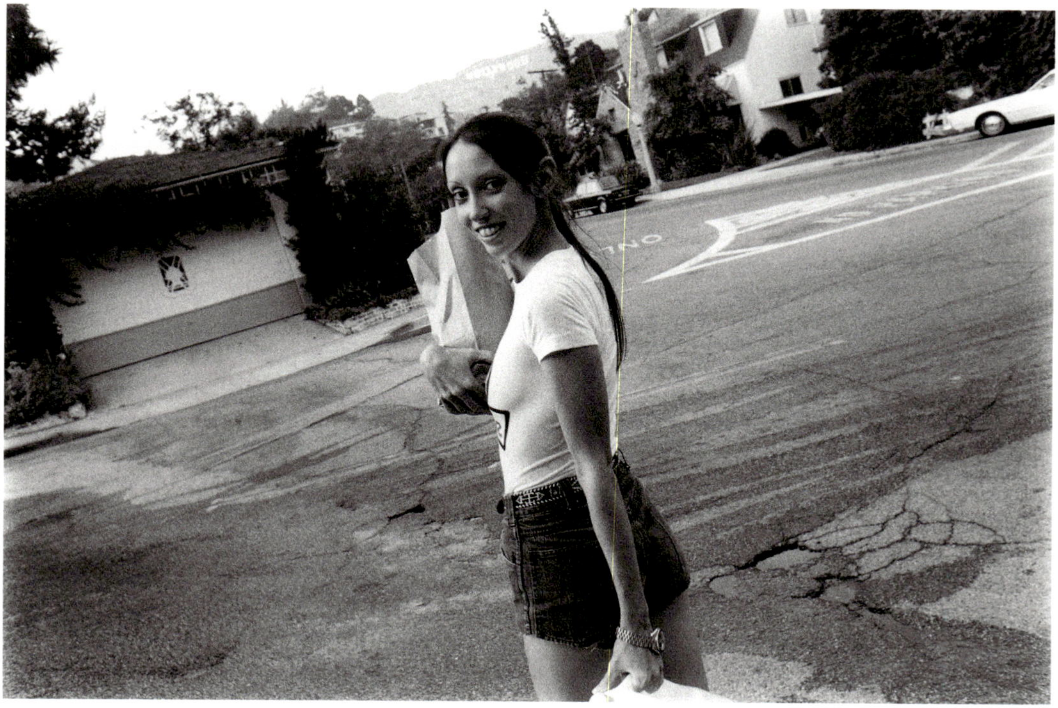

Marcia Resnick, "Shelley Duvall," 1975.

of a swimming pool in Philadelphia. At which point Resnick interrupted to ask, for clarification's sake, "Could you tell us very specifically, what is the New York Correspondence School?" **Yes**, Ray obligingly responded, only to go on to inform them that **I have received this year an NEA grant and I had to fill out forms to state very explicitly what it is, who I am, because I am an individual who is a group and I am me and I am you, and that was an example of my mind splitting into several parts.**

This was 1977. Johnson had just received the second of two consecutive yearly grants from the National Endowment for the Arts, as well as one from the New York State Council on the Arts. He had proposed to document the History of the New York Correspondence School, another synoptic project that never came to fruition. The money did, however, enable the artist to rent a Minolta photocopier, the kind of machine that lends an official look to any enterprise.

Ask me another question, Johnson commanded Resnick when he had run out of things to say about the NYCS, and after a moment's hesitation—it was hard to tell if he was really done, since, as he had just admonished her, **I'm trying to answer your question the way that I answer questions**—she complied. "What's the Spam Radio Club and what's the Shelley Duvall thing?" This query, a signal that Resnick was up to date on Johnson's doings, set the artist off on a twisting-turning story about the Spam Radio Club, **one division of my school**, that went on until he looked up and said **I'm here to talk about books and I am digressing and books are not my main concern, although everything I do can be put into a book in this fashion** and then he showed them a few more pages of **A BOOK ABOUT DEATH** and class was over, leaving the question of the Shelley Duvall thing unresolved.

XII

Only in the 1970s could Shelley Duvall have risen to stardom in American movies, and even then, she was only really a star in the eyes of director Robert Altman, who cast her in seven films between 1970 and 1980. (The only other director ever to cast Duvall in a leading role was Stanley Kubrick, who put the actress through torture both on screen and off to elicit her haunted and haunting performance in *The Shining*.) Altman's own career, for that matter, could probably only have gained traction just then, in the parenthesis between the end of the studio system and the rise of the blockbuster, when Hollywood seemed to slip its mercantile moorings and American screens filled with broken-backed stories of misfits and outlaws. Duvall had the type of looks—doe-eyed, buck-toothed, giraffe-necked—that the French call *belle laide* and had neither trained nor aimed for an acting career when Altman recruited her into the stock company of one-of-a-kind characters that gave his cinematic world its funky, lived-in texture. Marcia Resnick captured the actress's gawky charm in a 1975 picture, from the photographer's "Over the Shoulder" series.

Resnick was not the only Johnson friend-fan with a Duvall connection. Gerald Ayres was introduced to Ray Johnson in New York in the late '50s through Soren Agenoux, a poet, playwright, speed-freak, and petty thief whose given name was Frank Hansen, and whose louche charms spelled "chaos" for the then-married Gerry. Soon, Gerry started sending Ray "long poems, more or less about his work," and in return, the artist mailed him a remarkable series of moticos featuring the Lucky Strike logo, one each month for a year. Ayres would later move to Hollywood and make his name as the producer of *The Last Detail* (1973), a funny-melancholy period piece about two sailors assigned to transport a third one to the brig, who all then proceed to wander from their way. In 1976, when Ray gave a friend notice that **There will be a Shelley Duvall Fan Club Meeting on Feb. 28th at the Iolas Gallery on 57th Street**, the fanboy in him could not help adding, **I telephoned Gerry Ayres in Hollywood and he had just spent yesterday he said with Shelley, who is his best friend. Her dog had puppies.**

The thought that his friend is best friends with a *star* seems almost too much for the fanboy. But the artist in Johnson knew that Duvall was a peculiar sort of star, and that it was her peculiarity that qualified her to be a Fan Club figurehead. Duchamp, the object of Johnson's first Club's adulation, may have been a true star in the art world's estimation, but the names that appear on his subsequent stamps range from the not-quite-major to the never-heard-of. Cartoonist Ernie Bushmiller, creator of Nancy, gets a Fan Club stamp, as does the Symbolist painter Odilon Redon and the sixteenth century-trompe l'oeil master Giuseppe Arcimboldo. There are stamps for the talk show host Dick Cavett and for Sandra Bernhard, whose one star turn in film was as the crazed fan of a talk show host—and a stamp for Bernhard's agent, Irene Pinn, who blocked Johnson's efforts to contact her client. There is a cluster of Clubs dedicated to women whose fame, however merited, has been overshadowed by that of some starrier relation, like Nancy Sinatra, daughter of Frank, Edie Beale, cousin of Jacqueline Kennedy Onassis, Dorothea Tanning, wife of Max Ernst, and Pablo Picasso's lover, Dora Maar. Picasso's son, Claude, is also named on a stamp, while Claude's sister, Paloma, muse of the fashion designer Yves St. Laurent and herself a jewelry designer of note (her "graffiti" line was a hit for Tiffany's in the 1980s), was celebrated at an actual Meeting, held at the Ronald Feldman Gallery in 1974.

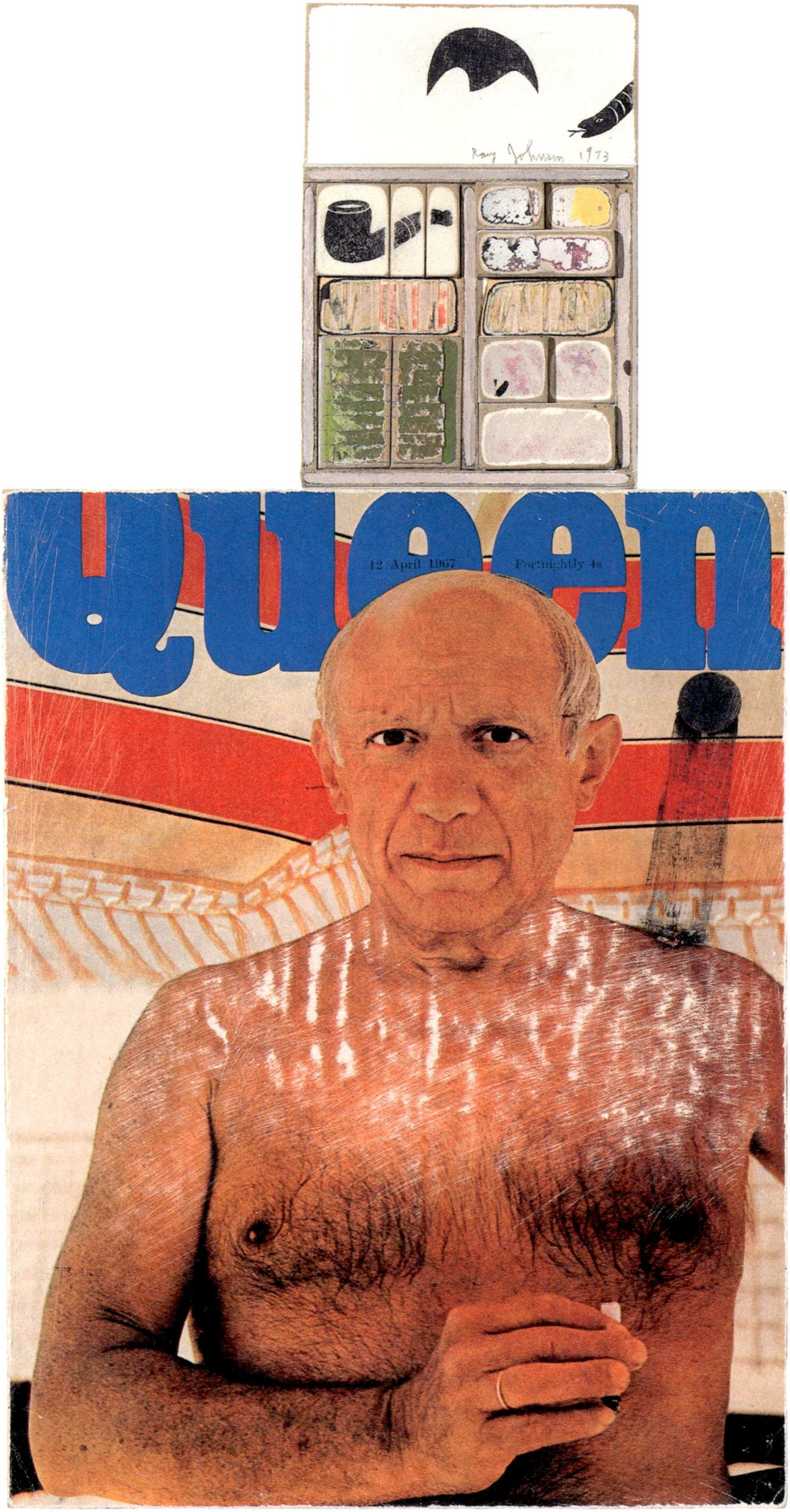

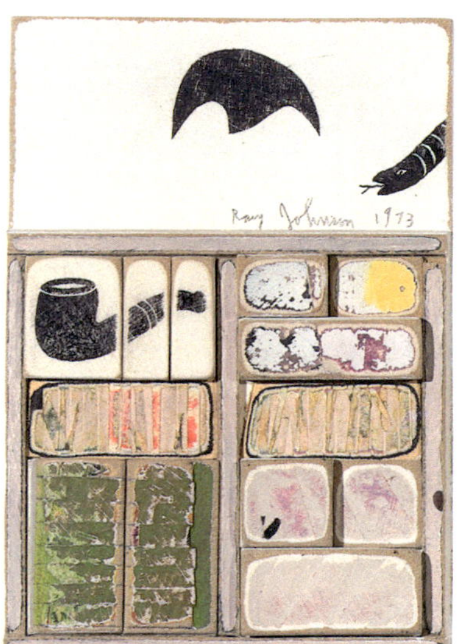

Ray Johnson, *Picasso Queen* (1973).

Picasso *fille* was among the few of Johnson's idols to make the transition from the stamped-on page to real, or at least real-ish, space, in part because she was game. **I am dining with Paloma Picasso this evening and will read to her Marianne Moore's list of probable names for the 1950's Edsel automobile**, the artist reported to poet Michael André in 1975, landing a namedropping triple lutz while marking his favorite spot on the map, the crossroads where the unlikeliest encounters occur. Johnson also seemed to develop a somewhat belated interest at this stage in linking himself to Paloma's father, who was after all the supposed inventor of collage. The artist's hesitation to add Picasso to his otherwise capacious list may have reflected the partisan divide that opened in the 1960s between the post-painterly Duchampians and those who still considered the Cubist conquest of painted space *the* historical pivot of modern art. Or it may have had something to do with Pablo's big-Daddy persona. In a 1973 collage, built around the cover of a conveniently named British women's magazine, the painter is portrayed as a hairy-chested Queen, crowned with a tesserae picture-in-picture that features a phallic Magrittean pipe and Johnsonian snake together with the vulval icon that Johnson alternately identified as Marianne Moore's hat and Marilyn Monroe's lips. Ray Johnson's crossroads is a place not just for meetings but for metamorphoses, where unlike things have way of turning into one another.

The Fan Clubs were termites that began to eat away at the foundation of Johnson's School as soon as he began to fear that he had gotten fixed into position as its head. It was all very well for his followers to joke that he was the Dada of correspondence art, but to stay alive he had to stay in motion, and to stay in motion he had to keep authority at one remove. Better eternally to shiver in the paternal shadow than to *be* the Father. Better still to seem to have sprung out of nothing, to be the only one of your kind. A flyer for the first Shelley Duvall Fan Club Meeting (there would be two more, in 1977 and 1980) pairs a Duvall bunny head with "Ferdinand Chevel," Johnson's slight

YOU ARE INVITED TO A NEW YORK CORRESPONDENCE SCHOOL SPAM BELT CLUB SHELLEY DUVALL FAN CLUB MEETING TO BE HELD ON FEBRUARY 28TH FROM 5 TO 7 PM AT THE IOLAS GALLERY BROOKS JACKSON, INC., 52 EAST 57 ST., N.Y.C. 10022 PL.56914.

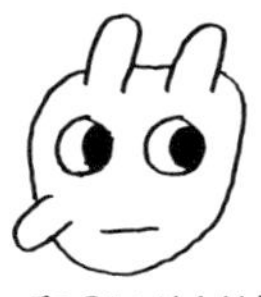

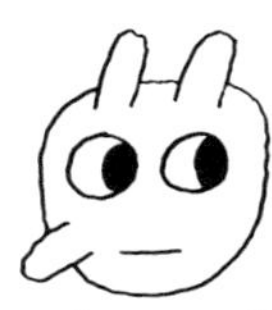

Ray Johnson, *Shelley Duvall Fan Club Meeting* flyer, 1976, detail.

misspelling of the name of perhaps the most famous of French outsider artists, also known, in reference to his day job, as the Postman Cheval. In the heyday of Surrealism, Cheval's homemade masterpiece of fantastic architecture, the *Palais Idéal*, had a vogue with art-world insiders like Picasso, who dedicated a series of drawings to Cheval, and Ernst, whose collage for the Postman includes an actual envelope. Did his embrace by insiders make Cheval less of an outsider? Was Altman's embrace of Duvall enough to cement her status as a star? Try asking Ray Johnson's bunnies these questions and they will just roll their eyes.

After that first Duvall meeting, Ray received a letter from "Chevel," as "dictated by Gerry Ayres," who "is too busy to write himself since he is currently organizing the Hollywood Hills chapter of the Fan Johnson Ray Club." Ayres's Chevel also tips Ray off that he knows Ray knows that his name is really spelled "cheval," French for "horse," by slipping in a crack about "a chevel of a different color." Chevel only half rhymes with Duvall. The moment Ray Johnson ceased to measure his exact distance from stardom is the moment he would start to fall.

XIII

If you were in New York and in the art world or wanted to be in the art world in the 1970s and '80s, you would go to Soho on Saturdays during the season and make the rounds of the galleries and see who was there. And if you were in Soho on a Saturday there was a good chance you might catch a glimpse of Ray Johnson moving purposefully from place to place, handing envelopes and packages to acquaintances he anticipated encountering along the way, or leaving things behind the desks at galleries to be picked up when the intended recipient came by. After some Saturdays, Johnson sent out flyers that seemed to suggest that he had held a Meeting of his usual sort. A 1976 duck-rabbit name-chart mailer (the icon recast here as a "disco duck," a creature featured in a campy novelty song that had recently hit number one on the charts), for example, gives all the details for **Each Time you Drag Me This Way/A New York Correspondence School Meeting/ For Katherine Kuh and Morris Graves/ By Ray Johnson and Robin Lee Crutchfield/ And Featuring the Erasers/ Saturday Afternoon, Three to Five, Nov 20th/ Soho, West Broadway, New York City**.

However, as Johnson noted afterwards, whereas previous **Meetings had been restricted to architecture interior space ... the Each Time happened on three city blocks and there was moving and not-meeting. It was a Graves landscape event.** The already minimal formal framework

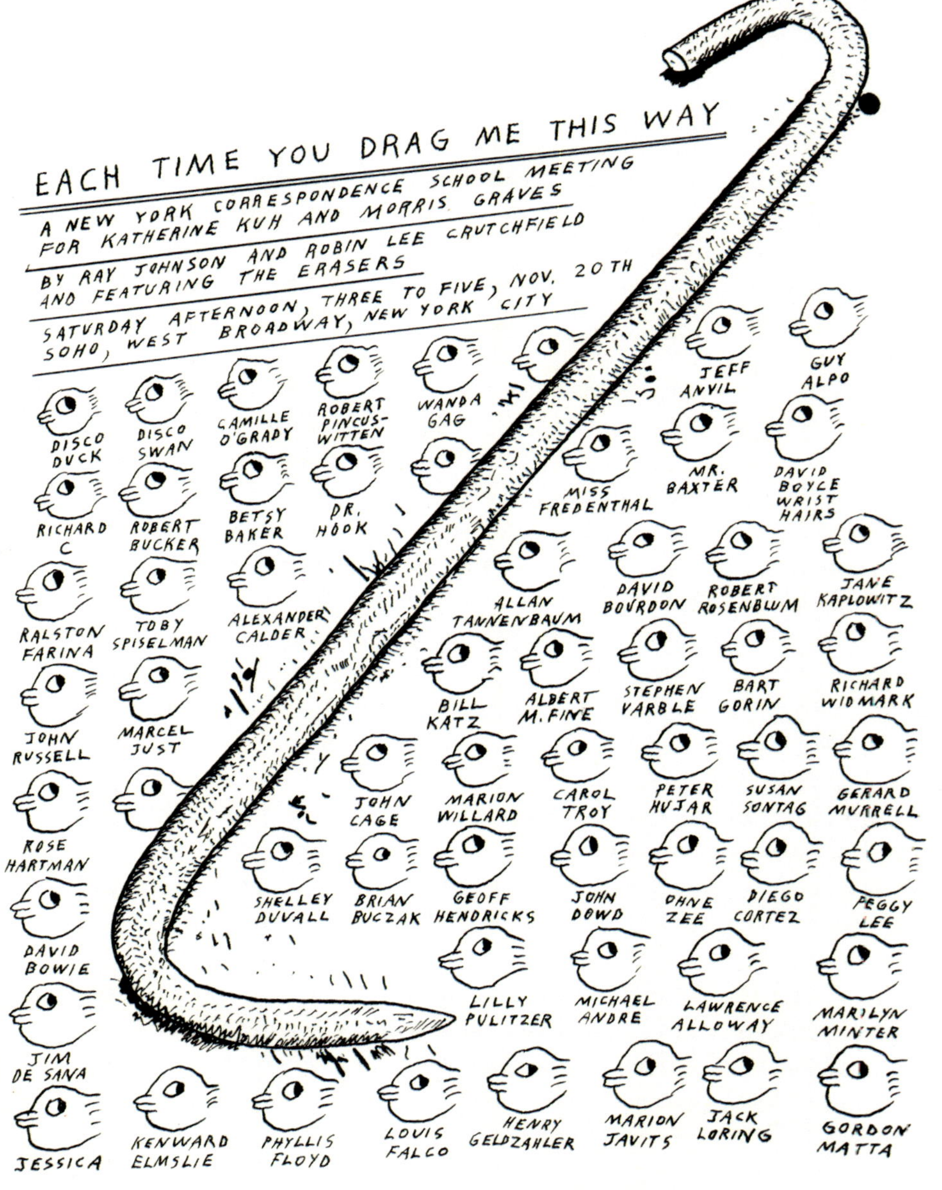

Ray Johnson, *Each Time You Drag Me This Way* meeting flyer, 1976.

that had defined other Meetings as events had been pared away to near invisibility. It was a Meeting as found object, like the grungy meat hook, picked up that day in an empty lot on Mercer Street, that cuts a zigzag path through the name chart on the flyer. Some passersby, knowing Ray, may have guessed as he engaged them that they had stepped into his frame, but it was not their knowing but their **moving and not-meeting** that gave life to Johnson's landscape. It was a picture that dissolved as it was made.

To the knowing observer on West Broadway, Ray Johnson might seem to have landed right back where he started. Once again, everyone on the New York art scene knew who he was but few knew what he did, other than indulge, in his attention-catching way, in what Wallace Stevens calls "the pleasures of merely circulating." The art world, though, had changed since Ray and his friends first foraged for debris on half-deserted downtown streets, had transformed from floating crap game to dauntingly respectable establishment, and many of the friends, too, had become established figures, bulwarked by galleries and studios and flocks of assistants. Johnson's elemental lightness of being, so costly to maintain, appeared all the more anomalous against this built-up backdrop.

This artist's undefended look, and the piquant contrast between that look and the unflagging conviction with which he executed his throwaway gestures, attracted a new set of friend-fans. At the time of the *Each Time* event, Robin Crutchfield, listed on the flyer as Johnson's co-host, was still aiming to make his name as a performance artist, but by the following year he had joined a band called DNA that would instead win him a place in punk rock history. Crutchfield's friends David Ebony, Jane Fire, and Susan Stringfield, members of the Erasers, the band featured on the *Each Time* flyer, also moved between the art and music scenes—Fire and Stringfield worked at a Soho gallery, and Ebony was an artist who would later do graduate work in art history with Rosalind Krauss. These twenty-something strivers had a sense that Ray Johnson was someone, yet unlike others of his generation, he was someone you could just walk up to and engage in conversation and then follow down the streets of Soho as he ran his enigmatic errands.

The gay men among this younger cohort—like Crutchfield and Ebony, the punk scene photographer Jimmy DeSana and his roommate, curator Diego Cortez, and Bart Gorin, assistant to art dealer Sam Green, Greta Garbo's frequent escort—you can find DeSana, Cortez, and Gorin on the *Each Time* flyer—would often continue on with Ray along his path once the galleries had closed. That path led to a different set of institutions, to Boots & Saddle and the International Stud, to the Anvil, Keller's, and the Mineshaft, all leather bars of varying sexual intensity, ranging from the companionable to the Hadean. To his young friend-fans it appeared that Johnson, who was, Ebony recalled, "a beloved figure in some of these places," went there "to socialize, not to cruise." Ray's nights in the West Village, by these lights, were in some respects much like his days in Soho. "He would do a circuit; he would have those Saturday nights so planned out. He had many stops on his itinerary."

Ray Johnson was no celibate. The bars must have played their part in the satisfaction of his needs and tastes. Yet as the young men moved with him from establishment to establishment, from the art world to the equally insular gay world, he gave them the impression that he was, in both these worlds, at once an echt-insider and a non-participant. The artist knew his audience, knew they were wondering, how will I find a place in the world without losing my sense of self? He was demonstrating the trick he had spent a lifetime mastering, the one-and-the-other trick. One Ray Johnson wants what he wants in art and sex, however weird or unacceptable his desires might seem to some, while the other Ray Johnson stands off a ways, like Walt Whitman's Me Myself, "Looking with side-curved head curious at what comes next / Both in and out of the game and watching and wondering at it." That's the kind of thing they teach you at Buddha University.

The title that Johnson came up with for his exhibition at Western Illinois University was **Detachment as Composition**, a joke about the instructions to "detach here & send" that he included in a set of mailings where the image is divided, coupon-style, into sections demarcated by dotted lines. But beneath the joke lay an abiding concern with the kind of psychic detachment that enables the cultivation of internal distance. **I am an individual who is a group and I am me and I am you, and that was an example of my mind splitting into several parts**, Johnson explained, meaning at once to satisfy and to deflect his friend's request that he define his practice. He was showing her students, as he showed the kids who trailed him through the galleries and bars, how "Je est un autre" feels in practice, how it feels to break the bonds that tie the ego to its objects.

To refuse to name those objects, though, is also a defensive gesture. In Ray Johnson's art and letters, one finds vanishingly few traces of the people he desired and what he felt about them and did with them. This artist never stopped moving, it seemed, never stopped performing and recording and constructing, and yet that part of his life within the life that we call private remained private. Is it frustrating to keep running up against this wall? Yes. But also edifying. Following Johnson on his path, one learns to tell the difference, however infrathin, between a life story and an art story.

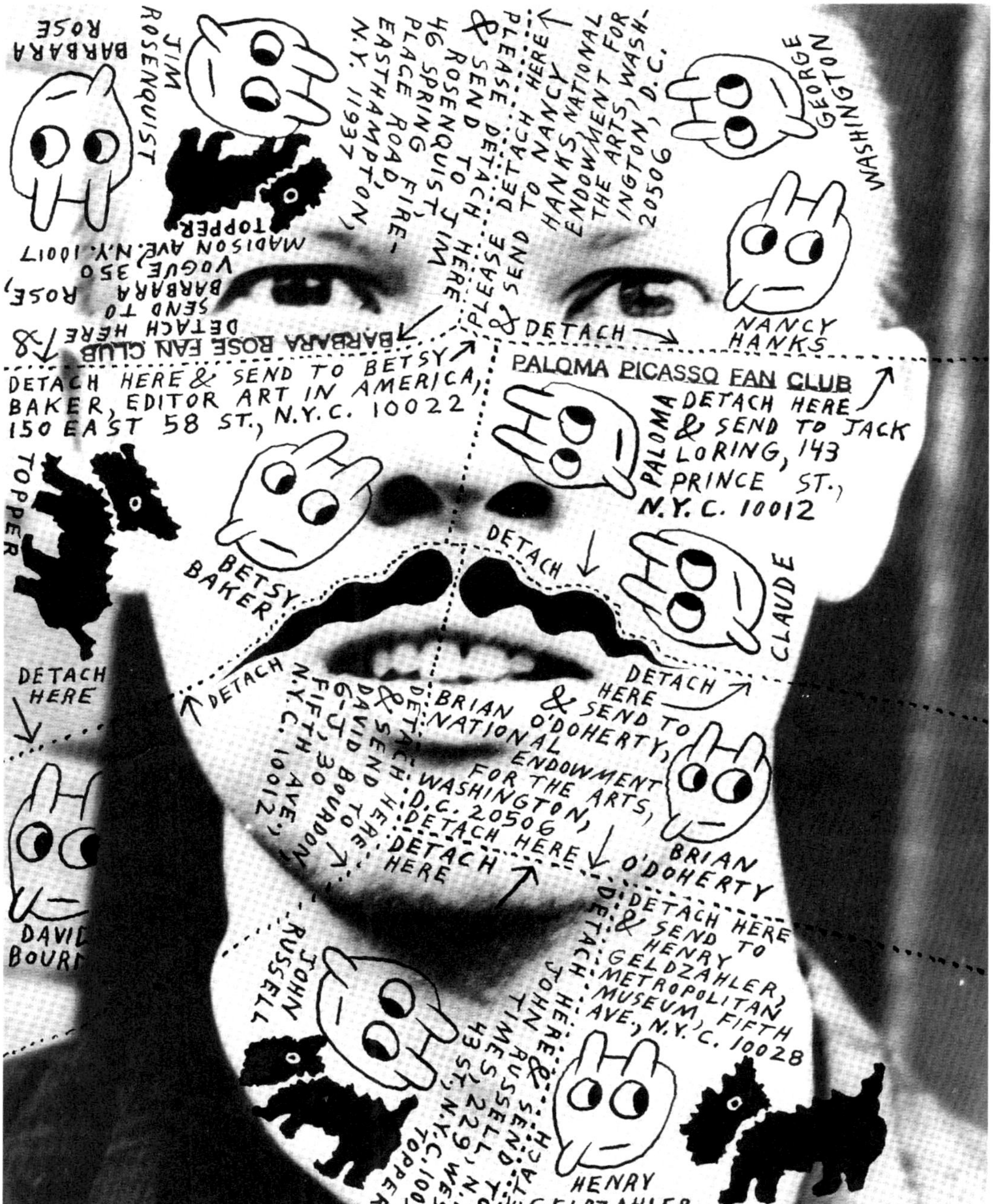

Ray Johnson, “detach here & send” mailer, ca. 1975.

XIV – AN ART STORY

AA Bronson, an editor of *FILE* magazine and one-third of the Toronto art group General Idea, corresponded with Ray Johnson for three years before he met him in the flesh, on a visit to New York in 1973. For their first rendezvous, "Ray offered to take me on an art tour," an offer the young out-of-towner naturally jumped at, only to find that "his art tour turned out to start at 1 a.m." They were joined on the tour by another recent arrival in the city, Jimmy DeSana, who had just published his first book of photographs, *101 Nudes*. When Johnson's little group assembled at the Spike, a gay bar by the river in the then-rough West 20s, Bronson's first thought was, "this doesn't really seem like an art tour," but "then we went to the Eagle and there was John Dowd and then I kind of understood."

The Eagle was another riverfront bar and John Dowd was its famously attractive bartender. Bronson knew him through the Canadian mail art network, into which Dowd had gotten looped after an encounter at Max's Kansas City, the New York artists' bar, with the Vancouver-based network member John Jack Baylin, a.k.a. Count Fanzini. Once back in Canada, Baylin founded the John Dowd Fan Club, which spawned mailings and meetings, and in 1972, the *John Dowd Fanny Club Fanzine*, the first in a series of zines produced collaboratively by Baylin and Dowd. Their model in this venture was, of course, Johnson, who in turn would contribute to an exchange of mailings published in the December 1973 issue of *FILE* celebrating the appointment of AA Bronson as "official liaison officer/Eastern Canada for the now infamous JOHN DOWD FAN CLUB." This chain of events would come full circle the following year, when Jimmy DeSana, now in the loop, took a photograph of Dowd with his pants down and Baylin and Dowd printed it with the caption "John Dowd bum shot by Jim DeSana in the role of Ray Johnson."

XV – SOCIAL NOTES

In a letter to Bart Gorin dated April 24, 1976, Ray Johnson thanks him **for the roll of strap** (sample attached) and **for the Michael Greer information.** (From *The New York Times*, April 20, 1976: "Michael Greer, a prominent interior designer who had helped decorate a room in the White House during the Dwight D. Eisenhower and John F. Kennedy Administrations, was found dead yesterday in his apartment at 525 Park Avenue at 60th Street, his feet bound by a red sash.") For Gorin's information, Johnson reports on sightings of **Kevin mustache at the Anvil** and of Peter Berlin, a self-invented superstar of gay erotica whose given name was Armin Hagen Baron Freiherr von

Hoyningen-Huene, lately spotted **on his bicycle in tiny white shorts and after midnight had switched to tiny red shorts. Is it possible he wears litmus paper?** Then there was a visit to Andy Warhol, who **asked lots of questions about the Anvil, etc., holding his tape recorder**. But that wasn't what Ray was there for. **I finally did Andy's silhouette this week and have done some terrific artworks based on it. Jamie Wyeth was there, naturally. "Don't forget, Jamie," said Andy, "that we have to have lunch with Paulette tomorrow."**

XVI

Haven't we all made shadow-pictures at one time? Ray Johnson asks, implicitly, in the lower left corner of a 1976 double portrait of May Wilson and Andy Warhol. A hand is moving its fingers to make a shape that will read either as a rabbit or a duck once it is turned just so and placed between a bright light and a wall. It is only a few steps removed from this nursery magic to the rudimentary form of portraiture called a silhouette, after "Etienne de Silhouette, an 18th century French minister of finance whose hobby was profile cutting," as Helen Harrison informs us in "Ray Johnson: Shadow and Substance," written in 1982. By then, Harrison calculates, Johnson had "been making silhouette portraits for about seven years."

One could say that society portraiture had long been Johnson's genre. The name-charts with their gridded icons are portraits, and so are the memorials, many of which commemorate the living as if they were dead (fame kills; skins shed). But Johnson had never dealt in likenesses until, as critic Nina Ffrench-Frazier tells us, the art dealer Holly Solomon sent him "a tiny silhouette portrait of herself that she had made in Disneyland," and "he was off and running, making silhouettes of everybody you could possibly imagine, a lot more you might never have thought of and a few you've never even heard of." Soon after the project got underway in 1976, the artist's correspondents started receiving "silhouette lists" with the names of those who submitted to having their profiles traced, arranged in numbered columns.

Johnson never did get Cher to pose for a silhouette, as he told editor Barbara Burn he had hoped to, but he did corral other notables, including writer William S. Burroughs (number one on the list), space oddity David Bowie, actor Joel Grey, playwright Edward Albee, poet John Ashbery (who resisted at first because "I try to conceal my profile as much as possible"), and porn star Harry Reems. Filling out the lists were assorted friends-of-Ray, dealers, critics, collectors, and artists, not only from New York, but from the art worlds of Detroit, where Johnson, long ignored in his hometown, finally had a solo gallery show in 1975, and Long Island, where Johnson's visibility increased as his presence on the Manhattan scene grew ever more phantasmatic.

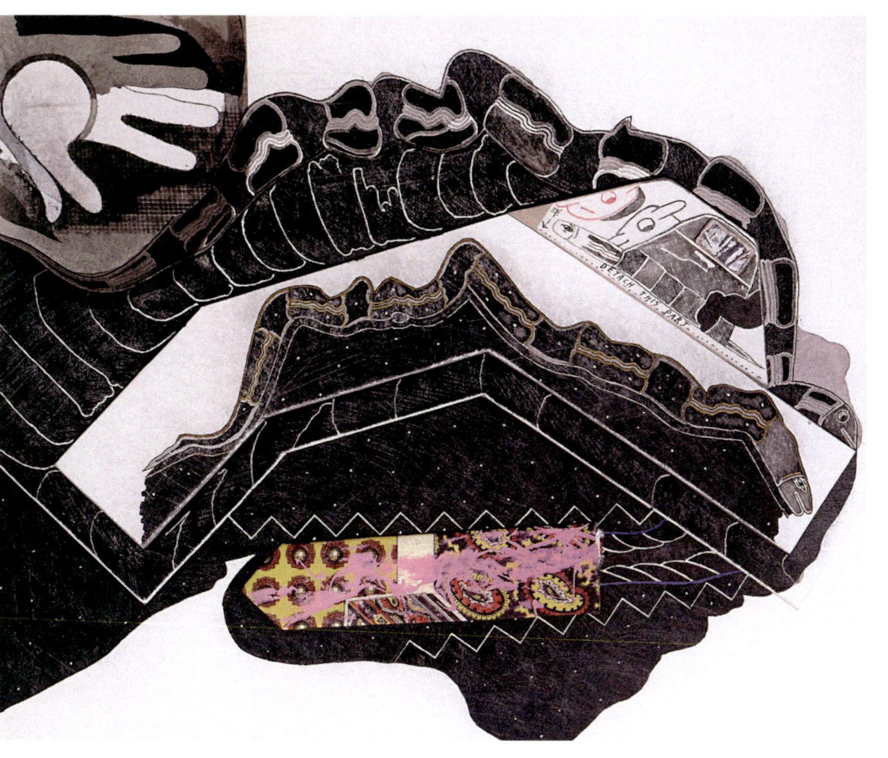

Ray Johnson, *May Wilson with Andy Warhol* (1976).

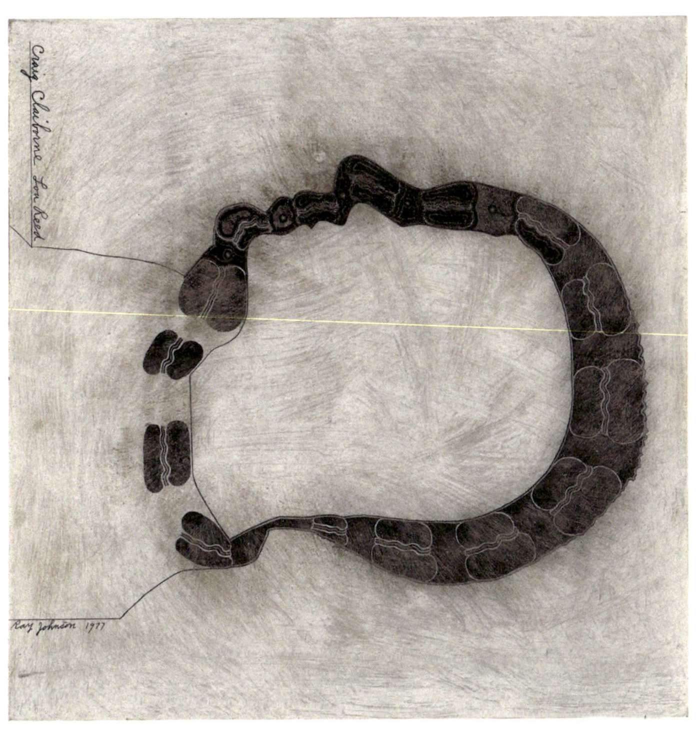

Ray Johnson, *Craig Claiborne Lou Reed* (1977).

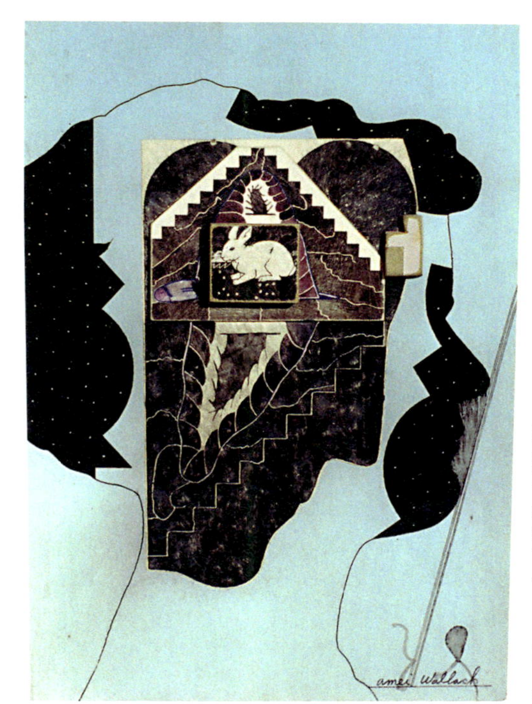

Ray Johnson, *Amei Wallach* (1977).

While the silhouette lists fueled the churning engine of the correspondence network, the tracing sessions were performances, staged one by one for Johnson's ideal audience of one. Helen Harrison, present at Johnson's session with portraitist Chuck Close, saw drama in the way the figure, placed just so by the artist between a bright light and a sheet of paper taped to the wall, "is conscious of its own breathing, heartbeat, eye movements, and all the tiny vibrations that betray its pent-up vitality." **I'm ruthlessly, relentlessly presenting myself to the person whose portrait I'm doing**, Johnson told her. **The aesthetic is that I'm doing it for the person. I'm trying record like a seismograph. It's a document of the rapport between my nervous energy and the person who's posing for me.** The artist makes precise use of the word "document" here. "You call that a drawing?" the fastidious Warhol scoffed, when he saw the results of his session with Ray. Harrison herself insists that "The surreal mood which permeates these 'standings' is somehow magically transmitted to the resulting drawings, in spite of their notational slightness." But Johnson simply shrugged and said, **They're all terrible drawings.** They're as close as something can get to being nothing.

Ray Johnson had been drawing with shadows ever since he began to build up tiles out of layered cardboard; now he was drawing shadows themselves. The tracings that came out of the sessions were mere indices, expressive only of the artist's inevitable failure to capture a subject that is fugitive by nature. But in the dusty light of Johnson's studio (**This house never gets cleaned**, he admitted to one of his rare visitors), these tremulous notations took on a new solidity. It was the first time Johnson had **worked on masonite**, as he informed a museum director who had expressed interest in doing a show—not quite canvas, but a step up from his usual illustration board, from the museal point of view—**and the collage work has become more "painterly," with painted scumbled surfaces. Size a bit larger too. It is a new snake direction.**

In the exceptionally austere double portrait *Craig Claiborne Lou Reed*, Johnson highlights the tension between the ghostliness of the profile tracings and the "painterly" textural effects he produces in the studio. The shadow-heads cast yet another shadow, created by rubbing through the white paint to the grainy Masonite, while a few added spidery lines sketch a notional bust and underscore the names of the artist and his subjects, both written in the same spidery hand. These barely-there elements are anchored by the thick tessellated ink outline of the outer profile, which, when it appears in other silhouette pictures, is often capped by a snake head; in *May Wilson with Andy Warhol*, for instance, both profiles are bounded by snakes. The spidery line is a throwaway gesture; the tessellated band is a portrait of the artist. **It is a new snake direction.**

Craig Claiborne was a best-selling cookbook writer and the food editor at the *New York Times*. Musician Lou Reed cofounded the Warhol Factory's house band, The Velvet Underground, before moving on to a starry solo career. The southern gentleman and the rock and roll animal make for a very odd couple, but subdued by the picture's foggy, almost gothic atmosphere, one hardly dares to laugh at the incongruity. Many of the silhouette pictures are, like this one, double portraits, with one head nested inside the other, as if each were thinking the other into existence. In the Claiborne/Reed picture, the May Wilson/Warhol picture, and in a portrait of art critic Amei Wallach, the lesser known of the two subjects frames the more famous one. The inner profile in the Wallach picture, however, is not one of Johnson's tracings but a version of *Self-Portrait in Profile* (1958), a torn-paper silhouette of and by Marcel Duchamp that would later be reproduced by Arturo Schwarz as an editioned print. There is also a third portrait in the Wallach picture, affixed to a tile that bursts from Johnson's Duchamp's brain: a drawing of a rabbit, not the artist's usual signature cartoon, but a creature that, like the tile itself, is almost but not quite fully three-dimensional. Like his model, Duchamp, Ray Johnson makes it hard to tell the realized from the notional.

He also makes it hard to tell a portrait from a self-portrait, not so much out of egotism as because he is an individual who is a group. Or as the artist put it when he wrote to gallerist Paula Cooper in April 1976 to request that she pose for her silhouette, **As Gertrude Stein in writing The Making of Americans said, " "** [*sic*], **I too want to create a work about everyone.** The project had just begun but, Johnson wanted Cooper to know, it was already official. **A rubber stamp is being made reading: SILHOUETTE UNIVERSITY.**

XVII

With the silhouettes, Johnson grasped the synthesis of image, message, and performance he had been reaching for. In 1977, fifty of the new works went on view at the Elaine Benson Gallery in Bridgehampton on Long Island and in April 1978, *37 Portraits* opened at the Brooks Jackson/Iolas Gallery on 57th Street, Johnson's first solo exhibition in Manhattan in five years. In September of that year, *Viewpoints: Ray Johnson*, a substantial one-man show, opened at the Walker Art Center in Minneapolis. By the end of 1979, there were over two hundred names on the silhouette list; the artist was working once again in an unbroken rhythm.

The following year, in October, around the time of his fifty-third birthday, Ray tore a page of gallery advertisements out of the *New York Times* and glued his own ad onto it and photocopied the result and put it into the mail. **Ray Johnson nothing/no gallery**, it said.

Beneath this ultimate advertisement for nothing lies an ad for the Robert Schoelkopf Gallery, which hosted exhibitions of Joseph Cornell's work toward the end of his life. (Like Johnson, Cornell had a genius for exasperating dealers and the "bookish and soft-spoken" Schoelkopf, as Cornell's biographer Deborah Solomon describes him, "known for championing realist and representative painters whose work most dealers dismissed," was the artist's last resort.) In 1966, Dore Ashton's review of a Cornell show at Schoelkopf was followed by her review of Johnson's show at Willard and in the accompanying photos, as Ray wrote to Richard Lippold, his collage **Pink Above was reproduced next to a Cornell and I am so very happy.**

That was then and this was now. **Ray Johnson nothing/no gallery** was a vow in the form of an advertisement. The artist's short, fraught life in the commercial gallery world had come to an end. Another death. Though not *just* another death. Once Ray had made this decisive throwaway gesture, the real life, the posthumous one, could begin.

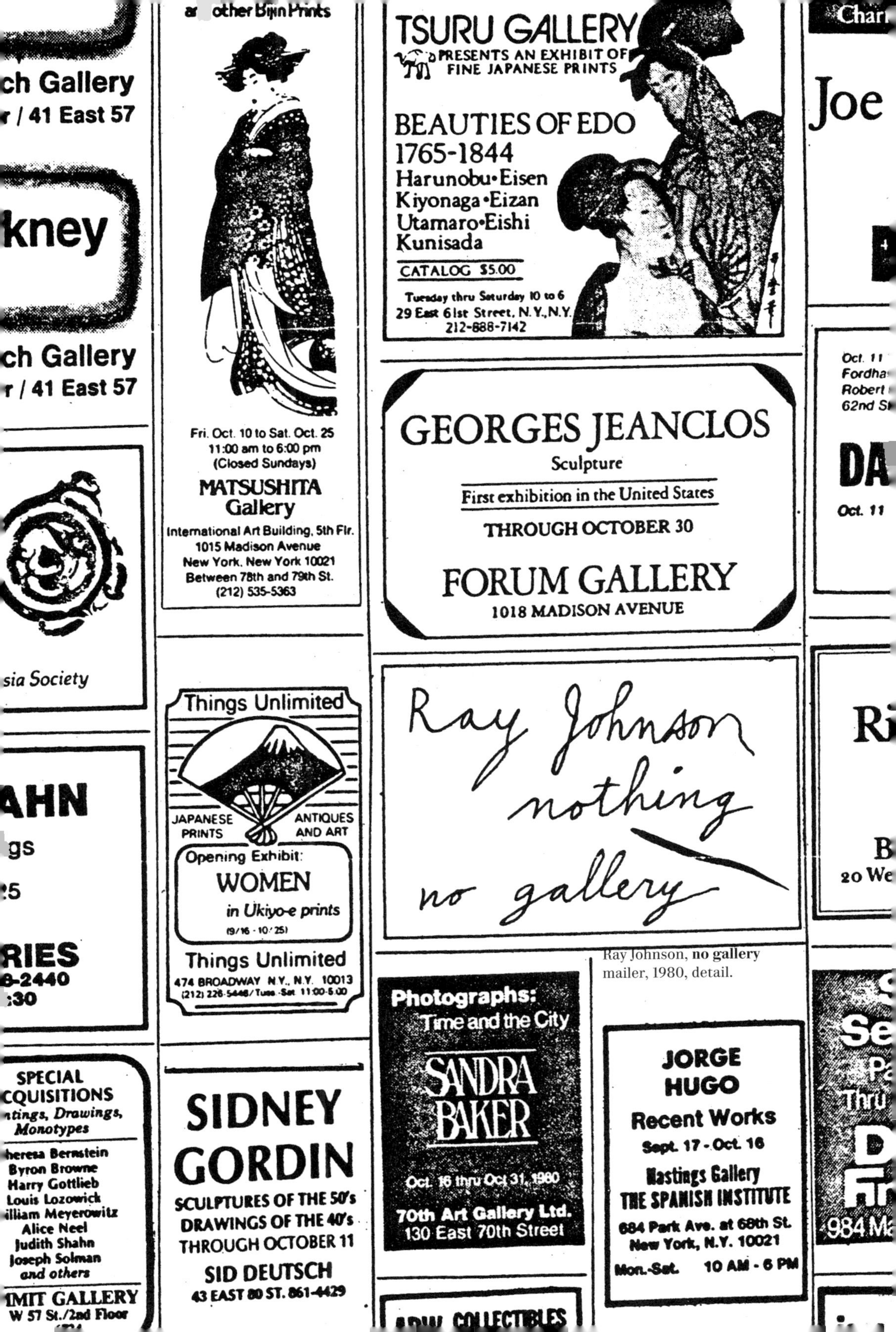

ch Gallery
r / 41 East 57

kney

ch Gallery
r / 41 East 57

sia Society

AHN
gs
25

RIES
6-2440
:30

SPECIAL
CQUISITIONS
ntings, Drawings,
Monotypes

heresa Bernstein
Byron Browne
Harry Gottlieb
Louis Lozowick
illiam Meyerowitz
Alice Neel
Judith Shahn
Joseph Solman
and others

MIT GALLERY
W 57 St./2nd Floor

other Bijin Prints

Fri. Oct. 10 to Sat. Oct. 25
11:00 am to 6:00 pm
(Closed Sundays)
MATSUSHITA
Gallery
International Art Building, 5th Flr.
1015 Madison Avenue
New York, New York 10021
Between 78th and 79th St.
(212) 535-5363

Things Unlimited
JAPANESE PRINTS
ANTIQUES AND ART
Opening Exhibit:
WOMEN
in Ukiyo-e prints
(9/16 - 10/25)
Things Unlimited
474 BROADWAY N.Y., N.Y. 10013
(212) 226-5446 / Tues.-Sat. 11:00-5:00

SIDNEY
GORDIN
SCULPTURES OF THE 50's
DRAWINGS OF THE 40's
THROUGH OCTOBER 11
SID DEUTSCH
43 EAST 80 ST. 861-4429

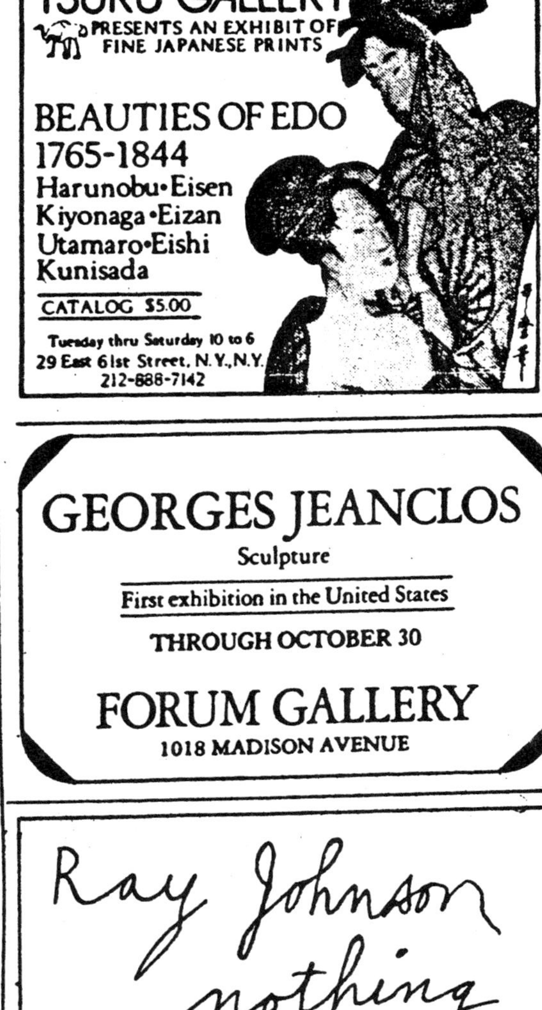

TSURU GALLERY
PRESENTS AN EXHIBIT OF
FINE JAPANESE PRINTS
BEAUTIES OF EDO
1765-1844
Harunobu•Eisen
Kiyonaga•Eizan
Utamaro•Eishi
Kunisada
CATALOG $5.00
Tuesday thru Saturday 10 to 6
29 East 61st Street, N.Y., N.Y.
212-888-7142

GEORGES JEANCLOS
Sculpture
First exhibition in the United States
THROUGH OCTOBER 30
FORUM GALLERY
1018 MADISON AVENUE

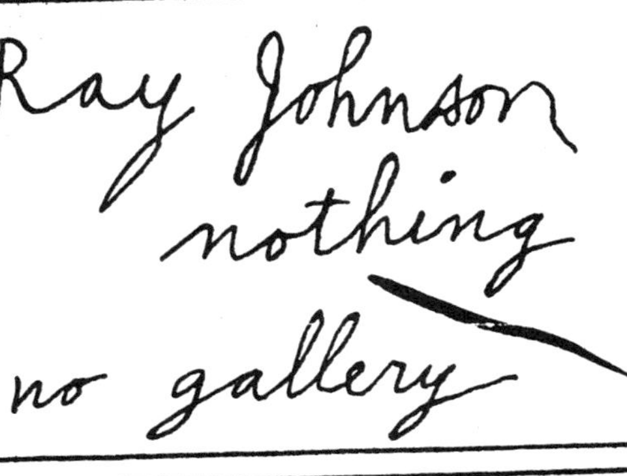

Ray Johnson, **no gallery** mailer, 1980, detail.

Photographs:
Time and the City
SANDRA
BAKER
Oct. 16 thru Oct 31, 1980
70th Art Gallery Ltd.
130 East 70th Street

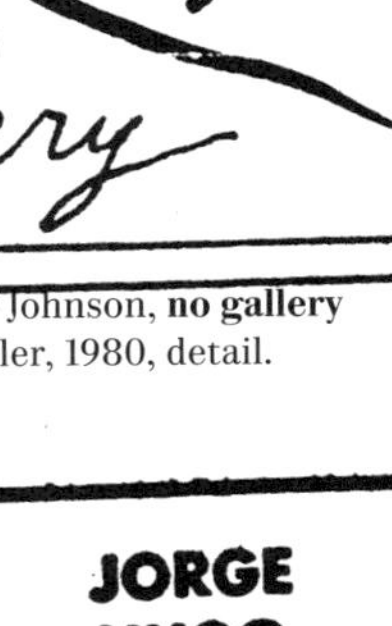

JORGE
HUGO
Recent Works
Sept. 17 - Oct. 16
Hastings Gallery
THE SPANISH INSTITUTE
684 Park Ave. at 68th St.
New York, N.Y. 10021
Mon.-Sat. 10 AM - 6 PM

ADW COLLECTIBLES

Char

Joe

Oct. 11
Fordha
Robert
62nd S

DA
Oct. 11

Ri
B
20 We

Se
Pa
Thru
D
Fr
984 M

"You mean, says J. Daley, that Ray sends you letters with real news ?!?" begins a newsy letter to Ray from Henry Martin. And it's true, the Ray of the letters to Henry is different from the Ray one finds in most of his other correspondences: more direct, franker, and more vulnerable. Like all great correspondents, Ray keyed his tone to the tone of his recipient, and Henry's epistolary character was expansive, expressive, witty, erudite, and warm. Martin's geographical remoteness and the prohibitively high cost back then of international phone calls may also be factored in, as should the fact that Johnson tended to be more direct when he had business to conduct, as he so often did with Henry, who kept hoping his many contacts in the Italian art world might be deployed to Ray's benefit. "We will make you rich and famous yet since of course I *already* love you."

Ultimately, though, Ray's openness with Henry was a matter of trust. Ray put trust in Henry's innocence, which matched his own. And, perhaps more than anyone else, Ray could trust Henry—an American in Europe, a black man in a white world, a brilliantly well-connected anti-careerist—to credit his ambivalence. No document I have come across in my siftings through **the boxes and boxes and boxes and boxes and boxes of material** has given me a better sense of what drove Ray Johnson to paste that advertisement for nothing in the *New York Times* than a letter from Ray to Henry dated March 1, 1976, a month before the silhouette sessions started.

Henry's last letter had contained the news that the collector Nicola Incisetto had just snapped up ninety of Johnson's collages in Italy and hoped to meet the artist on his next visit to New York, with the aim of acquiring still more work. Ray was grateful—**All your information is most valuable to me**—but also **in a state of shock hearing that Mr. I has purchased 90 works of mine. Having struggled on the NY City art scene for all these many years of no sales and appreciation, I cannot respond to this news except to be in shock. And delight. And fear**. As if to counter the fear, he turns to the subject of the **N.C. Letters show**: he is **rather touched** by some of the submissions, **Elaine de Kooning's especially**. And then:

Oh.

It's like I was dead.
The whole time displacement. Am I an exile? Was James Joyce?
Why was I not appreciated in my <u>own</u> cunt-try?

Yet Incisetto could hardly have appreciated him more. After the collector and his wife returned from their New York trip, Henry told Ray that "Mrs. Incisetto says that meeting Ray Johnson was one of the great experiences of her life, she finally feels that she has had the experience of meeting a truly great artist." Which made it all the more puzzling, even to sympathetic Henry, when the Incisettos reported that they had tried to work out an agreement with Ray to buy a series of his works going forward and the artist "turned them down on every count" and "just kept saying that there was nothing they were saying that could interest" him. Delight is fleeting. Fear is forever. Until you die, that is.

In the letter from March 1, Ray's response to Henry's news about the ninety collages is preceded by his account of the opening of an elegantly presented exhibition of Joseph Cornell's work at Leo Castelli, this artist's first showing at that prestigious Soho gallery. Cornell had been dead four years. **Leo was tailored. The works were gorgeous. I felt so bad for dead Cornell, who in his living his daily living as G. Stein put it couldn't relate to galleries like Leo. Remember Cornell showed in a frumpy Americana gallery after dealers did him in. He was so suspicious, had suffered so & after death so well-groomed when in life he hid in Utopia unrelated.**

If only Ray could live, as Cornell had, on a street with a poetic name like Utopia Parkway, instead of plain West 7th Street in Locust Valley. But one takes one's refuge where one can. **It's like I was dead**, without actually being dead. To maintain that kind of shadowy existence, to keep pursuing the flashes of delight while holding off the fear, that is the trick.

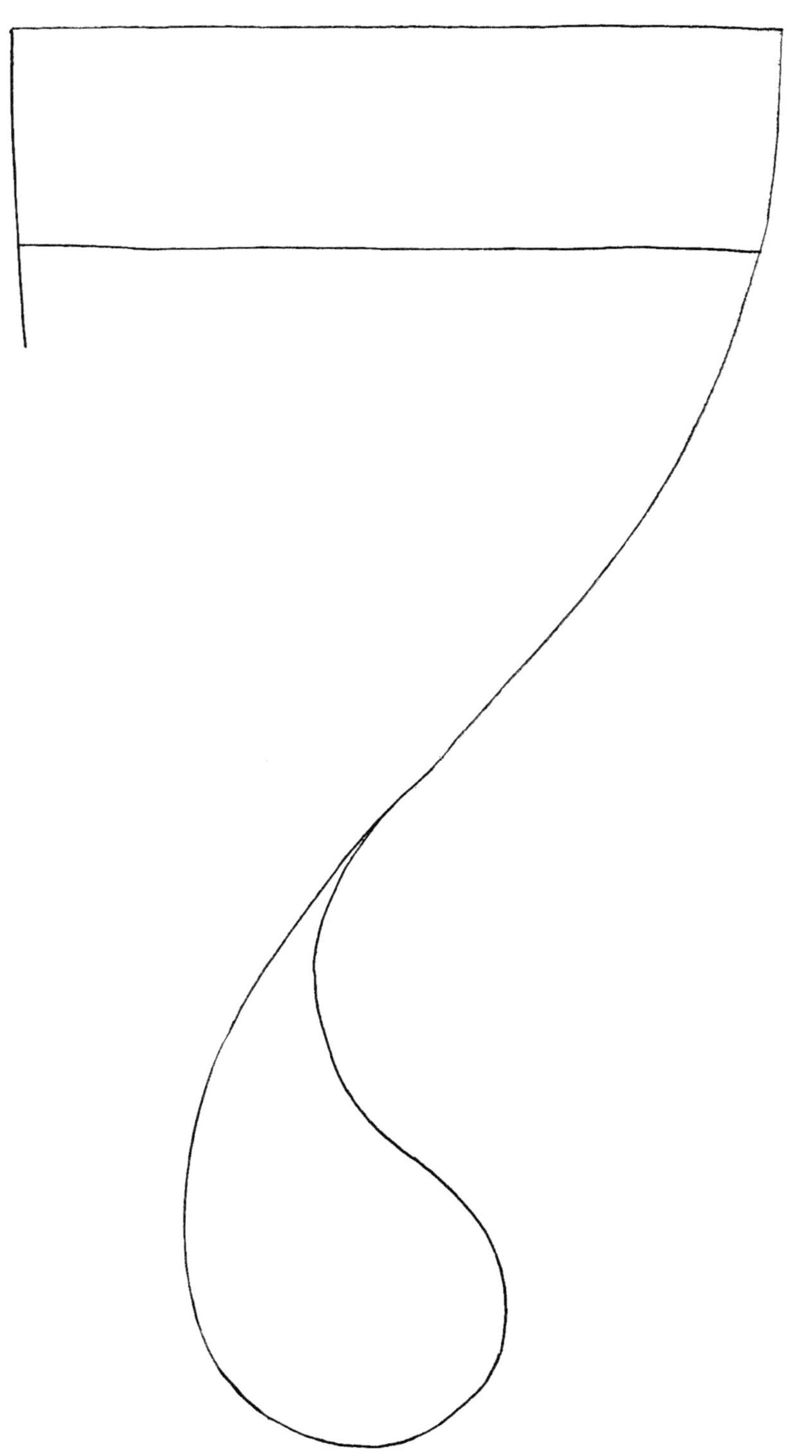

1980–1995

"I DO NOT EXITS": RAY JOHNSON'S MEMORY THEATER

**e.
dickin-
son said:
which is
the best,
the moon
or the
crescent?
neither,
said the
moon.
that is
best which
is not.
achieve
it, you
efface
the sheen.**

—Ray Johnson to Frances X. Profumo, written in the margin, ca. 1950

That is best which is not.

I

In a possibly unsent letter dated February 20, 1986, Ray Johnson records a vision that came to him that morning in **the time between getting up and getting to the john. This rectangle appeared and I knew as it took shape like something put into water a substance like a photographic negative an image appears I saw this shape and realized that it was important.** It seemed to him that **the Portrait work I have been working on for the past eleven years was summed up in the realization of that shape** and—that it might also help somehow with **the problems I have to solve** in connection with yet **another of those stage appearances next month for an art group in an auditorium.**

The private theater of the silhouette tracings and the public theater of the institutional performances fused at that moment into an icon that, as Johnson tells his correspondent, **relates to those puppet plays I did as a kid in school except this is now on a much larger stage and scale**. By which he does not mean a larger physical scale. The stages that would fill the artist's sketchbooks and pepper the collages from then on were postcard-sized or smaller, scaled for intimate viewing.

Some of the stages come accompanied by a laconic script. The player introduced in line three of each script varies, but the other elements—

title, stage direction, audience response—recur verbatim. It is the element of the audience, I think, that acts as a magnifier, shifting the work, in the artist's view, toward **a much larger stage and scale**. Which might seem ironic, given the deflationary nature of the response of Johnson's imaginary audience, the hollow echo of their "ha, ha, ha." Not to mention the **Ray Johnson/nothing/no gallery** business, which some years before had put what might look like a finishing flourish on the maddening game of fort-da that Johnson had been playing with audiences, both actual and potential, since the start of his art-life.

And yet, **although**, as Ray himself admitted to his possibly imaginary recipient, **it sounds silly**, the coming-into-focus of the little theater did herald **a profound development** in the artist's thinking. The curtain opens: player and audience, face to face, at last.

II

The salutation on the theater-vision letter reads "Hi Ma," which is odd, because Ray had always, since his college days, addressed his parents in letters by their first names, Lorraine and Eino. Another possibility is suggested in a small, spare collage, undated, but in the artist's early-1990s style, with a drawing of a hand that has just written **DEAR MA** and is poised to add another letter, which might turn **MA** into **MAY**. May Wilson, however, was also an unlikely recipient of the theater letter, since in early 1986 she was fading fast in both body and mind. She would die in October of that year, although Bill would receive please-send-to's addressed to May from Ray for several years after. Eino Johnson had died in 1984, and Lorraine had grown frail enough by the summer of 1986 to prompt Ray to turn to the now-experienced Bill for advice about putting his mother in a nursing home and ordering her affairs. Who else but Lorraine, though, would remember **those puppet plays I did as a kid in school**? Memory takes the shape of a theater as one's first audiences withdraw.

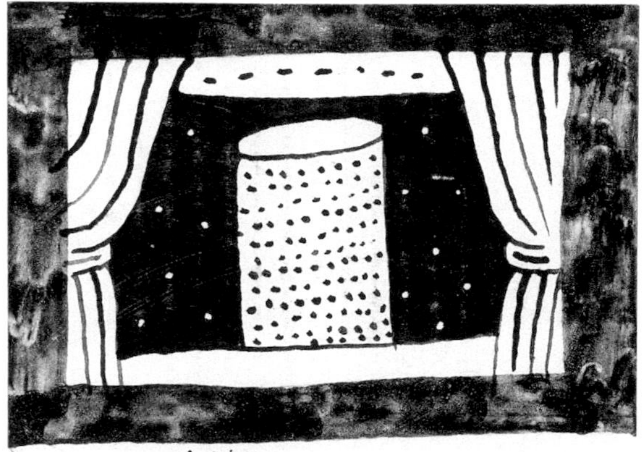

Ray Johnson, *Untitled (A Obera Can of Sand)* (1992).

In 1957, Ray Johnson wrote to Richard Lippold about their mutual friend **Merce's concert last night. I was so impressed by the complete devotion to dance of himself and his dancers that it didn't really matter if there was an audience there because they were beyond mere entertainment.** Maybe, Ray mused, it would be best, at that moment of perfect self-forgetfulness, **to lose them completely and no longer know them all. By forgetting they exist maybe in the future we can meet fresh and it will be like another life in which to find anew all these things we all seem to know through our experience.**

In 1958, Judith Malina and Julian Beck of the Living Theater commissioned Ray Johnson to decorate the stairway that led to their new performance space on 14th Street. "Ray's idea for the mural," as Malina remembered it, "was to paint around the hands of a little child, drawing an outline around them, the left hand on one side, the right hand on the other, and then to fill in the outlines with very bright colors." The mural was only half done when the child-model was killed in a fire and Malina thought it should be left as it was "as a kind of memorial, but Ray said he couldn't." So the mural was painted over. And then early one evening Johnson came to the theater and "he took a different colored crayon in each hand. And he went up and down the stairs with a crayon in each hand, creating a line as he went up and down." He went up and down until three in the morning, laying down layer after layer of crayon in what Ray's friend Malka Safro, who worked the theater's box office, described as "a slow and continual ritual or effort. It was beyond effort." The result, Safro thought, was "so thick and so rich and so fantastic." But Malina and Beck thought not and once again the mural was painted over. Decades later, after Ray was gone, Malina would express regret that "we couldn't yet understand this possibility. Ray was right, I think, that should have been the mural of the entrance to the Living Theater."

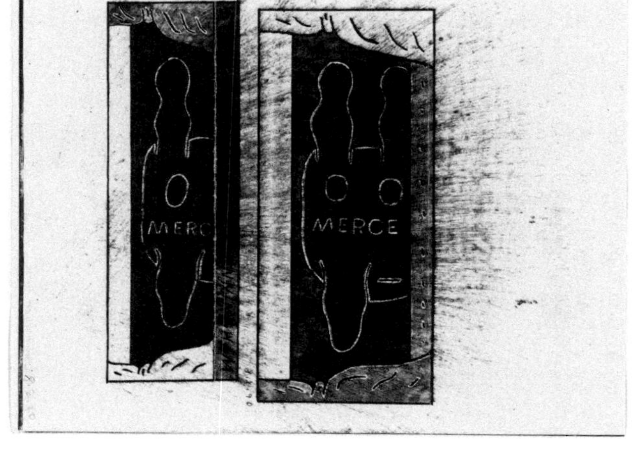

Ray Johnson, *Stage Set for Merce*, from *A BOOK ABOUT MODERN ART* (1990).

> **in the future we can meet fresh and it will be like another life in which to find anew all these things we all seem to know through our experience**

IV

The first and, as it turned out, only museum retrospective of Ray Johnson's work mounted during his lifetime took place in 1984 at the Nassau County Museum of Art in Roslyn, New York, which Johnson described in a letter to Henry Martin as **this local Museum on a former Frick Estate with lots of land and lots of historic old trees**. A far cry from MoMA or the Whitney; nonetheless, Ray told Henry, **I am very excited about all this**, excited to be exhibiting the work on a much larger stage and scale than heretofore and to see **the "fine art" works for the first time shown with letters—that north carolina show** was great, but really, just **the tip of the iceberg**. Critics and curators have found it exceptionally difficult to hold these two aspects of Johnson's practice together in mind. Even practiced dialecticians tend to land, in this artist's case, on one side or another of a dichotomy of taste: for every lover of the refined and the complex who thinks "the collages should come first" (per *New York Times* critic John Russell), there is another who dismisses them as "rather dull formal gallery works" in favor of the "amusing radical collage-communications" (Hilton Kramer). In the end, Janice Parente and Phyllis Stigliano, the curators of Johnson's Nassau County show, decided to focus on "his extraordinarily inventive collages," which filled the six second-floor gallery spaces, while relegating the correspondence pieces—just the graphic mailers, "no missives in envelopes"—to the hallway.

One wonders what it was about these **two young pretty curators** that enabled them to breach Johnson's formidable defenses and pull together a show that the raft of critics who ventured out to the suburbs for Ray all agreed made a convincing case that, as Grace Glueck wrote in the *New York Times* (which also published a second favorable review, by Phyllis Braff), "Mr. Johnson's fame as a collagist should equal his prominence as dean of the New York Correspondance [*sic*] School." Parente and Stigliano must have had the openness that comes with youth, that quality that Johnson maintained at such cost to himself and valued so highly in others. The out-of-the-way, only semi-official character of their institution may also have put the artist off his guard. In any case, seven months before the show was to open, Ray reported to Henry that **my Museum exhibition is proceeding splashingly**, that there had **been so far splendid willingness** on the part of private collectors—few museums yet owned his work—**to**

participate, so now it is starting to be fun. He was having **weekly sessions** with the game young curators **to show them stuff and endlessly tell them stories about the vast network of personalities involved over the years**.

My work as a result is exploding like wildfire in every direction, just as it had in the old days, when the prospect of a gallery show was in the offing. In his next letter, Ray is jazzed to tell Henry about **some really new work ideas, a new concept of it all. you have to see it, see it. all my white backgrounds are now black with tons of those tiny spaced out polka dots in the night sky. a hush of darkness over everything.** Over the underlined **black**, he has handwritten **BLACK SUN** with an arrow leading to the postscript, **am reading the Harry Crosby DIARIES**, assuming that Henry would get the reference. *Black Sun* was the title of Geoffrey Wolff's best-selling 1976 biography of Harry Crosby, a poet, publisher and icon of the Lost Generation, whose brief, wild life ended with a murder-suicide—as the book blurb has it, "a man who killed himself to make his life a work of art."

On January 30, 1984, one week before the show's opening, Ray wrote to Bill to thank him for offering to throw a party to celebrate the occasion, but **I think we should cancel it—I am not well in heart/mind because of this Nassau Museum exhibition It is difficult to have to write a sentence describing a "not well"** so instead, he tells Bill that he **drove past Joseph Cornell's house again late one evening**—Cornell had died in 1972 and the house had new occupants—and that on another such drive-by viewing **I noticed a wishing well in someone's front yard reminding me once of the advertisement I clipped from someone who had a wishing well they wanted to sell. I don't know how to write. Ray**

Ray got himself to the museum on opening night but never went inside, lurking instead in the darkness by the entrance all evening as the invitees streamed by. Several reviewers of the show, however, found the artist present and apparently eager to engage when they made their visits. Johnson took Gerrit Henry, from *Art in America*, "past *every* collage in each of the five rooms devoted to them, his patter about the collages—what they meant (possibly), who they referred to, how they came about—informatively non-stop"; while with Grace Glueck, he eschewed "lengthy exegetics,"

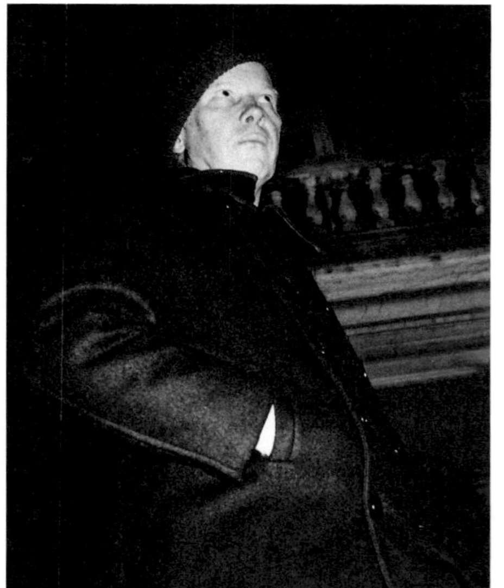

Ray Johnson outside the Nassau County Museum of Art, February 7, 1984, photograph by Richard P. Meyer.

explaining "**I'm the founder of the Deadpan Club**," and "plunge[d] instead into an account of how he keeps occasional watch on the home of the late Joseph Cornell on Utopia Parkway in Queens, now occupied by another family."

But the hush of darkness lingered. To Henry, one month and a day after the exhibition closed:

> **I have been in a very funny mood during that Nassau show, also after. I mean funny. I'll tell you about it sometime if I ever figure it out. It has so much to do with:**
>
> **I**
do not
exits. [*sic*]
>
> **Please tell g. brecht. I also don't do windows.**
>
> Ha, ha, ha.

V

To exits or not to exits, that is the question.

After announcing his exit from the commercial gallery circuit in 1980, Ray Johnson continued to try various back doors. Certain dealers had a couple of collages on consignment stashed away somewhere, if you knew to ask. Or if you were among the more determined collectors, you might still finagle a private showing of whichever array of works Johnson thought fit for you to see, although even then it was not simply a matter of making your choice and writing a check, you had to become a partner in the dance. The film *How to Draw a Bunny* features a couple of stories of baroque Johnsonian negotiations—Ray's artist-friend Peter Schuyff asking for a discount on a collage and receiving the piece with the requested percentage, translated from dollars into inches, neatly snipped off, literary agent Morton Janklow responding to Ray's offer of twenty-six collages for $21,000 with a counter of $13,000, a gesture whose minginess the artist underscored by changing his price to eighteen pictures for $12,700 or nineteen for $13,150.

Ray Johnson loved to play with numbers and hated to talk about money. But the math games threaten to distract from the most interesting aspect of the Janklow story, that is, the glimpse it offers into the chamber theater of Johnson's studio. The group of collages the collector was chasing all featured the tracing Johnson had done of Janklow's silhouette. Should he fail to respond to the artist's parodic counter-counter-offer within a month, Ray informed Morton, **I plan on January 1, 1982** to **start adding Paloma Picasso to each of the compositions of your**

26 portraits. Her head will appear next to yours, or as a larger head containing your head. I am not sure if her head will have to overlap yours. The portraits were duly encrusted with Palomas as negotiations corkscrewed on and finally Janklow walked away from the deal. But two years later, he couldn't resist asking Johnson what had happened to the portraits, which led to a series of missives detailing the further changes they had undergone and continued to undergo until in 1986 Morton admitted to Ray that he was "really sorry that there is no documentation of the original series of portraits, and even sorrier that I don't own a few of them." Another artist might have taken this as a cue to once again name his price. Ray only sent more teasing letters.

Once the artist knew he had his audience hooked, the point became the performance's sheer ongoingness, not just in the communications that were the visible tip of the iceberg, but also in the process that unfolded unseen day by day in the aqueous atmosphere of the house in Locust Valley. Their recycled materials, faded colors, and sandpapered surfaces had always lent Johnson's exhibition works a time-warped quality akin to the one Cornell had cultivated in his similarly sealed-off space out on Utopia Parkway. But it was not until Johnson went into the no-gallery business in earnest, and the usual career benchmarks ceased to apply, that time assumed a starring role in the pictures. **The works cannot be exhibited in the usual way because they constantly change, like the news in the papers or the images on a movie screen,** he explained, back when moticos rained down on the streets. The papers and the movies manifest the forward flow of time in sequence, edition after edition, frame after frame. Now Ray was wondering, as he wrote to Bill in 1988, if **all those movies**—referring now to Harold Edgerton's pioneering experiments in using strobe lights to capture on film movements too rapid for the naked eye—**could simply be shown backwards and where would logic be then I ask neht? ah ah ah.**

Johnson was holding on to his pictures, adding elements to them as ideas struck, scribbling dates to indicate that changes had been made, registering the flow of time within a single frame, not in sequence but in depth. As the collages migrated from the crammed storage spaces upstairs down to the first-floor worktable and back, the changes in one picture could reverberate in others, waves rippling through the charged atmosphere, a hush of darkness over everything.

Johnson left no instructions in his correspondence or notes-to-self on how to interpret the dates that litter these later works like so many fallen leaves. In his case as in Cornell's, another auto-collector who worked on pieces over long spans, the sedimented changes in each piece may equally obscure and highlight transformations in the artist's style over time: many clues, no solutions. For instance: *Untitled (Wed Dead Led)*, a collage dated "1968-88-89-92-94," contains wide stretches of white space that may signal that the rudiments of the composition were laid down in 1968, the first date marked on the picture, since by the second date, 1988, Johnson's *horror vacui* was once again in the ascendant and most new collages were either packed edge to edge with detail, or flooded with washes of black ink, or both. The added element marked **9.25.1988** seems just to be a salutation written in at the end of the printed caption below a cutout image of one of Picasso's *Minotaurs*: **DEAR ERIC SATIE.** Satie: the composer who collaborated with Picasso on the legendary proto-surrealist ballet *Parade*, and who was forever associated in Ray's mind with the time at Black Mountain when John Cage held his series of Satie concerts and Richard Lippold drove down in his hearse and Ray **walked with Bill and Elaine one sad evening up "the Road" when they had just heard about Gorky's death** and John, Merce, Richard, Elaine, Bill, and even baby Ray each had a hand in the production of Satie's *Ruse of Medusa* that brought the curtain down on that fateful summer. (Having suffered a devastating series of losses and setbacks, painter Arshile Gorky hung himself on July 21, 1948. In 1992, Johnson sketched two versions of a little theater on whose stage stands a shadowbox inscribed with Gorky's name.)

The date of "2.8.92" written over the corner of the Picasso cutout, along with the date of "2.17.92" just to the left, likely commemorate Johnson's addition of the net of thin ink lines overlaid with a thick wavy circle that at once frames and obscures the place in the drawing where the bull-man penetrates the writhing nymph. **LETTING PIN IN LETTING LET IN LET IN IN IN IN IN**, urge the merciless letters penned over the image. Here Johnson quotes the text of another legendary work of avant-garde theater, Gertrude Stein's *Four Saints in Three Acts*, a passage (see Act 2, Scene IX) from which the "wed-dead-led" phrase that runs around the little black frame above is also taken. Like the Picasso drawing, the Stein paragraph—really one long sentence—oscillates between dread and ecstasy, states that Stein deems, at the conclusion of the sentence, "the funniest in union."

There are two keys in the collage, one in ink, boxed by the little frame, one real, suspended over its ink-shadow, neither liable to unlock the picture's secrets. Both the key on the hook-chain and its spindly mate, a suspended fishhook, look like beach-walk finds. Ray Johnson to Ann Wilson, August 10, 1967: **I found a rusty fish hook and delighted to find later in the dictionary under barb the same fish hook not rusty** [here he inserts a drawing of a fishhook to show how it resembles] **the J of Johnson I had to swim back with it in my right hand.** A barb can make you say ouch or ha, ha, ha or both at once, the funniest in union.

First things last. The plaque at the bottom of the collage marks a birth rather than the artist's usual tombstone birth-to-death: **JAMES STEWART WAS BORN IN INDIANA, PENNSYLVANIA ON MAY 20, 1908**. This information is x-ed out—Johnson's late additions often take the form of negations—then written in again below the plaque in the same hand as the signature and string of dates, the last of which is **94**, placing this piece among the works the artist turned to in the months before he died. When the interviewer sent by the Smithsonian archives in 1968 asked Johnson where he was born and how he was raised, he first gave the non-answer, **Your beginning questions prompt a certain silence**, then told her about his recent experience with **an old nickelodeon** which **can go very slowly or very fast. You can make it stop and you can sort of go at it at your own rate of interest. So that, in a certain way, my childhood was like that. Many years later ...** Time runs in a wavy circle—like a snake with its tail in its mouth—from which, it seems, there is no exit.

When Morton Janklow died in 2022, his obituary in the *New York Times* featured a photograph of this "bold, risk-taking negotiator," as the headline has it, all twenty-six of the Janklow-Picasso silhouette portraits at his elbow. He had bought them from Johnson's estate not long after the artist's death for a sum the collector described as "considerably more than originally asked."

VI

The dowdy little house on Utopia Parkway was far enough outside Manhattan that you had to make a special pilgrimage to pay your respects to Joseph Cornell. Everyone who was anyone in the New York art world in the 1950s and '60s had a story about their visit, the awkward conversation over slices of tooth-achingly sugary cake, the stolen glimpses of a box or two, evidence of just enough eccentricity to reconfirm Cornell's status as the insiders' favorite outsider.

Ray's visits were no different—once he began to court Cornell in 1966, he was invited out and brought the chocolate cake from Ratner's that Cornell had asked for and was served in addition **memorable tepid canned peaches** as they listened to Dionne Warwick's sublime recording of "Message to Michael" and **one I never heard before Ragmop.** Having passed his host's test, on a second visit **Richard Lippold and I arrived and saw work room in the basement**; a few more visits and much

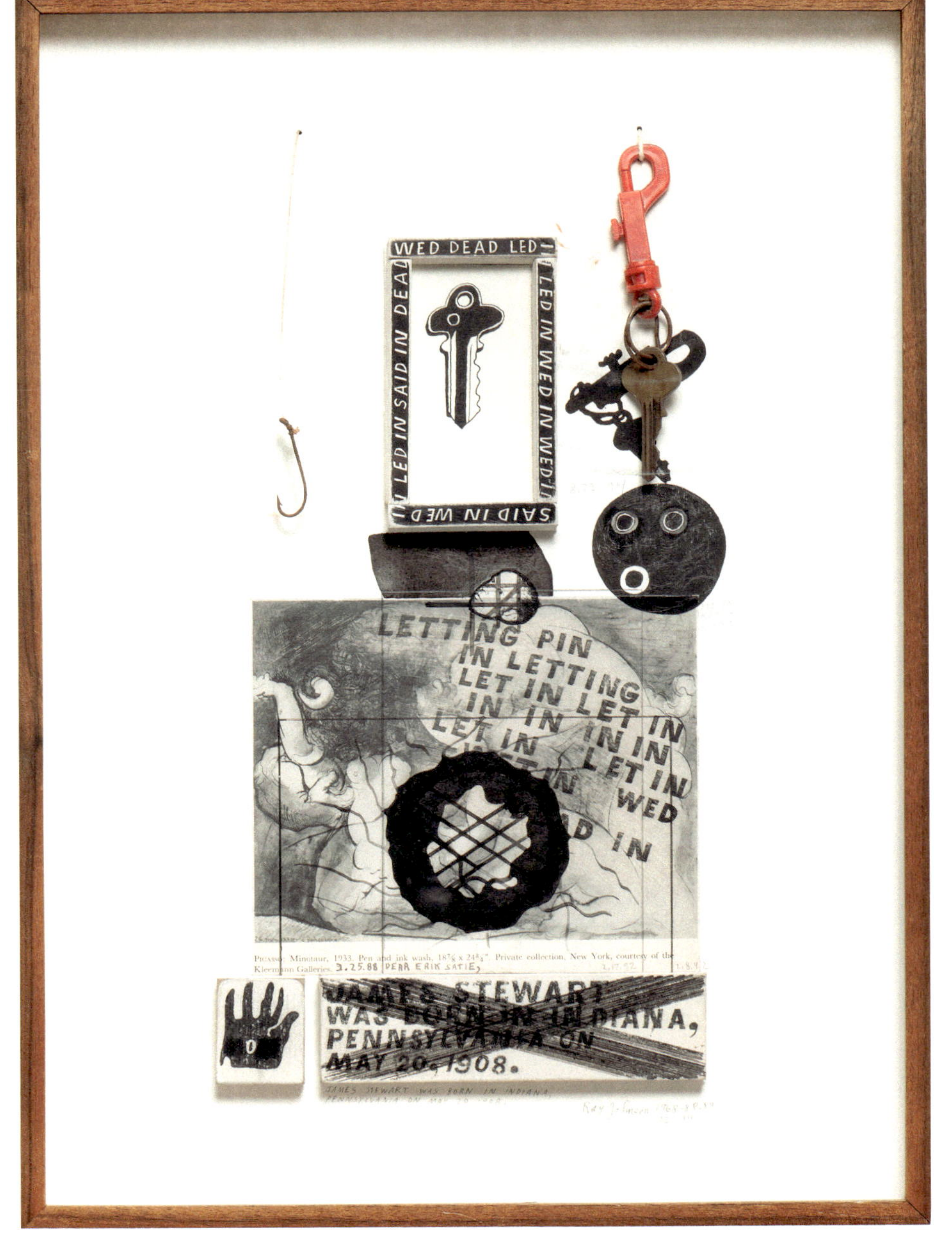

Ray Johnson, *Untitled (Wed Dead Led)* (1968-88-89-92-94).

correspondence followed. However, Ray's friend John Willenbecher, who made his name in the 1960s with poetic shadowboxes that were shown by the devoted Cornellian Richard Feigen, said that Cornell once told him that he found Ray's mailings confusing—was he really expected to *attend* all those Meetings?—because "of course, Cornell had *no* sense of humor."

Whereas, of course, Marcel Duchamp was all wit. Duchamp was like Cornell insofar as his reputation as an enigma was enhanced by the distance he kept from the art world, but in his case this distance devolved from conscious decision, rather than helpless eccentricity, on the artist's part. Nor was the distance physical, exactly, since his admirers would have found the Greenwich Village studios Duchamp maintained from 1943 until his death in 1968 easy enough to get to. Yet those who were admitted found little evidence there of new work, and the word during those years was that Duchamp had largely retired from art to devote himself to chess. Soon after his death, though, it was revealed that the artist had been working all that time, in a room accessible only through a hidden door in the studio wall, on a project that would prove as confounding and fascinating as anything he had ever done: *Étant Donnés*, whose full title in English is *Given: 1. The Waterfall, 2. The Illuminating Gas*. To view this piece now, one must peer through a peephole in a door set into a wall in the final room of the suite of Duchamp galleries in the Philadelphia Museum of Art. Beyond the hole is a theatrical scene, composed of three-dimensional objects set against a flat backdrop, which includes the two elements mentioned in the title. But the element that rivets the eye is a naked female torso visible from neck to knees, flat on her back on a bed of twigs, legs splayed wide to expose the split lips of the vulva, an opening beyond which the eye cannot penetrate.

Étants Donnés was installed at the Philadelphia Museum in 1969 in accordance with instructions left by the artist, under the supervision of Duchamp's widow, Alexina "Teeny" Duchamp, his stepson Paul Matisse, and a young assistant curator, Anne d'Harnoncourt, whose father, the former MoMA director René d'Harnoncourt, was the subject of one of Johnson's Dollar Bill portrait-collages. In 1973, Anne d'Harnoncourt, at that point the museum's curator of twentieth- century art (she would become its director in 1982), co-organized a major Duchamp retrospective and Ray Johnson started sending her Duchamp-themed mailings. (He also came to Philadelphia for the opening of the retrospective, but hung back in the museum parking lot throughout, watching the others go in, out of his usual inextricable mix of conscious decision and helpless compulsion.) By the time the museum mounted its next major Duchamp exhibition, honoring the centennial of the artist's birth in 1987, d'Harnoncourt had amassed enough Johnson sendings to fill a satellite show at the Philadelphia Print Club, which she titled "Ray Johnson: Prints After *Étant Donnés*." (**I didn't get down at all for my print exhibition there**, Ray let a friend in Philadelphia know, after the show closed.)

Curator Michael R. Taylor tells the story of d'Harnoncourt's dealings with Johnson in his essay for the catalogue of a 2009 Philadelphia Museum exhibition focused on the history and influence of *Étant Donnés*. Taylor also notes there that the schematic outline of a torso that appears in Johnson's tributes to Duchamp's installation seems not to have been derived from the finished work but "from a preparatory study on transparent Plexiglass in which the artist delineated the figure in gouache and perforated it with tiny pinholes." Beyond the scene beyond the peephole, another scene. Ray Johnson's history of *Étant Donnés* unfolds at a distance from the others, a distance only he can measure.

VII

Like the moticos icons, Ray Johnson's *Étant* shape is at once a quasi-alphabetic sign and a two-dimensional shade of a three-dimensional object. The artist makes this connection plain in a 1992 photocopied image sent to his friend Clive Phillpot with instructions to send it on to Anne d'Harnoncourt. **This is Mae West viewing Étant Donnés**, Johnson explains, in a note typed at the corner of the page. Both figures in the image, a photo of the star and a silhouette of the *Étant* torso, are tattooed with moticos, and West's shoulder is also adorned with what looks like a starfish but is in fact a detail from the 1919 photograph of Duchamp with a star shaved into his pate on which Johnson modeled his 1968 collage, *Duchamp with Star-Haircut*. One starfish-arm points toward the object of West's veiled gaze, a phallus composed of three black balls strung on a line, anchored in the *Étant* figure's crotch.

Is Johnson's phallic *Étant* a dirty joke? Yes, and so is Duchamp's peepshow. (If you doubt this, stand by in Philadelphia's *Étant Donnés* room and watch as visitor after visitor steps up to the hole, then jerks back, laughing). And yet, for the absorbed viewer of the scene, there may come a moment when, as art historian Molly Nesbit found, "the physical separates from the literal" and "the *Étant Donnés* siphons off its female and male material into light." No longer does one see the naked lady as "an object: all that is shed." And yet, and yet, one wonders if the shock of that initial peep will ever really fade away, if the stager of the scene would ever want it to. Duchamp once asked an audience to believe that

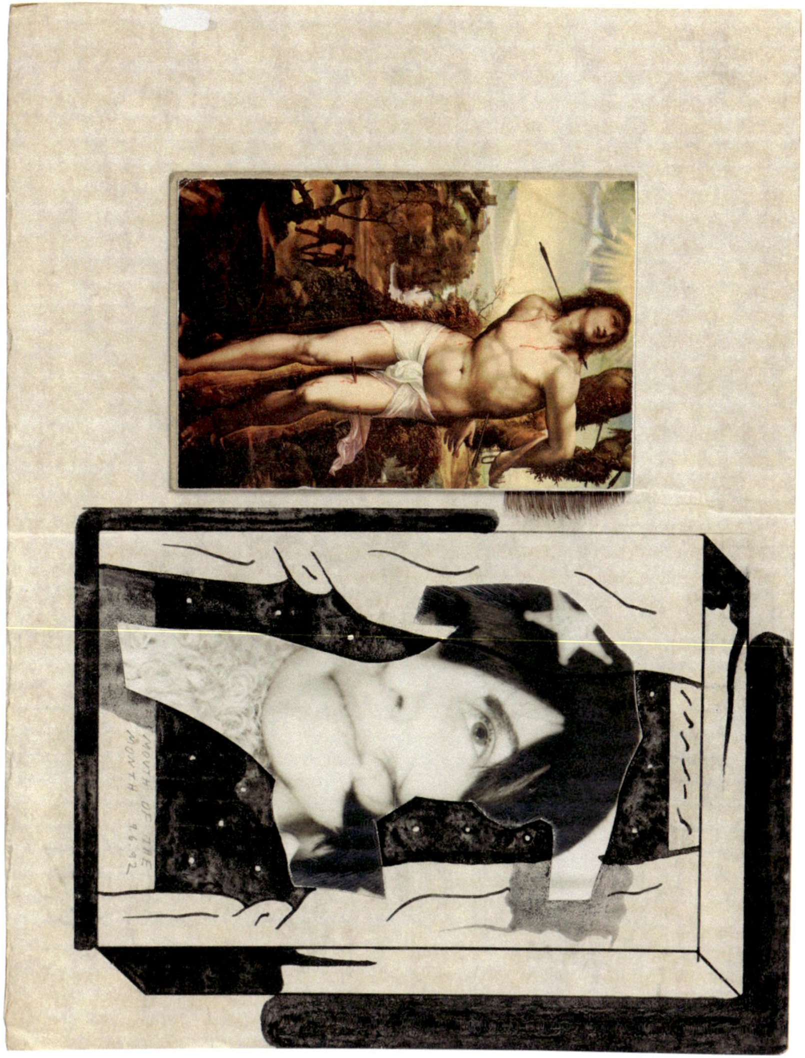

Ray Johnson, *Untitled (Étant Donnés with St. Sebastian)* (1992).

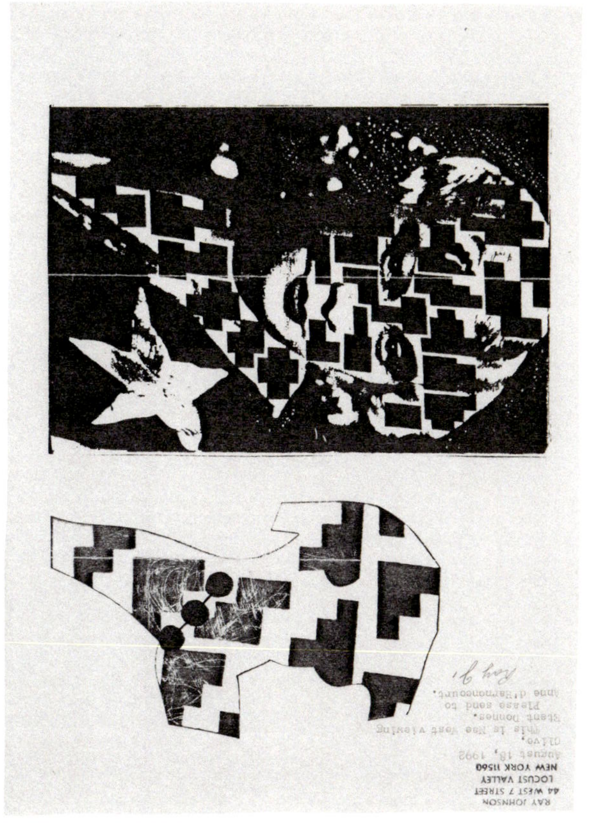

Ray Johnson to Clive Phillpot to Anne d'Harnoncourt, August 18, 1992, *Mae West Viewing Étant Donnés.*

his decision to present a urinal as a work of art was "based on a reaction of *visual* indifference with at the same time a total absence of good or bad taste." Should we take him at his word?

Yes. And yet. To get beyond taste, you cannot tiptoe around the questions your taste raises; you must work through them for yourself. You must go *through* the shock, titillation, disgust, amusement, horror, and dazed admiration that *Étant Donnés* provokes to reach the state of transcendence, or as its creator might say, indifference, that Nesbit claims to have attained in her viewing. And you never go through this process once and for all but must start again each time you engage with art in any form. "The peep was just a stage. There will be a thousand others," Nesbit sighs, at the end of her struggle to explain her attraction to a work that some call pornographic. A sign, meanwhile, that even as the critic turns away from the absorbing scene, she cannot quite shake the memory of her first glimpse of that vulnerable body: she casts her transcendence not in aesthetic but in gendered terms, as the dissolution of embodied femaleness and maleness "into light."

Star light, star bright. Gender as seen through the eyes of Ray Johnson's **Mae West viewing Étant Donnés** is an unending relay between the two sides of this double portrait. Here, the artist, figured as a phallic female torso; there, the actress, who stands in for a Johnson muse, the other May W. This Mae wears a sheriff's badge—a sign of authority taken from that other artist, the begetter of the torso—a badge that Ray once pinned on another of his muses, who appears in yet another double portrait, a collage dated "9.6.92," thirteen days after Johnson relayed the Mae West *Étant* via Phillpot to d'Harnoncourt.

On one side of the collage is St. Sebastian as painted by the Sienese artist known as Il Sodoma and on the other, the *Étant* shape, rendered as a cutout from a photograph of Toby Spiselman posing for *Duchamp with Star-Haircut*. The Toby-*Étant* steps out on one truncated leg from behind the curtains of one of Johnson's little theaters, which, unlike the others, is drawn in three dimensions, linking it to Duchamp's diorama, even if it looks more like a Cornell box. As Johnson doubtless knew, Sodoma's Sebastian also has its theatrical aspect, having originally been made for a gonfalon, a banner designed to be held on high above the crowd in public processions. Il Sodoma alludes to his banner's function on the painting's reverse side, which depicts the Virgin in glory, gawked at from below by a crowd of saints and patrons.

Johnson's diptych, by contrast, is a private devotional object, and Toby and the sexy saint (Sodoma owed his nickname, "the sodomite," to his preference for boys) are one another's audience of one. Could one say the same of Duchamp's eyeless *Étant* and her peeper? Ray Johnson seems to think so, seems to think that his predecessor, too, sees the positions of viewer and viewed, artist and muse, as reversible and perpetually mobile. Were the relay to end, both parties would cease to exist. Every portrait of the artist is a double portrait. Double or nothing.

VIII

Andy Warhol died in February 1987 at the age of fifty-eight after having his gallbladder removed, usually a routine operation, but complicated in his case by the injuries he sustained during the Solanas shooting and a long-standing fear of hospitals that kept the artist from receiving timely treatment. Later that year, Ray jotted down a list of landmarks in his long history with Andy. The **Elvis painting** is there, and, in shorthand, **The night Andy was shot and I almost**, and the **New Directions book jackets** that marked a point of convergence in their early careers as graphic designers. The cryptic **Haircut** stands for the day in 1963 that Ray brought Andy to one of Billy Linich's infamous haircut parties at Linich's silver-lined apartment. Later, Warhol returned with his camera and filmed *Haircut*, starring Linich, John Daley, Fred Herko, and James Waring, after which Billy moved into the Factory and silvered it over at Andy's request and changed his name to Name. Then there are the episodes only a historian like Johnson would record: **I crash a Warhol party as Norman Mailer**, **I go to Factory but refuse to appear in a group photo**, **I draw Andy's silhouette but not Jamie Wyeth's**.

At the center of the page of notes is a looping line that just barely describes a head in profile, enclosing a triangle-capped square inscribed with the phrase **FLOP art**, with a circle around the FLOP. The puffy square-plus-triangle looks a little like a house and a little like a turd (one of the meanings of "flop") and the profile could be a sketch—the kind one does from memory, with eyes closed—of Johnson's Elvis/Oedipus, only facing the reverse direction. Flop Art is the reverse of Pop Art, just as Ray is Andy, only facing the other way, facing away from the crowd, away from success. Or at least, away from success as it is usually measured. In an archival note regarding a postcard that he sent to Ray in 1988 and received back with additions, Bill Wilson explains that the phrase he inscribed on the card to Ray, "failure failure failure," is a reference to "a work of his that I have—on which writing 'failure failure' makes it a successful work." Perhaps, but successful in what sense?

The greatest example I can think of Flop art is the *Étant ∂onnés* of Duchamp, Ray wrote in December 1987 to his friend in Philadelphia, artist Charles Fahlen. **You must admit she is "flopped,"** sprawled out, exposed, subject to the prurient snickers of her peepers. **Flop art figures are on their backs—the submissive pose**, Ray explained on the phone to Clive Phillpot, who was preparing to give a talk on the subject (and who had begun to take notes on his calls with Ray). **Have you got a slide of Étant Donnés for your Flop Art lecture?** "I will have," Clive assured Ray.

I have started this "Art" season by coming on strong with Flop Art, Ray wrote to Henry in October 1988, implying that, by his standards, Flop Art was indeed a success. Then a few sentences later comes the complaint that **Nobody wants to write "the definite book on Ray Johnson." When I say "Flop art," people say, "What is that?"** Ray can say this to Henry because he knows that Henry, like his teacher Bill, had long wanted to write the definitive book on Ray Johnson. With Henry, as with Bill, Ray can expose his vulnerable side. At the same time, the artist is signaling to his would-be historian that he has reached a turn in his path.

New York's most famous unknown artist was now officially a flop, which is to say, a success, in his own terms. If Ray was right in thinking that, as he phrases it to Henry, **The sublime example of Flop Art is the Duchamp *Étant donnés***, then his own embrace of the submissive pose, his decision to conduct his business behind a hidden door, his determination to stay on the wrong side of history, would prove canny, just as Duchamp's maneuvers had. But no artist who emerged in Marcel Duchamp's wake could match his chess-player's mastery of the long game; his heirs would have to stay on history's good side, as Warhol had, or take their licks.

IX

After filling Charles Fahlen in on Flop Art, Ray mentions his visit to the big traveling **Pop Art show from Berkeley**, titled *Made in U.S.A.*, **that had my three movie star collages in it**. It was the second such exhibition in recent years to feature Johnson's proto-pop images of the mid-1950s, the first being 1985's *Pop Art 1955–1970*, curated by Ray's old friend Henry Geldzahler, who referred to Johnson's Elvis and James Dean as "the Plymouth rock of the Pop Art movement" in the show's catalogue. As Johnson proudly informed critic Marco Livingstone, the Berkeley Art Museum also **used the Elvis in their show of Pop for a subway poster and outdoor billboard 40 feet long**. Livingstone had just written to Johnson regarding his plans to curate yet another big Pop show, which would open in 1990 at London's Royal Academy, accompanied by Livingstone's book, *Pop Art: A Continuing History*.

What was it about the 1980s and Pop Art? For clues, one might look to a zeitgeist exhibition that made a splash early in the decade, 1981's *New York/New Wave*, curated by Diego Cortez, one of the kids who had followed Ray around the galleries and clubs not long before. The junk aesthetic and focus on glamor (albeit of an abject, punkish sort) that characterized much of the work in the show put off critics who had grown accustomed to the austerities of minimalism and conceptualism. But time runs in a wavy circle. What one reviewer described as *New York/New Wave*'s "appeal to our willingness to accept tabloid myth as truth," and refusal to make "demands on anything other than our ability to consume"—its ethos of "participatory narcissism," as critic Peter Schjeldahl put it—drew on aspects of Pop Art that *its* first critics also found distasteful. In a nod to this history, Polaroids by Warhol and mailings by Johnson could be found tacked up among the similarly offhand productions of dozens of the curator's peers.

Some artists in *New York/New Wave*, like Robin Lee Crutchfield, Jimmy DeSana, Marcia Resnick, and Cortez himself, were also old correspondents of Ray's, and two of its youngest and most ambitious participants, Jean-Michel Basquiat and Keith Haring, would soon be drawn into Warhol's orbit. The beautiful Basquiat fed the elder artist's hunger for glamour, but Haring was the more Warholian of the two. Funny-looking and unmistakably queer, he developed a streamlined repertoire of cartoonish figures that crystallized into a brand. In 1986, Haring gave a new twist to Warhol's paeans to consumer goods when he opened his Pop Shop, where for a few dollars anyone could buy a T-shirt or coffee cup emblazoned with Haring's signature icon, the Radiant Child. Never one to miss the chance to stake a historical claim, Ray Johnson had already sent a mailing in 1983 bearing the salutation **Dear Keith Haring**, followed by twenty-four of his signature cartoon bunny heads, with **Ray Johnson**, plus the years from 1955 to 1978 in sequence, written beneath each one.

X

In 1981, the year of *New York/New Wave*, the *New York Times* ran an article with the headline, "Rare Cancer Seen in 41 Homosexuals." It turned out that the cancer was a sign that the men had a condition soon to be known as Acquired Immune Deficiency Syndrome. By the middle of the decade, the effects of AIDS were killing gay men by the thousands. Hence Johnson's description to Marco Livingstone of his second Elvis, the one **with fingers**, as **a depressingly colorful disintegration-face of rot 1957 which I see as a pre-1980's AIDS image**. That was in May 1988. In July,

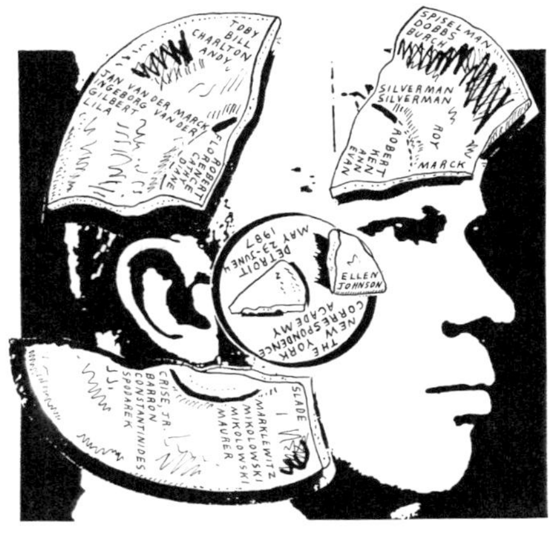

Ray Johnson, flyer, *New York Correspondence Academy Detroit, May 23–June 4, 1987.*

Ray informed Bart Gorin that their mutual friend **john dowd died in s.f.=aids**. Gorin himself would go that way within a few years, as would Jimmy DeSana and Keith Haring.

In the summer of 1987, Ray went to Detroit for a month to move his mother out of her house and settle her in a nursing home. While there, he sent out a series of flyers announcing an unspecified event to occur in the near future—the dates changed from flyer to flyer—under the auspices of the New York Correspondence Academy Detroit.

The flyers all include Johnsonian lists of names, most of them belonging to members of the Detroit art world of that period who had some link to Ray. On the flyer dated May 23–June 4, for instance, we find Charlton Burch, who often featured Johnson in his journal *Lightworks*; *Detroit Artists Monthly* editor Diane Spodarek, who had interviewed Johnson in 1977; Fluxus collector Gilbert Silverman, whose construction company had built the house Lorraine Johnson lived in; and Ray's curator friend, Jan Van Der Marck, then the director of the Detroit Institute of Arts, which had just acquired its first collage by Ray Johnson. The artist had long chafed at the meager recognition his work received in his hometown. He did have one solo show there, in 1975, at Gertrude Kasle, one of Detroit's leading galleries, but even then, the opening was followed by **an impossible disaster dinner with the In-crowd kids I adored,** after which the disaffected native son made his **hasty retreat from the City of crime statistics, unemployments, and abortion clinics.**

With the Detroit flyers, Ray stakes his tenuous claim to fame in the place where he was born as he faces the prospect of losing Lorraine, his strongest remaining tie to that place. But these mailings also have a more specific commemorative function, which is indicated in the heading on the third of the flyers, **A THROWAWAY GESTURE FOR BRIAN BUCZAK.** Brian Buczak was a high schooler in Detroit when he started corresponding with Ray. He went on to major in art at the city's College for Creative Studies, where he won a prize that came with a cash award and "to his parents' dismay," promptly "spent the money on a Ray Johnson collage that included a Marcel Duchamp silhouette." Buczak's future romantic partner, Fluxus artist Geoffrey Hendricks, recounts this incident in a dual memoir of Buczak and Johnson published in the Ray Johnson memorial issue of *Lightworks*. The closing date of the non-event

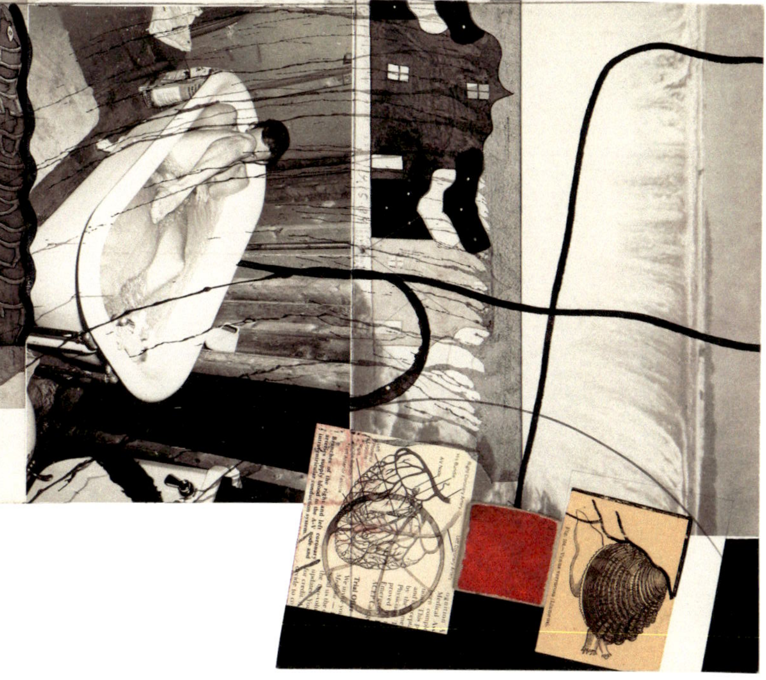

Ray Johnson, *Untitled (His Bundle)* (1990–94).

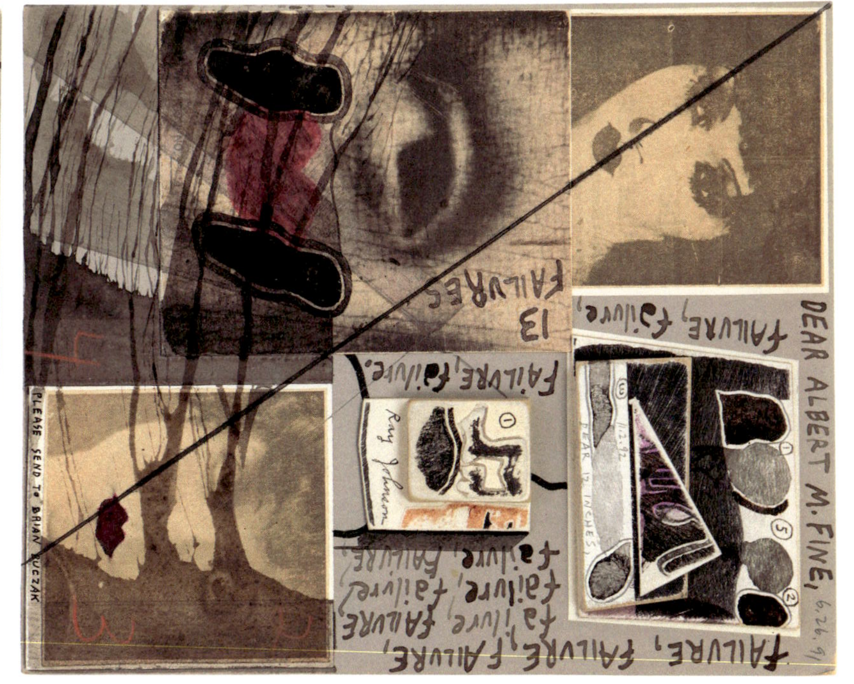

Ray Johnson, *Untitled (13 Failures)* (1991–92).

announced on the last of Johnson's Detroit flyers is July 4, 1987, the day that Brian Buczak died, of the effects of AIDS, at the age of thirty-three.

A directive to **PLEASE SEND TO BRIAN BUCZAK** is inscribed in the lower right-hand corner of a 1991–92 collage addressed, at the top, to Albert M. Fine, who also died in 1987, the first but certainly not the last member of his old gang whom Ray would lose to AIDS. Johnson's own name is suspended halfway between those of his two friends, signed on a tile that interrupts a litany composed, as the artist tells us, of **13 FAILURES. Failure, failure, failure**, the ghostly voice intones. But who has failed here, and how?

A friend of Ray's, Alvin Friedman-Kien, who was a doctor and a pioneer in the detection and treatment of AIDS, regularly tested Ray for HIV, the virus through which the disease is spread, so the artist would have known that he was not infected. (The autopsy conducted after Johnson's drowning showed him to be free not just of HIV infection, but of any significant signs of disease.) Disease is a kind of failure, and so is death, but unlike Brian and Albert, Ray was, strictly speaking, alive and well. Neither was he relentlessly self-destructive, like Albert, nor, as Brian had been when he fell ill, still full of youthful vitality and ambition. In the collage-memorial for Buczak and Fine, Ray Johnson's suspension between one death and another creates a tension that makes the thinned ink tremble as he writes and rewrites **failure**. Yet for this artist, failure is also a kind of success—the ink wash veils and x's out, imposing its hush of darkness, but as it does, it flows. **The fire melted the ice and there was a flow of water.** Where there is flow, there is openness to chance and the possibility of change.

We say that time flows, like water. As time went on, Ray dreamed of developing methods that would allow him to manipulate our perception of time's flow, as Harold Edgerton had in his stroboscopic films, which let us linger on the most elusive ephemera, like the reflection in a bubble before it pops. At the centerline of a collage in Johnson's late style, *Untitled (His Bundle)*, a date-notation from 1990 segues into another from 1994, eliding time just as the ink-wash flow elides the gulf that separates the rush of the waterfall at the top of the picture from the shimmer of the bathwater below. The raised foot of the beauty in the bath just barely shields what one might call "his bundle"; although a closer look reveals that "his bundle" is actually the caption to the medical illustration at center-right, depicting the tangle of arteries through which blood flows to the heart. Time rushes, and time pools and shimmers, and time flows beneath the surface unnoticed until it stops, with a shock. "His bundle," it turns out, refers to a blockage in the electrical pathways to the heart that may delay or halt its beating.

XI

After his mother died in 1988, Ray posted another of his paper memorials, a whirl of numbers that builds from 1 at the center to 1277 at the tip, then begins the count again at 1. Time stops for one, but memory spirals on.

Ray Johnson mailer, *Ray Johnson 1927–1989*, detail.

Time stops for Ray Johnson, not just once, but now and again. In 1989, he sent out yet another death notice, with his dates inscribed on an inverted triangle that is reminiscent of the logo adopted by activists in the fight against AIDS, a pink triangle with the phrase SILENCE=DEATH inscribed beneath.

Ray Johnson's last solo exhibition during his lifetime took place in late 1991 at the Goldie Paley Gallery of the Moore College of Art and Design in Philadelphia. The gallery's director, Elsa Longhauser, had intended to curate the exhibition herself. However, as planning got underway, Johnson reported to Clive Phillpot, who had been invited to write the catalogue essay, that Longhauser had come to him with some queries and he had responded that since **Ray Johnson died in 1989, there is no one who can supply you with the information you need.** After that, Janice Parente and Phyllis Stigliano, the organizers of Johnson's 1984 retrospective, were brought in as guest curators, because, as Ray told Clive, **I can—Mr. Deceased here—work with them. From the beginning, I told Elsa, "I'm difficult, impossible."** Lately, however, Mr. Deceased had been more recalcitrant than usual.

A note dated January 2, 1989, to Roni Feinstein, director of the Whitney Museum's branch facility in Connecticut, read, simply, perversely, **noitibihxe "egalbmessA" ruoy ni etapicitrap tonnac I**. As if the message were not clear enough, on a version of this missive that he sent to Bill to send to Toby Ray has added a photocopied postcard from 1981 over which he has written, **Ray Johnson/ nothing/ 1959–89**. He was slightly more gracious to the German gallerist Christel Schüppenhauer when he wrote in February 1989 to thank her for her **invitation to participate in your show titled "Wortlaut"** ["Text"], adding, **I submit this drawing**—at which point he stops typing and paints the word "nothing" in thinned ink that fades out toward the end, set off by a similarly faded ink-frame. Schüppenhauer displayed the letter in the show. Later that year came another invitation from Judith Van Wagner, whom Ray had found **always very kind**, to be her artist of choice for a "Curators' Choice" exhibition at a museum not far from Johnson's Long Island home. The artist soon reported to a friend that **I am doing a Nothing for the Heckscher Museum that has them in a tizzy I hear**, although they, too, ultimately accepted his offering, an empty plexiglass box on a wooden plinth.

Ray Johnson to Christel Schüppenhauer, February 1989, detail.

A young Ray Johnson had conceived his Nothing as a way of clearing a space in a crowded scene. It functioned then as what the philosophers call a determinate negation, one that threw into relief crucial features of the art that it was not: "not a happening," as Ray kept telling people, but also not the kinds of abstract paintings he and Allan Kaprow had been making until recently, nor the variously post-Duchampian takes on painting that peers like Johns, Rauschenberg, and Warhol had begun to develop. The no longer young Johnson was in a remembering mood, and Nothing was a numinous souvenir of those beginnings. But now it also functioned as a tool for clearing out the space that he himself had filled. This was Nothing with a vengeance. **etapicitrap tonnac I.** The film was running in reverse, as Ray had dreamed. But was the mechanism something that one could control, like an old nickelodeon? Or could one only sit in the audience and watch as the frames sped to their end?

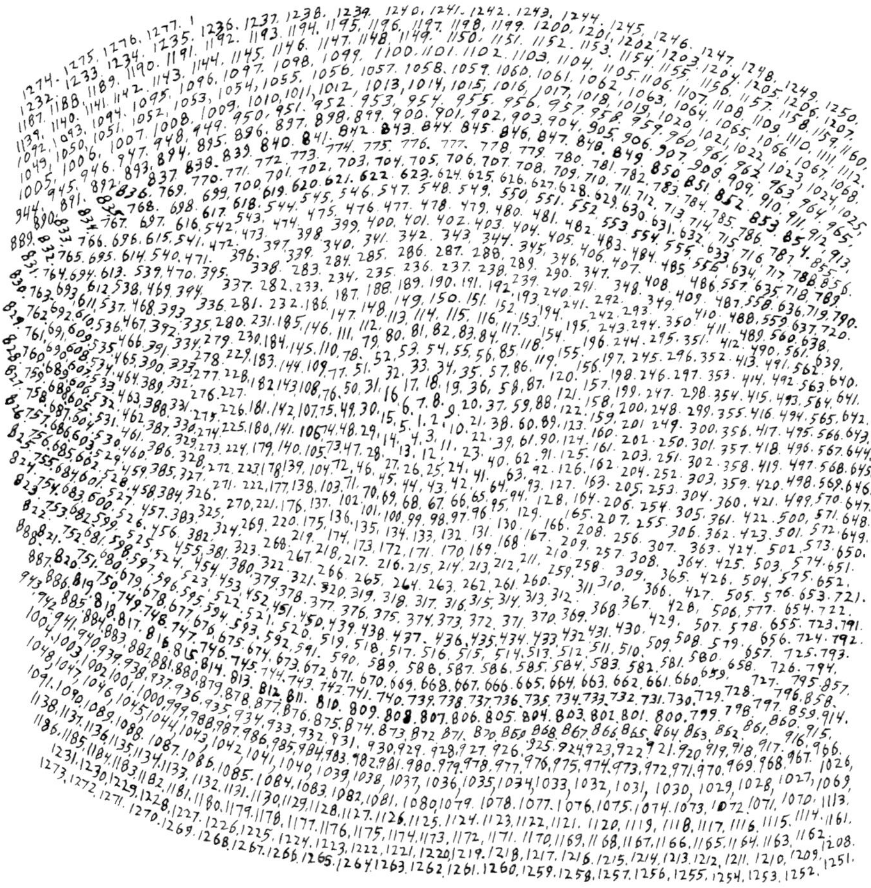

FOR LORRAINE SEPTEMBER 7, 1988

Ray Johnson, mailer, *For Lorraine September 7, 1988.*

When you run a film in reverse, it ends at the beginning. Beginning at the end of the 1980s, Ray Johnson reconceived his work as a theater of memory where he could perform continuously until the film ran out for an audience of one, or—it came to the same thing—of no one. In November 1989, he wrote to Toby about a **surprising theatre performance type dream** that he had had, **the realization being the isolation the vision of the artist and the performance in an area not the audience area of the artist whose costume and actions are nothing to do with those observing.** It is a theater dream, there is a designated performance space and an audience, yet not; they are there, but x-ed out. Around this time, Ray sent Clive Phillpot a book on conceptual art and when Clive opened it, he saw that Ray had drawn a little theater where, as the script below says, when **The Curtain opens:/ There is nothing**, just white space that glows between the black drapes.

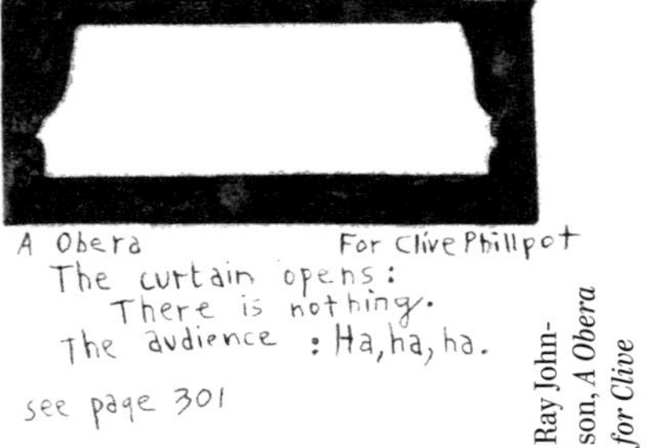

Ray Johnson, *A Obera for Clive Phillpot*, n.d.

Between July 2 and August 7, 1990, Ray Johnson sent thirteen envelopes to Clive Phillpot containing the fifty prints and thirteen letters that comprise the unique copy of Johnson's *A Book About Moðern Art* that now sits on a shelf in The Museum of Modern Art's library, where Phillpot was then head librarian. (There is also a twenty-eight page appendix to the book, consisting mainly of materials that Johnson sent to MoMA's director Kirk Varnedoe while Phillpot was on vacation, including, as Phillpot notes in the table of contents, "*Part Three* of *A Book About Moðern Art Nothing*, and other metamorphoses, leading to the death of *Book About Moðern Art*.") Although MoMA curators had been dutifully depositing their mailings from Johnson in the museum's archives since the mid-1950s, none had yet shown much interest in acquiring his work for the collection. *A Book About Moðern Art* opens with a tracing of Johnson's silhouette enclosing the word **NOTHING**, poised between his name above and **THE MUSEUM OF MODERN ART, NEW YORK CITY** below—a barbed comment on the artist's notable non-presence in an institution that wielded exceptional power to define what counted as canonical in the art of his time.

Yet simply by sending the pages of his book to Phillpot, Johnson also established a kind of presence at MoMA, via a back door, without the say-so of its curators. Clive was the perfect audience for Ray's act because, as the artist knew, the librarian loved artists' books, not least for the way they had of slipping past the gatekeepers of galleries and museums and falling into the hands of art-lovers equipped with more curiosity than money. As it happened,

Ray's first aim with this book was to get past Elsa Longhauser, the idea being that he would send the pages to Clive at the library to be sent on to constitute **the exhibition for Philadelphia, humorously loaned from MoMA to Philadelphia**. (Longhauser took the joke in stride, and the pages did appear in her exhibition, along with collages, mail art, and other Ray-books.) Then Ray told Clive that he had heard from his friend Chuck Close that Close had been invited to curate the next installment of MoMA's "Artist's Choice," a yearly show made up of an artist's selections from the museum's own collection. Chuck, who had chosen portraits, his painterly specialty, as his theme, wanted to include Ray but was stymied by the museum's lack of Johnsons.

Clive, though, had his own back door, for anything that had been accepted into the MoMA library's collection could be transferred, via an internal loan, into the museum proper. Thus portraits, also a specialty of Johnson's, became a subtheme of his book-in-progress. Eventually, after consultation with Chuck, Ray drew a bunny-head labeled **BILL DE KOONING** that Close would hang in his show—"fittingly," as Phillpot observed, facing "Van Gogh's head of the postman Roulin." The postman Johnson would enter the museum masked as one of the most canonical of postwar artists, **America's and the World's Greatest Painter**, as Ray once called Bill to his face. By that time, however, Bill was not what he once was. On page 21 of **A BOOK ABOUT MODERN ART**, vol. II, Johnson has photocopied a 1989 news article with the headline "De Kooning's Art Isn't Aging," which deals with the then-hot controversy over the artist's handling by his caretakers and promoters as he descended into dementia while continuing to paint. (In the accompanying photo, the outlines of a bunny head have somehow worked their way onto the canvas before which de Kooning stands, brush in hand.)

Then again, nothing, it seems, was what it once was. "We Remember MoMA," reads the headline on page 9 of *A Book About Modern Art*, vol. II. When the headline appeared in 1984 in the *Village Voice*, it was followed by a review that assessed the museum's reinstallation of its collection after a major renovation. The reviewer, Kim Levin, is disappointed to find that, instead of taking the redo as an opportunity to rethink the canonical order that Alfred Barr had diagrammed back in 1936, "MOMA is as traditionally modernist and as inflexible as ever." Of course, it is MoMA, so, despite the curation's sepulchral quality, it all looks beautiful, "embalmed so fastidiously that it actually seems to live and breathe again." It seems to live; but only because we remember what it once meant. The original story MoMA told was powerfully convincing, and the museum visitor nursed on that story—even, or perhaps, especially, one painfully aware of its omissions and suppressions—can still feel the ghostly absence-presence of the thing in whose reality she believed.

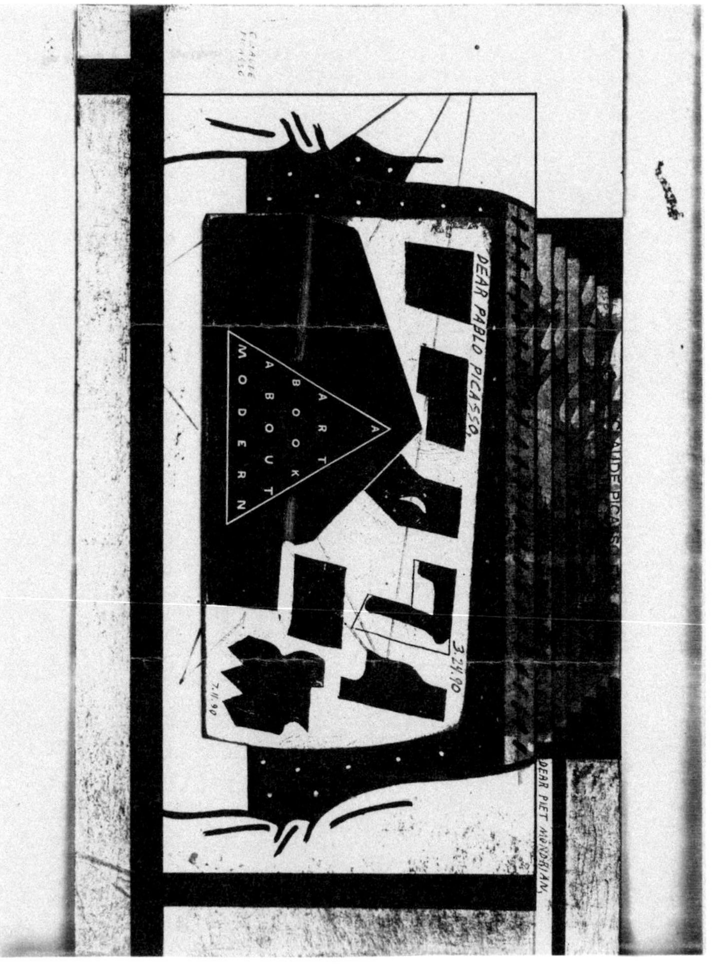

Ray Johnson, *A BOOK ABOUT MODERN ART* (1990), vol. I, page 14 (**Dear Pablo Picasso, DEAR PIET MONDRIAN**).

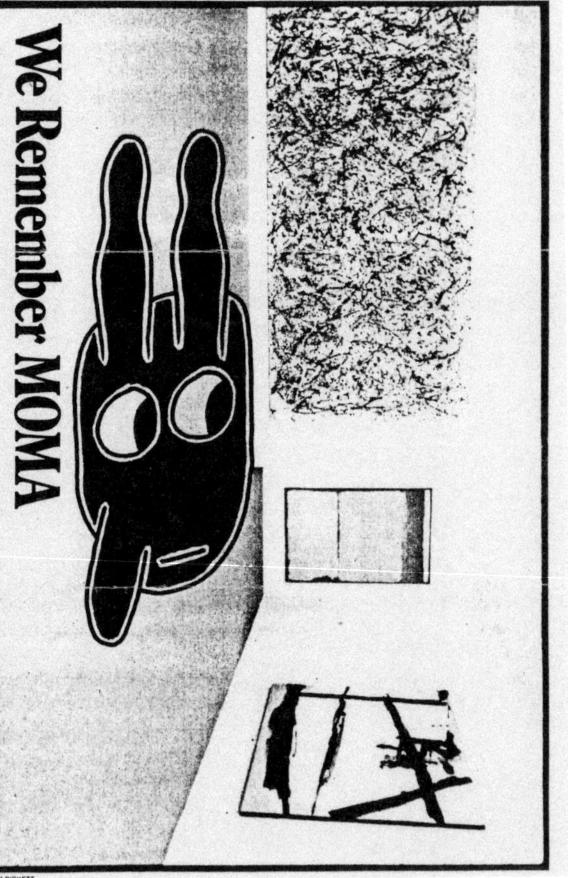
VOICE MAY 22, 1984

We Remember MOMA

KERI PICKETT

Pollock, Rothko, Kline, from the permanent collection

I. The Permanent Point of View

By Kim Levin

Seurat and the Douanier Rousseau (even in the absence of a major Seurat), but make a telling connection between Gauguin's exotic primitivism and Rousseau's, with Rousseau now seeming the more radically modern. In the gem of a Cubist room, a 1914 Picasso painting with Rus-

line dreams of modern times. I'm not crazy about the oval platform the Brancusis are on, but the Picasso room, the Matisse room, the Mondrian room, the De Chirico room (classic early modern ones with empty urban vistas and bottle green skies, of course) are all exquisite.

Ray Johnson, *A BOOK ABOUT MODERN ART* (1990), vol. II, page 9 (**We Remember MoMA**).

RAY JOHNSON

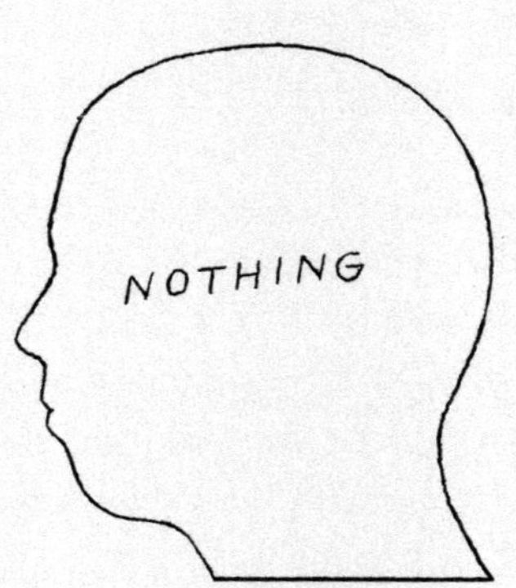

THE MUSEUM OF MODERN ART
NEW YORK CITY

Ray Johnson, *A BOOK ABOUT MODERN ART* (1990), vol. 1, page 1 (**Silhouette Face. Nothing**).

DEAR PABLO PICASSO, DEAR PIET MONDRIAN, calls out the man behind the curtain of the little theater on page 14, vol. I. At the center of the stage stands a triangular memorial inscribed with the words (which the tombstone-carver has ordered, not according to their sense, but to their size) **A ART BOOK ABOUT MODERN**. It is the MoMA story in a nutshell, or rather, given the rough quality of the print and the flimsiness of the copy paper, in the form of a throwaway gesture. Just as Clive in the fastness of his library was an ideal audience for Ray, Ray in his revivified Nothingness may have been an ideal audience for the thing that was modern art.

XIII

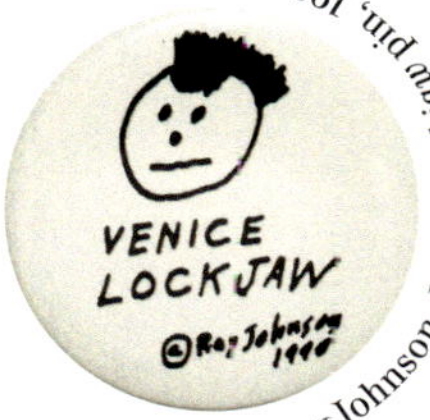

Ray Johnson, *Venice Lockjaw* pin, 1990.

The Ray Johnson exhibition at the Moore College of Art closed in December 1991. In January 1992, Ray Johnson conceived a new ambition. **I will be the Warhol of Locust Valley**, he told Clive Phillpot, referring to Andy Warhol's long-running practice of taking Polaroid glamour shots of the stars in all his worlds. Johnson did not mean by this that he was going to document the local socialites, who spoke with the archetypal upper-crust accent known as "Locust Valley Lockjaw" (although he did allude to that set in his "Venice Lockjaw" pins, which were handed out to fairgoers at the 1990 Venice Biennale).

In pursuit of his new art-thought, Johnson would, however, pull back the curtain that he had drawn across his life in Locust Valley, and he would take up a camera—not a Polaroid, which was an exceptionally expensive means of producing trashy-looking images, but the dirt-cheap Fuji QuickSnap, whose cardboard body and single-focus plastic lens signaled that it was in fact destined for the trash when its roll of film ran out. (The disposable camera was born in 1986, the year of Ray's first theater dream. It, too, may be seen now as a dream, a dream of a stream of hot and cold running images that anyone could tap, at low cost and with little skill, everyone an artist.) And with this throwaway machine, Ray would document the stars in all his worlds.

XIV

In the fall of 1994, Ray sent David Bourdon a copy of a photo that showed the young Ray perusing a wall of paste-ups in his **Early "Outdoor Movie Star Show" in Suzi Gablik's garden**, together with a recent QuickSnap of an assemblage, laid out on the ground, of graphic images of bunnies and other icons, centered around a magazine ad featuring Ray's old fan-club favorite Paloma Picasso, in blood-red gloves.

This later show, too, took place outdoors, in honor of events from the old days, like the one in Suzi's garden, and still more, like that other memorable time with Suzi, when she brought her photographer friend down to Ray's and they played in the streets with the moticos, which discovered then that **it likes those moments of being inside the box**. And yet, the artist warned after the shoot, much as it may have liked the sensation of being taken up by the picture-making machine, when the **film is printed and the moticos is finally seen, it will not be seen**. The events of that day with Suzi and the photographer all happened so fast; before Ray could grasp what they meant to him, they had receded deep into the past. Now the time had come to take the moticos-moment up into the box once more.

And so, one day in January 1992, Ray Johnson spread Elisabeth Novick's photos of the moticos on the ground and climbed a ladder with his camera and began to recast a happy accident from the past as a conscious project for the future. After Ray sent some moticos to Ruth Asawa in 1956 in the hope that she might sell them, she had to give him the bad news that "People don't want to buy them, because they're paper etc. and they curl up. Are they missing something?" They were, but so was he. In retrospect, the photographs revealed that the moticos came into their own when they relinquished their claim to be singular objects and became actors in a play, like **those puppet plays I did as a kid in school**, only **on a much larger stage and scale.** The world was their stage—the world of Lower Manhattan in the 1950s, with its loading docks stacked with pallets and its streets spread with debris. A relatively small world, in terms of space; but in terms of time, the play had no predetermined limits. In theory, Ray could keep his actors moving as long as he wanted, as long as he had breath.

One problem with the moticos photographs: it is hard to make out the details of the individual moticos because of their scale, small enough to slip into an envelope, small enough to hold in one hand. The exhibition collages that succeeded them, with their subtly changing levels and densely packed, miniaturized modules of information, are also a photographer's nightmare. But for the pictures he took with the throwaway cameras—which produce low-quality images, fuzzy on detail—Johnson created a new kind of moticos, of a scale and type that would register on camera as legibly as the bone structure of a born star. In letters to David Bourdon from this period, Ray referred to these collages, which, he specified to David, were **32 inches high. And vary from 7 ½ to 8 inches wide**, as his

MO ST
VE ARs.

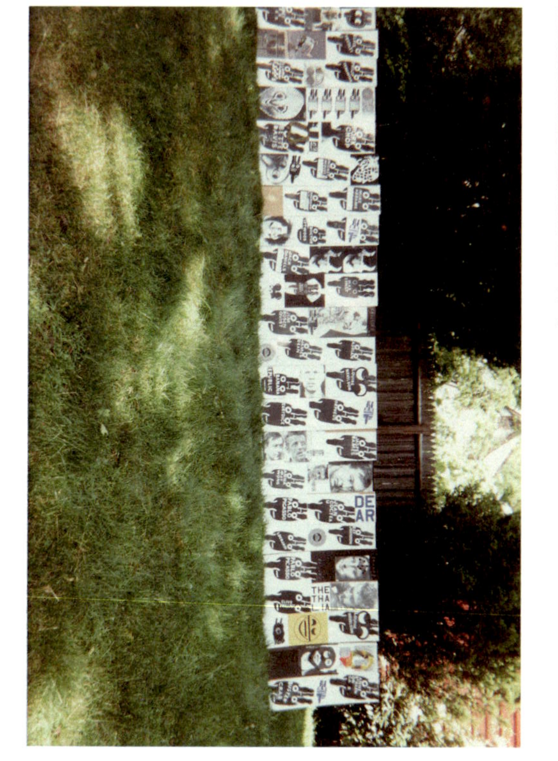

Ray Johnson, *Untitled (Move Stars with Paloma)* (1994).

Ray Johnson, *Untitled (Outdoor Movie Show)*, detail.

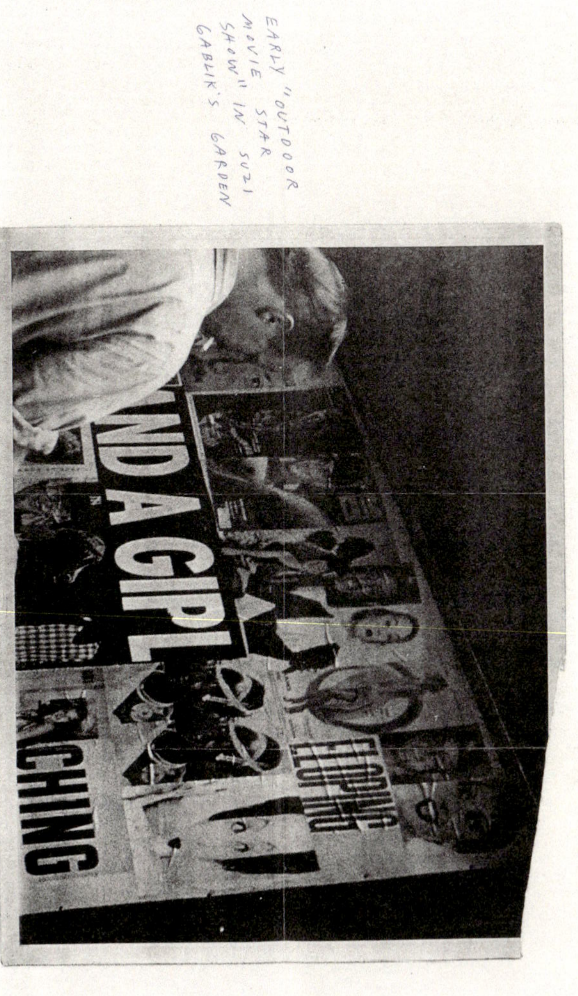

Ray Johnson to David Bourdon, September 28, 1994, inscribed **Early "Outdoor Movie Star Show" in Suzi Gablik's garden.**

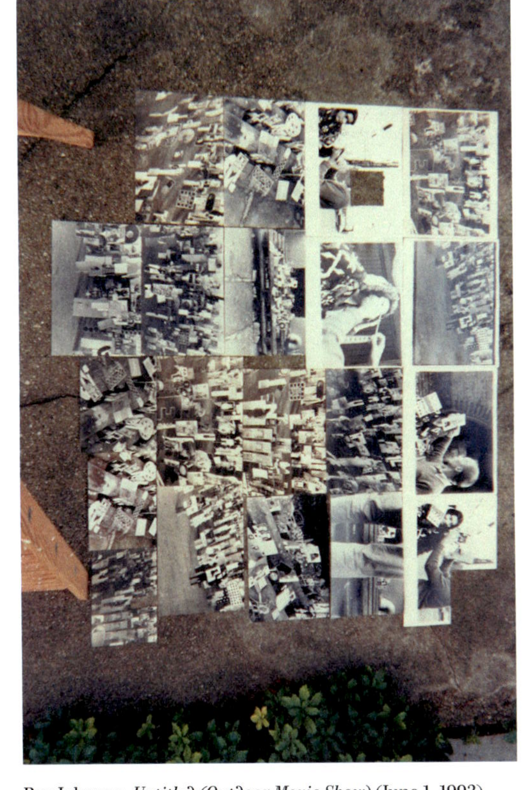

Ray Johnson, *Untitled (Outdoor Movie Show)* (June 1, 1993).

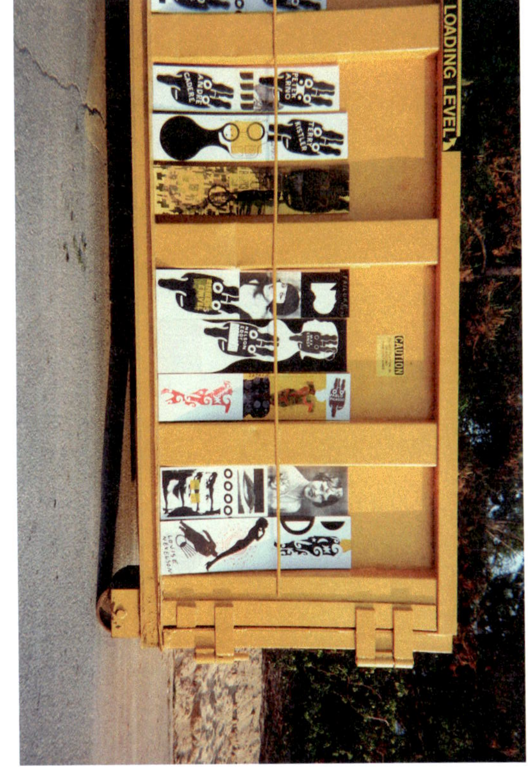

Ray Johnson, *Untitled (Move Stars and Dumpster)* (1993).

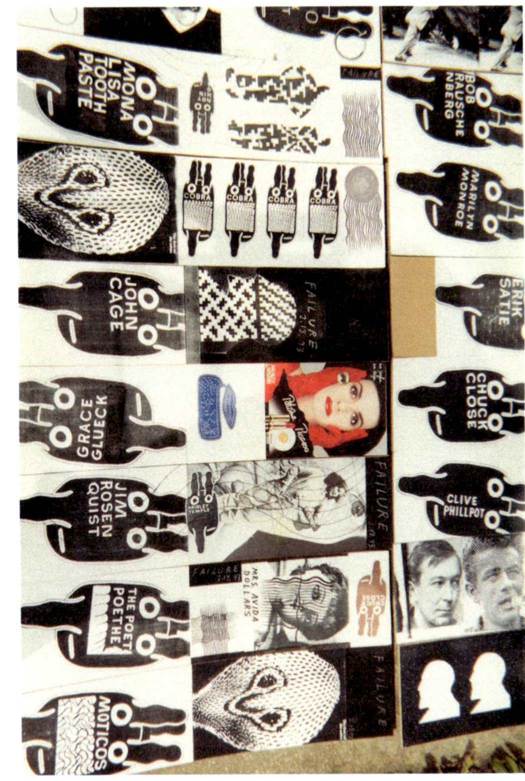

Ray Johnson, *Untitled (Move Stars with Paloma)* (1994).

Though larger than the moticos, the Move Stars were still small and light enough to be loaded by the dozens into the trunk of Johnson's car to be driven to various locations and arranged and rearranged for the stagings he called Moves. In the Moves, as in the moticos photos, Johnson's stars seem somehow at once out of place and very much of the place where he has set them. But instead of the ragged edges of the deindustrializing metropolis of 1955, we find the ragged edges of the suburbs to which the city folk had fled: cul-de-sacs and vacant lots and shady small backyards that, as seen through Johnson's eyes, have their own kind of trashy poetry. This had been Ray Johnson's day-to-day world since 1968, and it appears in gleams here and there in his letters, and in the bits of debris gleaned on what he called his "prison walks" (my studio, my prison) that made their way into his mailings and collages. It is startling nonetheless to see these quotidian scenes unroll in photo after photo in all their suggestive nothingness. Although, why should that be? Perhaps because, in both Ray Johnson's own mind and in the minds of others who seek to understand and place this artist, he is bound to the New York of a certain fertile moment, a moment that came back to him at this late date wearing the look of fate.

In a constellation within the spread of stars that Ray set up in his yard one summer day in 1993, one sees the past condensed. Nine heads form a tic-tac-toe square. The intense young man at bottom center and top right is Jasper Johns, who had an elfin look akin to Ray's; above and below him is James Dean, a Coke bottle glued—by Ray—to his temptingly parted lips. The connection between these two is clinched by the name on a companion bunny head, **JASPER JAMES**, set catty-corner from a head identified as Anna May Wong, a minor figure in Hollywood, but a major star in Ray-land. Johns makes frequent appearances in Johnson's late work, not just in the photos, but also in drawings and collages, often in the form of a name cached in an anagram that functions as a determinate negation: **NO RAY JOHNS**.

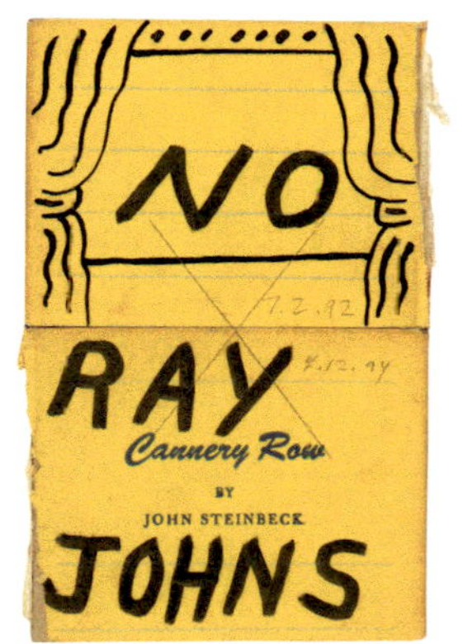

Ray Johnson, *Untitled (NO RAY JOHNS Theater)* (1992–94).

While Ray Johnson may have had mixed feelings about Robert Rauschenberg, he had nothing but admiration for Jasper Johns. His sense of connection to this artist comes, though, with painful intimations of a life unlived. Had he kept painting, could he have had a career like Jasper's? Who had maintained his privacy and his enigma and let the dealers and collectors do what they wanted with the work. The Orpheus and Eurydice bunnies to one side of the Jasper James quadrangle may serve as a warning: if we give in to the all-too-powerful desire to turn back and look, what we once wanted most will disappear before our eyes. In this scenario, the gone-too-soon James Dean plays Eurydice. Then again, if, in Johnson's schema, artist and muse do indeed keep changing places, he will find himself in the positions both of mourner and the mourned—of the one who stands there, looking back, and one who is always already gone.

XV

It was happening again. **When your film is printed and the moticos is finally seen, it will not be seen.** Apart from a few images that Johnson sent to select friends like Bourdon, the photographs that the artist had developed at a local shop from the rolls of film he pulled from his throw-away cameras would not be seen in his lifetime by anyone but him. For years after his death, no one took much interest in the boxes of these photos that remained at Johnson's estate, until finally, in 2019, Joel Smith, curator of photography at the Morgan Library, searched them out and went through them all and calculated that the artist had run through 137 cameras, from which he had printed over five thousand images. Smith also unearthed a set of collages that Johnson had begun to build around the photos, along with the full cast of Move Stars.

The Quicksnap series was the last of Johnson's synthetic projects, marrying image, message, and performance, and, in this period of retreat from galleries and museums, serving as a mode of exhibition, too. But as hermetic as his previous projects had been, with them one could still venture answers to the questions, message to whom? performance for whom? Whereas the Moves and their material traces remained outside the institutions through which, however deviously, Ray Johnson had reached his audience. Not only did the photo-project fail to appear in galleries or museums or college auditoriums, it never became fodder for the correspondence network. A photo taken at the outset of the project depicts a message in Ray's hand, with the date, the salutation **DEAR TOBY**, and a bit of the bunny head sign-off, but the letter is written in sand, addressed only to the waves that will efface it.

And yet, not only to the waves; to write is always to address someone. This is the paradox of Johnson's **performance in an area not the audience area of the artist whose costume and actions are nothing to do with those observing**: he has not left the theater. Exchanges between the artist and human actors do feature in certain of the photographs. A little boy met on a prison walk obligingly poses by a "NO EXIT" sign. (**I do not exits.**) A young man with a fuchsia mohawk tries to suppress a grin as he holds up a Move Star with a James Rosenquist bunny on one end and the word **FAILURE** on the other.

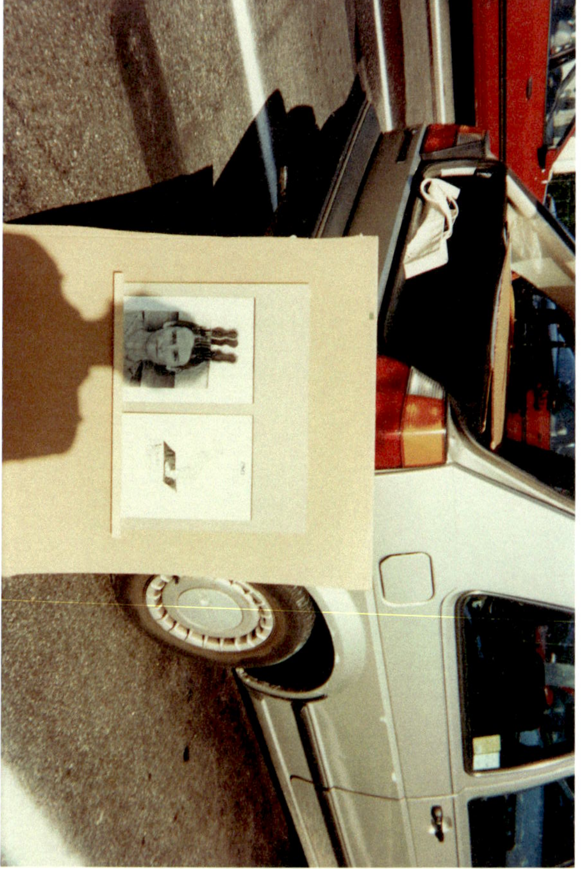

Ray Johnson, *Untitled (Sandra Gering's Shadow on Walker Evans Photograph)* (1992).

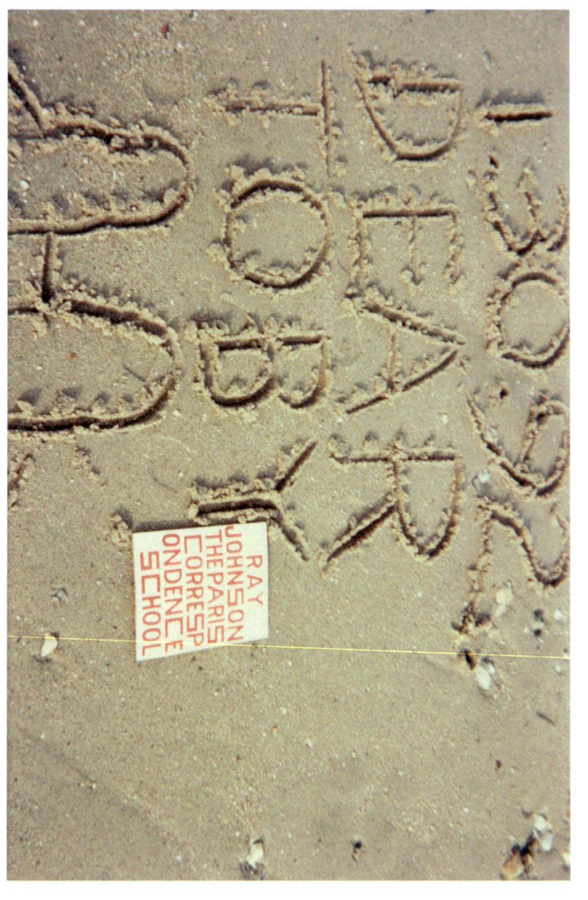

Ray Johnson, *Untitled (DEAR TOBY)* (1992).

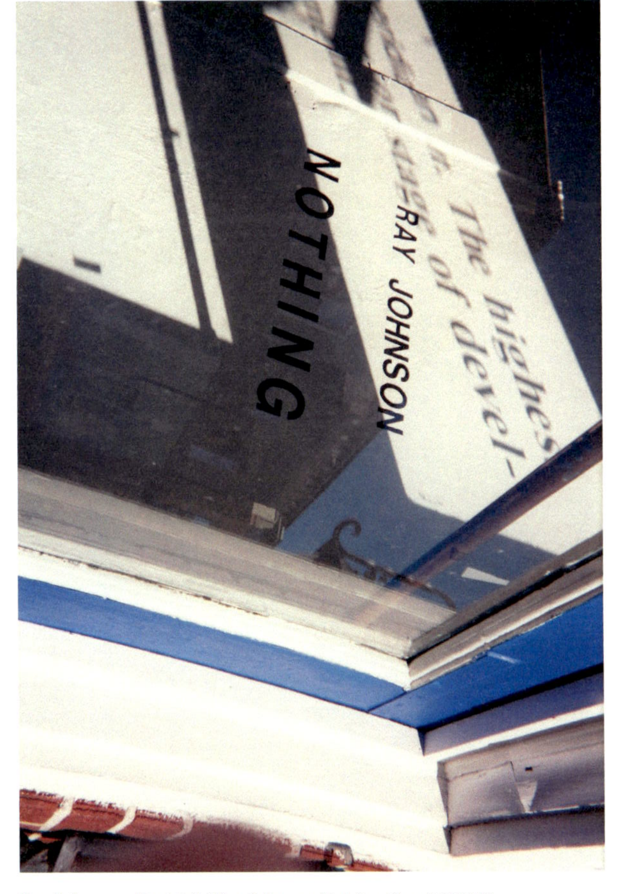

Ray Johnson, *Untitled (Ray Johnson Nothing Show)* (1994).

The shadow of a head that falls on a photograph by Walker Evans of Alabama sharecropper Allie Mae Burroughs turns out to have been cast by Manhattan gallerist Sandra Gering. Ray often referred to Gering during these years as *my dealer*, even though the big show she kept discussing—and discussing and discussing—"every time he called," Gering said, "it was a two hour conversation"—doing with him would never come to fruition.

The show that Gering wanted to do would have focused on Johnson's performances. On a day when Ray knew Sandra had an errand that would bring her to his part of Long Island, he said **I'm gonna do a performance for you, only you. Don't bring anybody**. "*Okay*," she said, but still, "I couldn't believe it that he actually came, and, in his car, he had different photographs and different drawings that he had done, and he lined them up in the parking lot. He walked around the photographs, maybe three times, then he picked them back up and put them back in his trunk." Later, she received the photo of her shadow in the mail. It was a portrait, of sorts, and an enigmatic message, and a souvenir of a performance that doubled as a fugitive exhibition.

Those letters in the sand addressed to Toby may also count, in the end, as a kind of exchange. Unlike Joseph Cornell, Ray Johnson was not given to encouraging his acolytes and city friends to make the pilgrimage out to the dowdy little house in Locust Valley. Even Bill Wilson never went there. But Toby had her own room in Ray's house. She was the only one to bridge Ray's two lives: the life where everyone knew him as New York's most famous unknown artist, and the life that no one, or at least, no one who was anyone by New York standards, knew much about. The message in the sand says that on some level everything he does is addressed to Toby, that without his muse he is nothing.

XVI

Ray Johnson cared about New York standards. If he hadn't, he could not have limned the pain inflicted by such standards in his art with such cold precision, and yet also with such pathos. But one charm of life in Locust Valley was that no one there was bound by those standards. The area of Long Island where Ray lived was full of artists and curators who taught in local colleges and showed in local galleries and programmed local museums and did beautiful work and visited each other's studios and collaborated and competed with one another and gossiped about one another. In short, this place where Ray lived for twenty-six years had an art world, and the longer Ray lived there, the more at home he felt in that world.

The town of Sea Cliff, a few miles from Locust Valley, had a cluster of galleries where Ray's artist friends would show, and he would go for the opening night festivities that spilled from gallery to gallery. At a gallery and frame shop called the Sea Cliff Photograph Company—the proprietor, Don Mistretta, framed some of Johnson's work for the Nassau County Museum exhibition—Ray would rummage through the collection of vintage photographs kept in the back room. In 1992, the year that Johnson began taking photos, an artist named Sheila Sporer left a child's chair there for Don to refinish and Ray began leaving envelopes and packages on the chair for friends he knew might drop by, just as he had done at gallery desks around Soho. This went on through 1994. Toward the end of that year, Ray left a package addressed to Don and to Will Farrington, a particular friend of Ray's who taught art at the New York Institute of Technology. When the two addressees opened the package, they found, recalled a still-unnerved Mistretta, "a glove that said 'Death' on it, okay?" Okay.

A QuickSnap from August 1994 shows a package addressed to Sheila Sporer, with **DO NOT OPEN** in red letters, leaning against a shop window behind which a ceramic bunny rears up on its hind legs. One from October 1994 shows a package from Sheila to Ray, to which Ray has tethered a helium balloon with a bunny face, tugged sideways by the wind. Ray became very close to Sheila, as close as he had been to anyone, after he saw an assemblage of hers in 1991 in a Sea Cliff gallery, which was inspired, she said, by "the poem 'Royalty' by Arthur Rimbaud, which was about a beautiful man and woman who both wanted to be queen." Ray loved Sheila's work and urged her to use his connections to get it seen in New York, but, flattered as she was by his confidence in her, "I didn't have that life where I could get into the city and do things and I was okay with it."

In December 1994, Ray told Sheila that he had just had a lunch to discuss the possibility of doing something with Sandra Gering, whom "I know he liked," Sporer said with a laugh, "because he always called her a 'classy dame.'" Nonetheless, when Johnson and Gering met, he did his Ray thing: **She ordered the champagne and I ordered the water. She ordered the shrimp cocktail and I ordered nothing and crossed my silverware.** And in the end, of course, he said no to the show. But Sheila intuited that "he was conflicted about that," so she made a suggestion. A place in Sea Cliff called the Meridian Gallery had nothing scheduled for the two weeks before Christmas and Sheila offered to talk to the gallery owners, but Ray said, no, he would do it, and they said he could use the space for a show. After that, however, Sporer said, "he would not take the key to the gallery; he wanted *me* to have the key to the gallery." Ray would deposit messages for Sheila and pieces for the show through the gallery's mail slot, using a grabber tool, and if he wanted to make changes to Sheila's installation, he would call her to be let in.

The gallery door was locked during the whole two weeks the show was up. (**DO NOT OPEN**) Don Mistretta remembers looking in and seeing a pile of cardboard boxes in the middle of the floor and Sheila Sporer remembers that there were bunny heads in the window, including a "good-sized" Harpo bunny. The photographs that Sporer took to document the installation were subsequently stolen from her studio, she thinks she knows by whom (small world). Ray took a few pictures, too, all taken from the outside looking in, including one of the Harpo bunny and another that shows his name and the title of the show painted on the gallery window but shot so that they seem to be suspended in mid-air.

XVII

What is an audience? At its root, the word means "a hearing," as in a courtroom. One's case was heard by a monarch or other singular authority, and later, by a jury of one's peers. But if one is an artist, one looks to one's audience not only for their judgment but for that most elusive of rewards, recognition. You look out, they look back, and you see that you are seen. "The mother's face, the purpose of the poem," writes Wallace Stevens, meaning that every glance of recognition takes one back to that initial downturned look.

In the script penciled in between the bars of the red letters that spell FAILURE in a tondo-shaped late collage, the artist does what he can to appease a judgmental crowd.

A OPERA
The curtain opens:
A large BONE.
Audience: Ha,
ha, ha,
6.14.92

What kind of bone does he throw them? Part of a sentence pops out from the block of prose pasted at the top of the tondo: "the story

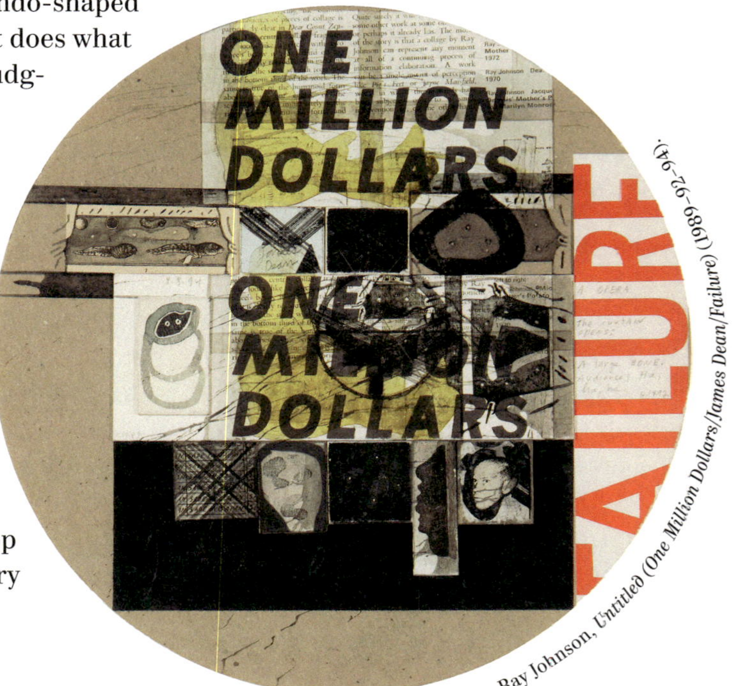

Ray Johnson, *Untitled (One Million Dollars/James Dean/Failure)* (1989–92–94).

is that a collage by Ray Johnson can represent any moment at all in a continuing process of information elaboration." (This is from Henry Martin's 1972 review of Johnson's Potato Masher show at Arturo Schwarz.) Living as we do in an Age of Information, perhaps this artist has something to teach us about how to thread our way through the deliberately confusing maze of words and images that endlessly unfolds before us wherever we step?

Then again, to get to this thought, we must lean in close to read the small print. Easier just to sit back and repeat the magic words inked across the surface in big block letters: **ONE MILLION DOLLARS ONE MILLION DOLLARS**. They, too, contain a lesson. The story—as told by Frances Beatty, who became director of Ray Johnson's estate, but who never could get Ray to show with her during his lifetime—is that Johnson had been invited by an old friend-fan, Robert Pincus-Witten, to meet with Pincus-Witten's employer at the time, gallerist Larry Gagosian, a power player in the New York art world since his arrival in the mid-1980s. Johnson prepared his usual carefully calibrated showing, but once he got to the gallery and set his box of collages before Pincus-Witten, the famously money-minded Gagosian just walked in and snapped, "Ask him how much he wants," and walked out. Soon afterward, Pincus-Witten received a flyer in the mail that read **RAY JOHNSON COLLAGES ONE MILLION DOLLARS EACH**. Which was not to say that this was their price, but that they were priceless.

The question for Ray Johnson was never, "How much do you want?" but always, "What, what on earth, do you want?" In 1992, Phyllis Stigliano approached Beatty on Johnson's behalf to talk about his doing a show at Richard Feigen's gallery, a discussion which

> went on for like three and half hours and I would say one thing and she, it was like she was channeling Ray. I said, "would Ray let us see any of the things that he's doing now?" And I remember she said, "that's a problem." And I said, "no it's not; it's not a problem. Whatever he's doing, we'll show." Then I said to her, "does he have any idea of the prices of these things?" I thought, might as well ask, and she said, "no." Finally I said, "you tell Ray that we will do a show of work that we haven't seen for prices that we don't know. Tell him that that is fine. That's fine."

It was not fine. There was no show. Then, in January 1995, Ray called Frances to say that he had finished doing Nothing and was going to do Something, and after that she could have her show. *Ray Johnson: A Memorial Show* opened at Richard L. Feigen & Co. in April of that same year. But the price that Frances had to pay—the price that everyone had to pay—to see all those Ray Johnsons together on the wall was far too high.

In the *FAILURE* tondo, Ray Johnson looks back at us from a square tile afloat on black space. Only, if you look very, very closely, you can see that the ground is not entirely flat black, that "James Dean" has been scratched in at left, in shaky cursive, and then covered over again. Dean's name also appears above in smaller letters, on a white square half-covered by a nascent X. Is the dead star the artist's intended audience? (**DEAD MAY WILSON,** reads the salutation on a silhouette collage from 1990. The mother's face ...) One tends to think of "audience" as a plural noun, but—like the moticos—an audience can also be singular. The recipient of a letter usually opens it alone, and she does so in the absence of the sender, whose envelope was sealed in another space, at another time.

It is a pity that Ray Johnson did not live to read *The Gorgeous Nothings*, an edition published in 2013 of Emily Dickinson's "envelope poems," so called because she wrote them on split-open envelopes and other paper scraps. One cannot help but think that the artist would have thought himself the ideal audience for the poem that an editor of the volume, Jen Bervin, cites as the inspiration for its title.

By homely gifts and hindered Words
The human heart is told
Of Nothing—
"Nothing" is the force
That renovates the World—

From his letters to his Black Mountain friend Frances X. Profumo, we know that Johnson was reading Dickinson in his twenties. And we know from the Quicksnaps that he was still thinking about her forty years later.

Four Move Stars lean against a tombstone in one of the local graveyards that were among the photographer's favorite settings for his shoots. Paired at the center are a New York Correspondence School bunny head and a silhouette of Emily Dickinson, done when she was fourteen years old, an image Johnson used in several of his silhouette collages. He likely knew enough about the poet to know that she resisted being painted or photographed, that the silhouette is only one of three known lifetime images made of her, making her a perfect subject for his portraits that are likenesses, and yet not. He certainly knew that Dickinson used correspondence to circulate her poems, as an alternative to publication, which she also vigorously resisted. One Dickinson silhouette collage includes a Nancy cartoon in which Johnson's favorite girl tells her Aunt Fritzi, "I was elected secretary of our correspondence club," to which the aunt replies, "Won't you have to answer an awful lot of letters?"

People ask as well of Emily Dickinson, what, what on earth, did she want? Did she want her poems to be published in her lifetime, despite her theatrical resistance, or at least, did she want them to be published after her death? The fact that these questions are and always will be unanswerable forms part of this poet's fascination for her audience. A poem of hers that Johnson quotes in a letter to Profumo suggests that what the poet may have wanted most was not to be had, on earth, at least. Here is the whole thing.

Which is the best—the Moon or the Crescent?
Neither—said the Moon—
That is best which is not—Achieve it—
You efface the Sheen.

Not of detention is Fruition—
Shudder to attain.
Transport's decomposition follows—
He is Prism born.

Ray Johnson, like Emily Dickinson, dreamed of an unworldly—a virtually world-less—art: the sheen without the moon. He wanted Nothing; the black square; the calm center. **all my white backgrounds are now black with tons of those tiny spaced out polka dots in the night sky. a hush of darkness over everything.** The darkness is not absolute, there are those dots that may be stars. Or maybe not. In the blackness between the curtains of the little theater near the center of the FAILURE tondo, the dots become eyes, the abyss that looks back.

Like Emily Dickinson, Ray Johnson dreamed of an audience that might grant him the recognition he craved—that we all crave. It was an audience that, for him as for her, took the form of a particular receiver, separated from the sender in space and time. The sender's and receiver's positions are reversible, they are equals, but the distance between them preserves their particularity. A perfect democracy, held in delicate, precarious balance. Unlike the other dream, not impossible on earth, for a moment, at least.

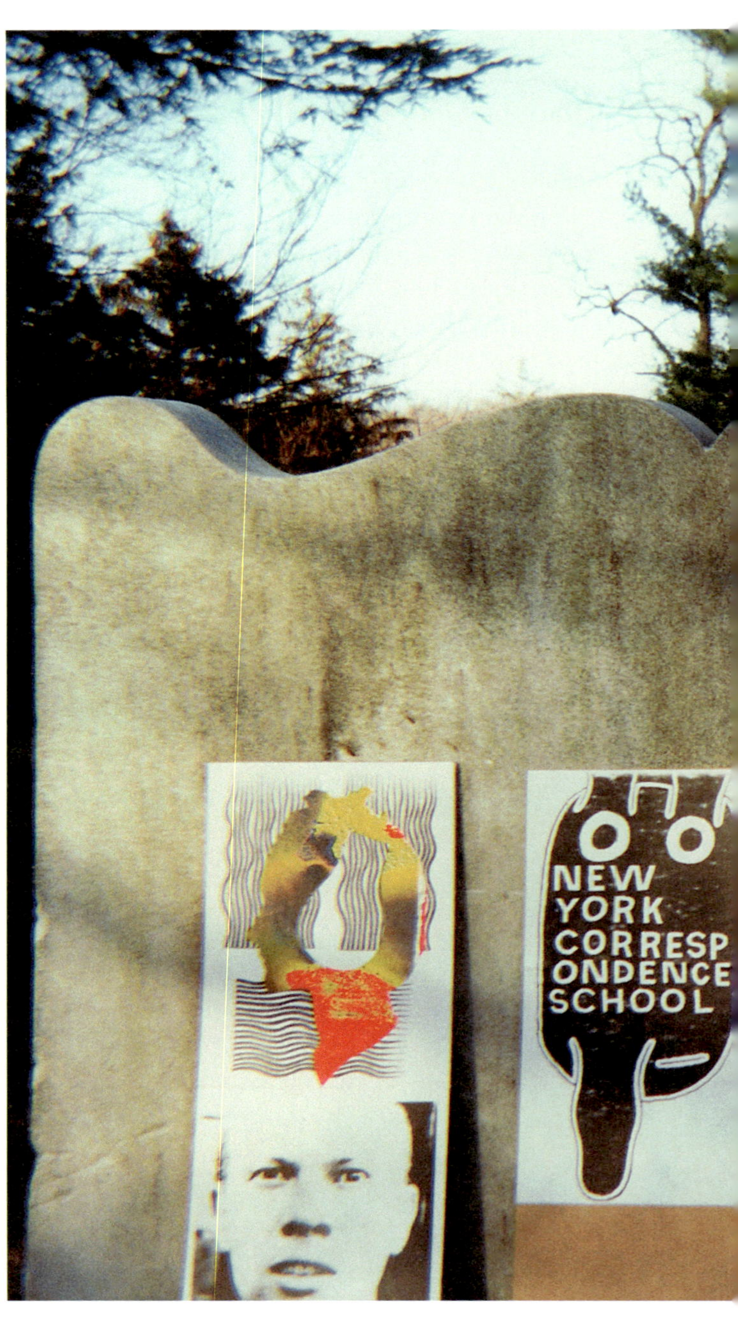
NEW
YORK
CORRESP
ONDENCE
SCHOOL

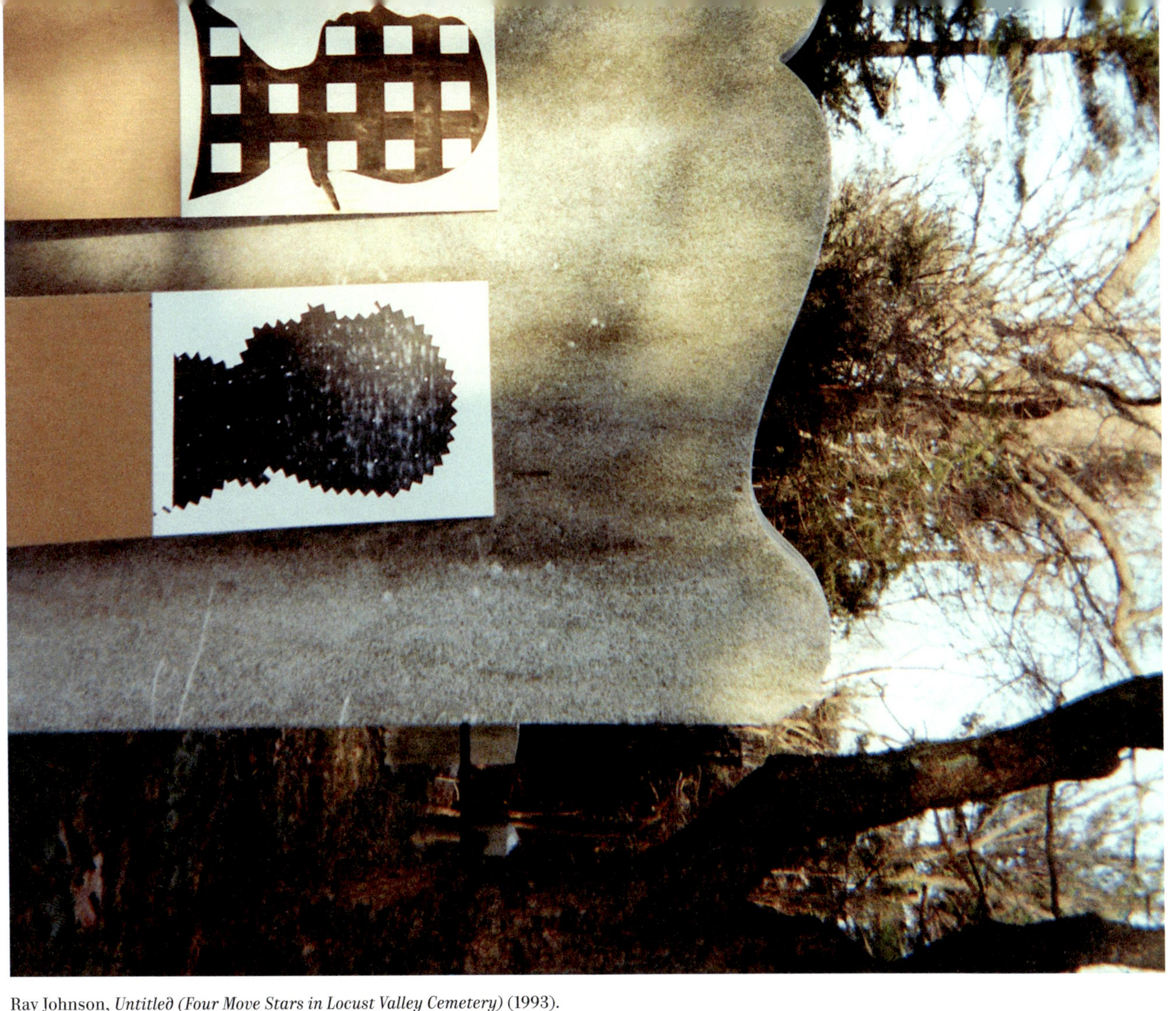

Ray Johnson, *Untitled (Four Move Stars in Locust Valley Cemetery)* (1993).

CODA

I

We know what we know about the circumstances surrounding the death of Ray Johnson because, after his body was found, on Saturday, January 14, 1995, floating offshore in a sea-cove, there was a police investigation. The investigators determined that Johnson had left home the previous day, an overdetermined Friday the 13th, and driven fifty miles west to Sag Harbor, near Long Island's easternmost tip. He checked into a room at the Baron's Cove Inn at 5:30 p.m., used the bathroom and lay on the bed, then went out to his car and drove until he got to a Seven-Eleven convenience store and parked the car in the lot. The Seven-Eleven was a short walk from the Sag Harbor-North Haven Bridge, from which, at 7:15 p.m., two teenage girls saw a man plummet into the wintry water and swim off, an occurrence alarming enough that they headed to the local police headquarters to report it, but finding the station closed, gave up and went on their way.

We know what Ray Johnson's house looked like when he left it because, once Frances Beatty saw what the artist had done, she brought people to photograph and film the meticulous installation of boxes and boxes and boxes of material and racks of art and stacks of phone books and book-books, arranged in rational-irrational grids like so many Johnson tesserae. All the art was sealed away or obscured from view, with the unmissable exception of a photo-portrait of Ray Johnson by Chuck Close,

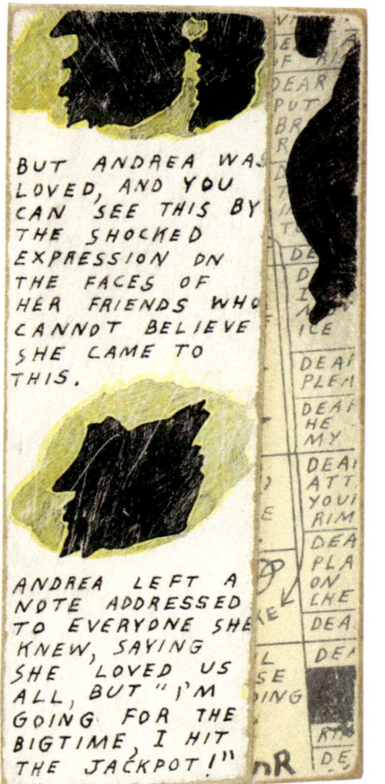

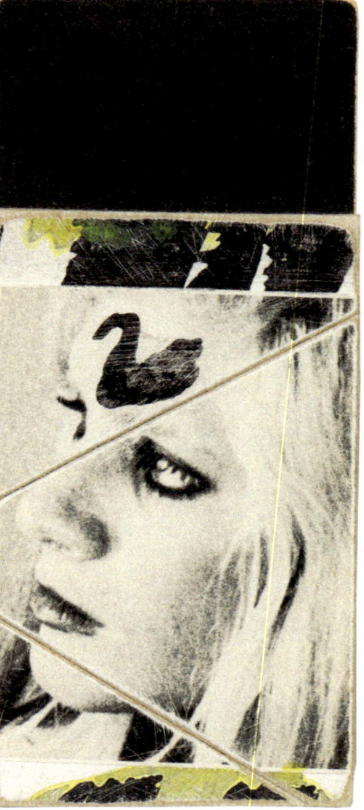

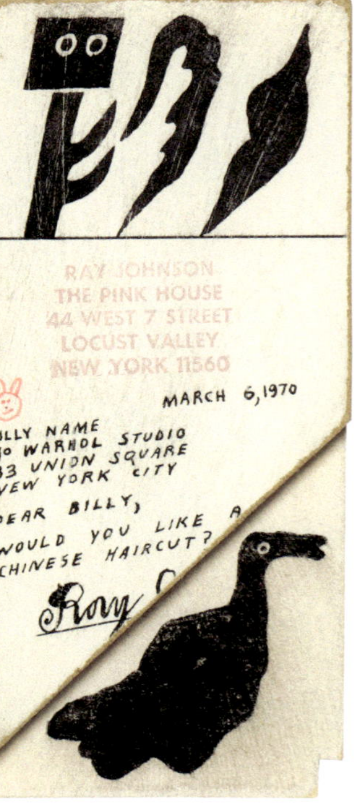

Ray Johnson, tesserae-collages from *Untitled (The Green Box)*, n.d.

which Johnson had placed facing outward to greet posthumous visitors. A few other things, Beatty thought, had also been arranged in ways meant to catch the eye. For instance, a Johnson drawing of a foot wielding a pen to inscribe the signature "John Hancock" (an editioned print commissioned by Richard Feigen in 1968), was draped over a green shoebox, which when opened turned out to enclose two more boxes, one of which contains forty three-by-six-inch moticos-style collages.

Many of these miniatures look to have been formed from fragments cut from one or more full-sized collages made shortly after the 1972 suicide of Warhol Superstar Andrea Feldman. Some pieces are directly related to Feldman—one tile bears her photograph, another, a bunny head with her name—while others have more oblique connections, like the tile with a note from Ray to Billy Name, asking if he **would like a Chinese haircut**, a backward glance at the haircut parties in the silver-lined apartment that marked an epoch in Ray's, Billy's, and Andy's intertwining lives. "He created in me an emotional imbalance that was painful and almost incapacitating," someone says of Warhol on another tile. This was true for Feldman and for Billy Name, but less so for Johnson, who kept his distance from the Factory scene, although the strain of being a sort of anti-Andy did tell on Ray from time to time throughout his life.

Other quotations on the tiles may be traced to an obituary of Feldman—also known to her friends as Andy—written by her friend and fellow Warhol Superstar Geraldine Smith and published in the *Village Voice*. Johnson obviously sees himself in the portrait that Smith draws, perhaps even envies the unselfconsciousness that allows her to voice sentiments he might feel but never utter.

We all stood by helpless watching her as her self-inflicted sufferings became reality and we were not able to do anything about it.

Andrea was tormented constantly by her fear of not being loved, of unrecognition, of ridicule and not being understood.

But Andrea was loved and you can see this by the shocked expressions on the faces of her friends who cannot believe she came to this.

This is why it is all the more tragic that her previous fears returned to torment her in her last days with us.

Before Feldman leapt from a fourteenth-floor window, Smith recounts, "Andrea left a note to everyone she knew, saying she loved us all, but 'I'm going for the big time, I hit the jackpot!'" To show that he, for one, may understand her, Johnson uses the second box within the box to house the jackpot. Lift up the sheet on which the artist has inked Feldman's silhouette, with a snake encircling it and a heart-shaped window cut out of it, and you see—stars.

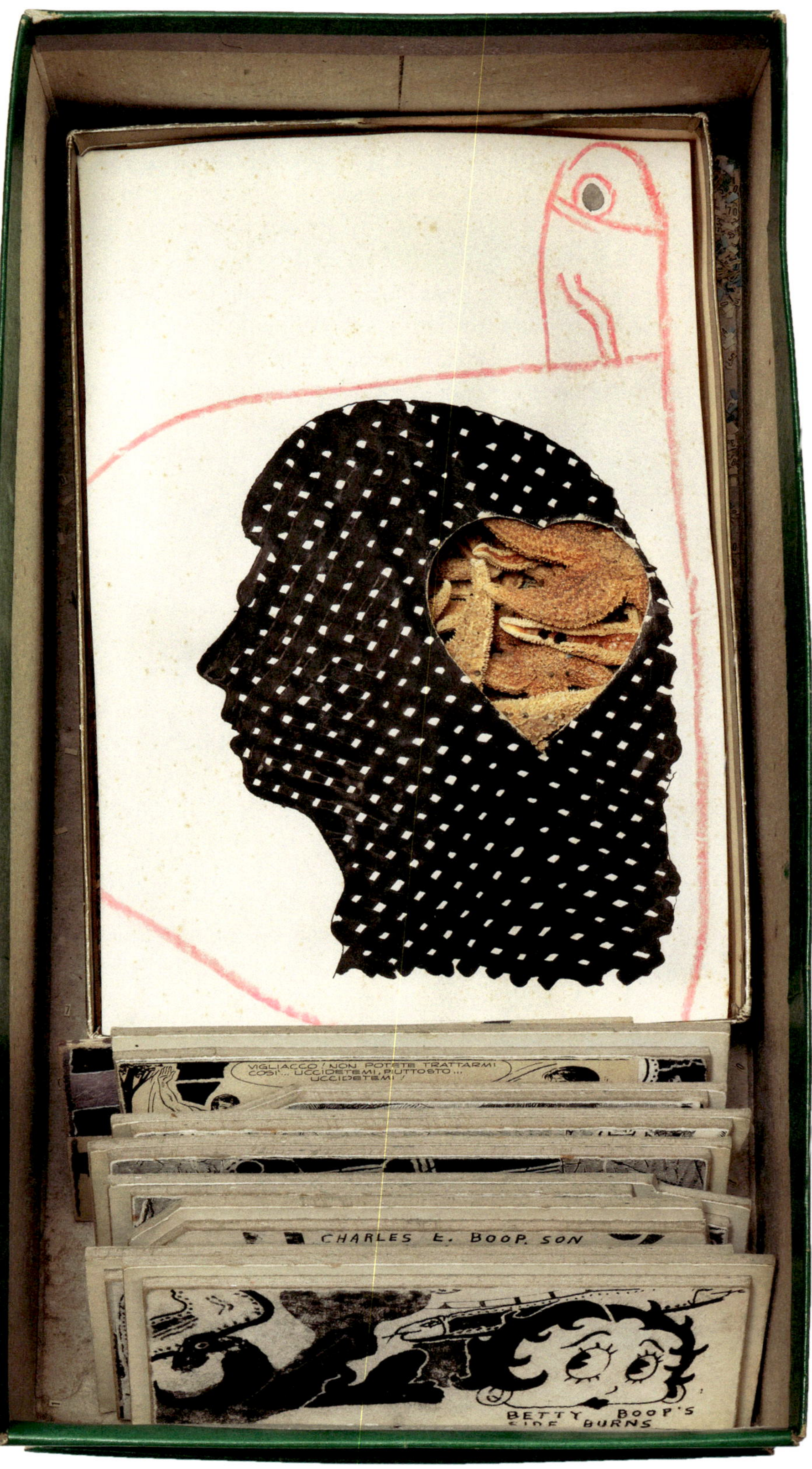
VIGLIACCO! NON POTETE TRATTARMI COSÌ... UCCIDETEMI, PIUTTOSTO... UCCIDETEMI!
CHARLES E. BOOP. SON
BETTY BOOP'S
BURNS

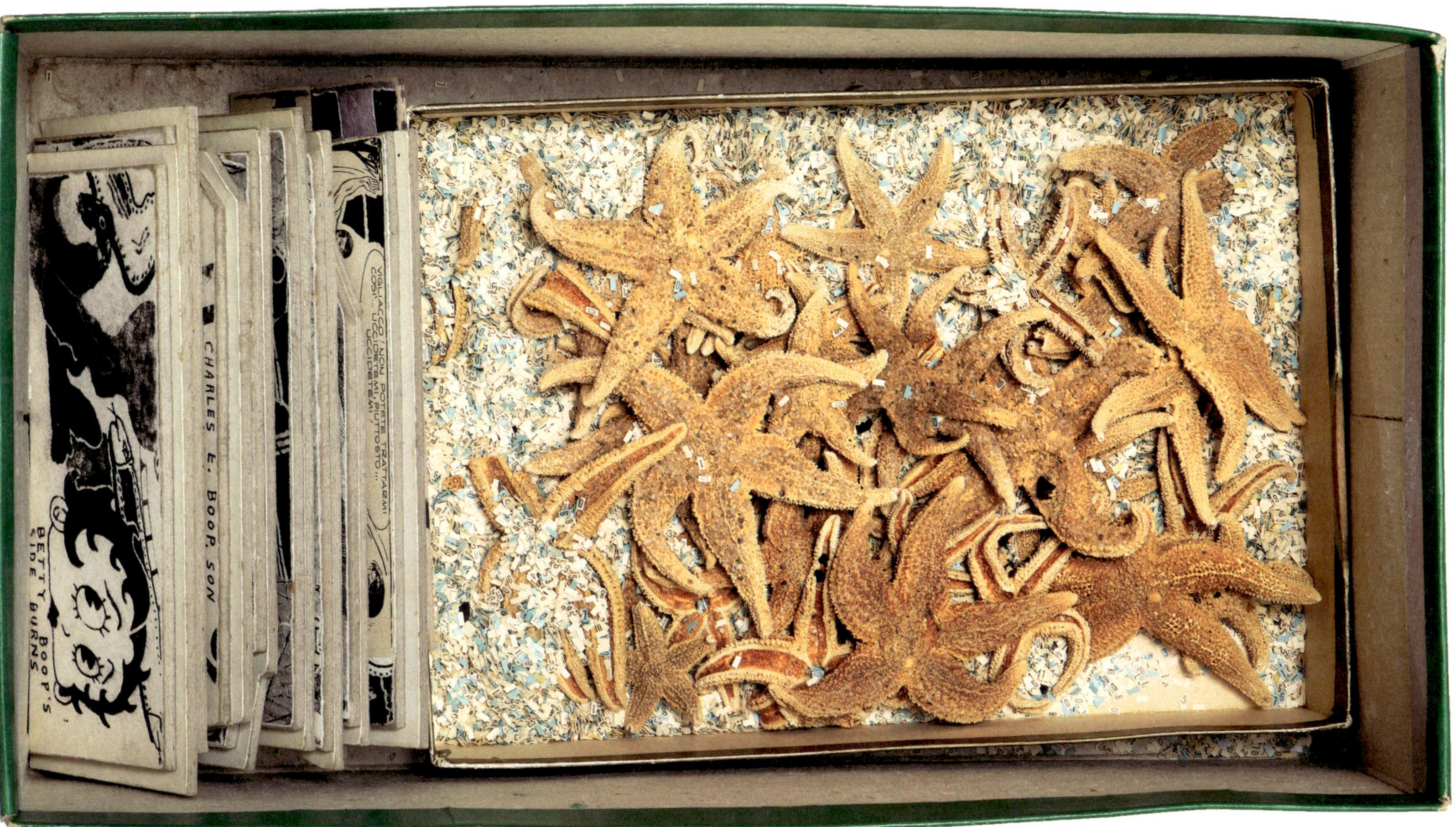

Ray Johnson, starfish box with and without Andrea Feldman silhouette, from *Untitled (The Green Box)*, n.d.

II

Ray Johnson did not leave a note of the kind one usually associates with suicides. One could read the obituary fragments in the green box as that kind of note placed in quotation marks. One could also read the entire contents of the house as he had left it as a kind of message, the kind one will never finish reading. Johnson's work is full of references to death, particularly to death under bizarre circumstances and to suicide, and most particularly, to death by drowning. A packet of scraps sent to Henry Martin in the mid-1960s includes the cover of a vintage Red Cross guide to "Life Saving and Water Safety." "Parisians Washed Up by Seine," reads the headline of a clipping sent to Bill Wilson in 1973, along with a notice of artist Robert Smithson's death in a plane crash and the famous photo of John F. Kennedy's assassin, Lee Harvey Oswald, recoiling from the impact of the bullet shot by his assassin Jack Ruby. In 1983, Bill received a card with a quotation from Tennessee Williams's memoirs, expressing the playwright's desire, when he dies, to be "Sewn up in a clean white sack and dropped overboard, twelve hours north of Havana, so that my bones may rest not too far from those of Hart Crane," the poet, who is presumed to have leapt to his death from a steamer carrying him home from Cuba. Another poet mysteriously lost at sea, Arthur Cravan, stars in the flyer for a throwaway gesture scheduled for January 13, 1979. Here, though, the pathos is cut with goofy wordplay: Cravan is misspelled Craven, the given surname of Richard C., who makes an appearance, along with those other crucial Arthurs, Rimbaud and Secunda, and Jean Author, one of the many star-name mash-ups that served as Johnson pseudonyms.

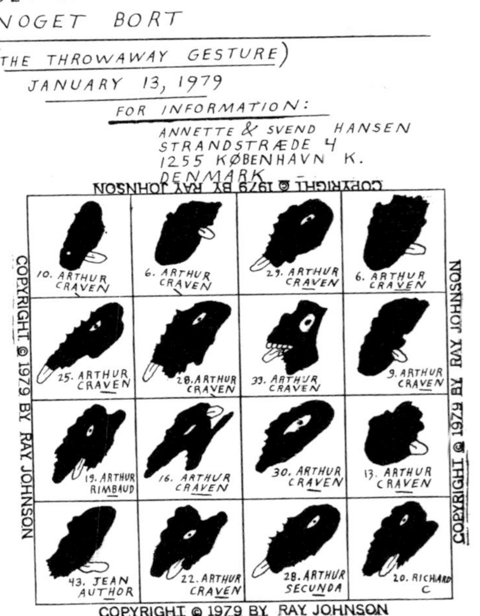

Ray Johnson, *The Throwaway Gesture* flyer, January 13, 1979.

"When a man in good health commits suicide it is, finally, because there is no one who understands him. After his death the incomprehension often continues because the living insist on interpreting and using his story to suit their own purposes. In this way the ultimate protest against incomprehension goes unheard after all," said John Berger of poet Vladimir Mayakovsky. "Andrea was tormented constantly by her fear of not being loved, of unrecognition, of ridicule and not being understood," said Geraldine Smith of Andrea Feldman. Ray Johnson was a sender of messages exquisitely fitted to the interests and sensibilities of their receivers and he was also, like Emily Dickinson, a writer of letters to a world that failed to respond, or at least, left him with the tormenting sense that he remained unrecognized. But to say even this much in this context is to interpret and use Ray Johnson's story to suit my own purposes.

We do not know and will never know just why Ray Johnson killed himself. People who are plagued by persistent thoughts of suicide, as Johnson was, often act on those thoughts. And clearly, his act was not impulsive: in the months before he died, he made calls and sent mailings to many in his wide circle of friends that in retrospect, they all said, they should have taken as warnings. In an article published in the *New York Times* in February 1995, a friend who spoke to him the day before he died, Edvard Lieber, reports Ray as having said, **I have a new project, the biggest one I've ever undertaken, the most important one in my life**, a declaration Lieber thought then was just Ray being Ray, but which now "haunted" him. Having heard other such stories in the course of his research, the writer of the *Times* piece concludes that "if there is any belief that unites his friends about the last days of his life, it is that Ray Johnson would never have passed up such a dramatic moment in which to impart a message."

It was a message, they said. And it was a performance, "Ray Johnson's Last Event," as one newspaper headline phrased it. Johnson himself led them to think so. **You'll read about it in the New York Times**, he told Sheila Sporer when she called during those last days, worried about the "desperate" tone of a note he had just sent her. "I'm going for the big time, I hit the jackpot!" Except, when Ray issued his warning to Sheila, he didn't sound ebullient, he sounded "very cold, so unlike him, he never spoke to me this way." If you love someone, there is something deeply wrong, something truly obscene, about conceiving of their death as a performance. Sheila's friend should have known that; but it was not Sheila's friend speaking.

Ray Johnson had a taste for the obscene. He also had a taste for jewel-box mosaic, and groan-worthy puns, and austere abstraction, and street debris, and literary allusion, and gossip both high and low, tastes he might exercise one at a time or, more often, all at once. Like Duchamp, Johnson wanted his receivers to see the testing of their taste against a given work not as a matter of preference, but of ethics, the question being not, What do I like? but, Who am I, that this is what I like? And—now that you ask—might I be something other than this "I" that I thought I was? For to make art is to see, over and over, that I is an *other*, the other that is this thing that comes from you, but is not exactly you. This is an art story, not a life story. Ray Johnson himself seems to say as much in a very late self-portrait.

It is a double portrait, as it says, of **The Poet** and **The Poem**. The one faces us ass-out, legs bound by cords that speak of purely private compulsions, the other is a jewel-like fragment, waiting to find its place in the larger mosaic. Or not. The fragment is adorned with a fringe of false eyelashes, a recurrent feature in the artist's late collages. When asked by Henry Martin if he thought of his collages as "a kind of final resting place" for his restless flow of gestures, thoughts, and images, Johnson answered with the question, **Should an eyelash last forever?** By which he meant, of course, that nothing lasts forever. Not even stars. Is it enough for the star that someone looked up once and said, I see it? Yes, the poet thought, that is what it means to be a star.

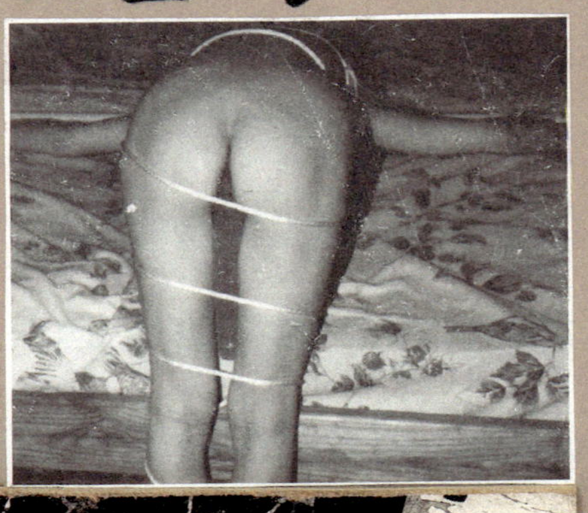

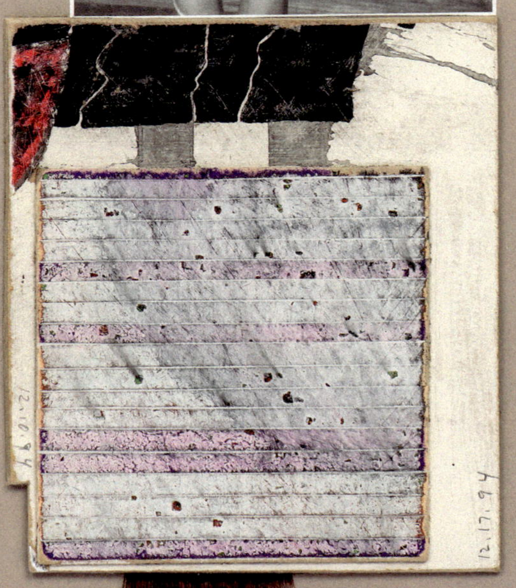

Ray Johnson, *Untitled (The Poet The Poem)* (1994).

ACKNOWLEDGMENTS

This book is dedicated to Frances F. L. Beatty and William S. Wilson—an unlikely pair on the face of it, but alike nonetheless in having devoted much of their lives and considerable energies to preserving as many traces as they could of Ray Johnson's fugitive existence. Without their collections of Johnsoniana and their tireless efforts to make those collections intelligible and available to virtually everyone who ever showed an interest in Ray Johnson, this artist's work might indeed have come to nothing, as it sometimes seemed he wished it would. When I conceived this project, I first approached Frances, who said, "ask Bill Wilson; if he says yes, then I will." He did, and I had the incalculable benefit and great honor of knowing the person John Ashbery referred to as "brainy Bill Wilson" in what turned out to be the last year of his life. Frances has seen this project through with incredible patience as well as her characteristic grace and wit, a measure of which I can only hope has been osmotically transmitted to these pages.

Bill Wilson's archivist and assistant, Michael Von Uchtrup, welcomed me into his parlor-floor realm and shared his wealth of knowledge, a trove shaped by the intimate collective wisdom of the tribe of Ray. When the Wilson archive went to the Art Institute of Chicago, it acquired a worthy interpreter in Caitlin Haskell, who surely never imagined when she went into museum work that she would one day bear the title, "Director of Ray Johnson Collections and Research" (imagine what RJ would have done with those words on a flyer!). Caitlin's encouragement and support have been essential, and her conversation, richly generative. Jessica Smith, of the Art Institute's Ryerson & Burnham Art and Architecture Archives, has been immensely helpful; thanks are owed as well to the RBAAA's Nathaniel Parks. I am grateful to Maria Ilario, archivist at the Ray Johnson Estate, not only for the gift of her time and assistance, but as an interlocutor, reader, and all-around fun companion through long days in the Ray-mines. And for his heroic forbearance, thanks to Alexander Adler, partner in Adler Beatty, the consultancy where the Estate is now housed.

At other institutions: special thanks to archivists Matt Gray at the Andy Warhol Museum, Sophie Haaser at Mumok in Vienna, and Anna Tidlund at the Morris and Helen Belkin Gallery of the University of British Columbia. Invitations to speak from Tommy Anderson at Mississippi State University, Tom Huhn at the School of Visual Arts in New York, Jonathan Neufeld at the College of Charleston, and Susan Rosenbaum at the University of Georgia nurtured the work in progress. The seeds of parts of chapter 2 were sown when Michael Stone-Richards invited me to write about Johnson and Detroit for his journal, *Detroit Research*. Through the shadow institution of Ray-Johnson-world I found myself enrolled in an absorbing floating seminar with (among others named here) Gerard Forde, Johanna Gosse, Julie Thomson, and Elizabeth Zuba. The students in my Collage & Poetry class at Pratt Institute were able collaborators in thinking through the ideas that undergird this story. Two of those students, Sav Hampton and Klara Vertes, went on to assist me in putting the pieces of this complicated puzzle of a book together. I already admired Sav's and Klara's smarts and curiosity; now I also marvel at their tolerance.

At the MIT Press, editors Thomas Weaver and Gabriela Bueno Gibbs provided unstinting support and sure-handed guidance, transmitted with tact and wit. Thanks to Judith Feldmann and the production team for their alert oversight of these unconventional pages. To design the book, Tom Weaver brought on Rosa Nussbaum of Studio Christopher Victor, a dream collaborator—which is to say, Rosa's version of this book realizes its unconscious wishes in ways its dreamer never could have.

"With Ray," said his friend Joan Harrison, "behind every door you open, there's another thousand people." Johnson's world was brought to life for me by the following interviewees, many of whom also shared their boxes of Ray-mail: Betsy Baker, Mary Bauermeister, Frances Beatty, AA Bronson, Charlton Burch, Michael Cooper, Richard Craven, Robin Lee Crutchfield, David Ebony, Michael Findlay, Alvin Friedman-Kien, Sandra Gering, Coco Gordon, Helen Harrison, Joan Harrison and Michael Ach, Robert Heide, Miani Johnson, Wynn Kramarsky, Ero Lippold, Tiana Lippold Benway, Gracie Mansion, Stephen Paul Miller, Don Mistretta, Judy Newman, Frank Olt and Meredith McRoberts, Clive Phillpot, Larry Poons, Henry Martin and Berty Skuber, Linda Rosenkrantz and Chris Finch, Peter Schuyff, Joel Smith, Sheila Sporer, Marie Tavroges Stilkind, Charles Stuckey, Robert Warner, John Walter, Daniel Wells, John Willenbecher, Karl Wirsum and Lorri Gunn Wirsum. Some are no longer here to receive thanks, but gratitude is a hard thing to keep to oneself. I also cannot help wishing that the extraordinary Henry Martin had lived to finally write his book about Ray.

A strange twist of fate turned Madison Smartt Bell from a friend into the agent who guided this book into print. A happy result, certainly, but the greater gift was his unflinching backing of the project, which nerved me to keep going. Gregg Horowitz, my in-house backer, is the only person to have read every word of every version—a distinction not to be wished for, perhaps, but one he has borne with the humor that makes life with him such a pleasure. He is a gentle editor but a tough questioner, and his questions made a difference at every step along the way. Heather Cass White also applied much-needed tough love to these pages, even as she supplied a steady flow of unconditional encouragement (supplemented by periodic hosannas from the Fowler-White chorus). Liza Lorwin and Vernon Shetley each cast an expert eye over multiple chapters.

More readers: Elizabeth Barnett, Michael Davis, Jody Davies, Carolyn Dever, Lisabeth During, Jonathan Galassi, Kenneth Gross, Karen Hornick, Alison Hughes, Tom Huhn, Suzanne Joelson, Ruby Johnstone (also the designer-manager of the book's website), Susie Linfield, Annabel Manning, Henry Martin, Andrew Moore (who shared his Ray-resources with me as well), Margot Spindelman, Nancy Steele, Kenneth Wampler, Liza White, John Willenbecher, and Mark Wollaeger, plus the generous souls who reviewed the project for MIT Press. And more encouragers: Jay Bernstein, Bianca Calabresi, Karen Cooper, Dirk Denison, Idit Dobbs-Weinstein, Lynn Duffy, Susan Frankel, Jonathan Gilmore, Karen Gratch, Nora Griffin, Michael Kelly, Linda Leavell, Carol Levy, Edward Levy, David Salkin, Rachel Saltz, Shelley Wanger, and Mike Zega. David Frankel had been telling me stories for years about this incredible teacher he had had in college, Bill Wilson, and suddenly, those stories came into startlingly sharp focus.

KEY TO ABBREVIATED REFERENCES

Some archival materials I cite also appear in one or more of the publications listed below; in those cases, archival notes are followed by publication references and page numbers.

RJE The Ray Johnson Estate.
RBAAA The William S. Wilson Archive of Ray Johnson, Ryerson & Burnham Art and Architecture Archives, Art Institute of Chicago.
C *Ray Johnson: Correspondences*. Ed. Donna de Salvo and Catherine Gudis. Paris and New York: Flammarion, 1999.
CNCMA *Correspondence: An Exhibition of the Letters of Ray Johnson*. Ed. Richard Craven. Raleigh, NC: North Carolina Museum of Art, 1976.
HSIAT *Ray Johnson: How Sad I Am Today ....* Texts by Michael Morris, Sharla Sava, Peter Schuyff and Muffet Jones. Vancouver, CA: Morris and Helen Belkin Gallery, 2001.
HTDAB *How to Draw a Bunny*. Dir. John Walter. Palm Pictures and Mr. Mudd Productions, 2002.
NN *Not Nothing: Selected Writings by Ray Johnson, 1954–1994*. Ed. Elizabeth Zuba. Los Angeles: Siglio, 2014.
RJCO *Ray Johnson c/o*. Ed. Caitlin Haskell with Jordan Carter. Chicago: Art Institute of Chicago, 2021.
TWTA *That Was the Answer: Interviews with Ray Johnson*. Ed. Julie J. Thomson. Chicago: Soberscove Press, 2018.
RJ Ray Johnson
BW Bill Wilson
DB David Bourdon
FXP Frances X. Profumo
HM Henry Martin
MW May Wilson
RL Richard Lippold
TS Toby Spiselman

NOTES

A NOTE ON THE TYPE

Philip Blocklyn, "'It's Right the Way It Is': Printing at Black Mountain College," *Journal of Black Mountain College Studies* 12 [Spring 2020], published May 2021: https://www.blackmountainstudiesjournal.org/blocklyn-printing

CHAPTER 1

I

"The Willard Gallery": Grace Glueck, "What Happened? Nothing," *New York Times*, April 11, 1965: X.18.
my ghost: RJ to BW, January 21, 1958, Binder *1958 01-07*, page *58 01 21*, The William S. Wilson Collection of Ray Johnson, RBAAA, Art Institute of Chicago.
"You'd be walking": author's interview with Henry Martin, June 11, 2017.
"Ray wasn't a person": Billy Linich (Name) in HTDAB.

II

"Wilson came into possession of a page": Author's digital archive. Original accessed at the home of William S. Wilson, New York City. Present location unknown.
"an immense archive of materials by, for, and about Ray Johnson": Graphic designer Irma Boom evokes the eccentric, expressive character of Bill Wilson's archive in her layouts for *Ray Johnson c/o*, the catalogue for the show of the same name held at the Art Institute of Chicago from November 26, 2021 to March 21, 2022. The catalogue and show were edited and curated by Caitlin Haskell with Jordan Carter and marked the acquisition of the Wilson materials by the Art Institute and Ryerson & Burnham Art and Architecture Archives.
"Where were you born?"/Your questions: Sevim Fesci, "Oral History Interview with Ray Johnson (1968)" in *TWTA*, 25–26. Also Archives of American Art, Smithsonian Institution: https://www.aaa.si.edu/collections/interviews/oral-history-interview-ray-johnson-13236.
"The father ... grandfather ... even the 'sugar dada'": Clive Phillpot, "The Mailed Art of Ray Johnson," *Eternal Network: A Mail Art Anthology*, ed. Chuck Welch (Calgary, Alberta: University of Calgary Press, 1995), 25.
"Ray Johnson plays": William S. Wilson, "Ray Johnson," in Ray Johnson, *The Paper Snake* (New York: Something Else Press, 1965), n.p.
"I was soon sending": Edward M. Plunkett et al., "Send Letters, Postcards, Drawings, and Objects: The New York Correspondence School," *Art Journal* 36, no. 3 (Spring 1977): 233–234.
"The Zen Master": Tim Keane, "Ray Johnson: The Zen Master of the Social Network," *Utne Reader*, Winter 2014, http://www.utne.com/media/ray-johnson-zm0z14wzsau.

III

Mail art has no history: RJ to DB, December 25, 1975. NN, 143; CNCMA, no. 18.
"Homogenous empty time": Walter Benjamin, "Theses on the Philosophy of History," *Illuminations*, ed. Hannah Arendt, trans. Harry Zohn (New York: Schocken, 1969), 261.
"they believe": Siegfried Kracauer, *The Mass Ornament: Weimar Essays*, ed. Thomas Y. Levin (Cambridge, MA: Harvard University Press, 1995), 49.
"can be seized": Benjamin, "Theses," 254.
"My own autobiography": Sue Gangel, "An Interview with John Ashbery," *Poets on Their Work*, ed. Joe David Bellamy (Urbana and Chicago: University of Illinois Press, 1984), 10.
"Ray Johnson likes to tell": Rosalind Constable, "The Mailaway Art of Ray Johnson," *New York Magazine*, March 2, 1970, 43.
"You are remarkably reticent": David Bourdon and Ray Johnson, "An Interview with nosnhoJ yaR," *Artforum* 3 (September 1964): 29.
i like STARS: *Th Thee For anð Lai Book*, ca. 1955. RJ, unique artist book made for Remy Charlip, n.p. Binder, *Unique Books*, The William S. Wilson Collection of Ray Johnson, RBAAA, Art Institute of Chicago.
So when you ask me about being born: Fesci, "Oral History Interview."

IV

"a New York opening without a show": "Mary Josephson" (Brian O'Doherty), "Ray Johnson at Betty Parsons," *Art in America* 61 (May–June 1973): 105.

V

"In Ray Johnson's collages, words and images": Lawrence Alloway, "Ray Johnson's History of the Betty Parsons Gallery," *The Nation*, February 5, 1973: 190.
"Mr. Rauschenberg's Soho friends ... bobby-pin over each ear": Charlotte Curtis, "Artist Redefines Black-Tie Dinner for a Princess," *New York Times*, October 9, 1972, 72.
"Johnson merely explained": Alloway, "Ray Johnson's History," 190.

VI

There is a Ray Johnson negro dancer: RJ to Michael Morris, May 11, 1968, RJE, box 48, folder 1968; NN, 73.

to stay out: RJ to Dorothy Miller, Binder *1955*, page *55 02 14A*, The William S. Wilson Collection of Ray Johnson, RBAAA, Art Institute of Chicago.

VII

"the Plymouth Rock": Henry Geldzahler, *Pop Art: 1955–1970* (Sydney: Art Gallery of New South Wales, 1985), 182.

IX

ONE TWO THREE: RJ to BW, January 1963. Binder *Book About Death 63-65*, page *undated*, The William S. Wilson Collection of Ray Johnson, RBAAA, Art Institute of Chicago.

I AM NORMAN: Binder, *Norman Solomon before 1995*, page *59 10 05*, The William S. Wilson Collection of Ray Johnson, RBAAA, Art Institute of Chicago.

X

"place him with such": "Cover," uncredited note on contents page, *ArtNews* 57 (January 1958): 5.

"The Grandma Moses": William S. Wilson, "Grandma Moses of the Underground," *Art and Artists*, May 1968, 16–17.

I have not seen Arts: Binder *1958 01-07*, page *58 01 19*, The William S. Wilson Collection of Ray Johnson, RBAAA, Art Institute of Chicago.

Bob Rauschenberg told me: RJ to BW. Binder *1958 01-07*, page *58 03 13*, The William S. Wilson Collection of Ray Johnson, RBAAA, Art Institute of Chicago.

XI

I went to Cy Twombly's: RJ to BW. Binder 1958 07-12, page *58 10 26*, The William S. Wilson Collection of Ray Johnson, RBAAA, Art Institute of Chicago.

XII

Rosalind Constable's presence at the When It Rains It Pours meeting was noted by May Wilson ("One look at Rosalind Constable's face, very impressive"), Binder *1969 09-12*, page *After 69 11 05*, The William S. Wilson Collection of Ray Johnson, RBAAA, Art Institute of Chicago.

"A letter from Ray Johnson"/"this was not the first time": Rosalind Constable, "Mailaway Art": 42.

XIII

"Time-Life's avant-garde specialist": "Between the Lines" (front material, no author given), *New York Magazine*, December 16, 1968, 4.

"'Rosie Constable,' says an admirer": John Wilcock, "The Whither Eye of Time Magazine." *Village Voice*, January 11, 1962, 2.

"which is a pity": Wilcock, "Whither Eye," 2.

Those Jasper Johns alphabetized: RJ, "Frankie & Me," *Village Voice*, June 4, 1964, 4.

"of questionable worth": Louis Calta, "Theater: 'Home Movies'; Off-Beat Musical Found Too Far Out to Grasp," *New York Times*, May 12, 1964, 32.

Living Theater program: Binder *1963 03-06 Yam Fest*, page *63 05 15*, The William S. Wilson Collection of Ray Johnson, RBAAA, Art Institute of Chicago.

Jasper Johns has a sell-out: RJ to BW. Binder *1958 01-07*, page *58 02 04*, The William S. Wilson Collection of Ray Johnson, RBAAA, Art Institute of Chicago.

Someone once asked: RJ to Nam June Paik. Binder *REJ Paik + Moorman, mid-1960s*, page *68 11 30*. The William S. Wilson Collection of Ray Johnson, RBAAA, Art Institute of Chicago. NN, 83.

XV

"forming a neat political cut ... we don't want to hear": "Josephson," "Ray Johnson at Betty Parsons," 104–105.

"Mary Josephson, one of my alter egos": Brian O'Doherty, *Postwar American Art: The Novak/O'Doherty Collection*, ed. Christina Kennedy (Dublin: Irish Museum of Modern Art, 2011), 97.

the Duchampian ethic: my references throughout the book to the Duchampian ethic that declares that everyone is an artist are informed by Thierry de Duve's discussion of this concept in *Kant after Duchamp* (Cambridge, MA: MIT Press, 1996).

"The Key Was on the Table": RJ to BW. Binder *1964 09-12*, page *64 10 09*, The William S. Wilson Collection of Ray Johnson, RBAAA, Art Institute of Chicago.

"first idea": Lewis Carroll, *Alice's Adventures in Wonderland* (New York: Doubleday, Page & Co., 1916), 7.

XVI

"A chronicler": Benjamin, "Theses," 254.

"In a more pedagogic mood": Robert Pincus Witten in Edward M. Plunkett et al., "Send Letters, Postcards, Drawings, and Object: The New York Correspondance School," *Art Journal* 36, no. 3 (Spring 1977): 239.

Remember what Asawa said: RJ to Lorna Blaine, 1947. Asheville Art Museum, Black Mountain College Collection, Gift of the Black Mountain College Project and Lorna Blaine.

"Richard and I tried ... performance": Frances Beatty, quoted in Amei Wallach, "Dear Friends of Ray, and Audiences of One," *New York Times*, February 28, 1999, Section 2, 45.

"The past can be seized only," "seize hold of a memory," "void ... irretrievably": Benjamin, "Theses," 255.

"He was so intent": William S. Wilson, *Ray Johnson En Rapport*, ed. Frances F. L. Beatty (New York: Richard Feigen & Co., 2006), n.p.

XVII

Bill, // A response immediately: Binder *1958 01-07*, page *58 01 21*. The William S. Wilson Collection of Ray Johnson, RBAAA, Art Institute of Chicago.

"I is some one else": Arthur Rimbaud, *Illuminations and Other Prose Poems*, trans. Louise Varêse (New York: New Directions, 1957), xxvii.

Dear Bill Wilson: RJ to BW. Binder 1966 08-12, page 66 12 30. The William S. Wilson Collection of Ray Johnson, RBAAA, Art Institute of Chicago; NN, 41.

I'm intrigued and interested: RJ, quoted in Richard Bernstein, "Ray Johnson's World," *Andy Warhol's Interview*, August 1972, 40. TWTA, 58.

CHAPTER 2

I

Wallace Stevens, "Connoisseur of Chaos," in *Wallace Stevens: Collected Poetry & Prose* (New York: Library of America, 1997), 194.

II

Did you ever read: RJ, *MO Questionnaire*. Binder *1955*, page *55 09 ??*, The William S. Wilson Collection of Ray Johnson, RBAAA, Art Institute of Chicago.

A shipping clerk: RJ, untitled moticos mailing, ca. 1955. Binder *Ray Johnson's Own Publications* B, The William S. Wilson Collection of Ray Johnson, RBAAA, Art Institute of Chicago; RJCO, 179.

I intended: cited in John Wilcock, "The Village Square," *Village Voice*, October 26, 1955: 3.

"i read": John Wilcock to RJ, August 26, 1955, transcribed by RJ. Binder 1955, page *After 58 09 00*, The William S. Wilson Collection of Ray Johnson, RBAAA, Art Institute of Chicago.

It's a good word: cited in Wilcock, "Village Square," *Village Voice*.

"made a mailing list": Norman Solomon to Marie Tavroges Stilkind. Binder *Norman Solomon Before 95*, page *55 08?? (96 08 05)*, The William S. Wilson Collection of Ray Johnson, RBAAA, Art Institute of Chicago.

III

Ever see any KURT SCHWITTERS: RJ to Lorna Blaine Halper, March 7, 1947, Asheville Art Museum, Black Mountain College Collection, Gift of the Black Mountain College Project and Lorna Blaine.

"My aim is the total," "Create it ourselves": Kurt Schwitters, "From Merz," in *PPPPPP: Kurt Schwitters, Poems Performance Pieces Proses Plays Poetics*, ed. and trans. Jerome Rothenberg and Pierre Joris (Cambridge, MA: Exact Change, 2002), 218, 221.

everyone is moving: RJ to MW. Binder *1959 01-05*, page *59 05 02*, The William S. Wilson Collection of Ray Johnson, RBAAA, Art Institute of Chicago.

"Do you want me": Ruth Asawa to RJ. Binder *1956 01-09*, page *56 07 11*, The William S. Wilson Collection of Ray Johnson, RBAAA, Art Institute of Chicago.

IV

"That day Ray": William S. Wilson, *Ray Johnson: The Early Years*, ed. Frances F.L. Beatty (New York: Richard L. Feigen & Co., 2007).

"Ray took the moticos": Wilson, *Early Years*.

V

On the Gutai-Pollock-Friedman connection, see Benjamin Genocchio, "Painting with Hands and Feet," *New York Times*, August 21, 2009; Hal Foster, "1955a," in *Art Since 1900: Modernism, Antimodernism, Postmodernism*, ed. Hal Foster, Rosalind Krauss, Yves-Alain Bois, and Benjamin H. D. Buchloh (London: Thames & Hudson, 2004), 373–375.

Bob Friedman showed me: RJ to Jiro Yoshihara, July 11, 1956. Transcribed by John Walter, Binder *1956 01-09*, page *56 07 11*, The William S. Wilson Collection of Ray Johnson, RBAAA, Art Institute of Chicago.

"from whose unseen": Percy Bysshe Shelley, "Ode to the West Wind," *Selected Poetry*, ed. Neville Rogers (London: Oxford University Press, 1968), 355.

"Like information": Suzi Gablik, "700 Collages by Ray Johnson," *Location* 1 (Summer 1964), 55.

VI

"the newest member": *ArtNews* 56, no. 9 (January 1958): 5.

I loaned my dear friend Suzi: RJ to MW. Binder *1958 01-07*, page *58 03 ??*, The William S. Wilson Collection of Ray Johnson, RBAAA, Art Institute of Chicago.

"protest … my collage": Robert Rauschenberg, *Art in Process: The Visual Development of a Collage*, prepared by Elayne H. Varian with statements by the artists (New York: Finch College, 1967), n.p.

"a short note": Elayne Varian to RJ. Binder *1967 01-02*, page *67 02 02*, accession # *2018.802.45.2*, The William S. Wilson Collection of Ray Johnson, RBAAA, Art Institute of Chicago; RJCO, 286. Johnson's reply to this letter was included in the *Art in Process* collage show, along with letters responding to similar requests sent by Varian to VanDerBeek and Weil.

"Also lost in that fire": See Roni Feinstein, "The Unknown Robert Rauschenberg: The Betty Parsons Exhibition of 1951," *Arts Magazine* (January 1985): 126–131.

"Rauschenberg found Albers's model": Robert Rauschenberg, "Statement on Josef Albers," unpublished typescript, n.d. Robert Rauschenberg Foundation website. Accessed November 27, 2022. www.rauschenbergfoundation.org/art/archive/albers.

"Four Pink Fish": RJ to Harry Torczyner, May 20, 1965, RJE, box 49, folder 1965.

VII

"Rauschenberg met": Calvin Tomkins, *Off the Wall: A Portrait of Robert Rauschenberg* (New York: Picador, 2005), 99.

“a filled-in, deep-water inlet … lofts”: Holland Cotter, “Where City History Was Made, a 50’s Group Made Art History,” *New York Times*, January 5, 1993, C1.

Little boats: RJ to Andy Oates. Binder *Autumn 1948–1952*, page *51 09 01*, The William S. Wilson Collection of Ray Johnson, RBAAA, Art Institute of Chicago.

Robert Indiana, “Coenties Slip,” published in *Richard Stankiewicz and Robert Indiana: An Exhibition of Recent Sculptures and Paintings* (Minneapolis, MN: Walker Art Center, 1963), n.p.

VIII

Program for the Black Mountain production of *The Ruse of Medusa*, available online in the State Library of North Carolina’s digital collections, accessed November 14, 2022, http://digital.ncdcr.gov/cdm/ref/collection/p249901coll44/id/1107.

How have I got through life: RJ to George Ashley. Binder *1974 05-12*, page *1974 Summer*, The William S. Wilson Collection of Ray Johnson, RBAAA, Art Institute of Chicago.

“Ray can tell you”: RL to FXP, October 21, 1948, RJE, box D360, folder 1.

my friends … albert and ruth: RJ to FXP, November 8, 1948, RJE, box D360, folder 1.

“Burn when read”: Ruth Asawa to FXP to RJ, January 16, 1949, RJE, box D360, folder 1.

Louise said: RJ to FXP, May 2, 1949, RJE, box D360, folder 1.

violets from Mrs. Cage: RJ to Andy Oates, Binder *Autumn 1948–1952*, page *51 09 01*, The William S. Wilson Collection of Ray Johnson, RBAAA, Art Institute of Chicago.

IX

John Cage, “Lecture on Nothing,” in *Silence* (Middletown, CT: Wesleyan University Press, 1961), 109–126.

“stood up part way through”: Cage, “Foreword,” in *Silence*, ix.

Norman Solomon’s Doberman: Binder *1973 01-07*, page *73 02 09*, The William S. Wilson Collection of Ray Johnson, RBAAA, Art Institute of Chicago; HSIAT, 67.

“airports for the lights”: Cage, “On Robert Rauschenberg, Artist, and His Work,” in *Silence*, 102.

X

influenced/who was: cited in Harvey Aronson, “What, You Never Heard from Ray Johnson?” *Newsday* (Long Island, NY), January 18, 1969, W12.

“Happenings are not”: Allan Kaprow, “Happenings in the New York Scene” (1961), in *Essays on the Blurring of Art and Life*, ed. Jeff Kelley (Berkeley and Los Angeles: University of California Press, 2003), 21.

An Interview: *A Tribute to John Cage: Prepared Box for John Cage*, ed. Allan Kaprow (Cincinnati: Carl Solway Gallery, 1987), 5B.

“anti-Brunelleschian … *legittima*”: Judith F. Rodenbeck, *Radical Prototypes: Allan Kaprow and the Invention of Happenings* (Cambridge, MA: MIT Press, 2011), 126.

XI

“Germans to Teach Art”: news item reproduced in Eva Diaz, *The Experimenters: Chance and Design at Black Mountain College* (Chicago: University of Chicago Press, 2015), 16.

“to open eyes”: Brenda Danilowitz and Frederick Horowitz, *Josef Albers: To Open Eyes* (New York: Phaidon, 2009).

“Attentiveness to details”: Diaz, 29.

“art was intelligible”: Diaz, 42.

In Design, RJ to Lorraine and Eino Johnson, Binder *Summer 1945–Summer 1948*, page *March 1946? ??*, The William S. Wilson Collection of Ray Johnson, RBAAA, Art Institute of Chicago.

XII

“Outstanding in the Art Department”: newspaper item reproduced in *Lightworks No. 22: The Ray Johnson Issue* (2000), 6.

There are lectures: CNCMA, no. 66, letter headed Thursday in my Art Comp. class.

what dance I was going to: Henry Martin, “‘Should an Eyelash Last Forever?’: An Interview with Ray Johnson (1982),” TWTA, 126; C, 188. The interview was originally published in *Lotta Poetica* (Verona, Italy) 2, no. 6 (February 1984): 2–24.

Friday morning: CNCMA: no. 66, letter headed, “Friday morning in my Art Comp. class.”

Dear Sirs: RJ to BW. Binder *1965 04-05*, page *65 04 ??*, accession # 2018.802.40.3, The William S. Wilson Collection of Ray Johnson, RBAAA, Art Institute of Chicago; RJCO, 156.

XIII

Pete—next Sat nite: Binder *Di Cresce*, page *undated*, The William S. Wilson Collection of Ray Johnson, RBAAA, Art Institute of Chicago.

“Twardowicz, Number 11”: RJ to BW. Binder *1964 07-09*, page *64 04 25*, The William S. Wilson Collection of Ray Johnson, RBAAA, Art Institute of Chicago.

XIV

“I met Ray”: Norman Solomon to Chuck Welch. Binder *Norman Solomon After 95*, page *95 07 18*, The William S. Wilson Collection of Ray Johnson, RBAAA, Art Institute of Chicago.

I sent this on a postcard to Dorothea: RJ to BW. Author’s digital archive. Original accessed at the home of William S. Wilson, New York City. Present location unknown.

the most complex painting: RJ to FXP, June 4, 1951, RJE, box D360, folder 3: Correspondence dated 1951–1953.

“prison”: Albers, cited on Whitney Museum of American Art webpage, https://whitney.org/

collection/works/4079; "The scheme of the *Homages* has no real esthetic consequences by itself. There were hundreds of possibilities, but since my main problem is color … let's have a scheme, a cooking pot that cooks for four people, and no more. Therefore, let the colors react in the prison in which I put them." Accessed January 10, 2021.

Twenty-seven squares, RJ to FXP, June 30, 1951, RJE, box D360, folder 3: correspondence dated 1951–1953.

"like looking at the underside": "L.C.," *Magazine Antiques* (March 1952): 44.

a riot of violent color: RJ to FXP, October 17, 1951, RJE, box D360, folder 3: Correspondence dated 1951–1953.

is painting an old salad bowl: RJ to Lorraine and Eino Johnson. Binder *Summer 1945–Summer 1948*, page *47 10. ??*, The William S. Wilson Collection of Ray Johnson, RBAAA, Art Institute of Chicago.

"left us," "Objects": Kaprow, "The Legacy of Jackson Pollock" (1958), in *Blurring*, 7–8.

XV

I am painting: RJ to FXP, March 28, 1953, RJE, box D360, folder 3: Correspondence dated 1951–1953.

XVI

"In order … are generated": Josef Albers, "Teaching Form Through Practice" (1928), http://www.albersfoundation.org/teaching/josef-albers/texts/. Accessed January 10, 2021.

albers garden: RJ to Lorna Blaine (Halper), ca. January 1947. Asheville Art Museum, Black Mountain College Collection, Gift of the Black Mountain College Project and Lorna Blaine.

"corrugated cardboard": Albers, "Teaching Form Through Practice."

"school with very little … waste bin": Fritz Horstman, "The Preliminary Course and the Matière," *Art Section*, August 2017: http://www.theartsection.com/albers---the-matire. Accessed December 10, 2021.

"nobody could see": cited in Michael Beggs, "Josef Albers: Photographs of *Matières*," *Leap Before You Look: Black Mountain College, 1933–1957*, ed. Helen Molesworth with Ruth Erickson (New Haven, CT: Yale University Press, 2015), 86.

"Longevity was not," "Instead of keeping": Beggs, 88.

XVII

"You have been extremely": William Carlos Williams to BW. Binder *1956 01-09*, page *56 04 27*, The William S. Wilson Collection of Ray Johnson, RBAAA, Art Institute of Chicago.

"Ray Johnson has not been wrong": BW to Terry Haller. Binder *1958 08-12*, page *58 11 19*, The William S. Wilson Collection of Ray Johnson, RBAAA, Art Institute of Chicago.

"Let me tell you": Julian Beck to RJ, September 21, 1955, sent by Ray Johnson to Bill Wilson, April 18, 1959. Binder *1959 01-05*, page *59 04 19*, The William S. Wilson Collection of Ray Johnson, RBAAA, Art Institute of Chicago.

XVIII

"the Plymouth Rock": Henry Geldzahler, *Pop Art: 1955–1970* (Sydney: Art Gallery of New South Wales, 1985), 182.

XIX

I'm the only painter: cited in Suzi Gablik and John Russell, *Pop Art Redefined* (New York: Praeger, 1969), 17. Johnson would reprint this phrase on a mail art flyer.

"I speak as one": Frank O'Hara, "For James Dean," in *The Collected Poems of Frank O'Hara*, ed. Donald Allen (Berkeley, CA: University of California Press, 1995), 228.

"The James Dean necrophilia": cited in Joe LeSueur, *Digressions on Some Poems by Frank O'Hara: A Memoir* (New York: Farrar, Straus and Giroux, 2003), 64.

"too out: cited in LeSueur, *Digressions*, 64.

the only extant copies: see Donald Allen's "Editor's Note" in O'Hara, *Collected Poems*, vi.

XXI

"that fancy form," "You are so new": Jiro Yoshihara to RJ. Binder *1957*, page *57 03 28*, The William S. Wilson Collection of Ray Johnson, RBAAA, Art Institute of Chicago.

The New York Correspondance School has no: RJ to DB, December 25, 1975, NN, 143; CNCMA, no. 18.

OLD MOTICOS: RJE, box 43, folder "Writings—early moticos," NN 2; CNCMA, no. 44.

"In a sense … apprehend," "the educator": William Empson, *Seven Types of Ambiguity* (New York: New Directions, 1966), 3.

I mean, all of these things: Shirley Samberg, "*That's Interesting* with Ray Johnson (1984)," TWTA, 191.

XXIV

"Ray, in coding": William S. Wilson, *A Book About A Book About Death* (Amsterdam: Kunstverein Publishing, 2009), 27.

"Ray had been told," "is pronounced as the word": Wilson, *A Book About A Book About Death*, 27.

XXV

"Ami": Wilson, *A Book About A Book About Death*, 50.

"Introduced by Ed": Author's interview with Karl Wirsum, February 17, 2017.

"wanted to see": Wilson, *A Book About A Book About Death*, 43.

XXVI

"an outsider," "I ran no risk": Dick Higgins, "The Hatching of the Paper Snake," *Lightworks No. 22: The Ray Johnson Issue* (2000): 26.

I got proofs: RJ to MW. Binder *1964 09-12*, page *64 11 04*, The William S. Wilson Collection of Ray Johnson, RBAAA, Art Institute of Chicago.
"what the book": Higgins, "Hatching," 28.

XXVII

You asked: RJ to Dorothy Miller. Binder *1964 04-05*, page *65 04 22*, accession # *2018.802.40.*7, The William S. Wilson Collection of Ray Johnson, RBAAA, Art Institute of Chicago.
It sheds, It is a very short space, It is for a moment, It is a person of 20 years, It is the hard: RJ, moticos mailing in the form of a letter with the salutation, Dear Lorraine. Binder *1958 01-07*, page *58 03 28*, The William S. Wilson Collection of Ray Johnson, RBAAA, Art Institute of Chicago.
"We met … drop out": Hilton Kramer, "The Sadness of Ray Johnson in Big New Whitney Show," *New York Observer*, February 8, 1999. Accessed November 23, 2022. http://observer.com/1999/02/the-sadness-of-ray-johnson-in-big-new-whitney-show/

CHAPTER 3

I

"Now could you tell me" … contend with: Sevim Fesci, "Oral History Interview with Ray Johnson" (1968), TWTA, 30–32. Also Archives of American Art, Smithsonian Institution: https://www.aaa.si.edu/collections/interviews/oral-history-interview-ray-johnson-13236.
I saw your beautiful ICE: RJ to Joseph Cornell, November 25, 1966, Joseph Cornell papers, box 2, folder 43, Archives of American Art, Smithsonian Institution, https://www.si.edu/object/ray-johnson-letter-joseph-cornell%3AAAADCD_item_8101.

II

There exists for me, At the moment I wish, There is obviously very little, carefully arranged in strict sequence, There are mostly no instructions, The problem will be solved, a true friend, Would sending the stuff, Should Mr. Alloway, The act of composing and distributing: "Correspondance Art," April 1, 1964, RJE, box 48, folder 1964; *NN*, 19.
add half hot tap water and mix. RJ to BW. I have been living on onion and cheese sandwiches washed down with what they call in this part of the world tomato soup. That is katsup stolen to-wich [*sic*] you add half hot tap water and mix. Binder *1962 01-05*, page *62 02 21*, The William S. Wilson Collection of Ray Johnson, RBAAA, Art Institute of Chicago.
"I want very much indeed": Lawrence Alloway to RJ, June 21, 1963, RJE, box 48, folder 1963.
"Johnson said of his correspondence school": Lawrence Alloway, "Ray Johnson," *Art Journal* 36, no. 3 (Spring 1977): 236.
"All of us are looped … text and reproduction": Lawrence Alloway, *Network: Art and the Complex Present* (Ann Arbor: UMI Research Press, 1984), 4, 6. For an extended consideration of the relation between Alloway's theory and Johnson's practice, see Stephen Moonie, "A Poet of 'Non-ressentiment'? Lawrence Alloway, Ray Johnson, and the Art World as a Network," *Getty Research Journal* 8 (2016): 161–175.

III

On Michael Malcé's business in the 1960s, see David Gordon, *60's Archiveography: part 2*, 2–4, http://davidgordon.nyc/decade/1960s, accessed November 26, 2022; and Ellery Akers, "The $100 Mickey Mouse," *New York Magazine*, April 29, 1968, 43–45.
"Michael, he's the pioneer of camp": quoted in David Bourdon, "Stacking the Deco," *New York Magazine*, November 11, 1974, 66.
Metaphysique d'ephemera: See Mary Ann Caws's editorial note regarding Cornell's use of this phrase in *Joseph Cornell's Theater of the Mind: Selected Diaries, Letters, and Files*, ed. Mary Ann Caws (New York: Thames and Hudson, 1993), 136.
"'toys for adults' … Christmas gifts": Deborah Solomon, *Utopia Parkway: The Life and Work of Joseph Cornell* (New York: Noonday Press/Farrar, Straus and Giroux, 1967), 67–68, 107.
"Ray Johnson is to the letter": Nicolas and Elena Calas, *Icons and Images of the Sixties* (New York: E.P. Dutton, 1971), 319; cited in Alloway "Ray Johnson," 235.

IV

"box of ice cubes": Joseph Cornell to Charles Henri Ford, July 27, 1940, in *Joseph Cornell's Theater of the Mind*, 90.
Lil Picard, "Death Rattle Art," *East Village Other*, February 15, 1967, 15.
I have this form. RJ to MW. Binder *1962 05-12*, page *62 11 09*, The William S. Wilson Collection of Ray Johnson, RBAAA, Art Institute of Chicago.
wearing an elegant English blue suit. RJ to Ann Wilson. Binder *Ray in Bellevue*, page *64 08? 09?*, The William S. Wilson Collection of Ray Johnson, RBAAA, Art Institute of Chicago.

V

"Ray at a very tender age": Janet Giffra, "The Early Beginnings in the Life of Raymond E. Johnson." Written for Johnson's memorial at Friends Meeting House, April 29, 1995. Binder *II Unpublished Type-Scripts 1995–2010*, page *95 04 29*, The William S. Wilson Collection of Ray Johnson, RBAAA, Art Institute of Chicago.
"meaningful colors": Richard Lippold, "Ray Johnson," Binder *I Unpublished Type-Scripts*, page *ca. 1967*, The William S. Wilson Collection of Ray Johnson, RBAAA, Art Institute of Chicago.
"sudden rightnesses": Wallace Stevens, "Of Modern Poetry," *Stevens: Collected Poetry & Prose*,

ed. Frank Kermode and Joan Richardson (New York: Library of America, 1997), 219.

"I spoke with Diane di Prima": RJ to George Brecht, letter dated "January 39th, 1963," Binder*1963 01-02*, page *63 01 39*, The William S. Wilson Collection of Ray Johnson, RBAAA, Art Institute of Chicago.

"STAN VAN DER BEEK, filmmaker ... hard to tell you about": George Ashley to MW. Binder *1966 01-07*, page *66 04 27*, The William S. Wilson Collection of Ray Johnson, RBAAA, Art Institute of Chicago.

VII

I'm not a painter: interview by Shirley Samberg for "That's Interesting," WCWP 88.1 FM, September 13, 1984, transcribed by John Walter, TWTA, 190.

"a founder ... intriguing in themselves": Dore Ashton, "New York Commentary," *Studio International* 172, no. 879 (July 1966): 46–47.

"A friend recalls being distracted": Author's interview with John Willenbecher, April 21, 2017.

Bill after you left. RJ to BW. Binder *1966 08-12*, page *66 10 10*, The William S. Wilson Collection of Ray Johnson, RBAAA, Art Institute of Chicago.

VIII

Merce's concert last night: RJ to RL. Binder *1957*, page *RL:GM ca. 1957*, The William S. Wilson Collection of Ray Johnson, RBAAA, Art Institute of Chicago.

Dear James Waring: RJE, box 48, folder 1965.

IX

Jill,/ Your dance last night: RJE, box 48, folder 1964.

My sister Jill: RJ, "Review by Ray Johnston [*sic*] (In the Style of Floating Bear): BOB Morris at Green Opening," *Floating Bear* no. 27 (November 1963): n.p.

"submit a petition": Jill Johnston, "Dance Journal," *Village Voice*, November 9, 1967, 24.

"I didn't correspond with Ray ... one noticed": *Artbreaking*, radio show hosted by Charlie Finch, WBAI FM, New York, March 30, 1995. Panel on Ray Johnson featuring Mark Bloch, Chuck Close, Richard Feigen, Jill Johnston, and Knight Landesman. Transcribed by John Walter. Binder *1995 01-05*, *95 03 30*, The William S. Wilson Collection of Ray Johnson, RBAAA, Art Institute of Chicago.

X

"She's too scary": Billy Name, cited in Randy Kennedy, "Dorothy Podber, 75, Artist and Trickster, Is Dead," *New York Times*, February 19, 2008, Section A, 22.

"a terrorist," "a marvelous, evil woman": William S. Wilson, cited in Charles Darwent, "Dorothy Podber: 'Witch' Who Shot Warhol's Marilyns," *Independent*, March 13, 2008.

"the wildest, most way-out": Millicent Safro in HTDAB (Walter, 2002), DVD.

XI

Another dream: RJE, box 49, folder 1967.

XII

Suzi sent the Dore Ashton: RJ to RL. Binder *1966 07-12*, page *66 10 8*, The William S. Wilson Collection of Ray Johnson, RBAAA, Art Institute of Chicago.

National Institute of Arts and Letters citation for Ray Johnson, May 25, 1966: Binder *1966 01-07*, page *66 05 25*, The William S. Wilson Collection of Ray Johnson, RBAAA, Art Institute of Chicago.

"Mooreiana": See, for example, RJ to FXP, July 26, 1949, November 2, 1953, May 21, 1954, January 24, 1963, RJE, box D360, correspondence folders 1948–49, 1951–53, 1954–57, 1958–74. Johnson mentions meeting Moore through Profumo, as well as his encounter with Moore at Charles Henri Ford's, in a letter to the poet. Binder *1964 09-12*, page *64 12 09*, The William S. Wilson Collection of Ray Johnson, RBAAA, Art Institute of Chicago.

"Thank you very much, Mr. Johnson": Marianne Moore to RJ. Binder *1967 03-12*, page *67 04 04*, The William S. Wilson Collection of Ray Johnson, RBAAA, Art Institute of Chicago.

"Some say the world": Robert Frost, "Fire and Ice," *The Poetry of Robert Frost*, ed. Edward Connery Lathem (New York: Holt, Rinehart, & Winston, 1969), 220.

My death notice. RJ to Soren Agenoux, February 10, 1967, RJE, box 49, folder 1967; NN, 43.

XIII

"The book, as a total expansion": Stéphane Mallarmé, "Le Livre, Instrument Spirituel," in *Divagations* (Paris: Bibliothèque-Charpentier, 1897), 276. Author's translation.

XIV

Today I turned "Dimple," Today I hung "Dimple," Last night I hit "Dimple": RJ to Sam Wagstaff, n.d., January 25, 1964, February 13, 1964; The "Balzhazzar's Feast" aspect: Johnson to Wagstaff, December 22, 1964, in Samuel Wagstaff Papers, box 2, folder 1, Archives of American Art, Smithsonian Museum. Miriam Kienle situates the story of Johnson's *Balzhazzar's Feast* in the context of network theory in "Facing Others: Ray Johnson's Portrait of a Curator as a Network," *Archives of American Art Journal* 59, no. 2 (Fall 2020): 24–45.

"wrote over against ... brought it to an end": *Daniel* 5.5–26 (JPS).

CHAPTER 4

I

Golly gee/"Gee, Ray": David Bourdon and Philip Leider, "The New York Correspondence School," *Artforum* 6, no. 2 (October 1967): 55.

"In 1970, Leider went": Thomas Crow, "On Philip Leider's 'How I Spent My Summer Vacation,'" *Artforum* 51, no. 1 (September 2012): 92–95.

II

a sampling of whimsical, poetic responses: Binder *Oversized Material Archives of the New York Correspondence School*, page *Carolee Schneemann, 2018.802.388 (p. 1)*, The William S. Wilson Collection of Ray Johnson, RBAAA, Art Institute of Chicago; RJCO, 190.

"Dear Miss Selznick": RJ to BW. Binder *1963 01-02*, page *63 02 19D*, The William S. Wilson Collection of Ray Johnson, RBAAA, Art Institute of Chicago.

A fan: RJ to Bill and Ann Wilson. Binder *1963 07-12*, Page *63 07 21*, accession # *2018.802.28.1*, The William S. Wilson Collection of Ray Johnson, RBAAA, Art Institute of Chicago; RJCO, 274.

III

That year, sociologists: Donald Horton and R. Richard Wohl, "Mass Communication and Para-Social Interaction: Observations on Intimacy at a Distance," *Psychiatry: Journal for the Study of Interpersonal Processes* 19 (1956): 215–229.

Ray Johnson became a fan of the cultish comedian: See Weslea Sidon, "*That's Interesting* with Ray Johnson," in TWTA, 155.

IV

"And what I assume": Walt Whitman, "Song of Myself," *Leaves of Grass and Other Writings*, ed. Michael Moon (New York: W. W. Norton, 2002), 26.

I am trying to find information: RJ to DB, February 26, 1963; sent to BW, May 2, 1974. Binder *1974 05-12*, page *74 05 02*, The William S. Wilson Collection of Ray Johnson, RBAAA, Art Institute of Chicago.

an interview with the artist: Francis Steegmuller, "Duchamp: Fifty Years Later," *Show: A Magazine of the Arts* 3, no. 2 (February1963): 28–29.

"based on a reaction": Marcel Duchamp, "Apropos of Readymades," lecture at the Museum of Modern Art, October 19, 1961, in *The Writings of Marcel Duchamp*, ed. Michel Sanouillet and Elmer Peterson (New York: Da Capo, 1989), 141.

V

"Will you please check who makes the combs (12 in a plastic bag for 29¢)? … Hoping that you will help me with this much more": Jan Van Der Marck to RJ, August 21, 1967, RJE, box 48, folder 1966.

a group of under-knowns: See *Pictures to Be Read/ Poetry to Be Seen: An Exhibition* (Chicago: Museum of Contemporary Art, 1967).

"explicitly dedicated," "known for the charming," "an impossible ideal": Harold Rosenberg, "The Art World: Museum of the New," *New Yorker*, November 18, 1967: 226–227, 231, 234.

"The mingling … forces and energies": Rosenberg, "Collage: Philosophy of Put-Togethers," in *Collage: Critical Views*, ed. Katherine Hoffman (Ann Arbor: UMI Research Press, 1989), 64.

"projections of ideas": Rosenberg, "Museum," 233.

VI

Dear Harold,/ Anything anyone: RJ to Harold Rosenberg. Binder *1967 03-12*, page *67 11 28*, The William S. Wilson Collection of Ray Johnson, RBAAA, Art Institute of Chicago; NN, 65.

I would be upset if: RJ to Rosenberg, November 17, 1967, RJE, box 49, folder 1967.

"I seem to remember … two hills": Rosenberg to RJ, November 25, 1967, RJE, box 49, folder 1967.

VII

It is interesting: RJ to Lotte Drew-Bear, June 21, 1971, RJE, box 49, folder 1971.

Section VIII

"The work strikes the eye": "T.M.," "Ray Johnson," *Arts Magazine*, May 1967: 58.

Got your envelope: RJ to TS, April 16, 1967, RJE, box 49, folder 1967.

"in my dictionary": TS to RJ n.d. Author's digital archive. Document accessed at the home of William S. Wilson, New York City. Present location unknown.

IX

Two hands veil: My discussion of *Duchamp with Star-Haircut* and the two persona-photographs of Duchamp draws on Kate Dempsey Martineau's account of the relation among these works in *Ray Johnson: Selective Inheritance* (Oakland, CA: University of California Press, 2018), 169–184.

The N.Y.C.S. is planning: RJ to Lotte Drew-Bear, February 15, 1968, RJE, box 48, folder 1968.

The New York Correspondence School held: RJ to Jan Van Der Marck, May 13, 1968, RJE, box 48, folder 1968.

"R.J. in white": document signed "Robyn Anderson, Fall 68," RJE, box 48, folder 1968.

not a party or a "happening": RJ to Jackson Mac Low, May 27, 1968, RJE, box 48, folder 1968.

X

"living sculpture": Billy Name in HTDAB.

XI

Pat dear: RJ to Patty Oldenburg (Mucha), March 23, 1964, RJE, box 48, folder 1964; CNCMA, no 38b. See also Dick Higgins's note on the occasion of this letter in CNCMA, front matter.

"What's that?": Barry Schwabsky, "First Break, Larry Poons," *Artforum* (February 2003): 23.

XII

IS MARIANNE MOORE MARIANNE MOORE? Binder *1966 08-12*, page *66 11 02*, accession # *2018.802.44.7*, The William S. Wilson Collection of Ray Johnson, RBAAA, Art Institute of Chicago. Also reproduced in facsimile, with annotations by William S. Wilson, in C, 168–175.

"like a ride on a roller coaster": John Ashbery, "Straight Lines Over Rough Terrain: Marianne Moore," in *Selected Prose*, ed. Eugene Richie (Ann Arbor: UMI Press, 2004), 110.

"Ray so disapproved"; "an expressive significance"; "twoness": William S. Wilson, "Ray Johnson: The One and the Other," C, 165.

"Looking at the letter *M*": Wilson, "The One and the Other," 168.

"was not famous enough": Linda Leavell, *Holding On Upside Down: The Life and Work of Marianne Moore* (New York: Farrar, Straus and Giroux, 2013), 349.

XIII

Marianne Moore certainly: RJ, IS MARIANNE, 1.

XIV

"his favorite word": Author's interview with Henry Martin, June 11, 2017.

"was brilliant but not ... real professionals": Cited in Paisid Aramphongphan, "Real Professionals? Andy Warhol, Fred Herko, and Dance," *Performing Arts Journal* 110 (2015): 3.

"everything Warhol was not": Aramphongphan, 12.

"the time and the place": Steven Watson, *Factory Made: Warhol and the Sixties* (New York: Pantheon, 2003), 172.

"the DY of Andy": William S. Wilson, *A Book About A Book About Death* (Amsterdam: Kunstverein Publishing, 1999), 52.

XV

"My mother, May Wilson ... the last act": William S. Wilson, "Preface" (2004) to reprint of Wilson's 1968 essay, "Prince of Boredom: The Repetitions and Passivities of Andy Warhol," Warholstars.org, ed. Gary Comenas: https://warholstars.org/prince-boredom-warhol-william-wilson.html. Accessed November 22, 2022.

to buy the papers to read: RJ to Bob Benson, June 4, 1968, RJE, box 48, folder 1968.

"some friends/ temporarily": RJ to unknown recipient, July 18, 1968, RJE, box 48, folder 1968.

5:10 pm/ Andy: RJ to Alvin Balkind, dated June 3, 1968 (unsent); Warhol Shot/Kennedy Shot added after June 5, 1968, RJE, box 48, folder 1968.

CHAPTER 5

EPIGRAPH

RJ to Suzi Gablik, April 28, 1973, RJE, box 49, folder 1973.

I

all quotations: RJ to John Gruen, June 8, 1971, RJE, box 49, folder 1971.

II

an exhibition ... "members": RJ to Marcia Tucker, November 9, 1969, RJE, box 48, folder: Whitney Museum 1970.

"an art that presents itself": Marcia Tucker, "Anti-Illusion: Procedures/Materials," in *Anti-Illusion: Procedures/Materials*, ed. James Monte and Marcia Tucker (New York: Whitney Museum of American Art, 1969), 25.

"gives one much to think about": Hilton Kramer, "Art: Melting Ice, Hay, Dog Food, Etc.," *New York Times*, May 24, 1969, 31.

"What you or I might deem ... is a museum": Hilton Kramer, "Art: Out of the Mailbox," *New York Times*, September 12, 1970, 18.

the gems ... on top of each other: RJ to Marcia Tucker, July 23, 1970, Getty Research Institute, Marcia Tucker Papers, box 60, folder 20.

III

"an image-word ... since the mid-60s": Kasha Linville, "Ray Johnson: Whitney Museum of American Art," *Artforum International* 9, no. 3 (November 1970): 86. Marcia Tucker thanks Linville for her help with the *Anti-Illusion* exhibition in *Anti-Illusion: Procedures/Materials*, 4.

IV

I have discussed ... bleak horizon: RJ to Lotte Drew-Bear, June 21, 1971, RJE, box 49, folder 1971.

were still singing ... stairs to Castelli gallery: RJ to Diana Epstein. Binder *Malka Safro with dates*, page *71 10 05*, The William S. Wilson Collection of Ray Johnson, RBAAA, Art Institute of Chicago.

"The logo, a four-holed black button": RJ to John Willenbecher, October 1971, Collection of John Willenbecher.

V

a Joseph Cornell attic: RJ to Philip Leider, September 16, 1968, RJE, box 48, folder 1968.

its like ... Miss you too: RJ, July 19, 1968, RJE, box 48, folder 1968.

Last night I delivered ... wonderful trees: RJ to Ben Vautier. Binder *1969 03-08*, page *69 06 01*, The William S. Wilson Collection of Ray Johnson, RBAAA, Art Institute of Chicago; NN, 86; CNCMA, no. 74.

VI

"as a 'get-well present'": Gary Comenas, "Mark Lancaster Interview, part 1," accessed October 22, 2022, https://warholstars.org/andywarhol/interview/mark/lancaster.html.

a T-shirt that read "MARK": Comenas, "Mark Lancaster Interview, part 2," accessed October 22, 2022: https://warholstars.org/andywarhol/interview/mark/lancaster.html.

rather Dubuffet or Klee-like: RJ to HM, July 13, 1966, mumok—Museum of Modern Art Ludwig Foundation Vienna, OL 434 010.

Richard Hamilton is in town: RJ to Jan Van Der Marck, dated "May 12th," RJE, box 48, folder 1966.

IX

Last Sunday: RJ to Lotte Drew-Bear, September 30, 1969, RJE, box 49, folder 1969.
For a brief description of VICE-Versand, see Deborah Wye and Wendy Weitman, *Eye on Europe: Prints, Books, and Multiples, 1960 to Now* (New York: Museum of Modern Art, 2006), 304.

X

"it is a mapping ... the realm of art": Rosalind Krauss, *The Originality of the Avant-Garde and Other Modernist Myths* (Cambridge, MA: MIT Press, 1985), 9, 17. RJ's personal library, now at RJE, contains a copy of *October* 9 (Summer 1979), in which "Grids" first appeared.
"so much the better": the VICE-Versand edition of Robert Filliou's *Optimistic Box #3* may be found in several museum collections, including those of the Fondazione Bonotto, the Kunstmuseum Liechtenstein, and New York's Museum of Modern Art.
tiny and strikingly ... there as well: Henry Martin, "Should an Eyelash Last Forever? An Interview with Ray Johnson," TWTA, 124. C, 187.
"anticoncept": "Down and Dirty: 'L'Informe' at the Centre Georges Pompidou. Lauren Sedofsky talks with Yves-Alain Bois and Rosalind Krauss," *Artforum* 34, no. 10 (Summer 1996): 92. See also: Yves Alain Bois and Rosalind Krauss, *Formless: A User's Guide* (New York: ZONE Books, 1997); Krauss, "'Informe' without Conclusion," *October* 78 (Autumn 1996): 89–105.

XI

"based on a 1930s": unpublished interview with Suzi Gablik, cited in Muffet Jones, "Selected Biographical Chronology and Exhibition History." C, 206.

XII

"Seeing as," "the flashing": Ludwig Wittgenstein, *Philosophical Investigations*, trans. G. E. M. Anscombe (Oxford: Blackwell, 1958), Bk. II, section xi, 197, 197.
Everybody is a member: RJ to Richard Feigen, April 5, 1970, RJE box 49, folder 1970.
"the grid extends ... fabric": Krauss, *Originality of the Avant-Garde*, 18.
Jones, "Selected Biographical Chronology," C, 205.

XIII

All quotations: Arthur Danto, "The Artworld," in *Aesthetics: A Critical Anthology*, ed. George Dickie, Richard Sclafani, and Ronald Roblin, 2nd ed. (New York: St. Martin's Press, 1989), 171–182.

XIV

Plan: NN, 108; C, 116.
REQUEST: HSIAT, 55.
Johnson had initiated: See Michael Morris, "Ray Johnson: An Appreciation," in HSIAT, 7, 17.
"looped together": Lawrence Alloway, *Network: Art and the Complex Present* (Ann Arbor: UMI Research Press, 1984), 4.

XV

Dear Deaths: RJE, box 49, folder 1973; NN, 120; CNCMA, no. 13.
I would be delighted: RJ to Thomas Albright, November 17, 1971, RJE, box 48, folder 1971.

XVI

After reading the New York Times: RJ to "Mary Josephson," May 23, 1973, RJE, box 49, folder 1973.
"A Delayed Obituary," Johnson photocopied this article and sent it, with various alterations, to multiple correspondents. See, for instance, RJ to BW, binder, *1973 01-07*, page *73 05 30*, The William S. Wilson Collection of Ray Johnson, RBAAA, Art Institute of Chicago; and RJ to Michael Morris, May 30, 1973, HSIAT, 81.

XVII

to suspect that everybody at Art in America: RJ to Brian O'Doherty, July 10, 1973, RJE, box 49, folder 1973.
"43 Seized at Artists' Ball": RJ to BW. Binder *1961 06-12*, page *62 11 10*, The William S. Wilson Collection of Ray Johnson, RBAAA, Art Institute of Chicago.
"long-desired ... stops speaking": *A Mental Masquerade: When Brian O'Doherty Was a Female Art Critic: Mary Josephson's Collected Writings*, ed. Thomas Fischer and Astrid Mania (Leipzig: Spector Books, 2019), 76.

XVIII

working on the last batch: RJ to Lotte Drew-Bear, May 24, 1970, RJE, box 49, folder 1970.
The filmmakers even went to the length: for production background on the party scene in *Midnight Cowboy*, see Glenn Frankel, *Shooting Midnight Cowboy: Art, Sex, Loneliness, Liberation, and the Making of a Dark Classic* (New York: Farrar, Straus and Giroux, 2021), 221–228.

XX

"I'm dictating this to Jamie Herlihy": James Leo Herlihy to RJ. Binder *1970 11-12*, page *70 11 06*, The William S. Wilson Collection of Ray Johnson, RBAAA, Art Institute of Chicago.
having long suffered: Glenn Frankel traces Herlihy's trajectory in *Shooting Midnight Cowboy*.

XXI

Karl August: RJ to Karl Wirsum, ca. 1969. Collection of Lori Gunn and Karl Wirsum.
I am an individual: Paul Schinkel, "Ray Johnson at Marcia Resnick's 1977 Symposium." Film made for ARTIFACTS.

“Walter K. Gutman”: Sophie Cras mentions Gutman in the context of a reading of *Midnight Cowboy Dollar Bill* as part of her analysis of the way Johnson’s work relates to economic trends of the 1970s; Cras, *The Artist as Economist: Art and Capitalism in the 1960s* (New Haven, CT: Yale University Press, 2019).

“a Proust in Wall Street”: John Brooks, “Profiles: A Proust in Wall Street [Walter Gutman],” *New Yorker*, June 20, 1959, 41–64.

XXII

Toby a most extraordinary: RJ to TS, October 11, 1972, RJE, box 49, folder 1972.

XXIV

“four horsemen,” “‘She is not, for me,’” “‘a fiction who exists’”: Calvin Tomkins, “Profiles: A Keeper of the Treasure [Betty Parsons], *New Yorker*, June 9, 1975, 46, 54.

the idea of exhibiting works … famous Vogue model: RJ to Betty Parsons and Jock Truman, April 27, 1972, RJE, box 49, folder 1972.

his letters to her are alternately addressed: see the Archives of American Art, Betty Parsons Gallery records and personal papers, 1916–1991, series 1, box 8, folder 12.

XXV

“infrathin”: Frances Naumann quotes Duchamp, speaking to Richard Hamilton: “It would be better to go into the infrathin interval that separates two ‘identicals’ than to conveniently accept the generalization which makes two twins look like two drops of water.” Francis Naumann, *Marcel Duchamp: The Art of Making Art in the Age of Mechanical Reproduction* (New York: Harry Abrams, 1999), 17.

XXVI

“All you have to know”: “Art in View,” *Andy Warhol’s Interview* 29 (January 1973): 46.

“whose embers still glow”: Lawrence Campbell, “The Ray Johnson History of the Betty Parsons Gallery,” *ArtNews International* 72 (January 1973): 56.

“death-car girl”: Brad Gooch, *City Poet: The Life and Times of Frank O’Hara* (New York: Harper Perennial, 1994), 288.

In Bill’s studio one day: Randy Kennedy, “Ruth Kligman, Muse and Artist, Dies at 80,” *New York Times*, March 6, 2010: D7.

“Kleenex History”: “Mary Josephson” (Brian O’Doherty), “Ray Johnson at Betty Parsons,” *Art in America* 61 (May–June 1973): 104.

“more than a series of glass”: Campbell, “Ray Johnson History of the Betty Parsons Gallery,” 56.

XXVII

“simply the most,” “‘I began playing’”: Philip Glass, *Words Without Music* (New York: Liveright, 2016), 92, 97.

“watched Elaine de Kooning”: Albert M. Fine, “Fear No Forks,” 1965, RJE, box 145; also https://digital.lib.uiowa.edu/islandora/object/ui%3Afluxus_11849.

“Fluxus-type performance”: *Artbreaking*, radio show hosted by Charlie Finch, WBAI FM, New York, March 30, 1995. Panel on Ray Johnson featuring Mark Bloch, Chuck Close, Richard Feigen, Jill Johnston, and Knight Landesman. Transcription, John Walter. Binder *1995 01-05*, page *95 03 30*, The William S. Wilson Collection of Ray Johnson, RBAAA, Art Institute of Chicago.

“symbolized that Albert”: cited in Charlton Burch and Gary S. Vasilash, “Maintaining a Lotus in a Snakepit: The Life and Art of A.M. Fine,” *Lightworks*, no. 19 (Winter 1988–89): 9.

“egregiously subordinate”: Hilton Kramer, “Tuttle’s Art on Display at Whitney,” *New York Times*, September 12, 1975, 21.

CHAPTER 6

I

“How many years,” “Milan abandoned,” “interminably”: HM to RJ, June 15, circa 1970, RJE, box 50, folder “Henry Martin.”

“the enormous good fortune,” “Ray was very,” “Ray liked me”: Author’s interview with Henry Martin, June 11, 2017.

II

“I showed your pictures to Schwarz”: HM to RJ, January 17, 1966, RJE, box 50, folder “Henry Martin.”

Mary Bauermeister … smuggled in a suitcase: Mary Bauermeister, letter to author, June 15, 2021.

I am so very tired: RJ to Thomas Albright, November 17, 1971, RJE, box 48, folder 1971.

“a continuous happening”: Thomas Albright, “New Art School: Correspondence.” *Rolling Stone* no. 106 (April 13, 1972): 32.

III

“The Ray Johnson Joseph Cornell”: RJE, box 49, folder 1973.

“a ream of paper … gravity of the art world”: Tom Bloomer and William Graham, “Return of the Native with a Mailbag of Tricks,” *New Art Examiner*, January 1979, 25.

IV

an artist-in-residence, Since my ideas about what I do: RJ to Francis Lassiter, October 30, 1974, RJE, box 49, folder 1974.

“impromptu”: “Ray Johnson Presentation at Oberlin College, October 15, 1974: A brief summary of ‘events’ to supplement tape transcription,” unsigned document. Binder *1 Unpublished Type-Scripts*, page *After 74 10 15*, The William S. Wilson Collection of Ray Johnson, RBAAA, Art Institute of Chicago.

I spin the bottle: "Ray Johnson speaks in a Long Island Kitchen to Two Women." Binder *1 Unpublished Type-Scripts*, page *77 01 ??*, The William S. Wilson Collection of Ray Johnson, RBAAA, Art Institute of Chicago.

"I simply cannot thank you": Ellen Johnson to RJ, October 25, 1974, RJE, box 49, folder 1974.

"an aggressively silly": *New Video and Performance Art in Detroit; Works in Progress V, The Detroit Institute of Arts*, preface by Jay Belloli, commentary by Peter Frank (Detroit: The Institute, 1979), 12.

V

a special group ... I hope the February thing is as nice: RJ to Daniel Wells, October 17, 1973, RJE, box 48, folder Illinois 1973–1974.

"it was kind of funny ... it was very strange": Daniel Wells, interview with author, October 6, 2021.

VI

"three women ... He didn't interrupt": Author's interview with AA Bronson, May 21, 2021.

with adhesive tape: RJ, mailer with letter to Rain-Rien, May 19, 1974, RJE, box 48, folder 1974,

"it would be really": HM to RJ, April 10, 1973, RJE, box 50, folder "Henry Martin."

I think they're pissed off: RJ to Colin Naylor, April 12, 1973, RJE, box 49, folder 1973.

"'We feel it' ... bought them from Arturo": HM to RJ, February 4, 1975, RJE, box 50, folder "Henry Martin."

Marian Goodman and Jaap Reitman: RJ to HM, January 19, 1976, mumok—Museum of Modern Art Ludwig Foundation Vienna, OL-Stg 434/122.

"rumor has it": HM to RJ, February 7, 1976, RJE, box 50, folder "Henry Martin."

VII

"*visual* indifference": Marcel Duchamp, "Apropos of Readymades."

"Invoice #4": RJE, box 48, folder 1965. For drafts of this document and background material related to it, see Binder *Invoice #4 650400*, The William S. Wilson Collection of Ray Johnson, RBAAA, Art Institute of Chicago.

VIII

attempt to obtain ... World's Greatest Painter: RJ, "Abandoned Chickens," *Art in America* 62, no. 6 (Nov.–Dec. 1974): 107–108.

I have started a silhouette: RJ to Barbara Burn, May 18, 1976, RJE, box 49, folder 1976.

"in principle": Burn to RJ, May 18, 1976, RJE, box 49, folder 1976.

IX

a Major Work: RJ to Anne Trueblood Brodsky, July 1, 1975, RJE, box 49, folder 1975.

after showing to an audience: RJ to "Alador" (Aladar Marberger), May 17, 1975, RJE, box 49, folder 1975.

the reality of money ... work to document: RJ to HM, February 14, 1975, RJE, box 50, folder "Henry Martin."

mailing to Arturo Schwarz: RJ to Arturo Schwarz, March 19, 1975, *Correspondence: An Exhibition of the Letters of Ray Johnson*, ed. Richard Craven (Raleigh, NC: North Carolina Museum of Art, 1976), no. 65.

X

A daily chore: RJ to Arturo Schwarz, March 28, 1975, RJE, box 48, folder 1975.

Richard Lippold died: RJ to BW. Binder *1974 05-12*, page *74 05 31*, The William S. Wilson Collection of Ray Johnson, RBAAA, Art Institute of Chicago.

"since the free-spending days": "Sculptor Has Party to Show Off Pipe Organ," *Chicago Tribune*, Monday, May 16, 1966, section 2, 16.

Lippold's golden *Orpheus and Apollo*: after an outcry from preservationists, the sculpture was restored and installed at LaGuardia Airport.

summer of severe love problems: RJ to George Ashley. Binder *1974 05-12*, page *74 Summer*, The William S. Wilson Collection of Ray Johnson, RBAAA, Art Institute of Chicago.

XI

The New York/Correspondence: RJ to HM, February 14, 1975. RJE. Box 50, folder "Henry Martin."

The New York Correspondence School has no history: RJ to DB, December 25, 1975, NN, 143; CNCMA, no. 18.

"fell to his knees": Richard Craven, interview with author, January 15, 2021.

which has my drawing on the front ... can be put into a book in some fashion: "Ray Johnson Performance-Lecture: Marcia Resnick's Book Art Symposium International Center for Photography, (1977)," video produced by Inner-tube Video LLC, directed by Paul Tschinkel for ARTIFACTS.

XII

"chaos," "long poems": Gerald Ayres, *The Apple Bites Back: A Memoir, the Early Years* (self-pub.: Middletown, DE, 2017), 178, 184.

There will be a Shelley Duvall: RJ to Diana Epstein, RJE, box 48, folder 21.

I am dining with Paloma: RJ to Michael André, July 14, 1975, CNCMA, no. 2.

"dictated by Gerry Ayres": Gerald Ayres to RJ. Binder *1976*, page *76 0229*, The William S. Wilson Collection of Ray Johnson, RBAAA, Art Institute of Chicago.

XIII

Meetings had been restricted: RJ to Michael Morris, November 23, 1976. Cited in Muffet Jones, "Selected Biographical Chronology and Exhibition History." C, 208.

"a beloved figure ... to cruise": David Ebony, "The Insider-Outsider," Artnet.com, January 22, 1999. Accessed March 30, 2022. http://www.artnet.com/magazine_pre2000/features/ebony/ebony1-22-99.asp.

"He would do a circuit": Author's interview with David Ebony, April 3, 2022.

XIV

"Ray offered": Author's interview with AA Bronson, May 21, 2021.

"official liaison": John Jack Baylin, letter to the editor, *FILE*, December 1973, 43.

"John Dowd bum shot": *Fanzini Goes to the Movies*, ed. John Dowd and John Jack Baylin (Vancouver: self-published, 1974), n.p.

XV

for the roll ... Paulette tomorrow: RJ to Bart Gorin, April 24, 1976. RJE, box 49, folder 1976.

XVI

"Etienne de Silhouette," "for about seven years": Helen Harrison, "Ray Johnson: Shadow and Substance," *Re-Dact, An Anthology of Art Criticism 1*, ed. Peter Frank (New York: Willis, Locker, and Owens, 1984), 78, 77.

"a tiny silhouette portrait": Nina Ffrench-Frazier, "Ray Johnson," *Arts Magazine* 52 (June 1978): 8.

"I try to conceal my profile": John Ashbery to RJ, October 17, 1979, RJE, box 118, folder B40, #1.

"is conscious," I'm ruthlessly, "The surreal mood," They're all terrible: Harrison, "Shadow and Substance," 77, 78.

"You call that": cited in Ffrench-Frazier, "Ray Johnson," 8.

This house never: Amei Wallach, "That Unmistakable, Personal Stamp," *Newsday*, Sunday, August 14, 1977, section II: 15.

worked on Masonite ... new snake direction: RJ to Thomas Leavitt, July 24, 1977, RJE, box 48, folder 1977.

As Gertrude Stein: RJ to Paula Cooper and Douglas Baxter, April 23, 1976, RJE, box 48, folder 1976.

XVII

underneath Johnson's nothing: the Schoelkopf ad appeared in the *New York Times*, Friday, October 10, 1980, C26.

"bookish and soft-spoken," "known for": Deborah Solomon, *Utopia Parkway: The Life and Work of Joseph Cornell* (New York: Noonday Press, 1997), 310.

Pink Above was reproduced: RJ to RL. Binder *1966 07-12*, page *66 10 8*, The William S. Wilson Collection of Ray Johnson, RBAAA, Art Institute of Chicago.

POSTSCRIPT

"You mean, says J. Daley ... I *already* love you": HM to RJ, September 11, 1971, RJE, box 50, folder "Henry Martin."

All your information ... Utopia unrelated: RJ to HM, March 1, 1976, RJE, box 50, folder "Henry Martin."

"Mrs. Incisetto ... that could interest": HM to RJ, May 24, 1976, RJE, box 48, folder "Henry Martin."

CHAPTER 7

EPIGRAPH

e. dickinson said: RJ to FXP ca. 1950, RJE, box D360, folder 2: Correspondence without envelopes.

I

the time between getting up, relates to those puppet plays, although it sounds silly: RJ to "Ma," February 20, 1986, RJE, box 18, binder 16, 1Q. *NN*, 181.

II

a small, spare collage: RJE, image #15714.

to prompt Ray to turn to the now-experienced Bill: Bill Wilson wrote Ray a letter of advice on dealing with aging parents on August 2, 1986. Binder *1985 1986*, page *86 08 02*, The William S. Wilson Collection of Ray Johnson, RBAAA, Art Institute of Chicago.

III

Merce's concert last night: Binder *1957*, page *RL:GM ca. 1957*, The William S. Wilson Collection of Ray Johnson, RBAAA, Art Institute of Chicago.

"Ray's idea for the mural," "a slow and continual," "we couldn't yet understand": "From the Cutting Room Floor," in HTDAB DVD special feature.

IV

this local museum, I am very excited, two young pretty curators: RJ to HM, May 17, 1983, mumok—Museum of Modern Art Ludwig Foundation Vienna, OL-Stg 434/136.

"the collages should come first": Edward M. Plunkett et al., "Send Letters, Postcards, Drawings, and Objects ..." *Art Journal* 36, no. 3 (Spring 1977): 237.

"rather dull formal gallery works": Hilton Kramer, "Mixing the Media," *New York Times*, October 29, 1967, 34.

"his extraordinarily inventive collages": Phyllis Stigliano and Janice Parente, "Acknowledgments," in *Works by Ray Johnson* (Roslyn, NY: Nassau County Museum of Art, 1984), 5.

"no missives in envelopes": Phyllis Stigliano, email to author, March 29, 2022. Phyllis Stigliano and Janice Parente both declined to be interviewed for this book, but Stigliano responded to questions by email.

"Mr. Johnson's fame as a collagist": Grace Glueck, "A Witty Master of the Deadpan Spoof," *New York Times*, February 19, 1984, 29.

my museum exhibition is proceeding, My work as a result,: RJ to HM, July 27, 1983, RJE, box 48, folder "Henry Martin."
some really new work ideas: Johnson to HM, August 16, 1983, mumok—Museum of Modern Art Ludwig Foundation Vienna, OL-Stg 434/143.
"a man who killed himself": jacket copy Geoffrey Wolff, *Black Sun: The Brief Transit and Violent Eclipse of Harry Crosby* (New York: NYRB Classics, 2003).
I think we should cancel it: RJ to BW. Binder *1984 01-08*, page *84 02 01*, The William S. Wilson Collection of Ray Johnson, RBAAA, Art Institute of Chicago.
"past every collage": Gerrit Henry, "Ray Johnson: Collage Jester," *Art in America* 72 (December 1984): 140.
"lengthy exegetics": Glueck, "Witty Master," 31.
I have been in a very funny mood: RJ to HM, May 9, 1984, mumok—Museum of Modern Art Ludwig Foundation Vienna, OL-Stg 434/144.

V

I plan on January 2, 1982: RJ to Morton Janklow. Binder *1981*, page *81 11 23*, The William S. Wilson Collection of Ray Johnson, RBAAA, Art Institute of Chicago.
"really sorry I don't": Phoebe Hoban, "Tantalizing Images, Lost and Found," *New York Times*, February 16, 2003: B37.
all those movies: RJ to BW, February 5. 1988, RJE, box 108, binder 9, #45.
I found a rusty fish hook: RJ to Ann Wilson, August 10, 1967, RJE, box 49, folder 1967; NN, 58.
"bold, risk-taking negotiator": Robert D. McFadden, "Morton Janklow, Agent for Best-Selling Authors, Dies at 91," *New York Times*, May 27, 2022: B10.
"considerably more": Hoban, "Tantalizing Images," 37.

VI

memorable tepid canned peaches, Richard Lippold and I: RJ, handwritten notes with heading, "3 Visits to Joseph Cornell," RJE, box 48, folder 1968.
"of course, Cornell had no": author's conversation with John Willenbecher, June 17, 2022.

VI

I didn't get down: RJ to Charles Fahlen, December 4, 1987, RJE, box 118, folder B40, #110.
"from a preparatory study": Michael R. Taylor, *Marcel Duchamp: Étant Donnés* (Philadelphia: Philadelphia Museum of Art, 2009), 220.

VII

"The physical separates ... a thousand others": Molly Nesbit, "Marcel Duchamp's *Étant Donnés*," *Artforum* 32, no. 1 (September 1993): 159.

VIII

The Elvis painting... FLOP art: RJ, untitled page of notes, dated October 28, 1987, RJE, box 118, Folder B40, #106.
"a work of his that I have": Binder *1988*, page *88 07 23*, The William S. Wilson Collection of Ray Johnson, RBAAA, Art Institute of Chicago.
The greatest example..."flopped": RJ to Charles Fahlen, December 4, 1987, RJE, box 118, folder B40, #110.
Flop art figures, Have you got a slide, "I will have": Clive Phillpot, *Ray Johnson on Flop Art* (London: Fermley Press, 2008), 14, 15.
I have started this season, Nobody wants, The sublime example: RJ to HM, mumok—Museum of Modern Art Ludwig Foundation Vienna. OL-Stg 434/147.

IX

Pop Art show from Berkeley: RJ to Charles Fahlen, December 4, 1987, RJE, box 118, folder B40, #110.
used the Elvis: RJ to Marco Livingstone, May 10, 1988, RJE, box 118, folder B40, #118.
"appeal to our," "demands on anything": Richard Flood, "Skied and Grounded in Queens: New York/New Wave at P.S. 1," *Artforum* 19, no. 10 (Summer 1981): 87.
"participatory narcissism": Peter Schjeldahl, "New York/No Wave No Fun," *Village Voice* March 4–10, 1981, 69.
Dear Keith Haring: RJ to Peter Schuyff, Archives of the Morris and Helen Belkin Art Gallery, University of British Columbia, Peter Schuyff Fonds 16.009.

X

"Rare Cancer": Lawrence Altman, "Rare Cancer Seen in 41 Homosexuals," *New York Times*, July 3, 1981, A20.
with fingers: RJ to Marco Livingstone, May 10, 1988.
john dowd died: RJ to Bart Gorin, July 12, 1988, RJE, box D363.
an impossible disaster dinner: RJ to HM, March 3, 1975, RJE, box 48, folder "Henry Martin."
Buczak flyers: Binder *1987*, pages *87 05 07*, *87 06 05*, The William S. Wilson Collection of Ray Johnson, RBAAA, Art Institute of Chicago.
"To his parents dismay": Geoffrey Hendricks, "Memories, Salt, Portraits, and Nothing." *Lightworks Magazine* #22 (*The Ray Johnson Issue*): 39.

XI

Ray Johnson died in 1989, I can—Mr. Deceased: Phillpot, *Ray Johnson on Flop Art*, 28, 31.
noitibihxe "egalbmessA": RJ to BW to Toby Spiselman, January 2, 1989. RJE, Box 118, folder B40, #119.
invitation to participate: the letter is reproduced in the show's catalogue: Christel Schuppenhauer, *Wortlaut* (Cologne: Galerie Schüppenauer, 1989), n.p.

always very kind: RJ to Judith Van Wagner, May 23, 1990, RJE, Box 118, folder B40, #123.

I am doing a Nothing: RJ to Coco Gordon, June 10, 1989, RJE, box 118, folder B40, #120.

XII

surprising theater performance type dream: RJ to TS. NN, 200.

Ray had drawn a little theater: the drawing is reproduced in Clive Phillpot, "Ray Johnson and Nothing," in *Voids*, ed. John Armleder, Mathieu Copeland, Gustav Metzger, Mai-Thu Perret, and Clive Philpott (Zurich: JRP/Ringier, 2009), 250.

A Book About Modern Art: the unique copy of this book is contained in three binders assembled by Clive Phillpot, which are housed in the Special Collections of the Museum of Modern Art library and listed in the catalogue as Ray Johnson, *Book About Modern Art* (1990).

"*Part Three* of *A Book*": Clive Phillpot, table of contents, *A Book About Modern Art*; included at the beginning of each of the book's three volumes.

the exhibition for Philadelphia, "fittingly": Clive Phillpot in "2 Printed Books by Ray Johnson," *Lightworks Magazine* 22 (*The Ray Johnson Issue*): 58.

"MoMA is as traditionally ... live and breathe again": Kim Levin, "We Remember MoMA: The Permanent Point of View," *Village Voice*, May 26, 1984, 88–89.

XIII

I will be the Warhol: Phillpot, *Lightworks* 22, 59.

Early "Outdoor Movie Star Show": RJ to DB. David Bourdon Papers, III.7. The Museum of Modern Art Archives, New York.

32 inches high: RJ to DB. David Bourdon Papers, III.5. The Museum of Modern Art Archives, New York.

"prison walks": RJ to Vince Grimaldi: Every afternoon I do my Prison Walk. Binder *1992 01-06*, page *92 01 13*, The William S. Wilson Collection of Ray Johnson, RBAAA, Art Institute of Chicago.

XV

in 2019, Joel Smith: see Smith's essay and acknowledgments in Joel Smith, ed., *Please Send To Real Life: Ray Johnson Photographs* (London: Mack Books, 2022), 188–195, 200.

"every time he called," I'm gonna do a performance, "*Okay* ... back in his trunk": Author's interview with Sandra Gering, June 26, 2022.

XVI

"a glove that said": Author's interview with Don Mistretta, September 1, 2022.

"The poem 'Royalty'," "I didn't have that life," "I know he liked," "he was conflicted," "he would not take the key": Author's interview with Sheila Sporer, January 6, 2021.

XVII

"The mother's face": Wallace Stevens, "The Auroras of Autumn," in *Collected Poetry & Prose*, 356.

"the story is that a collage": Henry Martin, "Mashed Potatoes," *Art and Artists* (May 1972), 23.

"Ask him how much he wants," "went on for like three and a half hours": Author's interview with Frances Beatty, September 21, 2021.

DEAD MAY WILSON: Johnson's *Dead May* (1990) is reproduced in HSIAT, 128.

"By homely gifts": quoted in Jen Bervin, "Studies in Scale," *Emily Dickinson: The Gorgeous Nothings*, eds. Jen Bervin and Marta Werner (New York: Christine Burgin/New Directions, 2013), 8.

One Dickinson silhouette collage: Johnson's *Untitled (Emily Dickinson with Ray, Comic Strips, and Bunny)* (1972–85–91–93) is reproduced in Achim Sommer and Jasper Hallmanns, *Kurt Schwitters & Ray Johnson: Merz & Moticos* (Bruhl, Germany: Max Ernst Museum Bruhl des LVR, 2011), 141.

CODA

I

"An obituary of Feldman": Geraldine Smith, "Andy Feldman, 1948–1972," *Village Voice*, August 17, 1972: 52.

II

"Life Saving and Water Safety": RJ to HM, ca. 1964–1965, mumok—Museum of Modern Art Ludwig Foundation Vienna, OL-Stg 434 0 Johnson 149.

"Parisians Washed Up by Seine": Binder *1973 08-12*, page *73 08 14*, The William S. Wilson Collection of Ray Johnson, RBAAA, Art Institute of Chicago.

"Sewn up in a clean": Binder *1983*, page *83 02 26*, The William S. Wilson Collection of Ray Johnson, RBAAA, Art Institute of Chicago.

"When a man in good health": John Berger, "Mayakovsky, his Language and his Death," *Night Wraps the Sky: Writings by and about Mayakovsky*, ed. Michael Almereyda (New York: Farrar Straus Giroux, 2008), 17.

I have a new project, "haunted," "if there is any belief": Peter Marks, "Friends of an Enigmatic Artist See a Riddle in His Death," *New York Times*, Sunday, February 12, 1995, I.37, 46.

"Ray Johnson's Last Event": Brian Boyhan, "Ray Johnson's Last Event," *Sag Harbor Express*, Thursday, January 19, 1995, 1–2.

"desperate," "very cold": author's interview with Sheila Sporer, January 6, 2021.

Should an eyelash: Henry Martin, "Should an Eyelash Last Forever? An Interview with Ray Johnson," TWTA, 141–142; C, 199.

ADDITIONAL WORKS CITED

Albers, Josef. "Teaching Form Through Practice" (1928). Accessed January 10, 2021. http://www.albersfoundation.org/teaching/josef-albers/texts/.

Albright, Thomas. "New Art School: Correspondence." *Rolling Stone* no. 106, April 13, 1972, 32.

Alloway, Lawrence. *Network: Art and the Complex Present*. Ann Arbor: UMI Research Press, 1984.

Alloway, Lawrence. "Ray Johnson's History of the Betty Parsons Gallery." *The Nation*, February 5, 1973, 189–190.

Altman, Lawrence. "Rare Cancer Seen in 41 Homosexuals." *New York Times*, July 3, 1981, A20.

Aramphongphan, Paisid. "Real Professionals? Andy Warhol, Fred Herko, and Dance." *Performing Arts Journal* 110 (2015): 1–2.

Aronson, Harvey. "What, You Never Heard from Ray Johnson?" *Newsday* (Long Island, NY), January 18, 1969, W10–12.

Ashbery, John. *Selected Prose*. Ed. Eugene Richie. Ann Arbor: UMI Press, 2004.

Ashton, Dore. "New York Commentary." *Studio International* 172, no. 879 (July 1966): 46–47.

Ayres, Gerald. *The Apple Bites Back: A Memoir of the Early Years*. self-published, 2017.

Beggs, Michael. "Josef Albers: Photographs of Matières." In *Leap Before You Look: Black Mountain College, 1933–1957*, ed. Helen Molesworth with Ruth Erickson. New Haven, CT: Yale University Press, 2015.

Benjamin, Walter. *Illuminations*. Ed. Hannah Arendt; trans. Harry Zohn. New York: Schocken, 1969.

Berger, John. "Mayakovsky, His Language and His Death." In *Night Wraps the Sky: Writings by and about Mayakovsky*, ed. Michael Almereyda. New York: Farrar, Straus and Giroux, 2008.

Bloomer, Tom, and William Graham. "Return of the Native with a Mailbag of Tricks." *New Art Examiner* (January 1979): 25.

Bourdon, David, and Philip Leider. "The New York Correspondence School." *Artforum* 6, no. 2 (October 1967): 50–55.

Bourdon, David. "Stacking the Deco." *New York Magazine*, November 11, 1974, 64–66.

Burch, Charlton, and Gary S. Vasilash. "Maintaining a Lotus in a Snakepit: The Life and Art of A.M. Fine." *Lightworks* 19 (Winter 1988/89): 6–9.

Cage, John. *Silence*. Middletown, CT: Wesleyan University Press, 1961.

Campbell, Lawrence. "The Ray Johnson History of the Betty Parsons Gallery." *ArtNews International* 72 (January 1973): 56.

Caws, Mary Ann, ed. *Joseph Cornell's Theater of the Mind: Selected Diaries, Letters, and Files*. New York and London: Thames and Hudson, 1993.

Comenas, Gary. "Mark Lancaster Interview." Accessed October 22, 2022. https://warholstars.org/andywarhol/interview/mark/lancaster.html.

Constable, Rosalind. "The Mailaway Art of Ray Johnson." *New York Magazine*, March 2, 1970, 43.

Cotter, Holland. "Where City History Was Made, a 50's Group Made Art History." *New York Times*, January 5, 1993, C1.

Crow, Thomas. "On Philip Leider's 'How I Spent My Summer Vacation.'" *Artforum* 51, no. 1 (September 2012): 92–95.

Curtis, Charlotte. "Artist Redefines Black-Tie Dinner for a Princess." *New York Times*, October 9, 1972, 72.

Danto, Arthur. "The Artworld." In *Aesthetics: A Critical Anthology*, ed. George Dickie, Richard Sclafani, and Ronald Roblin, 2nd ed., 171–182. New York: St. Martin's Press, 1989.

de Duve, Thierry. *Kant After Duchamp*. Cambridge, MA: MIT Press, 1996.

Diaz, Eva. *The Experimenters: Chance and Design at Black Mountain College*. Chicago: University of Chicago Press, 2015.

Dickinson, Emily. *The Poems of Emily Dickinson*. Ed. R. W. Franklin. Cambridge, MA: The Belknap Press of Harvard University Press, 1999.

Duchamp, Marcel. "Apropos of Readymades." In *The Writings of Marcel Duchamp*, ed. Michel Sanouillet and Elmer Peterson. New York: Da Capo, 1989.

Ebony, David. "The Insider-Outsider." *Artnet.com*, January 22, 1999. http://www.artnet.com/magazine_pre2000/features/ebony/ebony1-22-99.asp.

Empson, William. *Seven Types of Ambiguity*. New York: New Directions, 1966.

Feinstein, Roni. "The Unknown Robert Rauschenberg: The Betty Parsons Exhibition of 1951." *Arts Magazine* (January 1985): 126–131.

Ffrench-Frazier, Nina. "Ray Johnson." *Arts Magazine* 52 (June 1978): 8.

Flood, Richard. "Skied and Grounded in Queens: New York/New Wave at P.S. 1." *Artforum* 19, no. 10 (Summer 1981): 87.

Frankel, Glenn. *Shooting Midnight Cowboy: Art, Sex, Loneliness, Liberation, and the Making of a Dark Classic*. New York: Farrar, Straus, and Giroux, 2021.

Gablik, Suzi. "700 Collages by Ray Johnson." *Location* 1 (Summer 1964): 55.

Gablik, Suzi, and John Russell. *Pop Art Redefined*. New York: Praeger, 1969.

Gangel, Sue. "An Interview with John Ashbery." In *Poets on their Work*, ed. Joe David Bellamy. Urbana and Chicago: University of Illinois Press, 1984.

Geldzahler, Henry. *Pop Art: 1955–1970*. Sydney: Art Gallery of New South Wales, 1985.

Glass, Philip. *Words Without Music*. New York: Liveright, 2016.

Glueck, Grace. "What Happened? Nothing." *New York Times*, April 11, 1965, Section X, 18.

Glueck, Grace. "A Witty Master of the Deadpan Spoof." *New York Times*, February 19, 1984, Section II, 29.

Harrison, Helen. "Ray Johnson: Shadow and Substance." In *Re-Dact, An Anthology of Art Criticism 1*, ed. Peter Frank. New York: Willis, Locker, and Owens, 1984.

Henry, Gerrit. "Ray Johnson: Collage Jester." *Art in America* 72 (December 1984): 140.

Hoban, Phoebe. "Tantalizing Images, Lost and Found." *New York Times*, February 16, 2003, B37.

Horstman, Fritz. "The Preliminary Course and the Matière." *The Art Section*, August 2017. Accessed July 15, 2021. https://www.theartsection.com/albers---the-matire.

Horton, Donald, and R. Richard Wohl. "Mass Communication and Para-Social Interaction: Observations on Intimacy at a Distance." *Psychiatry: Journal for the Study of Interpersonal Processes* 19 (1956): 215–229.

Kaprow, Allan. *Essays on the Blurring of Art and Life*. Ed. Jeff Kelley. Berkeley and Los Angeles: University of California Press, 2003.

Keane, Tim. "Ray Johnson: The Zen Master of the Social Network." *Utne Reader*, Winter 2014. Accessed September 18, 2019. http://www.utne.com/media/ray-johnson-zm0z14wzsau/.

Kracauer, Siegfried. *The Mass Ornament: Weimar Essays*. Ed. Thomas Y. Levin Cambridge, MA: Harvard University Press, 1995.

Kramer, Hilton. "Art: Melting Ice, Hay, Dog Food, Etc." *New York Times*, May 24, 1969, 31.

Kramer, Hilton. "Art: Mixing the Media." *New York Times*, October 29, 1967, 34.

Kramer, Hilton. "Art: Out of the Mailbox." *New York Times*, September 12, 1970, 18.

Kramer, Hilton. "The Sadness of Ray Johnson in Big New Whitney Show." *New York Observer*, February 8, 1999. Accessed November 23, 2022. http://observer.com/1999/02/the-sadness-of-ray-johnson-in-big-new-whitney-show/.

Kramer, Hilton. "Tuttle's Art on Display at Whitney." *New York Times*, September 12, 1975, 21.

Krauss, Rosalind. *The Originality of the Avant-Garde and Other Modernist Myths*. Cambridge, MA: MIT Press, 1985.

Leavell, Linda. *Holding On Upside Down: The Life and Work of Marianne Moore*. New York: Farrar, Straus, and Giroux, 2013.

LeSueur, Joe. *Digressions on Some Poems by Frank O'Hara: A Memoir*. New York: Farrar Straus and Giroux, 2003.

Linville, Kasha. "Ray Johnson: Whitney Museum of American Art." *Artforum* 9, no. 3 (November 1970): 86.

"T.M.," "Ray Johnson," *Arts Magazine* (May 1967): 58.

Mallarmé, Stéphane. "Le Livre, Instrument Spirituel." In *Divagations*. Paris: Bibliothèque-Charpentier, 1897.

Marks, Peter. "Friends of an Enigmatic Artist See a Riddle in His Death." *New York Times*, February 12, 1995, Section I, 37, 46.

Monte, James, and Marcia Tucker. *Anti-Illusion: Procedures/Materials*. New York: Whitney Museum of American Art, 1969.

Nesbit, Molly. "Marcel Duchamp's Étant Donnés." *Artforum* 32, no. 1 (September 1993): 159.

O'Doherty, Brian. *A Mental Masquerade: When Brian O'Doherty Was a Female Art Critic: Mary Josephson's Collected Writings*. Ed. Thomas Fischer and Astrid Mania. Leipzig: Spector Books, 2019.

O'Doherty, Brian. *Postwar American Art: The Novak/O'Doherty Collection*. Ed. Christina Kennedy. Dublin: Irish Museum of Modern Art, 2011.

O'Doherty, Brian. "Ray Johnson at Betty Parsons." *Art in America* 61 (May–June 1973): 105.

O'Hara, Frank. *The Collected Poems of Frank O'Hara*. Ed. Donald Allen. Berkeley, CA: University of California Press, 1995.

Picard, Lil, "Death Rattle Art." *East Village Other*, February 15, 1967, 15.

Rauschenberg, Robert. *Art in Process: The Visual Development of a Collage*. Prepared by Elayne H. Varian with statements by the artists. New York: Finch College, 1967, n.p.

Rauschenberg, Robert. "Statement on Josef Albers," unpublished typescript, n.d. Robert Rauschenberg Foundation website. Accessed November 27, 2022. http://www.rauschenberg-foundation.org/art/archive/albers.

Rodenbeck, Judith F. *Radical Prototypes: Allan Kaprow and the Invention of Happenings*. Cambridge, MA: MIT Press, 2011.

Rosenberg, Harold. "The Art World: Museum of the New." *New Yorker*, November 18, 1967, 225–234.

Rosenberg, Harold. "Collage: Philosophy of Put-Togethers." In *Collage: Critical Views*, ed. Katherine Hoffman. Ann Arbor: UMI Research Press, 1989.

Schjeldahl, Peter. "New York/No Wave No Fun." *Village Voice*, March 4–10, 1981, 69.

Schwabsky, Barry. "First Break, Larry Poons." *Artforum* (February 2003): 23–24.

Schwitters, Kurt. *PPPPPP: Kurt Schwitters, Poems Performance Pieces Proses Plays Poetics*. Edited and translated by Jerome Rothenberg and Pierre Joris. Cambridge, MA: Exact Change, 2002.

Sedofsky, Lauren. "Down and Dirty: 'L'Informe' at the Centre Georges Pompidou. Lauren Sedofsky Talks with Yves-Alain Bois and Rosalind Krauss." *Artforum* 34, no. 10 (Summer 1996): 90–95.

Solomon, Deborah. *Utopia Parkway: The Life and Work of Joseph Cornell*. New York: Noonday Press/Farrar, Straus and Giroux, 1967.

Stevens, Wallace. *Collected Poetry & Prose*. New York: Library of America, 1997.
Taylor, Michael R. *Marcel Duchamp: Étant Donnés*. Philadelphia: Philadelphia Museum of Art, 2009.
Tomkins, Calvin. *Off the Wall: A Portrait of Robert Rauschenberg*. New York: Picador, 2005.
Tomkins, Calvin. "Profiles: A Keeper of the Treasure [Betty Parsons]." *New Yorker*, June 9, 1975, 44–48.
Wallach, Amei. "Dear Friends of Ray, and Audiences of One." *New York Times*, February 28, 1999, Section 2, 45.
Watson, Steven. *Factory Made: Warhol and the Sixties*. New York: Pantheon, 2003.
Wilcock, John. "The Whither Eye of Time Magazine." *Village Voice*, January 11, 1962, 2.
Wilcock, John. "The Village Square." *Village Voice*, October 26, 1955, 3.
Wittgenstein, Ludwig. *Philosophical Investigations*. Translated by G. E. M. Anscombe. Oxford: Blackwell, 1958.

A SELECTIVE BIBLIOGRAPHY OF WRITINGS ON AND BY RAY JOHNSON

RAY JOHNSON, WRITINGS AND INTERVIEWS

Higgins, Dick, ed. *The Paper Snake*. Los Angeles: Siglio, 2014.

Phillpot, Clive. *Ray Johnson on Flop Art*. London: Fermley Press, 2008.

Thomson, Julie, ed. *That Was the Answer: Interviews with Ray Johnson*. Chicago: Soberscove, 2018.

Zuba, Elizabeth, ed. *Not Nothing: Selected Writings by Ray Johnson, 1954–1994*. Los Angeles: Siglio, 2014.

MUSEUM EXHIBITION CATALOGUES

Ahrens, Carsten, ed. *Ray Johnson—I Like Funny Stories*. Bremen: Weserburg/Museum für Moderne Kunst Bremen, 2012.

Blom, Ina. *The Name of the Game: Ray Johnson's Postal Performance*. Oslo: The National Museum for Contemporary Art, Norway, 2003.

Craven, Richard, and Huston Paschal. *Correspondence: An Exhibition of the Letters of Ray Johnson*. Raleigh: North Carolina Museum of Art, 1976.

De Salvo, Donna, and Catherine Gudis, eds. *Ray Johnson: Correspondences*. Columbus: Wexner Center for the Arts, Ohio State University, 1999.

Haskell, Caitlin, with Jordan Carter, eds. *Ray Johnson c/o*. Chicago: Art Institute of Chicago, 2021.

Longhauser, Elsa, and Clive Phillpot. *More Works by Ray Johnson*. Philadelphia: Goldie Paley Gallery, Moore College of Art and Design, 1991.

Matthews, Sebastian, ed. *From BMC to NYC: The Tutelary Years of Ray Johnson*. Asheville, NC: Black Mountain College Museum & Arts Center, 2010.

Morris, Michael, et al. *Ray Johnson: How Sad I Am Today....* Vancouver, Canada: Morris and Helen Belkin Gallery, 2001.

Smith, Joel, ed. *Please Send to Real Life: Ray Johnson Photographs*. London: Mack Books, 2022.

Sommer, Achim, and Jasper Hallmanns. *Kurt Schwitters & Ray Johnson: Merz & Moticos*. Bruhl, Germany: Max Ernst Museum Bruhl des LVR, 2011.

Stigliano, Phyllis, and David Bourdon. *Works by Ray Johnson*. Roslyn Harbor, NY: Nassau County Museum of Fine Arts, 1984.

MONOGRAPHS AND BOOK CHAPTERS

Cras, Sophie. *The Artist as Economist: Art and Capitalism in the 1960s*. New Haven: Yale University Press, 2017.

Dempsey Martineau, Kate. *Ray Johnson: Selective Inheritance*. Oakland: University of California Press, 2018.

Muñoz, Jose Esteban. *Cruising Utopia: The Then and There of Queer Futurity*. New York: New York University Press, 2009.

Phillpot, Clive. "The Mailed Art of Ray Johnson," *Eternal Network: A Mail Art Anthology*, ed. Chuck Welch. Calgary: University of Calgary Press, 1995.

Phillpot, Clive. "Ray Johnson and Nothing." In *Voids*, ed. John Armleder, Mathieu Copeland, Gustav Metzger, Mai-Thu Perret, and Clive Philpott. Zurich: JRP/Ringier, 2009.

Wilson, William S. *Ray Johnson Ray Johnson*. New York: Between Books Press, 1977.

Wilson, William S. *A Book About A Book About Death*. Amsterdam: Kunstverein, 2010.

JOURNAL FEATURES AND SPECIAL ISSUES

Burch, Charlton, ed. "The Ray Johnson Issue," *Lightworks Magazine* 22 (1995–2000).

Dempsey, Kate, ed. "A Tribute to Ray Johnson," *Journal of Black Mountain Studies* 2 (Spring 2012).

Plunkett, Edward M., et al. "Send Letters, Postcards, Drawings, and Objects: The New York Correspondence School." *Art Journal* 36, no. 3 (Spring 1977): 233–241.

Von Uchtrup, Michael, ed. "Something Else Entirely: Ray Johnson, Dick Higgins, and the Making of The Paper Snake," *Journal of Black Mountain Studies* 8 (July 2015).

Wilson, William, et al. "Ray Johnson," *Black Mountain College Dossiers*, no. 4 (1997).

ESSAYS

Blom, Ina. "'Every letter I write is not a love letter': Inventing Sociality with Ray Johnson's Postal System." MACBA/*Quaderns portàtils* (digital publication), 2010.

Bourdon, David. "Cosmic Ray: An Open Letter to the Founder of the New York Correspondence School." *Art in America* 83, no. 10 (October 1995): 106–111.

Kahan, Benjamin. "Ray Johnson's Anti-Archive." *Angelaki: Journal of the Theoretical Humanities* 23, no. 1 (2018): 68–84.

Kienle, Miriam. "Facing Others: Ray Johnson's Portrait of a Curator as a Network" *Archives of American Art Journal* 59, no. 2 (Fall 2020): 24–45.

Kienle, Miriam. "Ray Johnson's Robin Gallery: Queer Publicity Network as Counterpublic." *Oxford Art Journal* 42, no. 2 (2019): 197–216.

Levy, Ellen. "Ray Johnson's History of the Detroit Art World." *Detroit Research* 3 (Spring/Summer 2022): 408–431.

Levy, Ellen. *What's In a Name: Ray Johnson's Free Associations*. New York: Richard Feigen & Co., 2011.

Joseph-Lowery, Frédérique. *Ray Johnson … Dali/Warhol/and Others*. New York: Richard Feigen & Co., 2009.

Martin, Henry. "Mashed Potatoes." *Art and Artists* (May 1972): 22–25.

Moonie, Stephen. "A Poet of 'Non-ressentiment'? Lawrence Alloway, Ray Johnson, and the Art World as a Network." *Getty Research Journal* 8 (2016): 161–175.

Stuckey, Charles. *Dear Ray Johnson*. New York: Richard Feigen & Co., 2007.

Wilson, William S. "Ray Johnson: NY Correspondence School." *Art and Artists* 1, no. 1 (April 1966): 54–57.

Wilson, William S. "Ray Johnson: Letters of Reference." *Arts Magazine* 44, no. 4 (February 1970): 28–30.

Wilson, William S. *Ray Johnson: En Rapport*. New York: Richard Feigen & Co., 2006.

Wilson, William S. *Ray Johnson: The Early Years*. New York: Richard Feigen & Co., 2007.

Wilson, William S. *Ray Johnson: Challenging Rectangles*. New York: Richard Feigen & Co., 2008.

Zuba, Elizabeth. *Ray Johnson's Art World*. New York: Richard Feigen & Co., 2015.

TEXT CREDITS

60 "Connoisseur of Chaos" from *The Collected Poems of Wallace Stevens*, by Wallace Stevens, copyright © 1954 by Wallace Stevens and copyright renewed 1982 by Holly Stevens. Used by permission of Alfred A. Knopf, an imprint of the Knopf Doubleday Publishing Group, a division of Penguin Random House LLC. All rights reserved.

340–41 "Which is the best—the Moon or the Crescent" J 1315/F 1376 and "By homely gifts and hindered words" J 1563/F 161 from *The Poems of Emily Dickinson: Reading Edition*, edited by Ralph W. Franklin, Cambridge, MA: The Belknap Press of Harvard University Press, Copyright © 1998, 1999, by the President and Fellows of Harvard College. Copyright © 1951, 1955 by the President and Fellows of Harvard College. Copyright © renewed 1979, 1983 by the President and Fellows of Harvard College. Copyright © 1914, 1918, 1919, 1924, 1929, 1930, 1932, 1935, 1937, 1942 by Martha Dickinson Bianchi. Copyright © 1952, 1957, 1958, 1963, 1965 by Mary L. Hampson. Used by permission. All rights reserved.

KEY TO IMAGE CREDITS

All works in all media by Ray Johnson are reproduced in this book credit of @ The Ray Johnson Estate, courtesy of Frances F. L. Beatty and Adler Beatty.

Images of Ray Johnson correspondence art and other archival materials provided courtesy of The William S. Wilson Collection of Ray Johnson, Ryerson & Burnham Art and Architecture Archives, Art Institute of Chicago are marked in captions as "RBAAA."

Images of works by Ray Johnson from the archives of the Ray Johnson Estate are marked in captions as "RJE."

Exhibition collages by Ray Johnson depicted here that are not identified in captions as belonging to a private collection or named public collection remain as of this writing at the Ray Johnson Estate.

The form used for references to materials housed in the William S. Wilson Collection of Ray Johnson in the Ryerson & Burnham Art and Architecture Archives at the Art Institute of Chicago derives from the system established by Wilson himself. In the Wilson Collection, all materials other than framed collages, three-dimensional objects and oversized pieces are filed in three-ring binders. Each item is identified by binder name and page number: for instance, "binder *1955*, page *55 02 14A*." Binders are often (although not always) named for years and sometimes also for a range of months within the year: for instance: "binder *1958 01-07*" (January–July 1958). Pages are usually (although not always) marked with a date: for instance: "page *59 10 05*" (May 10, 1959). These dates may be tied to a postmark, a time of publication, an event, or other clues. When Wilson was uncertain about the date of an item, he added question marks: for instance: "binder *Summer 1945–Summer 1948*, page *47 10. ??*." These marks are considered integral to the references. The final identification number in the caption is the Art Institute of Chicago accession number.

IMAGE CREDITS

4 RJE.

PRELUDE

10 CNCMA no. 71.

CHAPTER 1

15 Binder *1963 03-06*, page *63 03 06 A*, The William S. Wilson Collection of Ray Johnson, RBAAA, Art Institute of Chicago. 201812_B27-S6-001

16–17 The Detroit Institute of Arts.

18 Binder *1963 01-02*, page *After 63 02 28 B*, 2018.802.24.17, The William S. Wilson Collection of Ray Johnson, RBAAA, Art Institute of Chicago. 201812_B24-S100-001.

21 (top) Binder *1958 01-07*, page *58 06 09*, 2018.802.15.1, The William S. Wilson Collection of Ray Johnson, RBAAA, Art Institute of Chicago. 201812_B15-S100-001.

21 (bottom) RJE.

23 (top) RJE.

26 Private collection.

29 Binder *1955*, page *55 12 10*. The William S. Wilson Collection of Ray Johnson, RBAAA, Art Institute of Chicago. 201812_B10-S103-001.

30 David Bourdon Correspondence, The Museum of Modern Art Archives, New York.

31 The Art Institute of Chicago, Promised gift of The William S. Wilson Collection of Ray Johnson, Obj: 248595.

33 (top) Binder *1963 Undated 1964*, page *Prob. 1963*, 2018.802.29.1, The William S. Wilson Collection of Ray Johnson, RBAAA, Art Institute of Chicago. 201812_B29-S2-001.

34 © 2023 The Andy Warhol Foundation for the Visual Arts, Inc./Licensed by Artists Rights Society (ARS), New York.

35 Binder *Norman Solomon Before 95*, page *Undated*, The William S. Wilson Collection of Ray Johnson, RBAAA, Art Institute of Chicago. 201812_B122-001.

39 (bottom) Berkeley Art Museum.

40–41 RJE.

43 Binder *1965 01-03*, page *65 02 26*, The William S. Wilson Collection of Ray Johnson, RBAAA, Art Institute of Chicago. 201812_B36-S92-001.

45 Binder *1963 03 06*, page *After 63 06 21*, 2018.802.27.21, The William S. Wilson Collection of Ray Johnson, RBAAA, Art Institute of Chicago. 201812_B27-S129-001.

46 Private collection.

48 RJE.

49 RJE.

50 RJE.

50–51 Binder *REJ by WSW 1*, page *Sept. 1965: REJ at Tilghman Island*, The William S. Wilson Collection of Ray Johnson, RBAAA, Art Institute of Chicago. 045848.

54 (top) The Art Institute of Chicago, Promised Gift of The William S. Wilson Collection of Ray Johnson, Obj. 248611. 043784.

54 (bottom) 2018.802.208. The William S. Wilson Collection of Ray Johnson, RBAAA, Art Institute of Chicago. 044885.

55 RJE.

57 Binder *1973 01-07*, page *After 73 01 09*, 2018.802.61.4, The William S. Wilson Collection of Ray Johnson, RBAAA, Art Institute of Chicago. 046006.

CHAPTER 2

60 RJE.

61 Binder *Moticos Pix, Ca. 1955*, page *55 10? ??*, 2018.802.9.1, The William S. Wilson Collection of Ray Johnson, RBAAA, Art Institute of Chicago. 201812_230609-003.

62 2018.802.187, The William S. Wilson Collection of Ray Johnson, RBAAA, Art Institute of Chicago. 046959.

63 The Museum of Modern Art. © 2023 Artists Rights Society (ARS), New York.

65 Binder *1963 07-12*, page *63 09? ??*, 2018.802.25.5, The William S. Wilson Collection of Ray Johnson, RBAAA, Art Institute of Chicago. 201812_B28-S59-001.

66 Private collection.

69 (both) RJE.

72 The Art Institute of Chicago, Gift of Edlis Neeson Collection, 2015.122. IM008526.

73 Binder *1963 07-12*, page *63 09? ??*, 2018.802.25.5, The William S. Wilson Collection of Ray Johnson, RBAAA, Art Institute of Chicago. 201812_230609-004.

75 Binder *RJ Notable Collages. Writing No Dates*, page *Undated*, 2018.802.113.35, The William S. Wilson Collection of Ray Johnson, RBAAA, Art Institute of Chicago. 201812_B113-001.

78 RJE.

80–81 Binder *1961*, page *61 07 05*, 2018.802.20.10, The William S. Wilson Collection of Ray Johnson, RBAAA, Art Institute of Chicago. 046149.

82 RJE.

85 Courtesy of the Western Regional Archives, State Archives of North Carolina.

87 RJE.

88 Binder *Di Cresce*, page *unnumbered*, 2018.802.12.10, The William S. Wilson Collection of Ray Johnson, RBAAA, Art Institute of Chicago. 045881.
90 Private collection.
92 RJE.
93 RJE.
94 RJE.
95 RJE.
96–97 RJE.
100 (top) Photograph by Ted Dreier. The Josef and Anni Albers Foundation, 1976.34.108. Courtesy of the Josef and Anni Albers Foundation.
100 (middle) 2018.802.206, The William S. Wilson Collection of Ray Johnson, RBAAA, Art Institute of Chicago. 044883.
100 (bottom) Binder *1957*, page *57 11 25*, 2018.802.14.9, The William S. Wilson Collection of Ray Johnson, RBAAA, Art Institute of Chicago. J14274.
102 (top) Binder *1959 01-05*, page *59 03 ??*, The William S. Wilson Collection of Ray Johnson, RBAAA, Art Institute of Chicago. 201812_B17-S48-001.
102 (bottom) Binder *1958 08-12*, page *58 11 12*, The William S. Wilson Collection of Ray Johnson, RBAAA, Art Institute of Chicago. 201812_B16-S89-002.
103 Binder *1958 08-12*, page *58 11 12*, The William S. Wilson Collection of Ray Johnson, RBAAA, Art Institute of Chicago. 201812_B16-S89-001.
105 (bottom left) The Art Institute of Chicago, Promised gift of The William S. Wilson Collection of Ray Johnson, Obj: 248595.
105 (bottom right) The Art Institute of Chicago, Promised gift of The William S. Wilson Collection of Ray Johnson, Obj: 248596. 041912.
107 *Oversized Material, Moticos*, 1956, 2018.802.347, The William S. Wilson Collection of Ray Johnson, RBAAA, Art Institute of Chicago. 268531.
108 (top) RJE.
108 (bottom) *Oversized Material, Untitled [A Bird Can Do Easy Flying...]*, c. 1955-56, 2018.802.344, The William S. Wilson Collection of Ray Johnson, RBAAA, Art Institute of Chicago. 045698.
109 (top) *Oversized Material, Ray Johnson Drawings*, 1956, 2018.802.402, The William S. Wilson Collection of Ray Johnson, RBAAA, Art Institute of Chicago. 045916.
109 (bottom) *Oversized Material, Untitled (If Tears Are Dropped)*, c. 1961, 2018.802.358, The William S. Wilson Collection of Ray Johnson, RBAAA, Art Institute of Chicago. 045711.
111 RJE.
115 Binder *Malka Safro Wo Dates 2*, page *Undated*, 2018.802.131b.17, The William S. Wilson Collection of Ray Johnson, RBAAA, Art Institute of Chicago. 201812_B131-001.
117 *A Book About Death*, p. 1, Mar. 8, 1963, 2018.802.225, The William S. Wilson Collection of Ray Johnson, RBAAA, Art Institute of Chicago. 045644.
118 *A Book About Death*, p. 3, Sept. 10, 1963, 2018.802.226, The William S. Wilson Collection of Ray Johnson, RBAAA, Art Institute of Chicago. 045645.
120 *A Book About Death*, p. 4, Oct. 22, 1963, 2018.802.228, The William S. Wilson Collection of Ray Johnson, RBAAA, Art Institute of Chicago. 045647.
121 *A Book About Death*, p. 10, Oct. 1, 1964, 2018.802.220, The William S. Wilson Collection of Ray Johnson, RBAAA, Art Institute of Chicago. 045639.
122 *A Book About Death*, p. 9, July 8, 1964, 2018.802.219, The William S. Wilson Collection of Ray Johnson. RBAAA, Art Institute of Chicago. 045638.
125 *A Book About Death*, p. 15, Feb. 19, 1965, 2018.802.222, The William S. Wilson Collection of Ray Johnson, RBAAA, Art Institute of Chicago. 045641.
126 (top) Binder *1965 01-03*, page *65 02 26*, The William S. Wilson Collection of Ray Johnson, RBAAA, Art Institute of Chicago. 201812_B36-S92-001.
126 (middle) *A Book About Death*, p. 10, Oct. 1, 1964, 2018.802.220, The William S. Wilson Collection of Ray Johnson, RBAAA, Art Institute of Chicago. 045639.
126 (bottom) Binder *1965 04-05*, page *65 05? ??*, 2018.802.40.7, The William S. Wilson Collection of Ray Johnson, RBAAA, Art Institute of Chicago. 046161.
129 Courtesy of the Estate of Hazel Larsen Archer and Black Mountain College Museum + Arts Center.
130 Courtesy of the Estate of Hazel Larsen Archer and Black Mountain College Museum + Arts Center.
131 Courtesy of the Estate of Hazel Larsen Archer and Black Mountain College Museum + Arts Center.

CHAPTER 3

136 Collection of John Willenbecher.
138 Binder *1964 09-12*, page *64 10 09 A*, The William S. Wilson Collection of Ray Johnson, RBAAA, Art Institute of Chicago. 201812_B34-S15-001.
141 (top) Binder *1968 06-08*, page *68 07 18*, 2018.802.43.13, The William S. Wilson Collection of Ray Johnson, RBAAA, Art Institute of Chicago. 045664.
141 (middle) Binder *Mail Art No Dates (REJ Only) 1960s 2*, page *68 07 or Later*,

2018.802.114.1, The William S. Wilson Collection of Ray Johnson, RBAAA, Art Institute of Chicago. 045670.

141 (bottom) *A Book About Death*, p. 6, Mar. 17, 1964, 2018.802.227, The William S. Wilson Collection of Ray Johnson, RBAAA, Art Institute of Chicago. 045646.

144 Binder *1963 01-02*, page *63 02? ??*, The William S. Wilson Collection of Ray Johnson, RBAAA, Art Institute of Chicago. 201812_B24-S72-001.

144 The Museum of Modern Art, New York.

147 The Museum of Modern Art, New York. © 2023 The Joseph and Robert Cornell Memorial Foundation / Licensed by VAGA at Artists Rights Society (ARS), NY.

149 mumok—Museum of Modern Art Ludwig Foundation, Vienna. ÖL-Stg 434/0046.

150–51 The Metropolitan Museum of Art.

157 © 2023 Billy Name Estate / Artists Rights Society (ARS), New York.

160–61 RJE.

163 Binder *2 REJ By WSW*, page *Before 67 03 09: Finch College Pix*, The William S. Wilson Collection of Ray Johnson, RBAAA, Art Institute of Chicago.201812_B108-001.

165 © 2023 Estate of Pablo Picasso / Artists Rights Society (ARS), New York.

169 The Metropolitan Museum of Art.

CHAPTER 4

175 Binder *1963 07-12*, page *63 07 21*, 2018.802.28.1, The William S. Wilson Collection of Ray Johnson, RBAAA, Art Institute of Chicago. 048038.

177 Binder *Undated Sept. 61 through May 63*, page 61-63 7, The William S. Wilson Collection of Ray Johnson, RBAAA, Art Institute of Chicago. 201812_B21-S32-001.

178 (bottom) The Philadelphia Museum of Art. © Association Marcel Duchamp / ADAGP, Paris / Artists Rights Society (ARS), New York, 2023.

179 (top) The Philadelphia Museum of Art. © Association Marcel Duchamp/ADAGP, Paris/Artists Rights Society (ARS), New York, 2023.

179 (bottom) Binder *1974 05-12*, page *1974 05 02*, 2018.802.64.1, The William S. Wilson Collection of Ray Johnson, RBAAA, Art Institute of Chicago. 201812_B58-S5-001.

180 2018.802.21.1, Collection of Karl Wirsum & Lorri Gunn Wirsum.

181 Binder *Undated, Sept. 61 Through May 63*, page *After 63 01 11*, The William S. Wilson Collection of Ray Johnson, RBAAA, Art Institute of Chicago. 201812_B21-S6-001.

182 (top) RJE.

188 RJE.

190 Private collection.

191 (top) The Philadelphia Museum of Art. © Man Ray 2015 Trust/Artists Rights Society (ARS), NY/ADAGP, Paris, 2023.

191 (bottom) RJE.

193 RJE.

196 The Art Institute of Chicago, Promised Gift of The William S. Wilson Collection of Ray Johnson, Obj. 248657. 043809.

197 (top) Photograph by Tazio Secchiaroli, © David Secchiaroli.

197 (bottom) Binder *2 REJ By WSW*, page *Before 67 03 09: Finch College Pix*, The William S. Wilson Collection of Ray Johnson, RBAAA, Art Institute of Chicago. 201812_B108-002.

200 (top) The Museum of Modern Art, New York.

200 (bottom) The Whitney Museum of American Art.

201 Tate Gallery, London. © 2023 The Andy Warhol Foundation for the Visual Arts, Inc./Licensed by Artists Rights Society (ARS), New York.

203 Binder *1965 06-12 3 of 3*, page *65 10 05*, 2018.802.42.7, The William S. Wilson Collection of Ray Johnson, RBAAA, Art Institute of Chicago. 201812_B42-S102-001.

204 *A Book About Death*, p. 12, Dec. 22, 1964, 2018.802.331, The William S. Wilson Collection of Ray Johnson, RBAAA, Art Institute of Chicago. 201812_230609-002.

206 Binder *1966 01-07*, page *66 05 31*, 2018.802.43.7, The William S. Wilson Collection of Ray Johnson, RBAAA, Art Institute of Chicago. 201812_B43-S90-001.

209 RJE.

CHAPTER 5

216 Collection of John Willenbecher.

218 Private collection.

219 Private collection.

221 RJE.

224–25 Private collection.

226 RJE.

227 Private collection.

238 (left) Binder *1963 07-12*, page *63 11 06*, The William S. Wilson Collection of Ray Johnson, RBAAA, Art Institute of Chicago. 201812_B28-S118-001.

238 (right) Binder *1963 07-12*, page *63 11 06*, The William S. Wilson Collection of Ray Johnson, RBAAA, Art Institute of Chicago. 201812_B28-S118-002.

239 (top) Binder *1963 07-12*, page *63 11 06*, The William S. Wilson Collection of Ray Johnson, RBAAA, Art Institute of Chicago. 201812_B28-S118-003.

239 (bottom) Binder *1963 07-12*, page *63 11 06*, The William S. Wilson Collection of Ray Johnson, RBAAA, Art Institute of Chicago. 201812_B28-S118-004.

241 (top) Private collection.

241 (bottom left) Collection of John Willenbecher.
241 (bottom right) Binder *1965 02 15-65 04 ??*, page *65 02 15:18*, 2018.802.39.15, The William S. Wilson Collection of Ray Johnson, RBAAA, Art Institute of Chicago. 048014.
242 Private collection.
243 Collection of Karl Wirsum & Lorri Gunn Wirsum. © James Falconer, Art Green, Gladys Nilsson, Jim Nutt, Suellen Rocca, and Kirl Wirsum.
244 (top) The Art Institute of Chicago, Gift of Gladys Nilsson and Jim Nutt. 2018.26. AR184154.
244 (bottom) The Museum of Modern Art, New York.
245 Private collection.
251 Betty Parsons papers, box 8, folder 19. Archives of American Art, Smithsonian Institution.
252 The Museum of Modern Art, New York.
253 The Museum of Modern Art, New York.
259 The Museum of Modern Art, New York.

CHAPTER 6

263 (top) The William S. Wilson Collection of Ray Johnson, RBAAA, Art Institute of Chicago. 045982.
263 (bottom) Binder *1963 01-02*, page 63 02? ??, The William S. Wilson Collection of Ray Johnson, RBAAA, Art Institute of Chicago. 201812_B24-S72-002.
264 RJE.
265 RJE.
271 (top) The Virginia Museum of Fine Arts.
271 (bottom) Fondazione Bonotto, Colceresa, Italy.
276 CNCMA, no. 65.
277 RJE.
280 (bottom) Photo © Marcia Resnick.
283 Museum Frieder Burda, Baden-Baden, Germany.
284 RJE.
286 RJE.
289 RJE.
292 (bottom) Private collection.
293 Private collection.
297 Binder *1980*, page *80 10 16?*, 2018.802.72.6, The William S. Wilson Collection of Ray Johnson, RBAAA, Art Institute of Chicago. 201812_B72-001.

CHAPTER 7

304 Library of the Museum of Modern Art, NY
314 (top) The Philadelphia Museum of Art.
314 (bottom) The Philadelphia Museum of Art.
319 RJE.
322 (top) RJE.
322 (bottom) RJE.
323 RJE.
324 Collection of Clive Phillpot.
326 (both) Library of the Museum of Modern Art, New York.
327 Library of the Museum of Modern Art, New York.
328 (top) RJE.
330 (top) David Bourdon Correspondence, The Museum of Modern Art Archives.
330 (bottom) The Morgan Library & Museum.
331 (top) David Bourdon Correspondence, The Museum of Modern Art Archives.
331 (both) The Morgan Library & Museum.
334 (both) The Morgan Library & Museum.
335 The Morgan Library & Museum.
342–43 The Morgan Library & Museum.

CODA

350 RJE.

INDEX

JOHNSON, RAY

ARTISTIC MOTIFS AND SERIES

ARTIST'S BOOKS AND ESSAYS

EXHIBITION WORKS

FLYERS

PERFORMANCES

PHOTOGRAPHS

LIFETIME EXHIBITIONS

A BOOK ABOUT RAY
ELLEN LEVY

THE MIT PRESS WOULD LIKE TO THANK THE ANONYMOUS PEER REVIEWERS WHO PROVIDED COMMENTS ON DRAFTS OF THIS BOOK. THE GENEROUS WORK OF ACADEMIC EXPERTS IS ESSENTIAL FOR ESTABLISHING THE AUTHORITY AND QUALITY OF OUR PUBLICATIONS. WE ACKNOWLEDGE WITH GRATITUDE THE CONTRIBUTIONS OF THESE OTHERWISE UNCREDITED READERS.

PUBLICATION OF THIS BOOK HAS BEEN AIDED BY A GRANT FROM THE WYETH FOUNDATION FOR AMERICAN ART PUBLICATION FUND OF CAA.

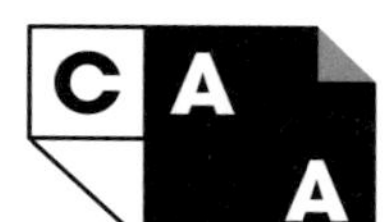

GRAPHIC DESIGN
STUDIO CHRISTOPHER VICTOR

REPROGRAPHICS
FLAVIO MILANI

PRINTED AND BOUND IN ITALY
BY MUSUMECI SPA

LIBRARY OF CONGRESS
CATALOGING-IN-PUBLICATION DATA

Names: Levy, Ellen (Ellen Sue), 1957- author.
Title: A book about Ray / Ellen Levy.
Description: Cambridge, Massachusetts : The MIT Press, [2024] | Includes bibliographical references and index.
Identifiers: LCCN 2023028860 (print) | LCCN 2023028861 (ebook) | ISBN 9780262048743 (hardcover) | ISBN 9780262377676 (ebook) | ISBN 9780262377669 (pdf)
Subjects: LCSH: Johnson, Ray, 1927-1995. | Artists—United States—Biography.
Classification: LCC N6537.J63 L48 2024 (print) | LCC N6537.J63 (ebook) | DDC 709.2 [B]—dc23/eng/20230901
LC record available at https://lccn.loc.gov/2023028860
LC ebook record available at https://lccn.loc.gov/2023028861

10 9 8 7 6 5 4 3 2 1